Applying
Educational
Research

FIFTH EDITION

Applying Educational Research

A PRACTICAL GUIDE

Joyce P. Gall

M. D. Gall
University of Oregon

Walter R. Borg
Late of Utah State University

PEARSON

Boston | New York | San Francisco
Mexico City | Montreal | Toronto | London | Madrid | Munich | Paris
Hong Kong | Singapore | Tokyo | Cape Town | Sydney

Senior Editor: Arnis E. Burvikovs
Series Editorial Assistant: Megan Smallidge
Marketing Manager: Tara Whorf
Editorial-Production Service: Omegatype Typography, Inc.
Composition and Prepress Buyer: Linda Cox
Manufacturing Buyer: Andrew Turso
Cover Administrator: Kristina Mose-Libon
Interior Design: Carol Somberg
Electronic Composition: Omegatype Typography, Inc.

For related titles and support materials, visit our online catalog at www.ablongman.com.

Between the time Website information is gathered and then published, it is not unusual for some sites to have closed. Also, the transcription of URLs can result in typographical errors. The publisher would appreciate notification where these errors occur so that they may be corrected in subsequent editions.

Library of Congress Cataloging-in-Publication Data

Gall, Joyce P.
    Applying educational research : a practical guide / Joyce P. Gall, M. D. Gall, Walter R. Borg.—5th ed.
        p. cm.
    Includes bibliographical references and index.
    ISBN 0-205-38078-6
    1. Education—Research—Handbooks, manuals, etc.   I. Gall, Meredith D., 1942–   II. Borg, Walter, R.   III. Title.

LB1028.B59 2005
370'.7'2—dc22

                                                                2003070684

Printed in the United States of America

10 9 8 7 6 5 4   09 08 07 06 05

CONTENTS

chapter 3   Using Preliminary Sources to Search the Literature   61

chapter 4   Reading Secondary Sources   82

part **III**: QUANTITATIVE RESEARCH IN EDUCATION   **121**

chapter **5** **Reading Reports of Quantitative Research Studies**   **122**

chapter **6** **Statistical Analysis of Research Data**   **149**

part IV: QUALITATIVE RESEARCH IN EDUCATION   303

chapter 10 Case Studies in Qualitative Research   304

part V: APPLICATIONS OF RESEARCH METHODOLOGY   451

chapter 14 Evaluation Research   452

chapter 15 Action Research   487

SELF-CHECK TEST ANSWERS   522

REPRINTED ARTICLES, by Chapter

The following articles are reprinted exactly as they appeared in the original source, except that the format of the original articles (e.g., column layout) has been standardized for presentation in this text.

CHAPTER 2   **Literature Review**
Kappa, S. (2002). Shifting the paradigm from "at risk" to "at promise": A review of the construct of resilience and its educational applications. Unpublished master's paper. Eugene, OR: University of Oregon.

CHAPTER 4   **Meta-Analysis**
Bayraktar, Sule (2001–2002). A meta-analysis of the effectiveness of computer-assisted instruction in science education. *Journal of Research on Technology in Education, 34*, 173–188.

Professional Review
Slavin, R. (1992). Cooperative learning. In M. C. Alkin (Ed.), *Encyclopedia of educational research* (6th ed., vol. 1, pp. 235–238). New York: Macmillan.

CHAPTER 7   **Descriptive and Causal-Comparative Research Study**
Conley, D. T., & Goldman, P. (1995). Reactions from the field to state restructuring legislation. *Educational Administration Quarterly, 31*, 512–538.

CHAPTER 8   **Correlational Research Study**
Cooper, H., Jackson, K., Nye, B., & Lindsay, J. J. (2001). A model of homework's influence on the performance evaluations of elementary school students. *The Journal of Experimental Education, 69*, 181–199.

CHAPTER 9   **Experimental Research Study**
Mills, P. E., Cole, K. N., Jenkins, J. R., & Dale, P. S. (2002). Early exposure to direct instruction and subsequent juvenile delinquency: A prospective examination. *Exceptional Children, 69*(1), 85–96.

PREFACE

GOALS OF THIS BOOK

As with the four preceding editions of *Applying Educational Research: A Practical Guide,* this new edition explains the primary methods for conducting and synthesizing educational research and demonstrates its relevance to educators' work in schools and other institutions.

The book has three audiences: graduate students in education who need to conduct a research study or write a paper reviewing the research literature on a particular problem; education professionals who wish to understand the research literature relating to specific educational issues; and university instructors who teach introductory courses about educational research.

Conducting a publishable research study or literature review requires extensive training and experience. This book introduces you to the basic skills involved in these endeavors. It provides a foundation on which you can develop more specialized skills if that is your goal. At the same time, the book contains sufficient information for you to do a literature review or research study that will develop your expertise as an education practitioner. If you can locate or collect research findings that relate to the problems that arise in educational practice, you will be able to make sounder decisions than someone who relies only on personal experience or others' opinions.

The contexts and tasks of education are diverse. Therefore, in explaining research methodology, we provide examples of research about elementary, secondary, and higher education; about varied areas of the curriculum, such as language arts, science, and health; and involving different educator roles, such as staff development, teaching, administration, special education, and education in the private sector. The common thread throughout the text is its focus on how educators can apply the methods and findings of educational research in making decisions about problems of practice.

NEW FEATURES

As in previous editions, a recent research article from the educational literature is reprinted in full to illustrate each major research method. Seven of the articles are new to this edition. They include an exemplary review of the literature prepared as a final paper by a student obtaining a master's degree in education and an action research paper published online. Also among the new articles are contributions by researchers in Canada and Turkey, reflecting the fact that educational research studies published in the United States have an increasingly international perspective. Of the six articles repeated from the previous edition, two contain new researchers' comments.

The thirteen research articles are easily identified by their two-column format. Each is accompanied by comments specially prepared by the individual(s) who conducted the research, and by footnotes that we prepared to explain technical terminology.

New to this edition is a form for outlining a research proposal. Its purpose is to develop your understanding of what is required to design a sound research study. The form is introduced in Chapter 1, and examples of its use are presented in most of the other chapters. These examples all relate to curriculum alignment, an increasingly important issue in this era of increased testing of student competencies required by state education agencies. In each chapter, we fill in parts of the form pertaining to the content of that chapter.

By studying the filled-in outlines, you will learn the many decisions and procedures involved in conducting a research study. This learning will stand you in good stead if you are asked to conduct a research project as a degree or work requirement. You will find that the essential first step in a research project is preparing a proposal, much like creating a blueprint is the essential first step in constructing a building. The proposal outline included in Appendix 1 is sufficiently broad to accommodate any of the research approaches covered in the book.

This edition continues its commitment to a balanced introductory treatment of quantitative and qualitative approaches to research. Resources for further study of each approach are included at the end of each chapter. They have been updated and annotated for this edition.

Each chapter has been revised to reflect new issues and changes affecting educational research. For example, the chapters in Part II describe the many new resources available on the World Wide Web for searching the education literature for particular types of publications. Chapter 5 describes the new conceptualization of test validity presented in the latest edition of *Standards for Educational and Psychological Testing*. In Chapter 12 we provide expanded coverage on critical pedagogy, and in Chapter 15 we include several new topics, such as action science, insider–outsider collaboration, and criteria to increase the validity of action research.

ORGANIZATION OF THE BOOK

Parts I through V

The body of the book is divided into five parts, each preceded by a brief introduction to orient you to its topics.

Part I consists of one chapter, in which we explain the important role that research plays in improving educational practice.

Part II covers the process of finding and synthesizing research studies in the published literature on any topic of interest. Chapter 2 explains the steps involved in conducting a review of the research literature. Chapter 3 focuses on how to search the literature using one of the major preliminary sources that index reports of educational research studies. Chapter 4 describes procedures for reviewing secondary sources, that is, syntheses of research literature on specific topics.

Several appendixes supplement the chapters in Part II. Appendixes 2 and 3 provide a comprehensive list of preliminary and secondary sources to support the process of doing a literature review. Appendixes 4 and 5 list questions that will help you judge the quality of research studies that you plan to include in your literature review.

Part III covers the concepts and procedures of quantitative research in education. Chapter 5 explains what to look for in each section of a typical report of a quantitative research study. Chapter 6 provides an overview of the statistical analysis of research data, which is central to quantitative research design. Chapters 7, 8, and 9 cover the main methods of quantitative research found in the research literature: descriptive and causal-comparative research in Chapter 7, correlational research in Chapter 8, and experimental research in Chapter 9.

Part IV covers commonly used approaches in qualitative research in education. Chapter 10 describes case study research and various qualitative research traditions. Chapters 11, 12, and 13 focus on three of these research traditions because of their special relevance to education: ethnographic research in Chapter 11, critical-theory research in Chapter 12, and historical research in Chapter 13.

Part V covers applications of educational research that can involve either quantitative or qualitative methods of inquiry: evaluation research in Chapter 14 and action research in Chapter 15.

Chapter Organization

Each chapter of the book begins with a vignette, followed by chapter objectives and key terms. Following the main text of the chapter is an example of how to outline a research proposal (except Chapter 1), a self-check test, chapter references, and resources for further study. An article from the education literature is reprinted in full at the end of most chapters, preceded by comments from the researchers who conducted the study and wrote the article. Chapters 4 and 9 both contain two reprinted articles, each illustrating different sets of concepts and procedures covered in the chapter.

SUGGESTED STUDY STRATEGY

Examine the book's organization. Before you start reading the book, explore its layout: table of contents, list of reprinted articles, introductions to each part, organization of each chapter, and end matter (self-check test answers, appendixes, glossary, and name and subject indexes).

Start each chapter by reading the vignette, objectives, and key terms. Each chapter begins with a brief vignette, followed by objectives and key terms. Reading these advance organizers will give you an overview of the chapter. The objectives are listed in approximately the same order in which they are covered in the chapter, and the key terms are listed alphabetically.

Read the body of the chapter. As you read the chapter, try to locate the main information relating to each objective and key term. Also, look for the examples that illustrate concepts and procedures. In addition to reading these examples, reflect on what each concept and procedure might mean in an educational context that is familiar to you. Where a key term is defined or described in the chapter, the term appears in boldface. All key terms that are general or conceptual in nature also appear in the glossary.

Read the reprinted article. As you read each reprinted article, consider how it employs the concepts and procedures described in the chapter. Also, consider how the findings of the study contribute to your understanding of education and the development of your expertise as an educator.

You will note that most of the reprinted articles contain footnotes. We prepared these footnotes to explain technical terms that might cause you difficulty in comprehending the article. The book's glossary and subject index also are sources of help for understanding technical terminology.

Check your mastery. After reading the chapter, go back to the objectives and see if you can define the concepts and describe the procedures stated in each objective. If you find anything that you have not mastered, engage in further study of the chapter or resources elsewhere in the book. Then take the self-check test in the chapter, which includes multiple-choice items related to each of the chapter objectives. If you wish to expand your understanding of particular topics, you can read the resources for further study listed at the end of the chapter.

Prepare for tests. You can prepare for the instructor's tests by rereading the chapter objectives and key terms, any chapter material that you underlined, and any notes that you took. Another useful strategy is to have a review session with one or more classmates. Each of you can alternate taking the role of the instructor by making up questions about the chapter content and asking your classmates to answer them.

Complete any assigned application problems. The Instructor's Manual for this text contains application problems for each chapter, along with suggested answers, which your instructor may choose to assign. We recommend that you work on these problems carefully. They will deepen your understanding of the research process, especially of the many problems and decisions that confront researchers in investigating educational issues and phenomena.

INSTRUCTOR'S MANUAL

An Instructor's Manual is available to accompany the text. It includes suggestions for designing an introductory or applied research course for graduate students in education and related fields; application problems that can be assigned for each chapter along with a suggested answer for each problem; teaching activities related to the chapter content; and a test-item bank with both closed- and open-form items covering the content of each chapter.

Thorough coverage has been given of the most recent computer search procedures for applying research. To further support research using technology, this text can be packaged with our free **Research Navigator**™ database of research publications, *New York Times* articles, and other resources. This package can be ordered by contacting your local Allyn and Bacon Representative.

ACKNOWLEDGMENTS

We thank our many colleagues who have shared with us their knowledge, insights, and experiences relating to educational research. In particular, we express deep appreciation to the following reviewers of portions of the manuscript: Dale I. Foreman, Shenandoah University; Deborah J. Hendricks, West Virginia University; Jean Krows, Emporia State University; and Marylin Lisowski, Eastern Illinois University. Thank you for spending time carefully reading chapter drafts and giving us feedback to help us refine this new edition of *Applying Educational Research.*

Joyce P. Gall
M. D. Gall

Applying
Educational
Research

part I

THE CONTRIBUTIONS
OF EDUCATIONAL RESEARCH

This part of the book provides an overview of educational research as an organized approach to inquiry about the many facets of teaching, learning, and schooling. You will find that the goals of this inquiry include the discovery of patterns in educational practice, the development of theories to explain such patterns, and the use of research knowledge in the creation and validation of methods to improve educational practice.

You also will learn that educational researchers face important, still unresolved, philosophical issues concerning the nature of social reality and the best means for acquiring knowledge about it. Researchers have taken different positions on these issues, and consequently, they have developed quite different approaches to the investigation of education. We introduce you in Part I of the book to the two main approaches, commonly known as quantitative and qualitative research. Subsequent parts of the book provide detailed explanations of how research studies are conducted according to each approach.

In reading Part I, you will find that research plays an important role in efforts to improve educational practice. At the same time, educational research is a very human process and, therefore, it is prone to error and bias. We describe various procedures that researchers have developed to minimize the influence of such factors on their findings.

chapter 1

Using Research to Improve Educational Practice

After studying this chapter, you will be able to

1. define research and explain its role in professional work.

2. explain how basic, applied, and action research each contribute to practice.

3. explain how an awareness of research findings and methods can benefit educational practitioners.

4. describe several ways in which practitioners in education can collaborate with researchers.

5. describe the key characteristics of research that differentiate it from other forms of inquiry.

6. describe how quantitative researchers and qualitative researchers differ in their views about the nature of knowledge, and how that difference affects their approach to data collection and analysis.

Mary Gomez has been an elementary school teacher for twenty years. She has taken classes about how to help different types of students learn to read, and has tried to apply this knowledge in her own classroom. She served on a reading curriculum committee for her middle school, but found it frustrating. "Nobody asked about the goals of the different reading programs we looked at, or how we could be sure they would really help our kids learn," she complained to her husband. "They were more concerned about which program looked nicest and would be easiest to use." To another teacher she confided, "We must find some way to improve students' reading skills before they get to middle school and fall further behind. But from now on I want my voice to be heard more. That's why I'm going back to the university for my master's degree. I want to find out what's really known about teaching reading. I want to be able to cite research, not just my experience or opinions."

Mary has designed her master's degree program so that she will learn in depth about research on the reading process and on reading instruction. To understand this body of research knowledge, she will need to develop general research skills. For this reason, she most likely will take a research methods course in which she will study this textbook or one like it. Perhaps there is some similarity between your situation as an educational practitioner and Mary Gomez's.

In this chapter we introduce you to the world of educational research and how it can be used to improve educational practice. Also, you will learn about different types of research and how each type contributes to our understanding of education. ●

THE NATURE OF EDUCATIONAL RESEARCH

Educators are members of a profession. Teachers, school psychologists, principals, and many other types of practitioners who work in the field of education must earn professional licenses or degrees in order to gain employment. Most belong to professional associations in their fields of specialization.

A major characteristic of a profession is that it has a base of research knowledge. For example, the medical profession has a base of research knowledge that derives from research in biology, chemistry, and other physical sciences. In the profession of business management, the knowledge base is informed by research in such disciplines as economics, psychology, and mathematics.

The education profession also has a base of research knowledge. This knowledge base derives primarily from disciplines in the social sciences, including psychology, history, anthropology, and sociology. In addition, many individuals receive training specifically to conduct research investigations of educational issues and practices. Educational research is a substantial enterprise, as evidenced by the large membership of the American Educational Research Association.

If you wish to be a fully informed member of the education profession, you will need to learn about the knowledge generated by researchers. You also will need to develop an understanding of their methods of inquiry and of the problems and practices that they are currently investigating. You would expect no less of a doctor, an engineer, a therapist, an airline pilot, or any other professional on whom you depend.

The Purpose of Educational Research

Educational research can be defined as the systematic collection and analysis of data in order to develop valid, generalizable descriptions, predictions, interventions, and explanations relating to various aspects of education. It is this reliance on carefully collected and analyzed data that most strongly distinguishes between research knowledge and the personal knowledge that we gain through experience.

Description.   The purpose of **descriptive research** is to make careful, highly detailed observations of educational phenomena. For example, Marilyn Adams's monumental synthesis of research on learning to read includes findings about how an individual's eyes move while reading text (Adams, 1990). Contrary to popular belief, researchers have found that good readers process every word in the text rather than engage in selective scanning. This finding has important implications for teaching children to read.

You will study methods of descriptive research in Chapter 7. These methods involve collection and analysis of numerical data. Other types of descriptive research rely primarily on verbal data, such as interview data, historical records, or ethnographic data. This form of research—often called qualitative research—is explained in the chapters of Part IV of the book.

Prediction.   The purpose of **prediction research** is to determine whether data collected at one point in time can predict behavior or events that occur at a later point in time. For example, a substantial amount of research has been done to identify the characteristics of young children that predict whether they are likely to drop out of school or do poorly in school as they become older.

Another common type of prediction research involves selection of students for admission to institutions of higher education or selection of individuals for jobs in the workplace. Tests have been developed to aid selection. To validate the tests, researchers conduct studies to determine how well the tests, administered at a particular point in time, predict subsequent performance in school or the workplace.

Prediction studies typically involve the use of causal-comparative or correlational methods, which are explained in Chapters 7 and 8.

Intervention.   Some research seeks to determine whether a phenomenon can be controlled or improved by a particular intervention. Research of this type involves the experimental method. For example, many researchers have conducted experiments to determine whether introducing cooperative learning into a classroom improves students' learning.

The findings of experimental research are particularly important to educators. Virtually everything they do is an "intervention" of some sort. For example, teachers "intervene" in students' lives in order to facilitate their learning. Administrators "intervene" by engaging in leadership behavior that facilitates the work of other individuals in the organization. Experiments can determine what types of interventions are most likely to be successful.

Methods of experimentation involving quantitative data are explained in Chapter 9. Some researchers study the effects of an intervention by in-depth exploration of a single case, or several cases, to which the intervention has been applied. This type of research involves the use of case study methodology, which is explained in Chapter 10.

Individual practitioners can do small-scale experiments to improve local practice. This approach, called **action research,** is explained in Chapter 15. Also, practitioners, working together or with a professional researcher, do studies to determine not only the effects of an intervention, but also the value or worth of the intervention. For example, they might wish to determine whether the intervention is cost-effective, better than other possible interventions, or valued by the community. This type of investigation, called **evaluation research,** is explained in Chapter 14.

Explanation. The purpose of some research is to explain individual or group behavior. Explanation, as we use the term here, involves the statement of cause-and-effect relationships. For example, a common explanation of the finding that students in some schools do better on state or national tests is that they come from families with higher socioeconomic status. In other words, socioeconomic status (the cause) is invoked as an explanation of students' academic achievement (the effect).

All of the research methods mentioned above, with the exception of purely descriptive methods, can be used to investigate cause-and-effect relationships. The researchers hypothesize that one or more factors are causes and one or more factors are the effects. They then collect data to determine whether variations in the presumed cause (e.g., schools with high teacher morale versus schools with low teacher morale) are associated with variations in the presumed effect (e.g., high student attendance rate versus low student attendance rate).

Researchers study cause-and-effect relationships to test a personal theory or just to satisfy their curiosity. However, some researchers investigate cause-and-effect relationships in order to develop and test theories. Indeed, some researchers believe that the ultimate goal of educational research is to develop theories that explain various aspects of education. A **theory** is an explanation of particular phenomena in terms of a set of underlying constructs and a set of principles that relates these constructs to each other. **Constructs** refer to structures or processes that are presumed to underlie observed phenomena.

For example, our local newspaper reported a new research finding with major significance for the teaching of motor skills (Recer, 1997). The researchers, led by a psychiatrist at Johns Hopkins University, used a device to measure blood flow in the brain. They observed consistent changes in the portion of research participants' brains where blood flow was most active during and after motor learning tasks. They used constructs from the information-processing theory of learning to explain these changes in blood flow and motor-skill learning.

The researchers found that it takes approximately six hours for a new motor skill that has been taught to move from short-term memory to long-term memory. If another new motor skill is taught during this six-hour interval, the first motor skill will not move into long-term memory. Short-term memory and long-term memory are constructs in information-processing theory. They are called constructs because they cannot be observed directly, but are inferred to exist on the basis of observed phenomena.

The possible applications of this finding are considerable. For example, say that a teacher is teaching students a new skill (e.g., cutting wood with a power saw). If the students then get a lesson shortly thereafter on another new skill (e.g., serving a volleyball), the memory of the first skill is not likely to be retained. More time must pass before the new skill is introduced, so that the skill studied in the first lesson is permanently learned.

Information-processing theory and other theories are powerful because they not only help to explain educational phenomena but also help educators make predictions and design better forms of instruction or other interventions. For example, information-processing theory has helped educators understand and improve students' ability to read with good comprehension and to prepare for school tests effectively. Some of the research articles that you will read later in this book draw from and in turn contribute to such theories.

Basic and Applied Research

Researchers do not use a single approach to inquiry. Some of their investigations can be characterized as basic research, whereas others can be characterized as applied research. The purpose of **basic research** is to understand basic processes and structures that underlie observed behavior. For example, medical research currently is making enormous advances by seeking to explain the occurrence of certain diseases (the observed behavior) in terms of underlying differences in gene composition (a basic structure) among individuals. The published article that you will read in Chapter 10 reports basic research on how teachers construct a personal knowledge base to inform their daily work.

In contrast to basic research, the purpose of **applied research** is to develop and test predictions and interventions that can be used directly to improve practice. In education, the development and testing of a new method to help students engage in mathematical problem solving would be an example of applied research. The published research articles that are included in Chapters 9 (Experimental Research), 14 (Evaluation Research), and 15 (Action Research) are examples of applied research.

Some practitioners believe that applied research is more valuable as a guide to their work than basic research, and that it should therefore have funding priority over basic research. A study of medical research by Julius Comroe and Robert Dripps (1976) raises doubts about this view. Comroe and Dripps studied the advances in research knowledge that were necessary for innovations in the treatment of cardiovascular and pulmonary disease (e.g., cardiac surgery and chemotherapy). Surprisingly, many more basic research studies were instrumental in these innovations than were applied research studies. Basic research leads to theoretical understanding of underlying processes and structures, and this understanding provides a necessary foundation for constructing interventions that are likely to be effective.

THE BENEFITS OF EDUCATIONAL RESEARCH

It is difficult to convince some educators that research benefits practitioners and students. For example, we might point to standardized tests (e.g., intelligence tests and college entrance tests) as products of research that are in wide use today. However, education and research are value-laden enterprises. While some educators believe that standardized tests are valuable, others believe that these tests are harmful to the teaching–learning process.

In another example, recent research reviewed by Beth Azar (1997) suggests that day care may have adverse effects on children's later social and academic development. These research findings might lead to beneficial changes in day-care practice, but some groups have decried the entire line of research as sexist.

These examples suggest that research can and does contribute to the practice of education, but only to practice based on a particular set of values. In this respect, education is no different than other professions. Research has identified various ways in which business managers can maximize profit. Some individuals might view this research as valuable, but others may view the profit motive as immoral and might therefore reject this type of research. Medical research keeps finding new ways to prolong life in seriously ill patients, but some individuals question the ethics of this goal.

Another reason it is difficult to claim that research has benefited educational practice is that its influence is rarely direct. The work of education professionals is influenced by many factors, only one of which is research. Also, it often takes a long time for research findings to find their way into practice. The change process in education is very slow.

As you read this textbook, you will study a variety of published literature reviews and research studies, along with comments from the researchers who wrote them. After reading each one, we invite you to consider whether it was worth doing. For example, you can ask yourself the question, "Did I learn anything of value from this study?" In our experience, professional educators who have read studies like these do find value in them. At the same time, they may be hard-pressed to find a *direct* application of these studies' findings to educational practice. Rather, the main benefit of the increased professional knowledge that they gain from reading such studies is that the findings inform their thinking about particular practices. Then they must combine this thinking with other factors (e.g., the budgetary and political realities of schools), and with their own creativity, in order to generate new solutions to problems of practice. In other words, research knowledge usually is a necessary, but not sufficient, condition for the improvement of practice.

Robert Slavin (1989) has demonstrated how the practice of education has swung like a pendulum from one fad to another and back again. The shift from phonics-based reading instruction to whole-language instruction, now reversing back to phonics-based instruction, is one example of the pendulum-swing phenomenon that is so common in educational practice. Although pendulum swings change education, they rarely result in lasting improvement. Slavin argues that practitioners need to learn about research so that they may start to base their decisions more on evidence and less on fads promoted by charismatic individuals.

The belief that educational practice should be based on research evidence had a major influence on the No Child Left Behind Act, which was signed into federal law in January 2002. Among other things, this law allows for grants to states that use instructional practices drawn from scientifically based research to improve the reading achievement of young children. Certain parts of the No Child Left Behind Act are controversial, including the meaning of "scientifically based research," but the act does signal a new level of commitment among policy makers to use research evidence as a guide for improving education.

APPLYING EDUCATIONAL RESEARCH TO PRACTICE

Using Research Knowledge to Inform Practice

Educators need a large amount of knowledge in order to carry out their work effectively. For example, they need knowledge about the learning process, knowledge about student characteristics, and knowledge about school management. Where does this knowledge come from? For example, how do teachers, in preparing for the first day of school, decide what to do when their first class of new students arrives?

Some teachers rely on their past experience, perhaps the experience gained during their student teaching. Other teachers base their decisions on the opinion or example of colleagues, or of people whom they consider to be experts. Still others might decide to do whatever occurs to them at the time, believing that they can only learn by trial and error what works and what doesn't work in the classroom.

Part II of this book will help you develop skills for reviewing and applying the education literature to help you solve the issues and problems that arise in your work. Some of this literature presents theory, opinions, or the personal experience of practitioners and others, but our focus is on the research literature. You will learn how to conduct a literature review (Chapter 2), and how to use preliminary sources to find literature on particular topics (Chapter 3). You will also learn how to obtain and evaluate published literature reviews on particular topic areas (Chapter 4).

Because there are many types of research studies, you need to understand the specific purposes and methods of each type. The chapters in Parts III, IV, and V will help you develop this understanding. In Chapter 7 and each subsequent chapter, you will read a description of each type of educational research and a published study that illustrates it. In addition, you will read comments written for this book by the authors of these studies. Reading their comments will give you a deeper understanding of how researchers think, why they decide to carry out a particular research study, how they go about designing their research, and what the relevance of their work is to educational practitioners.

Conducting Action Research

Action research is research carried out by practitioners to improve their own practice. There are at least two reasons why practitioners might want to conduct action research rather than relying on findings from others' research. One reason involves the generalizability of research findings, that is, the extent to which the findings are likely to apply to their particular work situation. For example, a program might have been found effective in urban schools, but you may work in a suburban or rural school. In this case you could carry out your own research to determine the program's effectiveness in your situation.

A second reason that practitioners might wish to conduct action research is that they have a question about an idea or method, and the research literature has not provided sufficient information to answer the question to their satisfaction. For example, suppose a counselor has been collecting anecdotes and newspaper articles about the growing problem of drug abuse among younger students. She has ideas for a program to address the problem but cannot find an existing program or set of research findings that relate to her ideas. By carrying out action research, she can develop the program and determine whether it is effective.

Action research does not need to be as formal as the studies that are reported in research journals. The reason is that an action researcher is not concerned with obtaining findings that can be generalized to other settings. Nonetheless, local action research can draw on the methods of data collection and analysis, including the techniques for minimizing bias, that professional researchers have developed.

You will learn procedures for conducting action research in Chapter 15. The placement of the chapter at the end of the book reflects the fact that action researchers can use any of the approaches to research that are presented in the previous chapters. Therefore, reading those chapters first will give you a better understanding of the variety of ways in which you can design your own action research projects.

Collaborating with Researchers

In order for research to inform and improve practice, practitioners need to participate in an ongoing dialogue with research professionals. Maintaining a dialogue can be a challenge, however. One reason is that researchers and practitioners tend to be very different in their views about knowledge and research. According to Lilian Katz and Dianne Rothenberg (1996), researchers' main interest in knowledge is scientific: When confronted with a problem, they seek to explore and discover the nature of the problem, no matter how long that might take. By contrast, practitioners' main interest in knowledge is clinical: When confronted with a problem, they seek information that will allow them to solve it, usually under the pressure of a time limit. Katz and Rothenberg add that effective practice:

> . . . depends to some extent on the certainty with which the practitioner approaches his or her task. And by definition, the researcher's task is to prize doubt and uncertainty and be open to being wrong. . . . (p. 8)

Researchers and practitioners can take steps to understand each other's needs and to communicate clearly with each other. For example, researchers can develop research agendas that are responsive to practitioners' needs and can prepare reports of their findings that are written in nontechnical language and that spell out the implications of the findings for practice. Practitioners in turn need to make an effort to understand the language and methods used by researchers. The researchers' comments that accompany the articles reprinted in this book were specially prepared by the articles' authors to give you a sense of how researchers think.

In addition to improving lines of communication, practitioners and researchers can strengthen the application of research to practice through collaboration. Several types of collaborative possibilities are described below.

Being a Research Participant. Researchers often ask practitioners to participate in research studies. The effort required might be minimal (e.g., filling out a questionnaire) or more extensive (e.g., volunteering your class to be part of the experimental or control group in an experiment). By volunteering to participate, you may find that you are eligible to receive special training or consultation, or curriculum materials that can be kept and reused. You also learn about how research is actually done and how it can contribute a fresh perspective about educational phenomena.

Participating in Program Evaluation. Educational institutions often obtain grants from private or government funding sources to implement experimental programs. These grants typically require the grantee to carry out an evaluation of the program during or at the end of the funding period. If your institution employs evaluation specialists, you can work alongside them to design an evaluation that is appropriate for your experimental program's intended objectives. For this collaboration to happen, however, you need to be knowledgeable about evaluation research. If no evaluation specialists are available to help you in securing a grant and satisfying its requirements for evaluation, you will need to know enough about evaluation research to deal effectively with this aspect of the grant.

Chapter 14 will explain how to conduct an evaluation study, and how to decide whether you can apply the findings of other evaluations to help you make a decision in your own practice. Because evaluation research may involve any of the research approaches described in Parts III and IV of this book, study of the chapters in those parts of the book will be helpful to you, too.

Influencing Policy Agendas. Various policy-making bodies, ranging from national and state legislatures to local school districts, are constantly proposing changes in educational practice that directly affect practitioners' work. (We described one such change, the No Child Left Behind Act, above.) Some changes are sound, but others make little sense to the practitioners who must implement them. For example, many states have implemented or are considering mandatory achievement testing of all students in order to make educators accountable for student learning outcomes. Teachers in particular are concerned about the validity of these tests and whether they respect the large individual differences in students' learning needs and family situations. However, without knowledge about research on achievement testing and student characteristics, teachers and other practitioners are in a poor position to influence statewide testing programs.

Ill-considered policies perhaps could be avoided if practitioners and researchers would collaborate to make their views and knowledge known to policy makers. For this to happen, though, researchers and practitioners must be familiar with each other's knowledge base and perspective.

CHARACTERISTICS OF RESEARCH

In recent years, some scholars have begun to question the relevance of research to understanding human behavior and society. Adherents of this movement, which is called **postmodernism,** acknowledge that science has contributed to an understanding and control of the physical world, but they argue that no one method of inquiry can claim to be true, or better than any other method, in developing knowledge about the human world (Graham, Doherty, & Malek, 1992). Thus postmodernists would argue that the methods of social science inquiry are not superior to personal reflection, or to other forms of inquiry such as artistic or religious study.

The postmodern critique of scientific inquiry has caused social science researchers (including educational researchers) to rethink their claims to authority in the pursuit of knowledge. They have identified several characteristics of research that establish its claim to authority and that differentiate it from other forms of inquiry. We describe these characteristics in the following sections.

Creation of Concepts and Procedures That Are Shared, Precise, and Publicly Accessible

Social science researchers have developed specialized concepts (e.g., test reliability) and procedures (e.g., purposeful sampling) to help them conduct studies of high quality. They accept responsibility for making their terminology and procedures public and explicit. Everyone is free to learn and use this terminology and these procedures. Indeed, most journals that publish research reports use a "blind" review procedure, meaning that the reviewers do not have access to the names of the authors or other identifying information about them.

Of course, there are power struggles in the arenas of funding and publicity for research findings, but it is highly unlikely that important theories or findings could be suppressed over the long term. This is because researchers generally are committed to **progressive discourse** (Bereiter, 1994), which means that anyone at any time can offer a criticism about a particular research study or research methodology, and if it proves to have merit, that criticism is listened to and accommodated.

If we compare educational research with practice, we find that many practitioners perform their work at a high level of excellence and have developed many insights from their personal inquiries. However, they lack concepts and procedures for making their ideas for effective practice publicly accessible.

Hence, their knowledge cannot be publicly debated, and it generally disappears when they retire. In contrast, new researchers are able to learn from experienced researchers, and the results are available in research journals for all to study.

Replicability of Findings

For researchers to have their findings published, they must make public the procedures by which the findings were obtained. Because the procedures are public, other researchers can conduct similar studies, called **replications,** to see whether they obtain the same results. Some researchers conduct their own replication studies, and publish the findings only if their original findings are replicated.

Individuals who engage in nonscientific inquiry may obtain potentially important effects and insights. However, their inquiries are of limited value because they do not make their procedures sufficiently explicit for others to replicate them. Thus, we have no way to know whether an individual's claimed effects and insights are unique to that individual or can inform the work of other individuals.

Refutability of Knowledge Claims

Karl Popper (1968) proposes a standard for testing knowledge claims that has won general acceptance among social science researchers. Popper argues that science advances through the process of **refutation,** which involves submitting its knowledge claims (theories, predictions, hunches) to empirical tests that allow them to be refuted, that is, challenged and disproved. If the data are inconsistent with the knowledge claim, we can say that it is refuted. The knowledge claim must then be abandoned or modified to accommodate the negative findings. If the data are consistent with the knowledge claim, we can conclude that it is supported, but not that it is correct. We can say only that the knowledge claim has not been refuted by any of the tests that have been made of it thus far.

The refutation test of knowledge claims is more rigorous than the way we test everyday knowledge claims. For example, suppose a school administrator visits a particular teacher's classroom one day and discovers that (1) the teacher has attended a recent workshop on behavior management, and (2) the teacher's class is unusually quiet and orderly. The administrator might conclude that the workshop is effective, and therefore she advocates that all teachers be required to take it. In effect, this administrator made an observation first and then formulated a broad knowledge claim. In contrast, researchers who follow Popper's logic make a knowledge claim first and then test it by making observations. The tests are cautious in that contrary data can disprove the knowledge claim, but confirmatory data do not prove it. Instead, if the data are confirmatory, we conclude that the knowledge claim thus far has withstood efforts to refute it.

Control for Researcher Errors and Biases

Researchers acknowledge the likelihood that their own errors and biases will affect the data that they collect. Therefore, they design research studies to minimize the influence of such factors. For example, in making observations, researchers often seek to reduce error by using multiple observers and training them beforehand in the system for collecting data on observational variables. In addition, they may use statistical procedures to estimate the observers' level of agreement. While the observations of different observers rarely agree perfectly, a satisfactory level of agreement can be accepted as an indicator of the accuracy of the observations.

Another approach often used in qualitative research to validate findings based on the study of particular cases is triangulation of data sources. **Triangulation** refers to the researchers' attempts to corroborate the data obtained with one data collection method (e.g., observation of individuals) by using other data collection methods (e.g., interviews of individuals or examination of documents).

Researchers are particularly careful to avoid the error of generalizing their knowledge claims beyond the bounds of what their research findings support. Many of these procedures involve sampling logic, which is explained in Chapter 5. For example, researchers who are interested in studying the effects of teachers' enthusiasm on student attendance might first define a population (e.g., fifth-grade teachers in urban school systems) and then study a sample that is representative of the population. The researchers would generalize the findings obtained from the data collected on this sample only to the population that they initially defined. To generalize knowledge claims beyond the defined population is considered speculative until those knowledge claims are supported by evidence from new studies that involve other populations.

Other research procedures that we describe in various chapters of this book are intended to minimize various researcher errors and biases in data collection and analysis. We invite you to compare the rigor of these procedures with the everyday procedures that individuals use in their personal lives or in the workplace to arrive at and justify their knowledge claims.

QUANTITATIVE AND QUALITATIVE RESEARCH

Educational research is not a unified enterprise. For example, the approaches to research described in Part III, called quantitative research, involve the study of samples and populations, and rely heavily on numerical data and statistical analysis. In contrast, the research traditions described in Part IV, called qualitative research, make little use of numbers or statistics, but instead rely heavily on verbal data and subjective analysis.

Why does educational research include such diverse approaches? To answer this question, we need to consider the different **epistemologies**—that is, views about the nature of knowledge—that guide educational researchers. Some researchers assume that features of the human environment have an objective reality, meaning that they exist independently of the individuals who created them or are observing them. The students in a teacher's first-period class are viewed as the same, regardless of what the teacher is thinking about them or doing with them at the moment. These researchers subscribe to a **positivist** epistemology.

Positivists believe that there is a real world "out there" and that it is available for study through scientific means similar to those that were developed in the physical sciences.

Most **quantitative research** is carried out by researchers who ascribe to the positivist epistemology. Thus they define their subjects of interest in terms of observable behavior (e.g., "feeling good about one's teacher" might become "students report positive attitudes . . ."). They attempt to define that behavior in terms of the specific operations used to measure it (e.g., "students with positive attitudes gave average ratings of 3 or higher on 5-point scales . . ."). They also are concerned about the probability that what they discover in a research sample would occur in the larger world from which that sample was presumably drawn.

Other researchers take the epistemological position known as **interpretivism** (Erickson, 1986). To them, aspects of the human environment are constructed by the individuals who participate in that environment. Interpretivists believe that aspects of social reality have no existence apart from the meanings that individuals construct for them. For example, the students in a teacher's first-period class might be constructed as "13 boys and 16 girls," or as 29 unique individuals, or as "easier to teach than students I've had other years," depending on when the teacher is thinking about them. If the principal steps into the teacher's classroom, his construction of the students in the class might vary depending on how they are behaving at the moment, how the principal is feeling, or many other factors.

Most **qualitative research** is carried out by individuals who subscribe to the interpretivist epistemology. These researchers believe that scientific inquiry must focus on the study of the different social realities that individuals in a social situation construct as they participate in it. Qualitative researchers usually study single individuals or situations, each of which is called a *case,* and generalize case findings mainly by comparing the case with other cases that also have been studied in depth.

Qualitative researchers also accept and acknowledge their own role in constructing the social realities that they describe in their research reports. For this reason they often include their own experiences in what they report. This focus on the researcher's self as a constructor of social reality is called **reflexivity.**

While some scholars use the terms *positivism* and *interpretivism* to distinguish these two approaches to research, the terms *quantitative research* and *qualitative research* are more commonly used. For this reason we will refer to quantitative and qualitative research in this book. The terms *quantitative* and *qualitative* highlight the differences in the kinds of data that typically are collected by the researchers, and the ways in which the data are analyzed. Table 1.1 provides a further elaboration of the distinguishing characteristics of quantitative and qualitative research.

Given that both quantitative research and qualitative research are conducted to investigate education, several questions arise. Is one approach better than the other? Do they complement each other in some way? Do they produce conflicting findings?

| TABLE 1.1 | Differences between Quantitative and Qualitative Research |

QUANTITATIVE RESEARCHERS	QUALITATIVE RESEARCHERS
Assume an objective social reality.	Assume that social reality is constructed by the participants in it.
Assume that social reality is relatively constant across time and settings.	Assume that social reality is continuously constructed in local situations.
View causal relationships among social phenomena from a mechanistic perspective.	Assign human intentions a major role in explaining causal relationships among social phenomena.
Take an objective, detached stance toward research participants and their setting.	Become personally involved with research participants, to the point of sharing perspectives and assuming a caring attitude.
Study populations or samples that represent populations.	Study cases.
Study behavior and other observable phenomena.	Study the meanings that individuals create and other internal phenomena.
Study human behavior in natural or contrived settings.	Study human actions in natural settings.
Analyze social reality into variables.	Make holistic observations of the total context within which social action occurs.
Use preconceived concepts and theories to determine what data will be collected.	Discover concepts and theories after data have been collected.
Generate numerical data to represent the social environment.	Generate verbal and pictorial data to represent the social environment.
Use statistical methods to analyze data.	Use analytic induction to analyze data.
Use statistical inference procedures to generalize findings from a sample to a defined population.	Generalize case findings by searching for other similar cases.
Prepare impersonal, objective reports of research findings.	Prepare interpretive reports that reflect researchers' constructions of the data and an awareness that readers will form their own constructions from what is reported.

Source. Table 1.2 on p. 25 in Gall, M. D., Gall, J. P., & Borg, W. R. (2003). *Educational research: An introduction* (7th ed.). Boston: Allyn & Bacon. Copyright by Pearson Education. Reprinted by permission of the publisher.

Some researchers (e.g., Biddle & Anderson, 1986) believe that the methods of qualitative research and quantitative research are complementary, and that researchers who use a combination of both types of methods can give the fullest picture of the nature of educational phenomena. One study that used this approach was conducted by Stephen Stoynoff (1990), who studied international students. English was the second language for the 77 students in his sample, who had just begun their freshman year at a U.S. university.

First Stoynoff conducted quantitative research to determine how well students' scores on the Test of English as a Foreign Language (TOEFL) and on the Learning and Study Strategies Inventory (LASSI) predicted their first-term grade point average (GPA). The results indicated that TOEFL and LASSI scores yielded only modest predictions of GPA. Stoynoff then conducted qualitative case studies of selected members of his sample to determine whether other factors might be more important to the academic success of international students. Stoynoff made the following discovery from the case studies:

> The LASSI does not measure the compensatory methods that students use to help them negotiate the system. Interviews revealed that students sought social assistance from a wide variety of persons. They used tutors and roommates to explain and review homework. They borrowed lecture notes, previous tests, and papers from classmates and friends. They asked teachers for extra help. Students also learned to carefully select their courses based on the recommendations of others. These compensatory methods are not measured by the LASSI. . . . (p. 112)

Stoynoff's discoveries from his qualitative research could be used to conceptualize what *compensatory method* means. Another researcher might then develop a measure of such compensatory strategies, and administer it to a sample in a quantitative research study to test Stoynoff's insights. Depending on the results, new studies might be done, again combining the approaches of qualitative and quantitative research.

Some researchers would argue that quantitative and qualitative research are incompatible because they are based on different epistemological assumptions. For example, they might argue that it is not possible to believe that social reality exists independently of the observer while also asserting that it is constructed by the observer. In our opinion, both approaches have helped educational researchers make important discoveries. Over time, philosophers of science may gain enough understanding to resolve the seeming contradictions in the epistemological assumptions that underlie qualitative and quantitative research.

STEPS IN DOING A RESEARCH STUDY

If you are in a university degree program, you might be required to complete an independent project, typically a research study. The project might consist of "library research," meaning that you conduct a review of the literature on a topic that you have selected. A step-by-step process for doing this type of library research—a literature review—is presented in Chapter 2. Several steps in the process are explained in more detail in Chapters 3 and 4.

You might be required instead to conduct your own research study as a degree requirement. An action research project (see Chapter 15) could be an option, particularly if you are in an undergraduate or master's degree program. Alternatively, you might do a study using one of the more formal research designs described in Chapters 7 through 14.

Doing a sound research study is a complex process. We will describe the basics of the process here. As you gain experience, you will be able to do more sophisticated studies. Be assured, however, that the findings of even a simple research study, if well designed and executed, can contribute much to local practice and perhaps even apply to other settings. Research studies typically go astray not because of subtleties of procedure, but because of flaws in the basics of research design, such as the selection of an ill-defined or trivial problem for investigation.

Doing a research study involves three major steps: (1) preparing a proposal describing the study to be done and its significance; (2) collecting and analyzing data; and (3) writing a report of the completed study. The first step, preparing the proposal, is the most crucial, because it largely specifies the process of data collection and analysis. Also, a well-prepared proposal can serve as an outline for the final report.

If you plan to conduct a research study as part of a degree program, your professors are likely to require that you prepare a formal proposal as the first step. Furthermore, you will be required to submit this proposal, in modified form, to an institutional review board, which will determine whether you have included adequate procedures to protect the rights of your research participants.

Because a research proposal is so central to the process of doing a study, we focus on proposal preparation in the next section. At the end of each subsequent chapter we give an example of how to outline a research proposal using concepts and procedures described in the chapter.

Preparing a Research Proposal

Although there are different types of educational research, they share many of the same features. In planning your own research study, you will need to consider each of these features and describe them in your proposal.

Appendix 1 includes a generic form that you can use to outline your research proposal. It is suitable for virtually any kind of research study that might be done in the field of education. The key elements of the form are summarized in Table 1.2 and explained here. In subsequent chapters, we highlight particular elements of the form and illustrate their use.

Purpose of Study.   A good self-test of whether you understand what you propose to study is to try stating your research purpose in one sentence. Suppose I am interested in how educators are reacting to the recent trend toward mandatory state testing of the academic achievement of students. My interests might go in various directions, such as wondering whether educators value these tests, whether administrators and teachers differ in their reactions to these tests, and how educators are using the test results to improve instruction. After study and reflection, I narrow my interests to a single purpose, such as: "The purpose of this study is to determine how teachers change their instruction after they receive state test scores for the students in their school."

Before you can state your research purpose in this concise a form, you will need to review relevant educational literature, including articles and books written for practitioners and reports of research studies. You are likely to find many publications on important topics, but typically just a few that strongly influence the design of your study. You should discuss these publications in some depth

TABLE 1.2   Summary of Form for Outlining a Research Proposal

1. Purpose of study
   - Statement of purpose
   - How your study builds on previous research
   - How your study will contribute to knowledge about education
2. Research questions, hypotheses, or objectives
   - Form in which study purpose is stated
   - Relationship to an existing theoretical framework
3. Literature search
   - List of descriptors
   - Preliminary and secondary sources
4. Research design
   - Type of research design
   - Internal validity and generalizability concerns
5. Sampling
   - Characteristics of the population or phenomenon that you plan to study
   - Procedures for selecting a sample or cases that represent the population
   - Sample size and subgroups
6. & 7. Variables & methods of data collection
   - List of variables and how you intend to measure them
   - Measurement concerns involving validity and reliability
8. Data analysis procedures
   - Use of descriptive and inferential statistical techniques
   - Use of qualitative analysis techniques
9. Ethics and human relations
   - Possible threats that your study poses to participants and steps you will take to minimize them
   - Procedures for gaining the cooperation of participants
10. Timeline
    - List of the major steps of your study and the date by which each step will be completed

to give the reader a sense of what is known about the topic and what you propose to study in order to advance knowledge about it.

Research Questions, Hypotheses, or Objectives.   Because of the complexity of most educational topics, you probably will want to pursue more than one question or hypothesis in your study. For example, you might want to compare how teachers at different grade levels or with different attitudes about testing change their instruction after receiving state test scores. The following questions might be stated:

1. What types of instructional changes do elementary teachers make after receiving state test scores for their students?
2. What types of instructional changes do middle school teachers make after receiving state test scores for their students?
3. Do elementary and middle school teachers make different types of instructional changes after receiving state test scores?
4. Do teachers with more favorable attitudes toward state-mandated testing make greater instructional changes after receiving state test scores for their students than do teachers with less favorable attitudes?

Literature Search.   A good research study is built on a strong understanding of the literature on the problem or topic that you wish to investigate. In fact, we recommend intensive reading of the literature as your initial step. As you read, you will discern patterns in the types of questions that have been posed and in the research findings. At some point, you may experience a moment of insight in which the seeds of your proposed study come to you. Often, students will say to us, "I like this study and want to do a study to follow up on it or extend it by doing. . . ." When students make such a statement, more often than not they are ready to generate a viable research proposal.

You will need to focus your reading, because the literature on education is vast. Fortunately, various professional organizations have indexed and categorized the literature into electronic or hard-copy databases. Also, researchers periodically prepare reviews of the literature on important topics. In your research proposal, you will need to inform the reader about which databases (sometimes called *preliminary sources* or *indexes*) you have consulted, or plan to consult. Also, you need to indicate what terms (sometimes called *descriptors*) you will use in searching the databases. If you plan to rely on published reviews of the literature (sometimes called *secondary sources*), they too need to be indicated in the proposal. Procedures for doing a literature review are described in Chapters 2, 3, and 4.

Research Design.   The fourth set of elements in the proposal summary shown in Table 1.2 involves the design of your research study. Over time, researchers have developed standard approaches (called *designs*) for answering their questions or testing their hypotheses. In fact, much of this book is concerned with explaining and illustrating the most commonly used or otherwise noteworthy research designs.

To illustrate how research designs can differ, consider the problem of investigating teachers' reactions to state test scores. We might use a case study design to study in depth a few teachers at one school. We could interview them extensively to learn how they think about the test scores and how this thinking relates to their belief systems about the students in their classroom and about various aspects of education. Alternatively, we might wish to create and test a program designed to teach teachers about test interpretation and the use of test data to individualize instruction for those students whose test performance is markedly low. In this instance, a controlled experiment probably is the most appropriate research design.

No research design is perfect. Each is susceptible to different flaws. You need to be aware of these flaws and take steps to avoid them. That is why we explain not only the features of each research design in this book, but also their potential weaknesses and how to minimize them.

Sampling. It is nearly impossible to study every instance of the phenomenon that interests you. For example, if you are interested in investigating teachers' reactions to state-mandated tests administered in their classroom, you cannot study the entire population of teachers. It simply would be too expensive and time-consuming. There are ways, though, to select a sample that is representative of the population, so that you can generalize your findings from the sample to the population. Sampling procedures are described in Chapters 5 and 10.

Variables and Methods of Data Collection. If you are planning to do a quantitative research study (see the chapters in Part III), you will need to identify each concept (e.g., self-esteem) that you plan to measure. When these concepts are measured, they are called *variables* because individuals or other entities are thought to vary in the extent to which they have them.

In the example we have been considering, "test scores" would be a variable. Because of the nature of the study, this variable would already have been measured by the individual or group that scored the test. However, more precision in defining the variable is needed. Will we have teachers examine the actual test score sheets that the school district receives from the state's scorers (perhaps a computer printout)? Will we have teachers examine the raw test scores or some transformation of these scores (e.g., percentile scores)? If the scores are available only for the classroom as a whole (i.e., a class average), will we attempt to get the scores of individual students in the classroom and present those to the teacher?

Educational terms such as "learning," "self-concept," and "leadership style" can be defined and measured differently by different researchers. That is why you need to pay careful attention when identifying variables and measures in your study. Also, measures of variables are susceptible to flaws, and therefore you need to be aware of these flaws and how to minimize them. Variables and measures, and procedures for determining whether measures are valid and reliable, are explained further in Chapter 5.

Qualitative researchers usually do not think in terms of variables and measures. Instead, they think about investigating particular *aspects* of a case, or different *perspectives* from which a case might be viewed, or the different *contexts* in which the case appears. If you are planning a qualitative study, you need to think about these aspects, perspectives, and contexts beforehand in order to ensure that you collect appropriate data about them. Case delineation and data collection procedures in qualitative research are explained further in Chapter 10.

Data Analysis Procedures. Whatever your research design may be, you will be collecting data. In fact, the collection of data to answer questions or test hypotheses represents the very essence of research. Raw data do not speak for themselves, however, so they need to be analyzed and interpreted. Therefore, your research proposal should include a section on how you plan to analyze your data.

This planning will help you determine whether your research design will result in data that are amenable to statistical analysis and relevant to your research questions and hypotheses. The analysis of quantitative data involves the use of statistical techniques, which are described in Chapter 6. Some qualitative data are also amenable to statistical analysis, but more likely you will use the analytical techniques described in Chapter 10.

Ethics and Human Relations.   As we explained above, the federal government requires that most research studies involving the study of humans need to be evaluated by an institutional review board (IRB) before data collection can begin. The IRB will ask you to include a section in your research proposal, or complete a special form, in which you describe the steps that you will take to protect your research participants from certain risks. For example, your data about the research participants might expose them to risk if they became public. This risk can be avoided by taking steps to ensure the participants' anonymity.

Each IRB has its own procedures for reviewing research proposals. If you are doing a research study as a university degree requirement, it is likely that the university has an IRB and that the IRB has published its procedures. Because these procedures vary, we do not describe this aspect of proposal preparation in detail.

Timeline.   The preceding discussion reveals that a research study involves many steps. The process may seem daunting, but you can be assured that most students are able to complete a successful research project if they are systematic in their approach.

To be systematic, it is helpful to analyze all the steps in your proposed study and estimate a completion date for each step. This process is particularly important if you plan to collect data in schools. For example, if you plan to collect data from teachers, you most likely will need to do it when school is in session. If you plan to collect data from students, you likely will need to do it on days when they are not involved in such activities as taking tests or going on field trips.

This concludes our explanation of how to conduct a research study. As you read the remaining chapters of the book, each step of the process should become clearer to you. Also, if you are planning to do a research study, we recommend that you use the detailed form for outlining a research proposal in Appendix 1. After reading each chapter, determine how its content pertains to a particular section, or sections, of the form. Then complete the sections, if they are relevant to your proposed study. Over time, you will see your study gradually take shape.

We recommend that you show the partially completed form to your research advisor for feedback and assurance that you are on the right track. It is much easier to revise an outline, or trash it and start over again, than to write a complete, polished proposal only to learn that it must undergo extensive revision or be scrapped.

SELF-CHECK TEST

1. An essential characteristic of educational research is its
   a. focus on description rather than prediction.
   b. assumption that control of human behavior is unethical.
   c. systematic collection and analysis of data.
   d. avoidance of qualitative methods of inquiry.

2. The role of theory in educational research is primarily to
   a. develop precise descriptions of educational phenomena.
   b. explain phenomena in terms of constructs and principles.
   c. evaluate the effectiveness of specific instructional interventions.
   d. provide a language that facilitates collaboration between educational researchers and educational practitioners.

3. Unlike applied research, basic research
   a. requires replication of findings prior to publication.
   b. seeks to develop interventions that can be used directly to improve educational practice.
   c. seeks to prove that knowledge claims are true or false.
   d. seeks to develop understanding of the processes and structures underlying observed behavior.

4. Action research is particularly appropriate when educators
   a. want to test a particular theory of education.
   b. are concerned about improving local practice rather than developing generalizable knowledge.
   c. wish to pinpoint the precise causes of an educational phenomenon.
   d. have minimal knowledge about the methods of basic or applied research.

5. For educational practitioners, the main benefit of reading research findings is that such findings
   a. provide the best basis for making professional decisions.
   b. can be applied directly to improve practice.
   c. are more effective than political advocacy in bringing about changes in educational policy.
   d. enrich their thinking about particular educational practices.

6. In order to collaborate successfully with researchers, educational practitioners will find it essential to
   a. suspend judgment as to the potential implications of the research for practice.
   b. obtain formal training in how to conduct research.
   c. volunteer as research participants.
   d. make an effort to understand research terminology and procedures.

7. Using multiple observers to collect observational data about a particular phenomenon illustrates researchers' concern for
   a. obtaining generalizable findings.
   b. obtaining different perspectives about the phenomenon.
   c. controlling for measurement error.
   d. predicting future behavior or events.

8. If the research data are consistent with the researchers' knowledge claim, Karl Popper would conclude that the knowledge claim
   a. has practical significance.
   b. is correct.
   c. has not been refuted.
   d. is generalizable beyond the defined population.

9. Qualitative researchers are much more likely than quantitative researchers to
   a. include their personal experiences in conducting the study as part of their research report.
   b. study samples rather than individual cases.
   c. assume a constant social reality.
   d. analyze social reality into variables.

10. Quantitative researchers tend to
    a. subscribe to the belief in an objective reality independent of the observer.
    b. believe that aspects of the human environment are constructed by the participants in that cnvironment.
    c. disregard description as a goal of scientific inquiry.
    d. disregard the possible effects of their own biases on the research findings.

CHAPTER REFERENCES

Adams, M. J. (1990). *Beginning to read: Thinking and learning about print.* Cambridge, MA: MIT Press.

Azar, B. (1997). When research is swept under the rug. *American Psychological Association Monitor, 28*(8), pp. 1, 18.

Bereiter, C. (1994). Implications of postmodernism for science, or, science as progressive discourse. *Educational Psychologist, 29,* 3–12. Quote appears on p. 6.

Biddle, B. J., & Anderson, D. S. (1986). Theory, methods, knowledge, and research on teaching. In M. C. Wittrock (Ed.), *Handbook of research on teaching* (3rd ed., pp. 230–252). New York: Macmillan. Quote appears on p. 239.

Comroe, J. H., Jr., & Dripps, R. D. (1976). Scientific basis for the support of biomedical science. *Science, 192,* 105–111.

Erickson, F. (1986). Qualitative methods in research on teaching. In M. C. Wittrock (Ed.), *Handbook of research on teaching* (3rd ed.) (pp. 119–161). New York: Macmillan.

Graham, E., Doherty, J., & Malek, M. (1992). Introduction: The context and language of postmodernism. In J. Doherty, E. Graham, & M. Malek (Eds.), *Postmodernism and the social sciences* (pp. 1–23). Basingstoke, England: Macmillan.

Katz, L. G., & Rothenberg, D. (1996). Issues in dissemination: An ERIC perspective. *The ERIC Review, 5,* 2–9.

Popper, K. (1968). *Conjectures and refutations.* New York: Harper.

Recer, P. (1997, August 8). Learning physical skill requires time. *The Register Guard,* pp. 1A, 10A.

Slavin, R. E. (1989). PET and the pendulum: Faddism in education and how to stop it. *Phi Delta Kappan, 70,* 752–758.

Stoynoff, S. J. (1990). English language proficiency and study strategies as determinants of academic success for international students in U.S. universities. *Dissertation Abstracts International, 52*(01), 97A. University Microfilms No. AAC-9117569.

Resources for Further Study

Beghetto, R. (2003). *Scientifically based research.* (ERIC Digest 167). Eugene, OR: ERIC Clearinghouse on Educational Management. Retrieved August 12, 2003, from http://eric.uoregon.edu/publications/digests/digest167.html

This article describes the recent history of the scientifically based research movement and its implications for education professionals.

Cooper, H. (1996). Speaking power to truth: Reflections of an educational researcher after 4 years of school board service. *Educational Researcher, 25*(1), 29–34.

The author describes his efforts to include knowledge of educational research as a legitimate component of his service as a member of the school board in a midwestern community. He explains the aspects of research that may have contributed to the skepticism of some board and community members toward research knowledge as a basis for policy making.

Kennedy, M. M. (1997). The connection between research and practice. *Educational Researcher, 26*(7), 4–12.

The author argues that both educational research and educational practice are parts of an educational system that has "multiple, competing, and often ill-defined goals." For this reason, it is difficult for research to influence educational practice or for educational practice to make fundamental improvements. Recognition of the shifting political and social context of the U.S. educational system may pave the way for research that is more persuasive and accessible to practitioners.

Shavelson, R. J., & Towne, L. (Eds.). (2002). *Scientific research in education.* Washington, DC: National Academy Press.

This book presents current views about the principles that guide sound educational research and the role that such research should play in educational policy making. It is a contribution to the growing literature on research evidence as a basis for determining how schools should operate.

THE RESEARCH LITERATURE
ON EDUCATION

The knowledge base in educational research continues to expand at an accelerating rate. Similarly, the technology designed to store and access that knowledge in the form of electronic or hard-copy databases is expanding and changing rapidly. Thus, you need to know the current status of these databases, and how to search them to identify research findings that can help guide and improve your educational practice. The chapters in Part II are designed to inform you about sources of research findings and how to search them effectively.

In Chapter 2 we discuss the value of preliminary, primary, and secondary sources of research literature, and how they differ from each other. The chapter also describes a generic strategy for finding educational literature that bears on a problem or question that concerns you. A master's paper that is a comprehensive literature review is reprinted in full at the end of the chapter.

Chapter 3 describes how to conduct either a hard-copy or computer search of preliminary sources, which are indexes to journal articles, book chapters, conference proceedings, technical reports, and other types of research literature. We place particular emphasis on ERIC, which is the preliminary source most often used by educators.

Chapter 4 explains the value of reading secondary sources, which are reviews of the literature that experts have prepared on particular topics or problems. We describe strategies for locating appropriate secondary sources early in your literature search. Two articles that illustrate different types of secondary sources are reprinted in full at the end of the chapter.

chapter 2

Conducting a Review of the Research Literature

For seven years, Clara Davis has taught career development and health classes at a community college. Clara wants to expand the career development program to give students more intensive preparation for careers involving technology.

Clara has decided to submit a grant proposal to a foundation that supports innovative educational efforts. The proposal will require her to demonstrate familiarity with research about adult education and technology. Clara recently made a trip to the library of the state university. She tried looking for books on her own, but could not find anything recent that dealt with both technology and adult education. That was when she decided to make an appointment with the reference librarian, David Conners.

David showed Clara how to select descriptor search terms that best reflected her information needs. Then he demonstrated how to use those terms to search the education literature quickly, by computer. With David's help, Clara was able to download more than twenty citations for recent publications that relate to both technology and adult education. After reading several of these publications, Clara's picture of the theory and previous research related to her topic area was much clearer. In particular, she sensed a great opportunity for, and unique problems in, teaching computer and technology skills to older adults.

In this chapter we present a general process that you can use to locate research findings and other information about any educational topic. We explain each step of the process, from identifying the questions that will guide a search of the educational literature to preparing a report of the literature review. Once you understand this general process, you can adapt it to meet your specific information needs. ●

After studying this chapter, you will be able to

1. describe the steps involved in carrying out a literature review, and the purpose of each step.

2. explain the value of contacting experts before you begin your literature review.

3. explain the value of reading a few secondary sources on your topic early in your literature search.

4. distinguish between preliminary, secondary, and primary sources, and explain how each type of source is used in the conduct of a literature review.

5. outline the information you need to include in writing a report of your literature review.

K E Y   T E R M S

abstract
bibliographic citation

bulletin board
chart essay
descriptor
preliminary source

primary source
publication
secondary source

 SYSTEMATIC PROCESS FOR CONDUCTING A LITERATURE REVIEW

As we explained in Chapter 1, research findings can help educators by inform-ing their thinking about the problems and questions that arise in their work. For research findings to be helpful, though, educators need some way to access them. They also need to be able to interpret and synthesize the findings, and re-port them to their colleagues in a meaningful, convincing manner.

The purpose of this chapter is to provide you with a general model for ac-cessing, synthesizing, and reporting research findings that you retrieve from the literature. The steps in the model are summarized in Table 2.1. Each step is de-scribed in this chapter, and reference is made to other chapters where certain as-pects of the steps are discussed in more depth.

In our explanation of how to conduct a literature review, we focus on iden-tifying research findings that can inform and improve educational practice. However, the education literature also includes theories, expert opinions on is-sues, descriptions of experimental programs, methods that individual practi-tioners have found useful in their work, and other information of potential value to you. The literature review process that we present in this chapter will be use-ful to you in accessing these types of information as well.

Educators do reviews of the literature for various reasons. It may be that conducting a substantial literature review is a requirement for completing an

TABLE 2.1   A Systematic Process for Reviewing
the Research Literature

1. Frame your information needs as a set of questions that will guide your literature search.
2. Contact experts who can answer your questions directly or guide you to relevant publications.
3. Read general secondary sources to obtain a broad overview of the research literature pertaining to your questions.
4. Select preliminary sources that index the type of research literature relevant to your questions.
5. Identify descriptors that reflect your information needs, and use these descriptors to search the preliminary sources for relevant publications.
6. Read and evaluate primary sources that are relevant to your questions.
7. Classify all the publications that you have reviewed into meaningful categories.
8. Prepare a report of the findings of your literature review.

advanced degree. This is the case for the literature review presented at the end of this chapter. If the requirement instead is to do one's own research study, conducting a literature review is one step of the process. Reviewing the literature will reveal what is already known about the problem that you wish to study and will help you generate ideas for framing new questions to investigate and for designing the methodology of the study. A master's thesis or doctoral dissertation typically has an entire section or chapter reporting the literature review.

Still another reason for doing a literature review is to answer questions that arise in educational practice. For example, class size has increased dramatically in some Oregon school districts because of budget cuts. A local TV news reporter called recently to ask for an expert who could comment on the effects of class size on young children's learning. One of us knew the research literature on this problem and volunteered for an interview. He was able to cite an authoritative review of the research literature, which concluded that when class size is less than fifteen, students' learning increases substantially. The same review synthesized research on average class size in countries around the world. The news reporter was informed that class size in some local schools was approaching that of some Third World nations. As one might expect, this "sound bite" made waves when it was broadcast on TV!

STEP 1: FRAMING QUESTIONS TO GUIDE THE LITERATURE SEARCH

The usual problem that you will encounter in seeking information about a particular topic is not a lack of information, but too much of it. For example, *Cabell's Directory of Publishing Opportunities in Education* (1998) lists hundreds of journals in education dealing with nearly every conceivable aspect of educational practice. Also, there are many different types of publications. Here we use the term **publication** to include any communication that has been prepared for dissemination, whether in print, on microfiche, on the Internet, or possibly in other forms. For example, there currently are more than one hundred electronic journals in education on the Internet (American Educational Research Association, n.d.). The disseminating agency may be a book publisher, professional association, government office, school system, or other type of organization.

To avoid being lost in the information explosion of our era, you will need to focus your literature search. One way to do this is to reflect on your information needs, and then frame them as a set of questions. Here are a few examples of this process:

An inner-city elementary school teacher is concerned about students fighting during and after school. She has heard that anger management and conflict resolution programs have been developed for schools, and wants to learn about them. She formulates the following questions to guide her literature search: "What anger management and conflict resolution programs, if any, have been developed for use at the elementary school level? What are the characteristics of these programs? Is there any evidence that they are effective?"

A committee of school superintendents met with officials from the state department of education to learn more about plans for statewide mandatory testing of students' achievement at selected grade levels. The superintendents expressed several concerns about the testing program. State officials worked with the superintendents to frame questions for which the state department agreed to seek answers. The following key questions were framed: "What have other states with mandatory testing programs done to ensure that the tests accurately reflected the school curriculum? What have other states done to ensure that the tests were administered and scored fairly? What is the range of students who failed to earn the states' criterion score on the tests? What remediation programs, if any, have these states developed to help students who failed to achieve the criterion score? How effective are these remediation programs?"

An educator from an Asian country is enrolled in a master's degree program at a U.S. university and wants to learn teaching methods that she can use in a private school that she operates. In particular, she is interested in the latest methods for teaching English as a Second Language (ESL), which is the subject of her final project for the master's degree. She frames the following questions for this project: "What methods are currently used to teach ESL in U.S. schools? What is the theoretical basis, if any, for these methods? How effective are these methods? Are there particular teaching resources that are needed in order to use these methods effectively? Are there any obstacles or disadvantages to using these methods?"

The preceding examples illustrate how framing specific questions can focus a literature search. The more focused your search, the greater the likelihood that you will obtain satisfactory answers to your questions within a reasonable time period. Also, framing your questions clearly will simplify the subsequent steps in the literature search process, especially the last step, which involves preparing a report of your literature review.

The approach of framing questions to guide a literature search can be modified for different circumstances. For example, as you start reading publications identified through an initial literature search, you may think of new questions for which you would like answers. These questions can be added to those that you framed initially, and you can then orient your literature search accordingly. Also, you may wish to find information to prove a point rather than to answer a question. As an example, you might be convinced that students would perform much better in college if they could take their course examinations without the pressure of time limits. In this case, the purpose of your literature search is to find evidence to support a belief—what technically we call a *hypothesis*—rather than to answer a question. You could therefore guide your literature search with a purpose statement, for example: "The purpose of this literature search is to determine whether there is research evidence that students perform better on tests under untimed conditions than under timed conditions." Alternatively, you could frame your information need as a question, for example: "Do students perform better on tests under untimed conditions than under timed conditions?"

STEP 2: CONSULTING WITH EXPERTS

Business managers who need information and advice frequently call in consultants who have expert knowledge. Educators, too, make use of experts when they have a pressing need for information and advice. Of course, expert consultants are often hired for a fee. However, many experts are willing to help you as a professional courtesy without charge if your information need is clearly focused and can be addressed quickly. They often are willing—even eager—to tell you their ideas, and can point you to the most important publications relating to your information needs. With their expert knowledge as an initial framework, you can carry out a literature search with greater confidence and efficiency.

Educators in your local community may know an expert in your area of interest, or they may be able to refer you to someone who might know of such an expert. For example, the principal of a high school in Portland, Oregon, recently was planning to switch to block scheduling. (In block scheduling, fewer classes are offered, but they meet for longer time periods than in conventional scheduling of classes.) He wanted information about how best to implement block scheduling so that teachers would "buy into it" and so that students' learning would benefit. He mentioned his information need to a member of his teaching staff, who in turn called us. We are not experts in the practice of block scheduling, but we knew a colleague who was. We referred the principal to our colleague, and he was able to obtain an orientation to block scheduling from her. Thus, he had a strong initial background of information prior to conducting his own search of the literature on this practice.

A good way to contact experts outside your geographic area is by sending an e-mail message by way of the Internet. Some printed directories now include the e-mail addresses of the individuals or organizations listed in the directory. If not, you can use various search engines available on the Internet (e.g., Yahoo) to help you find the types of people, or specific individuals, with whom you wish to communicate.

Computer users have formed many computer networks through which members carry on electronic discussions or post information of various types, like announcements of upcoming conferences. Called **bulletin boards** or *discussion forums*, these networks on the Internet are managed by a computer software program called *Listserv*. Some Listserv bulletin boards are moderated and others are unmoderated, depending on whether someone monitors the contributed messages to decide which will be posted.

One general bulletin board for educational researchers is the *Educational Research List (ERL-L)*, which is sponsored by the American Educational Research Association (www.aera.net). The topics of its specialized bulletin boards, with the *listname* stated in caps, are as follows:

AERA-A	Educational Administration
AERA-B	Curriculum Studies
AERA-C	Learning and Instruction
AERA-D	Measurement and Research Methodology

AERA-E	Counseling and Human Development
AERA-F	History and Historiography
AERA-G	Social Context of Education
AERA-H	School Evaluation and Program Development
AERA-I	Education in the Professions
AERA-J	Postsecondary Education
AERA-K	Teaching and Teacher Education
AERA-L	Politics and Policy in Education
AERA-GSL	Graduate Studies List

If you have access to the Internet, you can subscribe to any of these bulletin boards by going to a web site (www.aera.net/resource/listserv.htm).

STEP 3: READING GENERAL SECONDARY SOURCES

Once you have identified the questions that you want to answer through a literature review, it is a good idea to read some secondary sources in order to form a general picture of the research that has been done on your topic. A **secondary source** is a publication in which the author reviews research that others have conducted. Two publications in education are especially helpful for identifying secondary sources: the *Encyclopedia of Educational Research,* and the *International Encyclopedia of Education.* The articles in these sources cover a wide range of topics that are relevant to educators.

Chapter 4 describes these encyclopedias and other more specialized publications containing secondary sources. It may be that one of these sources will be sufficient for your information needs. If not, at least it may help you refine the questions that you want to answer. It will also help you develop a conceptual framework for making sense of the information that you retrieve when you carry out the subsequent steps of the literature-review process described below.

STEP 4: SELECTING A PRELIMINARY SOURCE

The education literature includes many thousands of publications—books, journal articles, technical reports, papers presented at professional conferences, curriculum guides, and so forth. Even if you limit your literature search to publications that have appeared in the past five or ten years, the number of such publications is overwhelming. For this reason, various preliminary sources have been created to help you navigate the literature. A **preliminary source** is an index to a particular body of literature. Because the body of literature in different fields grows continually, these indexes are updated periodically.

Chapter 3 explains how to use a preliminary source to identify publications that are relevant to your information needs. First, though, you will need to select an appropriate preliminary source, because each one indexes a different body of literature. For example, *Sport Discus* indexes literature on sport, physical education, physical fitness, and sport medicine; *Child Development Abstracts and Bibliography* indexes literature on child development; and *Educational Administration Abstracts* indexes literature on educational administration. There are also preliminary sources that seek to provide a very broad coverage of topics that are relevant to education. The most widely used of these sources are the indexes maintained by the Educational Resources Information Center (ERIC): the *Current Index to Journals in Education (CIJE)* and *Resources in Education (RIE)*. Appendix 2 contains a comprehensive list of preliminary sources. You may find it necessary to experiment with some of them before you find the ones that index the types of publications that are most relevant to your information needs.

STEP 5: SEARCHING A PRELIMINARY SOURCE BY USING APPROPRIATE DESCRIPTORS

A typical preliminary source indexes many thousands of publications. The individuals who keep the preliminary source updated have coded each of these publications by using a standard set of **descriptors,** that is, key terms. For example, consider the report *School and Family Partnerships,* written by Joyce Epstein and Lori Connery and published by the National Association of Secondary School Principals in 1992. This publication was coded by the preliminary source *Resources in Education* using the following descriptors from the *Thesaurus of ERIC Descriptors* (Houston, 1995): *educational cooperation, family role, family school relationship, middle schools, parent influence, parent role, parent school relationship, school community relationship*, and *secondary education.* Say that you were interested in how schools and parents might cooperate to improve students' learning. If you had used *Resources in Education* and any of these descriptors, you would have come across Epstein and Connery's report.

It requires skill to identify appropriate descriptors to use in identifying publications that are relevant to your information needs. If you use inappropriate descriptors, you will miss relevant publications. Chapter 3 teaches you how to use descriptors and other features of preliminary sources so that you identify a list of publications that is not unmanageably long, but is sufficiently complete to include all potentially relevant publications. Also, you will learn that some preliminary sources are available in both a computerized and hard-copy (that is, print) format. In Chapter 3 we focus on conducting a computer search of preliminary sources because of the advantages that computer searching provides. We also provide an explanation of how to conduct a manual search of the hard-copy version of a preliminary source, should you need or wish to use that approach.

STEP 6: READING PRIMARY SOURCES

Your search of a preliminary source will yield a list of publications that correspond to your descriptors. The **bibliographic citation** for each publication typically will include the authors, title, publisher, and publication date. If the publication is a journal article, the page numbers of the article will be included, too. Some bibliographic citations also include an **abstract,** which is a brief summary (typically, one hundred words or less) of the information contained in the publication.

Preliminary sources may also cite other preliminary sources, for example, an annotated bibliography of publications on a specified topic. However, most of the publications indexed by preliminary sources are either secondary or primary sources. As we explained, secondary sources are publications in which the author reviews research that others have conducted. In some secondary sources, the author may review educational programs, curriculum guides and materials, and methods that others have developed.

In contrast to secondary sources, a **primary source** is a publication written by the individual or individuals who actually conducted the work presented in that publication. The following are examples of primary sources: a journal article that reports a research study conducted by the author of the article, a curriculum guide in the form that its authors prepared it, a diary of reflections and experiences in the form that its author prepared it, and a report describing the author's opinions about a particular educational phenomenon or practice. In short, whereas a secondary source is a publication that is written by author A about the writings of authors X, Y, and Z, a primary source *is* the writing of author X, Y, or Z.

It sometimes is necessary to read primary sources directly rather than to rely on the summary of the primary source that is contained in a secondary source. For example, if you conduct a research study for a master's thesis or doctoral dissertation in education, you will be required to prepare a literature review as part of the thesis or dissertation. This literature review must include a detailed analysis of primary sources and their relationship to the problem that you investigated.

Other situations also require you to read primary sources. Suppose you read a secondary source that reviews research evidence relating to a program that you want your school or other organization to adopt. Because this research evidence may play a critical role in convincing others to adopt the program, you most likely will want to read the actual primary sources that produced this evidence rather than relying on a secondary-source review of these studies. Similarly, you most likely will want to read program materials and documents written by the program's developers (i.e., primary sources) rather than relying on others' description of them in secondary sources.

Unless you live near a university with a large research library, you will need to order research journals through interlibrary loan, or request a reprint of the article from the publisher. Publisher addresses are listed in the front of each issue of *Current Index to Journals in Education (CIJE)*. You also can order photocopies of journal articles from a reprint service such as ISI Document Solution (www.isinet.com/isi/products/ids/ids/index.html) or ProQuest (www.il. proquest.com/proquest/). Curriculum guides, program materials, and other publications of this type also may need to be ordered. After you obtain these types of primary sources, you may find that they require slow reading. Most primary sources are written in technical language and describe sophisticated research procedures. Therefore, this step of the literature search process typically is the most time-consuming.

It is frustrating to search for a primary source in a library, or to order it through interlibrary loan, only to find once you get hold of it that it is irrelevant to your information needs. Therefore, you need to study carefully the abstracts that are part of the bibliographic citations available from some preliminary sources. These abstracts usually contain sufficient information for you to decide whether particular publications are relevant to your information needs. In some cases, the abstract contains sufficient information that you do not need to obtain and read the actual publication.

Many journal articles start with an abstract of their contents. As with the abstracts in preliminary-source citations, the article's abstract can help you decide whether the article is relevant to your information needs, and may contain sufficient information so that it is not necessary to read the article itself. Even if you do decide to read the article, reading the abstract first gives you a conceptual framework that will facilitate your comprehension of the article's contents.

If you plan to read a set of research studies, it usually is a good idea to start with the most recent ones. The reason is that the most recent studies use the earlier research as a foundation, and thus are likely to help you understand what has been learned about the problem under investigation. It will then be much easier to see how older studies relate to this problem.

Most reports of research studies follow a standard format. As you learn this format, you can search more quickly for the information you need. The format typically follows this sequence: (1) an abstract; (2) an introduction that states the problem and discusses important previous research relating to it; (3) a statement of the research questions or hypotheses to be tested; (4) a description of the research method, including subjects, measures, and research design; (5) a presentation of statistical and/or qualitative analyses; and (6) a discussion of the research results that includes interpretations and implications for further research and practice. As you study Parts III, IV, and V of this book, you will learn more about this format and you will see it illustrated in the various reprinted studies.

The introductory and discussion sections of a research report might mention relevant previous studies that did not turn up in your search of preliminary sources. If this is the case, you can add the bibliographic data for these studies to the list that you compiled from your search of preliminary sources.

It is frustrating to take notes on primary and secondary sources while you are at the library, only to find later that your notes omitted important details. The only alternatives are to continue your review without knowing the detail or to make a return trip to the library. Therefore, if you think you will need to take a lot of notes on a particular publication, you should consider photocopying it instead. You can save time by marking relevant information on the photocopy rather than writing notes on a bibliography card or sheet of paper. Also, you can refer back to your photocopies whenever you wish.

STEP 7: CLASSIFYING PUBLICATIONS INTO MEANINGFUL CATEGORIES

While studying the publications identified in your literature search, you should consider developing categories for grouping them. For example, suppose you are reviewing the literature to help your school system plan a staff development program for its administrators. As you read the literature, you may observe that some publications concern school administrators specifically, whereas others concern administrators in business and industry or administrators generally. This observation suggests grouping the publications into three categories: (1) school administrators, (2) administrators in business and industry, and (3) general. You also may find that different publications concern different purposes of staff development, leading you to formulate the following subcategories under each of the three main categories: (a) staff development to help administrators improve staff morale, (b) staff development to help administrators lower their stress and maintain a healthy lifestyle, (c) staff development to help administrators improve organizational effectiveness, and (d) staff development for other purposes.

Developing a set of categories can help you set priorities for reading the publications that you identified in your literature review. It can also suggest the best way to synthesize your findings. A systematic approach to synthesis is important because your literature search can yield a large, and sometimes contradictory, set of findings. Developing a set of categories can help you organize your findings into meaningful clusters that facilitate the process of synthesis. In Chapter 4, you will learn several different approaches to literature synthesis, each of which benefits from having available a set of categories for grouping publications.

It is easier to use categories if you develop a code for each of them. The codes can be written on bibliography cards or photocopies of each publication. Here is a coding system developed by one of us for a review of the literature on ability grouping:

S   Studies dealing with social interaction among children within a particular ability group
A   Studies describing ability-grouping systems and their relationship to student achievement
G   Studies discussing problems involved in ability grouping, such as the range of individual differences within ability groups
B   Studies relating ability grouping to behavior problems in students
P   Studies relating ability grouping to students' social adjustment, personality, and self-concept

The appropriate code was placed in the upper right-hand corner of each bibliography card. Publications that covered several different topics were assigned multiple codes.

STEP 8: PREPARING A REPORT OF THE LITERATURE REVIEW

Depending on your purpose for conducting a literature review, you may or may not need to prepare a report of what you learned from it. First we suggest guidelines for preparing a written report, and then we describe a procedure that is suited to making a more visual and nontechnical presentation.

Preparing a Written Report of a Literature Review

A report of a literature review describes the state of knowledge about the questions that were investigated and makes recommendations based on that knowledge. A formal written report typically contains the following sections:

1. *Introduction.* A description of the situation that created a need for information, the questions that guided your literature search, and the literature search plan that was followed.

2. *Findings.* A presentation of the information that you learned from conducting your literature review. The findings should focus on what is most important and relevant to your information needs. This section of the report should be organized by meaningful categories or by the questions that guided the literature search.

3. *Discussion.* Your conclusions about the state of knowledge relating to the questions you investigated and your recommendations for a course of action.

4. *References.* Complete bibliographical information for all the primary and secondary sources that you cited in the report.

Each of these sections is described below.

Introduction.   The introduction of the report should state the problem or questions that motivated your literature review (step 1 in Table 2.1) and the reasons why you chose to investigate them. If the information gained from your literature search led you to redefine your problem statement or questions, you can present your new problem statement or questions in the introduction.

The introduction also should include a description of your literature search procedures. This description should indicate the preliminary sources that you consulted (step 4 in Table 2.1), the years that were covered, the descriptors that were used (step 5 in Table 2.1), and any special situations or problems that you encountered. If you read particular secondary sources that provided a historical background or conceptual framework for your literature review (step 3 in Table 2.1), they can be summarized in the introduction.

Findings.   You can organize the findings of your literature review by the questions that guided your literature search (step 1 in Table 2.1) or by the categories that you created to organize the publications identified in your search (step 7 in Table 2.1).

You will need to decide on the order in which to present your questions or categories. Then for each question or category, you can decide on the order in which to present relevant research studies, theories, programs, methods, and opinions. By grouping together closely related publications, you can emphasize areas of agreement and disagreement that would be of interest to your audience. A particular publication may be pertinent to several questions or categories, and thus might be cited several times in your report.

Recommendations for writing the findings section of your report are presented in Table 2.2. Also, this chapter includes a literature review by a graduate student in education, and Chapter 4 includes a reprint of two published literature reviews. Studying how each of these reviews is organized will give you additional ideas for organizing the findings of your literature review.

Discussion.   When you write the findings section of the literature review, it is important to be objective and therefore fairly literal in representing research findings, theories, program characteristics, and other types of information. In the discussion, however, you are free to provide your own interpretation and assessment of this information.

TABLE 2.2   Recommendations for Writing the Findings of a Literature Review

1. Use straightforward language that clearly expresses whether you are reporting someone's research findings, theories, or opinions. For example, an author may describe a new program and its advantages, but not report any empirical evidence. In this case you might write, "Jiminez (1991) claims that. . . ." If the author conducted a research study, you might write, "Jiminez (1991) found that. . . ." If the author developed a theory or referred to another's theory, you might write, respectively, "Jiminez (1991) theorized that . . ." or "Jiminez (1991) referred to Piaget's theory of. . . ."

2. Use frequent headings and subheadings to help the reader follow your sequence of topics more easily.

3. Describe the strengths and weaknesses of the methods used in important studies so that readers have enough information to weigh the results and draw their own conclusions.

4. Discuss major studies in detail, but devote little space to minor studies. For example, you might first discuss the most noteworthy study in depth and then briefly cite others on the same topic: "Several other studies have reported similar results (Anderson, 1989; Flinders, 1991; Lamon, 1985; Moursund, 1990; Wolcott, 1990)."

5. Use varied words and phrases, such as: "Chou found that . . .", "Smith studied . . .", "In Wychevsky's experiment the control group performed better on . . .", "The investigation carried out by Gum and Chew showed that. . . ."

6. Use a direct quotation only when it conveys an idea especially well, or when it states a viewpoint that is particularly worth noting.

As an example, suppose that your literature review was aimed at determining the effectiveness of programs to help teenage mothers complete their high school education. Now you must present a brief report of your literature review to state legislators, who are considering a bill to provide funds for such programs. In writing the findings section of your report, you would need to state objectively what researchers have discovered about these programs and what experts think about them. In the discussion section of your report, however, you need to reach your own conclusions based on what you learned in reviewing the literature. For example, you might conclude: "The research evidence shows consistently positive effects for high school completion programs for teenage mothers. However, it appears that programs that isolate them from students in the mainstream or that separate them from their children have lower retention rates."

A good procedure for writing the discussion is to start by listing the main findings of your review. You can compile this list by asking yourself, "What did I learn from this review?" and then attempting to answer this question without looking at your report of the findings. By relying on memory, you are more likely to focus on the prominent findings rather than on a variety of specific details. If necessary, you then can read over what you wrote to be sure you did not miss any important findings.

Now list the findings in order of importance, and reflect on each one. You might ask yourself questions such as these: "To what extent do I agree with the overall thrust of the research evidence, theories, descriptions, and expert opinions that I examined? Are alternative interpretations possible? How would I explain the contradictions in the literature, if any? What is the significance of a particular finding for the problem I need to solve or the question I want to answer?"

The discussion also should contain your recommendations regarding the problem or questions that initiated your literature review. The recommendations should be stated clearly and, if possible, without qualification. If you are tentative or indirect, readers of your report will not know where you stand. They want to know your opinions and recommendations because you did a review of the literature, so you are an expert compared to policy makers or colleagues who do not know the literature. For example, in the above example of programs for teenage mothers, you might make a recommendation such as the following: "I recommend targeted funding for programs that create a school within a school for teenage mothers and also an on-site day-care center for their children. These recommendations are based on research findings demonstrating that teenage mothers are likely to have better self-esteem if they go to classes with mainstream students and are less likely to drop out of school if they can check on their child occasionally during the school day."

References.   All the publications that you cite in your report should be included in the references section. Conversely, the list should not contain any publications that were not cited in the report. If you should wish to include noncited publications for some reason, you should present them in a separate list, with a heading such as "Supplemental References" and an explanatory note about why they are being cited.

Different preliminary sources use different bibliographic citation styles, and the bibliographies in the secondary and primary sources you read may also be in different styles. For example, in one style all the main words in the title are capitalized, while in another style only the first word is capitalized.

It is important that you convert all your citations to the same style before typing your reference list. Some institutions require that students writing dissertations or theses use a certain style for bibliographic citations, so if your report is being written for this purpose, you will need to check on what style to use. If no particular style is required, we recommend that you use the citation style of the American Psychological Association (APA), because it is the most widely used style in educational and psychological journals. The chapter references and recommended readings sections of this book are written in APA style. To learn APA style, obtain a copy of the fifth edition of the *Publication Manual of the American Psychological Association* (American Psychological Association, 2001).

Because typing errors are easy to make in citations, you should check the reference list once again for accuracy and consistency after it is typed.

Preparing a Visual Presentation of a Literature Review

Perhaps you plan to present the findings of your literature review to educational practitioners or to an audience that includes lay people. In such cases, it is helpful to present your findings in an interesting but nontechnical format that your audience will understand.

In Table 2.3 we give an example of a **chart essay,** which is a format that uses charts to focus the audience's attention on aspects of the literature review in which they are likely to be interested. The chart essay format was originally designed to summarize the findings of a single research study (Haensly, Lupkowski, & McNamara, 1987). Here we have adapted it to illustrate the value of a visual format for presenting the findings of a literature review in a nontechnical form. The chart essay in Table 2.3 presents graphically two findings from Robert Slavin's review of cooperative learning, which you will read in Chapter 4.

You can see that the chart poses one research question, immediately followed by the empirical research findings that pertain to it. The second research question is presented in similar fashion. The chart concludes with two trend statements, which are generalizations that can be inferred from the empirical findings. These statements are called *trends* because the evidence pertaining to each question was not always consistent. However, there was sufficient consistency to identify a trend that could serve as a guide to improving educational practice.

The chart essay presented in Table 2.3 is shown as a single chart. However, in showing the chart essay to an audience on overhead transparencies or handouts, the presenter might want to use three charts—one for each of the research questions and a third for the trend statements.

TABLE 2.3	Visual Presentation of Selected Findings from a Literature Review on Cooperative Learning

Research Question 1: How effective is cooperative learning relative to traditional instruction in fostering academic achievement?

In 60 studies, there were 68 comparisons of cooperative learning classes and traditional classes on an achievement measure. Achievement was:

significantly higher in the traditional classes in:	not significantly different in the cooperative learning and traditional classes in:	significantly higher in the cooperative learning classes in:
4%	34%	62%
of the comparisons.	of the comparisons.	of the comparisons.

Research Question 2: How important is it that group goals and individual accountability both be present for cooperative learning to be effective?

Percentage of studies showing significantly positive achievement effects for cooperative learning when group goals and individual accountability are:

Present	Absent
80%	36%

Trends

Cooperative learning is more effective than traditional instruction in promoting student achievement.

Cooperative learning is most effective when it includes both group goals and individual accountability.

Source. Based on data from Slavin, R. (1992). Cooperative learning. In M. C. Alkin (Ed.), *Encyclopedia of educational research* (6th ed., vol. 1, pp. 235–238). New York: Macmillan.

EXAMPLE OF OUTLINING A RESEARCH PROPOSAL

To illustrate the process of creating and outlining a research proposal, we will focus on curriculum alignment, which we define as the process of matching curriculum content with the content of classroom instruction and the content of tests. The assumption underlying curriculum alignment is that students will learn better if teachers teach what the curriculum specifies and if they test what they teach.

We selected curriculum alignment as our example in this and succeeding chapters because educators increasingly are turning to it in response to new federal and state policies holding them accountable for student learning, as measured by externally developed tests. Many educators believe that curriculum alignment will help them meet these accountability requirements. We want to learn whether they are correct.

Chapter 2 stresses the importance of having a clear purpose and clear research questions or hypotheses to guide your literature review. Below, you see how we filled out the parts of the outline form in Appendix 1 pertaining to these elements of a research study.

1. PURPOSE OF STUDY
    A. The purpose of this study is to determine whether curriculum alignment improves students' performance on achievement tests.
2. RESEARCH QUESTIONS, HYPOTHESES, OR OBJECTIVES
    B. The study seeks to answer the following questions:
        1. What percentage of high schools in Oregon have engaged in curriculum alignment?
        2. What procedures have administrators, teachers, and specialists used to align curriculum content with instruction and test content?
        3. Does students' performance on achievement tests improve after a curriculum-alignment process has been completed in their schools?

SELF-CHECK TEST

1. One of the most common problems that educational practitioners encounter in conducting a literature search is
    a. a lack of sufficient information relevant to their topic.
    b. an overabundance of information relevant to their topic.
    c. a shortage of preliminary sources pertinent to educational topics.
    d. a shortage of primary sources pertinent to educational topics.

2. Consulting an expert prior to conducting a literature review is particularly helpful for
    a. developing a theory relating to the topic of your review.
    b. identifying critical primary and secondary sources to include in the review.
    c. establishing the credibility of your review.
    d. determining an appropriate bibliographic citation style.

3. A publication that presents a theory that was developed by the author of the publication is a
    a. secondary source.
    b. preliminary source.
    c. literature review.
    d. primary source.

4. The most important criterion for selecting the preliminary source to search in conducting a literature review is that it
    a. is available in hard-copy (print) form.
    b. uses a bibliographic citation style with which you are familiar.
    c. indexes the types of publications that contain information about your topic or problem.
    d. includes citations of annotated bibliographies.

5. In choosing descriptors with which to search a preliminary source, you should try to specify terms that
   a. are used in coding publications that are indexed by that preliminary source.
   b. are unique to your topic area.
   c. are sufficiently nontechnical that policy makers will understand them.
   d. correspond closely to the research methods and procedures that you wish to apply.

6. Reading some of the primary sources identified in your literature search will be of greatest help to you in
   a. developing a conceptual framework for making sense of the publications that you identify through your literature search.
   b. choosing the best descriptors for searching the preliminary source that you have selected.
   c. checking whether the findings of the research studies are accurately reviewed in a secondary source on which you are relying.
   d. deciding whether the preliminary source you used was sufficiently comprehensive.

7. In writing a report of your literature review, the _____ section should describe the preliminary source searched, descriptors used, and range of publication years examined.
   a. introduction   c. discussion
   b. findings   d. references

8. The primary advantage of a chart essay over a written report of a literature review is that a chart essay
   a. identifies the particular studies upon which the findings of the literature review are based.
   b. focuses on the statistics that were used to test the significance of the research findings.
   c. highlights the categories that were used to cluster the publications included in the review.
   d. is presented in a form that is more easily comprehended by lay persons.

CHAPTER REFERENCES

American Educational Research Association. (n.d.). *Electronic journals in the field of education*. Retrieved August 11, 2003 from http://aera-cr.ed.asu.edu/links.html

Cabell, D. W. (1998). *Cabell's directory of publishing opportunities in education* (5th ed.). Beaumont, TX: Cabell.

Haensly, P. A., Lupkowski, A. E., & McNamara, J. F. (1987). The chart essay: A strategy for communicating research findings to policy makers and practitioners. *Educational Evaluation and Policy Analysis, 9,* 63–75.

Houston, J. D. (Ed.), (1995). *Thesaurus of ERIC descriptors* (13th ed.). Phoenix, AZ: Oryx.

Publication manual of the American Psychological Association (5th ed.). (2001). Washington, DC: American Psychological Association. See also the website: www.apastyle.org

Resources for Further Study

Dunkin, M. J. (1996). Types of errors in synthesizing research in education. *Review of Educational Research, 66*, 87–97.

> *The author identifies nine types of errors that sometimes occur in literature reviews. For example, reviewers might exclude relevant literature, report details of a study incorrectly, or draw unwarranted conclusions from the literature reviewed.*

Henson, K. T. (1998). *Writing for professional publication: Keys to academic and business success.* Boston: Allyn & Bacon.

> *This book provides useful guidelines for educators who wish to prepare their literature review as a manuscript to submit for publication. It includes a discussion of how to write journal articles, books, and grant proposals in education. An appendix describes the characteristics (e.g., circulation, percentage of accepted manuscripts, manuscript length) of a representative sample of education journals.*

In the following section of the chapter you will read a literature review prepared by a student as part of the requirements for a master's degree in educational leadership. It is preceded by comments written especially for this book by the author of the paper. Then the paper itself is reprinted in full, just as it appeared when submitted to the university awarding the degree. Where appropriate, we have added footnotes to help you understand the information contained in the paper.

Sample Literature Review
Shifting the Paradigm from "At Risk" to "At Promise": A Review of the Construct of Resilience and Its Educational Applications

Kappa, S. L. (2002). Shifting the paradigm from "at risk" to "at promise": A review of the construct of resilience and its educational applications. Unpublished master's paper. Eugene, OR: University of Oregon.

● **RESEARCHER'S COMMENTS,** *Prepared by Sandra Kappa*

I did this review of the literature on resilience to fulfill the University of Oregon's requirement of a capstone research project for a master's degree combined with initial administrator licensure. I began the review two months prior to the tragic events of September 11, 2001, and completed it about a year later. The resilience I observed in the United States in the face of growing insecurity and profound change in our collective way of life makes this time frame significant to my project.

I began by brainstorming about educational research topics I found interesting, followed by an initial meeting with my project guide, Joy Gall. Joy was quick to pinpoint the area (at risk students) about which I was most passionate. Joy shared my concern that so much emphasis was being placed on early interventions as the only viable course for changing the direction of an "at risk" student's life. This prompted me to look at the issue of "at risk" students in a wider sense that, in turn, helped me draw broader conclusions from the literature review that can be applied to students of any age.

As an aspiring school administrator, I recognize the importance of facilitating teacher growth and development. I want to foster student growth by nurturing teachers' professional development and ensuing continuous school improvement and reform (Henderson & Milstein, 2003). I felt that having a deeper understanding of how to help "at risk" students would provide me with a means to assist teachers in their endeavors in this challenging area of educational life. As I immersed myself in the literature, I came to realize that not only could I create a learning environment in the classroom that would help students build resilience, but I could, as an educational leader, help build teacher resilience, too.

The initial questions to which I wanted answers from the literature developed from my own childhood experiences with abuse, poverty, and neglect. As a child I succeeded brilliantly in school, and I have had a rich and happy personal life in spite of the adversity and hardships I faced in my childhood. Unfortunately, my younger brother, who was raised with the same hardships, has not "bounced back." I remember discovering the term "invulnerable" to describe children who flourish in spite of adversity. Are there such children, and had I been one, or was my resilience explainable in some other way?

I started with a very scattered set of questions about the impact I was potentially having on my students and the transformation that I hoped to bring about but did not see much evidence of, despite my best efforts. I felt that my personal experiences put me in a better position to understand others who had experienced adversity and connect with them. I postulated that this connection would help me to magically help them transform as I had transformed. Surely, I thought, caring deeply about the children should make a difference and should be a successful means to make such transformations happen.

My initial search keyword was "at risk," and I found a wealth of literature relating to that liberally used term. I wondered how I would ever wade through the mountain of books and journal articles and make some meaningful synthesis of it. In particular, I wondered whether I would find research-based methods for "fixing" the "at risk" students I care about so deeply.

I thought I would have plenty of time during the course of the year to go back and reread material for the purpose of highlighting ideas for possible citation in the report of the literature review. The truth is, an effective method of coding the "big ideas" early on would have saved me much time. On the other hand, because I cast my net very wide in my literature search, I was able to draw from other disciplines, such as rehabilitative studies. As a result, I stumbled upon the concept of salutogenesis, the idea that people who are sick or injured will naturally try to adapt or return to the initial state of health. Applying this concept to kids who are "at risk" led me to the discovery of the website of the National Resilience Resource Center (2003), where I first saw the term "at promise." I was already seeking to shift my thinking away from the idea that there was some hopeless group of children who, because of risk factors, were doomed to lifelong failure. I began to believe that even if there was no "magic bullet," there might be an innate push towards adaptation that could be fostered by focusing on children's strengths. The term "at promise" helped to crystallize this shift in my thinking.

Based on what I know now, I would have started this literature review by first trying to find and talk with experts in the field of at-risk and resilience research, noting the authors and seminal works they mentioned. I would then start my review with that background information. Then I'd go back to talk to the experts again. I believe that this approach would have helped me find more meaning in the literature and draw stronger conclusions from it. The prospect of actually writing the literature review was daunting in spite of my usual enjoyment of the writing process. I didn't feel I was enough of an expert in spite of the countless hours and numerous articles and books I had read. There were so many sources and related subjects that I could have kept reading for another year easily.

I found, though, that a deeper understanding of the literature began to develop as I started to write. The paper went through many drafts, and the collaborative style of my project guide, Joy, was invaluable because her questions helped me to clarify, expand, and relate the synthesis of the findings to my own experiences in a powerful way. Indeed, Joy fostered my own resilience as a researcher by asking questions that prompted a deeper view of the literature and, as important, demanded a personal connection between my experiences as a teacher and application of the research findings to those experiences. This dialogue profoundly affected my confidence as a writer, researcher, and educator, particularly at a time in my life when I could easily have been overwhelmed with all of the work I was simultaneously responsible for besides this project: mother, teacher, graduate student and aspiring educational administrator.

I found it helpful to evaluate and synthesize the literature around the question, "What can I do as an administrator to make my school one that fosters resilience?" Howard and Johnson's study, cited in my paper, was particularly relevant to this question. They found a "pervasive theme concerning the need for help with school work" (p. 328) when students were asked what schools could provide them to help overcome their hardships. Some of the suggestions students made for how the school could help them were to provide additional learning assistance programs, special tutors, individual attention, and patient help from teachers when tasks proved too difficult for the students. Ironically, the teachers who were surveyed had barely mentioned formal learning at all, focusing instead on the importance of social skills training and making children feel comfortable and secure within the school. These findings illustrate how research can help teachers question and improve their taken-for-granted practices.

Indeed, I've learned that research related to the improvement of one's professional practice never ends. Each research study leads to new questions and new understandings. As a researcher and educator, one must have a willingness to ask fresh questions, consider new directions, and shift paradigms in the face of research-based evidence.

As I researched and wrote this paper, my incredulity regarding the events of 9 11 gave way to a realization of the tremendous vulnerability we all share as Americans and as human beings on this planet. I concluded my paper with the idea that applying the paradigm shift of considering our society "at promise" rather than "at risk" may be a more constructive response to the troubling world climate. It stands to reason that applying the precepts of caring, authentic helpfulness, responsiveness to individual needs, and a shift in our thinking from a deficit model to one of possibility and promise will help our country continue to be resilient in the face of great challenges.

References

Henderson, N., & Milstein, M. (2003). *Resiliency in schools: making it happen for students and educators*. Thousand Oaks, CA: Corwin.

National Resilience Resource Center. Retrieved 1/17/03 from www.cce.umn.edu/nrrc/research.shtml

Shifting the Paradigm from "At Risk" to "At Promise": A Review of the Construct of Resilience and Its Educational Applications

Sandra Kappa
Unpublished Master's Paper
University of Oregon, Eugene, Oregon

Abstract

Teachers and administrators who seek to make a difference in the lives of students "at risk" of failure in schools can assist students by promoting protective factors within the school to foster students' resilience. This resilience building can affect school climate, student achievement and, potentially, successful adaptation in adult life. Research on independent variables associated with the study of resilience theory shows promising results, but more research and standardized definitions of terms and methodologies are needed to move education from the theoretical to the practical with valid interventions.

INTRODUCTION

This literature review began with the research question "How can I know if what I do is having a positive effect on kids in my classroom who are clearly 'at risk' of failure?" I wanted to focus on "problem" kids—those whose behavior is never quite transformed but is merely managed. I postulated that such "at risk" students must be victims of some sort of deficit, whether social, economic, emotional, behavioral or intellectual, which caused them not to fit within the normal boundaries of school achievement and participation. As a teacher I was frustrated to feel that the students I had the most trouble managing hadn't really changed over the course of a school year. I knew I had done my best to move them forward, but I had a gnawing sense that I had failed to do my job—transform their behavior. I wondered if anything I had done might at some point in their future emerge as having had a transformational positive impact, and if I could do anything differently that might be more effective with my future students.

I have served mainly in rural school districts since I began teaching ten years ago, teaching almost all levels from grades 1 to 6 during my career. Currently, I teach third grade and have taught at this level for the past four years. Given the population I am currently serving, the question of risk and its relationship to student performance and future prospects for success is compelling, The Peridot Elementary and Middle School where I teach (a pseudonym) is a small, rural school of about 300 students in a formerly prosperous logging town. Fifty-eight percent of the students qualify for free or reduced lunch. This indicator of poverty significantly exceeds the state average of 36 percent. Indeed, many of the children of the community are fed their only meals by the school. The population of ethnic minority students is quite low (approximately three percent), and only one English as a Second Language student is currently being served. The turnover rate for students is high, with many families moving and then returning to the area in an almost cyclical fashion. Rural schools tend to have, comparatively, more "at risk" conditions such as poverty and student attrition, along with a lack of resources (Helge, 1992). The idea of tapping into resilience-building protective factors to help "at risk" students succeed potentially fits the needs of this population.

Reflecting on the more challenging students I've had in my class over the years, I realized that the classroom management techniques I used were generally the same, and involved, in order of increasing severity, verbal reprimand, parent contact, or other punitive measures such as "time out" or office referrals. For continued transgressions, the student would receive a loss of privileges such as recess time. On the positive side, I also relied on reward systems such as giving extra time on the computer for work completed or additional recess time for consistently good behavior. In more severe individual cases, I would develop an individualized tracking system of specific goals that, when met, would result in some sort of treat or other reward. Often I have used preferential seating combined with close physical monitoring to help students stay on-task. My "bag of tricks" also included some proactive, whole group, small group and individual social skills training from the program *Tribes* (Gibbs, 2001).

Academically, I survey and carefully observe students in an effort to choose material that directly interests them for their use in reading, writing, science and art activities. I also use diagnostic, formative and summative assessments in varied ways to better individualize instruction by addressing individual needs.[a] I feel that it is very important to identify the academic or social strengths of students and to plan curriculum and classroom management to put such strengths to use.

As I reflected on my own experiences with "at risk" students, I began to assess my classroom management methods for protective characteristics. What I was aiming for was something beyond mere management of problematic behavior. I wanted to address the underlying risk factors to actually help these children transform into more productive, settled, purposeful and happy students.

As I reflected, three students came to mind who defined for me the three areas of concern I have encountered in the classroom: behavioral, academic, and, social. It is important to note that while the source of the risk factor can generally be categorized in this way, the actual presentation of the problem is primarily behavioral for all three categories. I've categorized them so that I can address the core problematic mechanism that I felt served as their greatest barriers to success in the classroom. It is interesting to note that for two of these students standardized academic measures revealed high scores, but for all three students regular classroom academic achievement showed significant deficits.

John (not his real name), a third-grade male, had been identified as emotionally disturbed. He was under the care of a psychiatrist, and his recommended placement was a self-contained behavior management classroom. The self-contained classroom in the area was full. Therefore John was placed in my classroom, with no additional interventions provided except for the after-school counseling program he attended with his mother and older brother, who himself was in the self-contained behavior management classroom mentioned earlier. Although John was on medication for the control of his temper, it seemed to have little or no effect on his behavior. Through my talks with John's mother, it came to

a. In formative assessment, the teacher uses students' performance on homework, tests, and other tasks as feedback to make decisions about next instructional steps (e.g., remediation or introduction of new curriculum content). In summative assessment, the teacher judges students' level of mastery at the end of instruction for the purpose of assigning course grades or other summary indicator of learning.

light that John had witnessed her being physically and verbally abused by the father. She had separated from the father and kept custody of the two boys. The family lived in a poverty situation in this small, rural area. Although John performed well on standardized tests, his behavior was so disruptive that he spent a great deal of time out of the classroom and, consequently, achieved very little success academically. He was very much in danger of failing. Examples of his acting out included threatening other students, shouting obscenities for no apparent reason, fighting, throwing chairs and other destructive behavior, and frequent, attention-seeking verbal outbursts.

I was afraid of John. I remember talking to anyone I could find about strategies I might put in place before school began so as to get off on the right track with him. Right off the bat, I made the decision to control my tone of voice and to give as much positive feedback as I could. Even the smallest actions on his part that were positive or appropriate, I rewarded with praise. I set up a reward system in which I would place colorful, die-cut paper shapes of computer disks in a large, transparent plastic jar on John's desk whenever he did anything remotely positive or in the absence of negative behavior. When the jar was full, John could go to the computer in the classroom and play a game of his choice for 15 minutes. We would then start the process again.

I also invited John's mother to help in the classroom. She and I had several very open and honest discussions about John. At first John was very rude to his mother in class, but we made the decision to ignore the rude behavior. She spent much of her time with other students, and John was able to see them treating her with respect. His behavior improved somewhat, but his rude manner toward his mother was never fully extinguished. After the winter break when I returned to school, I was told that John and his family had moved to another town several miles away. John's mother had often complimented me on my handling of her son and although his problematic behavior continued, it had, indeed, improved to some degree. That was six or seven years ago, and I often wonder if anything I did made any difference in John's life later on.

Steven, also a third grade male student but in a different year and school than John, had many behavioral issues in the classroom. At first I thought his severe behavioral outbursts and agitation were due to the poor circumstances of his life outside school. It wasn't until the spring of that school year that I came to realize that most of his difficulties, including his behavior problems, were more likely due to academic deficits. It puzzled me that I was unable to get Steven, a verbally capable child, to produce much written work of any quality or substance. Unlike John, he was rarely violent but could be impulsively aggressive with other students when provoked in some manner. Steven had numerous risk factors in his life. His mother gave birth to him when she was only 14 years old. He, like many of the children in the area, lived in poverty. His mother suffered ongoing problems with drug and alcohol abuse. Steven was often shuttled back and forth between his mother and his grandmother's home. I knew that he might not have been capable of achieving as high a scholastic standard as I set for him, but I was fairly relentless in my manner regarding the high expectations I had for him. I was fairly tough on him: redirecting his attention several times an hour to the work at hand; sending work back to be redone; and keeping him in at recess to finish work others had long since finished. I did all this in a warm and caring manner, although at times I would feel very frustrated with Steven. However, I truly felt that firm structure, high expectations and consistent follow-through would make a difference in helping him become a successful student. I welcomed his mother in the classroom and spent a lot of time helping her to understand how she could best help Steven at home.

In the spring, after reviewing the final reading scores, I finally decided to refer Steven to the special education teacher for testing to see if he had some discernible learning difficulty that was the root of his trouble in school. Testing revealed that Steven's IQ was in the high 70's. Because there was no discrepancy between his low performance and his low test scores, Steven was not eligible for special education services. Previously I hadn't considered Steven to be a slow learner. He had seemed capable and bright to me, and

I had honestly thought that he could do the work but chose not to. I often wonder if my relentlessly high expectations for him would have been lower but more realistic if I'd referred him for testing sooner. I wonder, too, though, if he is better off today because of my having had those high expectations of him.

Jenna was also a third grade student of mine. She could sometimes produce outstanding work, but usually she would simply sit and appear to be paying attention while not actually engaged in work. She was not disruptive to the other students and when called upon directly she would usually respond in some way, however minimal, but generally she did not participate in classroom activities. Jenna, too, lived in poverty. Her mother fought constantly with Jenna's father, who lived in another state, for custody of Jenna and her two younger sisters, with each parent accusing the other of child abuse and substance abuse. Jenna had been referred to the school's student services team almost every year of her school life. Testing showed that scholastically she was capable of a very high level of achievement. The state program involving services to children and families had been contacted numerous times regarding allegations of abuse and neglect but no action had yet been taken.

The passive-aggressive nature of Jenna's refusal to do work in the absence of any verbal refusals or other negative active behaviors was frustrating and puzzling, especially considering the few times she did choose to display her more than adequate skills. I tried using timers and rewards to get at least a minimal amount of work from her in order to keep her from failing.

Jenna's mother and stepfather were frequent visitors to the school but were inconsistent in their efforts to follow through on steps we agreed upon to help Jenna complete unfinished work that was sent home. The stepfather would often arrive unexpectedly to check up on Jenna, while clearly under the influence of alcohol. The mother, during meetings, would often forget details of previous meetings, especially regarding suggestions she had made to help Jenna and her own agreements for taking responsibility at home for encouraging Jenna to finish work sent home. It was difficult to maintain a consistent set of supports for Jenna under these conditions.

As with the other students I've described, my efforts with Jenna were largely focussed on management rather than effecting any kind of transformation of her behavior. Jenna is now in sixth grade and continues to struggle with work completion and on-task issues. There is a strong social risk component evident in her interactions with others. She would often mope around at recess time and rarely interacted with other students. At the end of the year, I wondered if any of my attempts at "dangling the carrot on the stick" in front of her in order to get her to complete the bare requirements of the grade had made any lasting difference. Even more, I wondered what other things I could or should have been doing to help Jenna.

All three of these students—John, Steven, and Jenna—represent many others with whom I have worked over the years. These students have caused me to question my efficacy as a teacher. I want to make a difference to children. That's why I am a teacher. That's why I want to be an administrator. These three students are symbolic of the types of challenges a caring teacher who wants to make a difference faces. The question remains in my mind: What can I do to help them more effectively to succeed?

WHY THE CONSTRUCT OF RESILIENCE?

In my review of the literature I found many research articles devoted to identifying vulnerabilities and testing corresponding remedial interventions for students "at risk." As I pondered the huge body of information about all the different things that can go wrong in a child's world and the desire on my part to be a teacher who can make a difference for every child in my care, I felt overwhelmed. I found it difficult to focus on a single risk factor, yet that seemed necessary if I was to have any reasonable chance of completing this master's paper.

It was the sense of feeling overwhelmed that caused me to choose the framework of a literature synthesis for my master's project. I knew I had some very important burning questions, but the questions themselves were quite unfocused and uninformed. I needed much more information, and a clearer focus for my research. I could have chosen to work on developing a model for applying resilience theory in the school or classroom. I felt my time would be better served to first learn all I could about the construct and its components through a thorough literature review. However, my review provides numerous suggestions for the promotion of resilience in the classroom and in the school. Indeed, my attitude toward teaching has been fundamentally affected by this literature review, such that my awareness of the protective mechanism school can afford students in need will surely have a positive effect on my current and future classroom teaching and schoolwide leadership endeavors. I feel so strongly about my findings that I fervently hope to continue working in this area.

In my literature review I was struck by the optimism of a few articles that referred to something called "resilience." I decided to pursue my research on this theoretical construct. Its holistic and optimistic nature appealed to me on a philosophical level. I was gratified to find a substantial and growing body of research, mostly theoretical but with some very important practical successes (Luther, Cicchetti & Becker, 2000a&b; Miller, Brehm & Whitehouse, 1998).

Some studies of resilience show the positive effects of teacher rapport on student achievement (Bowen & Bowen, 1998). In one study, abused students who were provided with a "supportive and nurturing network of services" in the school had a significantly lower likelihood of engaging in risky behaviors (Brown & Block, 2001). In another study, an early intervention program, with aspects similar to a mentoring program for young students (grades 1 to 4) identified as being "at risk" for social adjustment, resulted in significant and positive changes in social variables associated with adaptive behavior (Nafpaktitis & Perlmutter, 1998). An action research study designed to assess a resilience-building program for sixth graders showed promise for reducing violence and promoting resilience in youth who are "at risk" from environmental factors (Meyer & Farrell, 1998).

I found that the construct of resilience incorporates a multidisciplinary approach to a cluster of psychological, educational and emotional concerns. This approach can be likened to medical research on physical health concerns that seeks to promote health and prevent disease rather than simply prescribe treatments when ill health arrives (Howard & Johnson, 1999; Luther, et al., 2000a&b). This multidisciplinary approach promotes "out of the box" strategies to restructure the school environment, such that the school can act as a catalyst and an agent of resource management to meet the varying needs of students who would not otherwise be ready or able to participate in the fundamental activity of academic learning for which schools were built (Maeroff, 1998).

New research questions emerged as I followed this new path: What is resilience? What are protective factors? How can protective factors or processes be used in the classroom? Are the programs or models that operationalize protective factors supported by action research findings?

WHAT IS RESILIENCE?

Resilience is "the power or ability to return to the original form or position after being bent, compressed, or stretched" (*Random House Dictionary*, 1968, p. 1123). Resilience is further defined as, "the ability to recover readily from illness, depression, adversity or the like." Buffering or protective factors are commonly evident in resilient children, that is, students who seem to rise above the social, economic and environmental deficits in their lives and avoid the potential harmful effects of such adversity (Rak & Patterson, 1996). Studies suggest that by helping students develop or tap into such protective factors, schools enable students to help themselves achieve and succeed in school and in life.

Resilience has been shown to be a cluster or combination of protective factors that operate together during times when risk factors (such as illness, depression, and adversity) are present and offer the student the best chance to build a capacity for recovery. "Resiliency is more appropriately understood as a continuum" (Bradley, et al., 1994) and ". . . adaptive functioning is subject to change over time . . ." thus indicating the need for a process or set of processes that create a mechanism within which risks can be ameliorated depending on individual needs. "Just as risks seem to accumulate to the detriment of children's health and development, protective mechanisms seem to accumulate to their benefit" (Bradley, et al., 1994).

Resilience is not one single moment in time in which a person "bounces back" and is forever free from the negative effects of risk (Bradley, et al., 1994). Because the continuum of risk and resilience is fluid and ever-changing, because labeling students for the purpose of direct interventions that focus on deficiencies about which they may have little control poses dangers, and because of children's natural and innate advancement toward health, it would seem that a focus on promoting resilience and providing the means for children to build their resilience capabilities is an important and worthwhile goal for schools to adopt.

Resilience is related to the medical concept of salutogenesis: the origin of health. Salutogenesis refers to the time and place before which maladjustment begins to occur, as well as the consistent and innate push to grow in a healthy way in spite of trauma, disease or adverse conditions (Levenstein, 1994; Lustig, et al., 2000; Rak & Patterson, 1996; Strumpfer & Mlonzi, 2001). Resilience research involves efforts to glean understanding from this process and then search for practical applications through the promotion of such factors and processes to help children build their capacity for achieving good outcomes in the face of adversity (Luthar, et al., 2000a&b).

DEFINITIONS OF "AT RISK" AND ADVERSITY

The term "at risk" is reminiscent of medical terminology regarding the potential for poor health outcomes as a result of behaviors or conditions present in the patients' lives. It is a broad, loosely defined term that has a variety of negative predictive outcomes, including being "at risk" of dropping out of school several years down the road, being "at risk" for perpetrating violence in the classroom as a result of abuse suffered, and the prediction of a life lived in poverty and hopelessness as a result of social capital deficits.

Similarly, adversity, as defined by Irwin Sandler, is that which, ". . . threatens the satisfaction of basic human needs and the acquisitions of competencies to carry out valued social roles" (Sandler, 2001). Further, ". . . an adverse condition [is] a relation between children and their environments that threatens the satisfaction of basic human needs and goals and impedes the accomplishment of age appropriate developmental tasks" (Sandler, 2001, p. 20).

Adverse conditions include internal risk factors like learning disabilities and physical handicaps. External risk factors can include family violence, parental substance abuse, parental criminality, divorce, large family size, single parenthood, child abuse and neglect, poor child rearing skills and poverty (Howard & Dryden, 1999). Risk factors associated with institutions like schools include bullying by peers, unsympathetic teachers, inappropriate boundaries and rules, or doing little to invite or encourage parental/school communication (Howard & Dryden, 1999).

MOVING FROM REACTIVE TO PROACTIVE

The traditional "at risk" intervention model, wherein the school seeks to respond or react to deviant behavior, can actually increase student risk by placing students in a lose/lose situation (Osterman, 2000). If the student is acting out on the basis of some non-school related difficulty and the school's response is to further penalize or stigmatize the student, the school is then further harming the student and, consequently, contributing to the risk (Osterman, 2000).

For instance, one day Steven came to school wearing pink fingernail polish and eye shadow. I'm not sure exactly what the motive was, but I got the distinct impression that his mother and he had been playing "dress-up" together and he decided to wear the makeup to school. This could have been a disruptive event if I had chosen a course of action that would have escalated it, such as sending him to the office on a behavior referral. Needless to say, his behavior was inappropriate and unexpected, but to draw undue attention to it and/or to invite peer scorn would have done Steven a great disservice. I venture a guess that in a classroom not so forgiving this could have resulted in a traumatic event for Steven; school could have put him at further risk if he'd been teased or disproportionately punished.

Although there was some twittering from a few students in the class, all I had to do was remind the students of the rules we'd agreed upon, which included "no put-downs," and Steven's unusual appearance was dismissed quietly and without incident. The next day he came to school without makeup, and he did not repeat that behavior. What could have put him at greater risk, instead, became an experience of acceptance and kindness. This example is somewhat simplistic in nature, but it does illustrate the importance of having an environment set up such that strengths have been built up and children feel safe that even if they are different in some way, they will still be accepted members of the group.

To move to a more proactive strategy that would seek to help students succeed given the likelihood of problematic responses to certain behaviors (such as a boy wearing makeup to class), one must set up the environment so that the likelihood of these responses is decreased (Krovetz, 1999). For instance, if the culture of the school is such that teasing or making fun or put-downs are not permitted, if Steven shows up with nail polish on, we already have the means in place to diffuse the situation, keep the disruption to a minimum, and thus protect Steven's self-esteem and sense of belonging (Osterman, 2000).

SHIFTING THE PARADIGM FROM "AT RISK" TO "AT PROMISE"

The nature of the pathogenic term "at risk," especially when combined with the deleterious effects of labeling students, can operate as a self-fulfilling prophecy. Howard & Dryden state, ". . . students labeled by schools as vulnerable or "at risk" are often those whose appearance, language, culture, values, home communities, and family structures often do not match those of the dominant culture . . ." (Howard & Dryden, 1999). From this subjective ideological perspective, the effect of assigning a self-fulfilling label ("He's the trouble-maker" or "He's certainly going to wind up on the front

page of the crime section someday") can further alienate students identified as "different" and can work against the more inclusive provisions of promoting the protective mechanism (Osterman, 2000). Potentially, we all could be assigned the label of "at risk," given the nature of our stress-laden culture and current world events today. "Life inevitably entails threats, after all, no matter how comfortable one's circumstances" (Finley, 1994). In some ways, if the wrong combination of challenges and deficits in resources combined to prohibit or preclude success in any given instance, any student could potentially be "at risk" for failure in a given developmental task.

Identifying and labeling students as "at risk" focuses on intervening to change children and/or families in order to better fit into the school structure, rather than changing the school structure to accommodate the needs of the students (Howard & Dryden, 1999). Adopting a more proactive approach, in which the school assumes students have a diversity of needs, identifies students' strengths, and builds on those strengths by creating an environment of emotional safety, can better serve as a protection to those students who are facing adversity outside the school environment (Krovetz, 1999).

Werner and Smith, in their seminal longitudinal study of over 600 people in Kauai, Hawaii, over a 40-year period, found that most children have an innate push to develop positively even in the face of adversity, and that their caring relationships, competent behavior and positive self-concept can flourish even in the face of extraordinary life difficulties (Werner & Smith, 1982, 1992). Children who live in the shadow of major external challenges (like abuse, neglect, poverty), who have faced some overwhelming trauma (like the death of a parent or sibling) or who struggle with personal disadvantage (like physical or learning disabilities), frequently surmount such difficulties and succeed beyond the predicted inferior outcome one might expect would result from such bleak circumstances (Werner & Smith, 1982, 1992).

One compelling story is told in an article written by one of the "at risk" children originally identified in the Werner & Smith study (Kitashima, 1997). Mervlyn Kitashima, now grown, wrote about the things that made a difference to her that she believes are responsible for her having grown up into a successfully adapted adult. Of her childhood, she writes:

> We were "those children." You know what "those children" are?—the ones where you as parents say to your own, "I don't want you playing with 'those children.' I don't want you going to 'those people's house.'" We were the "those children" that nobody wanted around.

Mervlyn lists a number of factors that she feels made a difference in her life. One struck me as particularly poignant. From time to time her grandmother would look after her when her parents, both alcoholics, were incapacitated. Mervlyn writes, "My Grandma Kahuanaele never treated me like one of 'those children.'" When Mervlyn stayed at her Grandma's house during her mother's institutionalization, she suffered from nightmares. Mervlyn's Grandma, who had had a leg amputated in childhood, would crawl on her hands and knees down the hall to make sure that Mervlyn was okay in the night; she wouldn't even spare the time to put her wooden leg back on. Mervlyn writes of ". . . an example, a memory, of caring and support unsurpassed by anything else for me." This simple yet courageous act demonstrated the level of love and devotion this caregiver had for the child, and the child, long since grown, remembers. This child, born into poverty, surrounded by disadvantage, went on to become a successful adult and contributing member of society.

Even better news is that, of Mervlyn's seven siblings, six are doing well in their lives. Only one sister succumbed to drug abuse and a life on the streets. Mervlyn writes, "Six out of seven, not bad." This mirrors Werner and Smith's findings: Most "at risk" children overcame their adversity-filled childhoods to become successful adults (Werner & Smith, 1982, 1992). Considering children who are facing adversity to be "at promise" rather than "at risk" will help to prevent such children from fulfilling a negative self-concept imposed on them by others. It is amazing to realize how many people do succeed in life despite the challenges, trauma

and mistreatment they might have experienced as children, but it gives much hope to those of us who seek to make a difference for them.

KEY PROTECTIVE FACTORS

Studies of children who demonstrate resilience have found some common factors that are present either internally, as part of their personality or way of dealing with the world, and externally, from family, school and community influences that buffer the child (Anthony & Cohler, 1987; Seligman, 1995; Werner & Smith, 1982, 1992). Such protective factors seem to work together in a process whereby adverse conditions are ameliorated (Benard, 1997; Werner & Smith, 1982, 1992). This is not a prescriptive, step-by-step process (Bradley, et al., 1994; Christiansen, 1997; Doll & Lyon, 1998). Not all protective factors are present at all times in the resilient child (Bradley, et al., 1994). Development of resilience is fluid, complicated, and more an evolving process than a single experience. That is, the risk and protective factors interact in such a way that the outcome ends up being positive in spite of the risk factor or factors present, and the outcome is not a particular occurrence but, instead, a continual adjustment and growth mechanism operating in the face of challenges or traumas as they arise (Bradley, et al., 1994; Looper & Grizenko, 1999).

Protective factors or mechanisms ameliorate the effects of disadvantage or adversity (Dugan & Coles, 1989; Garmezy, 1991; Henderson, Benard & Sharp-Light, 2000; Krovetz, 1999). Protective factors work together to support the strengths the child possesses (Dugan & Coles, 1989; Garmezy, 1991; Krovetz, 1999). They come to the fore when risk factors might otherwise overcome. Focus on protective factors contrasts with a risk-management model for "at risk" students (Bowen & Bowen, 1998). The use of an approach that focuses on children's strengths rather than deficiencies, is flexible to address individual differences rather than seeking to fit the child to a preconceived mold, and changes school structures to serve individual needs can result in more positive outcomes (Bowen & Bowen, 1998; Howard & Dryden, 1999; Miller, 1997).

INTERNAL PROTECTIVE FACTORS

Internal protective factors include temperament, cognitive skills, and a special kind of persistence and positive responsiveness (Dugan & Coles, 1989).[b] Children who have an internal locus of control are less vulnerable to the outside influences of risk factors (Dugan & Coles, 1989). Children who have a sense of "power rather than powerlessness" seem to bounce back more readily than those who do not (Garmezy, 1991). Being active rather than passive, being persistent in a flexible manner such that the same mistakes are not made again and again, and garnering support from adults are all examples of internal attributes that act as protective factors in the face of adversity (Bowen & Bowen, 1998; Garmezy, 1991). Children who possess such internal protective factors tend to show social competence that invites positive relationships with others. Despite the difficulties in their lives, they tend to have an effective problem-solving approach to such situations and a sense of independence, purpose and future (Werner & Smith, 1982, 1992).

EXTERNAL PROTECTIVE FACTORS

External protective factors include the presence of a parental surrogate figure such as a neighbor, teacher or other authority figure in the absence of responsive parents. (Krovetz, 1999; Werner & Smith, 1982, 1992). A supportive family culture in which there are appropriate boundaries and rules also promotes resilience in children who are otherwise "at risk" (Garmezy, 1991).

INSTITUTIONAL PROTECTIVE FACTORS

Institutional structures can also serve as protective factors if the student finds warmth, cohesion and a sense of belonging to a larger community (Barton-Arwood, Jolivette & Massey, 2000; Bowen & Bowen, 1998; Guetzloe, 1997; Osterman, 2000). It is important for children's resilience that they have at least one caring and nurturing relationship with an adult in the community or school (Werner & Smith, 1982, 1992). Indeed, "Schools serve as a critical support system for children seeking to escape the disabling consequences of poor environments" (Garmezy, 1991). Schools can offer children "at risk" stimulation, emotional support, structure, and physical safety, all of which are important protective factors in overcoming adversity (Bradley, et al., 1994). Schools can offer plentiful opportunities for students "at risk" to participate meaningfully in activities and within groups (Benard, 1997; Werner & Smith 1982, 1992). School is an excellent place to promote "required helpfulness" in which "at risk" students find meaning and purpose to their lives as they authentically participate in helping others (Benard, 1997; Werner & Smith 1982, 1992).

Students who feel that teachers care about them and show an interest in them tend to have higher grades and to be more invested in their education (Bowen & Bowen, 1998). It is vitally important for teachers to become aware of how significant an impact we can have on "at risk" students' success. Having high expectations that are effectively and clearly communicated to the student is an important protective factor that teachers can provide (Benard, 1997). Research shows, unfortunately, that many "at risk" students already receive less teacher support than low risk students (Bowen & Bowen, 1998). It is imperative that teachers understand the importance of "conveying warmth, concern, respect and a desire to have students in attendance" and to specifically target "at risk" students to provide additional support and understanding (Bowen & Bowen, 1998).

SCHOOL AS A PROTECTIVE MECHANISM

In a qualitative study by Sue Howard and Bruce Johnson (Howard & Johnson, 2000), the students and teachers interviewed from several disadvantaged areas in South Australia expressed similar views on the role of family and the community pertaining to resilience but expressed different views on the role of the school. Teachers felt that they helped most by providing social and emotional support for children via both formal and informal contact. Surprisingly, only some of the children agreed with the importance of this aspect of support on

---

b. Individuals with an internal locus of control habitually believe their successes and failures are due to their own efforts or abilities rather than to luck or chance.

the part of the school. When they did speak about teacher social support as important, it was generally in the context of intervening in bullying situations. Both teachers and students agreed on the importance of the school's role in promoting a good link of communication between home and school as a means of improving a child's circumstances. Interestingly, students were most concerned with and felt the most important aspect of school support needed was in the area of the school's ability to supply additional assistance with learning difficulties and challenges.

Howard and Johnson's study reflects an interesting and unexpected viewpoint for teachers to consider when questioning the efficacy of their teaching philosophy. Their study highlights the importance of student perceptions of their own academic successes in the promotion of resilience in these students. As mentioned previously, one protective factor that has been identified is that of high academic expectations being communicated to the student. This, along with the students' indications of the importance of extra help for succeeding academically, and the danger of "at risk" students having lower expectations and less teacher-initiated contact, points to one very powerful component of resilience: individual teachers individualizing instruction to maximize academic success in a meaningful, relevant and achievable but realistically high way (Howard & Dryden, 1999).

Concern has been expressed about systemic efforts in schools to promote resilience as faddish and consequently short-lived (Doll & Lyon, 1998). Nevertheless, the strong success for students when such protective factors have been operationalized into programs promoting resilience in the classroom provide compelling reasons for educators to shift their paradigm and promote an atmosphere in schools that, to borrow from the medical field again, will ". . . help, or at least to do no harm" (Hippocrates in *Epidemics,* Bk. I, Sect. XI; tr. by W. H. S. Jones). While caution is needed in implementing programs designed to promote resilience, the developing body of research does support the concept of institutionalizing those protective factors that are preventive or promotional for building individual resilience (Henderson, et al., 2000; Krovetz, 1999).

For example, in my school, Jenna, who awaits identification for special education and/or some type of home intervention by the state program involving services to children and families, likes to draw and will do so when given the opportunity. Building on her strength, I can modify the classroom assignments such that her drawing can be incorporated. This particular institutionalizing effect for building resilience involves individualizing instruction to build on student strengths rather than singling the student out and penalizing her with some ineffectual punitive action. I think it is important to note here that I am not suggesting that Jenna's difficulties be ignored. Instead I mean that Jenna will be more likely to succeed in the future if the school first recognizes her strengths and builds upon them.

Promoting resilience should be a priority of schools (Krovetz, 1999). Teachers need to change their thinking such that they take pride in ". . . the most worthy of societal enterprises—the enhancement of competence in their children and their tailoring, in part, of a protective shield to help children withstand the multiple vicissitudes that they can expect of a stressful world" (Garmezy, 1991). This competence refers to the child's ability to successfully adapt and respond to adversity and difficulty (Finley, 1994). Teachers need to realize that their ". . . appropriate role is to think of oneself as a protective figure whose task is to do everything possible to enhance students' competence" (Garmezy, 1991). We as educators may rarely be able to transform students' lives or behavior, but we can always teach skills, provide a caring, supportive atmosphere, and communicate high, realistic standards, thus enabling students to build such competence and ultimately experience success as we tap into the innate salutogenic pursuit of health evident in all living things.

HOW CAN PROTECTIVE FACTORS BE OPERATIONALIZED SCHOOL-WIDE?

Resilience theory, when applied school-wide, effects change in the school climate (Krovetz, 1999). A list of suggestions for promoting resilience building in schools emerged from the Werner and Smith study (Werner & Smith, 1982, 1992) and is echoed in several other articles (Benard, 1997; Henderson, et al., 1999; Krovetz, 1999; Osterman, 2000):

- Provide authentic and meaningful opportunities for children to be helpful
- Provide optimistic leadership
- Address individual and intensive academic or social interventions for those in need
- Assess strengths and protective factors along with deficits and risks
- Maintain caring connections with children who leave the school
- Refer to children in positive terminology
- Create an authentic atmosphere of an extended family at school
- Provide plentiful opportunities for meaningful participation
- Communicate high expectations and the belief that such expectations can be met by the child

The literature suggests that we can do more for "at risk" students by taking a preventive, proactive approach to bolstering students' strengths rather than waiting for failure to occur and then applying, or attempting to apply, remedies that are beyond the scope of the usual school boundaries (Henderson, et al., 2000; Krovetz, 1999). School is a good place to operationalize protective factors. Individual teachers using effective teaching techniques can provide the best environment for protective mechanisms to operate (Garmezy, 1991; Howard & Dryden, 1999). Building a "mentoring structure" or "protective community" within the school will effectively enhance student success at school and in life (Guetzloe, 1997; Henderson, et al., 2000; Miller, 1997; Osterman, 2000; Terry, 1999; Young & Wright, 2001). A significant connection between the quality of the teacher-student affective relationship and subsequent student academic performance has been demonstrated (Bowen & Bowen, 1998). This suggests that even an effort by individual teachers to communicate positive affect and demonstrate willingness to support students who are struggling can improve student achievement and is thus clearly a protective factor that can be easily operationalized in the school to the benefit of many.

A school climate that promotes pro-social bonding promotes resilience in students (Henderson, et al., 2000). Examples of such bonding include encouraging supportive and caring relationships with others in the school community. Mentoring programs can be viewed as one aspect of the protective mechanism schools can provide for students. A school environment that sets clear and consistent boundaries is another protective mechanism (Henderson, et al., 2000). Current research on Effective Behavioral Support (EBS) programs shows that such programs succeed by focusing on the positive while actually providing articulated behavior training to students (Lewis, Sugai & Colvin, 1998).[c] This study suggests that, "Critical to the success of any school-wide system is the reduction of risk factors among children during their life spans." Clearly, EBS systems can be school-wide resilience-building instruments. Cooperative learning programs, such as the *Tribes* program, can provide a means for social skills training that is also an operationalized resilience-building approach (Gibbs, 2001).

SUGGESTIONS FOR FURTHER RESEARCH

One potential problem, perhaps mostly political in nature, is the question of whether resilience depends more on experience (nurture) or the innate qualities (nature) of the child. That is, is the ability of children to "right themselves" over time more a function of their internal qualities or is their recovery largely due to environmental factors? Critics of school resilience-building programs may argue that students who succeed must do so by ". . . pulling themselves up by their own bootstraps" (Gelman, 1991). It would be interesting to see if there is indeed any difference in the relationship between populations of "at risk" children and their successful or

---

c. Effective Behavioral Support is a research-based program that aims to improve student behavior and motivation. It involves a schoolwide effort to recognize and reinforce students' positive behaviors while extinguishing negative behaviors by reducing the attention given to them.

unsuccessful adaptation when viewed by the number or quality of resilience-building experiences.

Von Eye and Schuster (2000) developed several sample research designs that can be used to analyze the construct of resilience from different perspectives. They make several suggestions for the development of more "controlled causal analysis of resilience." They also give voice to the dilemma that, as compelling and hopeful as resilience theory and its potential for therapeutic interventions, "the conceptual, empirical, and methodological bases are far from clear." As in many other murky areas of educational research, it may be, as von Eye and Schuster suggest, that quasi-experimental research designs that seek to control confounding effects may be the most appropriate methodology.[d]

Several researchers focused on the need for further definition and clarity of terms in resilience research (Jew, Green & Kroger, 1999; Luther, et al., 2000a&b; von Eye & Schuster, 2000). Continued work in this area, particularly in identifying controllable independent variables and developing meaningful and quantifiable assessment tools, will help to bring greater focus and reliability to this area of study. Currently, interaction effects are "at the heart of resilience research" (Luthar, et al., 2000a).[e] With more universal and standardized terminology and methodology in place, the identification of causal and main effect relationships, and, potentially, respondent intervention strategies, will have more validity (von Eye & Schuster, 2000).

CONCLUSION

School was my "safe place." I am a person who bounced back or, more accurately, continues to bounce back from the adversity I faced in my childhood. I am successful today because of teachers and other adults who cared about me, mentored me, respected me and believed in me.

Emmy Warner, a pioneer in the field of resilience research, wrote:

Forget about getting results overnight (or within an hour!) Take a longer view! Just like the research on resiliency program building and evaluation take time and perseverance, but also an attitude of hopefulness. (Henderson, et al., 2000)

Through my life journey I've come to realize that my effect on students is not about big transformational successes skillfully manipulated by me, the idealistic and influential teacher. It is more about the little successes of the students themselves as they push forward with their strengths to grow in spite of adverse conditions. Focusing on the strengths and victories, no matter how small, can eventually lead to transformation (Benard, 1998). As a teacher or educational administrator, I can provide an environment in which such successes are more likely to happen. I can be, as Bonnie Benard (1998) puts it, a "turnaround teacher."

A key protective belief is that there are some things over which we have no control: ". . . the ultimate mystery of life . . . [we must] recognize that there are forces at work in all of our lives that are beyond human understanding" (Ridley, 1996). No matter how gifted we are as educators, we can only do so much to help students who are in need. On the other hand, if we're not there to "stand in the gap'" and if we don't at least do what we can, who else will?

I know from my own life experience how important school can be in providing a protective atmosphere for student growth. My school experience was not perfect and, indeed, there were times that school itself operated in a detrimental way in my life. Certainly, bullying, unresponsive teachers, and systemic barriers and obstacles can make school difficult for students already facing

---

d. Quasi-experimental research is a quantitative research method involving an experimental group that receives the treatment and a control group that does not receive the treatment. Unlike a true experiment, participants in a quasi-experiment are not randomly assigned to the treatment or control conditions.

e. An interaction effect is said to have occurred if an experimental intervention is found to be more effective than a control condition, but only for a certain type of individual. In other words, the intervention "interacts" with individual characteristics to produce certain outcomes. For example, a particular intervention might make boys more resilient, but have no effect on girls' resilience.

adversity in their personal lives. Still, even with its flaws, without the protective mechanism of school I am unsure what course my life would have followed but fairly certain it would not be the positive road I am now on.

Unfortunately, the pathogenic concepts of risk and deficit are more prevalent among educators and policymakers than the more salutogenic concepts of resilience and protective factors and mechanisms (Finley, 1994). What I discovered in conducting this literature review is that true transformation of troubled children's lives is not so much within my sphere of influence as is the transformation within myself as an educator to better understand and promote those protective processes that can and do help children build capacity for transforming themselves.

Karen Osterman (2000) writes, ". . . many of the changes necessary to satisfy students' needs for 'belongingness' involve drastic changes in the cultural values, norms, policies, and practices that dominate schooling . . ." According to Nan Henderson (1996), effective education and resilience-building strategies are strongly related. She writes, ". . . effective school restructuring produces a resiliency-building school and resiliency building in schools is actually the foundation of effective education."

I urge busy teachers not to think that school-wide reform to enhance resilience building is just "one more thing" they have to try to accomplish. In the course of addressing the steps to create a resilient learning community, effective teaching practices are symbiotic if not synonymous (Krovetz, 1999). Mary Finley (1994) writes:

> . . . educators need to understand more clearly what goes right even in risky circumstances, and why . . . [it's important to] regard students not as a problem to be "fixed," but as personalities to be protected—and in which to nurture internal resilience to the prevalent threats.

It is important, then, as educators, to change our thinking regarding students who are "at risk" if we truly want to make a difference in their lives—to view them as capable participants who aren't substandard or doomed to failure.

My reflection process has helped me find the commonalities between my own personal teaching philosophy and the articulated theory of resilience, and identify the protective mechanisms that my classroom management strategies mirrored. Some of the good things I did for the three children I mentioned as examples in the introduction include: showing a genuine concern and warmth for the students; inviting parents in and trying to work with them as equal partners in their child's education; setting the environment up for success; being proactive in my approach to potential problems and planning how to deal with them when they arise; and focusing on the positives while minimizing focus on the negatives.

The most obvious failure on my part was not coming to the realization that Steven really had some significant learning problems that needed to be identified and addressed outside the regular classroom setting. My assumption that his behavior was due entirely to his poor life circumstances rather than any learning disabilities or deficits, especially if I had merely passed him on to the next grade without referring him for identification in order to get him the assistance he needed, would have put him at greater risk for failure later. Indeed, in many ways, I was thinking of him as "one of those kids." One of the best things I did with these three students, and that I strive to do with all my students, is to tap into their strengths, communicate high expectations, and, most importantly, build a caring and authentic relationship with them.

Like other living things, schools as organizational entities have the same salutogenic tendency: a push towards organizational health and well-being. With all the stresses and responsibilities placed on public schools, resilience theory and its application to school climate is the key to effective school reform, especially at a time when society is more "at promise" than ever before.

References

Anthony, E. & Cohler, B. (1987). *The invulnerable child*. New York: The Guilford Press.

Barton-Arwood, S., Jolivette, K., & Massey, G., (2000). Mentoring with elementary-age students. *Intervention in School and Clinic, 36*(1), 36–40.

Benard, B. (1997). Turning it around for all youth: from risk to resilience. ERIC/CUE Digest, Number 126.

Benard, B. (1998). How to be a turnaround teacher/mentor. *Mentoring for Resiliency.* San Diego: Resiliency in Action.

Bowen, N. & Bowen, G. (1998). The effects of home microsystem risk factors and school microsystem protective factors on student academic performance and affective investment in schooling. *Social Work in Education, 20*(4), 219–232.

Bradley, R., Whiteside, L., Mundfrom, D., Casey, P., Kelleher, K., & Pope, S. (1994). Contribution of early intervention and early caregiving experiences to resilience in low-birthweight, premature children living in poverty. *Journal of Clinical Child Psychology, 23,* 425–434.

Brown, K. & Block, A. (2001). Evaluation of Project Chrysalis: A school-based intervention to reduce negative consequences of abuse. *Journal of Early Adolescence, 21*(3) 325–353.

Christiansen, J. (1997). Helping teachers meet the needs of students "at risk" for school failure. *Elementary School Guidance & Counseling, 31*(3), 204–211.

Doll, B. & Lyon, M. (1998). Risk and resilience: Implications for the delivery of educational and mental health services in schools. *School Psychology Review, 27*(30), 348–365.

Dugan, T., & Coles, R. (1989). *The child in our times: Studies in the development of resiliency.* New York: Bruner/Mazel.

Finley, M. (1994). Cultivating resilience: An overview for rural educators and parents. ERIC Digest: ED372904.

Garmezy, N. (1991). Resiliency and vulnerability to adverse developmental outcomes associated with poverty. *American Behavioral Scientist, 34*(40), 416–430.

Gelman, D. (1991). The miracle of resiliency. *Newsweek, 117*(22), 44–48.

Gibbs, J. (2001). *Tribes: A new way of learning and being together.* Windsor, CA: CenterSource Systems.

Guetzloe, E. (1997). The power of positive relationships: Mentoring programs in the school and community. *Preventing School Failure, 41*(3), 100–106.

Helge, D. (1992). Solving special education reform, problems in rural areas. *Preventing School Failure, 36*(4), 11–16.

Henderson, N., Benard, B., & Sharp-Light, N. (2000). *School-wide approaches for fostering resiliency.* San Diego: Resiliency in Action.

Henderson, N., Benard, B., & Sharp-Light, N. (1999). *Resiliency in action: Practical ideas for overcoming risks and building strengths in youth, families and communities.* San Diego: Resiliency in Action.

Henderson, N. (1996). Integrating resiliency building and educational reform: Why doing one accomplishes the other.

Resiliency in Action: A Journal of Application and Research, Spr. 1996, 35–36.

Howard, S. & Dryden, J. (1999). Childhood resilience: Review and critique of literature. *Oxford Review of Education, 25*(3), 307–324.

Howard, S. & Johnson, B. (2000). What makes the difference? Children and teachers talk about resilient outcomes for children "at risk." *Educational Studies, 26*(30), 321–340.

Jew, C. L., Green, K. E., & Kroger, J. (1999). Development and validation of a measure of resiliency. *Measurement and Evaluation in Counseling and Development, 32,* 75–89.

Kitashima, M. (1997). Lessons from my life: No more "children at risk" . . . all children are "at promise." *Mentoring for resiliency.* San Diego: Resiliency in Action.

Krovetz, M. (1999). *Fostering resiliency: Expecting all students to use their minds and hearts well.* Thousand Oaks: Corwin.

Levenstein, S. (1994). Wellness, health, Antonovsky. *The Journal of Mind–Body Health, 10*(3), 26–30.

Lewis, T., Sugai, G., & Colvin, G. (1998). Reducing problem behavior through a school-wide system of effective behavioral support: Investigation of school-wide social skills training program and contextual interventions. *School Psychology Review, 27*(3), 446–459.

Looper, K. & Grizenko, N. (1999). Risk and protective factors scale: Reliability and validity in preadolescents. *Canadian Journal of Psychiatry, 44*(2), 138–145.

Lustig, D., Rosenthal, D., Strauser, D., & Haynes, K. (2000). The relationship between sense of coherence and adjustments in persons with disabilities. *Rehabilitation Counseling Bulletin, 43*(30), 134–142.

Luthar, S., Cicchetti, D., & Becker, B. (2000a). Research on resilience: Response to commentaries. *Child Development, 71*(3) 573–575.

Luthar, S., Cicchetti, D., & Becker, B. (2000b). The construct of resilience: A critical evaluation and guidelines for future work. *Child Development, 71*(3), 543–562.

Maeroff, G. (1998). *Altered destinies: Making life better for schoolchildren in need.* New York: St. Martin's.

Meyer, A. & Farrell, A. (1998). Social skills training to promote resilience in urban sixth-grade students: One product of an action research strategy to prevent youth violence in high-risk environments. *Education & Treatment of Children, 21*(4), 461–480.

Miller, G., Brehm, K., & Whitehouse, S. (1998). Reconceptualizing school-based prevention for antisocial behavior within a resiliency framework. *School Psychology Review, 27*(3), 364–379.

Nafpaktitis, M. & Perlmutter, B. (1998). School-based early mental health intervention with at-risk students. *School Psychology Review, 27*(3), 420–432.

Osterman, K. (2000). Students' need for belonging in the school community. *Review of Educational Research, 70*(3), 323–367.

Rak, C. & Patterson, L. (1996). Promoting resilience in at-risk children. *Journal of Counseling & Development, 74*(4), 368–374.

Ridley, K. (1996). Protective beliefs are a key to professionals' and students' resiliency. *Resiliency in Action: A Journal of Application and Research,* Spr. 1996, 31–32.

Sandler, I. (2001). Quality and ecology of adversity as common mechanisms of risk and resilience. *American Journal of Community Psychology, 29*(1), 19–61.

Seligman, M. (1995). *The optimistic child.* New York: Houghton Mifflin.

Strumpfer, D. & Mlonzi, E. (2001). Antonovsky's sense of coherence scale and job attitudes: Three studies. *South African Journal of Psychology, 31*(2), 30–38.

Terry, J. (1999). A community/school mentoring program for elementary students. *Professional School Counseling, 2*(3), 237–241.

von Eye, A. & Schuster, C. (2000). The odds of resilience. *Child Development, 71*(3), 563–566.

Werner, E. & Smith, R. (1982). *Vulnerable, but invincible: A longitudinal study of resilient children and youth.* New York: McGraw-Hill.

Werner, E. & Smith R. (1992). *Overcoming the odds: High risk children from birth to adulthood.* Ithaca: Cornell University.

Young, C. & Wright, J. (2001). Mentoring: The components for success. *Journal of Instructional Psychology, 28*(3), 202–208.

chapter **3**

Using Preliminary Sources to Search the Literature

OBJECTIVES

After studying this chapter, you will be able to

1. explain how to conduct a literature search using a hard-copy preliminary source.

2. describe the usual types of information about a publication that a preliminary source provides.

3. explain the advantages of using an electronic rather than a hard-copy preliminary source to conduct a literature source.

4. explain how truncation and the use of the *and* and *or* connectors affect retrieval of publications when using an electronic preliminary source.

5. describe several options for focusing the search of an electronic version of the ERIC database.

6. understand the options available for displaying and downloading selected entries from an electronic database.

Jill Novotny is a psychologist who has worked in the field of education throughout her career. She feels that she learned the hard way (mostly by lonely trial and error) what it takes to be a good parent. Now she is writing a book about how parents can support their children's learning both in and out of school.

Jill recently read about research showing that children of authoritative parents—defined as parents who provide both a high level of structure and a high level of nurturance to their children—have more success in school and in their personal lives than other children. She wanted to find out what work was being done to help parents learn this type of parenting.

Jill looked for books on authoritative parenting, but found very little. Then she decided to do an electronic search of a preliminary source (ERIC) to identify journal articles and other reports on this topic. Her search yielded twenty-six publications that had been coded as having information about the topic of authoritative parenting. "I thought almost no one else was concerned about this," she confided to a friend. "Now I see that other professionals are working on this style of parenting, and I have much to learn from them."

This chapter takes you through the steps that are involved in using a preliminary source to search the education literature on parenting or any other topic of interest to educators. You will learn how to define your search terms, design and carry out a search, and obtain citations for the publications that appear most likely to contain information relevant to your needs. ●

THE PURPOSE OF PRELIMINARY SOURCES

As we explained in Chapter 2, the education literature includes many thousands of publications. For this reason, preliminary sources have been developed to help you conduct a **literature search,** which is the process by which you identify the publications that are relevant to your information needs. A preliminary source is an index to a particular body of literature, for example, journals that publish articles about education. The body of literature may contain both publications that have been formally published (e.g., scholarly books and professional journals) and publications that have not been formally published but are intended for distribution to a wide audience (e.g., papers presented at professional conferences and technical reports prepared by a school system). We use the term *publication* to refer to all the types of items that are indexed in a preliminary source.

A preliminary source provides a citation for each publication that it references. A **citation** typically includes the publication's authors, title, year of publication, publisher, and possibly an abstract, which is a brief summary of the information in the publication.

In Chapter 2, we described a general process for conducting a literature review. The first three steps of the process involve framing questions to guide the literature review, consulting with experts, and reading general secondary sources. The next two steps involve selecting and searching a preliminary source. This chapter explains how preliminary sources are constructed and how they can be used effectively to identify all the publications in the literature that are relevant to your information needs.

Some preliminary sources are available only in print (also called **hard-copy**) form. Others are available in **electronic** form, typically as a database accessible by the Internet. Still others are available in both hard-copy and electronic forms. We explain how to use both forms in this chapter. Although electronic preliminary sources are rapidly becoming the dominant format, we first explain how to search a hard-copy preliminary source because the process is simpler and easier to learn. Once you understand the logic of a hard-copy search, it is relatively easy to learn how to use electronic preliminary sources.

SEARCHING A HARD-COPY PRELIMINARY SOURCE

You will find it helpful to maintain a record of your search of preliminary sources. You can consult this record to remind yourself of the steps of your search strategy that you still need to complete and to make sure that you do not repeat steps needlessly. Also, you can consult this record if you prepare a report of your literature review and wish to include a description of your search strategy.

Figure 3.1 contains a form for recording the steps followed in conducting a search of a hard-copy preliminary source (also known as a *manual search*). It is

Search question(s): *What are effective ways to help parents of at-risk students increase their support of their children's academic efforts?*
Preliminary source(s) used: *RIE and CIJE*

	Time Period				
Descriptors	*1999*	*2000*	*2001*	*2002*	*2003*
1. ~~Parents~~					
2. ~~At risk students~~					
3. ~~Academic efforts~~					
4. *Parent**	✓	✓	✓	✓	✓
5. *High risk students*	✓	✓	✓	✓	✓
6. *Academic achievement*	✓	✓	✓	✓	✓
7.					
8.					
9.					
10.					

FIGURE 3.1   Manual Search Record for a Literature Search on Parent Involvement

filled in with information for a sample literature search described in this section of the chapter. (In the following discussion of the steps for searching a hard-copy preliminary source we explain why some terms in the Descriptors column are crossed out.) You might want to design a form like this, or adapt it as you wish, for conducting your own literature search of a hard-copy preliminary source.

Parent involvement in their children's schooling is currently a major concern of many educators. Therefore, we selected it as a topic for illustrating search procedures in using a hard-copy preliminary source. We framed a specific question to guide our literature search on this topic: "What are effective ways to help parents of at-risk students increase their support of their children's academic efforts?" As we explained in Chapter 2, the framing of questions is a critical step in conducting a literature review.

Once you have framed the question or set of questions that will guide your search, you are ready to begin the process of selecting and using a preliminary source. The steps of this process are described in the next sections.

Step 1: Selecting a Preliminary Source

There are many preliminary sources, each of which indexes a different range and type of publications, related to education. For example, *Children's Books in Print* indexes books for young readers, whereas *Psychological Abstracts* indexes journals and other types of publications covering a wide range of psychological topics, including topics that relate to education. Appendix 2 provides a list and description of preliminary sources that may be useful to you in your work as a professional educator.

The most comprehensive preliminary sources for educators are *Current Index to Journals in Education* (**CIJE**) and *Resources in Education* (**RIE**). Both are published by the Educational Resources Information Center (**ERIC**), which is funded by the U.S. Government. ERIC also provides many publications and services to educators at no cost (see www.eric.ed.gov/about/about.html).

In 2003, major changes to ERIC were announced. The Education Sciences Reform Act of 2002 eliminated the Office of Educational Research and Improvement (OERI), the agency that funded ERIC and various types of educational research. OERI was replaced by the Institute of Education Sciences, which will administer ERIC. The ERIC clearinghouses that managed different parts of the *CIJE* and *RIE* database and provided various information services are to be eliminated by the end of 2003. They will be replaced by a centralized agency that might change the scope and search mechanisms for the database.

Our description of the *CIJE* and *RIE* database and other ERIC services is based on the ERIC system that was in place up until the end of 2003. For information about changes to this system subsequent to 2003 and how they affect the database and services, you can log on to this website: www.eric.ed.gov.

CIJE indexes more than 1,000 articles in nearly 800 education-related journals each month. It has been in operation since 1969. If you need to identify journal articles and books published prior to 1969, *Education Index* is a useful preliminary source.

Whereas *CIJE* indexes journal articles, *RIE* indexes papers presented at education conferences, progress reports on ongoing research studies, technical reports on studies sponsored by federal research programs, and reports on projects conducted by local agencies such as school districts. These publications sometimes are called **fugitive literature** because they are not widely disseminated or easily obtained. *RIE* has indexed such publications since 1966.

If you choose an inappropriate preliminary source, you will miss many publications that are potentially important to your literature review. Therefore, it is important to select the most appropriate preliminary source. *CIJE* and *RIE* are quite adequate for most literature reviews in education. However, if you wish to do a comprehensive literature review, you most likely will need to search additional preliminary sources for publications not indexed by either *CIJE* or *RIE.*

Because *CIJE* and *RIE* are the preliminary sources most widely used by educators, we will refer to them to explain the next steps of conducting a search of a hard-copy preliminary source. Other preliminary sources generally are organized similarly, so you should be able to apply most of what we say about *CIJE* and *RIE* to them.

Step 2: Selecting Descriptors

The *Thesaurus of ERIC Descriptors* (Houston, 2001) is a reference book that helps you identify appropriate descriptors to use in searching *CIJE* and *RIE* for publications that are relevant to your problem. As we explained in Chapter 2, a **descriptor** is used to classify all publications that contain information about a particular topic. Keep in mind, though, that *CIJE* and *RIE* contain not the actual publications, but rather a citation for each publication. ERIC uses the term **entry** in *CIJE* and the term **resume** in *RIE* to refer to these citations.

To identify appropriate descriptors for your literature search, you can start by underlining the most important words or phrases in your problem statement. Using our example about parents, we underlined the following words: "What are effective ways to help *parents* of *at-risk students* increase their support of their children's *academic efforts*?" Next we listed the underlined words in pencil in the section labeled *Descriptors* of the manual search record (Figure 3.1).

The next step is to look up each of our three terms in the Alphabetical Descriptor Display of the ERIC *Thesaurus* to determine whether they are ERIC descriptors. When we look up the term *Parents,* we find the display shown in Figure 3.2. This display has the following nine features. (Two additional features, not used in this particular display but in other displays, are also described.)

1. *Main-entry designation.* The term **PARENTS** is shown in boldface capital letters. This designation indicates that *Parents* is a main-entry descriptor, meaning that it is used to classify *CIJE* entries and *RIE* resumes.

2. *Add date.* The notation *Jul. 1966* indicates when this term was entered into the *Thesaurus.*

3. *Postings.* The number 3,438 indicates the number of times, as of October 2000, that this term was used as a major or minor descriptor in *CIJE* and *RIE.*

FIGURE 3.2 Display for the Descriptor *Parents* in the Alphabetical Descriptor Display of *Thesaurus of ERIC Descriptors*

Source. Text on pp. 231–232 in Houston, J. E. (Ed.). (2001). *Thesaurus of ERIC Descriptors* (14th ed.). Westport, CT: Oryx.

PARENTS		*Jul 1966*
	Postings: 3,438	GC: 510
UF	Catholic Parents (1966 1980) #	
NT	Adoptive Parents	
	Biological Parents	
	Employed Parents	
	Fathers	
	Grandparents	
	Lower Class Parents	
	Middle Class Parents	
	Mothers	
	Parents As Teachers	
	Parents with Disabilities	
BT	Groups	
RT	Adults	
	Child Caregivers	
	Daughters	
	Early Parenthood	
	Family (Sociological Unit)	
	Family Environment	
	Family Life	
	Family Problems	
	Heads of Households	
	Home Schooling	
	Home Visits	
	Kinship	
	One Parent Family	
	Parent Aspiration	
	Parent Associations	
	Parent Attitudes	
	Parent Background	
	Parent Child Relationship	
	Parent Conferences	
	Parent Counseling	
	Parent Education	
	Parent Empowerment	
	Parent Financial Contribution	
	Parent Grievances	
	Parent Influence	
	Parent Materials	
	Parent Participation	
	Parent Responsibility	
	Parent Rights	
	Parent Role	
	Parent School Relationship	
	Parent Student Relationship	
	Parent Teacher Conferences	
	Parent Teacher Cooperation	
	Parent Workshops	
	Parenthood Education	
	Parenting Skills	
	Sons	
	Spouses	

4. *Descriptor Group Code.* The notation *GC: 510* indicates that the descriptor *Parents* is in Descriptor Group Code 510. This three-digit number indicates the broad category to which this descriptor belongs. The code is useful for identifying other descriptors that are conceptually related to a descriptor, but do not necessarily appear in the descriptor's display. When we look at the categories list on page xxv of the *Thesaurus*, we find that *GC* is the category *Groups Related to HUMAN SOCIETY,* and that *GC 510* concerns *THE INDIVIDUAL IN SOCIAL*

CONTEXT. The term *group,* as used here, refers not to groups of people, but to groups of conceptually related descriptors in the *Thesaurus.*

5. *Used for (UF) designation.* The *UF* designation preceding the term *Catholic Parents* indicates that the descriptor *Parents* should be used instead of the term *Catholic Parents* in doing an ERIC search. The information in parentheses after the term *Catholic Parents* indicates that this term was a descriptor only during the period 1966 to 1980. The # designation after the term *Catholic Parents* refers to a footnote at the bottom of the page of the Alphabetical Descriptor Display where the term appears. The footnote states that two or more descriptors are needed to represent this term. By looking in the *Thesaurus* for *Catholic Parents* as a descriptor, the reader can learn which descriptors to use instead of this term.

6. *Narrower term (NT) designation.* The *NT* designation identifies narrower descriptors that are included under the main-entry descriptor *Parents.* The ten narrower descriptors shown under *Parents* also can be searched for *CIJE* entries and *RIE* resumes relating to parents.

7. *Broader term (BT) designation.* The *BT* designation identifies broader descriptors that subsume the concept represented by the main-entry descriptor. Thus we see that the broader descriptor *Groups* includes the descriptor *Parents* as a subcategory.

8. *Related term (RT) designation.* The *RT* designation indicates related descriptors that also are main-entry descriptors in the *Thesaurus.* These related descriptors have a close conceptual relationship to the descriptor *Parents,* but do not fit the superordinate/subordinate relationship described by BT and NT. All the related terms listed under *Parents* appear elsewhere in the *Thesaurus* as main-entry descriptors. Thus, any of these descriptors can be used to search for *CIJE* entries and *RIE* resumes relating to parents.

9. *USE designation.* The information shown in Figure 3.2 does not exhaust the descriptors relating to the topic of parents in the *Thesaurus.* Over a page of the Alphabetical Descriptor Display lists main-entry descriptors that include the word *Parent* or *Parents,* from *PARENT ASPIRATION* to *PARENTS AS TEACHERS.* Another example is *Parent Absence USE ONE PARENT FAMILY.* The *USE* designation tells us that the term *Parent Absence* is not a main-entry descriptor in the *Thesaurus.* If we are interested in searching for entries or resumes relating to parent absence, we will need to use the descriptor *One Parent Family.*

10. *Scope note.* If we now check the Alphabetical Descriptor Display for our second term, *At-risk students,* we will find the term **At Risk Persons** as a main-entry descriptor, followed by the information shown in Figure 3.3. *SN* is an acronym for *Scope Note,* which is a brief statement of the intended usage of an ERIC descriptor. The scope note clarifies an ambiguous term or restricts the usage of a term, and it may give special indexing information as well. The scope note in this case directs us to a narrower term, *High Risk Students.* Therefore, we change the term *At-risk students* to *High risk students* on our manual search record (Figure 3.1).

Suppose that our main interest is how teachers can help parents as a group rather than one at a time. If we look at the descriptors under *Parents* in

FIGURE 3.3 Display for the Descriptor *At Risk Persons* in the Alphabetical Descriptor Display of the *Thesaurus of ERIC Descriptors*

Source. Text on pp. 24–25 in Houston, J. E. (Ed.). (2001). *Thesaurus of ERIC Descriptors* (14th ed.). Westport, CT: Oryx.

AT RISK PERSONS	*Apr. 1990*
Postings: 2,514	GC:120
SN	Individuals or groups identified as possibly having or potentially developing a problem (physical, mental, educational, etc.) requiring further evaluation and/or intervention (Note: if possible, use the more specific term "High Risk Students")
UF	High Risk Persons (1982 1990)
NT	High Risk Students
BT	Groups
RT	Developmental Delays
	Disabilities
	Disability Identification
	Early Identification
	Early Intervention
	Incidence
	Symptoms (Individual Disorders)

the Alphabetical Descriptor Display, we see four related terms that involve working with parents as a group: *Parent Education, Parent Workshops, Parenthood Education,* and *Parenting Skills.* However, there may be only a few or no citations under these subjects in any given monthly issue or cumulated volume of *CIJE* or *RIE.* For this reason, we decide to include in our literature search all the entries or resumes classified by any descriptor that begins with the word *Parent.* Hence we cross out the term *Parents* on the manual search record (Figure 3.1) and add the term *Parent*.* The asterisk signifies that we want to check all the entries or resumes that have been coded for any descriptors that begin with these six letters (e.g., *Parent Influence, Parenthood Education, Parents, Parenting Skills*).

In an electronic search of the ERIC database the asterisk has a similar, but slightly broader, meaning. The asterisk refers to a search procedure called *truncation,* which means that we want to see all instances of any term that includes the "trunk" of a given word, whether it occurs at the beginning of the term or not. For example, the terms *signify, insignificant,* and *resign* all contain the "trunk" *s-i-g-n.*

To determine whether *Academic efforts* is the appropriate descriptor for our search concerning parents of high-risk students, we refer to the Rotated Descriptor Display in the *Thesaurus.* A rotated descriptor display takes each descriptor in the *Thesaurus* and shows all other descriptors that share any word in common with it. For example, if we key on the word *Academic* in *Academic efforts,* the Rotated Descriptor Display will show all *Thesaurus* descriptors that also include that word, irrespective of position (e.g., *Summer Academic Classes* and *Academic Achievement*). We could do the same kind of search in the Rotated Descriptor Display for the word *Efforts.*

We scanned all the phrases in the Rotated Descriptor Display beginning with the word *Academic.* The phrase *Academic Efforts* was not listed, but a related phrase, *Academic Achievement,* was listed. Therefore we changed the term *Academic efforts* on our manual search record (Figure 3.1) to *Academic achievement.*

Most education topics of any significance are represented in the literature, so if you do not locate any publications in your area of interest, you should reconsider your descriptors and your choice of a preliminary source. Most likely you have framed your search question in terms that are different from the descriptors used by ERIC indexers. Keep in mind, too, that your descriptors might identify some relevant publications but miss others, if the **indexer** at ERIC, the individual who classified the publications, used different descriptors than the ones that you used to conduct your search.

Step 3: Using the Subject Index to Identify Entries or Resumes

The hard-copy version of *CIJE* is published as monthly issues and as semiannual cumulated volumes. The hard-copy version of *RIE* is published as monthly issues and as annual cumulated volumes. The semiannual volumes for *CIJE* provide a cumulated set of indexes and all the corresponding main entries. The annual volumes for *RIE* include only cumulated indexes, so you must check the appropriate monthly issue to find the corresponding resumes. Keep in mind that the month of a publication's first printing or presentation is not necessarily the month in which it will appear in *CIJE* or *RIE*. Several months may pass before the publication is processed for inclusion in a preliminary source.

After having selected appropriate descriptors, we are ready to search the subject index in issues of *CIJE* or *RIE* for the time period we wish to review. The headings in the subject index for a particular issue or volume of *CIJE* or *RIE* include all relevant descriptors from the *Thesaurus*, as well as other terms called **identifiers** (e.g., names of tests or organizations), that ERIC indexers used to code the publications that are indexed in that issue or volume. As we stated above, the information provided about each publication is called an **entry** in *CIJE* and a *resume* in *RIE*.

In *CIJE*, the entries constitute most of each issue or volume, and are in the front section labeled *Main Entry Section*. *CIJE* includes three other indexes besides the subject index that you can use to search for relevant articles. You can check the author index to determine whether particular authors have written publications relevant to your problem. The source journal index gives information about each journal from which articles were selected for indexing in that *CIJE* issue. In this index, the journals are grouped by the ERIC clearinghouse that reviews each journal, which helps you determine the journals that are most relevant to a given topic area. The journal contents index lists the titles of the articles in each journal issue that have been indexed in that issue of *CIJE*. For example, the *CIJE* July–December 1996 Semiannual Cumulation lists the titles and ERIC accession numbers for ten articles from the Spring 1996 and Winter 1996 issues of the journal *Review of Educational Research*.

In *RIE* the resumes constitute most of each issue, and are in the front section labeled *Document Resumes*. *RIE* includes four other indexes that you can use to search for relevant publications. If you think that particular authors or sponsoring agencies might be associated with publications relevant to your search, you can check them in the author index or the institution/sponsoring agency index, respectively. If you want to examine certain types of publications (for example, ERIC Digests, which are explained in Chapter 4), you can search for them in the publication type index. You can also examine the publications that have been reviewed by a particular ERIC clearinghouse by using the clearinghouse accession number index.

It is obviously to your advantage to search the cumulated volumes of *CIJE* or *RIE* whenever possible. By looking in the subject index of a *CIJE* semiannual volume, for example, you can find all the publications that were classified by a particular descriptor for that six-month period. All the entries or resumes for those publications are in that same volume. If you used the six monthly issues instead, you would need to repeat the process of searching the subject index and the main-entry section six times in order to cover the same time period.

All main entries in *CIJE* and document resumes in *RIE* are written in the same standard format. Because all *CIJE* main entries are from journals, they tend to have fewer format features than *RIE* document resumes. The publications indexed in *RIE* involve various publication formats (for example, papers presented at conferences and reports by government agencies). Therefore, we will use an *RIE* resume to explain the information that *CIJE* and *RIE* provide about a publication.

To initiate our search concerning parents of high-risk students, we turned to the subject index of the 1992 volume of *RIE*. We found two citations under *Parent Role* that appeared relevant to our search question.

Family Focus: Reading and Learning Together Packet   ED 347 498
School and Family Partnerships   ED 347 638

We decided to check just the second citation, so we copied down its ED number.

Next we turned to the *Document Resumes* section of the December 1992 *RIE* issue, where the resumes are arranged in numerical order. Reading the resume for ED 347 638, we found that indeed it is relevant to our problem. The document resume is shown in Figure 3.4. Below we refer to it as we explain the typical elements in an *RIE* resume. Understanding these elements will be a great help to you in identifying and reviewing literature that is relevant to your question or topic.

1. *ERIC accession number.* *ED 347 638* is the identification number for this publication. Accession numbers are sequentially assigned to publications as they are processed for indexing in ERIC. The *ED* indicates that this is a non-journal document rather than a journal article. (Journal articles begin with an *EJ* number instead.) Resumes are placed in the document resumes section of *RIE* in numerical order by their accession number. If a library maintains a microfiche file of ERIC documents, the microfiches also are stored in accession-number order.

2. *Clearinghouse accession number.* The number *EA 024 079* is an accession number assigned to publications by the specific clearinghouse that processed

ED 347 638   EA 024 079
Epstein, Joyce L.   Connors, Lori J.
School and Family Partnerships.
National Association of Secondary School Principals, Reston, Va.
Report No.—ISSN-0912-6160
Pub Date—Jun 92
Note—10p.
Available from—National Association of Secondary School Principals, 1904 Research Drive, Reston, VA 22091-1537 ($2; quantity discounts).
Journal Cit—Practitioner; v18 n4 Jun 1992
Pub Type—Collected Works - Serials (022) — Guides — Non-Classroom (055)
EDRS Price — MF101 Plus Postage. PC Not Available from EDRS.
Descriptors—*Educational Cooperation, Family Role, *Family School Relationship, Middle Schools, *Parent Influence, *Parent Role, *Parent School Relationship, School Community Relationship, Secondary Education
   Concerns about and characteristics of family/school partnerships are the theme of this issue of a "newsletter for the on-line administrator." Because of the changing natures of students, families, and schools, school administrators must take a leadership role in facilitating parent involvement in education. The six major types of involvement for comprehensive partnership programs are outlined. These include basic obligations of families; basic obligations of the school; involvement at the school; involvement in home learning; involvement in decision making, governance, and advocacy; and community collaboration. Questions to be considered for organization of partnerships are discussed; some of these include the development of a written policy, a leadership and committee structure, a budget, and an evaluation process. Examples of each type of partnership that has been implemented in middle and high schools are provided. A brief program description and contact information are included. (LMI)

FIGURE 3.4   **Document Resume from the Hard-Copy Version**
of *Resources in Education* (RIE)
Source. Resources in Education (1992, December), p. 61. Washington, DC: U.S. Government Printing Office.

them for entry into the ERIC system. Referring to the list of ERIC clearinghouses in the *Thesaurus of ERIC Descriptors,* we find that EA is the designation for the Clearinghouse on Educational Management, which was housed at the University of Oregon.

   3. *Author(s).* The names in italics below the ERIC accession number are the names of the authors of the publication. Thus we learn that this publication was written by Joyce Epstein and Lori Connors.

   4. *Title.* The title of the publication is shown next. In this example it is *School and Family Partnerships.*

   5. *Organization where publication originated.* If the publication was available in print form prior to being placed into the ERIC system, the organization where it originated is specified here. We find that our publication originated with the National Association of Secondary School Principals (NASSP) in Reston, Virginia.

   6. *Sponsoring agency.* If a different agency from the one in which the publication originated was responsible for initiating, funding, and managing the project described, it is listed after *Spons Agency.* No separate sponsoring agency is shown for this publication.

   7. *Report number.* If a report number is given, it is the number assigned to the publication by the originating organization. In this case, the report number ISSN-0912-6160 would be used to request the publication from NASSP.

   8. *Date published (Pub Date).* The Pub Date indicates the month and year in which the publication was entered in the ERIC system.

9. *Contract or grant number.* If a contract or grant number is given, it signifies the number assigned by the funding agency to the project or grant described in the publication. No contract or grant number is given for this publication.

10. *Note.* A descriptive note gives additional information about the publication, such as its page length and country of origin. We find that this publication is 10 pages long.

11. *Availability.* If the publication is available from a source other than ERIC, it is listed here. This publication is available from the National Association of Secondary School Principals. It costs $2.00 per copy, with quantity discounts available.

12. *Language of publication.* If the publication is available in a language other than English, this information is indicated. This publication is written in English only, so no language designation is included in the resume.

13. *Journal citation.* If the publication has been cited in a recent journal issue, the journal title and issue number are listed here. We checked the journal issue mentioned in the document resume shown in Figure 3.4, and found a published version of the document that was cited in *RIE.* This example illustrates that occasionally a publication is produced both as a journal article and as an *RIE* document available in microfiche form from the ERIC Document Reproduction Service (EDRS is explained in item 15).

14. *Publication type (Pub Type). Pub Type* is a three-digit code that classifies a publication by its form of publication. For example, there are separate codes for research/technical reports, dissertations and theses, and instructional materials for learners. The Pub Type code appears in the printed issues of *RIE,* but not in the printed issues of *CIJE.* Two Pub Types were assigned to our sample publication: *Collected Works—Serials (022)* and *Guides—Non-Classroom (055).*

15. *ERIC Document Reproduction Service (EDRS) availability.* This code indicates whether the publication can be ordered through ERIC's reproduction service facility. This service and other methods for obtaining ERIC-referenced publications are described later in the chapter (see step 5 of an electronic search).

16. *Descriptors.* The descriptors from the ERIC *Thesaurus* that were assigned to this publication by an indexer at an ERIC clearinghouse are listed here. These descriptors classify the substantive content of the publication. Up to six major descriptors, each preceded by an asterisk, are listed to cover the main content of the publication. Minor descriptors also are listed to indicate less important content of the publication, or nonsubject features such as methodology or educational level. A minor descriptor for educational level is mandatory for every publication and journal article indexed in ERIC, unless it is entirely inappropriate. If a publication covers a specific age range, a minor descriptor for age level also may be assigned. A publication is cited in the subject index of *CIJE* or *RIE* under its major descriptors, but not under its minor descriptors.

17. *Identifiers.* Identifiers are key words or "indexable" concepts intended to add depth to subject indexing that is not possible with the ERIC *Thesaurus* descriptors alone. They generally are either proper names or concepts not yet represented by approved descriptors. They appear in *CIJE* entries or *RIE* resumes

in a separate field just below the descriptors. Major identifiers are marked with an asterisk and appear in the printed subject indexes of *RIE* and *CIJE.* There are no identifiers for this publication.

18. *Target audience.* If a publication specifies an intended audience, this information is provided in the entry or resume. Eleven different audiences are identified by ERIC: policy makers; researchers; practitioners, which include the five subtypes administrators, teachers, counselors, media staff, and support staff; students; parents; and community members. If more than two practitioner groups are identified, only the generic target audience *practitioners* is catalogued. No target audience is specified for the resume shown in Figure 3.4.

19. *Abstract.* This is a brief summary of the publication's contents, written either by the author or by the indexer at the ERIC clearinghouse.

20. *Indexer's initials.* The initials of the person at the ERIC clearinghouse who indexed each publication are indicated in parentheses at the end of the resume. The indexer for our sample publication is LMI.

In doing a hard-copy search of *CIJE* and *RIE,* we can search for entries or resumes using only one subject heading at a time. In the preceding section, for example, we identified some relevant publications concerning parents, but we do not know if they also are relevant to our other descriptors, *High risk students* and *Academic achievement.* We will need to study each entry or resume to make this determination.

You can take notes on the bibliographic information and abstract of each *CIJE* entry or *RIE* resume that is relevant to your literature search. However, this is time-consuming, and you run the risk of making errors in copying bibliographic citations. A far simpler and more effective method is to make a photocopy of all relevant entries and resumes.

SEARCHING AN ELECTRONIC PRELIMINARY SOURCE

Searching a hard-copy preliminary source is not difficult if you have just a few descriptors and need to cover only a few years of the literature. Suppose, instead, that you are planning to write a master's thesis, a doctoral dissertation, or another type of major report, or that you want comprehensive information for making an important educational decision. In these situations, you need to be able to conduct a thorough review of the literature. The manual search process would be too time-consuming and unreliable to accomplish this task, so it is necessary to know how to conduct an electronic search using a computer.

Step 1: Selecting an Electronic Preliminary Source

An electronic preliminary source has two key components. One of them is the **database,** which consists of the citations for all the publications that the preliminary source indexes. The other component is the software that allows you to search the database. Many of the preliminary sources listed in Appendix 2 are available as electronic databases.

You will recall that we used *RIE* as the hard-copy preliminary source to be searched for publications related to our search question about parent involvement. In electronic versions of this preliminary source, *RIE* is integrated with *CIJE* into one database, hereafter referred to as the *ERIC database.*

The ERIC database is accessed through a **search engine,** which is specialized software that enables users to find citations satisfying certain criteria (e.g., all the publications of a particular author). Different versions of the ERIC database and ERIC search engines are available. The version that we will use to illustrate an electronic literature search is easily accessible on the Internet (www.searcheric.org). It is a comprehensive index of the educational literature and has many desirable search options.

Step 2: Selecting a Search Strategy

It is no easy task to sort through the more than one million documents in the ERIC database to find those that are relevant to your research questions. You will find it necessary to develop a systematic search strategy in order to focus your search. Also, you will need to keep careful records of your search procedures for two reasons: first, to avoid repeating them unnecessarily; and second, to use as a reference point when describing these procedures in your thesis, dissertation, or other report. In addition to reading the strategies described below, you might find it helpful to examine searches conducted by experts. Examples can be found at http://searcheric.org.

In describing strategies for an electronic search of the ERIC database, we will refer to the questions in the research proposal that we outline at the end of most chapters of this book. (The research proposal is introduced at the end of Chapter 2.) The three research questions are as follows:

1. What percentage of high schools in Oregon have engaged in curriculum alignment?
2. What procedures have administrators, teachers, and specialists used to align curriculum content with instruction and test content?
3. Does students' performance on achievement tests improve after a curriculum-alignment process has been completed in their schools?

We start our search for relevant literature by going to the home page for the search engine www.searcheric.org. We keep a record of our search using the form shown in Figure 3.5.

Searching by *Thesaurus* Descriptors.   At the top of the home page is a "Wizard" feature, which is an electronic version of the *Thesaurus of ERIC Descriptors.* Looking at our research questions, we decide to check these terms in the Wizard: *curriculum alignment, achievement test performance,* and *state achievement tests.*

SEARCH PROCEDURES FOR SEARCHERIC.ORG	NOTES
1. "curriculum alignment" in Wizard	Is not a descriptor.
2. "curriculum" in Wizard	Is a descriptor. "Curriculum-based assessment" is also a descriptor.
3. "achievement test performance" and "state achievement test" in Wizard	Neither is a descriptor.
4. "achievement test" in Wizard	"Achievement test" is a descriptor. "National competency tests" and "achievement gains" also are descriptors.
5. "achievement" in Wizard	"Achievement" is a descriptor. "Academic achievement" also is a descriptor.
6. "Oregon Department of Education" in Wizard	Is not a descriptor. Search as a keyword, but use the more general term "Oregon."
7. Research Question 1. Searched using "Oregon" and "curriculum alignment" as keywords	Many entries, but only one is relevant.
8. Research Question 2. Searched using "curriculum alignment" as keyword	More than 100 entries. Many are relevant.
9. Research Question 3. Did keyword search for: ("curriculum alignment") and ("achievement gains", "academic achievement", "national competency tests")	Search yielded many entries, not all of them relevant.

FIGURE 3.5   **Record of Procedures in an Electronic Search of Literature on Curriculum Alignment**

The Wizard tells us that *curriculum alignment* is not a descriptor. We decide to try a broader term *curriculum.* We find that it is a descriptor and that there are narrow and related descriptors associated with it. One of them is *curriculum-based assessment,* which seems relevant to our research questions.

We move on to check *achievement test performance* and *state achievement test* in the Wizard. Neither is a descriptor, but *achievement test* is. Among the narrow and related descriptors associated with it are *national competency tests* and *achievement gains,* so we add those terms to our list. We also check *achievement* in the Wizard, and find that it is a descriptor, as is *academic achievement.*

Conducting a Free-Text Search.   A **free-text search** (also called a *natural-language search*) involves requesting every entry in which a particular word or set of words appears anywhere in the entry. These words sometimes are called *keywords.* In the electronic version of ERIC we are using, the keywords can occur anywhere in the title, descriptors, identifiers, or abstract of the entry.

Free-text searching is particularly useful in searching for entries by or about a particular organization. For example, suppose we wished to know whether the Oregon Department of Education has any publications relating to curriculum alignment. The Wizard indicates that *Oregon Department of Education* is not a descriptor. However, we can still search for entries in the ERIC database using the keyword feature. For keywords that include more than one word, such as *Oregon*

Department of Education, we need to surround the entire phrase by quotation marks. Otherwise, the search might produce entries that have nothing to do with the Oregon Department of Education; it just happens that these words are scattered throughout the entry.

Combining Descriptors and Keywords. In describing the hard-copy search of *CIJE* and *RIE,* we noted the difficulty of searching for entries relevant to all three of our descriptors: *Parent*, High risk students,* and *Academic achievement.* This task is no problem in searching an electronic database. We can insert a term known as an ***and*** **connector** (in mathematics, a connector is called a *Boolean operator*) between each of the three descriptors: *"parent*" and "high risk students" and "academic achievement."* The search engine will only select those entries in the database that contain all three descriptors.

Conversely, we can use an ***or*** **connector** for our search: *"parent*" or "high risk students" or "academic achievement."* The search engine will select any entry in the database that has any one or more of these descriptors. Use of *or* connectors typically will expand the number of retrieved entries, because the entry need have only one of the descriptors in order to be selected. Use of *and* connectors typically will reduce the number of retrieved entries, because the entry must be coded by all the descriptors in order to be selected.

Using connectors and the descriptors/keywords that we identified (see Figure 3.5), we can proceed to search for relevant literature for the three research questions listed above. For the first research question, we decide to enter *Oregon and "curriculum alignment"* in the search window. We also exercise our option to limit the search to publications from 1990 to the present. (Our other option is to search for all publications in the ERIC database from 1966 to 1989.) This search yields more than one hundred entries, none of which is directly relevant to the first research question. However, one entry seems indirectly relevant:

> N. Golden & M. Lane (1998). *A seven-step process to align curriculum with Oregon state content standards* (ED 426 470).

We decide to read this publication and also contact the authors to determine whether they know about the status of statewide efforts to align curriculum.

For the second research question, we decide to enter "curriculum alignment" in the search window. The search yields more than one hundred entries, many of them relevant. For example, the following entry describes many curriculum-alignment procedures that educators have used or can use:

> F. W. Fenwick & B. E. Steffy (2001). *Deep curriculum alignment: Creating a level playing field for all children on high-stakes tests of educational accountability* (ED 454 587).

For the third research question, we decide to enter *("curriculum alignment") and ("achievement gains", "academic achievement", "national competency tests")* in the search window. This phrase tells the search engine to identify any entries that have the keyword *curriculum alignment* and either the descriptors *achievement gains* or (the *or* connector is indicated by a comma in this search engine) *academic achievement* or *national competency tests*. We designed the search this way because we think that entries that are about achievement gains, academic achievement, or national competency tests are likely to be relevant to our research question.

The search yields nineteen entries, only some of which we view as relevant. One of them is

D. Bergman et al. (1998). *Vertical alignment and collaboration* (ED 421 472).

The first sentence of the abstract states, "This study investigated whether vertical (grade level sequence) alignment of the curriculum in conjunction with teacher collaboration would enhance student performance on the Texas Assessment of Academic Skills (TAAS) in south Texas school districts of various sizes." This description is very much in the spirit of the third research question. Another entry also appears useful:

K. Cotton (1999). *Research you can use to improve results* (ED 432 048).

The author synthesizes 1,400 studies, some of which involve research on curriculum improvement.

We can continue our literature search using different descriptors and keywords in combination or singly. Because we have kept a record of our search procedures (see Figure 3.5), it is easier to reflect on our overall search strategy, refine it, and avoid repeating searches. We also can consider whether it might be desirable to search other databases. For example, it might be worthwhile to search the electronic database for *Dissertation Abstracts International,* because interest in curriculum alignment is increasing. Dissertations might report research studies that have not yet been revised for journal publication or that will never be published except as a dissertation.

Step 3: Displaying the Entries on a Computer Screen

After developing your search strategy, you will need to decide the amount of detail that you want about each entry on your computer screen.

ERIC and other databases offer various options for the level of detail that you can retrieve for each entry. The following are the two levels that the search engine at www.searcheric.org makes available:

1. *Title, author, and first two sentences of abstract.* If your search results in a substantial set of entries, it will be time-consuming to scan through them on your computer screen. Therefore, you may choose to examine just a few elements of a complete ERIC entry to decide which entries you wish to examine further.

Because these few elements require only a few lines of text, you can scroll through many entries in a matter of minutes.

2. *Complete ERIC entry.* By clicking on the title of the brief entry described above, the search engine will show you the complete entry. (A complete ERIC entry is shown in Figure 3.4.) This display option should be sufficient for you to decide whether the publication is relevant to your literature search.

Step 4: Downloading the Entries

As you review entries on your computer screen, the search engine typically will allow you to select certain ones or the entire list of entries yielded by the search. It would be extremely time-consuming to copy more than a few entries by hand from the screen. Therefore, the search engine has options for downloading them electronically so that you can view them again at your leisure and make a hard copy of them on a computer printer. For example, the search engine might allow you to copy the search results to your computer hard drive, disk, or other electronic storage device. Another possible option is for the search engine to send you the search results as an e-mail message or attachment to an e-mail message.

The most sophisticated option is to download the entries into a computer file created by bibliography software such as *Endnote* (www.endnote.com) or *ProCite* (www.procite.com). This software organizes each entry into a standard format and allows you to type your own notes about the entry and search through all the entries for those having certain features. Also, the software can format the entries into different styles (e.g., APA style) and can insert them into your report as you type it with a word processor (e.g., *Microsoft Word*). Keep in mind that bibliography software is powerful, but you might need the services of a reference librarian or tech support person to create the interface between it and the electronic preliminary source.

Step 5: Obtaining Publications after an Electronic Search

As you study the entries that you downloaded, you might find that the abstract included in the entry provides sufficient information about the publication. If the entry is particularly relevant to your research questions, however, you probably will want to study the actual publication.

A reference librarian at a university library should be able to help you locate journal articles and books in the library or through interlibrary loan. Some journals might be elusive, though, in which case you can consider using a fee-based article-reproduction service. Several of these services are listed at www.searcheric.org.

If you have done an ERIC search, some of the publications you might wish to read are unpublished documents. These documents are indicated by the accession-number prefix *ED*. Almost all of them are available on microfiche at more than 1,000 ERIC Resource Collections worldwide including most major universities. A list of their locations is at http://searcheric.org/derc.htm. For a fee you can read and print pages from an ED document with the institution's microfiche reader. Other options are to order the documents, if available, in hard-copy format through the ERIC Document Reproduction Service (www.edrs.com) or in Adobe Acrobat PDF format though *E*Subscribe* (www.edrs.com/products/subscription.cfm).

Still another option is to request a copy of the document from the author or from the institution that issued it. Address information for institutions usually can be obtained by a search engine such as *Google* or *Yahoo*. A good source of contact information for educational researchers is the online member directory of the American Educational Research Association (www.aera.net).

EXAMPLE OF OUTLINING A RESEARCH PROPOSAL

This feature of the chapter gives you an example of how to outline a research proposal using the form in Appendix 1. The example, involving a proposal to study curriculum alignment, is introduced in Chapter 2. Here we show how we filled out the parts of the outline having to do with preliminary sources.

3. LITERATURE SEARCH
   A. The descriptors are: "curriculum alignment"; "curriculum-based assessment"; "national competency tests"; "achievement gains"; "academic achievement"; "Oregon".
   B. PRELIMINARY SOURCE: ERIC (www.searcheric.org).

SELF-CHECK TEST

1. A preliminary source typically does not contain
   a. information about papers presented at professional conferences.
   b. abstracts summarizing the contents of publications.
   c. information about publications more than fifteen years old.
   d. the complete text of publications.

2. All the following are customary steps in searching the hard-copy ERIC preliminary source, except for
   a. identifying whether the information in monthly issues has been cumulated in semiannual or annual volumes.
   b. identifying relevant descriptors.
   c. taking note of the quality of each publication as rated by the preliminary-source indexer.
   d. using the subject index.

3. The elements of information about a publication that are contained in an *RIE* document resume are designed primarily to
   a. make it unnecessary for users to obtain and read the publication.
   b. suggest other publications about which users might want to get information.
   c. guide resume readers in making practical decisions relating to the publication's content.
   d. help users determine the relevance of the publication to their information needs.

4. A search engine enables an individual to
   a. look for relevant citations in a hard-copy database.
   b. find citations in a database that satisfy certain criteria.
   c. switch from one preliminary-source database to another.
   d. identify relevant citations in *CIJE*, but not in *RIE*.

5. One option that is available in an electronic version of a preliminary source, but not in a hard-copy version, is
   a. searching for publications over a span of many years.
   b. using standard descriptors established by the preliminary-source indexers.
   c. combining several descriptors so as to obtain only publications relevant to all of them.
   d. searching for publications by specific authors.

6. The use of truncation in searching an electronic preliminary source typically
   a. increases the number of entries retrieved.
   b. decreases the number of entries retrieved.
   c. has no effect on the number of entries retrieved.
   d. limits the search to standard descriptors and identifiers.

7. A good way to broaden the scope of a search of an electronic preliminary source is to
   a. connect several descriptors related to your topic by the *or* connector.
   b. connect several descriptors related to your topic by the *and* connector.
   c. ask for entries that are of a particular publication type.
   d. ask for entries that are directed to a specific target audience.

8. A free-text search of a specific set of words is most desirable when you
   a. are searching for a term that is likely to be an ERIC descriptor or identifier.
   b. want to find every entry that has mentioned the set of words for which you are searching.
   c. want to find entries for publications of a specific publication type.
   d. want to obtain complete citations for the retrieved entries.

9. *Endnote* and *Procite* are helpful for
   a. searching the hard-copy version of *CIJE* and *RIE*.
   b. downloading the results of an electronic search of the ERIC database into a standard format.
   c. ordering documents from the ERIC Document Reproduction Service.
   d. controlling the amount of ERIC entry information displayed on a computer screen.

CHAPTER REFERENCES

Houston, J. E. (Ed.), (2001). *Thesaurus of ERIC descriptors* (14th ed.). Westport, CT: Oryx.

RESOURCES FOR FURTHER STUDY

Brehm, S. K., & Boyes, A. J. (2000). Using critical thinking to conduct effective searches of online resources. *Practical Assessment, Research and Evaluation, 7*(7). Available online: http://PAREonline.net
   The authors demonstrate that the process of searching electronic preliminary sources requires critical thinking. As we identify references about a topic, we form hypotheses about the topic, and these hypotheses redirect the search. The authors provide examples of literature searching to illustrate the process.

Hertzberg, S., & Rudner, L. (1999). The quality of researchers' searches of the ERIC database. *Educational Policy Analysis Archives, 7*(25). Retrieved December 7, 2003, from http://epaa.asu.edu/epaa/v7n25.html
   This article describes an empirical study of ERIC search strategies used by various groups and concludes that many users use simplistic strategies. The authors describe strategies that are likely to result in more productive searches.

chapter 4

Reading Secondary Sources

Gene Letterman is a high school principal in a large urban school district that is facing a budget shortfall. Several teachers have been told that their contracts will not be renewed for the next school year, and the school board is considering further reductions in the teaching staff. The board chairman, Jane Rutledge, is worried about parents' reactions to the projected increase in class size, from 29 students to 31 students on average.

"Gene, we want to know how to respond if parents say we will be short-changing their kids," she says. "I know you try and keep up with research in education, so I wonder if you could get some information about whether increasing class size will affect our students' learning."

Gene promises to explore the issue, and agrees to make a presentation to the board at its next meeting. Like most school principals, Gene is pressed for time. Thumbing through the journals that he receives as part of his membership in professional associations, he finds nothing on the topic of class size. He also talks to a few other principals. They provide some ideas and information, but he doesn't feel that he yet has a solid answer for the school board.

At this point, he decides to look for a good secondary source, which basically is a review of the published literature. At a nearby university library he checks the second edition of the *International Encyclopedia of Education*, published in 1994, and reads the entry on "Class Size." It summarizes the important research findings, and concludes that a small change in class size appears to affect student achievement only under very limited conditions. It also notes that a substantial change in class size (an increase or decrease of five or more students) appears to have the greatest effect in the early grades, and for lower-achieving students.

Having read this article, Gene now feels ready to make a presentation to the school board about the effects of class size on learning, and to answer their questions with some confidence.

OBJECTIVES

After studying this chapter, you will be able to

1. explain how a secondary source differs from a primary source in a literature review.

2. explain how reading appropriate secondary sources can help you develop an understanding of the literature on an educational problem.

3. compare two types of secondary sources, primary source analyses and professional reviews, in their approach to the review and synthesis of research literature related to a topic.

4. compare the relative advantages of vote counting, the chi-square test, and meta-analysis for synthesizing quantitative research findings in a primary source analysis.

5. explain how to carry out a review of research that involves primarily qualitative research studies.

6. explain how to use a preliminary source to locate published literature reviews.

7. describe several major publications containing secondary sources and their usefulness in doing a literature search.

8. describe several criteria that you can use to evaluate a specific secondary source to determine its soundness and usefulness.

In this chapter, you will learn about the characteristics of a secondary source, such as the encyclopedia article that Gene Letterman used to meet his need for information about class size. You also will learn about different types of secondary sources, how to go about finding a secondary source for your particular information needs, and how to judge whether the secondary sources that you locate are sound. You also will read two illustrative secondary sources that are available in the professional literature. ●

KEY TERMS

Books in Print
cause-and-effect relationship
chi-square test
construct
control group
criterion measure
Current Index to Journals in Education (CIJE)
Educational Resources Information Center (ERIC)
effect size

Encyclopedia of Educational Research
ERIC clearinghouse
ERIC Digest
experimental group
exploratory case study method
fugitive literature
International Encyclopedia of Education
literature search
mean score
meta-analysis

NSSE Yearbooks
preliminary source
primary source
primary source analysis
professional review
Resources in Education (RIE)
Review of Educational Research
Review of Research in Education
reviewer bias
secondary source
standard deviation
statistical significance
vote counting

THE VALUE OF SECONDARY SOURCES

Secondary sources are publications in which the author reports on research that others have carried out, on theories and opinions that others have developed, or on experiences that others have had. Among the most common secondary sources in education are textbooks. For example, a book on educational psychology usually discusses the findings of classical and recent research in areas such as human development, motivation, learning, instructional methods, and assessment. Or an encyclopedia entry that synthesizes research on cooperative learning will summarize the findings of many researchers who have investigated this method. Authors of secondary sources may review their own research as well, but this research usually was originally reported in various primary sources.

Carrying out your own literature search of **primary sources** obviously has some advantages over relying on a secondary source. Searching the literature will give you an in-depth familiarity with the research findings that bear on your problem and a better understanding of the educational research process. If you are in a graduate degree or licensure program, you may be expected to conduct a thorough literature search as a program requirement.

There are several disadvantages, however, to conducting your own literature review "from scratch." The biggest problem is the time it takes to do a thorough literature review, especially when you are seeking an immediate answer to a pressing problem. As we described in preceding chapters, you must spend time defining your problem, selecting appropriate preliminary sources (that is, indexes to the professional literature), and using the preliminary sources to identify citations for primary and secondary sources. Next you must judge the relevance of each citation by reading the actual study, once you finish the time-consuming process of locating it. Then you must organize, evaluate, and interpret what each study found. Finally, you must synthesize the various findings, draw conclusions, and prepare a report.

The time and effort involved in this type of literature review are beyond the resources of many practitioners. Nonetheless, most educators, policy makers, and the public believe that educational practitioners should inform their decision making with research findings. Reading the most relevant secondary sources enables practitioners to accomplish this goal with much less effort. Even if you find a relevant secondary source that was written some years ago, you still will save a great deal of time, because you will only need to search for recent sources to update the information contained in the secondary source.

A published secondary source has a special advantage if its authors are well informed and experienced in the area they are investigating. You reap the benefits of their expertise in finding, organizing, and interpreting research, theory, opinion, and experience relevant to your problem. It is difficult for most practitioners to develop the same level of skill as a reviewer who is familiar with the range of methodologies, measures, and statistical tests that have been used to investigate a particular educational topic.

Still another advantage of reading a well-done, published secondary source is that it is authoritative, and so policy makers might view it as more credible than a search you do on your own. Furthermore, if you can cite well-documented research syntheses as the basis for your own opinions, policy makers and your colleagues are likely to give your opinions more weight.

Despite the advantages of good secondary sources, you cannot rely fully on them in forming your opinions. You still need to exercise independent judgment about the literature cited, and use your own reasoning to determine whether the conclusions reached are justified by the body of research evidence reviewed. You need to note any instances of **reviewer bias,** such as when reviewers omit important information from a primary source or interpret it in a way that reflects their own values. Therefore, it is wise to track down selected studies and read them yourself. Reading primary sources selectively will give you more detailed information than is contained in a secondary source, and will deepen your understanding of the research process.

There are two main types of secondary sources: primary source analyses and professional reviews. We discuss them in the following sections. As you will see, primary source analyses tend to focus either on quantitative research studies or on qualitative research studies. By contrast, professional reviews tend to analyze a wide variety of sources and focus on implications for practice.

PRIMARY SOURCE ANALYSES

Primary source analyses have a limited scope, involve a comprehensive search process, and focus on primary sources. As we explained in Chapter 3, primary sources are reports written by the individual or individuals who actually did the research study, developed the theory, or witnessed or participated in the experiences described in the report. The purpose of a primary source analysis, also known as a *research synthesis,* is to draw diverse findings together into a coherent picture of the state of research knowledge, theoretical understanding, and professional practice relating to a particular aspect of education.

Primary Source Analyses of Quantitative Research

Reviewers who do primary source analyses use various techniques to synthesize findings from quantitative research studies that have investigated the same problem, but with different types of participants, measures, and statistical techniques.

Vote Counting.   A simple technique is **vote counting,** which was recommended by Gregg Jackson (1980). First, studies are identified in which the effect of one variable on another variable, or the relationship between two variables, has been determined by statistical analysis. Then all the studies are classified into four categories depending on the statistical significance and direction of the results obtained. (As we explain in Chapter 6, if a result has **statistical significance,** it means that the result is probably true of the population, not just of the sample studied in the research.) Studies with statistically significant positive results (that is, in the direction hypothesized) are coded ++; studies with nonsignificant positive results are coded +; studies with statistically significant results opposite to the hypothesized direction are coded – –; and studies with nonsignificant results opposite to the hypothesized direction are coded –.

Barak Rosenshine (1971) used a form of vote counting in his review of the relationship between specific teaching behaviors and student achievement. Before vote counting, he made careful judgments about which studies were relevant to a particular teaching behavior. Once this determination was made, Rosenshine designed tables to show the significant and nonsignificant results from each relevant study. He then discussed the overall trend of the results, and drew conclusions. For example, having examined nine studies that concerned teachers' use of student ideas, Rosenshine concluded that

> . . . not one yielded a significant linear correlation between the use of this variable and student achievement. However, there was a positive trend . . . in eight of the nine studies. . . . Although a great deal has been written about the importance of teacher use of student ideas . . . the significance of this variable alone is not as strong as has been claimed. (p. 71)

Chi-Square Analysis. Other approaches to quantitative research synthesis are more mathematically precise than vote counting. N. L. Gage (1978) recommended a procedure called the **chi-square test.** It involves use of a particular statistical measure (chi-square) to test the statistical significance of two or more results across studies of a particular program or method. This procedure takes into account both the size of the sample and the magnitude of the relationship or difference reported in each study. Gage reviewed individual studies of how teaching techniques such as teachers' praise, criticism, and acceptance of student ideas affect student learning. Gage demonstrated that while individual studies tended to show weak, nonsignificant effects for these techniques, combining the results across studies using the chi-square test led to strong, generalizable conclusions about their effectiveness.

Meta-Analysis. In recent years, meta-analysis has become the most widely used method for combining results from different quantitative research studies. **Meta-analysis** involves translating the findings of a set of research studies on the same phenomenon into a statistic called an **effect size.** Most meta-analyses in education follow the procedures developed by Gene Glass (1976).

Suppose that the individual studies are experiments that test the effectiveness of a particular program. In this case the effect size indicates the degree to which participants in the **experimental group** show superior performance compared to a comparison group, called the **control group,** that receives either no treatment or an alternative program. The effect size typically is computed by this formula: The numerator is the difference between the mean score of the experimental group and the mean score of the control group on a **criterion measure** (for example, an achievement test). Here the **mean score** refers to the average of the scores of the experimental group or the average of the scores of the control group. The denominator is the average of the two groups' **standard deviations** (a measure of score variability) on the criterion measure.

For example, imagine a study of the effect of small cash rewards on the achievement of students in an inner-city high school. For one school year, experimental students receive cash rewards for passing weekly quizzes, and control students receive no rewards. At the end of the year both the experimental and control group students take the XYZ Mathematics Test, which is the criterion measure. For the experimental group the mean score is 46.2 and the standard deviation is 4.0. For the control group the mean score is 41.2 and the standard deviation is 3.6. The effect size would be 46.2 minus 41.2 divided by 3.8, or 1.32. An effect size of 1.32 means that a student who scores at the 50th percentile in the experimental group has a score equivalent to a student who scores at the 91st percentile in the control group. Thus, based on the findings described here, we would conclude that giving students cash rewards for passing quizzes is substantially more effective than not giving them cash rewards.

There is some consensus among practitioners and researchers that an effect size of 0.33 or larger has practical significance. An effect size of 0.33 indicates that a student in the group with a higher mean score whose score is at the 50th percentile would be at the 63rd percentile of the other group's score distribution.

Calculating an effect size for every relevant study included in a primary source analysis transforms the results from various studies into a comparable unit of measure. It does not matter that one study used the XYZ Mathematics Test, on which scores can vary from 0 to 70, and another study used the ABC History Test, on which scores can vary from 0 to 100. An effect size can be calculated for the results of both studies, and these effect sizes can be directly compared. An effect size of 1.00 is twice as large as an effect size of 0.50, regardless of the measures and scoring systems that were used. The mean of the effect sizes from different studies can be calculated to yield an estimate of the average effect that the experimental program or method produces relative to a comparison intervention.

Not all studies in the research literature report the means and standard deviations for calculating effect size in the manner described above. However, there are procedures for estimating effect size from virtually any statistical data reported in the primary sources included in the meta-analysis.

Meta-analysis has gained much popularity in different disciplines, among them medicine, psychology, and education. (One of the articles reprinted at the end of this chapter is a meta-analysis of research on the effectiveness of computer-assisted instruction in science education.) However, you should be aware of the potential limitations of this technique. One of them is the reviewer's basis for selecting studies. For example, in a meta-analysis of the effects of metacognitive instruction on reading comprehension, Eileen Haller, David Child, and Herbert Walberg (1988) state that they examined 150 references but limited their analysis to 20 studies. These 20 studies met certain criteria: the use of metacognitive intervention, employment of a control group for comparison, and provision of statistical information necessary to compute effect sizes. Gene Glass, one of the primary developers of meta-analysis, probably would have advised Haller and her colleagues to include as many of the 150 original studies as possible in their analysis, even though some are methodologically more sound than others. Glass argues that either weaker studies will show the same results as stronger studies and thus should be included, or that a truer picture will emerge if weak studies are also analyzed.

By contrast, Robert Slavin (1986) argues against including every possible study in a meta-analysis. Slavin examined eight meta-analyses conducted by six independent teams of reviewers and compared their procedures and conclusions against the studies they analyzed. Slavin reported that he found errors in all eight meta-analyses that were serious enough to invalidate or call into question one or more of the major conclusions of each study. Slavin therefore recommends including in a meta-analysis only studies providing "best evidence," that is, those that meet criteria such as methodological adequacy and relevance to the issue at hand. He also makes a strong case for calculating not only an overall mean effect size, but also separate effect sizes for subsets of studies—for example, those that used the same measure of the dependent variable or those that studied a specific ethnic group.

Consistent with Slavin's recommendations, we advise you not to accept an effect size in a meta-analysis at face value, but to examine at least a few of the primary sources that contributed findings to the calculation of the effect size. By taking this extra step, you can check exactly how the primary source investigated the particular educational practice or issue of interest to you.

Primary Source Analyses of Qualitative Research

Thus far we have considered procedures for reviewing primary sources that involve quantitative research. As we explained in Chapter 1, qualitative research represents another approach to scientific inquiry. It involves the study of individual cases in an effort to understand the unique character and context of each case. Rodney Ogawa and Betty Malen (1991) suggested a method for synthesizing qualitative research studies that enables the reviewer to acknowledge the unique characteristics of each case, but also to identify concepts and principles that are present across cases. Although the primary focus is qualitative studies, Ogawa and Malen's method, called the **exploratory case study method,** allows reviewers to include quantitative studies and nonresearch accounts of a phenomenon in their synthesis of the literature on a particular educational topic.

A literature review by Nathan Bos, Joseph Krajcik, and Helen Patrick (1995) illustrates several of the procedures that Ogawa and Malen recommend for reviewing qualitative research. Their review article appeared in a special issue of the *Journal of Computers in Mathematics and Science Teaching,* devoted to the topic of telecommunications. It was intended to clarify the potential role of computer-mediated communications (CMC) in improving teaching practice in mathematics and science. The report describes research on a selective number of projects (thirteen) about which sufficient research was available. The research consisted primarily of case studies of the projects, but some quantitative survey data were collected and analyzed, too.

One procedure recommended by Ogawa and Malen is to clarify the focus of the review and define key constructs used in the review. A **construct** is a concept that is inferred from commonalities among observed phenomena and that can be used to explain those phenomena. Consistent with this recommendation, Bos and his colleagues state a specific focus for their literature review: "This review will focus on computer networking projects that have been designed to support teacher practice" (p. 188). They define computer-mediated communications (CMC) as "e-mail networks, bulletin boards, listservers, and ftp libraries for teachers" (p. 188).

Ogawa and Malen recommend that reviewers classify the types of documents that they have identified in their search of the literature, for example: qualitative case studies, quantitative research experiments, and position statements. Bos and his colleagues do not present a document classification scheme in their article, probably because all the documents were similar in nature, being descriptions of specific CMC projects.

Qualitative case studies typically are reported in narrative form. Ogawa and Malen recommend that reviewers analyze the case studies by developing narrative summaries and coding schemes that take into account all the pertinent information in the documents. The literature review on CMC includes a table containing three columns: (1) the name of each CMC network, (2) the network's uses and purposes, and (3) research findings relating to the network.

According to Ogawa and Malen, the goals of a review of qualitative research are to increase understanding of the phenomena being studied and guide further research. These goals are achieved by searching the documents included in the review for relevant constructs and **cause-and-effect relationships.** A quantitative research review also has the goal of guiding further research, but its other goal is quite different, namely, to make generalizations based on statistical findings.

Bos and his colleagues identified several key constructs that helped them understand the potential benefits of CMC networks for teachers. Among these constructs are *reflective practice, support for innovation, professional isolation,* and *communities of learning.* In addition, the authors developed several cause-and-effect propositions from their analysis of findings reported in the documents that they reviewed. For example, they proposed that CMC (the presumed causal agent) helps to create "a uniquely egalitarian online 'classroom' for mutual reflection and idea-sharing" (p. 190), which is the presumed effect.

Ogawa and Malen caution reviewers of qualitative research to be aware of possible bias in their literature review procedures. For example, various statements in the literature review on CMC networks make evident that the authors strongly believe that these networks have great potential as a support for teachers. The reviewers therefore needed to be careful not to overlook or minimize any limitations of the positive effects, or possible negative effects, reported by the researchers. To provide an unbiased account, Bos and his colleagues include highlighted sections called "issues" that draw the reader's attention to several such limitations. They also suggest future directions for CMC development and research.

PROFESSIONAL REVIEWS

Some primary source analyses draw implications for educational practice, but this is not their main purpose, as they generally are written for researchers, not practitioners. By contrast, **professional reviews** draw this type of implication, because they are intended for practitioners and policy makers. Many of them are intended for a particular audience of practitioners, such as elementary school teachers.

Professional reviews typically use nontechnical language to describe research findings. They also tend to be brief and selective in their citations of primary sources. For example, the *Encyclopedia of Educational Research* consists primarily of professional reviews. Each review is about four pages and lists ten to fifteen references.

The article by Robert Slavin that is reprinted later in this chapter originally appeared in the 1992 edition of the *Encyclopedia of Educational Research* as the entry on the topic of cooperative learning. Slavin presents a brief review of the research that has been carried out to test the effects of cooperative learning on various student outcomes.

The reviewers who are invited to write articles for a publication like the *Encyclopedia of Educational Research* typically are recognized as experts on particular topics. For example, Slavin's research and development in the area of cooperative learning is well known among educational practitioners. In the article, Slavin summarizes not only his own work, but that of several other researchers and practitioners who have extensively promoted and studied cooperative learning strategies.

Authors of professional reviews generally examine published research studies, primary source analyses, and theoretical writings to determine their implications for improving professional practice. Slavin, for example, cites a number of research studies that found positive effects of cooperative learning methods on various student outcomes, and notes the conditions that are necessary to produce these effects in actual classrooms.

A good professional review can be beneficial to you because it contains both research evidence and explicit implications and recommendations for practice. Unless a professional review is recent, however, it may not provide a good basis for making a decision about practice. The reason is that, over time, new advances in research and the changing conditions of educational practice might invalidate the reviewer's conclusions. Even so, a professional review can be useful as a reflection of the state of knowledge and practice that prevailed at the time it was prepared. You can supplement it by conducting your own literature search for publications that appeared subsequent to the review.

As with primary source analyses, some professional reviews focus on quantitative research, others focus on qualitative research, and still others review both types of research. Whatever their research focus, most professional reviews rely primarily on a narrative approach to synthesize the varied findings in the literature. The value of the implications for practice presented in professional reviews thus depends almost entirely on the authors' judgment and experience and their understanding of conditions in real-world educational settings.

Slavin's article includes an example of vote counting, and he also refers to an effect size in an earlier literature review that he conducted. For the most part, however, Slavin states findings about cooperative learning in general terms, without giving specific information about the statistical results that formed the basis for those findings.

Professional reviews generally lack the rigor of a good primary source analysis, so you need to consider whether the reviewer's conclusions and recommendations are warranted. Also, some professional reviews are written by individuals with limited experience in the conduct or interpretation of research. Therefore, you are advised to read for yourself some of the primary and secondary sources cited in a professional review before basing important educational decisions on the review's conclusions.

How to Locate Secondary Sources

To identify relevant secondary sources, you may need first to consult preliminary sources. As we explained in Chapter 3, **preliminary sources** are indexes to the literature on education and other disciplines. Among the many preliminary sources listed in Appendix 2, two are particularly useful for finding published literature reviews: ERIC and *Books in Print.* They are described in the next section, followed by descriptions of publications that provide literature reviews on particular topics.

Using Preliminary Sources to Locate Published Literature Reviews

ERIC.   As we explained in Chapter 3, the **Educational Resources Information Center (ERIC)** publishes two of the main preliminary sources in education: *Resources in Education (RIE)* and *Current Index to Journals in Education (CIJE).* If you do an electronic search of these sources, you can combine *meta-analysis* or *literature reviews* as descriptor terms with your primary descriptor terms to identify relevant secondary sources. For example, we entered the followed terms and Boolean connectors (explained in Chapter 3) to search for published reviews of the literature on curriculum alignment: ("meta-analysis", "literature reviews") and ("curriculum alignment"). The search yielded some ERIC Digests (described below) and one additional entry:

ED 223 008 Considering the Research: What Makes an Effective School

This literature review was published in 1982, but might be helpful in giving us a historical perspective on the curriculum-alignment movement in education.

Until 2004, ERIC also operated clearinghouses focused on different educational topics. Each **clearinghouse** was responsible for cataloging, abstracting, and indexing relevant documents in its subject area. The clearinghouses also published newsletters, bulletins, annotated bibliographies, and literature reviews on high-interest topics.

The clearinghouses produced **ERIC Digests** on a regular basis. These are brief literature reviews and discussions of important current topics and problems in education. Many hundreds of them, extending back a period of years, have been published. As of August 2003 and perhaps subsequently, too, you could search for them, and view them online, at www.ed.gov/databases/ERIC_Digests/index/. We entered the search term "curriculum alignment" at this website and obtained a list of seven ERIC Digests. One of them appeared particularly relevant:

ED 458 288 Alignment of Standards and Assessments as an Accountability Criterion

Reading this ERIC Digest, we came across a reference to another publication that contains a review of relevant literature:

LaMarca, P. M., Redfield, D., & Winter, P. C. (2000). *State standards and state assessment systems: A guide to alignment.* Washington, DC: Council of Chief State School Officers.

This example illustrates how you can get a quick overview of the literature on your research questions by reading ERIC Digests. They in turn can guide you to other literature syntheses.

Books in Print. Some of the major secondary sources described in the next section, such as encyclopedias, are not published sufficiently often to present the current status of a particular educational practice or issue. If this is true of the topic you wish to review, your best chance of finding an up-to-date secondary source may lie in checking recent scholarly books, monographs, and textbooks.

A good source for locating such publications is ***Books in Print.*** Most major libraries and bookstores have either a hard-copy set or an online version. We conducted an online search for books about curriculum alignment and obtained five entries. One of them seemed particularly relevant:

English, F. W., & Steffy, B. E. (2001). *Curriculum alignment: Creating a level playing field for all children on high-stakes tests of educational accountability.* Lanham, MD: Scarecrow Press.

A good alternative to *Books in Print* is the Library of Congress catalog system. The Library of Congress is a repository for virtually every book published in the United States and also for various media. It can be accessed online at this web address: http://catalog.loc.gov/.

Publications Containing Secondary Sources on Specific Educational Topics

An extensive list of publications containing secondary sources is provided in Appendix 3. The following is a description of some of the most important of these publications.

Encyclopedia of Educational Research. The sixth edition of this monumental work, published in 1992, includes hundreds of literature reviews and analyses of important topics in education. The contents are organized in alphabetical order by such broad topic headings as educational measurement and assessment, levels of education, and teachers. If your topic is not in the alphabetical listing, you can check the extensive index. This is an excellent source for getting a brief review of topics related to your area of interest. Older editions of this publication also are helpful if you wish to obtain a historical perspective on the research questions you are investigating.

International Encyclopedia of Education. Published in 1994, the second edition of this encyclopedia presents an overview of research and scholarship on educational problems, practices, and institutions worldwide. The encyclopedia entries are grouped into twenty-one major clusters, such as administration of education, organization of schools, and teaching. Many of the entries on major aspects of education have been grouped together and republished as handbooks, e.g., the *International Handbook of Teaching and Teacher Education.*

NSSE Yearbooks. Each year the National Society for the Study of Education (NSSE) publishes two yearbooks. (Recent yearbooks are listed at www.press. uchicago.edu/Complete/Series/NSSE.html.) Each covers recent research and theory related to a major educational topic and contains ten to twelve chapters that deal with different aspects of that topic. The chapters are written by experts in their field. The titles of recent yearbooks of the NSSE are:

2003	Part I	*American Educational Governance on Trial: Change and Challenges*
	Part II	*Meeting at the Hyphen: Schools-Universities-Communities-Professions in Collaboration for Student Achievement and Well Being*
2002	Part I	*The Educational Leadership Challenge: Redefining Leadership for the 21st Century*
2002	Part II	*Educating At-Risk Students*
2001	Part I	*From the Capitol to the Classroom: Standards-Based Reform in the States*
2001	Part II	*Education across the Century: The Centennial Volume*

Review of Educational Research. This journal consists entirely of reviews of research literature on educational topics. It is published quarterly, and each issue typically contains four to seven reviews. Each review includes an extensive bibliography, which may list primary source articles relevant to your problem. For example, the Spring 1997 issue includes a review of research by Kathleen V. Hoover-Dempsey and Howard M. Sandler titled "Why Do Parents Become Involved in Their Children's Education?" The text of this article covers 40 pages and cites more than one hundred publications.

Review of Research in Education. This is an annual series of books that was started in 1973. Each volume contains chapters written by leading educational researchers who provide critical surveys of research on important problems and trends in education. For example, Volume 26, published in 2002, includes chapters that review research on welfare reform and education, educational transitions, educational reform, and the relationship between the economy and schooling.

Handbooks. An increasing number of handbooks (listed in Appendix 3) have been published to address specific areas of education. For example, the *Handbook of Research on Teaching* (4th ed.) has chapters on such topics as Paulo Freire's theory of education, teacher assessment, research on history teaching, special education, teachers' knowledge, and teaching in middle schools.

A good way to find professional reviews in the educational literature is to examine the types of journals that are intended for education professionals. For example, *The Reading Teacher* periodically publishes reviews that synthesize research findings relevant to school teachers. *Phi Delta Kappan* contains articles citing research and drawing practical implications on many important educational issues, such as standards-based schooling, educational technology, school choice, and recent trends in national assessments of student achievement.

CRITERIA FOR EVALUATING SECONDARY SOURCES

The following criteria are intended to help you judge the merits of secondary sources in your area of interest.

1. *Reviewer's credentials.* The reviewer's reputation and experience with the topic are factors to consider when reading a secondary source. One way to make this determination is to examine the reference list at the end of the source to see whether the author has done research on the topic, and if so, where and when it was published. You can also check for information in the article itself about the author's affiliation, title, and experience related to the topic.

2. *Search procedures.* In older published reviews, it was not customary for reviewers to specify their search procedures. Thus, it was difficult for readers to determine whether the research cited in the review resulted from a comprehensive search or whether it was selected haphazardly. Now reviewers often identify the preliminary sources examined, the descriptors used, and the years covered. This is more likely to be the case in a primary source analysis than in a professional review.

3. *Breadth of the search.* Research reviews vary widely in their breadth, from an exhaustive search for all primary sources on a topic to a highly selective search. The advantage of a comprehensive search is that you have some assurance that no significant research evidence or theoretical framework has been overlooked. A narrower search may be just as useful for your purposes, but in this case it is even more important to know how the reviewer selected the documents included in the review. The following dimensions reflect the breadth of the reviewer's search of the literature.

   a. Period of time covered by the search. The publication dates of the most recent and oldest sources provide an indication of this time period. Keep in mind, though, that the time period may span beyond these dates, but the search may not have yielded older or more recent publications that were relevant to the topic.

b. Types of documents reviewed. For example, the report might include only published journal articles, or it also may include dissertations and so-called **fugitive literature,** such as technical reports produced by a research team for its funding agency.

c. Geographical scope of the search. Some reviewers examine only studies carried out in the United States, whereas others also include studies conducted in other countries.

d. Range of grade levels and types of students, teachers, educational institutions, or other entities that were studied in the reviewed research.

e. Range of theoretical or ideological perspectives on the topic. For example, did the reviewer consider both studies based on behavioral theory and studies based on cognitive theory? Were different ideological perspectives, such as critical theory (see Chapter 12) and the accountability movement, considered?

f. Use of criteria to exclude any of the reports that were initially examined. For example, the reviewer might exclude research studies that involved atypical students or experiments that did not employ random assignment procedures. (Random assignment is explained in Chapter 9.)

4. *Amount of information provided about the studies reviewed.* Authors of research reviews have a challenging task: to summarize findings of a large number of studies briefly so as to be readable, yet in sufficient detail that the basis for their conclusions and interpretations is reasonably clear. Simply citing a reference or two in parentheses after making a sweeping generalization does not accomplish this goal. A better approach is for the reviewer to describe briefly the relevant information from a research study that demonstrates how it supports the generalization.

5. *Exercise of critical judgment.* Research reviews range from those that reflect uncritical acceptance of research findings to those in which the reviewer finds flaws in every research study and asserts that no conclusions can be drawn from them. Neither extreme is likely to be justified for topics that have been extensively researched.

Another aspect of critical judgment is whether the reviewer tended to lump studies together or discriminated among studies that appeared to deal with the same question, but that were actually quite different in design or purpose. The latter approach generally reflects better critical judgment.

6. *Resolution of inconsistent findings.* Nearly every research review will reveal that the results obtained in some studies do not agree with those found in other studies. You should examine carefully how the reviewer dealt with these inconsistencies. Earlier we described several approaches that can be used to synthesize varied findings from quantitative and qualitative research studies. These approaches are used most commonly in primary source analyses. Another approach is to make more holistic judgments based on one's expertise. This approach is used more commonly in professional reviews.

Example of Outlining a Research Proposal

This feature of the chapter gives you an example of how to outline a research proposal using the form in Appendix 1. The example, involving a proposal to study curriculum alignment, is introduced in Chapter 2. Below, we show how we filled out the parts of the outline having to do with secondary sources.

    3. LITERATURE SEARCH
       B. Published literature reviews:
- Cotton, K. (1999). *Research you can use to improve results.* Portland, OR: Northwest Regional Educational Laboratory. (ERIC Document Reproduction Service No. ED432048)
- English, F. W., & Steffy, B. E. (2001). *Curriculum alignment: Creating a level playing field for all children on high-stakes tests of educational accountability.* Lanham, MD: Scarecrow Press.
- Fuhrman, S. (Ed.). (2001). *From the capitol to the classroom: standards-based reform in the states* (National Society for the Study of Education Yearbook, 100th, Part I). Chicago: University of Chicago Press.
- LaMarca, P. M. (2001). *Alignment of standards and assessments as an accountability criterion* (ERIC Digest). College Park, MD: ERIC Clearinghouse on Assessment and Evaluation. (ERIC Document Reproduction Service No. ED458288)
- LaMarca, P. M., Redfield, D., & Winter, P. C. (2000). *State standards and state assessment systems: A guide to alignment.* Washington, DC: Council of Chief State School Officers.
- Westbrook, J. D. (1982). *Considering the research: What makes an effective school?* Austin, TX: Southwest Educational Development Laboratory. (ERIC Document Reproduction Service No. ED223008)

Self-Check Test

1. In contrast to primary sources, secondary sources
    a. do not describe the findings of research studies.
    b. are often technical and difficult to read.
    c. are not indexed in preliminary sources.
    d. are written by someone other than the person who carried out the research being described.

2. Reading a secondary source is particularly helpful when
   a. no original studies have been carried out on your research topic.
   b. you want to learn the meaning of research findings from the perspective of those who obtained them.
   c. an authoritative reviewer has summarized the literature related to your topic.
   d. all of the above.

3. Unlike a primary source analysis, a professional review
   a. tends to rely on secondary sources.
   b. is written mainly for other researchers.
   c. does not draw implications for practice.
   d. is written by someone who writes reviews for a living.

4. Unlike vote counting, meta-analysis
   a. relies primarily on interpretation to synthesize findings across research studies.
   b. examines the statistical significance of the findings of different research studies.
   c. provides a standard unit of measure for comparing the results of different studies.
   d. enables researchers to determine the cause of an observed effect.

5. In a review of research involving primarily qualitative research studies, the reviewer typically seeks to
   a. discover the unique characteristics of each case.
   b. identify concepts and principles that are present across cases.
   c. avoid limiting the focus of the literature review.
   d. accomplish all of the above.

6. To synthesize the findings of research studies, the author of a professional review usually
   a. employs a narrative approach.
   b. conducts a meta-analysis.
   c. employs vote counting.
   d. counts the frequency of each identified concept and theme.

7. To locate recent scholarly books and textbooks relating to your topic, probably the most useful preliminary source is
   a. ERIC.
   b. *Education Index.*
   c. *Psychological Abstracts.*
   d. *Books in Print.*

8. Of the following publications, the one containing the most literature reviews is
   a. any four issues of *Review of Educational Research.*
   b. any annual publication of *Review of Research in Education.*

    c. the *Encyclopedia of Educational Research.*

    d. the fourth edition of *Handbook of Research on Teaching.*

9. All of the following except _____ are relevant criteria for judging the usefulness and validity of a secondary source.

    a. specification of the reviewer's credentials

    b. identification of the search procedures

    c. breadth of the search

    d. exclusion of fugitive documents from the literature review

CHAPTER REFERENCES

Bos, N. D., Krajcik, J. S., & Patrick, H. (1995). Telecommunications for teachers: Supporting reflection and collaboration among teaching professionals. *Journal of Computers in Mathematics and Science Teaching, 14,* 187–202.

Gage, N. L. (1978). *The scientific basis of the art of teaching.* New York: Teachers College Press.

Glass, G. V. (1976). Primary, secondary, and meta-analysis of research. *Educational Researcher, 5*(10), 3–8.

Haller, E. P., Child, D. A., and Walberg, H. J. (1988). Can comprehension be taught? A quantitative synthesis of "metacognitive" studies. *Educational Researcher, 17*(9), 5–8.

Jackson, G. B. (1980). Methods for integrative reviews. *Review of Educational Research, 50,* 438–460.

Ogawa, R. T., & Malen, B. (1991). Towards rigor in reviews of multivocal literatures: Applying the exploratory case study method. *Review of Educational Research, 61,* 265–286.

Rosenshine, B. (1971). *Teaching behaviors and student achievement.* London: National Foundation for Educational Research in England and Wales.

Slavin, R. E. (1986). Best-evidence synthesis: An alternative to meta-analytic and traditional reviews. *Educational Researcher, 15*(9), 5–11.

RESOURCES FOR FURTHER STUDY

Cooper, H., & Hedges, L. V. (Eds.). (1994). *The handbook of research synthesis.* New York: Russell Sage Foundation.

    Includes thirty-two chapters in which various authors cover quantitative approaches to research synthesis and describe the procedures, benefits, and limitations of these approaches. Organized by the stages of research synthesis, from formulating a problem to reporting the results.

Lipsey, M. W., & Wilson, D. B. (2000). *Practical meta-analysis.* Thousand Oaks, CA: Sage.

    The authors explain how to decide which research reports to include in a meta-analysis, how to code information about each study's characteristics, and how to use computer software to analyze the resulting data.

In the following section of the chapter you will read a research article that illustrates a form of quantitative research review called meta-analysis. It is preceded by comments written especially for this book by the author of the article. Then the article itself is reprinted in full. With the permission of the author and the publisher, we have corrected various errors that occurred in the published article. Where appropriate, we have added footnotes to help you understand the information contained in the article.

Sample Meta-Analysis
A Meta-Analysis of the Effectiveness of Computer-Assisted Instruction in Science Education

Bayraktar, S. (2001–2002). A meta-analysis of the effectiveness of computer-assisted instruction in science education. *Journal of Research on Technology in Education, 34,* 173–188.

● RESEARCHER'S COMMENTS, *Prepared by Sule Bayraktar*

I undertook this meta-analysis because I was highly interested in understanding the effects of computers on student learning, particularly in science subject areas. When searching literature about this subject I had encountered various meta-analytic studies on the effectiveness of computers in general. However, I found very few studies in science subject areas. Also, many of the studies had been published many years earlier, and many newer research studies needed to be taken into consideration in my research synthesis.

To see overall trends clearly I decided to conduct a meta-analysis involving studies of the achievement effects of computer-assisted instruction (CAI) specifically in science subject areas over a three-decade period. Reading the meta-analytic studies in the literature had given me a general idea of the techniques of a meta-analysis. However, before I could conduct my own meta-analysis I needed a deeper understanding of this research method. To learn the method I benefited primarily from the publications by Hunter & Schmidt (1990); Glass (1976); Hedges (1998); and Rosenthal (1991).

The first step of a meta-analysis is to set up inclusion criteria. I decided to study a three-decade period, from 1970 through 1999. I limited the studies to be included to those done at either the secondary or college level and conducted in the United States. Also, because of the requirements of meta-analysis I excluded any studies that did not use either experimental or quasi-experimental research methods.

After setting the criteria for inclusion I began my search for every article meeting those criteria. Primarily I utilized electronic databases such as ERIC, PsycINFO, SSCI, Education Abstracts, Digital Dissertation Index, and PROQUEST, which are the most comprehensive databases dealing with science education. Database keyword and subject searches yielded hundreds of articles that seemed to be related to the subject. However, after looking up the abstracts I realized that some were not directly related to the topic and thus could not be used for the meta-analysis. A careful examination of the remaining articles revealed that a vast number of them also were not suitable. The reason was mostly that many studies had not specified the required statistics, such as effect size or standard deviation, mean, and number of research participants.

Examining all these research studies took a great deal of time and effort. However, I continued with determination to locate as many studies as I could. I looked through the references section of each reviewed article to find any other research that might relate to my subject. I also undertook a manual search of journals related to science education. Overall, my search yielded forty-two studies with one hundred eight effect sizes.

Having completed the selection process, I proceeded to set up coding criteria. After I instructed two graduate students on how to code each study, the students and I coded every specified coding criterion and item of effect size information for each study onto coding sheets. For assessing inter-rater reliability all three of us coded a random sample of five research studies. We obtained a .88 agreement rate. Using the statistical package Meta Win, we analyzed all the coded information.

I must state here that conducting a meta-analysis is a demanding task. I had to be meticulous at every step. I had to make sure that I had found all related published and unpublished research, or as close to that as possible. I had to make sure that the graduate students who helped me in coding thoroughly understood the process. I had to be careful in transforming statistical information to effect sizes when effect sizes were not given in an article directly. Coding the studies, recording all coded information without mistakes, and analyzing the data was time-consuming. However, the result was worthwhile. By integrating the results of existing studies, my study determined the overall effectiveness of CAI in science education and determined what study characteristics correlate with effect sizes, thus making it possible to know how CAI could be made more useful in promoting student learning. This study is the most comprehensive and up-to-date study on the effects of CAI on science education at the secondary and college levels. The precise and general conclusions provided by this meta-analysis will allow educators to make decisions about the implementation of CAI in science education with greater confidence.

Throughout my conduct of this research my research professor, Dr. George Johansen, provided me helpful comments. I would like to take this opportunity to express my deepest gratitude to him for his guidance, valuable suggestions, and contributions.

References

Cooper, H. (1998). *Synthesizing research* (3rd ed.). Thousand Oaks, CA: Sage.

Glass, G. V. (1976). Primary, secondary, and meta-analysis of research. *Educational Researcher, 5*(11), 3–8.

Hunter, J. E., & Schmidt, F. L. (1990). *Methods of meta-analysis: Correcting error and bias in research findings.* Newbury Park, CA: Sage.

Rosenthal, R. (1991). *Meta analytic procedures for social research* (rev. ed.). Newbury Park, CA: Sage.

A Meta-Analysis of the Effectiveness of Computer-Assisted Instruction in Science Education

Sule Bayraktar

Yuzuncu Yil University, Turkey

Abstract

This meta-analysis investigated how effective computer-assisted instruction (CAI) is in raising student achievement in secondary and college science education when compared to traditional instruction. An overall effect size of 0.273 was calculated from 42 studies yielding 108 effect sizes, suggesting that a typical student moved from the 50th percentile to the 62nd percentile in science when CAI was used. The results of the study also indicated that some study characteristics such as student-to-computer ratio, CAI mode, and duration of treatment were significantly related to the effectiveness of CAI. (Keywords: academic achievement, computer-assisted instruction, instructional effectiveness, meta-analysis, science education.)

Computer use in classrooms as an aid to teaching and learning processes has become increasingly popular during the last two decades. According to National Assessment of Educational Progress (NAEP, 1996) statistics, in 1996 more than 80% of the K–12 students in the United States reported using computers for learning purposes in school or at home, though this proportion was just above 50 percent in 1984.[a] The number of computers used in education is consistently increasing. Research on the effectiveness of computer-assisted instruction (CAI), however, does not provide consistent results.

Educational research often produces contradictions. Even frequent replications might produce diversified results. Thus, research review has been a common practice to resolve this kind of conflict. A research review provides an overall conclusion by bringing separately published studies together and investigating if some study characteristics were related to outcomes of the studies (Kulik, Bangert, & Williams, 1983).

A quantitative research review method introduced by Glass (1976) is called meta-analysis. Meta-analysis typically follows the same steps as primary research. A meta-analyst first defines the purpose of the review and develops the research question(s) of interest. Second, the meta-analyst locates research studies conducted on the topic that meet the specified criteria. Typically, meta-analyses are comprehensive reviews of a full population of relevant research studies. Third, the meta-analyst collects data from studies in two ways: (1) study features are coded according to the objectives of the review and (2) study outcomes are transformed to a common metric so that they can be compared. A typical metric in education is effect size (d), the standardized difference between the treatment and control group means. Effect sizes provided from each study are then combined to obtain an overall effect size (grand mean effect size). Finally, statistical procedures are used to investigate relationships among study characteristics and findings.

Although several meta-analyses (e.g., Flinn & Gravat, 1995; Kulik & Kulik, 1991; Liao, 1992; Niemiec & Walberg, 1985) focused on the effectiveness of computers in general, only two studies (Christmann & Badget,

Bayraktar, Sule (2001–2002). A meta-analysis of the effectiveness of computer-assisted instruction in science education. *Journal of Research on Technology in Education, 34,* 173–188. Reprinted with permission from the *Journal of Research on Technology in Education, 34*(2), Copyright © 2001, ISTE (International Society for Technology in Education), 1.800.336.5191 (U.S. & Canada) or 1.541.302.3777 (Int'l), iste@iste.org, www.iste.org. All rights reserved.

a. The NAEP is a congressionally mandated project of the U.S. Department of Education. It is a large-scale, continuing assessment of what a representative sample of students in the United States know and can do in various subject areas.

1999; Wise, 1988) focused exclusively on science education. Wise included 26 studies reflecting the situation of computer-based instruction prior to 1988. However, in that study, nearly half of the effect size measures came from studies investigating the effects of computer applications other than computer-assisted instruction.[b] Moreover, in the 12 years since that study, there have been enormous advances in computer technologies. Many other studies have been done and need to be taken into consideration in the research synthesis. In a more recent meta-analysis, Christmann and Badget compiled a total of only 11 studies consisting of CAI in the areas of chemistry, biology, physics, and general science. Thus, a comprehensive meta-analysis on the effectiveness of computer-assisted instruction in the science subject areas, covering a three-decade period, is needed to evaluate the status of this instructional method and to see overall trends clearly.

The purpose of the present meta-analysis is to determine the overall effectiveness of CAI on student achievement in secondary and college science education in the United States between 1970 and 1999 when compared to traditional instruction, by using meta-analysis as a research tool. In addition, the study also examines the effects of variables such as school level, CAI mode, and student-to-computer ratio on the effectiveness of CAI.

METHOD

The procedures used to conduct this meta-analysis will be described in detail in the following sections. First, criteria for studies included in the meta-analysis will be presented. Then, procedures for locating studies and coding study characteristics will be described. Finally, statistical techniques for investigating the relationships between study characteristics and effect sizes will be provided.

Inclusion Criteria

This study synthesized the research that investigated the effectiveness of CAI in the areas of physics, chemistry, biology, general science, and physical sciences at secondary and college levels. Studies included in this analysis were chosen from the experimental and quasi-experimental studies comparing the achievement of students who were taught science with a form of CAI and students who were taught science with traditional instruction.[c] The studies included in the synthesis were limited to those conducted in the United States. Designs including no comparison group were not used in the analysis. Studies that did not report effect sizes or adequate statistics for transformation into effect sizes were not included. Necessary statistics for these transformations are means, standard deviations, and number of subjects, or a variety of parametric statistics such as t and F test results where effect sizes were not reported.[d]

Locating the Studies

Studies included in the analysis were located by several approaches. A search was first conducted using electronic databases, including Educational Resources Information Center (ERIC), Social Science Citation Index (SSCI), PsycINFO, Education Abstracts, and Digital Dissertation Index PROQUEST.[e]

---

b. An effect size is a statistic based on a formula involving both the mean scores and standard deviations of the scores of two groups. It allows a precise calculation of how different the score distributions of the two groups are, and is adjusted so that it can be compared directly to effect sizes involving other samples or based on other measures.

c. A quasi-experiment is a type of experiment in which research participants are not randomly assigned to the experimental and control groups. Quasi-experiments are often contrasted with "true" experiments, which do involve random assignment of research participants to the experimental and control groups.

d. The mean is the average of a set of scores. The standard deviation is a measure of how much a set of scores deviates from the mean score. Parametric statistics make certain assumptions about the distribution and form of scores on the measured variable. A t test is a test of statistical significance that is used to determine whether the null hypothesis that two sample means come from identical populations can be rejected. An F test is similar to a t test, but is used when the null hypothesis involves more than two sample means.

e. These electronic databases are indexes to the education literature. (See Appendix 2.)

I also manually undertook a journal search for articles that may not have been included in the computer search databases. This search was conducted in the journals in which most of the studies on the effectiveness of CAI have been published: *Journal of Research in Science Teaching, Journal of Computers in Mathematics and Science Teaching, Computers in the Schools, Journal of Research on Computing in Education* (now *Journal of Research on Technology in Education*), *Science Education, The American Biology Teacher, School Science and Mathematics,* and *Journal of Chemical Education.*

Coding Process

A coding sheet was prepared for translating critical study information into coded form. By using these sheets, variables and effect size information were coded for each study by two coders and me. Both coders were Ph.D. students who had taken a graduate course on meta-analysis before this study.

Assessing the Reliability

To determine reliability, a random sample of 5 of 42 studies were duplicated and distributed among the coders. Each coder was given a copy of the articles, coding forms, and instructions for coding. To assess the inter-coder reliability, *agreement rate* (AR), also called the *percent agreement index,* was used.[f] The formula for AR, as represented by Orwin (1994), is:

$$AR = \frac{\text{Number of observations agreed}}{\text{Total number of observations}}$$

An agreement rate of 0.85 or greater was predetermined to be considered sufficient. An agreement rate of 0.88 was obtained for my study.

Variables

The following variables were coded for each study:

- Course content: general science, biology, physics, chemistry
- CAI type: drill and practice, tutorial, simulation
- Instructor effect: studies were classified as either having the same teachers instructing both the experimental and comparison group or having different teachers instructing both groups.
- Duration of treatment: less or equal to four weeks, greater than four weeks
- School level: college, secondary
- Student-to-computer ratio
- Software: commercial, teacher or researcher designed
- Instructional role of computers: substitute, supplement
- Publication year: 1970–1999
- Publication source: journal article, ERIC document, dissertation, master's thesis

Statistical Analysis

The Unit of Analysis. The unit of analysis for the present research was the effect size (*d*). Effect size was calculated by using the formula derived by Hunter and Schmidt (1990) for posttest comparisons of control and treatment groups. The formula is:

$$d = \frac{Xe - Xc}{SDp}$$

Xe is the experimental group mean, *Xc* is the control group mean, and *SDp* is the pooled standard deviation of the two groups.[g]

The formula for corresponding pooled standard deviation is:

$$SDp^2 = \frac{(Ne - 1)Se^2 + (Nc - 1)Sc^2}{(Ne + Nc - 2)}$$

f. Inter-coder reliability is the degree to which two or more individuals are consistent in their coding of a document or other communication.

g. The pooled standard deviation is the average of the standard deviation of the mean for the treatment group (also called the experimental group) and the standard deviation of the mean for the control group. If the size of the treatment-group sample differs from the size of the control-group sample, the computation of the pooled standard deviations typically takes this difference into account.

Ne is the number of subjects in the experimental group, Nc is the number of subjects in the control group, Se^2 is the experimental group variance, and Sc^2 is the control group variance.[h]

In many cases, the primary researchers did not report the standard deviations or means of the separate groups; instead, they used t, F, or r values. For such cases, these values were converted to d statistics by using the following conversion formulas provided by Rosenthal (1991):[i]

For t test $d = \dfrac{2t}{\sqrt{df}}$

For F test $d = \dfrac{2\sqrt{F}}{\sqrt{df}\ (\text{error})}$

For r test $d = \dfrac{2r}{\sqrt{1 - r^2}}$

Calculation of Mean Effect Sizes and Hypothesis Testing. MetaWin (Rosenberg, Adams, & Gurevitch, 1997), a statistical package designed to perform meta-analysis, was used to analyze the data. The variables and classes as well as the effect size information were recorded for each study. This particular software provides mean effect sizes with confidence intervals for each class of variable as well as the between-class homogeneity, Q_{Bet}, which allows one to compare classes.[j] Finally, MetaWin calculates the grand mean effect size, which is the mean effect size for all the effect sizes for all studies included in the meta-analysis.

The hypothesis that there are no effect size differences between classes of a variable was tested by utilizing the test of homogeneity between classes effect sizes (Q_{Bet}). Rejecting the Q_{Bet} implies that the effect sizes from the classes may not measure the same population parameter. In other words, there is a statistically significant difference in the mean effect sizes for each class of a variable.

RESULTS

The first purpose of this study was to determine the overall effectiveness of CAI in science instruction. The literature search yielded 42 studies meeting the inclusion criteria, including 5 ERIC documents, 20 journal articles, 2 master's theses, and 15 dissertations (Table 1). Some studies performed multiple comparisons—that is, multiple experiments within the same study—thus producing multiple effect sizes. Thus, 108 effect sizes from 42 studies were included in the meta-analysis.

Only one of the 42 studies showed no difference between CAI and the traditional instruction group ($ES = 0$) in terms of science achievement outcome. The range of the ES's was from −0.685 to 1.89.

Grand mean effect size for all 42 studies with 108 ES's was 0.273, considered to be a small difference. This effect size can be interpreted as: an average student exposed to CAI exceeds the academic achievement of 62 percent of the students in the traditional classroom. Ninety-five percent confidence limits were from 0.240 to 0.305.[k]

Seventy of the 108 effect sizes included in this analysis were positive, favoring the CAI group, and 38 were negative, indicating that traditional instruction was found more effective than the CAI. Twenty-eight of the

---

h. The variance is a measure of the extent to which the scores in a distribution deviate from the mean score. It is equal to the square of the standard deviation.

i. A d statistic is a measure of effect size. Various statisticians have developed different formulas for calculating d. The larger the d value, the greater the difference between the two groups on the statistic (e.g., the mean) being compared.

j. A confidence interval is a set of values, derived by computing statistics for a sample, that is likely to contain the actual population value. For example, the mean for a sample on a particular measure might be 5.1, but the actual mean for the population from which the sample was drawn might be different. The confidence interval indicates a range of scores within which the population mean is likely to fall. The Q test is a test of statistical significance that is used to determine whether the null hypothesis that two sample effect sizes come from identical populations can be rejected.

k. Confidence limits define the lower and upper limits of a confidence interval. Confidence limits at the 95 percent level of statistical significance define a range of scores that are very likely to contain the actual population score on the measure that was administered.

TABLE 1	The Primary Studies Included in the Meta-Analysis with Effect Sizes		
Study	**Subject Area**	**_n_ of _ES_**	**_ES_ Range**
Akpan & Andre, 1999	Life sciences	1	1.295
Ayoubi, 1985	Chemistry	6	−0.487 − 0.077
Bennett, 1985	Biology	2	0.253 − 0.719
Bobbert, 1982	Chemistry	4	−0.087 − 0.893
Castleberry, Montague, & Lagowski, 1970	Chemistry	1	1.89
Cavin & Lagowski, 1978	Chemistry	4	0.152 − 1.124
Chien, 1997	Physics	1	−0.685
Choi & Gennaro, 1987	General	1	0.005
Cracolice, 1994	Chemistry	4	−0.272 − 0.345
Duffy & Barowy, 1995	Biology	1	−0.288
Eisenkraft, 1986	Physics	12	0.136 − 1.246
Faryniarz & Lockwood, 1992	Biology	1	0.672
Ferguson & Chapman, 1993	Biology	4	0.439 − 0.815
Fox, 1986	Earth science	1	−0.557
Hauben & Lehman, 1988	Chemistry	4	−0.245 − 0.683
Hoge, 1995	Biology	5	−0.49 − 0.215
Hounshell & Hill, 1989	Biology	1	0.406
Jackman, Mollenberg, & Brabson, 1987	Chemistry	2	0.279 − 0.375
Jensen, Wilcox, Hatch, & Somdahl, 1996	Biology	1	0.523
Jones, 1972	Chemistry	1	−0.171
Kelly, 1997–1998	Earth science	1	−0.276
Kromhout, 1972	Physics	1	0.702
Lasater, 1971	Chemistry	2	0.284 − 0.472
Leece, 1982	Biology	1	0.877
Lehman, 1988	Biology	10	−0.384 − 0.679
Milkent & Roth, 1989	Physical science	5	−0.453 − −0.201
Miller, 1986	Biology	1	−0.220
Morrel, 1992	Biology	1	−0.566
Nicholls, Merkel, & Cordts, 1996	Biology	5	−0.016 − 0.439
Nishino, 1993	General science	1	0.457
Podell, Kaminsky, & Cusimano, 1993	Physical science	1	0.522
Rivers & Vockell, 1987	Biology	8	0.395
Shaltz, 1982	Biology	1	0
Shaw, 1984	General science	1	0.709
Stringfield, 1986	Biology	1	0.335
Summerlin & Gardner, 1973	Chemistry	1	−0.436
Tauro, 1980	Chemistry	4	−0.314 − 0.573
Tylinski, 1994	Biology	1	−0.472
Wainwright, 1985	Chemistry	2	−0.335 − −0.148
Williamson & Abraham, 1995	Chemistry	1	0.54
Wyman, 1988–1989	Physics	1	−0.453
Ybarrando, 1984	Biology	1	0.051

108 effect sizes were equal to or greater than 0.5, which indicates moderate to large effects of CAI in science education. Forty-two of the effect sizes were positive and small in magnitude. A summary of the analysis results is presented in Table 2.

DISCUSSION OF FINDINGS

This study synthesized the results of 108 effect sizes included in 42 studies. The mean of the 108 effect sizes was determined to be 0.273 standard deviation, indicating that computer-assisted instruction has a small positive effect on student achievement in science education when compared to traditional instruction. An effect is considered to be small when $ES = 0.2$ standard deviation, medium when $ES = 0.5$ standard deviation, and large when $ES = 0.8$ standard deviation (Cohen, 1977). However small, the positive effect indicates that incorporating computers in science instruction can be beneficial.

An effect size of 0.273 standard deviation indicates that an average student exposed to CAI exceeded the performance of 62 percent of the students who were taught using traditional instructional methods. This finding can also be interpreted as: the typical student moved from the 50th percentile to the 62nd percentile in science when CAI was used.

This finding is consistent with the Christmann and Badget (1999) study. The authors found an effect size of 0.266 standard deviation when they synthesized the results of 11 studies comparing the effectiveness of CAI and traditional instruction in science. Although the number of studies included in this analysis was four times larger than their sample size, this study showed very similar results, a fact that points to an overall trend. Similar results have been reported in earlier studies. Flinn and Gravat (1995), for example, reported an effect size of 0.26 standard deviation for CAI in science plus medicine. Niemiec and Walberg (1987) reported the effect size for science from two studies as 0.28 standard deviation. Smaller effects ($ES = 0.13$) for science were reported by Bangert-Drowns, Kulik, and Kulik (1985).

The results of this analysis also indicated that all variables except educational level were related to effect size. The strongest relationships were found for the following variables: length of treatment, student-to-computer ratio, and publication year. Effect sizes did not vary by publication status and educational level. The relationships between effect size and each variable will be discussed in the following sections.

TABLE 2   Summary of Analysis Results

Variables and Classes	Between-Classes Effect (Q_{Bet})	Number of Effect Sizes (N)	Mean Effect Size ($d+$)
Subject matter	178.16****		
Biology		45	0.167
Chemistry		36	0.108
Physics		16	0.555
General science		3	0.335
Physical science		5	0.025
Earth science		2	−0.507
Mode of CAI	115.60****		
Drill and practice		22	−0.107
Simulations		43	0.391
Tutorials		26	0.369
Combination		16	0.122

TABLE 2 Continued

Variables and Classes	Between-Classes Effect (Q_{Bet})	Number of Effect Sizes (N)	Mean Effect Size (d+)
School level	0.003		
Secondary		53	0.273
College		55	0.272
Instructor effect	10.434****		
Same instructor		33	0.218
Different		37	0.328
Unspecified		36	0.226
Length of treatment	40.18**		
0–4 weeks		34	0.378
More than 4 weeks		72	0.219
Unspecified		2	0.632
Student-to-computer ratio	46.647****		
1		40	0.368
2		9	0.168
3 or more		23	0.096
Unspecified		36	0.273
Software author	7.01*		
Researcher/teacher		60	0.318
Commercial		41	0.229
Unspecified		7	0.251
Role of computer	5.32*		
Supplementary		81	0.288
Substitute		27	0.178
Publication date	93.13****		
1970–1979		10	0.615
1980–1989		69	0.212
1990–1999		29	0.159
Publication type	14.27****		
ERIC documents		16	0.337
Journal articles		44	0.293
Dissertations		42	0.229
Theses		6	0.013

*$p < .05$. **$p < .01$. ***$p < .001$. ****$p < .0001$.[1]

---

1. A p value (i.e., a probability value) represents the likelihood that a statistical result was obtained by chance. The lower the p value (e.g., .0001 is lower than .05), the less likely it is that the result was obtained by chance.

The present meta-analysis detected significant differences in effectiveness for different CAI implementations. The results indicated that the most effective mode of CAI was simulation in science subject areas, followed by tutorial. A striking result of the analysis was that drill-and-practice CAI had a negative effect. This study supported the results of two previous meta-analyses (Liao, 1992, 1998) reporting that drill and practice is not as effective as simulation or tutorial. However, this finding was completely opposite that of earlier findings. Niemiec and Walberg (1985), for example, reported that CAI was most effective in drill and practice (ES = 0.47) and least effective in problem solving (ES = 0.12), with a moderate effect for tutorials (ES = 0.34). Similarly, Bangert-Drowns (1985) found that CAI is more effective in drill-and-practice form, followed by tutorial. However, it should be noted that these studies did not limit their primary studies to science and that these results were for all subjects in general.

This finding suggests that drill and practice might not be a good choice for science, although it might be beneficial in other subject areas. The higher effect sizes associated with studies using simulation might be partly because simulations create a more active learning environment, thus increasing student involvement and enhancing achievement. Drill and practice, on the other hand, is generally associated with rote learning. Science requires students, however, to be involved in higher-level cognitive processes such as questioning, hypothesizing, problem solving, analyzing, and synthesizing.

The majority of studies located for this meta-analysis were in the subject areas of biology and chemistry. The effects reported for these two subjects, however, were barely noticeable. Little research investigating the effectiveness of CAI in physics was available in the literature. However, the largest mean effect was found for physics (ES = 0.555), suggesting that CAI is most effective in physics. This result, however, should be viewed with caution, because the number of studies included was limited and the majority of them were conducted before 1990. Clearly, more research needs to be conducted to evaluate with confidence the effectiveness of CAI in physics teaching.

The majority of past meta-analyses reporting effect sizes for science did not distinguish between the subject areas. This analysis was consistent with the results of the only meta-analysis reporting the difference in effect sizes for different science subject areas, conducted by Christmann and Badget (1999). By synthesizing the results of 11 studies, the researchers concluded that CAI is most effective in general science (ES = 0.707), followed by physics (ES = 0.280), chemistry (ES = 0.085), and biology (ES = 0.042).

This study concluded that experimenter/teacher-developed software was relatively more effective than commercial software. Similar results were reported by several meta-analysts (Kulik et al., 1983; Niemiec & Walberg, 1985; Ryan, 1991). The explanation for this particular finding might be that an experimenter or teacher is more conscious of the specific objectives and desired outcomes of a course.

The results of this study suggested that the effects are smaller (ES = 0.218) when the same teacher taught both CAI and traditional classes and larger (ES = 0.328) when different instructors taught experimental and control classes. This result is consistent with the majority of research in the CAI literature. For example, Flinn and Gravat (1995) reported that, if the same teacher taught both groups, the effect size was 0.23 standard deviation; if different teachers taught, the effect size was 0.30 standard deviation. The instructor effect on CAI effectiveness was more impressive in a more recent study. Liao (1998) reported that the effect size was 0.782 for different and 0.068 for the same teachers. This finding is very crucial because it brings up the question of whether the instructional medium or the teachers' instructional effectiveness makes the difference in student achievement. As Kulik and Kulik (1991) suggested, assigning more effective teachers to the CAI group might account for higher effects found in different teacher experiments. However, this analysis showed that even when the same instructor was assigned to the control and treatment groups, student achievement was higher in the CAI groups, which shows a clear effect of CAI on student achievement.

This study detected a significant relationship between CAI effectiveness and the instructional role of computers. Effect sizes were higher ($ES = 0.288$) when computers were used as a supplement to the regular instruction and lower when the computer entirely replaced the regular instruction ($ES = 0.178$). This finding was consistent with the previous meta-analyses (Kulik et al., 1983; Liao, 1998), suggesting that using the computer as a supplement to regular instruction should be the preferred choice instead of using it as a replacement.

The results of the present study suggested a strong relationship between CAI effectiveness and student-to-computer ratio. The effect size difference between individual ($ES = 0.368$) and group ($ES = 0.096$) implementations was remarkable, suggesting that an individualized version of CAI would be preferable in educational settings. However, this finding is tentative, because some studies of the 36 relevant effect sizes did not specify the student-to-computer ratio. This variable has not been investigated extensively in the previous meta-analyses. One of the few studies reporting effect size differences with respect to the student-to-computer ratio was conducted by Liao (1998). That study, however, reported no significant relationship between effect size and the student-to-computer ratio.

This meta-analysis indicated that there were no significant effect size differences at different school levels. This result supports the meta-analysis conducted by Flinn and Gravat (1995), reporting an effect size of 0.26 standard deviation for elementary grades, an effect size of 0.20 standard deviation for secondary grades, and an effect size of 0.20 standard deviation for college. However, this finding is not consistent with the majority of meta-analyses (Bangert-Drowns, 1985; Burns & Bozeman, 1981; Liao, 1998; Roblyer, 1989), which report significant effect size differences for different school levels.

The results of this study indicated that the length of the treatment was strongly related to the effectiveness of CAI for teaching science. CAI was especially effective when the duration of treatment was limited to four weeks or less. The average effect of CAI in such studies was 0.378 standard deviation. In studies where treatment continued longer than four weeks, the effects were less clear ($ES = 0.219$). A similar relationship between length of treatment and study outcome has been reported in previous meta-analyses. Kulik et al. (1983), for example, reported an effect size of 0.56 for 4 weeks or less, 0.30 for 5–8 weeks, and 0.20 for more than 8 weeks. The higher effect sizes associated with shorter studies could be explained by the *Hawthorne effect*. A Hawthorne, or novelty, effect occurs when students are stimulated to greater efforts simply because of the novelty of a treatment. On the other hand, if the treatment extends over a long time period, it loses its attractiveness over time and the effects become less clear.

This study concluded that the results found in ERIC documents were more positive ($ES = 0.337$) than results found in journal articles ($ES = 0.293$) and dissertations ($ES = 0.229$). This variable was studied to investigate whether there is a publication bias in the research literature on the effectiveness of CAI. Publication bias is an alleged tendency of the editors or reviewers rejecting studies showing no significant results. This study did not show signs of any such bias, because the results found in ERIC documents were the most positive. The reason the results found in dissertations were remarkably smaller than journal or ERIC documents, however, remained unclear.

Year of publication was one of the most significant variables in this meta-analysis. A strong relationship between the effect size and the year of publication was determined. Results revealed that CAI was most effective ($ES = 0.615$) in science education between 1970 and 1979 and least effective ($ES = 0.159$) between 1990 and 1999. This finding is particularly surprising and contradictory to the earlier prediction that the effects of CAI on student achievement would be greater over the years, because software would be of better quality due to advances in computer technology. The result could be partly because computer use in schools was so new in the 1970s that a Hawthorne effect occurred.

CONCLUSION

The present meta-analysis detected a small positive effect for CAI use in science and determined that some characteristics of the study were related to the effectiveness of CAI. The small effect size seems to suggest that using CAI in the science classroom may not be highly effective at this point. However, investigation of effectiveness by variables revealed that CAI is more effective under particular conditions. CAI could be more beneficial in student learning in science when these conditions are fulfilled. The present analysis, for example, revealed that computers are more effective when used in simulation or tutorial modes. Consequently, tutorial and simulation CAI programs could be used in science classrooms to enhance student learning. This meta-analysis also revealed that CAI is more effective when computers are used individually. Supplying classrooms with a sufficient number of computers, thus allowing students to work individually rather than in groups, would be beneficial and is recommended for a higher level of effectiveness. According to the results of this study, CAI is more effective when used as a supplement to traditional instruction rather than as a substitute. Therefore, instead of devoting the entire class time to the use of computers, use of such technology in conjunction with other teaching strategies could be more beneficial for student learning in science subject areas. This analysis also revealed that experimenter- or teacher-developed programs were more effective than commercial software programs. This finding seems to indicate that teacher- or experimenter-developed software is more focused on the specific educational objectives of the lesson and the curriculum goals. Devoting more attention to these factors when designing software is recommended for a higher level of effectiveness.

Recommendations for Future Research

Although this analysis indicated that CAI was most effective in teaching physics, this finding is tentative. Because most studies investigating the achievement effects of CAI were done before 1990, this finding does not reflect recent trends. Therefore, more research on the effects of CAI in physics education is needed to reach a confident conclusion.

This research could not make use of some research studies because of the lack of necessary statistics, which are important elements of a meta-analysis. Educational researchers are advised to report all necessary statistics, such as number of subjects in treatment and control groups, standard deviations, and means, as well as significance levels.

Contributor

Sule Bayraktar received her Ph.D. in curriculum and instruction with an emphasis on science education from Ohio University. She is currently affiliated with Yuzuncu Yil University in Turkey. Her research interests include (1) effects of computer technologies and constructivist teaching methods on student achievement in science and (2) gender differences in science education. (Address: Sule Bayraktar, Yuzuncu Yil Universitesi, Egitim Fakultesi, Zeve Kampusu, VAN/TURKEY; sulebayraktar@yahoo.com.)

References

References marked with an asterisk (*) indicate studies included in the meta-analysis.

*Akpan, J. P., & Andre, T. (1999). The effects of a prior dissection simulation on middle students' dissection performance and understanding of the anatomy and morphology of the frog. *Journal of Science Education and Technology, 8*(2), 107–121.

*Ayoubi, Z. R. (1985). The effect of microcomputer assisted instruction on achievement in high school chemistry. (Doctoral dissertation, The University of Michigan, 1985). *Dissertation Abstracts International, 46,* A3310.

Bangert-Drowns, R. L. (1985, March–April). *Meta-analysis of findings on computer-based education with precollege students.* Paper presented at the annual meeting of the American Educational Research Association, Chicago. (ERIC No. ED 263 905)

Bangert-Drowns, R., Kulik, J. A., & Kulik, C. (1985). Effectiveness of computer-based instruction in secondary schools. *Journal of Computer Based Instruction, 12*(3), 59–68.

Bennett, R. F. (1985). The effects of computer-assisted instruction and reinforcement schedules on physics achievement and attitudes toward physics of high school students. (Doctoral dissertation, Boston University, 1985). *Dissertation Abstracts International, 46,* A3670.

*Bobbert, L. C. (1982). The effects of using interactive computer simulated laboratory experiments in college chemistry courses. (Doctoral dissertation, University of Cincinnati, 1982). *Dissertation Abstracts International, 43,* A2300.

Burns, P., & Bozeman W. (1981). Computer-assisted instruction and mathematics achievement: Is there a relationship? *Educational Technology, 10*(2), 32–39.

*Castleberry, S. J., Montague, E. J., & Lagowski, J. J. (1970). Computer-based teaching techniques in general chemistry. *Journal of Research in Science Teaching, 7,* 197–208.

*Cavin, C. S., & Lagowski, J. J. (1978). Effects of computer simulated or laboratory experiments and student aptitude on achievement and time in a college general chemistry laboratory course. *Journal of Research in Science Teaching, 15*(6), 455–463.

*Chien, C. C. (1997). The effectiveness of interactive computer simulations on college engineering student conceptual understanding and problem solving ability related to circular motion. (Doctoral dissertation, Ohio University, 1997). *Dissertation Abstracts International, 58,* A2589.

*Choi, B., & Gennaro, E. (1987). The effectiveness of using computer simulated experiments on junior high students' understanding of the volume displacement concept. *Journal of Research in Science Teaching, 24*(6), 539–552.

Christmann, E. P., & Badget, J. L. (1999). A comparative analysis of the effects of computer-assisted instruction on student achievement in differing science and demographical areas. *Journal of Computers in Mathematics and Science Teaching, 18*(2), 135–143.

Cohen, J. (1977). *Statistical power analysis for the behavioral sciences* (rev. ed.). New York: Academic Press.

*Cracolice, M. S. (1994). An investigation of computer-assisted instruction and semi-programmed instruction as a replacement for traditional recitation/discussion in general chemistry and their relationships to student cognitive characteristics. (Doctoral dissertation, University of Oklahoma, 1994). *Dissertation Abstracts International, 55,* A2335.

*Duffy, M., & Barowy, W. (1995, April). *Effects of constructivist and computer-facilitated strategies on achievements in heterogeneous secondary biology.* Paper presented at the annual meeting of the National Association for Research in Science Teaching, San Francisco. (ERIC No. ED 406 207)

*Eisenkraft, A. J. (1986). The effects of computer simulated experiments and traditional laboratory experiments on subsequent transfer tasks in a high school physics course. (Doctoral dissertation, New York University, 1986). *Dissertation Abstracts International, 47,* A3723.

*Faryniarz, J. V., & Lockwood, L. G. (1992). Effectiveness of microcomputer simulations in stimulating environmental problem solving by community college students. *Journal of Research in Science Teaching, 29*(5), 453–470.

*Ferguson, N. H., & Chapman, S. R. (1993). Computer-assisted instruction for introductory genetics. *Journal of Natural Resources Life Sciences Education, 22*(2), 145–152.

Flinn, C. M., & Gravatt, B. (1995). The efficacy of computer assisted instruction (CAI): A meta-analysis. *Journal of Educational Computing Research, 12*(3), 219–242.

*Fox, J. A. (1986). A comparison of lecture based instruction and computer based individualized instruction. (Doctoral dissertation, University of Northern Colorado, 1986). *Dissertation Abstracts International, 47,* A2132.

Glass, G. V. (1976). Primary, secondary, and meta-analysis of research. *Educational Researcher, 5*(11), 3–8.

*Hauben, M. H., & Lehman, J. D. (1988). Computer assisted instruction for problem solving by dimensional analysis. *Journal of Computers in Mathematics and Science Teaching, 7*(3), 50–54.

*Hoge, P. S. (1995). The effect of computer-assisted instruction on the achievement levels of secondary biology students. Unpublished master's thesis, Central Missouri State University, Warrensburg.

*Hounshell, P. B., & Hill, S. R. (1989). The computer and achievement and attitudes in high school biology. *Journal of Research in Science Teaching, 26*(6), 543–549.

Hunter , J. E., & Schmidt, F. L. (1990). *Methods of meta-analysis: Correcting error and bias in research findings.* Newbury Park, CA: Sage Publications.

*Jackman, L. E., Mollenberg, W. P., & Brabson, D. G. (1987). Evaluation of three instructional methods for teaching general chemistry. *Journal of Chemical Education, 64*(9), 794–796.

*Jensen, M. S., Wilcox, K. J., Hatch, J. T., Somdahl, C. (1996). A computer assisted instruction unit on diffusion and osmosis with a conceptual change design. *Journal of Computers in Mathematics and Science Teaching, 15*(1/2), 49–64.

*Jones, J. E. (1972). Computer-simulated experiments in high school physics and chemistry. (Doctoral dissertation, Iowa State University, 1972). *Dissertation Abstracts International, 33,* A4200.

*Kelly, P. R. (1997–1998). Transfer of learning from a computer simulation as compared to a laboratory activity. *Journal of Educational Technology Systems, 26*(4), 345–351.

Kinzie, M. B., & Sullivan, H. J. (1989). Continuing motivation, learner control, and CAI. *Education Technology Research and Development, 37*(2), 5–14.

*Kromhout, O. M. (1972). *Effect of computer tutorial review lessons on exam performance in introductory college physics. Tech memo number 64.* Tallahassee: Florida State University. (ERIC No. ED 072 654)

Kulik, C., Kulik, J., & Bangert-Drowns, R. (1984, April). *Effects of computer-based education on elementary school pupils.* Paper presented at the annual meeting of the American Educational Research Association, New Orleans, LA. (ERIC No. ED 244 616)

Kulik, C. C., & Kulik, J. A. (1991). Effectiveness of computer-based instruction: An updated analysis. *Computers in Human Behavior, 7*(1–2), 75–94.

Kulik, J., Bangert, R., & Williams, G. (1983). Effects of computer-based teaching on secondary school students. *Journal of Educational Psychology, 75*(1), 19–26.

*Lasater, M. E. (1971). The development and evaluation of a computer assisted instructional program involving applications of selected chemical principles. (Doctoral dissertation, University of Texas, 1971). *Dissertation Abstracts International, 32*(10A), 5535.

*Leece, C. G. (1982). *The development and evaluation of the microcomputer modules entitled photophosphorylation.* Houghton: Michigan Technological University. (ERIC No. ED 223 469)

*Lehman, J. D. (1988, April). *Integrating computers in the biology education of elementary teaching majors.* Paper presented at the annual meeting of the National Association for Research in Science Teaching, Lake of the Ozarks, MO. (ERIC No. ED 291 579)

Liao, Y. C. (1992). Effects of computer-assisted instruction on cognitive outcomes: A meta-analysis. *Journal of Research on Computing in Education, 24*(3), 367–381.

Liao, Y. C. (1998). Effects of hypermedia versus traditional instruction on students' achievement. *Journal of Research on Computing in Education, 30*(4), 341–359.

*Milkent, M., & Roth, W. M. (1989). Enhancing student achievement through computer generated homework. *Journal of Research in Science Teaching, 26*(7), 567–573.

*Miller, D. G. (1986). The integration of computer simulation into the community college general biology laboratory. (Doctoral dissertation, Florida Atlantic University, 1986). *Dissertation Abstracts International, 47,* A2106.

*Morrel, P. D. (1992). The effects of computer assisted instruction on student achievement in high school biology. *School Science and Mathematics, 92*(4), 177–181.

National Assessment of Educational Progress. (1996). *Trends in academic progress, 1996.* Washington, DC: U.S. Department of Education, National Center for Education Statistics.

*Nicholls, C., Merkel, S., & Cordts, M. (1996). The effect of computer animation on students' understanding of microbiology. *Journal of Research on Computing in Education, 28*(3), 359–371.

Niemiec, R. P., & Walberg, H. J. (1985). Computers and achievement in the elementary schools. *Journal of Educational Computing Research, 1*(4), 435–440.

*Nishino, A. K. (1993). An exploratory investigation to determine the effects of a multimedia computer-based science learning environment and gender differences, on achievement, and attitudes and interests of students in an eighth-grade science classroom. (Doctoral dissertation, University of Southern California, 1993). *Dissertation Abstracts International, 54,* A4414.

Orwin, R. G. (1994). Evaluating coding decisions. In H. Cooper & L. V. Hedges (Eds.), *Handbook of research synthesis* (pp. 139–162). New York: Sage Publications.

*Podell, D. M., Kaminsky, S., & Cusimano, V. (1993). The effects of micro-computer laboratory approach to physical science instruction on student motivation. *Computers in the Schools, 9*(2/3), 65–73.

*Rivers, R. H., & Vockell, E. (1987). Computer simulations to stimulate scientific problem solving. *Journal of Research in Science Teaching, 24*(5), 403–415.

Roblyer, M. D. (1989). *The impact of microcomputer-based instruction on teaching and learning: A review of recent research.* Syracuse, NY: ERIC Clearinghouse on Information Resources. (ERIC No. ED 315 063)

Rosenberg, M. S., Adams, D. C., & Gurevitch, J. (1997). MetaWin: Statistical software for meta-analysis with resampling tests [Computer software]. Sunderland, MA: Sinauer Associates.

Rosenthal, R. (1991). *Meta analytic procedures for social research* (rev. ed.). Thousand Oaks, CA: Sage Publications.

Ryan, A. W. (1991). Meta-analysis of achievement effects of microcomputer applications in elementary schools. *Educational Administration Quarterly, 27*(2), 161–184.

*Shaltz, M. B. (1982). *Development and Evolution of SUMIT microcomputer module entitled "Predator Functional Response."* Report submitted in partial fulfillment of the requirements for the degree of Master of Science in Biological Sciences, Michigan Technological University, Houghton. (ERIC No. ED 229 249)

*Shaw, E. L., Jr. (1984). Effects of the use of microcomputer simulations on concept identification achievement and attitudes toward computers and science instruction of middle school students of various levels of logical reasoning ability. (Doctoral dissertation, University of Georgia, 1984). *Dissertation Abstract International, 45,* A2827.

*Stringfield, J. K., Jr. (1986). The effects of reasoning ability and computer based instructional materials on the achievement and attitudes of high school students in a genetics unit in general biology. (Doctoral dissertation, University of North Carolina at Chapel Hill, 1986). *Dissertation Abstracts International, 48,* A1165.

*Summerlin, L., & Gardner, M. (1973). A study of tutorial type computer assisted instruction in high school chemistry. *Journal of Research in Science Teaching, 10*(1), 75–82.

*Tauro, J. P. (1980). A study of academically superior students' response to particular computer assisted programs in chemistry. (Doctoral dissertation, Syracuse University, 1980). *Dissertation Abstracts International, 42,* A643.

*Tylinski, D. J. (1994). The effect of a computer simulation on junior high students' understanding of the physiological systems of an earthworm (dissection). (Doctoral dissertation, Indiana University of Pennsylvania, 1994). *Dissertation Abstracts International, 55,* A923.

*Wainwright, C. L. (1985, April). *The effectiveness of a computer assisted instruction package in supplementing teaching of selected concepts in high school chemistry: Writing formulas and balancing chemical equations.* Paper presented at the annual meeting of the National Association for Research in Science Teaching, French Lick Springs, IN. (ERIC No. ED 257 656)

*Williamson, V. M., & Abraham, M. R. (1995). The effects of computer animation on the particulate mental models of college chemistry students. *Journal of Research in Science Teaching, 32*(5), 521–534.

Wise, K. C. (1988). The effects of using computing technologies in science instruction: A synthesis of classroom research. In J. D. Ellis (Ed.), *1988 AETS Yearbook* (pp. 105–118). Colorado Springs, CO: Office of Educational Research and Improvement, U.S. Department of Education.

*Wyman, N. R. (1988–1989). A computer-aided unit to teach reduction of experimental data to a functional relationship. *Computers in Mathematics and Science Teaching, 8*(2), 41–46.

*Ybarrando, B. A. (1984). *A study of the effectiveness of computer assisted instruction in the high school biology classroom.* (ERIC No. ED 265 015)

In the following section of the chapter you will read a published secondary source that illustrates a professional review. It is preceded by comments written especially for this book by the author of the article. Then the article itself is reprinted in full just as it appeared when originally published. Where appropriate, we have added footnotes to help you understand the information contained in the article.

SAMPLE PROFESSIONAL REVIEW
Cooperative Learning

Slavin, R. (1992). Cooperative learning. In M. C. Alkin (Ed.), *Encyclopedia of educational research* (6th ed. vol. 1, pp. 235–238). New York: Macmillan.

● RESEARCHER'S COMMENTS, *Prepared by Robert Slavin*

Research on cooperative learning represents one of the greatest success stories in the history of educational research—and also one of its greatest failures. As recently as the 1970s, cooperative learning methods were rarely used, little known, and considered "fringe" methods by most educators. By 1993, a national survey (Puma et al., 1993) found that 79 percent of third-grade teachers and 62 percent of seventh-grade teachers reported making sustained use of cooperative learning methods in teaching mathematics. The proportions in reading/language arts were 74 percent at both grade levels. Even though these figures are certainly overestimates, it is true that hundreds of thousands of teachers are making daily use of cooperative learning methods. Research rarely has anything like this impact on practice.

The research itself is an extraordinary success story. Field experiments comparing experimental and control groups using different teaching methods are relatively rare in educational research. Yet for a recent review (Slavin, 1995) I was able to locate ninety-nine experimental studies of cooperative learning in elementary and secondary schools that met high methodological standards, including a duration requirement of at least four weeks. Further, the research has been remarkably consistent in showing the benefits of cooperative learning on a broad range of student outcomes, including achievement.

The problem with this success story, however, is that the cooperative learning methods most often used in classrooms are not those that the research has found to be effective. Teachers generally use quite informal forms of cooperative learning, in which students may be assigned common tasks or projects with a single product, or may simply be allowed to sit together and help each other as needed. The problem with these structures is fairly obvious. Often, one group member can do all the work for the group. In some project groups, for example, some members do most of the thinking, while other members cut and paste, color, or type—and may even be *assigned* such nonthinking tasks by the teacher. Sometimes low-status members whom other members feel have little to contribute to the group are ignored or shut out of group activities or discussions. These forms of so-called "cooperative learning" fail to meet the criteria that have been established and validated, through considerable research, as necessary for the effectiveness of cooperative learning.

Since the 1970s, researchers have generally agreed that for cooperative learning to be effective, especially in promoting student achievement, two elements must be in place so that cooperative learning does not degenerate into one or a few students doing the work for other students.

One element is *group goals*. Group goals means that recognition is provided for, small rewards are given for, or a small proportion of students' grades are based on, the performance of the entire group.

The second element is *individual accountability*. Individual accountability means that the success of the group requires individual learning by all the members of the group. For example, effective methods may recognize groups based on the sum or average of individuals' scores on quizzes that are taken with group mates' help. Alternatively, effective methods can recognize a group's success based on the quality of a group report or book to which each group member contributes a (signed) chapter or distinct portion. The goal here is to motivate students to be concerned about the learning of all the members of the group, and to make it impossible for the group to succeed unless all group members learn satisfactorily. For cooperative learning to be effective, the interaction within each group should focus on teaching and learning, discussing and debating, assessing and filling in gaps in understanding, and so forth. It should *not* consist of students sharing unexplained answers, students doing work for each other, or students simply carrying out make-work tasks that do not foster their learning. See Webb & Palincsar (1996), which reviews research on behaviors associated with achievement gain in cooperative learning.

My own research on cooperative learning has moved toward the development and evaluation of comprehensive school-based programs that build curriculum, instruction, school organization, and support elements around a cooperative learning base. I have had many disappointments observing the way cooperative learning is usually structured in classrooms. My experiences have led me to try to create cooperative learning approaches that are so well worked out and complete, from student materials to teachers manuals to professional development procedures, that teachers can use them with confidence and integrity on a consistent basis. I have come to believe that instructional reform must be tied to curriculum reform so that teachers will fully understand how instructional ideas like cooperative learning can play out in practice.

To give readers a picture of what the result might be, imagine an elementary school built around the notion that cooperative learning is a regular feature of the curriculum in all classrooms throughout the school year. As part of this notion, students, teachers, administrators, and community groups are all committed to working *cooperatively* to make the school a better place for working and learning. Here is a brief list of the major components of the school's operation that follow from this commitment, with some examples of what each might involve (see Slavin, 1987).

1. *Cooperative learning in the classroom.* On any school day, cooperative learning methods can be observed in most classrooms and in all or most of the basic subjects. Learning is based more on cooperation among students than on competition between them.

2. *Integration of special education and remedial services with the regular program.* Special education and regular teachers team-teach on a regular basis. Students with handicaps are integrated with nonhandicapped students in cooperative learning teams.

3. *Peer coaching.* Teachers learn new cooperative learning methods together. Experienced teachers get release time to visit one another's classes and give assistance and exchange ideas when teachers implement new methods.

4. *Cooperative planning.* Teachers plan goals and strategies together and prepare common libraries of instructional materials. Teachers make joint decisions about cooperative learning activities that involve more than one class.

5. *Building-level steering committees.* Teachers and administrators work together through a steering committee to determine the direction that the school takes. Parents and other staff are represented on the committee.

6. *Cooperation with parents and community members.* The school supports the notion that children's school success is everyone's responsibility. Parental and community participation in school is SOP (standard operating procedure).

This set of practices was the basis for what we called the Cooperative Elementary School, which we successfully evaluated in the mid-1980s (Stevens & Slavin, 1995). They were then incorporated into our Success for All program, which as of the fall of 1997 will be in use in more than 700 elementary schools serving 350,000 children (see Slavin, Madden, Dolan, & Wasik, 1996, for more details). Research on Success for All finds substantial positive effects on student achievement.

In closing, let me return to cooperative learning as it exists in most schools today. Despite the lack of correspondence between the forms of cooperative learning found to be effective in research and the forms used in most classrooms, this has still been an exciting and fruitful area of research that has had an enormous impact on practice, and that will undoubtedly continue to do so for many years. If nothing else, kids love to work together, and it's great to be involved in research on something that makes so many kids (and teachers) so happy!

A more comprehensive and recent summary of my work in the field of cooperative learning and its impact on achievement is available in Slavin, Hurley, & Chamberlain (2003).

References

Puma, M. J., Jones, C. C., Rock, D., & Fernandez, R. (1993). *Prospects: The congressionally mandated study of educational growth and opportunity*. Interim Report. Bethesda, MD: Abt Associates.

Slavin, R. E. (1987). Cooperative learning and the cooperative school. *Educational Leadership, 45*(3), 7–13.

Slavin, R. E. (1995). *Cooperative learning: Theory, research, and practice* (2nd ed.). Boston: Allyn & Bacon.

Slavin, R. E., Hurley, E. A., & Chamberlain, A. M. (2003). Cooperative learning and achievement: Theory and research. In W. M. Reynolds & G. E. Miller (Eds.), *Handbook of Psychology,* Volume 7 (pp. 177–198). Hoboken, NJ: Wiley.

Slavin, R. E., Madden, N. A., Dolan, L. J., & Wasik, B. A. (1996). *Every child, every school: Success for All.* Thousand Oaks, CA: Corwin.

Stevens, R. J., & Slavin, R. E. (1995). The Cooperative Elementary School: Effects on students' achievement, attitudes, and social relations. *American Educational Research Journal, 32,* 321–351.

Webb, N. M., & Palincsar, A. S. (1996). Group processes in the classroom. In D. C. Berliner & R. C. Calfee (Eds.), *Handbook of educational psychology* (pp. 841–873). New York: Simon & Schuster Macmillan.

Cooperative Learning

Robert Slavin

Cooperative learning refers to instructional methods in which students of all levels of performance work together in small groups, usually toward a group goal. The many cooperative learning methods differ considerably from one another. The most extensively researched are described.

Slavin, R. (1992). Cooperative learning. In M. C. Alkin (Ed.), *Encyclopedia of educational research* (6th ed., vol. 1, pp. 235–238). New York: Macmillan Library Reference. © 1992, Macmillan Library Reference. Reprinted by permission of the Gale Group.

COOPERATIVE LEARNING METHODS

Student Teams-Achievement Divisions (STAD). In STAD (Slavin, 1986), students are assigned to four-member learning teams that are mixed in performance level, gender, and ethnicity. The teacher presents a lesson, and then students work within their teams to make sure that all team members have mastered the lesson. Finally, all students take individual quizzes on the material, at which time they may not help one another.

Students' quiz scores are compared to their own past averages, and points based on the degree to which students can meet or exceed their own earlier performance are awarded. These points are then summed to form team scores, and teams that meet certain criteria earn certificates or other rewards. The whole cycle of activities—from teacher presentation to team practice to quiz—usually takes 3–5 class periods.

The STAD method has been used in most subjects, from mathematics to language arts to social studies, and has been used from Grade 2 through college. It is most appropriate for teaching well-defined objectives with single right answers, such as mathematical computations and applications, language usage and mechanics, geography and map skills, and science facts and concepts.

Teams-Games-Tournament (TGT). The TGT method (De-Vries & Slavin, 1978; Slavin, 1986) uses the same teacher presentations and team work as in STAD but replaces the quizzes with weekly tournaments, in which students compete with members of other teams to contribute points to their team scores. Students compete at three-person *tournament tables* against others with similar past records in mathematics. A *bumping* procedure keeps the competition fair by changing assignments to tournament tables each week based on student performance. As in STAD, high-performing teams earn certificates or other forms of team rewards.

Team Assisted Individualization (TAI). The TAI method (Slavin, 1985a; Slavin, Leavey, & Madden, 1986) shares with STAD and TGT the use of four-member, mixed-ability learning teams and certificates for high-performing teams. But whereas STAD and TGT use a single pace of instruction for the class, TAI combines cooperative learning with individualized instruction. The TAI method is designed specifically to teach math-

ematics to students in Grades 3–6 (or older students not ready for a full algebra course).

In TAI, students enter an individualized sequence according to a placement test and then proceed at their own rates. In general, team members work on different units. Teammates check each others' work against answer sheets and help each other with any problems. Final unit tests are taken without teammate help and are scored by student monitors. Each week, teachers total the number of units completed by all team members and give certificates or other team rewards to teams that exceed a criterion score based on the number of final tests passed, with extra points for perfect papers and completed homework.

Cooperative Integrated Reading and Composition (CIRC). In CIRC (Stevens, Madden, Slavin, & Farnish, 1987), teachers use basal readers and reading groups, much as in traditional reading programs. However, students are assigned to teams composed of pairs of students from two different reading groups. While the teacher is working with one reading group, students in the other groups are working in their pairs on a series of cognitively engaging activities, including reading to one another, making predictions about how narrative stories come out, summarizing stories to one another, writing responses to stories, and practicing spelling, decoding, and vocabulary. Students work in teams to master main idea and other comprehension skills. During language arts periods, students write drafts, revise and edit one another's work, and prepare for "publication" of team books.

Jigsaw. In the original jigsaw method (Aronson, Blaney, Stephan, Sikes, & Snapp, 1978), students are assigned to six-member teams to work on academic material that has been broken into sections. For example, a biography might be later divided into early life, first accomplishments, major setbacks, later life, and impact on history. Each team member reads a section. Next, members of different teams who have studied the same sections meet in "expert groups" to discuss their sections. Then the students return to their teams and take turns teaching their teammates about their sections. Because the only way that students can learn sections other than their own is to listen carefully to their teammates, they are motivated to support and show interest in one another's work. Several modifications of Jigsaw have also been designed (Slavin, 1986; Kagan, 1989).

Learning Together. The learning together model of cooperative learning (Johnson & Johnson, 1987) was developed at the University of Minnesota. The methods that they researched involve students working in four- or five-member heterogeneous groups on assignment sheets. The groups hand in a single sheet, and receive praise and rewards based on the group product.

Group Investigation. Developed at the University of Tel Aviv (Sharan & Shachar, 1988), group investigation is a general classroom organization plan in which students work in small groups using cooperative inquiry, group discussion, and cooperative planning and projects. Students form their own two- to six-member groups. After choosing subtopics from a unit being studied by the entire class, the groups further break their subtopics into individual tasks and carry out the activities necessary to prepare group reports. Each group then makes a presentation or display to communicate its findings to the entire class.

RESEARCH ON COOPERATIVE LEARNING

More than 70 high-quality studies have evaluated various cooperative learning methods over periods of at least 4 weeks in regular elementary and secondary schools; 60 of these have measured effects on student achievement (Slavin, 1990). These studies compared effects of cooperative learning to those of traditionally taught control groups on measures of the same objectives pursued in all classes. Teachers and classes were randomly assigned to cooperative or control conditions, or they were matched on pretest achievement level and other factors.

Academic Achievement. Overall—of 68 experimental–control comparison studies of the achievement effects of cooperative learning in 60 different studies—42 (62%) found significantly greater achievement in cooperative than in control classes.[a] Twenty-three (34%) found no differences, and in only three studies did a control group outperform the experimental group. However, the effects of cooperative learning vary considerably according to the particular methods used. Two elements must be present if cooperative learning is to be effective: group goals and individual accountability (Davidson, 1985; Newmann & Thompson, 1987; Slavin, 1990). That is, groups must be working to achieve some goal or earn rewards or recognition, and the success of the group must depend on the individual learning of every group member. In studies of methods of this kind (e.g., STAD, TGT, TAI, and CIRC), effects on achievement have been consistently positive; 32 of 40 such studies (80%) found significantly positive achievement effects with a median effect size of +0.30 (Slavin, 1990).[b] In contrast, only 10 of 28 studies (36%) lacking group goals and individual accountability found positive effects on student achievement, and only 3 studies (11%) found effects favoring control groups, with a median effect size of only +0.06.

Research on behaviors within groups that contribute to learning gains has found that students who provide and receive elaborated explanations are those who gain the most from the activities (Webb, 1985). Successful forms of cooperative learning have generally been equally effective with high-, average-, and low-achieving students (Slavin, 1990).

a. The word *significantly* refers to statistical significance (see Chapter 6). A research study typically investigates a small sample that is intended to represent a much larger population. If a statistically significant difference is found between the experimental and control groups, one can conclude with some confidence that a similar difference will be found in the population represented by the sample.

b. A median effect size of +0.30 means that half of the 40 studies found an effect size of +0.30 or lower. In other words, an effect size of +0.30 corresponds to the 50th percentile in the distribution of effect sizes.

Intergroup Relations. Social scientists have long advocated interethnic cooperation as a means of ensuring positive intergroup relations in desegregated settings. The famous social science statement submitted as part of the *Brown v. Board of Education* school desegregation decision strongly emphasized that positive intergroup relations would rise from school desegregation if and only if students were involved in cooperative equal-status interaction sanctioned by the school (Slavin, 1985b, 1990). Research has borne out this expectation. Positive effects on intergroup relations have been found for the STAD, TGT, TAI, jigsaw, learning together, and group investigation models (Slavin, 1985b). Two of these studies, one on STAD and one on jigsaw II included follow-ups of intergroup friendships several months after the end of the studies. Both found that students who had been in cooperative learning classes still named significantly more friends outside their own ethnic groups than did students who had been in control classes. Two studies of the group investigation method found that students' improved attitudes and behaviors toward classmates of different ethnic backgrounds extended to classmates who had never been in the same groups.

Mainstreaming. The research on cooperative learning and mainstreaming has focused on the academically handicapped child. In one study, STAD was used to attempt to integrate students performing two years or more below the level of their peers into the social structure of the classroom. The use of STAD significantly reduced the degree to which the normal-progress students rejected their mainstreamed classmates and increased the academic achievement and self-esteem of all students—mainstreamed and normal progress. Similar effects have been found for TAI, and other research using cooperative teams has also shown significant improvements in relationships between mainstreamed academically handicapped students and their normal-progress peers (see Madden & Slavin, 1983).

Self-Esteem. Several researchers working on cooperative learning techniques found that use of teams increases students' self-esteem. Students in cooperative learning classes have more positive feelings about themselves than do students in traditional classes. These improvements in self-esteem have been found for TGT, STAD, and jigsaw, for the three methods combined, and for TAI (Slavin, 1990).

Other Outcomes. In addition to effects on achievement, positive intergroup relations, greater acceptance of mainstreamed students, and self-esteem effects of cooperative learning have been found on a variety of other important educational outcomes. These effects include liking of school, development of peer norms in favor of doing well academically, feelings of individual control over the student's own fate in school, time on task, and cooperativeness and altruism (Slavin, 1990).

Current Research. Research on cooperative learning is proceeding in several directions. One involves research on schoolwide applications of cooperative learning principles, including peer coaching, mainstreaming, and teacher collaboration, as well as widespread use of cooperative learning methods (Madden, Slavin, Karweit, & Livermon, 1989; Slavin, 1987). Another involves continuing research on the cognitive and motivational bases for the achievement effects of cooperative learning (Dansereau, 1988). Applications of cooperative learning to the education of Hispanic and Native American children are being studied. Some of the many topics in need of further study include methods for training, maintenance, and institutionalization of cooperative learning in schools and why cooperative learning increases student achievement and critical elements contributing to this effect. Further applications of cooperative learning to complex problem solving and to senior high schools are needed.

CONCLUSION

The positive effects of cooperative learning methods on a variety of student outcomes are not found in every study or for every method. The overall conclusion to be drawn from this research, however, is that when the classroom is structured to allow students to work cooperatively on learning tasks, students benefit academically as well as socially.

Robert E. Slavin

See also Deinstitutionalization and Mainstreaming, Exceptional Children; Grouping Students for Instruction; Minorities, Education of; Peer and Cross-Age Tutoring; School Desegregation.

References

Aronson, E., Blaney, N., Stephan, C., Sikes, J., & Snapp, M. (1978). *The jigsaw classroom*. Beverly Hills, CA: Sage.

Dansereau, D. (1988). Cooperative learning strategies. In C. E. Weinstein, E. T. Goetz, & P. A. Alexander (Eds.), *Learning and study strategies: Issues in assessment, instruction, and evaluation* (pp. 103–120). New York: Academic Press.

Davidson, N. (1985). Small-group learning and teaching in mathematics: A selective review of the research. In R. E. Slavin, S. Sharan, R. Hertz-Lazarowitz, C. Webb, & R. Schmuck (Eds.), *Learning to cooperate, cooperating to learn* (pp. 211–230). New York: Plenum.

DeVries, D. L., & Slavin, R. E. (1978). Teams-Games-Tournament (TGT): Review of ten classroom experiments. *Journal of Research and Development in Education, 12,* 28–38.

Johnson, D. W., & Johnson, R. T. (1987). *Learning together and alone* (2nd ed.). Englewood Cliffs, NJ: Prentice-Hall.

Kagan, S. (1989). *Cooperative learning resources for teachers.* San Juan Capistrano, CA: Resources for Teachers.

Madden, N. A., & Slavin, R. E. (1983). Mainstreaming students with mild academic handicaps: Academic and social outcomes. *Review of Educational Research, 53,* 519–569.

Madden, N. A., Slavin, R. E., Karweit, N. L., & Livermon. B. J. (1989). Restructuring the urban elementary school. *Educational Leadership, 46*(5), 14–18.

Newmann, F. M., & Thompson, J. (1987). *Effects of cooperative learning on achievement in secondary schools: A summary of research.* Madison: University of Wisconsin, National Center on Effective Secondary Schools.

Sharan, S., & Shachar, C. (1988). *Language and learning in the cooperative classroom.* New York: Springer-Verlag.

Slavin, R. E. (1985a). Team Assisted Individualization. In R. E. Slavin, S. Sharan, S. Kagan, R. Hertz-Lazarowitz, C. Webb, & R. Schmuck (Eds.), *Learning to cooperate, cooperating to learn* (pp. 77–209). New York: Plenum.

Slavin, R. E. (1985b). Cooperative learning: Applying contact theory in desegregated schools. *Journal of Social Issues, 41,* 45–62.

Slavin, R. E. (1986). *Using student team learning* (3rd ed.). Baltimore: The Johns Hopkins University, Center for Research on Elementary and Middle Schools.

Slavin, R. E. (1987). Cooperative learning and the cooperative school. *Educational Leadership, 45*(3), 7–13.

Slavin, R. E. (1990). *Cooperative learning: Theory, research, and practice.* Englewood Cliffs, NJ: Prentice-Hall.

Slavin, R. E., Leavey, M. B., & Madden, N. A. (1986). *Team Accelerated Instruction—Mathematics.* Watertown, MA: Charlesbridge.

Stevens, R. J., Madden, N. A., Slavin, R. E., & Farnish, A. M. (1987). Cooperative Integrated Reading and Composition: Two field experiments. *Reading Research Quarterly, 22,* 433–454.

Webb, N. (1985). Student interaction and learning in small groups: A research summary. In R. E. Slavin, S. Sharan, S. Kagan, R. Hertz-Lazarowitz, C. Webb, & R. Schmuck (Eds.), *Learning to cooperate, cooperating to learn* (pp. 148–172). New York: Plenum.

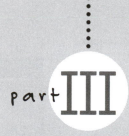

part **III**

QUANTITATIVE RESEARCH IN EDUCATION

To apply relevant research findings to your practice, you need a basic understanding of quantitative research methods. Therefore, Part III shows you how quantitative researchers design, analyze, and report an educational research study. It also introduces you to the major quantitative research designs used in educational research.

Chapter 5 explains how a typical report of a quantitative research study is organized into sections. We describe the topics covered in each section and how to evaluate the quality of the study based on the information that the researcher includes or fails to include.

Chapter 6 provides an introduction to the statistical techniques that researchers use to describe educational phenomena, to determine the validity and reliability of their research measures, and to test whether their findings generalize to a population of interest.

Chapter 7 and all the remaining chapters of the book include a reprinted research article to illustrate the research design described in that chapter. Chapter 7 shows how researchers conduct investigations that yield precise quantitative descriptions of educational phenomena. It also explains causal-comparative research, which involves comparing two or more groups that naturally differ in order to explore possible cause-and-effect relationships among phenomena.

Correlational research, the subject of Chapter 8, also has the purpose of exploring possible cause-and-effect relationships, but it involves different statistical techniques than those used in causal-comparative research.

In Chapter 9 we discuss various types of experimental research. Unlike causal-comparative and correlational research, experimental research involves the manipulation of variables to determine their effects on other variables. This chapter contains two reprinted research articles.

chapter 5

Reading Reports of Quantitative Research Studies

Bill Calvecchia is a student counselor who has worked in schools and colleges. He has been asked to do an extensive review of the literature on attention-deficit disorders in order to receive credit toward renewal of his counseling license. Most of his previous reading in the counseling field has been in textbooks and practitioner journals. Understandably, he is anxious about his ability to read and evaluate studies about attention-deficit disorders published in research journals. These journal articles have a format that he has not seen previously, and they include unfamiliar terminology and statistics.

Bill's apprehension about reading research articles will be reduced greatly once he learns how these articles are organized and the meaning of the technical terms commonly used in them. In this chapter, we explain the organization of quantitative research reports and their technical features. We also provide criteria and questions for evaluating the soundness of the studies they report. ●

OBJECTIVES

After studying this chapter, you will be able to

1. describe how a typical report of a quantitative research study is organized.
2. explain the purpose served by constructs, variables, and hypotheses in a quantitative research study.
3. explain how a researcher's biases might adversely affect the literature review and findings in a quantitative research study.
4. describe the characteristics of simple random sampling and stratified random sampling, and their advantage over nonrandom sampling.
5. explain how an analysis of the target population, accessible population, and research sample is used in judging the population validity of findings obtained from a nonrandom sample.
6. describe the distinguishing features of paper-and-pencil tests and scales, questionnaires, interviews, direct observation, and content analysis in quantitative research.
7. explain the meaning of test validity, and distinguish between types of evidence that can be used to demonstrate the validity of inferences made from test scores.

OBJECTIVES *continued*

8. explain the meaning of test reliability, and distinguish between four procedures for estimating a test's reliability.

9. describe the types of information that are included in the research-design section, results section, and discussion section of a quantitative research study.

KEY TERMS

abstract
accessible population
concurrent evidence of test
  validity
consequential evidence of
  test validity
constant
construct
content analysis
content-related evidence
  of test validity
convergent evidence of test
  validity
correlation coefficient

direct observation
face validity
high-inference variable
hypothesis
inter-observer agreement
inter-rater reliability
interview
item consistency
item response theory
low-inference variable
measurement error
parameter
performance measure
population validity
predictive evidence
  of test validity

proportional random sampling
questionnaire
reliability
sampling error
scale
simple random sampling
standard error of measurement
stratified random sampling
target population
test
test–retest reliability
test stability
test validity
true score
variable
volunteer sample

ORGANIZATION OF A QUANTITATIVE RESEARCH REPORT

Chapter 1 described quantitative research and qualitative research as two different approaches to scientific inquiry in education. Among the primary characteristics of quantitative research are an epistemological belief in an objective reality, the analysis of reality into measurable variables, the study of samples that represent a defined population, and a reliance on statistical methods to analyze data.

These characteristics of quantitative research affect the way in which researchers write their research reports. Quantitative research reports generally are much more impersonal and objective than reports of qualitative research. You will read several quantitative research reports—reprinted articles from research journals—in this part of the book. This initial chapter shows you how to read these reports and, in the process, develops your understanding of the main procedures of quantitative research.

Most reports of quantitative research studies are organized similarly. This is because researchers typically follow the style guidelines in the *Publication Manual of the American Psychological Association* (2001). These guidelines specify the sections of a quantitative research report and the order in which they are to be presented, as follows:

> Abstract
> Introduction
> Methods
>   Sampling Procedures
>   Measures (or Materials)
>   Research Design and Procedures
> Results
> Discussion

Each of these sections is explained in this chapter.

Of course, it is not sufficient to be able to read a research report with good comprehension. You also need to be able to evaluate the soundness of the study that it reports. Therefore, as we explain the parts of a research study that are reported in each section of the report, we also will explain how to judge whether each part is sound or flawed. To make these judgments, it is helpful to ask yourself questions as you read each section of the report. A set of questions for this purpose is presented in list form in Appendix 4. You can use this list to guide your evaluation of any quantitative research study.

ABSTRACT AND INTRODUCTORY SECTION

A research report begins with an **abstract,** which is a brief summary (typically about one hundred words) of the content of the report. Reading the abstract first will give you an idea of the purpose of the study, the method of inquiry that was used, and the major findings. With this information in mind, reading the full report will be substantially easier.

The introductory section of a quantitative research report explains the purpose of the study, the relevant variables, and the specific hypotheses, questions, and objectives that guided the study. In addition, the introductory section includes a review of previous research findings and other information that is relevant to the study. You also may be able to learn something about the researchers' qualifications. These different types of information are explained in the following sections.

Constructs and Variables

The introductory section of a research report should identify and describe each of the concepts that was studied. Examples of the concepts studied in educational research are learning style, aptitude, academic achievement, intrinsic motivation, top-down management, and implicit curriculum. Researchers usually refer to these concepts as constructs or variables.

A **construct** is a structure or process that is inferred from observed phenomena. For example, social scientists have observed that some individuals tend to speak about themselves in consistent ways, such as, "I'm very good at sports," "I am ambitious," "I don't like to draw attention to myself." The consistency of these self-perceptions over time and situations led the social scientists to infer that individuals have a psychological structure that they called *self-concept*. Self-concept, then, is a construct inferred from observed behavior; it cannot be observed directly. Other related constructs have been inferred as well, such as positive self-concept, negative self-concept, and self-esteem. Some constructs are tied to a particular theory. For example, logical operations and sensorimotor intelligence are key constructs in Piaget's theory of human development.

Quantitative researchers generally use the term *variable* rather than *construct*. A **variable** is a quantitative expression of a construct. For example, we can think of self-concept as ranging from highly negative to neutral to highly positive. In thinking this way, we are viewing self-concept as a variable. Variables usually are measured in terms of scores on a measure, such as an achievement test or attitude scale. Variables also can take the form of categories, for example, tall versus short, public versus private schools, or authoritarian versus democratic versus laissez-faire styles of leadership.

If a construct is part of the design of a research study but does not vary, it is called a **constant.** For example, suppose an experiment compares the effectiveness of teaching method A and teaching method B for community college students. The educational level of the students (that is, community college) is a constant because no other educational level is included in the research design. Suppose, however, that the experiment compares the effectiveness of the two teaching methods to see which is most effective for community college students and which is most effective for high school students. In this experiment, educational level is a variable because it takes on two values: community college and high school.

In reviewing a research report, you should examine carefully how each of the variables is defined and measured. If the definitions are unclear or nonexistent, the significance of the research results is cast into doubt. Similar doubts are created if the definitions of the variables are inconsistent with the methods used to measure them.

Research Hypotheses, Questions, or Objectives

A **hypothesis** in a research study is a reasoned speculation about how two or more variables are related to each other. For example, researchers might hypothesize that birth order of children is related to their level of leadership in school activities, or that method A is more effective than method B for promoting the academic achievement of students involved in distance education. After formulating a hypothesis, researchers collect data to test it and then examine the data to decide whether or not to reject it.

Hypotheses usually are formulated on the basis of theory and previous research findings. If theory or previous research do not provide an adequate basis for formulating specific hypotheses, many researchers instead will formulate questions or objectives to guide their investigation. For example, suppose a research team wondered about the effect of higher-cognitive questions on students' learning in social studies classes, but had no basis for formulating a hypothesis about what that effect might be. In this case they could pose a question such as "What is the effect of higher-cognitive questions on students' learning in social studies classes?" Or they could state an objective: "The objective of this study is to determine whether higher-cognitive questions improve students' learning in social studies classes."

The choice of research questions or objectives is generally a matter of personal preference. Both formats guide the study design, but neither expresses a prediction about what the research findings will show. By contrast, a research hypothesis makes a specific prediction before data are collected. If the researchers are willing to make predictions about some of the phenomena they are studying but are unwilling to make predictions about other phenomena, they might specify both hypotheses and questions (or objectives).

Formulating hypotheses, questions, or objectives is one of the first steps researchers take in planning a quantitative research study. These formulations guide the rest of the planning process, data collection, and data analysis. Therefore, you should look for hypotheses, questions, or objectives in the introductory section of the report. If none are present, you have reason to be concerned about the quality of the study and the validity of its findings. You also should be concerned if you find that hypotheses, questions, or objectives are stated, but the research design and statistical analyses do not deal with them directly.

The variables and their relationship to each other should be made explicit in the hypotheses, questions, or objectives. For example, consider this hypothesis: "There is a positive relationship between peer-group acceptance and attitude toward school among sixth-grade boys." This is a good hypothesis because the two variables (peer-group acceptance and attitude toward school) are made explicit. Furthermore, the hypothesized relationship between the two variables is made explicit: The researcher expects a positive relationship, meaning that boys who have greater peer-group acceptance will have better attitudes toward school, and boys who have less peer-group acceptance will have more negative attitudes.

This example can be contrasted with the following hypothesis: "The lecture method will have a different effect than the discussion method on students' performance on essay tests." Only one of the variables in this example is explicit: teaching method (lecture versus discussion). The other apparent variable, essay test performance, is actually a measure, but the variable being measured is not identified. Furthermore, the predicted effects of the teaching methods on essay test performance are not made explicit.

If the researchers have done a good review of the literature, they should be able to provide a good rationale for each of their hypotheses, questions, or objectives. This rationale should be made explicit. For example, Randall Eberts and Joe Stone (1988) did a research study, the objective of which is included in the following statement: "Using nationally representative data . . . we tested the major conclusions drawn from case studies regarding principal effectiveness" (p. 291). This objective developed from their observation that published case studies showed that school principals who displayed certain behaviors (e.g., setting clear priorities and organizing and participating in staff development programs) had a positive effect on the learning of students in their school. However, Eberts and Stone noted a weakness in the case studies:

> Case studies have many advantages in generating hypotheses, in evaluating the implementation of new techniques, and in providing detailed explanations and backgrounds for observed phenomena, but they are not necessarily representative and often suffer from weak controls for individual student and teacher attributes. (p. 291)

These researchers' rationale for their objective, then, was that nationally representative data would provide a stronger test of the principals' influence on student achievement than that provided by case studies.

Hypotheses, questions, and objectives that lack a rationale pose a problem for interpretation. For example, suppose a study is done to identify teachers' testing practices. If no rationale for this objective is provided, the readers have no basis for understanding why particular testing practices were studied or whether testing practices identified as important in previous research were ignored in this study. Also, the readers, as well as the researchers who conducted the study, will find it difficult to judge whether the observed testing practices are desirable or undesirable.

Literature Review

If you are doing a comprehensive review of the research literature on a particular problem, you will soon notice that a few key studies are cited in most research reports. If these key studies are not reviewed in a particular research report, it might indicate that the researchers were careless in reviewing the literature. If important studies that disagree with the researchers' findings are omitted, bias may be involved.

Most research journals allow researchers limited space for reviewing previous research, so you should not expect detailed reviews. However, the five to ten most relevant previous studies should be discussed, if only briefly. Significant syntheses of the literature also merit discussion. Research reports not appearing in journals, such as doctoral dissertations, usually provide much more detailed reviews because they are not subject to space limitations.

The Researchers' Qualifications

Because quantitative researchers strive to be objective, they generally reveal little or nothing about themselves in their reports. Their institutional affiliation typically is listed beneath their name at the start of the report, and there may be a note indicating their title. The literature review may refer to reports of other studies or scholarly work that they have written.

Knowledge about the researchers might provide some indication of whether researcher bias affected their study. For example, some research studies involve experimental tests of the effectiveness of an educational program or method. If we know that the researchers have a stake in the program or method (which is often the case), we should be on the alert for any indications that the design of the experiment was slanted in favor of it.

Whenever researchers have reason for wanting their research to support a particular viewpoint, the likelihood of bias is greatly increased. Occasionally, the bias becomes so great that the researchers slant their findings or even structure their research design to produce a predetermined result. A famous case of emotional involvement is the research into intelligence based on studies of twins that was conducted by Sir Cyril Burt. It appears that Burt was so intent on proving that intelligence is inherited that he slanted, or even fabricated, research data to support his hypothesis (Evans, 1976).

METHOD SECTION: SAMPLING PROCEDURES

In conducting a study, researchers ideally would investigate all the individuals to whom they wish to generalize their findings. These individuals constitute a **target population,** meaning that they make up the entire group of individuals having the characteristics that interest the researchers. Because of the great expense involved in studying most populations of interest, researchers are limited to studying a sample of individuals who represent that population.

For example, suppose the researchers wish to study the effect of a new reading program on the reading comprehension of visually impaired children in U.S. elementary schools. Because the researchers cannot try out the new reading program with the entire population, they must first define an accessible population and then select a sample from this population. The **accessible population** is the entire membership of a set of people, events, or objects that can feasibly be included in the research sample. The researchers now have solved the problem of making the study feasible to conduct, but they have created a different problem in the process, namely, whether they can generalize their findings from a limited sample to the entire population. As we explain below, researchers can use various sampling procedures to make their findings more generalizable.

Samples very rarely will have the exact same characteristics as the populations from which they are drawn. For example, suppose that you randomly select three male students from each class in a large high school and measure their height. Your sampling procedure is random, because each member of the population has an equal and independent chance of being included in the sample. Nonetheless, it is unlikely that the mean height of this sample would be identical to the mean height of all male students in the school (defined to be the population in this example). The difference between the sample's mean height and the population's mean height is a random sampling error. In technical terms, a **sampling error** is the difference between a statistic (e.g., a mean score) for a sample and the same statistic for the population. (The technical term to describe a statistic for the population is **parameter.**)

Sampling errors are likely to occur even when the sample is randomly drawn from the population. The size of the errors tends to become smaller as we select a larger random sample. For this reason, we can be more confident in generalizing results from studies with a large random sample than studies with a small random sample. The likelihood of sampling errors for a sample of a given size can be estimated by using a mathematical procedure (Kraemer & Thiemann, 1987).

Despite the advantages of a random sample, researchers often must study nonrandom samples. Sampling errors in nonrandom samples cannot be estimated by mathematical procedures. Therefore, generalizations about populations based on nonrandom samples need to be viewed as tentative.

Types of Sampling

Researchers have developed various techniques for drawing random samples from a defined population. Two of the most common techniques are simple random sampling and stratified random sampling.

Simple Random Sampling.   In **simple random sampling,** all the individuals in the defined population have an equal and independent chance of being selected as a member of the sample. By *independent,* we mean that the selection of one individual does not affect in any way the chances of selection of any other individual. A simple random sample can be selected by assigning a number to each individual in the population and using a computer-based random number generator, or a hard-copy table of random numbers, to select the needed number of individuals.

Simple random sampling is most feasible in survey research. For example, if researchers wish to know the opinion of psychologists on some educational issue, they can obtain a directory of a national organization for psychologists, such as the American Psychological Association. They then can draw a simple random sample of psychologists from the directory list, and request the sample to complete a mailed questionnaire or phone interview. Not everyone in the sample may agree to participate, however. In this case, the resulting sample of participants is no longer a random sample. If the response rate to the questionnaire or phone interview is below 70 percent, you should be concerned about the randomness of the sample.

Stratified Random Sampling.   **Stratified random sampling** is a procedure for ensuring that individuals in the population who have certain characteristics are represented in the sample. By constructing the sample in this manner, the researchers ensure that they will study these characteristics and their relationship to other variables. For example, suppose researchers are interested in whether boys and girls from three different home environments (single parent, mother; single parent, father; both parents together) have different attitudes toward mathematics. If the researchers draw a simple random sample from a school district's list of students, there is a chance that they will get few or no students in one of these six classifications: (1) boys with single parent, mother; (2) girls with single parent, mother; (3) boys with single parent, father; (4) girls with single parent, father; (5) boys with both parents together; and (6) girls with both parents together.

To ensure that all six groups are represented in the sample, the researchers can use stratified random sampling. They would consider each group (called *strata* in sampling terminology) as a separate population. They then would draw a random sample of a given size from each group, thereby ensuring that each population is represented adequately in the sample. Another option is to draw random samples of different sizes (but each size being an adequate number) so that the proportion of students in each group in the sample is the same as their proportion in the population. This procedure is called **proportional random sampling.**

Volunteer Samples

Educational research usually requires face-to-face interaction with individuals, as when the researcher needs to administer tests under standardized conditions or to try out a new instructional method. However, it is expensive to define a population that covers an extensive geographical area, to randomly select a sample from that population, and then travel to the individuals in the sample in order to collect the necessary data. Therefore, researchers typically work with nonrandom samples.

Sampling is further complicated by the fact that researchers have the legal and ethical requirement to obtain informed consent from individuals or their legal guardians before involving them in a research project. An individual can refuse to participate for any reason. As a result, nearly all educational research is conducted with **volunteer samples,** that is, samples based on individuals' expression of willingness to participate in a research study rather than on systematic sampling strategies.

Population Validity

The main difficulty with volunteer samples is that systematic sampling errors can occur such that members of a sample have different characteristics from the population that the sample is intended to represent. If the sampling error is large, the sample is said to have low population validity. The term **population validity** refers to the degree to which the sample of individuals in the study is representative of the population from which it was selected.

Population validity is established by showing that the selected sample is similar to the accessible population, which is the immediate population from which the researchers drew their sample. The researchers also must demonstrate that the accessible population is similar to the target population, which is the population to which the researchers want to generalize or apply their research findings. For example, if researchers were interested in investigating career planning among high school seniors, the target population could be defined as all seniors in U.S. public and private high schools. This target population most likely would be too large from which to draw a sample. The researchers might then limit themselves to their local community—let's say, Denver, Colorado. In this case, Denver high school seniors would be the accessible population from which the sample would be drawn.

To establish population validity, the researchers must show how (1) the sample, (2) the accessible population (Denver high school seniors), and (3) the target population (all U.S. high school seniors) are similar on variables that are relevant to their research problem. For example, it seems reasonable to expect that career planning would vary by gender, socioeconomic status, and ethnicity. Therefore, the researchers should determine the extent to which their sample, the accessible population, and the target population are similar on these variables. Evidence of similarity helps to establish the population validity of their sample.

In making a critical evaluation of a research report, you should pay close attention to the accessible population and to the sample. It also is important to determine the degree to which students, teachers, or other groups in the research sample are similar to the groups in the local setting to whom you wish to apply the research findings. As the similarity between the research sample and the local group decreases, the research results are less likely to apply.

Comparison of the research sample with your local group is a difficult task for several reasons. First, researchers often include very little information in their reports about the sample and the accessible population from which it was drawn. Second, local educational organizations often can provide only limited information about the characteristics of the local group that is of interest to you. Third, it is difficult to decide which differences between the research sample and the local population would actually affect the applicability of the research findings.

Given these problems, the best test of population validity may be to try out the educational practices suggested by the research findings and collect data to see how well they generalize to your local groups. This approach involves action research, which we discuss in Chapter 15.

METHOD SECTION: MEASURES

Research results can only be as sound as the measures used to obtain them. For this reason, you should pay special attention to the description of the measures in a research report. This description hopefully will give you basic information about the measures: the constructs that they are intended to measure, scoring procedures, and their validity and reliability. If the measures are ones that have been commonly used in educational practice or research, you can obtain more information about them by examining the resources for further study listed at the end of this chapter or by searching a preliminary source (see Chapter 3 and Appendix 2). Among the most useful of these sources is *Mental Measurements Yearbook: Test Reviews Online,* which is listed in Appendix 2.

Another way to learn about a measure used in a research study is to examine a copy of it. Some school systems and universities maintain collections of commonly used tests and the manuals that accompany them. Otherwise you may be able to order a copy from the publisher. In the case of a measure developed specifically for a research study, you can write the researchers to request a copy of the measure. They should be willing to send you a copy if you state a reasonable purpose for your request and if you provide assurances that you will maintain the confidentiality of the measure.

Types of Measures

Four types of performance measures are commonly used in quantitative research studies: (1) paper-and-pencil tests and scales; (2) questionnaires; (3) interviews; and (4) direct observation. Each type is described in the following sections.

Paper-and-Pencil Tests and Scales. **Tests** measure an individual's knowledge, depth of understanding, or skill within a curriculum domain. They typically yield a total score, which is the number of items answered correctly. **Scales** measure an individual's attitudes, personality characteristics, emotional states, interests, values, and related factors. They typically yield a total score, which is the sum of the individual's responses to item scales. For example, a Likert-type scale item typically has five response options (e.g., 5 points for "strongly agree" and 1 point for "strongly disagree").

Paper-and-pencil measures can be contrasted with **performance measures,** which involve evaluating individuals as they carry out a complex real-life task. An example of a performance measure is the driving test, during which you drive a car while being evaluated by a state examiner. Performance measures typically must be individually administered. Paper-and-pencil measures are used much more frequently in educational research than performance measures because they generally are cheaper to administer and require less time. Also, because of the huge number and variety of paper-and-pencil measures, researchers usually can find at least one such measure for virtually any variable.

Paper-and-pencil tests and scales also have limitations. First, most of them require that the person being tested be able to read and write. Thus, individuals who are lacking in these abilities will be unable to show what they know or think about the variables measured by tests and scales. Another limitation of these measures is that they rely on self-report. This is not a serious problem when measuring academic achievement, but in attitude measurement, for example, individuals may wish to hide their true attitude in order to get a more socially acceptable score. The third limitation is that many tests and scales are group-administered. Thus, it is difficult for the researcher to determine the physical and mental state of the persons being assessed. If they happen to be ill, tired, or emotionally upset, they are likely to perform atypically on the measure.

Questionnaires.   Paper-and-pencil tests and scales usually measure one or two variables, such as knowledge of vocabulary or attitude toward school. In contrast, **questionnaires** typically measure many variables. For example, a questionnaire might ask respondents about the type of computer they use, the software programs they use, the frequency of use of each program, their previous training in computers, and their intentions to expand their use of computers in the future. The response to each question may constitute a separate variable in the research study.

In evaluating the use of a questionnaire in a research study, you should consider the following questions.

1. *Was the questionnaire pretested?* It is impossible to predict how the items will be interpreted by respondents unless the researcher tries out the questionnaire and analyzes the responses of a small sample of individuals before starting the main study. Results of this pilot study should be used to refine the questionnaire and locate potential problems in the interpretation or analysis of the data. If a pilot study was done, you can have more confidence that the findings reported in the main study are valid.

2. *Did the questionnaire include any leading questions?* A copy of the questionnaire sometimes is included in the research report. You should check it carefully for leading questions, which are questions framed in such a way that individuals are given hints about the kind of response that is expected. Results obtained from leading questions are likely to be biased, so they should be interpreted with caution.

3. *Were any psychologically threatening questions included in the questionnaire?* In constructing items, the researcher should avoid questions that may be psychologically threatening to the respondents. For example, a questionnaire sent to school principals concerning the morale of teachers at their schools would be threatening to some principals, because low morale suggests that they are failing in part of their job. Many individuals who receive a questionnaire containing threatening items will not return it. If they do return it, little confidence can be placed in the accuracy of their responses because of their ego involvement in the situation.

4. *Were the individuals who received the questionnaire likely to have the information requested?* Researchers inadvertently may send a questionnaire to a group of persons who do not have the desired information. For example, a researcher seeking data on school financial policies sent questionnaires to a large number of elementary school principals. Many of the questionnaires returned were incomplete and contained few specific facts of the sort that the researcher wanted. This problem occurred because the trend in recent years has been for superintendents and their staffs to handle most matters concerning school finance.

Interviews.   Unlike paper-and-pencil tests, scales, and questionnaires, **interviews** involve the collection of data through direct interaction between the researcher and the individuals being studied.

The main advantage of interviews is their adaptability. The well-trained interviewer can alter the interview situation at any time in order to obtain the fullest possible response from the individual. For example, if the individual makes an interesting remark, the interviewer can ask a follow-up question on the spot. Another advantage of interviews is that they elicit data of much greater depth than is possible with other measurement techniques. For example, most questionnaires tend to be shallow; that is, they fail to probe deeply enough to produce a true picture of the respondents' opinions and feelings.

The major disadvantage of interviews is that the direct interaction between researcher and interviewee makes it easy for subjectivity and bias to occur. The eagerness of the interviewee to please the interviewer, a vague antagonism that sometimes arises between interviewer and interviewee, and the tendency of interviewers to seek out answers that support their preconceived notions are a few of the factors that may contribute to biasing of interview data. As a result, the validity of findings based on the interview method is highly contingent on the interpersonal skills of the interviewers.

The following questions will help you evaluate research studies that use interviews to collect data.

1. *How well were the interviewers trained?*   The level of training required for interviewers is related directly to the type of information being collected. Less training is required in structured interviews, because the interviewer asks specific questions from an interview guide and does not deviate from these questions. More training is required in semistructured and unstructured interviews, because the interviewer does not employ a detailed interview guide but instead has a general plan and decides on the spot what questions and comments to use in order to lead the interviewee toward the interviewer's objectives. Information on the training of interviewers should be included in the research report.

2. *How was information recorded?*   Audiotaping is the most accurate method of recording interview information. If interviewers take notes instead of audiotaping the interview, they may overlook important information or take biased notes.

3. *Were the interview procedures tried out before the study began?*   Because interviewing tends to be highly subjective, the researcher must use many controls and safeguards to obtain reasonably objective and unbiased data. A careful pilot study is necessary to develop these controls and safeguards before data for the main study are collected. The pilot study should be described in the research report.

4. *Were leading questions asked?*   As with questionnaires, leading questions can invalidate interview data.

If an interview was a primary measure in a research study, the report should include at least the main questions that were asked. You should study these questions for signs of bias.

Direct Observation.   **Direct observation,** as its name implies, involves collecting data while an individual is engaged in some form of behavior or while an event is unfolding. Standard observation forms generally are used for this purpose. If the forms are well developed, the variables listed on the forms will be carefully defined. Also, there will be evidence that the researchers' inferences from the observational data are valid and reliable.

Direct observation tends to yield more accurate data about particular variables than can be obtained from questionnaires or interviews. However, a disadvantage of direct observation is that it tends to be very time-consuming. Also, the observer tends to change the situation being observed, albeit unintentionally.

In evaluating the use of observational procedures in a research study, you should consider the following questions.

1. *Were **high-inference** or **low-inference variables** observed?* Observational variables differ in the amount of inference required by the observer. For example, an observer will need to use a greater degree of inference to decide how much enthusiasm a teacher is exhibiting during a lesson than to decide how many verbal praise statements the teacher made. Thus, the validity of the observer's data will be more of an issue if the observational variables are high-inference than if they are low-inference.

2. *Were observers trained to identify the variables to be observed?* The researcher should describe the kind and extent of training given to the observers, and whether they used a standard observation form or procedure.

3. *How long was the observation period?* The observation period should be sufficiently long to obtain a representative sample of the behaviors being studied. Otherwise the observation data could yield atypical results. The necessary period of observation will depend on such factors as the nature of the behaviors being observed, the circumstances under which the behavior occurs, and its frequency of occurrence.

4. *How conspicuous were the observers?* Observers ideally would be stationed behind a one-way screen, and their presence would not be known to the research participants. A few researchers are able to achieve these conditions, but, for ethical reasons, most need to be visible to the individuals being studied. Consequently, they are likely to have some impact on the persons being observed. This problem can be overcome to a certain extent if the observers do not record any observational data initially. In many situations, individuals—for example, students in a classroom—become accustomed to the observers after a while and engage in their customary behavior. It also helps if the observers remain as unobtrusive as possible. You should examine the research report to determine whether the researchers were sensitive to this problem in direct observation and took steps to minimize it.

Content Analysis.   Most observational data involve the direct study of individuals and groups. However, educational researchers sometimes focus their observations on documents produced or used by such individuals and groups. The collection and analysis of data based on close observation of documents is called **content analysis.** For example, researchers might study how males and females are portrayed in textbooks or the issues that are mentioned in the minutes of school board meetings.

In quantitative research, a content analysis involves the development of categories and a frequency account of the occurrence of each category in the document. For example, a researcher might form the following categories for the analysis of elementary mathematics textbooks: number-calculation problems; word problems involving situations that children might encounter; and word problems involving situations that children are not likely to encounter. The researcher might show the frequency and percentage of each type of problem in different textbook series.

In evaluating the soundness of this type of content analysis, you should look for evidence that (1) the categories are clearly defined and worthwhile; (2) the procedure for selecting a sample of documents was sound; and (3) the different observers could use the categories reliably.

Validity of Measures

The definitive guide for determining the quality of tests and other measures is the book *Standards for Educational and Psychological Testing* (American Educational Research Association, 1999). (We refer to this book hereafter as the *Standards*). According to the *Standards*, a good test is one that yields reliable test scores from which we can make interpretations that have strong validity. The key concepts in this view of test quality are reliability and validity. We discuss validity in this section and reliability in the next.

Test validity refers to the "degree to which evidence and theory support the interpretation of test scores entailed by proposed uses of tests" (*Standards*, p. 9). For example, if we administer a science achievement test to a group of students, each student earns a score on the test. We then might *infer* that this score represents how much each student has learned about science relative to other students. It is helpful to think about this inference as a "claim" that we make about the test scores.

Five types of evidence and theory can be used to demonstrate the validity of inferences we might wish to make from individuals' scores on a test or other measure:

1. evidence from test content
2. evidence from internal structure
3. evidence from relationship to other variables
4. evidence from response processes
5. evidence from consequences of testing

Some types of evidence might be more important than others for judging the validity of a test used in a research study. To make this judgment, you need to be familiar with all five types. Also, you should be aware that older research studies used different terms to refer to these types of evidence. The terms used in the 1999 edition of the *Standards* are intended to convey the fact that there are not different types of test validity, only different types of evidence to support test validity, which is a unitary construct.

Evidence from Test Content.   Validity evidence of this type involves a demonstration that the content of the test's items matches the content that it is designed to measure. For example, researchers might claim that the XYZ Test is a valid measure of how much students have learned about algebra in high school. To substantiate this claim, the researchers must provide evidence that the content of the test items represents the content of high school algebra curricula.

Content-related evidence of test validity is particularly important in achievement testing and various tests of skill and proficiency, such as occupational skills tests. It should not be confused with **face validity** evidence, which involves the degree to which the test *appears* to measure what it claims to measure. For example, we might examine the items of the XYZ Test and conclude that the test is valid because its items correspond to our view of what high school students typically are taught in an algebra course. The evidence for test evidence would be much stronger if we went beyond appearances (i.e., the "face" of the test) by systematically comparing the test content with course content. This comparison is time-consuming, because we need to analyze painstakingly teachers' course textbooks, lesson plans, handouts, classroom assignments, and tests, as well as each item on the XYZ Test.

Content-related evidence of test validity is particularly important in research in which the effect of different teaching methods on students' learning is investigated. The test of learning should measure as precisely as possible the curriculum content that was taught in the method under investigation.

Evidence from Internal Structure.   Nearly all tests and other measures have multiple items. (The most common exception is questionnaires, which often have a single item to measure a concept, e.g., the individual's age.) An analysis of the multiple items can yield evidence about a test's validity.

Suppose that researchers claim that a particular test, which has ten items, measures a teachers' desire to engage in continuous professional development. If this claim is true, each of the ten items should measure this concept. This means that if a teacher responded to an item in a certain way, he should respond to all the other items the same way; conversely, a teacher who responded to the item a different way should respond to the other items the same way. The claim can be tested by correlational statistics (see Chapter 8).

Suppose that a test was developed on the basis of a theory that there are five distinct learning styles. The test contains items purporting to measure each of these learning styles. The validity of this claim can be tested by correlational statistics, in particular, factor analysis (see Chapter 8). These statistics can be used to determine whether individuals who score high on an item measuring one learning style also score high on other items measuring that learning style and lower on items measuring the other learning styles.

Evidence from Relationship to Other Variables.   The *Standards* describes several types of validity evidence that have a common feature: the evidence is based on the degree of relationship between individuals' scores on the test and their scores on another measure. We consider some of these types of validity evidence in this section.

Suppose that the developers of a test claim that it measures skill in reading comprehension among students in the upper grades. **Predictive evidence of test validity** could be used to support this claim. For example, the researchers might hypothesize that if the test in fact measures reading comprehension, eighth-grade students who earn higher scores on it should also earn higher grades in their high school courses, because good reading comprehension is necessary for success in these courses. The researchers could do a study to test this hypothesis; if the results support the hypothesis, they can serve as evidence of the test's validity.

The collection of **convergent evidence of test validity** is another option. For example, the developers might examine the relationship between individuals' test scores and their scores on another test that purportedly measures reading comprehension. One possibility might be a test of reading comprehension included in a battery of tests required for college admission (e.g., the SAT). If students who earn higher scores on the developer's test also earn higher scores on another test measuring the same construct, this can serve as evidence of both tests' validity. The evidence is even stronger if the other test has a well-established body of evidence supporting its validity.

Some tests are rather long, so developers might wish to create a shorter version. Evidence supporting the validity of the longer test might be strong, but this does not mean that the shorter version also has validity. The developers need to do studies in which a sample of individuals take both versions. If individuals who earn higher scores on the long version also earn higher scores on the short version, this can serve as evidence of the short test's validity. This type of evidence sometimes is called **concurrent evidence of test validity,** because both tests are administered at about the same time.

Evidence from Response Processes.   Taking a test involves particular cognitive and evaluative processes. Sometimes the processes engaged are consistent with the construct the test is designed to measure, but other processes may not be. Response-processes evidence of test validity would demonstrate that the processes used by testees in taking the test are consistent with the particular construct or constructs underlying the test.

For example, a test of critical thinking might be designed to engage students' higher-order reasoning processes to solve certain types of mathematical problems. Suppose that some students obtain high scores on the test because they had received extensive instruction on these problem types and were thus able to solve them by applying specific algorithms, rather than by engaging in higher-order reasoning processes. In that case, the validity of interpretations that test scores reflect higher-order reasoning would be compromised.

Evidence from Consequences of Testing. Individuals' scores on a test can have consequences for them. **Consequential evidence of test validity** is the extent to which the value implicit in the constructs measured by a test and in the intended uses of the test are consistent with the values of test takers, those who will use the test results to make decisions, and other stakeholders. For example, students' low scores on a standardized achievement test might affect their chances of being admitted to the college of their choice. Children's scores on a test battery might affect whether they are identified as having a learning disability. These consequences need to be examined carefully to determine whether they are warranted. Evidence resulting from this examination can and should be used in making judgments about a test's validity.

The examples that we just used represent direct consequences for individuals resulting from interpretations of their test scores by others. At a more general level, policies about testing also have consequences. For example, some policy makers argue that preservice teachers should take and pass competency tests in order to obtain a teaching license. They claim that this requirement will result in a more effective teacher workforce. Evidence relating to this claimed consequence of testing needs to be collected. This evidence can be used to judge the validity of the competency tests for their intended use by policy makers.

Reliability of Measures

A test or other measurement tool is reliable to the degree that it is free of measurement error. In classical test theory, **measurement error** is construed as the difference between the scores that individuals actually obtain on a test and their true scores if it were possible to obtain a perfect measure of their performance. For example, if two testers score an individual's test and obtain different total scores, measurement error has occurred. Less obviously, suppose a student takes the same achievement test on two different days and obtains two different scores. These different results also constitute measurement error. They are not errors in the usual sense of the word, that is, mistakes resulting from students' lack of skill. Instead, they reflect shortcomings in the test's ability to accurately measure the students' performance.

It is difficult to develop a measure that is perfectly reliable, meaning that it is completely free of error, because a variety of factors can create error. Possible factors are differences in the skill of persons who administer the test or other measure, changes in testing conditions from one day to the next, temporary fluctuations in how individuals respond to the testing situation, and features of the test items that affect different individuals differently. It is virtually impossible to eliminate all these sources of error.

Tests and other measurement tools with very low reliability will produce large errors of measurement. These errors will obscure the effects of methods and programs, or the extent of a relationship between variables. This problem can be understood by considering the case of a completely unreliable test. After the test is administered, the resulting scores will consist entirely of measurement error, meaning that they are essentially random numbers. Random numbers obviously cannot reveal the true effects of educational programs or the true relationships between variables. For this reason you need to check how reliable a measure is before you reach conclusions about findings based on its use.

The degree of reliability of an educational measure is usually expressed by a **correlation coefficient.** For present purposes it is sufficient for you to know that reliability coefficients range from 0, which indicates no reliability, to 1.00, which indicates perfect reliability. In other words, a reliability coefficient of .00 means that the test scores are meaningless because they consist entirely of measurement error; in contrast, a reliability of 1.00 means that the measure has absolutely no measurement error. As a rough rule of thumb, a measure is considered reliable for most research and practical purposes if its reliability coefficient is .80 or higher. (In the case of one type of reliability coefficient, Cronbach's alpha, a value of .70 or higher usually is sufficient.)

Procedures for Estimating Test Reliability. Procedures have been developed to estimate the extent of the different types of measurement errors in a test. In describing each procedure, we use the term *test* to refer generally to various forms of measurement, such as achievement tests, attitude scales, and direct observation.

1. *Item consistency.* One type of measurement error is caused by inconsistencies in the items that make up the test. For example, if a test of visual creativity contains some items that measure this construct and other items that measure a somewhat different construct, the total score will be an inaccurate indicator of visual creativity. Therefore, test developers want all the items on the test to measure the same construct. In other words, they want the items to be consistent. If the items are perfectly consistent, individuals who score one way on an item should score the same way on all the remaining items. The test's reliability reflects the extent to which the test items are consistent with one another, and it can be determined by several statistical methods.

2. *Stability of measurement.* As we observed above, measurement error will occur if the individuals being tested vary in their performance from one testing occasion to the next. These variations can occur for many reasons. For example, an individual may be fatigued on one testing occasion and rested on the next. Or an individual may have reviewed a relevant item of information just before one testing occasion, but not just before the next.

If a test is free of this type of measurement error, individuals should earn the same score on each testing occasion. To determine the extent to which this is the case, researchers administer the test to a sample of individuals, and then after a delay they administer the same test again to the same sample. Scores obtained from the two administrations are then correlated to determine their reliability. This type of reliability is called **test–retest reliability** or **test stability.**

3. *Consistency of administration and scoring.* Individuals who administer or score tests can cause measurement errors because of carelessness or for some

other reason, such as not knowing the correct procedures. Highly objective measures, such as multiple-choice tests, tend to be free of this type of measurement error. However, even test-scoring machines have been known to make scoring mistakes because of mechanical defects. Less objective measures, such as individually administered intelligence and personality tests or direct observation, are more subject to administration and scoring errors.

The presence of test-administration errors can be determined by having several individuals administer the same test, or alternate forms of the same test, to the same sample. Their scores are then correlated with one another to yield a reliability coefficient. The presence of scoring errors can be determined quite simply by having several individuals or machines score the same set of tests. A reliability coefficient is calculated on the sets of scores to determine how well they agree. The degree of reliability among the individuals who administer or score measures is sometimes called **inter-rater reliability** or **inter-observer agreement.**

4. *Standard error of measurement.* Another approach to expressing the degree of reliability of a test is to calculate the standard error of measurement. This reliability statistic is based on the assumption that each individual's score on a test has two components: the individual's true score and the measurement error.

Suppose that the test measures knowledge of vocabulary. The individual's **true score** would be a perfect measure of the amount of this ability that the individual actually possesses. The difference between the individual's obtained score on the test and the individual's true score is construed as measurement error. Although we cannot know the individual's true score (except on a perfectly reliable test), the **standard error of measurement** is an estimate of the probable range within which the individual's true score falls.

The calculation procedures and rationale for the standard error of measurement are fairly sophisticated. For present purposes, it is sufficient to know that the calculation of a standard error of measurement enables the researcher to make a statement like, "The chances are about 95 in 100 that this sample's true score on the test lies between 12.75 and 16.63." It is advantageous for researchers to use a highly reliable test, because it reduces the range of values that is likely to contain the true score.

Evaluating Researchers' Determination of Reliability. We discussed above four procedures for estimating a test's reliability: calculation of item consistency, stability of measurement, consistency of test administration and scoring, and the standard error of measurement. It is unlikely that researchers will determine all these types of reliability for each measure used in a study. One type of reliability is typically of most concern, depending on the measure involved and the research situation. You will need to determine whether the researcher made the appropriate reliability check for each measure.

Item Response Theory. Most tests and other measures used in educational research are based on the reliability approaches described above. However, these approaches are imperfect. One of the main problems is that it is very difficult to develop a test that is reliable for all individuals. For example, consider the measurement of mathematical problem-solving ability. This ability ranges on a long continuum, from none at all, through the ability to solve the types of mathematical problems taught in school, to, at the end of the continuum, the ability to solve complex problems in theoretical mathematics.

If we developed a test that contained primarily items in the mid-range of this ability, it would be unsuitable for estimating the true score of individuals with the most rudimentary problem-solving skills or the true score of individuals with highly sophisticated problem-solving skills. Also, even for individuals in the mid-range of this ability, the test might have satisfactory reliability for individuals at some points in this mid-range but not for individuals at other points.

These problems can be overcome to a large extent by developing tests based on **item response theory** (IRT). This theory assumes, among other things, that individuals with different amounts of an ability will perform differently on an item measuring that ability. For example, suppose we have a large sample of items that represents the entire continuum of mathematical problem-solving ability and a large sample of individuals that also represents the entire continuum of this ability. Most of the individuals will be able to answer the simplest items. As the items become more difficult, fewer individuals—the ones with more problem-solving ability—will be able to answer them.

By using individuals' item responses and IRT procedures, test developers can order the items by difficulty level so that they can determine the level at which a particular individual "tests out." By this we mean that the individual is able to answer most of the items below that difficulty level and few or none above that difficulty level. Once we find the difficulty level at which the individual tests out, we can administer more items at that difficulty level in order to improve the reliability of measurement.

Test development using IRT procedures is complex and expensive. Also, test administration typically requires a computer that presents items one at a time and that adjusts item difficulty based on the individual's responses to preceding items. However, because of the superior reliability of tests based on IRT, this approach is being used increasingly to develop high-stakes tests, such as those used to assess students' academic achievement or potential for success in university studies and different occupations. Scores from such test administrations are likely to be used increasingly in educational research studies.

Limitations to Tests of Validity and Reliability

Researchers sometimes determine the validity and reliability of their measures by using evidence from other studies. If these studies involve a different population from the one used in the researcher's study, the validity and reliability evidence may not be applicable. In other words, a measure may be valid and reliable for one population, but not for another. Therefore, you need to check the source of the validity and reliability evidence that is presented in a research report.

METHOD SECTION: RESEARCH DESIGN AND PROCEDURES

Research reports should describe the research design that was used to obtain the data needed to test the research hypotheses, answer the research questions, or achieve the research objectives. Depending on the research design, the description of the procedures might be brief or it might need to be quite detailed. Descriptive research designs (see Chapter 7) generally are simple. The researchers might consider it sufficient to mention who administered the measures and how and when they were administered. If descriptive data were collected periodically, as in longitudinal research, the time intervals should be specified.

Other research designs, especially experimental designs (see Chapter 9), require more detailed explanations. For example, the report should indicate the timeline of the experiment so that readers know when the various measures and treatments were administered. Also, each of the experimental treatments (for example, a new teaching method) should be described so that other researchers could implement them as intended, if they wish to replicate the study. It is especially important that the researcher describe how long the treatments (e.g., different teaching methods) were implemented. In some experiments, the treatments are of such brief duration that it is not reasonable to expect an effect on the research participants' learning or other outcomes. Any flaws in the research design and procedures will weaken the conclusions that can be drawn from the statistical findings.

You will need a basic understanding of various research designs in order to evaluate the adequacy of the research design used in a particular quantitative research study. The next chapters in Part III are intended to help you develop this understanding. In addition to explaining each design, we present a report of an actual research study that used it.

RESULTS SECTION

The results section of a quantitative research report presents the results of the statistical analyses of the data generated from the researchers' administration of measures to their sample.

We explain commonly used statistical techniques and conditions for their appropriate use in Chapter 6. Then in Chapters 7, 8, and 9, we explain the statistical techniques that are commonly used in conjunction with particular quantitative research designs.

DISCUSSION SECTION

The final section of a quantitative research report is the discussion section (sometimes called "Conclusions"). The purpose of the discussion section is to explain the meaning and implications of the results. Thus, the researchers are expected to express their interpretations of the results; evaluate shortcomings in the design and execution of the study; draw conclusions about the practical and theoretical significance of the results; and make recommendations for further research. Although the results section should present an objective account of the statistical analyses, a more personal perspective is necessary in the discussion section.

In evaluating the discussion section, you must decide whether you agree with the researchers' judgments about how the results should be interpreted and their implications for theory and practice. The most critical factor in this evaluation is whether you think the researchers' judgments are supported by their research results and the results of the previous research that they cite. Your ability to make this evaluation will improve as you develop an understanding of research methodology and knowledge of the research literature to which a particular study contributes.

EXAMPLE OF TAKING NOTES ON A QUANTITATIVE RESEARCH REPORT

The form for outlining a research proposal in Appendix 1 also can be used to make descriptive and evaluative notes on quantitative research studies. To illustrate this use of the form, we used it to take notes on a study that was identified in our literature review on curriculum alignment (see the section Conducting a Free-Text Search in Chapter 2). The citation for the study is:

Bergman, D., Calzada, L., LaPointe, N., Lee, A., & Sullivan, L. (1998). *Vertical alignment and collaboration*. Prepared under Texas A&M University Corpus Christi/Kingsville Joint Doctoral Program in Educational Leadership. (ERIC Document Reproduction Service No. ED421472)

We downloaded a copy of this report using a subscription service available at our university's library. The study is relevant to our example of a proposal to study curriculum alignment, which is introduced in Chapter 2. Below, we show how we filled out relevant parts of the form in Appendix 1 for this study.

1. PURPOSE OF STUDY
   A. The purpose of this study was to investigate "whether vertical (grade-level sequence) alignment of the curriculum in conjunction with teacher collaboration would enhance student performance on the Texas Assessment of Academic Skills (TAAS) test" (Document Abstract).
   B. The researchers cite twenty-two publications, twelve of them since 1995. They cite two previous studies that investigated the effect of vertical alignment (aligning curriculum so that each grade's curriculum builds on the curriculum of the grades preceding it): Betz, 1995; Aguilera, 1996.

2. RESEARCH QUESTIONS, HYPOTHESES, OR OBJECTIVES
   B. The researchers state one question: "Does vertical alignment of the curriculum in conjunction with teacher collaboration enhance student performance on standardized tests?" (p. 21).
   C. This study does not appear to have a theoretical basis.
4. RESEARCH DESIGN
   A. The researchers used a correlational design. They determined the degree of relationship between two independent variables (amount of vertical alignment and teacher collaboration) and two dependent variables (students' scores on TAAS and percentage of students passing all parts of the TAAS).
   B. Because the researchers did not do an experiment, we cannot be sure whether correlations between the independent and dependent variables reflect a cause-and-effect relationship. For example, even if the amount of teacher collaboration is correlated with students' test scores, this does not mean necessarily that if we got teachers to collaborate more, students' test scores would improve. Also, other variables could influence the findings (see 6.A below).
   C. The generalizability of the findings is limited by the fact that the study was done entirely in Texas. Educators in other states might have different views about high-stakes testing of students. If so, their willingness to align curriculum and collaborate might be different, and they might use different alignment and collaboration processes.
5. SAMPLING
   A. The report contains no description of the school districts included in the sample, only that they are in South Texas Regions 1 and 2 (p. 20).
   C. The researchers used random sampling, which is good except that there is no information about the population from which the random sample was drawn.
   D. The researchers state, "Of the forty-seven surveys sent, twenty-seven were returned" (p. 19). The sample size seems sufficient, but the response rate is a concern. We don't know whether the twenty-seven responding school districts are representative of the school districts in the two regions.
6. VARIABLES
   A. The independent variables are (1) amount of vertical alignment and (2) amount of teacher collaboration. The two dependent variables are (1) students' growth on a standards-based achievement test ("the difference between the 1997 Grade 10 percent passing all tests and the 1994 Grade 10 percent passing all tests"—p. 22) and (2) percentage of students passing all parts of the test. It seems that the researchers assume that any growth in the pass rate from 1994 to 1997 is due to vertical alignment and collaboration. However, it could be that Grade 10 students in 1997 have different characteristics than Grade 10 students in 1994; thus, any observed growth could be due to changes in

student characteristics rather than to alignment and/or collaboration. Note, too, that the researchers do not indicate whether the dependent variable of "percentage of students passing all parts of the test" is based on 1994 or 1997 data, although the latter seems more likely.

7. METHODS OF DATA COLLECTION
   A. Amount of vertical alignment was measured by a Likert-scale questionnaire, with response options from 1 (disagree) to 7 (agree). Amount of teacher collaboration was measured the same way as amount of vertical alignment. (It appears, though, that the researchers collapsed both variables into a single variable "vertical alignment/collaboration"—see p. 22). Student performance and pass rates were measured by the Texas Assessment of Academic Skills (TAAS).
   B. No validity or reliability data are provided for the questionnaire. It would be desirable to see evidence that responses on the questionnaire correspond to the educator's actual behavior with respect to aligning curriculum and collaboration. No validity or reliability data are presented for the TAAS, but the researchers refer the reader to another report that contains "statistical data for this assessment" (p. 21).

8. DATA ANALYSIS PROCEDURES
   A. The researchers showed the actual data for each school district on each variable. Product-moment correlation coefficients were calculated to determine the degree of relationship between the independent and dependent variables.

RESULTS (Note: This is not part of the form in Appendix 1, but it can be easily added when using the form to review published studies.) The researchers' findings indicate that districts with less effort devoted to vertical alignment and collaboration among educators had the same improvement in student test scores from 1994 to 1997 as districts that exerted more effort. The researchers offer several explanations for these findings, all of which seem reasonable.

SELF-CHECK TEST

1. Reports of quantitative research studies typically
   a. are written in a more personal style than are reports of qualitative research studies.
   b. follow the style guidelines of the American Psychological Association.
   c. do not include an abstract.
   d. begin with a description of the research design that was employed.

2. Some research studies have found that direct instruction is more effective than other instructional styles. In this research, direct instruction is a
   a. constant.
   b. hypothesis.

    c. construct.

    d. stratified variable.

3. In reporting a quantitative research study, researchers typically
    a. include a statement of their qualifications to conduct the study.
    b. include a brief list of their work history and publications.
    c. do not mention their institutional affiliation.
    d. provide few details about their professional lives.

4. In simple random sampling, researchers
    a. select a sample of individuals who are easily accessible in the population of interest.
    b. identify a sample of populations, and select one of them at random to be studied.
    c. ensure that each individual in the population has an equal chance of being in the sample.
    d. do all of the above.

5. To evaluate population validity, researchers must analyze
    a. the selected sample, the accessible population, and the target population.
    b. the selected sample and the target population.
    c. the accessible population and the target population.
    d. the membership list used to define the target population.

6. A research questionnaire typically
    a. begins with a leading question.
    b. measures many variables.
    c. does not require pretesting.
    d. is ideal for obtaining psychologically threatening information.

7. A test's validity can be determined by collecting evidence based on
    a. an examination of its content.
    b. its internal structure.
    c. its relationship to other variables.
    d. all of the above.

8. If a measure has high reliability, it means that
    a. it has been endorsed by the editors of the *Standards for Educational and Psychological Testing.*
    b. all the items on the test measure the same construct.
    c. it has yielded valid results for a variety of users.
    d. it is relatively free of measurement error.

9. All of the following typically appear in the discussion section of a quantitative research report, except
    a. the statistical results.
    b. an interpretation of the results.
    c. the practical significance of the results.
    d. recommendations for further research.

CHAPTER REFERENCES

American Educational Research Association, American Psychological Association, and National Council on Measurement in Education. (1999). *Standards for educational and psychological testing*. Washington, DC: American Educational Research Association.

Eberts, R. W., & Stone, J. A. (1988). Student achievement in public schools: Do principals make a difference? *Economics of Education Review, 7,* 291–299.

Evans, P. (1976). The Burt affair: Sleuthing in science. *APA Monitor, 12,* pp. 1, 4.

Kraemer, H. C., & Thiemann, S. (1987). How many subjects? Statistical power analysis in research. Thousand Oaks, CA: Sage.

Publication manual of the American Psychological Association (5th ed.). (2001). Washington, DC: American Psychological Association.

RESOURCES FOR FURTHER STUDY

Evertson, C. M., & Green, J. L. (1986). Observation as inquiry and method. In M. C. Wittrock (Ed.), *Handbook of research on teaching* (3rd ed., pp. 162–213). New York: Macmillan.

The authors describe methods of observation and how observation has been used in educational research. They also discuss issues that arise in making observations and in selecting or designing observational instruments.

Fontana, A., & Frey, J. H. (2000). The interview: From structured questions to negotiated text. In N. K. Denzin & Y. S. Lincoln (Eds.), *Handbook of qualitative research* (2nd ed., pp. 645–672). Thousand Oaks, CA: Sage.

The authors describe various types of interviews, including structured interviews, unstructured interviews, group interviews, oral-history interviews, and electronic interviews. They also discuss various issues that should be considered in designing and conducting interviews and in analyzing interview data.

Fowler, F. J., Jr. (2001). *Survey research methods* (3rd ed.). Thousand Oaks, CA: Sage.

A basic guide for designing and conducting research surveys. Among the topics covered are methods for constructing survey questions, obtaining high response rates, and using computers and the Internet to collect and analyze data.

Henry, G. T. (1997). Practical sampling. In L. Bickman & D. J. Rog (Eds.), *Handbook of applied social research methods* (pp. 101–126). Thousand Oaks, CA: Sage.

The author explains the major methods of sampling and how sampling relates to the overall design of a research study.

Weber, R. P. (1990). *Basic content analysis* (2nd ed.). Thousand Oaks, CA: Sage.

The author explains the types of research problems for which content analysis is appropriate. Methods for collecting, analyzing, and interpreting content-analysis data are described.

Worthen, B. (1998). *Measurement and evaluation in schools* (2nd ed.). Boston: Addison-Wesley Longman.

The authors explain assessment principles and procedures for judging the quality of specific tests. Recent trends, such as authentic assessment and the use of microcomputers in testing, are also discussed.

chapter 6

Statistical Analysis of Research Data

Åfter many years of teaching, Henry Wu has returned to the university to obtain an administrator's license. His scheduled course work includes classes on educational statistics, assessment, and research methods.

New state assessment tests are scheduled to be given throughout Wu's state to students at three grade levels. Henry has some concerns about the upcoming state assessment. For example, he wonders whether repeated administrations of state tests can be used to measure learning gains, and whether administering the tests to samples of students—even large samples—will yield results that can be generalized to all students in the state at those grade levels. His deepest concern is whether statistics such as mean scores and percentile scores can present an honest picture of what students know, and whether they will reflect the large individual differences among students. Henry hopes that these concerns will be addressed in his licensure courses.

In this chapter, you will learn how educational researchers use statistics to summarize and describe the data obtained from administering tests and other measures to groups of individuals. You also will learn how researchers use statistics to help them make valid generalizations of statistical results obtained from a small sample to a much larger population. ●

149

THE PURPOSE OF STATISTICAL ANALYSIS

Most research studies, whether quantitative or qualitative, generate data that can be expressed in numerical form. For example, if researchers administer an aptitude test to their sample, the analysis of the sample's performance on the test will generate numerical scores. There might be a total test score for each individual in the sample, as well as scores for subsections of the test (e.g., verbal aptitude and mathematical aptitude). In addition, the researchers might have collected numerical data about each individual's personal background (e.g., age and number of years of professional work experience).

Qualitative research studies usually yield verbal data (e.g., transcripts of interviews) or visual data (e.g., videorecordings of events). These data typically are analyzed in their original state by the researchers. However, this method of analysis sometimes is supplemented by transforming the data into numerical form. For example, suppose that the researchers made transcripts of a set of interviews. The transcripts can be analyzed by counting the frequency with which certain words or themes are mentioned. These frequency counts constitute numerical data.

Even though statistical procedures sometimes are used in qualitative research, they are used much more intensively in quantitative research. For this reason, we introduce the use of statistical analysis in educational research in this part of the book.

The numerical data in a quantitative research study can be subjected to various statistical analyses. One purpose of these analyses is to summarize the scores on a particular measure that are obtained by all the individuals who constitute the sample. In some research studies, the sample includes hundreds or even thousands of individuals. Without statistical tools for summarizing their data, it would be virtually impossible to make sense of them. Other statistical tools, as you will learn in this chapter, help researchers determine whether conclusions based on the numerical data for a sample can be generalized to the population that the sample is intended to represent.

Statistical analysis is a branch of mathematics, and therefore you need to have some understanding of mathematics in order to make sense of the assumptions and computational procedures for the statistical tools used in educational research. Development of this understanding typically requires taking one or more courses in statistics and its applications in educational research. Coursework in statistics will also help you make better judgments about the appropriateness of the statistics that are used in published research studies, and to use appropriate statistical techniques in your own research.

Because you might not yet have taken statistics courses, we have minimized presentation of the mathematical basis for statistical analysis in this chapter. Each statistical procedure is described in nontechnical rather than in mathematical terms. We focus on the purpose of each statistical procedure, its appropriate use in research studies, and the information that it yields. You might be able to follow the discussion better if you have scratch paper handy as you read, so that you can see for yourself how we did certain calculations with the data that are presented in tables.

TYPES OF SCORES IN STATISTICAL ANALYSIS

In reviewing statistical analyses in a research report, you should start by determining what type of score was used in each analysis. These scores will be of different types depending on the type of variable that was measured. For example, a student's score on a typical achievement test is of a different type from the student's "score" on the variable of gender.

Three types of scores are computed in educational research studies: (1) continuous scores, (2) gain scores, and (3) categorical scores. You need to understand each of these types of scores, because different statistical analyses are appropriate for each type.

Continuous and Derived Scores

Continuous scores are values of a measure that has an indefinite number of ordered points. Most achievement and aptitude tests, attitude scales, and personality measures yield scores of this type. For example, suppose a test has fifty items, with a score of 1 point for each item answered correctly. Thus, scores on this test have 51 continuous points, ranging from 0 to 50. The points are ordered so that each value is greater than the value preceding it. The points are not truly indefinite in number but only approximately so, because on most standardized tests the continuous scores are limited to whole numbers. To be truly indefinite, the test would need to yield fractional values, such as 41.25.

One type of continuous score is the **raw score,** which is simply the total score obtained by following the test developers' scoring procedures. Raw scores by themselves are difficult to interpret. For example, a score of 30 on a fifty-item test might be interpreted as high or low, depending on how difficult the test is and on how well other individuals in the research sample performed on it. Therefore, researchers often report derived scores in addition to raw scores. **Derived scores** provide a quantitative comparison of each individual's performance relative to a comparison group. Five types of derived scores are commonly reported: age equivalents, grade equivalents, percentiles, standard scores, and rank scores.

Age Equivalents. A student's **age-equivalent** score is the age level of other students who typically earn the same raw score that the student did. This type of derived score is commonly used with academic achievement tests. The other students to whom the student's score is compared usually are a large sample, called a **norming sample,** which typically represents a national, regional, or state population. The raw score of each student in the research sample can be found in the table of norms, which will report the age of students in the norming sample who earned that score, on average. For example, if the age equivalent for a student who earned a raw score of 30 is 12.0, it means that this student earned the average raw score of students in the norming sample who were 12 years old. (Later in this chapter, you will find that *average* in this context refers to a statistic called the *mean.*)

Grade Equivalents. These derived scores are similar in meaning to age equivalents. The only difference is that the table of norms reports the average raw score earned by students at each grade level in the norming sample. For example, if the **grade equivalent** for a student who earned a raw score of 20 is 3.5, it means that this student performed at the average level of students in the norming sample who were in the middle of the third grade.

Percentile Scores. **Percentile scores** represent the percentage of individuals whose raw score falls at or below the raw scores of other individuals in the research sample. For example, suppose that 40 percent of the students in the research sample earn a raw score of 27 or below. In this case, a raw score of 27 would represent a percentile score of 40. More commonly, we would state that the student scored at the 40th percentile of the research sample.

Test developers often construct a table of norms in percentile form. If such a table is available, researchers can use percentile scores in addition to, or instead of, age and grade equivalents to express how well individuals in their sample performed relative to the norming sample. In the above example, a raw score of 27 might be at the 40th percentile in relation to other students in the research sample but at, say, the 35th percentile with respect to the norming sample.

Standard Scores.   These derived scores are similar in meaning to percentiles. However, they have mathematical advantages over percentile scores, and therefore are commonly used in statistical computations. An individual's **standard score** is derived by subtracting his or her raw score from the mean score earned by the research sample and then dividing that result by the standard deviation of the scores of the research sample. (Mean scores and standard deviations are explained later in the chapter.) Some test manuals include a table of norms in which the sample's raw scores can be converted to standard scores derived from a norming sample.

Intelligence test scores are a common example of standard scores. For example, the mean score on the Stanford-Binet Intelligence Scale is set at 100, meaning that half of the norming sample obtained a score that is at or below this standard score. The standard deviation is set at 16. By referring to the normal probability curve (discussed later in this chapter), you can determine the percentage of individuals in the sample who earned at or below a particular IQ score.

Rank Scores.   A **rank score** expresses the position of an individual on a measure relative to the positions held by other individuals. Rank scores are used by educators for various purposes. For example, a school might rank the students at a particular grade level with respect to academic achievement, or athletes might be ranked with respect to performance in a sports contest (e.g., first place, second place, and third place). These examples illustrate the educational or social significance of some measures that yield rank scores. Because of their significance, rank scores sometimes are collected and analyzed by educational researchers.

Rank scores typically have unequal intervals. For example, in one classroom there might be very little difference in academic achievement between the first-ranked and second-ranked student. In another classroom, however, these two ranks might reflect substantial differences in academic achievement. This limitation of rank scores should be kept in mind when interpreting statistical results based on this type of score.

Gain Scores

Individuals' learning and development are the focus of much educational research. Both processes involve change in an individual from one time to another. These changes can be detected by administering the same measure to individuals at two or more points in time. A **gain score** is simply the difference in an individual's score on the measure from one time to the next. Gain scores often are positive, but they also can be negative, as when an individual forgets information learned earlier.

Gain scores are sometimes reported by researchers, but you should view them with caution. For example, they are subject to a **ceiling effect**. To understand this effect, suppose that a student scores 95 out of 100 possible points on initial testing. The student can improve by a maximum of only 5 points on this test when it is readministered. These 5 points might be inadequate (the ceiling is too low) to measure all the new information or skills that the student has learned during the intervening time interval.

Another limitation of gain scores is that most tests tend to have unequal intervals. For example, suppose a test has fifty items, and each item answered correctly earns a score of 1. Suppose, though, that the items vary in difficulty. Now consider the case of two students who earn the same gain score of 5, but one goes from a raw score of 10 to a raw score of 15, whereas the other goes from a raw score of 40 to a raw score of 45. It probably is more difficult for the second student to make a gain score of 5 than it is for the first student, because he or she will need to answer correctly more difficult items on the test. Thus the gain score does not have the same meaning for both students.

Still another problem is that most tests contain different types of items. For example, suppose that two students earn the same gain score on a subtraction test, but they do it by making gains on different types of subtraction items. Once again, the gain score is the same, but it does not mean the same thing for the two students.

Despite these problems and others not described here, gain scores continue to be used in educational research and practice. To determine whether they provide meaningful information, you need to check for possible ceiling effects and determine whether similar gain scores for different individuals reflect similar learning or development.

Categorical Scores

Categories are variables that yield values that are discrete and nonordered when measured. An example would be students' parental status. We could assign categorical scores for different types of parental status, such as: (a) two parents together, (b) mother only, (c) father only, and (d) other. These categories are discrete, meaning that each student can be assigned to only one category; the categories do not overlap. Note, too, that the categories do not form an ordered continuum. For example, it would not make sense to say that a father-only family is "more" or "less" than a mother-only family or that either is "more" or "less" than a family categorized as "other." Because categories cannot be ordered, categorical scores must be analyzed by different statistical techniques than continuous or rank scores.

A **dichotomy** is a special type of categorical variable. It yields only two values. Gender, for example, is a dichotomous variable because only two values are recognized: male and female. Gender is a natural dichotomy, but other dichotomies are artificial, meaning that the values are defined by the researchers or by other individuals. For example, researchers might classify school districts as having a centralized or a decentralized administration, or students might classify themselves as college bound or not college bound.

DESCRIPTIVE STATISTICS

Research studies often yield a large amount of numerical data. **Descriptive statistics** serve a useful purpose by summarizing all the data in the form of a few simple numerical expressions, called statistics. A **statistic** is a number that describes the characteristic of a sample's scores on a measure. To illustrate, we created data for a hypothetical research study, which is shown in Table 6.1. The main purpose of this study was to determine whether there is a relationship between employed and nonemployed students' interest in history and their final grade in a history course.

The data in Table 6.1 constitute the raw data of the study. The students were classified as having part-time jobs or as not having any jobs, and the scores of these groups are shown separately. Data for employed students are shown on the left side of the table, and data for nonemployed students are shown on the right

TABLE 6.1 Interest in History and History Course Grade for Employed and Nonemployed Students

	EMPLOYED STUDENTS			NONEMPLOYED STUDENTS	
ID	Interest in History	Course Grade	ID	Interest in History	Course Grade
01	31	2	11	25	2
02	30	3	12	37	3
03	27	0	13	41	3
04	38	2	14	42	3
05	18	1	15	32	3
06	34	3	16	47	4
07	29	3	17	33	3
08	25	2	18	38	4
09	33	1	19	44	1
10	42	4	20	37	2
	$M = 30.70$	$M = 2.10$		$M = 37.60$	$M = 2.80$
	$SD = 6.73$	$SD = 1.20$		$SD = 6.43$	$SD = .92$

Total Sample ($N = 20$)

Interest in History	Course Grade
$M = 34.15$	$M = 2.45$
$SD = 7.32$	$SD = 1.10$

side. The ID column in this table is an identification code to distinguish each individual in the sample from the others. The ID numbers are in consecutive order, from 01 to 20.

The first data column of the table shows students' scores on the interest measure, with higher scores indicating greater interest. The second data column shows students' course grades (A = 4; B = 3; C = 2; D = 1; F = 0).

Raw data like these seldom are included in a research report. Journals, which are the primary medium in which research reports are published, lack space to include raw data. Even if they had space, however, they would not do so, because conclusions drawn from raw data tend to be imprecise. For example, one would be limited to statements such as, "It appears that students who are more interested in history tend to do better in a course on this subject," or, "Employed students tend to be less interested in history than nonemployed students." These statements do not tell us precisely how strong the tendency to do better is or precisely how much less interested employed students are than nonemployed students. Therefore, descriptive statistics are reported instead. They lead to mathematically precise statements such as, "There is a positive correlation of .49 between students' interest in history and their grades in a course on this subject," or, "Employed students scored an average of seven points less than nonemployed students on a twenty-item measure of interest in history."

The following is an explanation of the descriptive statistics that are commonly used in educational research.

Mean, Median, and Mode

Mean. Researchers are interested in the individuals who make up their sample, but they also are interested in the sample as a whole. In our hypothetical study, they would want to know the typical interest level of the sample and whether the typical interest level of employed students differs from that of nonemployed students. A statistic known as the mean usually is computed to represent the typical score in a distribution of scores. The **mean** is calculated by summing the individual scores of the sample and then dividing the total sum by the number of individuals in the sample. Table 6.1 reports the means (represented by the symbol M) for the total sample and separately for employed students and nonemployed students for the two variables: interest in history and course grade. The mean is misleading as a typical score if the distribution of scores is markedly asymmetrical. (A symmetrical distribution is shown in Figure 6.1.)

Median. The median is another statistic that can be used to describe a sample's typical score on a measure. The **median** is the middle score in the distribution of scores, meaning that half the individuals in the sample score at or below the median score. (If there is an even number of individuals in a sample, the median is the score halfway between the scores of the two middle individuals.)

The median for the total sample on the interest measure is 33.5, and the median course grade is 3.0. The median grade for the employed students is 2.0, and for the nonemployed students it is 3.0. You will note that the medians are similar to, but not identical with, the corresponding means. If the distribution of scores is markedly asymmetrical, the median provides a better representation of the typical score than does the mean.

Mode.   The **mode** is simply the most frequently occurring score among the scores for the sample. It is seldom reported, because it usually has little meaning. For example, the mode for course grades in our hypothetical study is 3, which corresponds to a grade of B. Without further information, we do not know whether this grade was assigned to slightly more students, or to many other students, than any of the other grades.

The mean is most often included in research reports because it is more stable than the median or mode. In other words, if one selected many samples at random from a population with scores on a certain measure, the means for the samples would be more similar to one another than would the medians or the modes.

The mean, median, and mode are appropriate descriptive statistics for continuous scores and rank scores.

Frequency Counts and Percentages

Suppose that the data for our hypothetical sample include the variable of type of employment. The three categories are (1) food service worker, (2) gas station attendant, and (3) store clerk. The mean, median, and mode are inappropriate statistics for data of this type. Instead, the frequency or percentage of individuals in each category is determined. Table 6.2 reports these statistics for the employed students in our hypothetical sample. The **frequency** is simply the total number of individuals in the sample who fit a particular category. The **percentage** is the frequency of individuals in a particular category divided by the total number of individuals in the sample. (For example, for food service workers, 5 divided by 10 = 0.5, or 50 percent.) Some research reports include only frequencies or only percentages rather than reporting both, because the other statistic can be calculated easily by readers if they wish to know it.

Range and Standard Deviation

The mean provides a mathematically precise and succinct description of the sample's average performance on a measure. This information, however, is not sufficient. We also want to know how much variation is present in the individual

TABLE 6.2   **Type of Employment for Employed Students**

TYPE OF EMPLOYMENT	FREQUENCY	PERCENTAGE
Food service worker	5	50
Store clerk	4	40
Gas station attendant	1	10

scores. Did most of the individuals in the sample obtain scores at or near the mean, or did they vary widely from the mean?

Range. One way to answer this question is to determine the range of scores. The **range** is calculated as the difference between the lowest and highest score plus 1 in the distribution of scores for a measure. Referring to Table 6.1, we see that the range for the interest measure is 30 (47 – 18 + 1), and the range of course grades is 5 (4 – 0 + 1).

Standard Deviation. Some research reports include the range of scores for each measure, but if so, they also should report the standard deviation of scores, which is a more stable and mathematically meaningful measure of variability. The **standard deviation** is a statistical expression of how much individual scores vary around the mean score. Table 6.1 reports the standard deviation (abbreviated as *SD*) for each mean that was calculated.

A simple way to understand the standard deviation is to imagine taking each individual score and subtracting it from the mean score of the sample. Following this procedure for the first student (ID = 01), we calculate a variation of 4.15 points from the total sample mean (34.15 – 31.00). Suppose we followed this procedure for the entire sample, ignoring whether the subtraction process yielded a negative or positive score. We then could sum these difference scores and divide the total sum by the number of individuals in the sample. The result is called the **average variation**, that is, the average amount by which individual scores deviate from the mean score. This result approximates the standard deviation. (The actual formula for calculating the standard deviation involves squaring the individual difference scores, and a few other procedures.)

Normal Curve. The standard deviation is a particularly useful statistic if the individual scores on the measure form a normal probability distribution. A **normal probability distribution** of scores, known more commonly as a **normal curve,** is shown in Figure 6.1. To understand this figure, suppose that a large number of individuals were measured on a particular variable. The height of the curve at any point along the horizontal line would indicate the number of individuals who obtained the score represented by that point. You will note that the mean of the sample's scores is indicated on the horizontal line. If the sample's scores are normally distributed, more individuals will obtain the mean score than any other score in the distribution of scores.

You will note, too, that actual scores for a measure are not shown in Figure 6.1. Instead, the scores are represented immediately below the curve as standard deviation units (–3, –2, –1, etc.). To understand what these units mean, consider the hypothetical data set shown in Table 6.1. The standard deviation for the total sample on the interest measure is 7.32, and the mean is 34.15. If an individual scored 1 standard deviation unit above the mean, it indicates that he or she obtained a score of 41 (34.15 + 7.32 = 41.47, rounded to the whole number of 41). This score corresponds to the +1 in Figure 6.1. Individuals who score 1 **standard deviation**

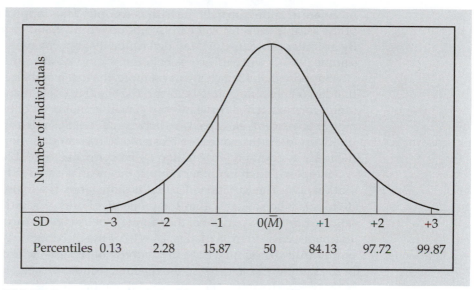

FIGURE 6.1   **Normal Probability Distribution of Scores**

Source. Adapted from Figure 5.1 on p. 179 in Gall, M. D., Borg, W. R., & Gall, J. P. (1996). *Educational research: An introduction* (6th ed.). Boston, MA: Allyn and Bacon. Copyright by Pearson Education. Adapted by permission of the publisher.

unit below the mean score would obtain a score of 27 (34.15 – 7.32 = 26.83). This score corresponds to the –1 in Figure 6.1.

Now consider the case of an individual who scores 2 standard deviations (7.32 × 2 = 14.64) above the mean. That individual's score would be 49 (34.15 + 14.64 = 48.79). This score corresponds to the +2 in Figure 6.1. No individual in the sample actually obtained that score, because the distribution of scores did not follow the normal curve perfectly.

The standard deviation units immediately beneath the normal curve shown in Figure 6.1 include a zero (0). The zero is the mean score of the sample or population. In our hypothetical study, the mean score of the sample on the measure of interest in history is 34.15. There is no deviation of a mean score from itself. Therefore, it has a value of zero when expressed in standard deviation units.

The advantage of the standard deviation units shown in Figure 6.1 is that scores for any measure can be represented by them, assuming that the scores are normally distributed. It does not matter whether one measure has 100 possible points and another has 20 possible points. The standard deviation units for each measure have the same meaning with respect to the normal curve.

The normal curve has practical value in interpreting the results of research studies. If you know the mean and standard deviation for the scores on a measure, you can use these two bits of information to determine the amount of variability in the scores (assuming the scores are normally distributed). Referring to Figure 6.1, you will see that scores 1 standard deviation below the mean are at approximately the 16th percentile, and scores 1 standard deviation above the mean are at approximately the 84th percentile. Thus, approximately 68 percent of the sample (84 – 16) will earn scores between +1 and –1 standard deviation. By a similar procedure, we can determine that approximately 96 percent of the sample (98 – 2) will earn scores between +2 and –2 standard deviations.

Suppose that, for a particular sample, the mean of their scores on a measure that has 50 possible points is 25 and the standard deviation is 2. Assuming the scores form a normal curve, we can conclude that most of the sample (approximately 96 percent) earned scores between 21 (–2 *SD* units) and 29 (+2 *SD* units). In other words, the scores are clustered tightly around the mean score, and so the mean is a good representation of the performance of the entire sample.

Suppose that, for another sample, the mean is again 25 but the standard deviation is 10. The variation in scores is quite large. If we consider only those individuals who scored within the range of +1 and –1 standard deviation units (approximately 68 percent of the sample), their scores are expected to vary from 15 (that is, 25 – 10) to 35 (that is, 25 + 10) if the distribution of scores follows the normal curve. In this case the mean does not represent closely the performance of the sample. In interpreting the research results, we need to keep in mind that in this research sample the individuals are more different than alike with respect to the variable that was measured.

The mean and standard deviation are mathematically elegant, because these two statistics together provide a succinct summary of the raw data. Even if the sample includes 1,000 individuals, we can tell much about how they performed on a measure just by knowing the mean and standard deviation.

Limitations of the Standard Deviation.   The standard deviation is interpretable only if the scores are normally distributed (as shown in Figure 6.1) or approximately so. If the distribution of scores deviates substantially from normality, the standard deviation cannot be interpreted in terms of the normal curve. For this reason, researchers should state in their reports whether scores for any measure deviate substantially from the normal curve. Fortunately, it seems to be a law of nature that most variables of educational significance are normally distributed.

The range and standard deviation are meaningful descriptive statistics for continuous scores and gain scores. They are not appropriate for categorical scores. The variability in distribution of these scores can be determined simply by looking at the frequency counts or percentages in each category. For example, if the variable being measured has five categories, you need only inspect the frequency counts or percentages to determine whether individuals are evenly distributed across the categories or whether a disproportionate number are in a few of the categories.

Bivariate Correlational Statistics

A major purpose of research is to explore the relationship between variables. In the case of our hypothetical research study, the purpose is to determine the relationship between high school students' interest in history and their final grade in a history course. **Correlational statistics** can be used to describe the extent of this relationship in mathematically precise terms. If only two variables are involved, a **bivariate correlational statistic** is calculated. This type of statistic is discussed at length in Chapter 8, which is concerned with the correlational research method. Therefore, we provide only a brief description of this topic here.

Correlational statistics involve the calculation of a correlation coefficient, such as that represented by the symbol *r*, for the **r value.** Larger *r* values indicate greater magnitudes of relationship between the variables that have been measured. Different types of correlation coefficients can be calculated, depending on whether continuous scores, rank scores, dichotomous scores, or categorical scores are involved.

The two variables in Table 6.1 both involve continuous scores, so the product-moment correlation coefficient is appropriate for describing the magnitude of their relationship. Positive values of this coefficient can vary between 0 and 1.00. The obtained coefficient (*r* = .49) for this sample indicates a moderately positive relationship, meaning that students with more interest in history tend to earn somewhat higher grades in a history course than students with less interest. For example, the student with ID 05 has an interest score of 18 and a course grade of D (numerical value = 1), whereas the student with ID 10 has a higher interest score of 42 and a higher course grade of A (numerical value = 4). The relationship between the two variables is less than perfect, however, as illustrated by the student with ID 19, who has a high interest score (44) but a course grade of D.

Multivariate Correlational Statistics

Advances in research methodology have enabled researchers to explore the relationship between more than two variables at the same time. In our hypothetical study, students' scores on a measure of interest in history were used to predict their grades in a history course. Suppose that we included several more measures to make this prediction, for example, measures of students' verbal aptitude and their study habits. It might be that a combination of the three measures (interest in history, verbal aptitude, and study habits) yields a better prediction of course grades than any one measure alone. A correlational procedure known as **multiple regression** can be used for this purpose. It determines which measure, or combination of measures, to use and how to weight students' scores on each measure to produce the best prediction of the criterion variable (in this case, students' course grades).

Multiple regression and other multivariate correlational techniques are discussed in Chapter 8.

INFERENTIAL STATISTICS

In Chapter 5 we explained procedures for selecting samples for quantitative research studies. The ideal procedure is to select a sample at random from a defined population. If random selection is not possible, researchers still should attempt to select a sample that represents a population of interest. In either case, the goal is to generalize from the sample to the population, that is, to make inferences about the population from the results obtained with the sample.

As the name implies, inferential statistics help in the process of making inferences. More specifically, **inferential statistics** enable researchers to make inferences about a population based on the descriptive statistics that are calculated on data from a sample that represents this population. Inferential statistics are commonly used in causal-comparative research (see Chapter 7), correlational research (see Chapter 8), and experimental research (see Chapter 9).

The mathematical basis for inferential statistics is complex. Therefore, we will provide a nontechnical explanation here by considering one of the results of the hypothetical study shown in Table 6.1.

If you examine this table, you will see that the mean of employed students on the measure of interest in history ($M = 30.70$) is lower than the mean of nonemployed students ($M = 37.60$). The question we must ask is whether a similar difference would be found if we studied the entire population of students taking this type of history course. In other words, can we generalize the results from our small sample to the population of students that it represents? (Let's assume that the population is all U.S. high school students, and that this sample is representative of that population.)

To conclude that the results are generalizable, we first must reject the possible explanation that the results are a chance finding. One way to reject this explanation would be to conduct **replication studies,** that is, to carry out the same study repeatedly with different samples representing the same population. If these replication studies consistently yielded approximately the same direction and degree of difference between employed and nonemployed students, this would constitute strong evidence of generalizability.

Replication studies, in fact, are commonly carried out for important findings. In medicine, for example, positive findings about a new drug obtained by one group of researchers rarely are accepted. Other laboratories around the world must test the drug to confirm the original results. The consequences of using a drug claimed to be effective, but actually not so, are far too serious to rely on the results of a single research study. In education, too, important findings are replicated across many studies. For example, hundreds of research studies on the effects of class size have been done, because class size is an important consideration in educational policy and budgetary decisions.

Chance Findings.   Inferential statistics are not as strong a test of generalizability as replication studies. However, they require only a tiny fraction of the effort required for a single replication study. As with replications, inferential statistics test the possible explanation that an observed result for a sample is a chance finding. What do we mean by a chance finding? To answer this question, imagine that we have two populations whose members have identical sets of scores on the measure of interest in history. These sets of scores are shown in Table 6.3. We

TABLE 6.3	Hypothetical Populations of Employed Students and Nonemployed Students with Identical Mean Scores on a Measure of Interest in History

POPULATION OF EMPLOYED STUDENTS ($N = 100$; $M = 32.28$)

27	31	29	28	40	42
26	32	37	36	39	21
31	29	38	33	26	39
28	36	31	26	27	32
28	30	43	32	40	36
35	37	37	24	24	33
30	29	26	27	27	35
45	36	37	29	28	30
29	32	40	31	23	19
38	34	32	34	28	25
22	29	40	39	25	28
35	39	35	23	34	42
37	31	41	29	38	41
38	37	21	38	36	33
34	36	35	33	28	25
35	34	32	26	27	44
20	41	30	30		

POPULATION OF NONEMPLOYED STUDENTS ($N = 100$; $M = 32.28$)

27	37	36	30	23	36
26	38	34	28	29	28
31	34	41	36	38	27
28	35	29	33	33	42
28	20	37	26	26	21
35	31	38	32	30	39
30	32	31	24	28	32
45	34	43	27	23	36
29	29	37	29	28	33
38	39	26	31	25	35
22	31	37	34	34	30
35	37	40	39	38	19
32	29	41	39	27	41
29	36	21	26	25	33
36	32	35	27	28	25
30	40	32	40	42	44
37	35	40	24		

labeled one population "employed students" and the other, "nonemployed students." Because the populations are identical with respect to interest in history, the mean of the scores for each population must be identical.

Now let's draw a random sample of ten individuals from one population and then do the same with the other population. Then we can compute the mean score of each sample on the measure of interest in history and determine the difference. The results of these computations are shown in the first row of Table 6.4. Note that even though the population means are identical, the two sample means differ from each other. In this case the mean score of the employed students, by chance, is greater than the mean score of the nonemployed students.

Table 6.4 shows the results of repeatedly drawing new samples of size ten from each population and computing their mean scores. In some samples the employed students score higher; in other samples the nonemployed students score higher; and in one sample there is no difference. The important thing to note, though, is that whenever a difference between employed and nonemployed students is obtained, it is a chance difference. Even though the population means are identical, differences between samples drawn from the two populations can and do occur simply by chance.

Testing for Chance Findings.   We see, then, the possibility that the difference between the mean scores of employed and nonemployed students shown in Table 6.1 could have occurred by chance. Now the question arises, just how likely is it that the result occurred by chance? The answer to this question is obtained by using inferential statistics. In nonmathematical terms, inferential statistics are the equivalent of creating identical populations and then drawing

TABLE 6.4   Results from Random Samples of Size Ten from Populations of Employed and Nonemployed Students Having Identical Scores on a Measure of Interest in History

EMPLOYED *M*	NONEMPLOYED *M*	DIFFERENCE
33.2	31.4	+1.8
32.0	35.4	−3.4
34.0	29.8	+4.2
32.3	32.3	0.0
34.4	30.3	+4.1
30.4	35.0	−4.6
31.8	32.9	−1.1
29.2	31.1	−1.9
32.0	31.1	+0.9
31.3	29.6	+1.7

many pairs of samples of a given size—just as we did in Table 6.4—and computing the difference between the mean scores. These difference scores will form a normal probability distribution, also known as a normal curve (an example is shown in Figure 6.1).

Researchers can determine how often the difference they obtained in their sample occurs in the normal distribution. Suppose we calculated this number for our hypothetical study and found that our obtained difference of 6.90 points (employed students' M minus nonemployed students' M) occurs only once in one hundred times when we draw samples of the same size as our samples from two identical populations. In this case, we can conclude that our obtained difference in mean scores might be a chance finding, but that this is not very likely. Therefore, we reject the explanation that our obtained result occurred by chance. Instead, we accept the alternative explanation that our obtained result came about because the two samples (employed students and nonemployed students) represent different populations, and the population mean of nonemployed students is greater than the population mean of employed students.

In reflecting on this deductive process, you might come to the realization that it is by no means perfect. Even though our obtained difference between employed and nonemployed students would occur by chance only once in one hundred times if the populations were identical, our samples might constitute that once-in-a-hundred-times occurrence. Also, even if we are correct in concluding that the obtained difference reflects real population differences, our sample means might not be the actual population means. For example, the mean score of the employed students in our sample on the measure of interest in history might not be the actual population mean score. The actual mean score might be somewhat higher or lower than the obtained mean score. (A particular inferential statistic, called a *confidence limit*, can be used to determine the range of mean scores within which the population mean score is likely to fall.)

Null Hypothesis.   The foregoing explanation of inferential statistics should be sufficient to help you understand several technical terms that you are likely to encounter in research reports. One term is **null hypothesis,** which simply is the explanation that an observed result for a sample is a chance finding. The basic purpose of any inferential statistic is to test the null hypothesis. The findings of this test are used to accept the null hypothesis (that is, attribute the obtained result to chance) or to reject the null hypothesis (that is, conclude that the obtained result can be generalized to the population).

Statistical Significance.   Other technical terms you are likely to see in research reports are p and statistical significance. In the example that we have been considering, a **p value** refers to the percentage of occasions that a chance difference between mean scores of a certain magnitude will occur when the population means are identical (see the previous discussion). The lower the p value, the less often a chance difference of a given magnitude will occur; therefore, the more likely it is that the null hypothesis is false. For example, a p value of .001 indicates that it is much more likely that the null hypothesis is false than would a p value of .01. A p value of .001 indicates that a mean score difference as large as the obtained mean score difference would occur only once in 1,000 drawings of two samples from identical populations. A p value of .01 indicates that a mean score difference as large as the obtained mean score difference would occur only once in 100 drawings.

In educational research, a p value of .05 generally is considered sufficient to reject the null hypothesis. This high a p value makes it fairly easy to reject the null hypothesis because the researcher's obtained difference between mean scores would need to exceed the difference that would occur only once in 20 times in samples drawn from identical populations. Therefore, some obtained results with $p = .05$ might be chance findings. For this reason, you should be cautious about generalizing results from a sample to a population if the p value is .05 or higher. You have less need for caution, though, if other research studies in the literature reported similar findings, that is, replicated the study results.

Some researchers will report p as $< .05$ rather than $= .05$. Usually the p value is not exactly .05 but rather some value less than that. The symbol "<" means "less than," and is a shorthand way of expressing this information.

When the obtained result is statistically significant, the null hypothesis is rejected. For this reason the various inferential statistics sometimes are called **tests of statistical significance.** In reading research reports, you should be careful not to confuse statistical significance with practical significance. A statistically significant result means only that it is likely to be generalizable beyond the sample, or in other words, that it is not a chance finding. Although generalizable, the obtained result might reflect such a small difference between groups that it has little **practical significance.**

We describe below the main types of inferential statistics used in educational research. Different types are necessary to test the generalizability of the different types of results obtained in research studies. In the above example, we considered only one of many possible results, that is, the difference between two mean scores.

The *t* Test

The *t* **test** is used to determine whether an observed difference between the mean scores of two groups on a measure is likely to have occurred by chance or whether it reflects a true difference in the mean scores of the populations represented by the two groups. In our hypothetical study of high school history instruction, the *t* test could be used to determine whether the mean score of employed students on the interest measure is truly different from the mean score of nonemployed students. Similarly, the *t* test could be used to determine whether the mean course grade of these two groups is truly different.

The computations involved in a *t* test yield a *t* **value.** Researchers look for this value in a table of the *t* distribution. A *t* value of 2.10 is statistically significant at the .05 level for a sample of twenty individuals, meaning that only 5 times in 100 will a difference in mean scores as large as or larger than the observed difference occur when drawing samples of a given size from identical populations. Researchers generally agree that *t* values yielding a *p* of .05 or lower (5 ÷ 100 = .05) are sufficient to conclude that a difference in mean scores of two groups can be generalized to the populations represented by the samples used in the study.

In our hypothetical study, the *t* value for the difference in mean scores on the interest measure for employed students (*M* = 30.70) and nonemployed students (*M* = 37.60) is 2.35. Because our obtained *t* of 2.35 exceeds the *t* value of 2.10 required for statistical significance at the .05 level, we would reject the null hypothesis that this is a chance finding. Instead, we would conclude that nonemployed students in other settings with characteristics similar to those of the research sample would display more interest in history than employed students.

The distribution of scores for one or the other group being compared sometimes deviates substantially from the normal curve (see Figure 6.1). The *t* test cannot be used under this set of conditions. Alternative tests of statistical significance can be used instead: the **Mann-Whitney *U* test** or the **Wilcoxon signed-rank test.** They do not require the same assumptions about score distribution as the *t* test.

The *t* test also can be used to determine whether observed correlation coefficients occurred by chance. For example, we could determine whether the correlation coefficient value of .49, representing the level of relationship between interest in history and history course grade in Table 6.1, occurred by chance. The null hypothesis to be tested is that the true relationship between interest and course grade in the population represented by the sample is .00 and that the observed coefficient of .49 is a chance deviation from that value. The test of this null hypothesis yields a *t* value of 2.39 (*p* < .05), and therefore we conclude that the relationship between interest and course grade would be found in other groups similar to the research sample.

Analysis of Variance

In our hypothetical study, the students were classified as employed or as nonemployed. Suppose, instead, that we had three classifications: (1) nonemployed, (2) working 10 hours a week or less, and (3) working 11 hours a week or more. This research design would yield three mean scores on the measure of interest in history, one for each of the three groups. The *t* test can compare only two means at a time. Therefore, another test of statistical significance, known as **analysis of variance,** must be used. This test determines the likelihood that the differences between the three mean scores occurred by chance, in other words, that they are chance values generated by drawing repeated samples from three populations having identical scores. (Analysis of variance also can be used to compare four or more mean scores.)

Analysis of variance yields an inferential statistic called an **F value.** If the *F* value exceeds a certain value determined by examining a particular statistical table (a table of the *F* distribution), we would reject the null hypothesis and conclude that the difference between the three mean scores is generalizable to a population. However, analysis of variance does not tell us which of the differences between the three mean scores is generalizable. If we represent the three mean scores by the symbols A, B, and C, we see that three comparisons are possible: A versus B, A versus C, and B versus C. One or more of these comparisons might be generalizable. To make these comparisons, a special form of the *t* test is applied to each comparison. The most common of these special tests are **Tukey's test** and **Scheffé's test.**

Another application of analysis of variance is to determine the likelihood that differences in the standard deviations of two or more groups occurred by chance. For example, we could use analysis of variance to test whether the standard deviations of the interest scores for the two groups of employed students (*SD* = 6.73) and nonemployed students (*SD* = 6.43) differ by chance. More accurately, we would be testing whether the variances in the two sets of scores differ by chance. (**Variance** is a measure of the variability in a set of scores; it is calculated by squaring the standard deviation.)

Analysis of Variance in Experiments.   Analysis of variance plays an important role in drawing conclusions from data yielded by experiments. To understand its role in this context, we constructed data for a hypothetical experiment comparing two types of text. Two groups of students were formed prior to the experiment: (1) students with high reading ability and (2) students with low reading ability. Students in each group were randomly assigned to the experimental and control treatments. Students in the experimental treatment read a text passage with inserted questions inviting them to relate the information being presented to something they already knew. Students in the control treatment read the same text passage but with no inserted questions. A multiple-choice test covering the content of the text passage was administered a day before students read the passage (the pretest) and a day after (the posttest).

Table 6.5 shows descriptive statistics for each subgroup (e.g., high-reading-ability students in the experimental group) on the posttest. Also shown are descriptive statistics for combinations of subgroups, for example, the mean score and standard deviation for all experimental-group students, whether they have high or low reading ability.

Many comparisons are possible for the mean scores shown in Table 6.5, for example, all experimental-group students versus all control-group students; high-ability students versus low-ability students in the experimental group; high-ability students in the experimental group versus high-ability students in the control group. One could do *t* tests for all these comparisons. However, not only is this procedure tedious, but as the number of comparisons increases so does the likelihood of false conclusions. (It can be shown mathematically that,

| TABLE 6.5 | Posttest Scores for Students Classified by Reading Ability and Experimental-Group or Control-Group Assignment in Hypothetical Experiment on Inserted Questions in Text |

EXPERIMENTAL GROUP		CONTROL GROUP	
High Reading Ability	Low Reading Ability	High Reading Ability	Low Reading Ability
23	18	19	3
14	17	12	7
16	9	16	1
18	10	14	6
16	17	7	4
17	19	8	7
19	8	13	6
20	20	10	5
17	15	19	3
17	16	9	2
$M = 17.70$	$M = 14.90$	$M = 12.70$	$M = 4.40$
$SD = 2.50$	$SD = 4.33$	$SD = 4.32$	$SD = 2.12$

	SUBGROUP STATISTICS		
Subgroup	N	M	SD
Experimental Group	20	16.30	3.73
Control Group	20	8.55	5.39
High Reading Ability Group	20	15.20	4.29
Low Reading Ability Group	20	9.65	6.33

as the frequency of inferential statistics calculated for a set of data increases, so does the likelihood of falsely rejecting the null hypothesis.) Analysis of variance is a more elegant and accurate method of making all the comparisons at once to determine which ones are likely to be chance differences.

Table 6.6 shows a summary of the F values generated by the analysis of variance of the data presented in Table 6.5, and whether each F value is statistically significant ($p = .05$ or less). The first line of results shows the F value (49.88) for the comparison of all experimental-group students ($M = 16.30$) and all control-group students ($M = 8.55$) on the posttest, ignoring whether the students have high or low reading ability. This F value is statistically significant ($p < .001$), meaning that the difference is generalizable. The second line shows the F value (25.58) for the comparison of all high-reading-ability students ($M = 15.20$) and

TABLE 6.6	Summary of Analysis of Variance for Posttest Scores in Hypothetical Experiment on Inserted Questions in Text

SOURCE	F	p
Treatment (T)	49.88	< .001
Reading Ability (R)	25.58	< .001
T × R Reaction	6.28	< .05

all low-reading-ability students ($M = 9.65$) on the posttest. This F value, too, is statistically significant ($p < .001$).

Interaction Effects.   The next line of Table 6.6 shows an F value of 6.28 ($p < .05$) for the interaction effect. In educational practice, an **interaction effect** is implied when we claim that different instructional methods are effective for different types of students. In statistics, an interaction effect is said to have occurred when the difference between two groups on variable B varies according to the value of variable A. To understand what this means, consider the research results shown in Table 6.5. For students with low reading ability (one level of variable B), the difference in the posttest mean scores of the experimental and control groups (variable A) is substantial ($14.90 - 4.40 = 10.50$ points). For students with high reading ability (the other level of treatment variable B), the difference in the posttest mean scores of the experimental and control students (variable A) is much smaller ($17.70 - 12.70 = 5.00$ points). Thus, it appears that the experimental text passage helped poor readers much more than it helped good readers. The inclusion of both variables in the experimental design yielded a better understanding of the experimental treatment's effectiveness than if the design had only compared an experimental group and a control group.

The experiment described above is fairly simple. There are two levels of each variable (sometimes called a **factor**). The first factor is the type of reading passage, and it has two levels: inserted questions versus no inserted questions. The other factor is reading ability, and it also has two levels: high versus low. Some experiments reported in the research literature have more complex designs, for example, three factors with three or more levels of one or more of the factors. Analysis of variance is capable of testing the statistical significance of group differences on each factor and also the statistical significance of the various interaction effects.

Analysis of variance is widely used in educational research because of its versatility. However, it can produce inaccurate results if the distribution of scores for any of the measures deviates substantially from the normal curve. Another condition that can produce inaccurate results is large differences in the size of the groups being compared.

Analysis of Covariance

We have ignored up to this point the pretest results for our hypothetical experiment. (The pretest was administered in order to determine how much students knew about the text passage content prior to the experiment.) The pretest mean scores for each group are shown in Table 6.7. These results complicate our interpretation of the posttest results, because they show that the experimental group had higher scores on the pretest than did the control group. The experimental group's superior knowledge of the text passage content beforehand, rather than the inserted questions in the text passage, might be responsible for its higher score on the posttest.

We could eliminate superior preknowledge as an explanation for the results by doing another experiment in which the students selected for the experimental and control groups were equivalent on the pretest. This solution, however, is time-consuming and expensive. Another solution is to use gain scores, which are computed by subtracting the pretest score from the posttest score for each student in the experiment. However, as we discussed earlier in the chapter, gain scores have several limitations, and so they are rarely used to analyze experimental data.

The best solution to the problem is to make the groups equivalent on the pretest by applying a statistical technique known as **analysis of covariance.** In this method, each student's posttest score is adjusted up or down to take into account his or her pretest performance. Statistical tables in research reports sometimes show both the actual posttest means and the adjusted posttest means after analysis of covariance has been applied. There is no need to do an analysis of variance if an analysis of covariance has been conducted. Analysis of covariance yields F values similar in meaning to those described above.

The procedure used in analysis of covariance is somewhat similar to the handicapping procedure used in sports such as golf. Poor golf players can compete with good golf players by being assigned a handicap based on their past performance. Each golf player's score in a tournament is determined by how much better or worse she does than her handicap (that is, her previous performance).

Analysis of covariance requires certain conditions and mathematical assumptions to yield valid results. If the research data do not satisfy these

TABLE 6.7	Pretest Means for Students in Hypothetical Experiment on Inserted Questions in Text	
	EXPERIMENTAL GROUP *M*	CONTROL GROUP *M*
High Ability Readers	10.10	7.70
Low Ability Readers	4.30	2.90

assumptions, the results of the analysis of covariance are likely to be invalid. In reading a research report, you should look for a statement by the researchers that they checked at least the key assumptions before using this statistical method. If there is no such statement, you should view the F values and p values associated with them with caution.

We explained analysis of covariance and analysis of variance by referring to hypothetical experiments. The same techniques can be used to test the statistical significance of results yielded by research designs that do not involve experimentation. These designs are explained in Chapter 7.

The Chi-Square Test

The t test, analysis of variance, and analysis of covariance are appropriate inferential statistics for data that are in continuous or rank score form. They are not appropriate for categorical data. The **chi-square test** is the appropriate test of statistical significance in this case.

To illustrate the use of this test, suppose that we want to determine whether urban school districts are more likely to employ female school superintendents than are rural school districts. A random sample of 100 urban school districts and 100 rural school districts is drawn from a population of school districts. The gender of each district's superintendent is determined.

The two variables involved in this study are gender (male versus female) and type of school district (urban versus rural). Both variables are categorical because they cannot be ordered on a continuum. For example, a rural district is neither "more" nor "less" than an urban district.

Table 6.8 shows hypothetical data relating to our research question. The descriptive statistics are in the form of frequencies, each frequency being the number of superintendents in each gender category for a particular type of district. Table 6.7 shows that the distributions of male and female superintendents vary across districts. We need to determine whether these differences occurred by chance or are characteristic of other districts similar to those used in the study.

The chi-square test is used to make this determination. It yields an inferential statistic known as *chi*, which is squared and represented by the symbol χ^2. The χ^2 value for the distributions shown in Table 6.8 is 7.42. This value is associated with a p value that is less than .01. Therefore, we reject the null hypothe-

TABLE 6.8	Distribution of Male and Female Superintendents in Urban and Rural School Districts

	URBAN	RURAL
Males	65	82
Females	35	18

sis that these results occurred by chance. Instead, we conclude that they can be generalized to the population of districts having similar characteristics to those in the study.

Parametric versus Nonparametric Tests

All the tests of statistical significance described above, with the exception of the chi-square test, are **parametric tests of significance.** These tests make several assumptions about the measures being used and the populations that are represented by the research samples. These assumptions are that there are equal intervals between the scores on the measures, that the scores are normally distributed about the mean score, and that the scores of the different comparison groups have equal variances.

Suppose the assumptions underlying parametric tests, especially the assumption of equal intervals, cannot be satisfied. In this case, researchers might use a parametric test anyway if the assumptions are not violated seriously. They could instead use a **nonparametric test of significance.** The chi-square test is the most commonly used nonparametric test, because many variables are in the form of categories, which do not form an interval scale. An **interval scale** is a measure that lacks a true zero point, and for which the distance between any two adjacent points is the same.

Other nonparametric tests sometimes found in the research literature are the Mann-Whitney U test and the Wilcoxon signed-rank test. These are nonparametric counterparts of the t test. Another nonparametric test is the **Kruskal-Wallis test,** which is the nonparametric counterpart of analysis of variance.

PRACTICAL SIGNIFICANCE AND EFFECT SIZE

As previously noted, statistical significance should not be confused with practical significance. If a result is statistically significant, it means only that the result probably did not occur by chance, and so one can generalize from the sample to the population that it represents. Even a trivial result can be statistically significant if the sample is sufficiently large, because the calculation of inferential statistics is affected by sample size. The larger the sample, the smaller the observed result required for statistical significance.

The practical significance of statistical results is a matter of judgment. For example, an experimental treatment might have only a small effect on learning relative to conventional instruction, but the type of learning might be so important that even small increments of learning are worthwhile.

Researchers have developed a statistical approach to determining practical significance. This approach involves the calculation of a statistic known as **effect size.** It is discussed in Chapter 4, which concerns procedures for synthesizing research findings. For present purposes, we will note only that the effect size statistic is most commonly used as an aid in determining the practical significance of the results yielded by experiments. It provides a numerical expression of how well the experimental group learned or otherwise performed relative to the control group. Effect sizes of 0.33 or larger generally are considered to have practical significance.

Although the effect size statistic provides useful information, it should not be the sole basis for making judgments about the practical significance of statistical results. You should examine the total context of the research study, especially the measures that were used and the scores they generated, in judging whether an observed result is sufficiently large to have implications for practice.

PROCEDURES IN STATISTICAL ANALYSIS

Some descriptive and inferential analyses can be done by hand, especially if the data set is small. Certain handheld calculators also can do these analyses. All you need to do is enter the data and then press the appropriate function key.

More complicated statistical analyses require software that is run on a personal or mainframe computer. The most commonly used software in educational research is the Statistical Package for the Social Sciences, the acronym for which is SPSS. (Information about SPSS is available at www.spss.com.) SPSS enables you to do any of the statistical analyses described in this book.

Because of its widespread use, you should be able to find someone in the research community who can help you learn how to use SPSS if needed. Another option is the Statistical Analysis System, the acronym for which is SAS (www.sas.com). SAS is more difficult to use than SPSS, but has more capabilities.

Errors can easily occur while conducting a statistical analysis. Therefore, you should run checks on your data entry and software operations. One helpful check is to do a few statistical analyses by hand and compare the results with those generated by your statistical software.

EXAMPLE OF OUTLINING A RESEARCH PROPOSAL

This feature of the chapter gives you an example of how to outline a research proposal using the form in Appendix 1. The example, involving a proposal to study curriculum alignment, is introduced in Chapter 2.

The first research question stated in the Example section of Chapter 2 is, "What percentage of high schools in Oregon have engaged in curriculum alignment?" We might restate this question by asking, "Is there a difference between large and small school districts in the percentage of high schools that have engaged in curriculum alignment?" For present purposes, we will suppose that we can form a random sample of thirty large and thirty small school districts, with one high school randomly selected from each district. We will further suppose that engagement in curriculum alignment is measured as a dichotomous variable: A district either has, or has not, engaged in curriculum alignment.

Given these suppositions, we show below how we filled out the part of the proposal outline pertaining to data-analysis procedures.

8. DATA ANALYSIS PROCEDURES
    A. The percentage of high schools in each type of district that has engaged (or not engaged) in curriculum alignment will be presented in a table. A table with made-up data is shown below.

CURRICULUM ALIGNMENT	FREQUENCY OF LARGE DISTRICTS	FREQUENCY OF SMALL DISTRICTS
Engaged	21	13
Not Engaged	9	17

The differences in these frequencies will be tested for statistical significance to determine whether the null hypothesis of no difference in frequencies between large and small districts can be rejected. Because the data are in the form of frequencies, the chi-square test is appropriate.

SELF-CHECK TEST

1. Statistics
    a. are never used in qualitative research.
    b. are frequently used in quantitative research.
    c. are only used to analyze achievement test data.
    d. cannot be used to analyze interview and video data.

2. Percentile scores
    a. are a type of derived score.
    b. are a type of raw score.
    c. yield the same information as grade equivalents.
    d. are used in educational practice, but not in educational research.

3. Ceiling effects are most likely to be found when
    a. the median is used as an indicator of average performance on a test.
    b. a large percentage of the sample scores low on a test.
    c. the distribution of scores deviates from the normal curve.
    d. raw scores are converted to gain scores.

4. If a distribution of test scores deviates substantially from the normal curve, the average score is best represented by the
    a. mean.
    b. median.
    c. mode.
    d. average variation.

5. A student who scores two standard deviation units above the mean on a test would be approximately
   a. between the 50th and 60th percentiles of the score distribution.
   b. between the 61st and 75th percentiles of the score distribution.
   c. between the 76th and 90th percentiles of the score distribution.
   d. above the 90th percentile of the score distribution.

6. If researchers wish to know how well the combination of students' high school GPA and college aptitude test scores predicts their college GPA, they most likely would use
   a. analysis of variance.
   b. analysis of covariance.
   c. multivariate correlational statistics.
   d. bivariate correlational statistics.

7. The purpose of inferential statistics is to determine whether
   a. a set of scores forms a normal distribution.
   b. the sample size is sufficiently large to detect real differences between the experimental and control group.
   c. an observed result is a chance finding.
   d. the results of one study constitute a non-chance replication of the results of another study.

8. The likelihood that the null hypothesis is false is greatest when the p value is
   a. .001.
   b. .01.
   c. .10.
   d. 1.00.

9. If the pretest scores of two groups in an experiment differ, researchers usually can compensate for this problem by
   a. using analysis of covariance.
   b. using analysis of variance.
   c. converting the pretest and posttest scores to gain scores.
   d. using a nonparametric test of statistical significance.

10. Nonparametric tests of statistical significance
    a. assume that the scores to be analyzed form an interval scale.
    b. do not assume that the scores to be analyzed form an interval scale.
    c. must be used even if the scores constitute a minor violation of the assumptions underlying analysis of variance.
    d. can be used only with continuous scores.

11. Decisions about the practical significance of research findings are aided by the calculation of a(n)
    a. p value.
    b. F value.
    c. standard deviation.
    d. effect size statistic.

RESOURCES FOR FURTHER STUDY

Bruning, J. L., & Kintz, B. L. (1997). *Computational handbook of statistics* (4th ed.). White Plains, NY: Longman.

> *This book shows how to compute commonly used statistics. For each statistic, the authors explain its purpose, provide an actual set of data, and then show, step by step, how the data are manipulated to yield the desired statistic. The book can be used as a computational guide or as a resource for understanding a particular statistical technique.*

Jaeger, R. M., & Bond, L. (1996). Quantitative research methods and design. In D. C. Berliner & R. C. Calfee (Eds.), *Handbook of educational psychology* (pp. 877–898). New York: Macmillan.

> *The authors provide an overview of appropriate statistical techniques for commonly used designs in quantitative research.*

Morgan, G. A., Griego, O. V., & Gloeckner, G. W. (2001). *SPSS for Windows: An introduction to use and interpretation in research*. Mahwah, NJ: Lawrence Erlbaum Associates.

> *This book explains how to use one statistical software package, SPSS, for one operating system, Windows. Other books, similar in design, are available for other statistical software packages and other operating systems.*

Vogt, W. P. (1998). *Dictionary of statistics and methodology: A nontechnical guide for the social sciences* (2nd ed.). Thousand Oaks, CA: Sage.

> *This dictionary provides definitions of approximately 2,000 terms. Its comprehensive nature means that you are likely to find a definition of any statistical or methodological term that you encounter in reading research reports.*

chapter 7

Descriptive and Causal-Comparative Research

Sue Griffin is a middle school teacher whose daughter Bethany started high school two months ago. Bethany has always loved school, and done well. But now she's staying up late, and Sue has to coax, threaten, and shake her to get her out of bed each morning. Bethany's first-period teacher noted on her midterm report card, "Sleeping in class."

Then Sue read a newspaper article titled, "Your teenager might not be lazy, just sleepy." It described the research of several professors showing that most adolescents need more sleep than adults, but do not become sleepy until later at night. It quoted a principal who noted positive effects on students' energy and learning after his school district shifted its start time two hours later for its middle schools and high schools.

Sue suggested that Bethany adjust her class schedule to keep first period free so that she can sleep longer in the morning. Next she plans to do a literature search on the professors who were mentioned in the article. Sue thinks, "I'll look for other ideas to help my own kids. And if what I learn convinces me that a later start time really works, I may ask my principal to consider it for our middle school."

In this chapter you will learn how educational researchers conduct descriptive studies to help educators like Sue understand more about the behavior and needs of the groups involved in education, including students, teachers, administrators, and policy makers. You also will learn about causal-comparative research, in which researchers explore possible cause-and-effect relationships among variables (like the relationship between the amount of sleep that teenagers get and their school achievement) that are difficult to manipulate experimentally. ●

OBJECTIVES

After studying this chapter, you will be able to

1. distinguish between descriptive, relationship, and experimental research.

2. describe the purpose and data collection methods of survey research.

3. state an advantage of direct observation as a method of gathering descriptive information.

4. describe procedures that can be used to increase the validity and reliability of research findings based on direct observation.

5. explain the purpose and methods of longitudinal research.

6. name and give an example of each of the two types of descriptive statistics that are used to analyze research data.

7. explain why causal-comparative research sometimes is used instead of experimental research to examine possible cause-and-effect relationships between two variables.

8. explain why the selection of comparable groups is important in causal-comparative research.

9. name and give an example of each of the two types of inferential statistics that are used to analyze causal-comparative or experimental research data.

O B J E C T I V E S   *continued*

10. describe three possible interpretations that can be made when causal-comparative research finds a significant relationship between two variables.

11. describe two conditions under which inferences about cause-and-effect relationships from causal-comparative research are nearly as sound as those from experimental research.

12. describe the similarities and differences between causal-comparative and correlational research.

K E Y   T E R M S

causal-comparative research
cause-and-effect relationship
central tendency
comparison group
correlational research
cross-sectional research
dependent variable
descriptive research

direct observation
experimental research
independent variable
inferential statistics
inter-observer agreement
interview
longitudinal research
nonparametric statistics
observer bias

panel study
paper-and-pencil test
parametric statistics
questionnaire
relationship research
sampling bias
self-report
survey research
variability

THE NATURE OF DESCRIPTIVE, RELATIONSHIP, AND EXPERIMENTAL RESEARCH

Most quantitative research studies can be placed in one of three broad categories: descriptive, relationship, and experimental research. **Descriptive research** aims to provide a clear, accurate description of individuals, events, or processes. For example, descriptive research might identify how reading teachers plan their lessons and how much time they spend in planning.

Relationship research includes both causal-comparative research, which is described in this chapter, and correlational research, the subject of Chapter 8. **Relationship research** is more complex than descriptive research because it explores observed relationships among variables that have not been manipulated by the researchers. An example would be a study to determine whether parents' occupations (variable 1) are related to students' choice of electives in school (variable 2).

Experimental research is the most complex type of research, because the researchers manipulate one or more variables and measure the effect on another variable or set of variables. For example, an experiment might involve training one group of teachers (the experimental group), but not training another group of teachers (the control group), in effective lesson planning techniques (the independent variable). Then the effects of lesson planning on students' reading comprehension skills (the dependent variable) might be measured.

DESCRIPTIVE RESEARCH

Descriptive research involves the collection and analysis of quantitative data in order to develop a precise description of a sample's behavior or personal characteristics. (Qualitative descriptive research is discussed in Chapter 10.) Researchers can describe a sample at one point in time only, or they can use longitudinal or cross-sectional research designs to describe a sample over time. Below we explain the various methods used in descriptive research.

Survey Research

Survey research is a form of descriptive research that involves collecting information about research participants' beliefs, attitudes, interests, or behavior through **questionnaires, interviews,** or **paper-and-pencil tests.** Opinion polls are a well-known example of survey research. Surveys can be used to explore many topics of interest to educators, for example: the extent to which cooperative learning occurs in elementary school classrooms, school district policies for serving students for whom English is a second language, and parents' preferences for various alternatives for schooling their children.

Descriptive studies that deal with highly sensitive topics, such as students' attitudes about sexuality, or that attempt to elicit deeper responses than can be elicited by questionnaires, frequently employ interviews. Some surveys use both questionnaires and interviews, the former to collect basic descriptive information from a large sample and the latter to follow up the questionnaire responses in depth with a smaller sample.

Because survey research is based on **self-report,** respondents can conceal information that they do not want others to know. Also, even if respondents want to give accurate information, they may not have the self-awareness to do so. For these reasons, the data obtained through survey research are likely to be distorted or incomplete to an unknown degree.

If researchers establish good rapport with the research participants and demonstrate that they are using some system to ensure the confidentiality of responses, self-report data will produce more accurate results. In addition, researchers can use the strategies described in Chapter 5 to design questionnaires, interviews, or tests so as to minimize leading questions or questions that give respondents clues as to what answers are socially desirable.

The procedure that is used to select the research sample is very important in survey research. For example, if survey researchers drew their sample from the telephone directory to predict the outcomes of a bond election, the resulting sample would be biased, because many individuals have unlisted telephone numbers or do not have telephones. **Sampling bias** also occurs when the response rate is low, because nonrespondents tend to differ from respondents, as explained in Chapter 5.

In some descriptive studies, tests of ability or achievement are administered to the research participants. The test scores provide a picture of individuals' ability to perform particular intellectual tasks. However, intellectual performance is dependent to some extent on motivation. For example, if students do not have a good reason to perform at their best level, they may not take the test seriously.

Some descriptive studies involve the administration of measures of personality and other personal characteristics. Most of these measures involve self-report and thus, like questionnaires or interviews, they may provide biased responses. Therefore, in reading descriptive research studies, you must consider the question of whether any conclusions about individuals based on self-report data are likely to be accurate.

Direct Observation

You were introduced to direct observation as a measurement procedure in Chapter 5. **Direct observation** involves gathering "live" data about individuals' behavior as the behavior occurs. Observations are more objective than surveys because they do not depend on research participants' self-report. For example, we probably could learn much more about students' racial attitudes by observing students of different ethnic groups during actual interactions with one another than by analyzing their answers to questions on a paper-and-pencil test about how they would behave in various situations involving interracial interactions.

Direct observation is especially effective when researchers want to study specific aspects of human behavior in detail. For example, the following questions are well suited for study by observation: How do school psychologists interact with parents when reporting their children's test results? How do preschool children behave after watching a television program that contains a large number of violent acts? How do parents interact with their children when discussing homework assignments?

In reviewing studies that employ direct observation, you should pay particular attention to the procedures used by the researchers to avoid the potential for **observer bias.** For example, suppose that observers record the social behavior of kindergarten children during free play. They might perceive more social behavior in those children who the observers know have higher verbal aptitude. The best approach to reduce observer bias is to design the observational procedures so that observers do not have prior knowledge of the research participants' backgrounds or characteristics.

To increase the validity of observational research data, researchers should use narrow, specific definitions of the behavior to be observed rather than broad, general definitions; measure low-inference variables (e.g., counting the number of times that specific actions occur during a game instead of rating each individual's sports performance from poor to excellent); and require observers to record only as many aspects of behavior as they can effectively attend to.

To collect reliable observational data, it is desirable to train observers carefully. Most good reports of observational research describe the procedures that were used to train the observers. They also include information on **interobserver agreement,** that is, the extent to which the observations of two or more observers agree when the observers have independently observed the same events.

Description of a Sample over Time

Most descriptive research involves reporting the characteristics of a sample at one point in time. In some descriptive studies, however, researchers want to examine patterns of stability or change in individuals from one point in time to another. This type of study is called **longitudinal research.** It helps us understand changes within individuals due to maturation or significant life experiences, or changes common to many individuals from one time period to another.

Panel Studies.   Longitudinal studies vary in their sampling strategies. One strategy is to select a sample and follow it over time. Because a **panel study** involves surveying the same sample at each data collection point, the researchers can explore changes in specific individuals and the possible reasons for such changes.

C. C. Carson, R. M. Huelskamp, and T. D. Woodall (1993) studied a cohort of high school students who were projected to complete their senior year in 1982. The researchers contacted the individuals in the sample in 1982 and again in 1984 and 1986, in order to determine how many had completed high school by then. At the first data-collection point (1982), only 82.7 percent of the students had completed high school, which represents a dropout rate of 17.3 percent. However, by 1984, 5.2 percent more of the students had completed high school, either by returning to high school or by earning a General Equivalency Degree (GED). By 1986, another 2.8 percent of the students had completed high school. On this expanded time frame, a total of 90.7 percent of the students had completed high school. The 9.3 percent dropout rate found in this cohort study is substantially lower than the rate reported in nonlongitudinal studies (typically, 25 to 30 percent).

Cross-Sectional Studies.   Another common sampling strategy in longitudinal research is to select samples that represent different stages of development and study all samples at the same point in time. Longitudinal studies of this type are called **cross-sectional research.**

Let's say that researchers want to examine changes in female students' attitudes toward mathematics as they mature. It would take a long time to follow a group of first-grade girls through twelve years of education and measure their attitudes every few years. Instead they could select samples of girls in, for example, the first, fourth, eighth, and twelfth grades, and, on a given date, measure each sample's attitudes toward mathematics. Differences between mean attitude scores at different grade levels could be interpreted as reflecting developmental changes in female students' attitudes toward mathematics. However, in order to reach this conclusion it is important to ensure that the samples do not differ on some other key characteristic besides grade level. For example, if instructional practices changed over time, the samples also would differ in the nature of their mathematics instruction. Perhaps the twelfth graders received no instruction in estimation during elementary school, for example, whereas the current sample of fourth graders may have been taught estimation as part of their instruction in mathematics.

Data Analysis in Descriptive Research

The procedures used to analyze descriptive research data are fairly simple to understand. Table 7.1 summarizes common statistics that are often presented in descriptive research reports. You will note that all of the statistics are measures of **central tendency** or measures of **variability.**

Several of these descriptive statistics were used in the study reprinted at the end of this chapter. The two researchers, David Conley and Paul Goldman, sent a 99-item questionnaire to over 2,000 educators in twenty Oregon school districts, to assess their reactions to state legislation mandating new high school graduation requirements and other reforms.

TABLE 7.1   Statistical Techniques Used to Analyze
Descriptive Research Data

PROCEDURE	PURPOSE
Measures of Central Tendency	**Provide a quantitative measure of the most representative or typical score in a score distribution**
Mean (M)	Equals the sum of the scores divided by the number of scores (N). Reported in almost all descriptive research studies.
Median (Med)	The middle score in the score distribution. Used when extreme scores would distort the mean.
Mode	The most frequently obtained score in the score distribution. A crude measure of central tendency that is seldom used in research.
Measures of Variability	**Provide a quantitative measure of the distribution of individual scores around the mean**
Range	The difference between the lowest and highest scores in the distribution, plus 1.
Standard deviation (SD)	Based on the deviations of individual scores from the mean. Most widely used measure of group variability.
Variance	The square of the standard deviation.

Table 7.2 shows several of the descriptive statistics that are reported in the article. The main columns of the table show the sample's responses to four scales: (1) change orientation (the belief that the schools need to change and that the legislation will foster that change), (2) resistance to change (skepticism about and opposition to the mandated changes), (3) learning outcomes (belief that specific features of the legislation will lead to increased student learning), and (4) changes in practices (belief that the legislation will lead to specific changes in educators' practices in the schools).

Each scale is composed of 5 to 16 items in the questionnaire. For example, the Change Orientation scale consists of five items. The researchers summed the number of items to which each respondent expressed agreement, and divided the sum by the total number of items (in this case, five) to yield a percentage score for each respondent. Thus if a respondent agreed with three of the five items concerning change orientation, that respondent's percentage score would be 60 percent. The percentage scores for all 2,257 educators in the sample then were summed and divided by 2,257 to yield the mean percentage score.

Looking at Table 7.2, we find that, on average, the educators' mean percentage of agreement with the items in the Change Orientation scale was 41.0 percent, and the mean percentage of agreement with the items in the Resistance to Change scale was 34.7 percent. We find, too, that, on average, the educators showed greater agreement with the items in the Learning Outcomes scale (63.9 percent) and the Changes in Practices scale (60.7 percent).

The researchers reported another descriptive statistic, the standard deviation, for most of the mean scores presented in their article. The standard deviation is a measure of how much the individuals in a sample vary in their scores. Looking at Table 7.2, we find that the standard deviation for the educators' percentage-of-agreement scores on the Change Orientation scale is 30.3. This is a rather large standard deviation. It indicates that many of the educators in the sample had a much higher percentage of agreement, or a much lower percentage of agreement, with the items on the Change Orientation scale than the mean percentage of 41 percent.

TABLE 7.2 Scale Means for Educators' Reactions to State Restructuring Legislation

	CHANGE ORIENTATION	RESISTANCE TO CHANGE	LEARNING OUTCOMES	CHANGES IN PRACTICES	N
Sample					2,257
Mean	41.0	34.7	63.9	60.7	
SD	30.3	22.7	23.2	32.2	

Source. Taken from Table 3 on p. 525 in Conley, D. T., & Goldman, P. (1995). Reactions from the field to state restructuring legislation. *Educational Administration Quarterly, 31,* 512–538. Copyright © 1995 by Sage Publications, Inc. Reprinted by permission of Sage Publications, Inc.

The descriptive statistics in Table 7.2 might strike you as abstract and "cold." However, keep in mind that these statistics summarize an enormous amount of data, namely, over two thousand educators' responses on four different scales. It would be very difficult to make sense of these data by considering them for one educator at a time. By examining the means and standard deviations that the researchers used to condense the data, we quickly can see the main patterns in these educators' attitudes toward state legislative methods for school reform.

CAUSAL-COMPARATIVE RESEARCH

In many research projects, investigators want to examine the possible effects of variables that are difficult or impossible to manipulate experimentally. A study by Gary Green and Sue Jaquess (1987) illustrates this point. These researchers were interested in the effect of high school students' part-time employment on their academic achievement. The sample included 477 high school juniors, some of whom were unemployed and some of whom were employed at least ten hours a week. It would not be feasible to manipulate student employment experimentally, requiring some students to work part time and others not to work at all. Instead, through careful sampling, the researchers were able to select two comparable groups of students and then assess the effects of natural variations in their employment.

Independent and Dependent Variables

In **causal-comparative research,** a variable that is hypothesized to cause an observed difference is called an **independent variable.** The variable in which the difference is observed is called the **dependent variable.** In the study described above, employment is the independent variable because it is hypothesized to affect students' academic achievement, which is the dependent variable.

In reviewing causal-comparative studies, you should examine whether there is any evidence that the two groups are similar except for the independent variable on which they are being compared. If two groups are formed because they differ on independent variable X, but they also happen to differ on variable Y, the researchers will not know whether group differences on the dependent variable are caused by variables X or Y. In the study by Green and Jaquess, the employed students were found to have lower scores on a measure of scholastic aptitude. Thus, we do not know whether their lower academic achievement (the dependent variable) is the result of their employment (independent variable X) or their lower academic aptitude (independent variable Y). To rule out independent variable Y, the researchers would have to select groups of employed and nonemployed students with similar aptitude. Another possibility is to use a statistical technique that can determine the relative effects of independent variable X and independent variable Y on the dependent variable. (Analysis of covariance or multiple regression typically is used for this purpose.)

Examples of other situations amenable to causal-comparative research include comparisons of the academic motivation of adolescent boys and girls, the test performance of students with adequate nutrition and students with inadequate nutrition, and the duties and work satisfaction of special educators who work in large school districts and those who work in small school districts.

In these examples, each of the causal-comparative research designs permits study of the effects of variables that are difficult to manipulate experimentally with human research participants. Even if it were possible to manipulate such variables, it might be unethical to do so. For example, researchers could not ethically withhold adequate nutrition from one group of research participants in order to study the effect of nutrition on academic performance.

Forming Comparison Groups

Sometimes the independent variable used to form **comparison groups** is in the form of discrete categories. Gender is an example of such a variable; an individual is either male or female. In the world of work, job classifications are typically discrete. For example, an individual might be classified as a custodian, teacher, secretary, or counselor.

In other situations, the independent variable forms a continuum, and researchers select comparison groups depending on which parts of the continuum they wish to study. For example, suppose that some researchers are interested in whether there is a relationship between students' nutrition (the hypothesized independent variable) and school performance (the hypothesized dependent variable). The researchers might obtain a measure of the nutritional adequacy of the diets of all the students in a school. The scores probably would range along a continuum of high to low. The researchers might choose to compare students at the extremes of the continuum, that is, students with very good nutrition and students with very poor nutrition. Alternatively, they could form multiple comparison groups that sample the entire continuum, for example, students with excellent nutrition, students with adequate nutrition, and students with poor nutrition.

Data Analysis in Causal-Comparative Research

In causal-comparative research, the typical first step in data analysis is to compute the mean score of each group on the dependent variable. Next, **inferential statistics** are used to determine whether differences between the mean scores are statistically significant. (Inferential statistics are explained in Chapter 6.)

Table 7.3 summarizes the inferential statistics that are most widely used in causal-comparative research. The same statistics also can be used to analyze data from experimental research, which is discussed in Chapter 9. Table 7.3 shows both **parametric** and **nonparametric statistics** for analyzing the data from causal-comparative or experimental research. As we stated in Chapter 6, nonparametric statistics are appropriate when the sets of data to be compared do not meet three assumptions: equal intervals between scores, normal distribution of

| TABLE 7.3 | Statistical Techniques Used to Analyze Causal-Comparative and Experimental Research Data |

TEST OF STATISTICAL SIGNIFICANCE	PURPOSE
Parametric	
t test	Used primarily to determine whether two means differ significantly from each other; also used to determine whether a single mean differs significantly from a specified population value.
Analysis of variance	Used to determine whether mean scores on one or more variables differ significantly from each other and whether the variables interact significantly with each other.
Analysis of covariance	Similar to analysis of variance but permits adjustments to the posttreatment mean scores of different groups on the dependent variable to compensate for initial group differences on variables related to the dependent variable.
Nonparametric	
Mann-Whitney *U* test	Used to determine whether two uncorrelated means differ significantly from each other.
Wilcoxon signed-rank test	Used to determine whether two correlated means differ significantly from each other.
Kruskal-Wallis test	Used to determine whether the mean scores of three or more groups on a variable differ significantly from one another.
Chi-square test	Used to determine whether two frequency distributions or sets of categorical data differ significantly from each other.

scores about the mean score, and equal variances in the scores of the different comparison groups.

The study of school reform by Conley and Goldman that is reprinted in this chapter made extensive use of inferential statistics. For example, Conley and Goldman used analysis of variance to examine differences between elementary, middle, and high school educators in the responses to the four scales measuring beliefs and attitudes about school reform. Table 7.4 shows the mean score of each of these groups on each of the four scales. (You will note that the middle school group also included some junior high school educators, who serve a similar age range of students.) In general, high school educators express more positive attitudes and beliefs about state-legislated school reforms in Oregon than do elementary- or middle-school educators.

The *F* value below each column of mean scores in Table 7.4 indicates the results of an analysis of variance. The purpose of this statistical analysis is to determine whether the mean scores of the groups on a particular variable are significantly different from each other. Two asterisks after an *F* value denote

TABLE 7.4	Scale Means by School Level for Educators' Reactions to State Restructuring Legislation				
	CHANGE ORIENTATION	**RESISTANCE TO CHANGE**	**LEARNING OUTCOMES**	**CHANGES IN PRACTICES**	**N**
High school	45.0	32.1	64.3	64.8	802
Junior high and middle	38.7	35.1	63.3	54.0	596
Elementary	39.1	38.5	63.1	61.0	768
F	9.2**	10.3**	0.3	16.1**	

*$p < .05$; **$p < .01$.

Source. Taken from Table 3 on p. 525 in Conley, D. T., & Goldman, P. (1995). Reactions from the field to state restructuring legislation. *Educational Administration Quarterly, 31,* 512–538. Copyright © 1995 by Sage Publications, Inc. Reprinted by permission of Sage Publications, Inc.

statistical significance at the .01 level. If an observed difference is statistically significant, that means that it probably did not occur by chance. (Statistical significance is explained in more detail in Chapter 6.)

When three or more mean scores are being compared, the finding of a significant F value can be followed by a statistical test to determine which pairs of means differ significantly from each other. Conley and Goldman used one of these tests (Tukey's HSD test) for this purpose. For example, on the Change Orientation scale, they found that the difference between the mean scores of high school educators (45.0) and middle school educators (38.7) was statistically significant. The difference between the mean scores of high school educators and elementary school educators (39.1) also was statistically significant. However, the difference between the mean scores of the middle school educators and the elementary school educators was not statistically significant.

Interpreting Causal-Comparative Research Findings

Causal-comparative research is valuable in identifying possible causes or effects, but it usually cannot provide definitive support for the hypothesis that one of the variables being studied caused the observed differences in the other variable. When we find that different scores on variable A are associated with different scores on variable B, three possible interpretations can be made: that differences in variable A caused the observed differences in variable B; that differences in variable B caused the observed differences in variable A; or that the differences in both variables A and B were caused by differences in a third variable, C.

Under certain conditions, the findings from causal-comparative research can be accepted as supporting a hypothesized cause-and-effect relationship with nearly the same level of confidence as experimental findings. These conditions are:

1. When the variables are time-ordered, meaning that variable A always occurs before variable B. In this sequence of events, variable A could cause variable B, but it is impossible for variable B to have caused variable A. For example, consider studies of the relationship between cigarette smoking and lung cancer. In such studies, the researchers investigate individuals who have a history of smoking behavior (variable A) and whose lung cancer (variable B) occurs subsequently. Therefore, it is possible to rule out the hypothesis that lung cancer caused the smoking. Thus, we can conclude that if a causal relationship exists, it can occur in only one direction.

2. When many causal-comparative studies have been conducted by different researchers working with different samples in different settings, and consistent results emerge from these studies. Again, this is the case with causal-comparative research on smoking and lung cancer. When the combined evidence from these studies is considered, the probability that these results could occur if smoking does not cause lung cancer is so slight that most scientists who have worked in the area have accepted the combined results as compelling evidence of a causal relationship.

Example of Causal-Comparative Interpretation.   The interpretation of causal-comparative findings can be illustrated by examining one finding of the study reprinted in this chapter. As shown in Table 7.4, Conley and Goldman found that educators who work in high schools had a more positive orientation toward school change and expected more positive results from the mandated changes than educators who work in junior high, middle, or elementary schools. These findings contradicted the researchers' predictions, based on earlier research, "that high school educators would be more wary than those in elementary schools" (Conley & Goldman, 1995, p. 523 in the original article). Their data led them to conclude that there is apparent support for large-scale change in high schools.

What are the possible causal implications of high school educators' greater apparent willingness to undertake the changes required by these legislated reforms? One might reason that it is in high school that the current system of education breaks down most severely for many students. If so, the high school educators in this research sample might have had more direct experience with the problems of the current system, and hence could be expected to have greater openness to proposed changes. The presumed cause-and-effect relationship, then, is that level of schooling (variable A) directly affects attitudes toward proposed school reform (variable B). However, if this hypothesis is true for this sample, the results might not generalize to school districts in which only a small proportion of high school students were dropping out or experiencing other learning problems or personal difficulties.

A second possibility is that variable B (attitudes toward proposed school reform) causes variable A (level of schooling). Because of the time-ordered nature of variables A and B (that is, specific proposals for school reform came after the educators who were surveyed had been hired into their current positions), this presumed cause-and-effect relationship is not realistic.

Another possibility is that educators who generally are more flexible and open to change are attracted to work at the high school level. In this case, variable *C* (flexibility and openness to change) can be hypothesized to cause both variable *A* (level of schooling) and variable *B* (attitudes toward proposed school reform). If this were true, even educators in high schools in which students were experiencing very few learning problems or personal difficulties would presumably be supportive of the proposed school reforms.

How researchers interpret their findings with respect to the presumed cause-and-effect relationship between variables such as school level and the respondents' survey responses will influence the direction of their future research. Indeed, Conley's comments preceding the reprinted article suggest that he and his colleagues have shifted to qualitative research methods (e.g., focus groups) in order to examine more closely the causal connections between educators' characteristics and their receptivity to school reform.

Differences between Causal-Comparative Research and Correlational Research

Like correlational research, which you will study in Chapter 8, causal-comparative research involves the determination of a relationship between two or more variables. However, causal-comparative research is more often used to examine variables that involve dichotomies (such as male and female) or categories (such as administrators of elementary, middle, and high schools). **Correlational research** is designed to discover the direction and degree of relationship among variables, including those that can be scored on a dimension from high to low (such as most measures of personality traits or aptitude).

In addition, causal-comparative research typically involves examining the relationship between only two variables at a time. By contrast, correlational techniques enable researchers to study and precisely quantify the nature of the relationship between three or more variables at the same time.

EXAMPLE OF OUTLINING A RESEARCH PROPOSAL

This feature of the chapter gives you an example of how to outline a research proposal using the form in Appendix 1. The example, involving a proposal to study curriculum alignment, is introduced in Chapter 2.

In Chapter 6, we took the first research question stated in the Example section of Chapter 2 and restated it as follows: "Is there a difference between large and small school districts in the percentage of high schools that have engaged in curriculum alignment?" Given this research question, we show below how we filled out the part of the proposal outline pertaining to the research design.

4. RESEARCH DESIGN
    A. *Research design.* The research design is causal-comparative. The independent variable is school district size, and the dependent variable is extent of curriculum alignment. Variations in the independent variable (school district size) occur naturally without researcher manipulation, so the research design is not experimental.

    We are studying a potential cause-and-effect relationship, because we hypothesize that the size of a school district (the presumed causal factor) has an influence on how much curriculum alignment has occurred in its schools (the presumed effect). Our rationale for this hypothesis is that larger districts have more resources that they can allocate for the process of curriculum alignment, and therefore are more likely to be further ahead in the process than small districts.

    B. *Threats to internal validity.* We are aware that other independent variables, besides the one we have chosen to study (school size), also might have an effect on the extent of curriculum alignment. For example, it might be that parents of students in large districts are more likely to put pressure on local educators to improve student performance on high-stakes tests. This pressure might compel the educators to make curriculum alignment a high priority.

    If this is true, parental pressure—not internal factors in the school system—would be the key causal factor influencing the extent of curriculum alignment. The study that we are proposing will not measure this variable.

    C. *Threats to external validity.* The accessible population from which the sample will be drawn is school districts in Oregon. High-stakes testing and curriculum alignment are relatively recent movements in education, so different states are likely to have different budgets and strategies for implementing them. Therefore, generalization of findings from the study must be cautious.

    In reporting the study, we will provide a detailed description of Oregon's state-level context for high-stakes testing and curriculum alignment so that educators in other states can compare it with their context. To the extent that the contexts are similar, they might be more confident about generalizing our findings to their state.

SELF-CHECK TEST

1. Researchers plan to study whether students whose teachers ask more higher-cognitive questions are more attentive in class than other students. This study is an example of
    a. relationship research.   c. experimental research.
    b. survey research.   d. descriptive research.

2. Survey data are likely to be distorted primarily because the data
    a. are obtained only from census reports.
    b. are based on self-report.
    c. involve direct observation.
    d. cannot be analyzed by inferential statistics.

3. Direct observation is especially effective for studying
    a. research participants with highly developed verbal skills.
    b. research participants' beliefs and interests.
    c. specific details of human behavior.
    d. variables that form natural categories.

4. The best way to minimize the effects of observer bias in collecting observational data is to
    a. provide broad, general definitions of the behaviors to be observed.
    b. prevent the observers from having contact with one another.
    c. use observers who are well known to the research participants.
    d. ensure that observers have no prior knowledge about the research participants.

5. Researchers send a questionnaire to the parents of all the first graders in one school to measure their interest in participation in school site management activities. Two years later they send the same questionnaire to the same parents. This study is most clearly an example of
    a. observational research.   c. causal-comparative research.
    b. experimental research.   d. longitudinal research.

6. Researchers examine the distribution of scores on a test that was administered to a sample, and they determine the score that was most commonly obtained. This score is an example of a
    a. measure of central tendency.   c. measure of variability.
    b. standard score.   d. percentage.

7. Experimental research is preferable to causal-comparative research primarily when
    a. the researchers have not stated a hypothesis about which of two behaviors is the cause and which is the effect.
    b. the groups to be compared are known to be widely different on a number of variables.
    c. the variables being investigated are easily manipulated.
    d. it would be viewed as unethical to withhold an intervention from one of the comparison groups.

8. In forming comparison groups for causal-comparative research, researchers usually
    a. take steps to ensure that the groups are similar except with respect to the dependent variable.
    b. take steps to ensure that the groups are similar except with respect to the independent variable.

    c. select individuals whose scores on the independent variable are within one standard deviation above or below the mean score.

    d. select individuals whose scores on the dependent variable fall at the extreme of possible scores.

9. A nonparametric test of statistical significance should be used to analyze data from a causal-comparative study whenever
    a. the independent and dependent variables are time-ordered.
    b. the researchers hypothesized in advance that differences in one variable are the probable cause of differences in another variable.
    c. the variances in the scores of the different comparison groups on the dependent variable are grossly unequal.
    d. there are equal intervals between possible scores on the independent variable.

10. A researcher finds that parents who earned good grades in high school more often attend social activities at their sons' and daughters' high school than parents who earned poor grades in high school. What is the least plausible interpretation of this finding?
    a. Parents' scholastic achievement in high school influences them to value their children's school activities.
    b. Participating in their children's school activities causes parents to do better in high school.
    c. Both parents' scholastic achievement and their participation in their children's school activities are caused by a third variable—for example, parents' socioeconomic status.
    d. There is a positive relationship between parents' own scholastic achievement and their participation in their children's high school activities.

11. Accepting causal-comparative research findings as supportive of a hypothesized cause-and-effect relationship is most questionable when
    a. the comparison groups differ on a variable other than the independent variable that could affect the dependent variable.
    b. the researchers did not state their research hypothesis before collecting data.
    c. the independent variable necessarily occurs before the dependent variable in given individuals.
    d. other researchers have investigated the same phenomena and have obtained similar results.

12. Unlike correlational research, causal-comparative research
    a. studies possible cause-and-effect relationships between variables.
    b. is ideal for examining relationships between continuous variables.
    c. enables researchers to study the relationship between three or more variables at the same time.
    d. focuses on independent variables that are formed into meaningful categories.

Chapter References

Carson, C. C., Huelskamp, R. M., & Woodall, T. D. (1993). Perspectives on education in America. *Journal of Educational Research, 86,* 259–311.

Green, G., & Jaquess, S. N. (1987). The effect of part-time employment on academic achievement. *Journal of Educational Research, 80,* 325–329.

Resources for Further Study

Blaikie, N. (2003). *Analyzing quantitative data.* Thousand Oaks, CA: Sage.

The author explains the analysis of data resulting from use of descriptive research designs. Also, the relationship between descriptive analysis and other forms of data analysis is clarified.

Johnson, B. (2001). Toward a new classification of nonexperimental quantitative research. *Educational Researcher, 30*(2), 3–13.

The author clarifies the differences between various quantitative research designs, including descriptive and causal-comparative designs. Each design is analyzed in terms of its purpose (description, prediction, or explanation) and its time perspective (cross-sectional, longitudinal, or retrospective).

Menard, S. (2002). *Longitudinal research* (2nd ed.). Thousand Oaks, CA: Sage.

The author explains the purposes of longitudinal research, the various longitudinal designs that are available to researchers, and methods for analyzing longitudinal data.

In the following section of the chapter you will read a research article that illustrates the use of both the descriptive and causal-comparative research methods. It is preceded by comments written especially for this book by David Conley, the first author of the article. Then the article itself is reprinted in full, just as it appeared when originally published. Where appropriate, we have added footnotes to help you understand the information contained in the article.

Sample Descriptive and Causal-Comparative Research Study
Reactions from the Field to State Restructuring Legislation

Conley, D. T., & Goldman, P. (1995). Reactions from the field to state restructuring legislation. *Educational Administration Quarterly, 31,* 512–538.

● RESEARCHER'S COMMENTS, *Prepared by David Conley*

The following study reports data on the perceptions of Oregon educators in late 1992 concerning school reform legislation passed by the Oregon legislature in 1991. I became interested in this research because of my concurrent work with schools in Oregon that were engaged in educational redesign, and my personal involvement in the formulation and passage of the legislation. I was most interested in how schools would react to the state's call for what amounted to fundamental restructuring.

The legislation, termed the Oregon Educational Act for the 21st Century, or House Bill 3565, has several components that would dramatically affect schools. It mandates Certificates of Mastery, one to be obtained by all students at age 16 and the other at age 18, that are to be based on demonstrated student performance in comparison to state standards. The Certificate of Initial Mastery (CIM) focuses on skills that are cumulative throughout a student's educational career, to be assessed via "benchmarks" at grades 3, 5, and 8. The Certificate of Advanced Mastery (CAM) focuses the last two years of high school around work readiness in the form of six broad "endorsement" areas, or career pathways. Students are expected to have experiences in the world of work before leaving high school.

The law specifies numerous changes to be made in school operations, including an extended school year, a statewide "report card" in which school performance would be reported annually, and site councils at every school. In terms of instruction, it mandates more emphasis on preschool programs to increase readiness, alternative learning centers for students who do not achieve certificates through traditional programs, and the use of different instructional strategies for students not making adequate progress toward benchmark performance levels. This was to be educational reform on a grand scale.

Passed quickly, with little dissent or amendment, the law sprung upon Oregon educators with suddenness and surprise when they returned to their schools in the fall of 1991. I was interested in how they would react to such a comprehensive blueprint for change and challenge to existing practice. I hoped that my research might inform the policy development process and be influential as future modifications to the law were considered.

In response to the proposed legislation, other, more partisan groups were conducting their own surveys. By contrast, my purpose was not to advocate through my research, but to establish some clear reference point for determining how educators perceived the law. With my coauthor, Paul Goldman, I took pains to report simplified versions of our results in formats much more accessible to practitioners and policy makers than research journals. We sent summaries to each school that we surveyed and published articles with graphs and summary tables in an in-state publication, the *Oregon School Study Council Bulletin*.

I consider my research to be in the area of policy analysis. While descriptive research studies fall within this category, policy analysis has, by definition, an interpretive strain that may go beyond what the data at hand support. In this article we tie all conclusions directly to the data that we report, consistent with the descriptive/causal-comparative research method. However, that method leaves out a good deal. As I worked with the legislature, key interest groups, and a range of schools, I developed my own hypotheses that sometimes exceeded our data but were consistent with already available data. We supplemented our survey data with comments and focus groups to provide more texture. But at a certain point, the researcher's ability to synthesize and hypothesize becomes an additional dimension of the study.

Policy analysis requires more than formulating a question, developing a data collection strategy, and reporting the data. There is a crucial "value-added" dimension that derives from the researcher's deep understanding of the phenomenon that she or he is studying. Of course, this understanding must be tempered with an awareness of one's individual biases and assumptions. For this reason I often conduct my research with a colleague, and I depend heavily on outside readers to detect possible biases.

The editors of the journal in which this article appeared pushed us toward a tight quantitative focus. Most of the questions and critiques we received during the revision process had to do with our statistical methods for interpreting the data, not with our conclusions. As a result, the study makes several significant generalizations about the dangers of stereotyping educator reactions to reform based on age, gender, or grade level taught. We also uncovered some important information on differences between school buildings and reaffirmed the importance of individual school sites as the locus of educational reform and restructuring. But we are aware that some important observations may have been lost in the process, and we ourselves question whether our study had any effect on policy making.

Although this article reports one year's data, the study is longitudinal. We have equivalent data for each year through 1995. We found that the same general trends we identified in 1992 continued through 1994, but that educators' support for the proposed reform dropped precipitously in 1995. We have reported the results from each year's surveys in state publications and at national conferences. In addition, I have provided personal briefings to key educators and members of the state education agency.

I have come to several conclusions about the overall effects of this research and our reports about it to the field. In general, I find that few individuals outside the research community seem to be interested in using empirical data to do anything other than justify the point of view they already hold. Little in the way of policy modification was undertaken based on the opinions from the several thousand Oregon educators whose views we recorded and analyzed over four years.

However, interest can arise suddenly and without warning. Recently, some key work groups who are attempting to implement reform have requested reports of the results from our studies. At the same time, concern has been expressed that our reports of a decrease in support for reform while the state legislature is in session could be "dangerous," because such information might jeopardize legislative support for reform.

I should hasten to add that we are continuing this line of research, but have directed it toward a new series of questions that arose from the conclusions presented in this study. I have now focused my investigations on how and why a school site responds to state restructuring legislation. I ask the more fundamental question: Can state legislatures effect fundamental change in schools via legislative programs? I also seek to understand in greater depth how teachers process state mandates. I want to know why it is that educators, who would be expected to respect authority and comply readily with government dictates, feel free to resist or ignore state legislation that directs them to change their practices toward new state goals for education.

In almost every research study that I have conducted, I have sought to incorporate a wide range of data sources. This study is no exception. More and more, I realize the need to capture subtleties and highlights in reporting my research—facets that would be obscured if only broad outlines and contrasts are allowed to be viewed. The nature of the phenomenon under investigation here necessitates a wider palette of data from which to paint the picture that emerges. In subsequent reports, Paul Goldman and I have included comments, focus group data, and document analysis in order to help readers better appreciate the complexity of educational reform efforts.

Reactions from the Field
to State Restructuring Legislation

David T. Conley
Paul Goldman

Can state legislatures mandate fundamental school reform when local control is prevalent and other legislative actions and policies may not be consistent with the goals of reform? This article examines teacher reactions to an Oregon law (H.B. 3565) designed to restructure public education around Certificates of Initial and Advanced Mastery and other changes. Over 2,000 educators in 92 schools completed surveys to determine their attitudes toward mandated reforms. Their reactions can be categorized as cautious support for the ideas contained in the reforms tempered with skepticism that the reforms can be implemented successfully. Individual schools varied greatly in their responses, but demographic groupings did not. States that mandate change may have to provide systematic supports—funding, demonstration projects, networks, consultation services—that enable educators to interpret, adapt, and act upon state mandates at the site level, and that are compatible with and supportive of the structures and strategies that emerge in schools.

In this article we explore educator reactions to the Oregon Educational Act for the 21st Century, known also as the "Katz bill" or as House bill 3565. We attempt here to understand the reactions of teachers and administrators to this comprehensive educational restructuring legislation, which portends fundamental changes in Oregon's K–12 educational system, especially for secondary schools. We pose one basic question in two parts: (a) Can a state legislature mandate educational restructuring when evidence suggests large-scale educational change is a school-by-school phenomenon? and

Authors' Note: Partial funding for this study was provided through a grant from the University of Oregon's Scholarly and Creative Development Award program.

(b) What are the factors that may be related to site-specific responses to such legislation?

TWO VIEWS ON THE STATE'S ROLE IN REFORM AND RESTRUCTURING

There are two basic views on the state's role in school reform and restructuring. One focuses on the state's ability to set standards and mandate the context and procedures of schooling. The other emphasizes the individual school site as the nexus for restructuring and argues that the state has difficulty effecting the conditions necessary for this site-based transformation to take place. We consider each of these perspectives as they help to frame the interactive relationship between state and school site actions, intentions, and goals.

In reaction to the issues raised by *A Nation at Risk* (U.S. Department of Education, 1983) and rising public concern, a significant amount of state-level education reform legislation was enacted during the 1980s. Key questions have been raised regarding the degree to which such legislation actually improved student learning (Wilson & Rossman, 1993). Studies of these reforms conclude that they have tended to mandate more of the same at the school site level, meaning more required courses in academic core areas, heightened teacher certification requirements, a lengthened school day or year, or more defined teacher evaluation practices (Center for Policy Research, 1989; Conley, 1986; Fuhrman, 1988; Grossman, Kirst, & Schmidt-Posner, 1986). This type of reform requires little change in fundamental practices or organizational structures. Teachers can merely continue their current practices or adapt them incrementally. Underlying assumptions and beliefs about teaching and learning are not challenged or modified. School structures need change little.

Many state legislatures have also noted the relatively weak effect of these mandated reform programs. State lawmakers have heard the steady call for large-scale redesign of schools from the business community, educational reformers, and, most recently, even the federal government. Simultaneously, many legislatures have gained much greater control over school finance as a result of lawsuits challenging or overturning local funding of school districts. As legislators revisit school reform in the 1990s, they often have much greater control over education and more responsibility for financing it than they did during the round of reforms in the 1980s. Increasingly centralized funding generally leads to greater scrutiny of schooling and a more activist stance by state lawmakers who feel more entitled (and obligated) to set statewide educational policy when they are providing the funds.

Although educational policy scholars have posited the relative merits and limitations of state intervention as the engine for fundamental school reform (Elmore, 1983; Elmore & McLaughlin, 1988; Firestone, Fuhrman, & Kirst, 1990, 1991; Fuhrman, Clune, & Elmore, 1991; Fuhrman & Elmore, 1990; Kirst, 1992; Smith & O'Day, 1991), there are relatively few studies that systematically examine the process by which educators interpret reform and mediate state-level initiatives. Although many reformers believe that real restructuring must be initiated at the state level, there is little evidence that current programs will actually lead to significant change in individual schools. To the contrary, 20 years of research on educational innovations beginning with Berman and McLaughlin's 1974 study suggests the opposite; educational change is idiosyncratic and uneven, regardless of the initiating source. Schools respond opportunistically, not systemically, to externally designed and mandated reform or improvement programs.

Fuhrman and her colleagues (Fuhrman, 1993; Fuhrman et al., 1991) have presented evidence that state-level initiatives can lead to change at the level of the school district, but the issue of whether and how these initiatives get translated to individual school sites remains largely unanswered. Although it is possible to achieve adherence to clearly stated rules or regulations, particularly at the district level (special education being a prime example), compliance to regulations does not necessarily translate into significant change within schools, or, more important, achievement of the goals that the regulations were designed to achieve. School sites and individual teachers may adapt to the new requirements without changing their educational practices in any significant fashion.

Fuhrman and others examined the adaptive incremental reforms of the 1980s. Larger scale, more fundamental programs of educational restructuring remain largely unexamined, primarily because states have just begun to initiate such programs. Mazzoni (1991) stated that "scholars have had little opportunity until recently to analyze the legislative initiation of structural reforms, because relatively few laws of this sort were enacted" (p. 115). There is evidence that a number of states are implementing or considering more fundamental structural reform, making it possible to consider the effects of large-scale changes initiated at the state level.

A second body of research examines how individual school sites are self-starting engines of school restructuring (Conley, 1991; David, 1990; Eberts, Schwartz, & Stone, 1990; Elmore, 1988; Glen & Crandall, 1988; Goldman, Dunlap, & Conley, 1991; Hallinger, Murphy, & Hausman, 1991). These researchers tend to report that educators who are restructuring view state intervention as a problem, nuisance, or barrier to change rather than as an initiator or facilitator of it. These studies focus on how educators at individual school sites develop unique, nonstandardized solutions to educational problems (Goldman, Dunlap, & Conley, 1993), and how educators at individual school sites are interpreting and responding to the restructuring movement (Conley, Dunlap, & Goldman, 1992; Goldman & Conley, 1994).

The data we have gathered provide us with an opportunity to examine and assess how state legislation designed to foster site-level restructuring is being perceived by those charged with the transformation. These perceptions can suggest the effect state legislation is having on the site-level school restructuring process which the legislation mandates. These data do not tell us whether or how much schools are changing, but do provide valuable insight into the first stage of what most Oregon educational leaders anticipate will be a multistep process of educational redesign. To provide a better sense of the magnitude of the changes being attempted, we begin with a brief overview of the legislation's major provisions.

MAJOR PROVISIONS OF THE OREGON EDUCATIONAL ACT FOR THE 21ST CENTURY

In 1991, the Oregon legislature passed House bill 3565, laying out a new vision of schooling for the state's 1,200 public elementary and secondary schools. Oregon's educators were neither prepared for nor participated in the development of this legislation. Instead, their attention had been focused on the state's recently enacted tax limitation measure and its implications for education funding. Oregon's reform legislation is far reaching, encompassing policies from early childhood to postsecondary education, from accountability to school governance. The act presents a complex framework for systemic redesign of education, preschool through postsecondary. Its stated intention is to create a "restructured educational system . . . to achieve the state's goals of the best educated citizens in the nation by the year 2000 and a work force equal to any in the world by the year 2010" (Oregon Educational Act, 1991).

Oregon's reforms are not incremental changes to be implemented gradually and sequentially year by year from early childhood to secondary education. In this regard, they differ fundamentally from legislation in other states. The Oregon legislation's emphasis on secondary education departs dramatically from major reform efforts elsewhere that have mandated changes first and foremost in primary education. The best examples of those approaches are Kentucky's Education Reform Act and British Columbia's Year 2000 Program (which began to lose provincial government commitment about 5 years after its 1988 enactment). House bill 3565's author and primary sponsor, Vera Katz, had been deeply influenced by the National Center for Education and the Economy's (1990) report "America's Choice: High Skills or Low Wages," which dealt explicitly with high schools and the school-to-work transition. Although the act contains provisions for full funding of early childhood education programs, it offers little more that relates to presecondary education.

The act emphasizes two performance- and skill-based milestones, the Certificate of Initial Mastery (CIM) and the Certificate of Advanced Mastery (CAM). The new educational system is designed to work downward as elementary and middle schools look specifically to ways in which they can adapt their programs to the requirements of the CIM and the CAM. Every student will have the opportunity to obtain the CIM by age 16 or the end of 10th grade. Students are then expected to pursue the CAM, which might take anywhere from 2 to 4 years to achieve.

To obtain a CIM, a student must demonstrate mastery in 11 performance areas at approximately 16 years of age. Benchmarks at Grades 3, 5, and 8 track student progress. Assessments must include "work samples, tests and portfolios . . . culminating in a project or exhibition that demonstrates attainment of required knowledge and skills" (Oregon Educational Act, 1991, p. 54). Performances are to be geared to world-class levels.

The CAM follows the CIM and is organized around six broad occupational categories. The CAM is designed to facilitate school-to-work transition by causing students to give more thought to their career choices as well as to investigate the world of work firsthand while still in school. There is an emphasis on professional-technical programs in addition to college preparation. Students are provided "opportunities for structured work experiences, cooperative work and study programs, on-the-job training and apprenticeship programs in addition to other subjects" in combination with "a comprehensive educational component" (Oregon Educational Act, 1991). The CAM can be earned in a high school or community college up to the age of 21.

There are several other provisions of interest and concern to Oregon educators. Site-based school councils were to be established in every school no later than September 1995. Teachers will form a majority, but parent and classified employees must be represented as well. These councils are to set school goals, approve school staff development programs, and support implementation of the act. Enhanced public accountability for education is achieved through the Oregon Report Card, a comprehensive report on performance on a school-by-school basis, accompanied by an increase in the frequency of external accreditation team visits, coupled with local school and district self-evaluations every 2 years, and increased parental involvement. The act contains provisions for lengthening the school year from the current 175 days to 185 in 1996, 200 in the year 2000, and 220 days by 2010.

The act defines how help and assistance will be provided to students who are not succeeding in public education. Included are requirements that schools identify in the primary years students who are not succeeding and employ alternative instructional approaches with them. Additional support for at-risk students is mandated through alternative learning centers. Social service agencies are required to coordinate their services with those of the public schools and to offer them at the site closest to the client. Learning centers will offer "teaching strategies, technology, and curricula that emphasize the latest research and best practice" to help students develop mastery in defined areas.

In essence, the act lays out a framework of expectations for student performance and calls on schools to redesign their programs to enable students to meet performance standards. The law does not prescribe the means or structures educators should employ to achieve the act's goals. Its sponsors envisioned it as a "trigger mechanism" to engage educators in serious redesign of schools. The law's principal sponsor stated she was attempting to use top-down legislation to catalyze bottom-up school restructuring. Hence Oregon would seem to provide a strong test of this top-down/bottom-up model of reform as well as of a state's capacity to mandate fundamental educational reform. Our data shed light on how educators interpret this type of reform legislation, and whether they are likely to initiate new programs and practices in school districts, buildings, and classrooms as a result of such legislation.

DATA COLLECTION AND METHODOLOGY

The methodology and design of this study applies a policy analysis perspective to this investigation. Although

no formal hypothesis is posed per se, we are attempting to shed light on a specific issue, that is, the relationship between state policy and teacher reactions as aggregated into various demographic groupings and school-by-school findings. We did enter this study with certain untested assumptions that did not have the structure of hypotheses. These assumptions were based on our previous research in the state over several years (Conley, 1991; Conley et al., 1992; Conley, Goldman, & Dunlap, 1993; Goldman et al., 1991, 1993) and conversations, formal and informal, that we had regularly with a wide range of Oregon educators and policymakers through our professional relationships and other ongoing research projects we were conducting. Furthermore, we sought to examine some of what passed for common knowledge in the state and, to some degree, nationally, regarding teacher attitudes toward school reform.

Data come from a self-administered questionnaire distributed and returned during fall 1992, approximately 15 months after the passage of the act. The eight-page questionnaire consisted of 99 forced-choice items, one open-ended question, a comments section, three items on personal characteristics, and five items describing the respondent's school building and school district. The forced-choice items were grouped into the following areas: (a) knowledge of the legislation's major provisions; (b) beliefs about the law's *intent;* (c) assessment of the law's potential *effects;* (d) predictions about the success of implementation; (e) personal reactions, including how much each respondent might have to *change;* (f) what resources would be required for the law to be implemented; and (g) whether specific provisions will improve student learning. We pretested the survey on Oregon educators during summer 1992.

We employed a stratified sampling technique in which the sampling units were school districts and school buildings.[a] This strategy provided a correction factor to overcome the extreme skewness in the size distribution of Oregon's 297 school districts, many of which are extremely small. Based on the number of students

---

a. Stratified sampling is a sampling strategy to ensure that certain subgroups are adequately represented in the sample. As the researchers explain, they used stratified sampling to ensure that larger school districts were adequately represented, and also to give proportional representation to elementary, middle (or junior high), and high schools.

served, the state was divided into four groups each having roughly the same number of students, plus Portland, the one large urban district. Within each of the four categories, districts were randomly selected so that each category would proportionally represent its share of the state's student population. Hence two districts each were selected in the two largest categories, four from the medium-sized group of school districts, and nine from the smallest ones. Within each school district, individual school buildings were randomly selected as follows: one high school, two middle schools or junior highs, and three elementary schools. In districts with fewer schools, all buildings were included in the study. We also designated two midsized districts as "case study districts," in which we surveyed all schools in the district.[b] A total of 92 schools were included in the sample, 64 from the state sample and an additional 28 from

those two districts. Except where otherwise noted, statistical tabulations present data from both the 18 randomly sampled districts and the 2 case study districts. Table 1 illustrates the parameters of the sample.

In each school, questionnaires were distributed to all certified staff. The principal was first approached with a request that the school participate in the study. In some cases, the request was referred to the district office. After permission was granted, appointments were scheduled so that a member of the research staff could make a brief presentation at a faculty meeting. In some cases, the principal personally requested faculty participation in a meeting or through a letter to the staff. Staff returned the anonymous completed questionnaires to a drop box in the school office, and members of the research team either picked them up or they were mailed directly to the researchers' university office.

TABLE 1   **Sample Description and Response Rates**

District Size (ADM)	Total Oregon Districts	Number Sample Districts	ADM in Oregon	Percentage Oregon ADM	Total Surveys	Total Surveys Returned	Percentage Returned Surveys	Return Rate (Percentage)
30,000+	1	1	53,700	11.6	225	140	9.2	62.2
10,400–29,999	4	2	83,100	17.9	562	374	24.7	66.5
5,000–10,399	15	2	113,300	24.4	504	271	18.0	53.8
2,000–4,999	35	4	113,700	24.5	757	478	31.7	63.1
Under 2,000	242	9	100,200	21.6	390	247	16.4	63.3
State of Oregon sample	297	18	464,000	100	2,438	1,510	100	61.9
Case study districts (5,000–10,000 ADM)					1,007	747		74.2
Total		20			3,445	2,257		65.6

Note. ADM is the average daily membership.

b. The researchers use the term "case study" in a different sense than the way in which this term is used in qualitative research (see Chapter 10). Here it means that these two school districts were surveyed comprehensively, with questionnaires being sent to every school in the district. As Table 1 indicates, the response rate was higher for the case study districts than for other districts, which might indicate that the researchers had greater involvement with the educators in those districts before or during the research study.

The questionnaires were distributed, completed, and collected between October 1, 1992 and December 15, 1992. No district refused to participate, but one school did decline to participate and was replaced by another from the same district. Of the 3,445 questionnaires distributed, a total of 2,260 were returned, a rate of just under 66%. Return rates were above 60% for all but one of the subsamples. The subsample proportions closely approximate the distribution of the state's teachers and schoolchildren. It is worth noting that response rates exceed by a substantial margin those from a similar type of survey conducted in British Columbia during the first year of that province's mandated school reform. Researchers surveying teachers there reported an individual response rate of 30% (2,547 distributed, 770 returned) and a school participation rate of 67% (Silns, 1992).

Four separate additive scales were distilled from the 99 individual questions.[c] The scales were developed through careful analysis of the language of individual items and through statistical analysis, specifically item correlations and factor analysis.[d] The scales and the individual questionnaire items they contain are displayed in Table 2. Scale scores were derived first by calculating the mean number of affirmative responses to the total number of items in each scale, then converting this score into a percentage figure. Each of the scales displays internal consistency, and this is reflected by the alpha statistic shown in Table 2.[e]

TABLE 2   Scales and Scale Items

ITEM Number	Item Description	Mean (Percentage Agree)	SD
Change Orientation			
39	It is time for fundamental change in education	56.1	49.6
42	Many schools are already doing much of what law mandates	30.4	46.0
43	Ideas make sense	32.7	46.9
44	Current system isn't working for many kids	58.8	49.2
67	Opportunity to do things I've always wanted to do	27.0	44.4
	Scale alpha		.68
Resistance to Change			
50	Unrealistic	34.3	47.5
51	Not good ideas for education	10.0	30.0
52	Unfair to some types of student	34.4	47.5
54	Too much change too fast for schools	43.4	49.6
63	Am skeptical	51.5	50.0
70	Will take it seriously when it is adequately funded	65.3	47.6

c. The scales shown in Table 2 are additive in that each individual's responses to all the items on the scale were summed to yield a total scale score for that individual.

d. Item correlations and factor analysis are statistical techniques for determining which subsets of items in a total set of items elicit a consistent response from a sample of individuals. A consistent response suggests that the subset of items measure the same construct. Four subsets of items in the 99-item questionnaire to which the educators responded consistently were identified in this manner, and these items defined the four scales shown in Table 2.

e. The alpha statistic is a means of testing whether the items comprising a measure (in this case, the items in the four scales shown in Table 2) consistently measure the same attitude, ability, or other construct. If a scale has a high alpha coefficient (typically, .60 or higher, with the highest possible coefficient being 1.00), it means that individuals who respond in a certain way to one item on the scale are likely to respond in the same way to the other items on that scale.

TABLE 2 Continued			
ITEM Number	Item Description	Mean (Percentage Agree)	*SD*

Resistance to Change *(continued)*

72	Have too much else to do to give it much thought	24.9	43.2
84	Rewrite it to make timelines more reasonable	41.8	49.3
	Scale alpha		.73

Learning Outcomes

15	Will benefit all students	40.5	49.1
16	Will benefit college bound	62.9	48.3
17	Will cause more children to enter kindergarten prepared	45.1	49.8
25	CIM will lead to decrease in dropouts	45.0	49.8
27	Alternative learning centers will help decrease dropouts	69.4	46.1
89	Site councils will lead to learning	69.1	46.2
90	Increased accountability will lead to learning	66.8	47.1
91	Funding for preschool will enable all students to enter school ready to learn	84.1	36.6
92	Extended school year will lead to learning	35.1	47.7
93	CIM will lead to learning	65.9	47.4
94	CAM will lead to learning	65.4	47.6
95	Alternative learning centers will lead to learning	86.0	34.7
96	Parental choice for students who are not succeeding in a school will lead to learning	61.8	48.6
97	Coordination of social services at the school site for those who need such services will lead to learning	80.5	39.6
98	Mixed age classrooms in Grades 1–3 will lead to learning	58.9	49.2
99	Educational philosophy of developmentally appropriate practices in Grades 1–3 will lead to learning	79.9	40.1
	Scale alpha		.82

Changes in Practices

11	Will promote more developmentally appropriate practice in elementary schools	66.4	47.3
14	Will increase teacher control over instructional program at school	38.6	48.7
18	Will cause teachers to increase number of instructional strategies they employ	61.8	48.6
19	Will lead to greater integration of social services in schools	60.7	48.9
20	Will lead to greater curriculum integration	74.3	43.7
21	Will lead to new and diverse ways to organize or group students for learning	77.0	42.1
22	Will lead to increased teacher involvement in decision making	55.5	49.7
23	Will lead to increased teacher collegiality and cooperation	51.3	50.0
	Scale alpha		.72

Note. CIM = Certificate of Initial Mastery. CAM = Certificate of Advanced Mastery.

Scale 1 is change orientation, consisting of items that suggest a general sense that schools should be changing and that the Oregon act provides an opportunity for change to occur. Scale 2, resistance to change, reflects both skepticism and disengagement. Although negatively correlated with change orientation ($r = -.31$), this scale seems to measure slightly different attitudinal dimensions, reflecting doubts that changes should or can be made.[f] Scale 3, learning outcomes, is taken directly from specific consecutive questions in one section of the questionnaire. These items asked educators whether, in their opinion, specific features of the act would lead to increased student learning. Scale 4 measures anticipated changes in practices, specifically in such areas as developmentally appropriate practices, integrating curriculum, and increased teacher collegiality and cooperation. Scales 3 and 4 are strongly intercorrelated ($r = .60$), but appear to measure somewhat different dimensions of response to House bill 3565.[g] Moreover, the two correlate with somewhat different demographic variables.

Statistically significant and conceptually interesting findings consisted primarily of comparisons of scale means between different values of categorical variables.[h] Statistical significance was assessed using F tests, and these are reported, as appropriate, in individual tables as recommended by Blalock (1972).[i] The F values reported in Table 3 have been verified by a post hoc pairs analysis using Tukey's Honest Statistical Difference test.[j] Readers should note, however, that with large sample size,

statistical significance may be reported when actual differences are small and, conversely, the lack of statistical significance where sample means show little difference between them may indicate "nonfindings" that are nonetheless suggestive or important (Cohen, 1990).

RESULTS AND INTERPRETATIONS OF THE DATA

We thought that teachers would be opposed to, or at the least suspicious of, state-level restructuring legislation, because the objection that teachers had not participated in the design of House bill 3565 in any significant fashion had been voiced by many teacher representatives. Furthermore, we assumed that some demographic groups might be more resistant to the requirements and intent of the legislation than others. For example, recent surveys elsewhere suggest that high school educators would be more wary than those in elementary schools, and that more veteran staff would be less receptive than younger or less experienced teachers (Auriemma, Cooper, & Smith, 1992; Harris & Wagner, 1993; King & Peart, 1992). In particular, we thought male high school teachers in the 45- to 50-year range might be expected to be less enthusiastic or supportive of such large-scale change.

Teachers in rural districts might be more critical because elements of the reform such as the CAM seemed much more difficult for small schools to implement. Correspondingly, staff in larger districts might be more

---

f. When two measures are negatively correlated, individuals with higher scores on one measure tend to have lower scores on the other measure. The magnitude of the relationship is indicated by a correlation coefficient such as *r*. The *r* value of −.31 indicates that educators with higher scores on the Change Orientation scale tend to have lower scores on the Resistance to Change scale. Conversely, educators with lower scores on the Change Orientation scale tend to have higher scores on the Resistance to Change scale.

g. An *r* value of .60 indicates that there is a positive correlation between these two measures. Educators with higher scores on Scale 3 also tend to have higher scores on Scale 4. Conversely, educators with lower scores on Scale 3 tend to have lower scores on Scale 4.

h. If a difference between groups is statistically significant, it means that we can generalize beyond this sample and conclude that a similar difference would be found in other samples from the same population as this sample.

i. *F* test is another term for the statistical technique of analysis of variance.

j. The Tukey Honest Statistical Difference (HSD) test is used when an analysis of variance reveals that the differences among three or more groups on a measure can be generalized to a larger population. The Tukey procedure enables researchers to determine which pairwise comparisons are generalizable in this sense. (If there are three groups, A, B, and C, there are three possible pairwise comparisons: A versus B, A versus C, and B versus C.)

responsive because Oregon's larger school districts see themselves as lighthouses. They tend to keep abreast of important state (and federal) legislation and could be expected to be more likely to make sure teachers and administrators understood the act and its implications.

Because we had previously conducted research at schools that had received competitive school improvement grants from the state through its "2020" program, we believed these schools would be more receptive to the act (Goldman et al., 1993). And, finally, we felt that the attention educators were paying to budget cuts brought on by the phased implementation of a property tax reduction measure passed in 1990 might seriously affect educators' willingness to take on anything new. Cuts were being made in nearly all districts, and we wondered if a district's relative wealth would be a factor in its professional staff's reactions to the act.

The results of the data analysis parallel these issues. The data suggest the ways in which educators are interpreting the legislation, as well as the types of action that a state might take to enhance the ability of sites to implement this and similar reforms. Policy analysis of this sort is designed to serve an "enlightenment function" (Majchrzak, 1984; Weiss, 1977), the purpose of which is to highlight the effects, both intended and unintended, of policy as it is put into practice. Therefore, we present an analysis of the data and provide an interpretation of its meaning and implications first in a more limited statistical sense, and then in a broader policy context.

In presenting the study's findings, we first lay out the highlights of the frequency distributions, summarizing previously reported findings (Conley et al., 1993) and setting the context for more detailed analysis. Second, we discuss and analyze the four scales in the context of individual, school, and district demographic characteristics. Third, we move from an individual to an organizational level of analysis, presenting and discussing how school buildings and school districts seem to differ from one another.

Questionnaire responses indicate that educators believed the act was well intended and had student interests at heart, but 15 months after enactment, they did not yet feel fully informed about the bill's details and its implications. A substantial majority believed that the most innovative programs, the CIM and CAM, would be implemented (88% and 86%, respectively), and almost as many (82%) expected site-based decision making would become the norm. They were very skeptical that preschool programs and the extended school year, the most expensive components of the act, would actually come to pass. Moreover, with virtual unanimity (92%), they believed that funding and time for staff development were essential prerequisites for successful implementation of the act.

Three quarters of the respondents thought the act would result in new ways to group students as well as greater curriculum integration, and that the new alternative learning centers for failing or at-risk adolescents would decrease dropout rates. A majority of educators believed both that the current system is not working for many kids (59%) and that it is time for fundamental change in education (56%). About half the respondents considered themselves skeptical but, at the same time, 66% expected to make at least a "little" change and another 29% expected to change "a lot."

In general, Oregon's educators seem more positive about the concepts embodied in the reform legislation than their counterparts who have been experiencing systemic educational reform elsewhere in North America (Harris & Wagner, 1993). Both the general intent of the law and its specific elements are apparently not in conflict with the ways educators perceive both current problems and the potential solutions to them. This conclusion is consistent with the findings of Fuhrman et al. (1991) that "suggest strongly that policy maker and educator support for reform, which is key to successful implementation, does not depend on participation in reform initiation and design" (p. 215). Our analysis tends to validate the proposition that most teachers and administrators in Oregon are ready philosophically to address the broad restructuring implied by Oregon's legislation. They are, however, quite skeptical that the state will follow through with either the funding or the sustained commitment over time necessary to put these changes into practice.

Individual Differences

Table 3 displays one-way ANOVAs for each of the scales as they are distributed among individual and organizational

TABLE 3   Scale Means by Individual, Building, and District Demographics

	Percentage Agree Responses				
	Change Orientation	Resistance to Change	Learning Outcomes	Changes in Practices	*N*
Sample					2,257
Mean	41.0	34.7	63.9	60.7	
SD	30.3	22.7	23.2	32.2	
Individual Characteristics					
Position					
Teachers	39.6	36.4	62.5	58.7	1,750
Other certified staff	44.0	34.2	66.7	63.7	317
Administrators	55.4	32.6	73.2	76.9	153
F	20.1**	29.0**	23.5**	17.9**	
Gender					
Men	40.6	33.3	60.8	58.5	872
Women	42.0	35.8	65.9	62.4	1,310
F	0.2	6.7*	22.8**	7.4*	
Age					
20–29	37.4	38.4	63.1	59.2	162
30–39	40.0	35.2	63.3	62.2	526
40–49	42.9	33.7	64.9	61.8	1,009
50–59	41.5	35.2	63.6	58.9	478
60+	43.0	40.9	54.4	49.4	27
F	1.6	2.2	1.7	1.5	
Building characteristics					
School level					
High school	45.0	32.1	64.3	64.8	802
Junior high and middle	38.7	35.1	63.3	54.0	596
Elementary	39.1	38.5	63.1	61.0	768
F	9.2**	10.3**	0.3	16.1**	
Student SES					
Highest quartile	41.9	34.8	62.8	62.4	476
2nd quartile	42.8	32.7	66.1	62.6	454
3rd quartile	39.9	35.5	62.4	58.9	475
4th quartile	40.8	35.3	64.9	60.9	498
F	0.9	0.7	1.3	2.7	

TABLE 3   Continued

| | Percentage Agree Responses | | | | |
	Change Orientation	Resistance to Change	Learning Outcomes	Changes in Practices	N
2020 Grant					
Yes	44.2	36.1	63.5	59.1	673
No	39.7	31.8	64.7	64.2	1,549
F	10.2**	16.7**	1.2	10.8**	
District Characteristics					
Size					
15,000+	38.9	37.5	63.5	55.6	458
5,000–14,999	41.9	33.5	64.3	62.1	928
2,000–4,999	41.6	32.3	63.7	65.7	440
100–1,999	40.9	38.7	63.9	55.9	234
F	1.3	8.1**	0.2	9.9**	
Region					
Portland Metro	38.3	37.4	62.1	55.9	933
Willamette Valley	46.6	32.0	67.8	67.6	728
Southern Oregon	41.4	30.2	65.2	63.0	246
Central/Eastern Oregon	31.8	41.2	56.5	55.3	137
Oregon Coast	39.4	33.0	61.2	59.4	210
F	9.0**	11.8**	10.3**	13.9**	
Per student expenditure					
Highest quartile	30.4	38.8	63.2	60.3	484
2nd quartile	37.1	38.3	67.0	66.0	518
3rd quartile	34.1	35.6	64.9	65.0	504
4th quartile	28.7	42.0	60.3	51.5	518
F	13.6**	13.9**	22.6**	7.66**	

*$p < .05$; **$p < .01$.

characteristics.[k] The table is organized in three sections: characteristics of individuals, characteristics of school buildings, and characteristics of school districts.

There are substantial differences in attitudes between classroom teachers and administrators. Each scale showed a differential of at least 10 points between the

k. Analysis of variance is a statistical procedure to determine the likelihood that a difference in the mean scores of two or more groups on a measure would also be found if the researchers studied the entire population. A one-way analysis of variance (ANOVA) involves one independent variable. For example, one of the first comparisons shown in Table 3 involves the independent variable of position, which includes three categories: teachers, other certified staff, and administrators. The F values show the effect of this independent variable on each of the four scales. For example, on the Change Orientation scale the analysis of variance yields an F value of 20.1, which is statistically significant. This means that if the three populations represented by these three sample groups had been studied, they likely would differ in a similar way on this scale.

TABLE 3A **Statistically Significant Pairs**[1]

	Change Orientation	Resistance to Change	Learning Outcomes	Changes in Practices
Position	All	All	All	All
School level	HS:MS HS:ELEM	All	HS:MS	HS:ELEM
District size		15K:5–14.9K 15K:2–4.9K 2–4.9K:.1–1.9K	15K:5–14.9K 15K:2–4.9K 2–4.9K:.1–1.9K	
Region	Metro:Valley Metro:South Valley:East Valley:Coast South:East East:Coast	Metro:Valley Valley:East Valley:Coast South:East	Metro:Valley Valley:East Valley:Coast South:East	Metro:Valley Metro:South Valley:East Valley:Coast South:East
Per student expenditure	1st:2nd 1st:3rd 2nd:4th 3rd:4th	1st:2nd 1st:3rd 2nd:4th 3rd:4th	1st:2nd 1st:3rd 2nd:4th 3rd:4th	1st:2nd 1st:3rd 2nd:4th 3rd:4th

Note. Post hoc paired comparisons were computed employing Tukey's HSD test with a significance level of .05.

two. Teachers appear to be less oriented to change generally and less likely to believe reformers' pleas that the educational system is in crisis; correspondingly, teachers are more resistant to change, at least the changes embodied in the act. A much lower proportion of teachers believe that the restructuring program will either change educational practices or make significant improvements in outcomes. Certified staff who are not classroom teachers present intermediate attitudes, but these specialists, counselors, and special educators have outlooks similar to teachers. A note of caution may be in order. These differences are relative: The typical teacher still thought 60% of the reform proposals would change practices and improve outcomes.

Comparisons between Oregon's female and male educators reveal only very small differences. Women express marginally more agreement with statements that describe resistance to change. However, this finding runs in the opposite direction from the differences on the outcomes and practices scales. Women are more optimistic both about the possible beneficial effects of the act on student learning and about the likelihood that teachers will change their instructional practices. These differences may be partially explained by differences between elementary and secondary teachers, but this is probably only part of the story. Note that there are virtually no differences in the response pattern between schools with male and female principals.

1. The authors of the article informed us of two corrections that should be made to Table 3A: (1) for School level, under Learning Outcomes, HS:MS should be deleted; (2) for School level, under Changes in Practices, HS:ELEM should be deleted, and HS:MS and MS:ELEM should be inserted.

Contrary to both conventional wisdom and to recent findings by Auriemma and colleagues (1992) and the Canadian Teachers Federation (King & Peart, 1992), there appears to be virtually no relationship between reactions to Oregon's restructuring legislation and educator age or experience. Oregon's teaching force is predominantly middle aged (median age is 45) and experienced. This sample seems to be a reliable approximation of the state; almost one half are in their 40s. Except for teachers in their 60s who present views less favorable to Oregon's educational reforms, no age group is noticeably more or less change oriented or change resistant.

If individual responses are not correlated with personal demographic characteristics, does the fact that the school serves elementary or secondary level children make a difference? As Table 2 indicates, high school and elementary school teachers do differ somewhat from one another, especially in the degree to which they embrace change.[m] Middle school and junior high teachers are in the middle. For example, two thirds of high school teachers but only one half of elementary teachers agree that "the system isn't working for many kids." Differences narrow when we ask whether teachers will change their instructional practices and whether this set of school reforms will improve learning outcomes. In addition, the gradation running from elementary to middle to high school breaks down when we consider how much teachers say they know about the act and how much they expect their own practices to change. Middle-level teachers believe they are less informed than both other groups and less likely to anticipate changed practices. The act does not specify or mandate program changes for the middle level, but many are clearly implied by other sections of the act, such as the CIM and the alternative learning centers.

We investigated whether school averages on student socioeconomic status might be related to how teachers view school reform. In general, schools with middle- and upper middle-class students have had somewhat more resources of all kinds, whereas schools with students from working and lower class families contain a higher proportion of children with learning problems who may have to be educated with relatively fewer resources. Whatever the differences between these types of schools in practices, workloads, or morale, we found no differences in their faculty's beliefs about school reform. These similarities were echoed by comparisons of district-level differences in funding. In our sample, educators in the poorest districts are a bit less optimistic about the act and its possible effects, but their responses are more similar to those of educators in the richest districts than to those in the middle.

Geography and district size appear to explain some differences. Over 80% of Oregon's population is within an hour's drive of I-5, the interstate highway that bisects the state from Portland to the California border. Educators in districts on the I-5 corridor are more knowledgeable about, and more receptive to, reform than those in less populated and more remote areas of the state. The findings for eastern Oregon indicate that these districts are less supportive of reform and see it as less relevant to them. The possible sources of these differences, and whether the apparent skepticism actually results from geographic isolation, or from a real and perceived distance from state policy makers, are discussed in the Conclusions section.

The data on district size reveal some differences as well. The largest and smallest districts are very similar to one another on two of the four scales: resistance to change, and the expectation that the legislation's consequences will include changed classroom practices. Teachers in the largest districts are on the lower extreme of the change orientation scale. If these results reflect a larger reality, they suggest that large districts may be having more difficulty translating broad policy initiatives, especially those originating externally, to staff in the schools, than medium-sized districts, that is, those below 15,000 students.

One final factor appears to have had an impact on attitudes: Educators in schools that had previous and current state-funded school improvement grants were more receptive to the restructuring legislation. These staffs

---

m. This information is shown in Table 3A, a supplement to Table 3, not in Table 2. It notes only the specific pair comparisons that were found to be statistically significant.

were also more likely to expect that the school reform legislation might have an effect on instructional practice. Between 1987 and 1993, Oregon's State Department of Education funded competitive school improvement and professional development grants. The funding, called 2020 grants after the legislative bill number, allowed schools considerable latitude but required that the monies be managed by a committee where teachers comprised the majority. Among the wide range of funded projects were those focused on creating readiness for restructuring, developing new assessment techniques, creating programs for at-risk students, implementing cooperative learning, developing new decision-making or governance structures, designing interdisciplinary curriculum, enhancing multiculturalism, improving school climate, addressing needs of special education students, and integrating technology (Conley, 1991). Schools that had already experimented with restructuring, whether or not they were successful, were more favorable to reform.

School Districts and School Buildings as Units of Analysis

What the data above suggest is that, aside from differences that seem to stem from job titles and job responsibilities, demographic factors are not strong predictors of individual responses. Even where the literature suggests possible individual explanatory factors—for instance, those associated with age, experience, or gender—personal characteristics appeared to have little effect. Similarly, at a broader more contextual level, district size and even the economic status of the district's students and the money the district spent on those children made little difference. When districts, and especially school buildings, are taken as units of analysis, however, the findings are different. Table 4 presents a nested analysis of variance comparing school and district effects in the 12 districts for which we collected data in five or more schools.[n]

Between district differences on all four scales are large and statistically significant, indicating that district

variations may nurture attitudes that are receptive to or skeptical about Oregon's school restructuring legislation. The range in expectations about whether schools will change their practices was especially large: In one large district, the mean was 48; in another (less large) the mean was 73, a substantial difference when we consider that these were measures aggregated over 210 and 125 respondents, respectively. Comparable differences on the three other scales were less dramatic: from 30 to 41 on resistance to change, 31 to 47 on change orientation, and 58 to 71 on expectations for learning outcomes. There were, however, no patterns suggesting that particular types of districts—larger or smaller, richer or poorer, close to or distant from the state capital and the major metropolitan center—produce environments that encourage staff to be more or less positive or optimistic about the restructuring legislation.

School-level data demonstrate similar patterns. In some districts, differences between schools are also large. Although overall school effects are smaller than district effects, there are several districts in which variation between individual schools is large enough to generate questions about how districts interpret state policy for schools. One example illustrates this phenomenon. One district near the Portland metropolitan area had school means ranging from 32 to 84 on change orientation, from 62 to 85 on expectation of changed practices, and from 48 to 85 on outcome expectations.

OBSERVATIONS, CONSIDERATIONS, AND IMPLICATIONS

We discuss these findings in three subsections: general observations from the survey; demographic, district, and site-level considerations; and implications.

General Observations from the Survey

The first year of the Oregon experience suggests that legislation mandating fundamental school reform can,

---

n. Analysis of variance can determine the effect of several independent variables on a dependent variable. In Table 4, the two independent variables are school district and school building. These two independent variables are not independent of each other, however, because the schools are located in (that is, nested in) specific school districts. The analysis of variance is designed to reflect the nested relationship between these two independent variables.

TABLE 4	Multischool Districts: Nested Building and District Effects			
District/School	Change Orientation	Resistance to Change	Changed Practices	Learning Outcomes
Model				
df	53	53	53	53
Mean square	1,551.05	1,203.05	3,265.07	1,180.75
F value	2.88**	2.47**	3.57**	2.41**
Error				
df	1,230.0	1,203.0	1,129.0	1,120.0
Mean square	538.8	486.62	913.8	489.3
R^2	.11	.10	.14	.10
District				
df	9	9	9	9
Mean square	2,527.67	2,950.74	8,311.95	2,327.92
F value	4.69**	6.06**	9.10**	4.76**
School (District)				
df	44	44	44	44
Mean square	1,351.3	845.6	2,232.8	946.1
F value	2.51**	1.74*	2.44**	1.93**

*$p < .01$; **$p < .001$.

at the very least, cause considerable reflection and self-examination by teachers. One indication was the fact that about 55% of responding teachers completed an optional comments section where they identified those activities they personally would have to change in their teaching practice as a result of passage of the act. Furthermore, the Oregon experience suggests that, even without teacher input, states can develop school restructuring legislation that teachers will accept if, and perhaps only if, it captures key themes that respond to concerns already felt by teachers. Fuhrman and colleagues (1991) reached similar conclusions.

The conventional wisdom, expressed frequently by administrators, policymakers, and policy pundits, and seemingly felt by the general public, that teachers are unresponsive to the need to change schooling may be somewhat overstated. A sizable number of teachers in

Oregon seem to be very ready to enter into discussions about school restructuring and to consider changing what they do and how they do it. In the same breath, it is worth noting that our data do not capture the intensity of feeling very well. Subsequent research we conducted using focus groups (Goldman & Conley, 1994) suggests there is a group of teachers who oppose reform strongly. Although smaller in number, their impact may ultimately be disproportionally large.

Oregon's educators believe strongly that fiscal issues will influence their ability to remake schooling on a large scale. However, the state policy-making and policy-implementation structures, experienced by educators as legislative mandates translated and enforced by state officials, have not sent coherent or consistent messages to the field about the relationship between funding and reform. In practice, there is no relationship, or even an inverse relationship: Funding decreases whereas expectations for enhanced performance, professional development, and systems redesign increase.

Teachers express skepticism that the act can be implemented without additional targeted funding to buy the time and expertise they perceive as necessary for their own training, learning, and changing. Teachers view the state's lack of financial commitment as a reason to wait before jumping onto the reform bandwagon. This suggests the interconnection between school finance reform and school restructuring programs. Radical school finance reform continues at a rapid pace in a number of states. Any new funding strategy and formula is likely to have significant interaction effects with any program of restructuring. Rarely are these finance reforms being designed and implemented in concert with educational restructuring programs. Our data suggest that a potentially strong magnifying or multiplier effect could be achieved if the two were linked, and if teachers in particular perceived the connection, a possibility suggested by Verstegen (1994).

Educators in this study express a willingness to entertain change, but do not believe they will necessarily be given the authority or resources they need to adapt successfully. Their ambivalence fosters a wait-and-see attitude. As they wait, the deadline for implementing key provisions of the act draws nearer. This creates a situation where more change will be required in less time. Few teachers plan for the changes; instead, they wait to see what each new legislature does to provide time, money, and guidance. Will teachers be able to adapt to the requirements of a standards-based system with extensive performance assessment requirements within the time remaining and with the resources that are currently available?

Demographic, District, and Site-Level Considerations

Our data suggest that both researchers and policymakers must be cautious when generalizing about the relationships between resistance to change and demographic factors such as age, gender, and locality, or distinctions between elementary and secondary schools. Resistors and enthusiasts exist in most schools and districts, but do not seem to come disproportionately from specific demographic categories. However convenient generalizations might be, it appears educator attitudes toward large-scale reform defy simple categorization.

Equally significant is the apparent potential support for large-scale change in high schools. We found this particularly striking, given the widely held view that the high school level is most resistant to change. This finding suggests that it may be more possible than supposed to redesign high schools. Current thinking on reform often emphasizes a focus on preschool and early childhood as the starting point for system redesign. Such an approach implies grade-by-grade restructuring as a student cohort moves through the system.

Our findings hint that it may not be necessary to take 12 or more years to reshape education by redesigning curriculum and instruction one grade level at a time, as was planned in the British Columbia Year 2000 design (Sullivan, 1988). The finding that a majority of teachers at all levels indicate support for fundamental change suggests that elementary, middle, and high schools might engage in reform and redesign more or less simultaneously. Interestingly, one of the several factors that contributed to a reappraisal of the Year 2000 program in British Columbia was resistance from secondary teachers, who expressed more concerns as the time approached for them to receive students educated under the Year 2000 program (Kuehn, 1993).

Differences in reaction that appear to be based on geography suggest that smaller schools, especially those in rural areas, may view reform with a cautious eye. Aside from possible staff selection factors, educators in the smallest districts may have problems scanning externally generated initiatives because administrative staffs are already stretched in so many directions. The problem would be exacerbated for those located at a distance from policy centers. People in these districts may also be more suspicious of state-level initiatives that they perceive as threatening to local autonomy. These educators apparently do not see the reforms the way the Department of Education presents them—as an opportunity to exercise more discretion in the operation of their schools. They do not interpret the act as an invitation to greater local control of their educational programs in exchange for improved student performance as defined by state standards.

Lower levels of support in larger districts may be attributable to the law's lack of procedural specificity. Schools in these districts could not simply wait to be told how to implement the law by central administration. Many of the large districts in this sample have an administrative structure and organizational culture that emphasizes strong central authority and standardization across schools within the district. Individual schools in these districts have less of a capacity to interpret and respond locally to broad policy frameworks. For these schools, a generalized call to restructure with few specific required activities will be viewed with much greater caution, particularly if large-scale change is implied. It would not be surprising if educators at the school level had difficulty taking initiative instead of waiting to be directed how to respond, which has been their previous practice.

Small districts may have had concerns regarding the lack of specificity, but for a different reason. The smaller districts have indicated they will be unable to meet some of the law's requirements, such as offering CAM programs in six "broad occupational categories" for all students or identifying work-based experiences for all students.

The lack of distinctive differences among almost all demographic groupings contrasted with clear differences among school sites. These findings reinforce the conclusions of many others over the past decade and a half that schools are the appropriate unit of analysis when considering policy implementation or reform in public education (Berends, 1992; David, 1990; Mortimore & Sammons, 1987; Muncey & McQuillan, 1993; Purkey & Smith, 1983). As difficult and inconvenient as it is to conceive of a public school system as thousands of individual school buildings rather than as one integrated system, it seems necessary to consider policy development from this perspective. In fact, well-constructed policy would require that sites be both able and expected to engage in a process of interpreting policy. State bureaucracies tend to prefer standardized reforms, whereas contextual effects and efforts at the building level tend to create nonstandardized responses. Resistance to and acceptance of change is more complex and subtle than demography or status suggest and is probably as connected to contextual as to personal characteristics.

Differences among schools may flow from the interaction among individual characteristics rather than organizational effects. Although demographic characteristics may not seem important when viewed in the aggregate, these same characteristics and others not sampled in this study may create dynamics—essentially an interaction effect—that does not occur when people express themselves individually. Characteristics such as a comparatively old or young staff, one that is predominantly male or female, or one where the principal has a strong vision can have a powerful effect individually or in combination within the context of a school building. Understanding how attitudes about school restructuring are formed at the school site is important because there are strong indicators that educational restructuring is a building-by-building process, not primarily a state phenomenon (Goldman et al., 1993; Louis & Miles, 1990; Murphy & Hallinger, 1993).

These findings taken in their entirety suggest that some combination of district-level actions and factors specific to each school affects attitudes toward the act. Possibly factors at the school such as history and culture, staff composition, leadership, and experience with school improvement combine to provide filters through which both state mandates and district policy pass as they are being understood, interpreted, and adapted. In other districts where school differences are much smaller, it is most likely that the school-level contextual factors described above are being influenced, at least modestly, by actions at the district level. Although restructuring is and likely will continue to be primarily a school-by-school phenomenon, districts do apparently influence attitudes toward reform at the site level as well. State actions merely initiate a series of complex interactions leading to a wide range of interpretations and responses.

Implications

Schools may serve as the locus for change, but the more crucial issue is whether they can create or sustain staff willingness and energy for change without external pressure for reform and improvement. Based on our findings, states that mandate change may have to provide systematic supports—funding, demonstration projects, networks, consultation services—that enable educators to interpret, adapt, and act on state mandates at the site level, and that are compatible with and supportive of the structures and strategies that emerge in schools. This observation is consistent with the findings of Teddlie and Stringfield's (1993) longitudinal study of school effects.

The movement toward national and state standards only sharpens the need to focus on the capacity of individual schools to meet externally imposed performance expectations. The national standards model is based on the assumption that once standards are developed, individual schools will have both the capacity and will to reshape their educational programs so that more students meet the standards. Oregon educators do not appear to accept this premise. They seem concerned that *any* action by the state will result in reduced local control. There is little evidence that teachers currently feel capable of making changes of the magnitude required for all students to reach high standards, nor that they even feel the most important factors could ever be under their control. For example, a common teacher response to poor student performance is to cite unsupportive or dysfunctional family environments. Serious resistance can be expected if teachers feel they are being given an impossible task.

Teachers may be more likely to accept the notion of externally designated learning standards if they believe that the conditions under which they teach and their students learn will somehow be modified substantially. The extent to which teachers participate in the decisions that operationalize restructuring may be key in determining their acceptance of externally designed frameworks for school organization (Conley & Goldman, 1994; Merwin, 1993). States may find themselves in the unfamiliar position of nurturing rather than mandating policy implementation.

If a state were to develop educational restructuring policy that responded to these findings, the policy would contain provisions to require or at least encourage individual school sites to respond to the state's pol-

icy in at least four ways: (a) by creating provisions that ensured each school determined the policy's likely effects on that school; (b) by enabling the site to tailor its responses or implementation in some important ways; (c) by making sure there were exemplars or models that showed educators how the new policy might play out in practice; and (d) by demonstrating to teachers that they will likely be able to adapt successfully to the demands of the policy.

Can states restructure their public education systems through comprehensive legislative programs, particularly when traditions of local control and school-based change are strong? Can legislative action spur and support change at school sites? Our data suggest that educators are much more receptive than might be expected, particularly considering their lack of involvement and the state's fiscal crisis. But they are realists. They are unlikely to proceed too far down this path if they believe there is little probability of success. Reform legislation has initiated a profound reexamination of current practice and has opened the door to a new vision of education. In that sense it has served the catalyst function desired by its initiators. It remains unclear whether policymakers and educators are now poised to walk through the door, or to close it after glimpsing what lies ahead.

References

Auriemma, F., Cooper, B., & Smith, S. (1992). *Graying teachers: A report on state pension systems and school district early retirement incentives.* Eugene, OR: ERIC Clearinghouse on Educational Management.

Berends, M. (1992). *A description of restructuring in nationally nominated schools.* Madison, WI: University of Wisconsin, Center on Organization and Restructuring of Schools.

Berman, P., & McLaughlin, M. (1974). *Federal programs supporting educational change: Vol. 8. Implementing and sustaining innovations.* Santa Monica, CA: RAND.

Blalock, H. (1972). *Social statistics.* New York: McGraw-Hill.

Center for Policy Research. (1989). *The progress of reform: An appraisal of state education initiatives.* Rutgers, NJ: Author.

Cohen, J. (1990). Things I have learned (so far). *American Psychologist, 45*(12), 1304–1312.

Conley, D. (1986). *Certified personnel evaluation in Colorado: A policy study of practices and perceptions at the time* of the implementation of the Certificated Personnel Performance Evaluation Act (H.B. 1338). Unpublished doctoral dissertation, University of Colorado, Boulder.

Conley, D. (1991). Lessons from laboratories in school restructuring and site-based decision-making: Oregon's 2020 schools take control of their own reform. *OSSC Bulletin, 34*(7), 1–61.

Conley, D., Dunlap, D., & Goldman, P. (1992). The "vision thing" and school restructuring. *OSSC Report, 32*(2), 1–8.

Conley, D, & Goldman, P. (1994). Ten propositions for facilitative leadership. In J. Murphy & K. S. Louis (Eds.), *Reshaping the principalship: Insights from transformational reform efforts* (pp. 237–262). Newbury Park, CA: Corwin.

Conley, D. T., Goldman, P., & Dunlap, D. M. (1993, April 14). *Radical state legislation as a tool for fundamental educational reform and restructuring: Reactions from the field to Oregon's H.B. 3565*. Paper presented at the annual conference of the American Educational Research Association, Atlanta, GA.

David, J. (1990). Restructuring in progress: Lessons from pioneering districts. In R. Elmore (Ed.), *Restructuring schools: The next generation of educational reform*. San Francisco: Jossey-Bass.

Eberts, R., Schwartz, E., & Stone, J. (1990). School reform, school size, and student achievement. *Economic Review (Federal Reserve Bank of Cleveland), 26*(2), 2–15.

Elmore, R. F. (1983). Complexity and control: What legislators and administrators can do about implementing public policy. In L. S. Shulman & G. Sykes (Eds.), *Handbook of teaching and policy*. New York: Longman.

Elmore, R. F. (1988). *Early experience in restructuring schools: Voices from the field*. Washington, DC: Center for Policy Research, National Governors' Association.

Elmore, R. F., & McLaughlin, M. W. (1988). *Steady work: Policy, practice, and the reform of American education*. Santa Monica, CA: RAND.

Firestone, W., Fuhrman, S., & Kirst, M. (1990, February). Implementation, effects of state education reform in the '80's. *NASSP Bulletin*, pp. 75–84.

Firestone, W., Fuhrman, S., & Kirst, M. (1991). State educational reform since 1983: Appraisal and the future. *Educational Policy, 5*(3), 233–250.

Fuhrman, S. (1993). The politics of coherence. In S. Fuhrman (Ed.), *Designing coherent policy: Improving the system*. San Francisco: Jossey-Bass.

Fuhrman, S., Clune, W., & Elmore, R. (1991). Research on education reform: Lessons on the implementation of policy. In A. Odden (Ed.), *Educational policy implementation* (pp. 197–218). Albany: SUNY Press.

Fuhrman, S., & Elmore, R. (1990). Understanding local control in the wake of state education reform. *Educational Evaluation and Policy Analysis, 12*(1), 82–96.

Fuhrman, S. O. (1988). Research on education reform: Lessons on the implementation of policy. *Teachers College Record, 90*(2), 237–57.

Glen, H., & Crandall, D. P. (1988). *A beginning look at the what and how of restructuring*. ERIC Document Reproduction Service No. ED 294 326.

Goldman, P., & Conley, D. (1994, April 4). *School responses to state-level restructuring legislation*. Paper presented at the annual conference of the American Educational Research Association, New Orleans.

Goldman, P., Dunlap, D., & Conley, D. (1991, April). *Administrative facilitation and site-based school reform projects*. Paper presented at the annual conference of the American Educational Research Association, Chicago.

Goldman, P., Dunlap, D., & Conley, D. (1993). Facilitative power and non-standardized solutions to school site restructuring. *Educational Administration Quarterly, 29*(1), 69–92.

Grossman, P., Kirst, M., & Schmidt-Posner, J. (1986). On the trail of the omnibeast: Evaluating omnibus education reforms in the 1980s. *Educational Evaluation and Policy Analysis, 8*(3), 253–266.

H.B. 3565: Oregon Educational Act for the 21st Century (1993). In *Oregon Laws Relating to Public Schools and Community Colleges*, pp. 43–80. Salem, OR: Oregon Department of Education.

Hallinger, P., Murphy, J., & Hausman, C. (1991, April). *Restructuring schools: Principals' perceptions of fundamental educational reform*. Paper presented at the annual conference of the American Educational Research Association, Chicago.

Harris, L., & Wagner, R. F. (1993, September). *Testing assumptions: A survey of teachers attitudes toward the nation's school reform agenda*. Ford Foundation.

King, A. J. C., & Peart, M. (1992). *Teachers in Canada: Their work and quality of life*. Ottawa, Ontario: Canadian Teachers Federation.

Kirst, M. (1992). The state role in school restructuring. In C. Finn & T. Rebarber (Eds.), *Education reform in the 90's*. New York: Macmillan.

Kuehn, L. (1993). *Teaching in the '90s: Rep. No. 1. Changing teaching practice: Teachers' aspirations meet school realities*. Vancouver: British Columbia Teacher's Federation.

Louis, K. S., & Miles, M. (1990). *Improving the urban high school: What works and why*. New York: Teachers College Press.

Majchrzak, A. (1984). *Methods for policy research*. Beverly Hills, CA: Sage.

Mazzoni, T. (1991). Analyzing state school policymaking: An arena model. *Educational Evaluation and Policy Analysis, 13*(2), 115–138.

Merwin, G. (1993). *Facilitative power: Strategy for restructuring educational leadership*. Unpublished doctoral dissertation, University of Oregon.

Mortimore, P., & Sammons, P. (1987). New evidence on effective elementary schools. *Educational Leadership, 45*(1), 4–8.

Muncey, D., & McQuillan, P. (1993). Preliminary findings from a five-year study of the coalition of essential schools. *Phi Delta Kappan, 74*(6), 486–489.

Murphy, J., & Hallinger, P. (Ed.). (1993). *Restructuring Schooling: Learning from ongoing efforts*. Newbury Park, CA: Corwin.

National Center for Education and the Economy, Commission on the Skills of the American Work Force. (1990). *America's choice: High skills or low wages!* Rochester, NY: Author.

Purkey, S., & Smith, M. (1983). Effective schools: A review. *Elementary School Journal, 83,* 427–452.

Silns, H. C. (1992). Effective leadership for school reform. *Alberta Journal of Educational Research, 38*(4), 317–334.

Smith, M. S., & O'Day, J. (1991). Systemic school reform. In S. H. Fuhrman & B. Malen (Eds.), *The politics of curriculum and testing: The 1990 yearbook of the politics of education association* (pp. 233–267). Philadelphia: Falmer.

Steffy, B. (1993). *The Kentucky Education Reform Act: Lessons for America*. Lancaster, PA: Technomics.

Teddlie, C., & Stringfield, S. (1993). *Schools make a difference*. New York: Teachers College.

U.S. Department of Education. (1983). *A nation at risk: The imperative for educational reform*. Washington, DC: Author.

Verstegen, D. A. (1994). Reforming American education policy. *Educational Administration Quarterly, 30*(3), 365–390.

Weiss, C. H. (1977). Research for policy's sake: The enlightenment function of social research. *Policy Analysis, 3,* 531–545.

Wilson, B., & Rossman, G. (1993). *Mandating academic excellence*. New York: Teachers College Press.

chapter 8

Correlational Research

Joseph Wright heads the history department of a large urban high school. He believes that many of his students do poorly in history because they lack good study skills. In talking with a professor of education at a nearby university, Joseph learned about a measure of study skills that is appropriate for high school students. The professor encouraged Joseph to test his theory by giving this measure to all the students enrolled in his history classes at the beginning of the term. According to the professor, if Joseph's theory is correct, the students' scores on the study skills measure should be related to their history course grades. This sounds reasonable to Joseph, but he does not fully understand the logic of the research design and how to analyze the data in order to test his theory.

By reading this chapter, you will develop an understanding of the data-collection procedures that were recommended for Joseph's study of the possible relationship between his students' study skills and their history course grades. These procedures constitute a type of investigation called correlational research. You will learn how correlational research makes it possible to investigate the precise extent of the relationship between two or more variables, or to predict an important criterion from variables that are related to the criterion. A reprint of a published correlational study is included at the end of the chapter. ●

OBJECTIVES

After studying this chapter, you will be able to

1. explain how calculation of a correlation coefficient is used to describe the relationship between variables.

2. describe the advantages and limitations of correlational research compared to causal-comparative or experimental research.

3. understand scattergrams and the possible interpretations of a correlation between variables *A* and *B*.

4. explain the difference between bivariate and multivariate correlational statistics, and give an example of each.

5. explain how characteristics of the research data affect researchers' choice of a correlational statistic for analyzing the data.

6. describe how relationship and prediction studies differ in design and in their interpretations of the significance of correlational research findings.

THE NATURE OF CORRELATIONAL RESEARCH

Both correlational research and causal-comparative research investigate relationships between variables. As you learned in Chapter 7, causal-comparative studies determine relationships by examining whether groups that differ on a specific characteristic (typically an independent variable) also differ on another characteristic (typically a dependent variable). For example, students scoring high on a variable such as popularity with peers might be compared with students scoring low on the variable. Having selected groups that differ on this independent variable, the researcher then determines whether these groups also differ on other variables, such as academic achievement and attitude toward school.

By contrast, correlational research examines all the levels of the variables that are measured. For example, popularity with peers is not actually dichotomous. Although some students are high in popularity and others are low, there are many students whose score on a measure of popularity would fall at various points between these extremes. In **correlational research,** the relationship of all these scores (not just high versus low) to students' scores on other variables is calculated. The statistical procedure used for this purpose is correlation.

Correlation Coefficients

To determine the degree of the relationship between two variables, researchers calculate a statistic called a correlation coefficient. To understand the correlation coefficient, it is helpful to think about individual differences. For example, students differ in their level of artistic ability. If everyone had the same level of artistic ability, there would be little interest in studying its determinants or in predicting it. Yet people do differ in this ability, and these variations can have important personal and social consequences. If researchers could discover the causes of individual differences in artistic ability, this knowledge might prove useful in helping individuals maximize their artistic potential.

Let us consider the role of the correlation coefficient in this kind of investigation. Imagine that a random sample of students earned scores varying from 40 to 100 on a measure of artistic ability. We want to determine whether students' scores on another variable, such as intelligence as measured by an IQ test, are related to their scores on the measure of artistic ability. Suppose that all students who received a score of 40 on artistic ability had an IQ score of 85, whereas those with an artistic ability score of 41 had an IQ score of 86. Imagine that this pattern continued through the entire range of scores, so that students with an artistic ability score of 100 had IQ scores of 145. In this case we would have reason to believe that there is a **positive correlation** between artistic ability and intelligence in the general student population.

Suppose, by contrast, that students obtaining a particular artistic ability score, indicated by a **positive correlation** between these two variables, had widely varying IQ scores. For example, students with scores of 40 on the artistic ability measure had IQ scores ranging from 85 to 145, and students with scores of 100 on the artistic ability measure also had IQ scores across the same range. Thus there is no relationship between the two variables. Still another possibility is that students with progressively higher artistic ability scores could earn progressively lower IQ scores. In this case, there is a **negative correlation** between artistic ability and intelligence.

A **correlation coefficient** is a precise mathematical expression of the types of relationships between variables described above. In other words, the coefficient indicates the extent to which scores on one variable covary with scores on another variable.

Advantages and Limitations of Correlational Research

Advantages

1. Determining the Extent of a Relationship.   Correlational research allows researchers to determine not only whether a relationship between variables exists, but also the extent of the relationship between them. For example, if we find in a study that the correlation between variable A and variable B is close to 1.00 (the highest possible positive correlation between two variables), then we can confidently say that in the sample we studied variables A and B are highly related.

2. Comparing Relationships.   Another advantage of correlational research is that we can compare one correlation coefficient to another. By doing so we can readily see whether variable A and variable B are more closely related to each other than variable A and variable C (or variable C and variable D). For example, suppose the correlation between GPA and amount of time spent studying is .45, and the correlation coefficient expressing the relationship between GPA and parental income is .23. By comparing these coefficients we can readily conclude that study time is more closely related to GPA than parental income is.

3. Determining Relationships among More Than Two Variables.   Correlational research also makes it possible to analyze the relationships between more than two variables at a time. Thus it enables researchers to investigate how several variables, either singly or in combination, might affect a particular pattern of behavior, such as attention deficit disorder or mathematical aptitude. By contrast, causal-comparative or experimental research are best suited to studying the effects of only one or two variables at a time. Suppose that we wish to study the relationship between specific teaching behaviors and elementary school students' mathematics achievement. We could conduct a correlational research study in which observers record the degree to which a sample of elementary teachers uses ten different teaching techniques while teaching mathematics over a period of several weeks. At the end of the observation period, each teacher would have been scored on each of the ten specific techniques that were observed. Achievement tests would be administered to the students in these teachers' classrooms before and after the observation period. To estimate the degree to which each technique predicted students' achievement in mathematics, a correlation coefficient would be computed between each **predictor variable** (that is, a particular teaching technique) and students' postobservation achievement, which is the **criterion variable.** (The researchers might use partial correlation, a special form of correlation, to correct for initial differences in students' preobservation mathematics achievement.) Thus, the researchers can study the potential effects of ten teaching techniques in a single correlational study, whereas only a few of these techniques feasibly could be manipulated in an experimental study.

Limitations

1. Difficulty of Causal Inferences.   Many correlational studies are done to investigate cause-and-effect relationships between variables. However, it is difficult to make inferences about cause and effect from the results of a correlational study. When variables *A* and *B* are correlated, researchers cannot definitively conclude that *A* caused *B*, that *B* caused *A*, or that both *A* and *B* are caused by some third variable, *C*. After the fact, researchers usually can give plausible explanations for any correlational result, be it positive or negative in direction; high, low, or near-zero in extent; and involving two or more than two variables. The best opportunity for concluding a cause-and-effect relationship based on correlational research is when the variables that are correlated were selected on the basis of a theoretical rationale. Two multivariate correlational statistics that involve generating hypotheses based on theory, and thus are useful for investigating possible causal links among correlated variables, are described later in the chapter.

2. Chance Findings.   When a large number of variables are correlated with each other, some variables will correlate significantly with each other by chance alone. If the study were repeated, these chance findings would not be replicated. Say that researchers found a positive, significant correlation between weight and GPA, for example. If the researchers studied another sample specifically on the relationship between these two variables, a nonsignificant correlation between them is quite likely to occur.

SCATTERGRAMS

The correlation between two variables can be represented pictorially by a scattergram. A **scattergram** plots each individual's score on one variable on the horizontal, or x, axis of a chart and plots each individual's score on another variable on the vertical, or y, axis. The two scores of each individual in the sample are thus represented by a single point on the scattergram, the point where that individual's scores on the two variables intersect.

Figure 8.1 presents several scattergrams. The first shows a perfect positive correlation. Each point marks one individual's scores on the two variables. All the points fall on a straight diagonal line, which is called the **line of best fit.** The

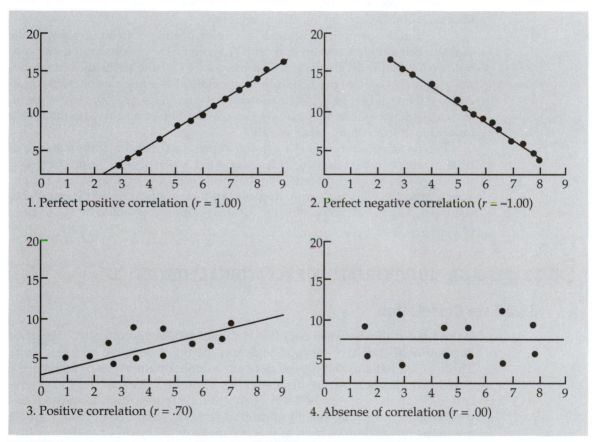

FIGURE 8.1   Scattergrams Showing Different Degrees and Directions of Relationship between Two Variables

Source. Adapted from Figure 11.1 on p. 410 in Gall, M. D., Borg, W. R., & Gall, J. P. (1996). *Educational research: An introduction* (6th ed.). Boston, MA: Allyn and Bacon. Copyright © 1996 by Pearson Education. Adapted by permission of the publisher.

line starts at the low end of both the x axis and the y axis, and it moves up at a 45-degree angle to the high end of both the x axis and the y axis. This graph indicates that each unit of increment, or increase, in the x-axis variable is accompanied by a unit of increment in the y-axis variable. The correlation coefficient is 1.00, meaning that if we know the individual's score on one variable, we can predict perfectly that individual's score on the other variable.

The second scattergram indicates a perfect negative correlation. Here again, as in scattergram 1, all the points fall on a straight diagonal line. In this case, however, the line starts at the high end of the y axis and the low end of the x axis and moves down at a 45-degree angle to the low end of the y axis and the high end of the x axis. This scattergram corresponds to a correlation coefficient of –1.00, indicating that each unit of increment on the y axis is accompanied by a decrement, or decrease, of one unit on the x axis. As with a perfect positive correlation, we can predict perfectly an individual's score on one variable if we know that individual's score on the other variable.

The third scattergram indicates a fairly high positive correlation between the two variables. If we know an individual's score on the x-axis variable, we cannot predict that individual's score on the y-axis variable perfectly, but we can make a fairly accurate prediction. A mathematical formula can be used to calculate the line of best fit, which is shown on the scattergram. If we know the individual's score on one variable, we can use the line of best fit to estimate the individual's score on the other variable.

The fourth scattergram is a graphic representation of a complete lack of relationship between two variables. Knowing a person's score on the x-axis variable is of no value in predicting that person's score on the y-axis variable. This relationship is graphically depicted by a line of best fit that is parallel to the x axis. The correlation coefficient for this relationship would be .00, or close to it.

Bivariate and Multivariate Correlational Statistics

Bivariate Correlation

If the relationship between only two variables is being investigated, **bivariate correlational statistics** are used to determine the correlation between them. The specific statistic that is used depends mainly on the types of scores to be correlated. (Score types are discussed in Chapter 6.) The data for many educational variables are in the form of continuous scores, such as individuals' total score on an achievement test containing many items. Sometimes the data are in the form of ranks, such as placing students in the order of their overall GPA. Some data are available in the form of a *dichotomy*, meaning that individuals are classified into two categories based on the presence or absence of a particular characteristic. For example, students can be classified as passing or failing a course, which is an artificial dichotomy because selection of the cut-off point for passing is arbitrary. Individuals also can be classified as female or male, which is a true dichotomy because it is based on a naturally occurring difference. Finally, some data are available in the form of categories. For example, students could be classified by the sport they most like to play: volleyball, football, soccer, tennis, and so on. These sports cannot be placed on a scale from high to low or less to more; rather, each sport is a separate, discrete category.

Table 8.1 briefly describes the most widely used types of bivariate correlational statistics. Probably the best-known bivariate correlational statistic is *r*, also called the *Pearson product-moment correlation coefficient*. Because *r* has a small standard error, researchers often compute *r* for any two sets of scores, even if they are not continuous scores. The other bivariate correlational statistics in Table 8.1 are used less frequently, but are more appropriate under the conditions listed in the "Remarks" column. Although a correlation coefficient theoretically can vary only from −1.00 to +1.00, for some of these statistics its value may be greater than 1.

TABLE 8.1 Bivariate Correlational Techniques for Different Forms of Variables

TECHNIQUE	SYMBOL	VARIABLE 1	VARIABLE 2	REMARKS
Product-moment correlation	r	Continuous	Continuous	The most stable technique, i.e., smallest standard error
Rank-difference correlation (*rho*)	ρ	Ranks	Ranks	A special form of product-moment correlation, used when the number of cases is under 30
Kendall's *tau*	τ	Ranks	Ranks	Preferable to *rho* for numbers under 10
Biserial correlation	r_{bis}	Artificial dichotomy	Continuous	Values can exceed 1, and have a larger standard error than *r*; commonly used in item analysis
Widespread biserial correlation	r_{wbis}	Widespread artificial dichotomy	Continuous	Used when researchers are interested in individuals at the extremes on the dichotomized variable
Point-biserial correlation	r_{pbis}	True dichotomy	Continuous	Yields a lower correlation than r_{bis}
Tetrachoric correlation	r_{t}	Artificial dichotomy	Artificial dichotomy	Used when both variables can be split at critical points
Phi coefficient	ϕ	True dichotomy	True dichotomy	Used in calculating inter-item correlations
Contingency coefficient	C	Two or more categories	Two or more categories	Comparable to r_{t} under certain conditions; closely related to chi-square
Correlation ratio, *eta*	η	Continuous	Continuous	Used to detect nonlinear relationships

Source. Adapted from Table 11.3 on p. 428 in Gall, M. D., Borg, W. R., & Gall, J. P. (1996). *Educational research: An introduction* (6th ed.). Boston, MA: Allyn and Bacon. Copyright by Pearson Education. Adapted by permission of the publisher.

Multivariate Correlation

If the relationship between more than two variables is being investigated, **multivariate correlational statistics** are used. Table 8.2 provides a brief summary of the major multivariate correlational statistics and their uses.

Multiple Regression.   Multiple regression probably is the most commonly used multivariate correlational statistic. It is appropriate in situations where researchers have scores on two or more measures for a group of individuals and want to determine how well a combination of these scores predicts their performance on an outcome or criterion measure. For example, suppose that researchers have the scores of a group of teachers working overseas on three measures: number of years of teaching experience, extent of travel while growing up, and tolerance for ambiguity. The researchers wish to know whether these measures can accurately predict the teachers' scores on a measure of adaptation to the overseas culture in which they are working. One approach to this question is to compute a separate correlation coefficient between each of the three predictor variables and the outcome measure. A more precise approach is a **multiple regression** analysis, which will determine whether some combination of the three predictor measures correlates better with the outcome measure than any one predictor variable alone.

Discriminant Analysis.   **Discriminant analysis** is a specialized form of multiple regression. Suppose that the outcome measure in the above example were a dichotomous variable (e.g., adapted well to the overseas culture versus adapted poorly) rather than a continuous variable (e.g., degree of adaptation to the over-

---

TABLE 8.2   **Multivariate Correlational Statistics and Their Uses**

Multiple regression	Used to determine the correlation (R) between a criterion variable and a combination of two or more predictor variables
Discriminant analysis	Used to determine the correlation between two or more predictor variables and a dichotomous criterion variable
Canonical correlation	Used to predict a combination of several criterion variables from a combination of several predictor variables
Path analysis	Used to test theories about hypothesized causal links between variables that are correlated
Structural equation modeling	Used to test theories about hypothesized causal links between variables that are correlated; yields more valid and reliable measures of the variables to be analyzed than does path analysis
Factor analysis	Used to reduce a large number of variables to a few factors by combining variables that are moderately or highly correlated with one another
Differential analysis	Used to examine correlations between variables among homogeneous subgroups within a sample; can be used to identify moderator variables that improve a measure's predictive validity

seas culture). In this case the researchers would use discriminant analysis to determine the correlation between teachers' scores on the three predictor variables and their adaptation to the overseas culture.

Canonical Correlation. **Canonical correlation** is another specialized form of multiple regression. It is used when there are multiple measures of the outcome variable. For example, suppose that the researchers administer several measures of adaptation, each assessing adaptation to a different aspect of the culture (e.g., the food, the climate, or the local customs). Canonical correlation enables researchers to determine which combination of predictor measures best correlates with a composite factor that represents the various outcome measures.

Investigation of Causal Links. **Path analysis** and **structural equation modeling** are sophisticated multivariate techniques for testing causal links among the different variables that have been measured. For example, suppose that the researchers hypothesize that, among teachers, (1) childhood travel experiences lead to (2) tolerance for ambiguity and (3) desire for travel as an adult, and that (2) and (3) make it more likely that a teacher will (4) seek an overseas teaching experience and (5) adapt well to the experience. Path analysis and structural equation modeling are methods for testing the validity of the hypothesized causal links involving these five factors. The study that is reprinted in this chapter involves the use of structural equation modeling to investigate the influence of homework on children's grades in elementary school.

Factor Analysis. Researchers sometimes wish to determine whether the variables they have measured reflect a smaller number of underlying factors. **Factor analysis** is a multivariate correlational statistic that allows them to do so. For example, suppose that researchers have developed measures of eight study skills: (1) organizing one's study materials, (2) time management, (3) classroom listening, (4) classroom note-taking, (5) planning for assigned papers, (6) writing assigned papers, (7) preparing for tests, and (8) taking tests. The researchers wonder whether these are related skills, meaning that students who are high on one skill are likely to be high on all or some subset of the other skills. Factor analysis is a correlational technique that can examine all eight measures and determine whether they cluster into a smaller number of factors. Perhaps the eight study skills reflect three underlying factors: (1) skills that involve writing, (2) skills that involve planning, and (3) skills that involve recall of learned information. Factor analysis can reveal this underlying structure of factors, if indeed it exists.

Differential Analysis. The final multivariate technique shown in Table 8.2 is differential analysis, which sometimes is used in prediction research. **Differential analysis** is the technique of using moderator variables to form subgroups when examining the relationship between two other variables. For example, suppose that we have reason to believe that self-esteem has more effect on school performance for students of lower socioeconomic status (SES) than for students of higher SES. Socioeconomic status, then, is a third variable—called a **moderator variable**—that is thought to mediate the relationship between the first two variables. Let's say that the correlation coefficient for the relationship between self-esteem and school performance is .40 for low-SES students and .25 for high-SES students. These results demonstrate that SES moderates (or mediates) the relationship between self-esteem and school performance.

RELATIONSHIP STUDIES AND PREDICTION STUDIES

Correlational statistics are used for two primary purposes in educational research: (1) to explore the nature of the relationship between variables of interest to educators, and (2) to determine variables that can be used to predict important educational or personal characteristics of individuals that will not occur until later. Correlational research studies usually have one or the other of these purposes, and differ in design accordingly. We use the terms **relationship study** and **prediction study** to distinguish these two purposes.

In some relationship studies, researchers use the correlational method to examine possible cause-and-effect relationships between variables, such as whether parents' educational level affects their children's success in school. In other relationship studies, the researchers want to gain a better understanding of factors that contribute to a complex characteristic, such as artistic ability. For example, if researchers were to find that observational skills, visual acuity, small-muscle dexterity, and creative imagination are all related to artistic ability, they would have gained some insight into the nature of this complex characteristic.

Relationship studies usually explore the relationships between measures of different variables obtained from the same individuals at the same point in time. By contrast, in prediction studies, some variables (the predictor variables) are measured at one point in time, and other variables (the criterion variables) are measured at a later point in time. This procedure is followed because the goal of prediction studies is to forecast important future behavior.

Good predictor variables are important whether or not we understand why they predict well. For example, the U.S. Air Force has developed a battery of tests that can be given to applicants for pilot training. Prediction studies have shown that each of these tests is correlated with later success in pilot training. By administering this battery of tests and studying the correlations obtained in previous research, the researcher can predict the likelihood that any given individual will complete the pilot-training program successfully.

STATISTICAL AND PRACTICAL SIGNIFICANCE OF CORRELATION COEFFICIENTS

Any correlation coefficient can be tested to determine whether it has **statistical significance.** If it is statistically significant, we can conclude that a correlation coefficient this great is unlikely to have occurred by chance if there is in fact no relationship between variables A and B in the population from which the sample was drawn. Whether or not a correlation coefficient of a particular size is statistically significant depends on several factors, including the significance level selected, the number of participants in the research sample, whether the researchers predicted the (positive or negative) direction of the relationship, and the variability of the scores.

Because its focus is on exploration and understanding, a relationship study is meaningful whether the correlation coefficient obtained is low or high, positive or negative. Any correlation coefficient contributes to an understanding of the educational phenomena involved. Therefore, in a relationship study the statistical significance of the correlation coefficient is far more important than its practical significance.

In prediction studies, researchers are concerned with both the statistical significance of the correlation coefficient and its practical significance. If the coefficient is sufficiently large to achieve statistical significance, we can be fairly confident that the observed relationship is not a chance finding. If the predictor variable is highly correlated with an important criterion variable, it will be useful for improving educational practice, and thus the correlation coefficient also has **practical significance.** For example, an aptitude measure that has been shown to relate to later school performance has many practical applications. School counselors could use students' scores on the aptitude measure to counsel students about what subjects to take or what careers they might want to explore. Scores also could be used to identify children who might need special education or to assign students to remedial or advanced classes.

EXAMPLE OF OUTLINING A RESEARCH PROPOSAL

This feature of the chapter gives you an example of how to outline a research proposal using the form in Appendix 1. The example, involving a proposal to study curriculum alignment, is introduced in Chapter 2.

In Chapter 7, we took the first research question stated in the Example section of Chapter 2 and restated it as follows: "Is there a difference between large and small school districts in the percentage of high schools that have engaged in curriculum alignment?" Note that the independent variable, school district size, is treated as dichotomous (large or small), even though size is a continuum. For this reason, the research design is causal-comparative.

We could decide, instead, to determine the actual size of each district—measured, let's say, as the number of enrolled students—and use that number in the statistical analyses. In other words, we could decide to treat school district size as a continuous variable. Now our research design is correlational, because all the levels of each variable (school district size and extent of curriculum alignment) are measured and included in the statistical analysis.

We show below how we filled out the part of the proposal outline pertaining to the research design. You will note that the statements are virtually the same as those in the example at the end of Chapter 7, because causal-comparative designs and correlational designs both explore the relationship between natural variations in two or more variables without experimenter manipulation.

4. RESEARCH DESIGN
   A. *Research design.* The research design is correlational. The independent variable is school district size, and the dependent variable is extent of curriculum alignment. Variations in the independent variable (school district size) occur naturally without researcher manipulation, so the research design is not experimental.

   We are studying a potential cause-and-effect relationship, because we hypothesize that the size of a school district (the presumed causal factor) has an influence on how much curriculum alignment has occurred in its schools (the presumed effect). Our rationale for this hypothesis is that as districts increase in size, they have more resources that they can allocate for the process of curriculum alignment and, therefore, are likely to be further ahead in the process.

   B. *Threats to internal validity.* We are aware that other independent variables, besides the one we have chosen to study (school size), also might have an effect on the extent of curriculum alignment. For example, it might be that parents of students in larger districts are more likely to put pressure on local educators to improve student performance on high-stakes tests. This pressure might compel the educators to make curriculum alignment a high priority.

   If this is true, parental pressure—not internal factors in the school system—would be the key causal factor influencing the extent of curriculum alignment. The study that we are proposing will not measure this variable.

   C. *Threats to external validity.* The accessible population from which the sample will be drawn is school districts in Oregon. High-stakes testing and curriculum alignment are relatively recent movements in education, so different states are likely to have different budgets and strategies for implementing them. Therefore, generalizations of findings from the study must be cautious.

   In reporting the study, we will provide a detailed description of Oregon's state-level context for high-stakes testing and curriculum alignment so that educators in other states can compare it with their context. To the extent that the contexts are similar, they might be more confident about generalizing our findings to their state.

SELF-CHECK TEST

1. A researcher finds that in her research sample, as particular students score higher than other students on variable *A*, they tend to score lower on variable *B*. The researcher can conclude that
   a. variables *A* and *B* are positively correlated in this sample.
   b. variables *A* and *B* are negatively correlated in this sample.
   c. there is a curvilinear relationship between variables *A* and *B*.
   d. the correlation between variables *A* and *B* is statistically significant.

2. Correlational research is superior to causal-comparative research in
   a. determining the causal relationship between two variables.
   b. determining the precise extent of the relationship between two variables.
   c. studying the effects of only one variable at a time.
   d. studying variables that involve discrete categories.

3. Researchers calculated correlations between each pair of twenty variables and found several statistically significant correlations. When they repeated the study, none of these pairs of variables were significantly correlated. This occurrence is most likely due to the
   a. selection of variables to be correlated based on a theoretical rationale.
   b. likelihood that when many variables are intercorrelated, some statistically significant correlations will occur by chance.
   c. failure to hypothesize in advance which variables had a causal effect on which other variables.
   d. selection of inappropriate predictor variables.

4. A scattergram is helpful in indicating all of the following except
   a. the direction of the relationship between two variables.
   b. the extent of the relationship between two variables.
   c. the relationship between more than two variables.
   d. whether there is no relationship between two variables.

5. A perfect negative correlation between variables *A* and *B* means that
   a. there is no relationship between individuals' scores on variable *A* and their scores on variable *B*.
   b. the higher an individual's score on variable *A*, the higher that individual's score on variable *B*.
   c. the higher an individual's score on variable *A*, the lower that individual's score on variable *B*.
   d. variations in individuals' scores on variable *A* caused the observed variations in individuals' scores on variable *B*.

6. Unlike multivariate correlational statistics, bivariate correlational statistics
   a. involve correlations between only two variables.
   b. are useful for determining causal relationships.

    c. are appropriate for measuring the relationship between more than two variables.

    d. are suitable for use in prediction studies.

7. The most important consideration in choosing a bivariate correlational statistic is
   a. the form of the scores for each variable.
   b. the number of variables to be correlated.
   c. whether one is trying to study a cause-and-effect relationship or predict a criterion variable.
   d. the size of the research sample.

8. If researchers wish to determine whether ten measured variables cluster into a smaller set of underlying characteristics, they are likely to use
   a. multiple regression.
   b. structural equation modeling.
   c. path analysis.
   d. factor analysis.

9. If variable *A* is significantly correlated with variable *B* in the research sample, we can conclude that
   a. there is likely to be a relationship between variables *A* and *B* in the population.
   b. variable *A* is a suitable predictor of variable *B*.
   c. no other variables are likely to correlate positively with variable *A*.
   d. variable *A* causes variable *B*.

10. The primary goal of a relationship study in correlational research is to
   a. determine cause-and-effect relationships between variables.
   b. forecast important future behaviors.
   c. discover statistically significant relationships between variables.
   d. discover practically significant relationships between variables.

Resources for Further Study

Grimm, L. G., & Yarnold, P. R. (Eds.). (2000). *Reading and understanding more multivariate statistics.* Washington, DC: American Psychological Association.

    This book and its predecessor, Reading and Understanding Multivariate Statistics *(1995), provide an overview of multivariate statistical techniques and the types of research questions they can answer. Among the covered techniques are correlation, multiple regression, path analysis, factor analysis, multivariate analysis of variance, and discriminant analysis.*

Jacoby, W. G. (1997). *Statistical graphics for univariate and bivariate data.* Thousand Oaks, CA: Sage.

    The author shows how graphical displays can enhance researchers' understanding and presentation of data. Among the graphical displays discussed in the book are histograms, scatterplots, and box plots.

Pedhazur, E. J. (1997). *Multiple regression in behavioral research: Explanation and prediction* (3rd ed.). Belmont, CA: Wadsworth.

> *The author provides an advanced treatment of the mathematical basis for multiple regression, the assumptions underlying its use, its role in research studies, and computational procedures.*

In the following section of the chapter you will read a research article that illustrates a correlational research study. It is preceded by comments written especially for this book by two of the article authors. Then the article itself is reprinted in full, just as it appeared when originally published. Where appropriate, we have added footnotes to help you understand the information contained in the article.

SAMPLE CORRELATIONAL RESEARCH STUDY

A Model of Homework's Influence on the Performance Evaluations of Elementary School Students

Cooper, H., Jackson, K., Nye, B., & Lindsay, J. J. (2001). A model of homework's influence on the performance evaluations of elementary school students. *The Journal of Experimental Education, 69,* 181–199.

● **RESEARCHER'S COMMENTS,** *Prepared by Harris Cooper*

Homework is an integral part of every child's schooling experience. It is also a frequent source of friction between schools and families. As a result, when I began to explore the relationship between homework and achievement in the early 1980s, I was surprised to discover how sparse and scattered the research literature was. Even more surprising was that many teachers told me when I began to speak about this topic that learning what made for a good homework assignment was rarely, if ever, covered as part of their teacher education. This led me to believe that pursuing homework as a research topic would allow me to make an important contribution both to the research literature and to how children were taught in schools. I was also not unmoved by the fact that my first child was a toddler at the time, and thus homework would soon become an important part of my family's life!

Of course, the lack of evidence-based knowledge about homework did not mean that many educators and educational pundits had not opined on the value of homework and how homework could be used most effectively. My first job, then, was to gather up all the literature on homework and attempt to devise a scheme to help me make sense of it. Ultimately, I read over 200 articles on homework before I put pencil to paper.

My training as a social psychologist led me to think about organizing the literature with a focus on the relationships between the actors in the homework process, that is, the teacher, student, and parents. It also led me to give the concept of *attitudes,* a central idea in the history of social psychology, a prominent place in the conceptual model that guided the research. Many social psychological explanations of behaviors follow a sequence in which interpersonal environments are conceived as setting the stage on which people engage in mutual influence. This perspective and sequencing are expressed in the model depicted in Table 1 of the article.

The data used in the article were part of a larger data set we collected that were meant to shed light on many different aspects of the homework process. For instance, in other articles we asked questions regarding why young children seemed to benefit less from homework than older children (Mulhenbruck, Cooper, Nye & Lindsay, 1999), what types of parent involvement were most helpful (Cooper, Lindsay & Nye, 2000), and how homework fit into the other activities that students pursue after school (Cooper, Valentine, Nye & Lindsay, 1999). We used the same data set to help answer all these questions, focusing on different variables for each.

Collecting large data sets also involves the cooperation of many researchers. For example, Barbara Nye, the Director of the Tennessee State University Center for Excellence in Basic Skills, was primarily responsible for obtaining the cooperation of the school districts and schools that took part in the study. Jim Lindsay, at the time a graduate student at the University of Missouri, managed the data collection and data entry.

In addition, the analyses used in this study involved the application of structural equation modeling. This is an advanced statistical technique that requires considerable specialized training to be employed successfully. Because this technique was outside my and the other team members' areas of expertise, I approached a colleague, Kristina Jackson, who was at the time a post-doctoral fellow at the University of Missouri and knew much more about structural equation modeling than we did. This is not an unusual circumstance when researchers collaborate to collect and analyze large, multipurpose data sets. Different researchers will take responsibility for those aspects of the project that are of greatest interest to them and/or for which they have specialized expertise. Without Kristina, the insights we learned from conducting the analyses contained in the article reprinted below could not have been realized.

● RESEARCHER'S COMMENTS, *Prepared by Kristina Jackson*

Structural equation modeling is an advanced statistical technique that has become increasingly popular with researchers. Its value lies in the opportunity to examine the relationships between a number of constructs all at once. We live in a complex world where behaviors are multiply determined, so research that examines only two or three constructs in isolation can be misleading. For example, although other researchers have shown that student norms are associated with classroom grades, our results suggested that this association may be due to positive parent involvement in homework.

The purpose of structural equation modeling is to generate a model based on a theory (and often depicted by a figure) that best fits the data. Typically, the researcher tries different models to determine the one that best fits the data (because we can't change our data!). When we applied structural equation modeling to the data in this study, we found that we had to make some modifications to our original theoretical model. For example, one modification was to combine student and parent reports of parent facilitation. We found that both these constructs had similar associations with student norms, student ability, and parent attitude, and when we combined them the resulting model better fitted the data.

Structural equation modeling has some additional requirements that we had to meet. One requirement is that there must be a sufficient number of respondents to reliably estimate the model's parameters. A problem that we had was that we would have liked to include teacher attitude and experience in our model; however, many of the students in our study had the same teacher. Although we had 214 student participants, we had only twenty-five teachers, which wasn't enough for the model. Yet despite the restrictions and complications of its use, the flexibility of structural equation modeling permits researchers to draw conclusions from correlational data that far outweigh its costs. We summarize these findings and their implications in our discussion.

References

Cooper, H., Lindsay, J. J. & Nye, B. (2000). Homework in the home: How student, family and parenting style differences relate to the homework process. *Contemporary Educational Psychology, 25,* 464–487.

Cooper, H., Valentine, J. C., Nye, B. & Lindsay, J. J. (1999). Relationships between five after-school activities and academic achievement. *Journal of Educational Psychology, 91,* 1–10.

Mulhenbruck, L., Cooper, H., Nye, B. & Lindsay, J. J. (1999). Homework and achievement: Explaining the different relations at the elementary and secondary school levels. *Social Psychology of Education, 4,* 295–317.

A Model of Homework's Influence on the Performance Evaluations of Elementary School Students

Harris Cooper
University of Missouri—Columbia

Kristina Jackson
University of Missouri—Columbia

Barbara Nye
Tennessee State University

James J. Lindsay
Behavioral Health Concepts

Abstract

This study was the first to test a model of the influence of homework on classroom performance using a sample of elementary school students. A total of 28 teachers in Grades 2

Cooper, H., Jackson, K., Nye, B., & Lindsay, J. J. (2001). A model of homework's influence on the performance evaluations of elementary school students. *The Journal of Experimental Education, 69,* 181–199. Reprinted with permission of the Helen Dwight Reid Educational Foundation. Published by Heldref Publications, 1319 Eighteenth St., NW, Washington, DC 20036-1802. Copyright © 2001.

and 4 took part in the study, along with 428 students and parents. The authors used structural equation modeling to examine relationships among variables. Student norms were positively related to the elimination of distractions from homework by parents. Positive student norms, higher student ability, and positive parent attitudes toward homework were all related to greater parent facilitation. Student's attitude toward homework was unrelated to home and community factors but was related positively to parent attitudes toward homework. Classroom grades were unrelated to student's attitude toward homework but were predicted by how much homework the student completed (even after the use of homework in grading was controlled), by student ability, and by the amount of parent facilitation. More generally, parent facilitation was an important mediator of the relation between student norms, student ability, and parent attitudes toward homework, and the outcome of classroom grades.

Key words: elementary school students, homework, structural equation modeling

The completion of a homework assignment involves the complex interaction of more influences than any other pedagogical technique. Teachers structure and monitor homework assignments in a multitude of ways. Student individual differences play a significant role because—more so than classroom instruction—homework allows students considerable discretion about whether, when, and how to complete an assignment. Parents and siblings often participate in assignments—sometimes voluntarily, sometimes by design. The home influences the process by creating an environment that either facilitates or inhibits study. Students take cues from peers about how much importance to place on homework. Finally, the broader community plays a role by providing other leisure-time activities that compete for the student's time.

Research involving thousands of students shows little correlation between homework and test scores in elementary school, but the relationship grows positive and strong in secondary school (Cooper, 1989). There are several reasons why that might be the case (Mulhenbruck, Cooper, Nye, & Lindsay, in press). First, young children who are struggling in school probably take longer to finish assignments. Second, young children have limited ability to keep their attention focused. Distractions at home entice them away from the books spread out on the kitchen table. Third, young children have not yet learned good study skills. They do not know how to apportion their time between easy and hard tasks or how to engage in effective self-testing.

In light of the complex pattern of influences that can affect the value of a homework assignment, it seems necessary to propose models of the homework process that include multiple variables in sequential relation to one another. Our first purpose in the present article was to examine previous attempts to build and test models

of educational outcomes that use homework as an integral part of the achievement process. In carrying out that review, we found that few such models exist and that those that do exist are either untested or have been tested on high school samples only. Therefore, our second purpose was to propose and test a model of homework's influence on the classroom performance of elementary school students.

A REVIEW OF MODELS THAT INCLUDE HOMEWORK AS AN INFLUENCE ON ACHIEVEMENT

Coulter (1979) presented a temporal model of the homework process that was divided into three phases. In the first phase, teachers acted to motivate, structure, and facilitate the completion of assignments, and greater efforts on the teacher's part were assumed to lead to more successful assignments. Those efforts, along with the student's personal characteristics, determined whether students chose to do homework or to engage in other activities. During the home–community phase, several factors that affect performance—including whether the home learning environment was facilitative, the types of tutoring resources available, and whether community resources were available—combined to influence the student's actual performance on the assignment. Finally, Coulter's results suggested that during classroom follow-up, the amount of teacher feedback on homework, the correspondence of tested material to material included on homework, and the relating of homework assignments to other class work positively affected classroom test results, attitudes, and ultimately academic achievement.

Keith and his colleagues have used several large national data sets to test various models of academic achievement that included homework among the predictors. For example, Keith (1982) used the High School and Beyond data set to test a model that included the amount of time spent on homework as a predictor of high school grades. That model proposed that student's race and family background (i.e., parent's education and father's occupation) were exogenous variables affecting student's ability and field of study (i.e., academic or vocational).[a] Time spent on homework was seen as a function of those three variables, with higher ability students from higher socioeconomic status (SES) families expected to spend more time on homework. Student's grades in high school was the final variable in the model.

Keith, Reimers, Fehrman, Pottebaum, and Aubey (1986) also used the High School and Beyond data set, but in that analysis, student's gender was added as an exogenous variable, parental involvement was added as a second-stage variable, and time spent watching television was added concurrently with time spent on homework. They expected that more parental involvement in homework and less television watching would be positive influences on student achievement. The outcome measure was an average of reading and math scores on tests designed for the study. Keith et al. (1993) applied a similar model to data from the National Educational Longitudinal Study. Keith and Cool (1992) added the variables of quality of instruction and student motivation to a new analysis of High School and Beyond data set.

Keith's models included none of the initial classroom or classroom follow-up variables contained in Coulter's model, undoubtedly because information on those variables was not included in the longitudinal data sets he used. On the other hand, Keith's models are clearly richer in representation of student background factors. Also, Coulter never put his model to empirical test, whereas Keith used sophisticated path analysis and structural equation modeling (SEM) procedures to test his models.[b] In all Keith's analyses, homework was found to have significant direct effects on the performance measure, even after spurious effects (i.e., those effects attributable to homework's and achievement's common association with prior variables in the model) were taken into account.

Cooper (1989) presented a modified and expanded temporal model of the homework process (see Table 1).

That model was meant to provide a comprehensive account of the variables mentioned in educational research that might influence homework's impact on a list of educational outcomes. Cooper's (1989) model retained the notion that the homework process could be divided into two classroom phases, with a home–community phase separating them. Borrowing from Keith (1982), Cooper's model viewed student ability and other individual differences as exogenous to the process. However, the student characteristics of race and family background were not among the initial variables because they are typically used in research as proxy variables meant to assess indirectly differences in home environments. In the Cooper model, differences in home environments were directly represented under home–community factors. Homework assignment subject matter and student grade level were also included as exogenous factors.

Neither the Coulter (1979) nor the Keith (1982) models included a set of influences relating to the characteristics of the assignment. The Cooper (1989) model contained such a set, distinguishing assignments according to their length, purpose, skill area, degree of choice and individualization, and completion deadlines, and the social context in which homework was to be performed. Finally, the broad set of outcomes that Cooper suggested are influenced by the homework process are delineated in Table 1.

THE PRESENT STUDY

One glaring omission in research to date is that models of the homework process have yet to be tested on data obtained from elementary school students. Neither Coulter (1979) nor Cooper (1989) tested the models they proposed, and both data sets used in Keith's research included only students who were in the eighth grade or above.

a. In a model of cause-and-effect relationships between specified variables, an exogenous variable is one for which no other variable in the model is hypothesized to influence it. In Figure 1, which appears later in the article, "student ability" is an exogenous variable because no other variable is hypothesized to influence it.

b. Path analysis and structural equation modeling are similar statistical methods for testing the validity of a theory about causal linkages between three or more variables. These two methods can be contrasted with simple correlation, which only determines linkages between two variables. Table 2, which appears later in the article, shows simple correlations between each pair of variables that were studied.

TABLE 1   A Temporal Model of Factors Influencing the Effects of Homework

Exogenous Factors	Assignment Characteristics	Initial Classroom Factors	Home–Community Factors	Classroom Follow-Up	Outcomes or Effects
Student characteristics	Amount	Provision of materials	Competitors for student time	Feedback	Assignment completion
Ability	Purpose	Facilitators	Home environment	Written comments	Assignment performance
Motivation	Skill area used	Suggested approaches	Space	Grading	Positive effects
Study habits	Degree of individualization	Links to curriculum	Light	Incentives	Immediate academic
Subject matter	Degree of student choice	Other rationales	Quiet	Testing of related content	Long-term academic
Grade level	Completion deadlines		Materials	Use in class discussion	Nonacademic
	Social context		Others' involvement		Parental
			Parents		Negative effects
			Siblings		Satiation
			Other students		Denial of leisure time
					Parental involvement
					Cheating
					Increased student differences

Given that the relation between homework and achievement appears to be different at different grade levels, that omission is of great consequence. The present study, then, is the first to test an SEM model of the influences on homework and homework's subsequent influence on classroom performance with a sample of elementary school students.

The data for our analyses were drawn from a larger study of the homework process (Cooper, Lindsay, Nye, & Greathouse, 1998). In choosing the variables to include in the model, we used two considerations to guide our decisions. First, we wanted to include variables that were suggested by previous models. However, including all the variables in Figure 1 would make the model prohibitively large. Therefore, we focused on variables related to student individual differences and parent, home, and community influences. We left out of the model the initial classroom and classroom follow-up factors. That decision also simplified our task because, similar to Keith's model tests, we could conduct the analyses using the student as the unit of analysis. Had classroom factors been included, the classroom would have been the appropriate unit. Second, and also similar to Keith's work, we were constrained by the variables represented in the data set. That constraint primarily influenced the measured variables that were available. There were no instances in which we felt an unobserved factor had to be left out of the model because the data set included no indicator of it.

Following the several models we have described, we included in our model three exogenous variables: student ability level, parent attitudes toward homework, and the homework norm created by the behavior of other students in the class. The second stage, or home and community variables, included (a) distractions present in the home environment; (b) level of positive parent facilitation, lack of interference, or both (hereinafter referred to as parent facilitation); and (c) amount of time the student spent in other after-school activities. The exogenous home and community variables were posited to influence the student's attitude toward homework, which, in turn, would influence amount of homework the student completed. All the variables were then viewed as influencing the student's classroom performance. The observed variables used to represent each unobserved factor are described in the Method section.

We used SEM to examine relationships among our variables. SEM is similar to multivariate regression in

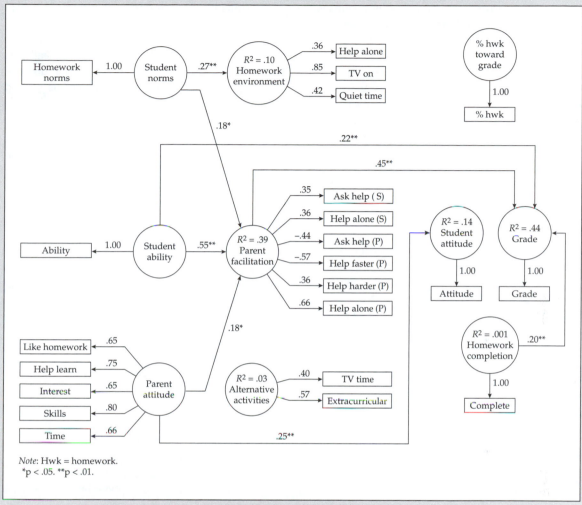

FIGURE 1 Student and Family Background Model of Student's Attitude toward Homework, Homework Completion, and Final Grade

its ability to examine relationships after accounting for relationships with other variables.[c] Moreover, SEM allows for the simultaneous estimation of direct and indirect effects and also provides overall fit indices for the model.

METHOD

Sample Size and Composition

To have a usable data unit, we obtained complete data from the teacher, at least 1 student in that teacher's

---

c. *Multivariate regression* is another term for multiple regression, which is a statistical method for determining the magnitude of the relationship between a criterion variable and a combination of two or more predictor variables. Multiple regression is less well suited for testing models of cause-and-effect relationships between variables than is structural equation modeling.

class, and 1 of that student's parents or guardians. A total of 28 teachers in Grades 2 and 4 agreed to take part in the study. When the data were analyzed, a total of 570 students and parents completed the questionnaires. However, only 428 respondents had no missing data and could be used in this analysis. Because a student's and that student's parent's responses formed a single data unit (about that student), the actual number of independent data units in the analyses was 214.

The response rate for students and parents was approximately 35%, somewhat lower than that obtained in other homework studies that required parents to complete and return questionnaires (Epstein, 1988; Bents-Hill et al., 1988). There may be several reasons for our lower response rate. First, our questionnaire was considerably longer than those used in previous research; therefore, it required parents to commit more time to complete and return it. Second, our response rate was based on completed questionnaires by both a student and 1 of the student's parents. Thus, our response rate was lowered if either the parent or the student did not participate. Although we would have liked to pursue nonresponding parents beyond the second mailing procedure, doing so was beyond the resources of our study. In 85% of the cases, the student's mother completed the parent questionnaire.

The vast majority of the teachers in our sample were White women, and more than half had over 10 years' teaching experience. About half of the teachers had advanced degrees (Master's level or beyond).

Three school districts agreed to take part in the research:

1. A large metropolitan public school district in Tennessee. The district serves nearly 65,000 students. About 58% of the students were White, and 39% were African American. About 45% of the students received free lunch. The participating teachers were drawn from one elementary school.
2. A suburban school district. Adjacent to the urban district, the suburban district served about 12,000 predominately White (94%) middle-class families; 6.5% of the students qualified for free lunch. Par-

ticipating teachers were drawn from two elementary schools.
3. A rural school district. This district served about 2,200 students, 90% of whom were White and 25% of whom were eligible for free lunch. The rural district participants came from five schools serving Grades K through 8.

When we compared the school-district descriptions with the characteristics of the respondents, we found that the respondents were not a random sample drawn from the districts; they were more likely to be White and less likely to be receiving free lunch than students in the districts as a whole. Therefore, care must be taken in generalizing our results to populations containing percentages of Whites and disadvantaged families that differ markedly from our sample statistics. However, minorities and low-SES families were already somewhat overrepresented in the three school districts when compared with national statistics.

Instruments

The homework survey, which we titled the Homework Process Inventory (HPI), was developed explicitly for this study. The questionnaire is a multi-item survey that has six different versions, one each for lower and upper grade students, their teachers, and their parents. The different versions include parallel questions, so that consistency of responses across the six versions can be examined. More complete descriptions of all the versions can be found in Cooper et al. (1998).

The HPI was pilot tested with small but heterogeneous samples of students, teachers, and parents before the actual data collection began. The pilot testing led to revisions in wording and the addition of questions. Consultants from the Academic Resource Center at the University of Missouri also examined the instrument.

For Grades 2 and 4, the HPI was completed with reference to homework in general, without regard to subject area. At those grade levels, students in the study had a single teacher and probably could not give reliable estimates of the amount of homework they were given or had completed in multiple subject areas. Likewise, we surmised that parents might be able to judge how much time their child spent on homework in general but not be able to distinguish reliably between homework in different subject areas.

Student and Family Background Factors. The presence of positive student norms was assessed with a single teacher item asking, "In general, how many of your students do you think actually finish their homework?" We used a 5-point scale, ranging from *all of them* to *none of them.* (All items were coded such that high scores represented the more positive or more frequent end of the dimension or behavior.)

We used a standardized achievement test, the Tennessee Comprehensive Assessment Program (TCAP), to assess student ability. The TCAP was given to all students in the second and fourth grades. The TCAP included both a norm-referenced and a criterion-referenced component.[d] The norm-referenced component consisted of the fourth edition of the Comprehensive Test of Basic Skills (CTBS/4; CTB, 1988). The criterion-referenced component was also developed by CTB but was customized for the Tennessee curriculum. We devised standardized raw score measures of achievement based on total TCAP score, standardized within grade level (with a mean of 0 and a standard deviation of 1). In that way, we were able to combine our scores across grade levels because each student's score was expressed as a departure, in standard deviation units, from the grade-level sample mean. The standardized raw scores ranged from −3.68 to 2.10.

We used three items to assess the availability of economic and time-related parent resources: (a) low or middle SES, which was based on a proxy variable of whether the student was eligible for free school lunch; (b) student and parent reports of whether an adult was usually at home when the student returned home from school; and (c) student and parent reports of the number of other individuals living in the home.[e] However,

during model development we found low correlations between SES and whether an adult was at home after school. Furthermore, the initial models revealed no significant relations involving the free-lunch and parent-at-home measures, so we dropped that variable from the analyses reported in the Results section.

We used five parent-report items to assess the extent to which the parent (a) liked homework, on a 5-point scale ranging from *like it very much* to *don't like it at all;* (b) thought homework helped their child learn, on a 3-point scale ranging from *helps very much* to *doesn't help at all;* (c) thought homework increased versus decreased interest in school, on a 5-point scale ranging from *increases it a lot* to *decreases it a lot;* (d) thought homework helped study skills, on a 3-point scale ranging from *helps very much* to *doesn't help at all;* and (e) thought homework helped the child learn how to manage time, on a 3-point scale ranging from *helps very much* to *doesn't help at all.*

Home and Community Factors. To assess the availability of a homework environment lacking distractions, we used three parent report items that tap the extent to which the homework environment is structured so as to minimize distractions. Those included (a) a binary item assessing whether the child was usually alone or with other people when homework was done; (b) an item assessing whether the television was generally on or off while the child did homework, on a 4-point scale ranging from *the television is always on* to *the television is always off* and (c) an item assessing how often the parent made the child set aside quiet time for doing homework, on a 5-point scale ranging from *all the time* to *never.* Although we also assessed student reports of those three items, the student items exhibited low interitem correlations among themselves and also with parent responses. An additional student report item that assessed where homework was completed (e.g., at school, in the kitchen, in the bedroom) was dropped

---

d. In a norm-referenced test, an individual's score is interpreted by comparing it to the scores earned by a norming group. In a criterion-referenced test, an individual's score is interpreted by comparing it to a prespecified standard of performance.

e. A proxy variable is an indirect measure of the variable that the researcher wishes to study. Proxy variables typically are specified when it is difficult to obtain a direct measure of the variable of interest. For example, socioeconomic status (SES) typically is determined by measures of parental income and occupation. Because it was not possible to obtain data on these measures, the researchers measured a similar variable (i.e., the proxy variable), which was student eligibility for a free school lunch.

because it was not clear how it would relate to the presence or absence of distractions.

To assess parent facilitation, we used three student and parent items asking how often (a) the student asks for help with homework from a family member, on a 5-point scale ranging from *all the time* to *never;* (b) someone else's help made it harder for the student to do homework, on a 5-point scale ranging from *all the time* to *never* (and reverse scored); and (c) someone else helped with homework by doing things the student should do him- or herself, on a 5-point scale ranging from *every night* to *never.* In addition, the parent facilitation assessment included a parent report of how often the student's homework required help from another, on a 5-point scale ranging from *every night* to *never,* and how often somebody helped so the child could finish faster, on a 5-point scale ranging from *all the time* to *never.* During model development, we dropped student reports of the extent to which the student asked for help with homework from a family member because that item had a low and nonsignificant factor loading, and we dropped the item asking how often the student asked for help because he or she did not understand the homework, again because of its low intercorrelation with the other items measuring parent facilitation.

We used two items to assess alternative activities. The first item was a student report of how much time was spent watching television every day, on a 4-point scale ranging from *I don't watch TV* to *I watch five or more shows every day.* The second item was a composite of two parent items, including the number of hours per week that the child spent on organized activity groups outside of school, on a 5-point scale ranging from *none* to *more than 10 items,* and the number of hours the student watched television every day.

Homework Outcome Variables. We used a single item to assess the student's attitude toward homework: "Do you think homework helps you learn?" Homework completion was assessed by a single student item, "How much of your homework do you finish?" Although parent reports of homework completion were assessed, those were uncorrelated with the student report ($r = .02$) and hence were not included in the analyses. We expected that the student would have greater awareness of the amount of homework completed than would the parent.

Finally, teachers provided the class grade the student would receive if the class ended on the day the teacher completed the questionnaire. For all analyses that included the grade variable, the extent to which homework counted in grade computation (on a 4-point scale ranging from *it does not count* to *more than 20%*) was controlled statistically.[f]

Procedures

Recruitment of Schools and Teachers. In October 1994, a meeting was held between the investigators and administrative personnel from each of the three participating school districts. At the meeting, the background and nature of the study were explained. After the meeting, each of the district administrators asked school principals if they were interested in allowing the study to be conducted in their schools. Names and addresses of consenting principals were then forwarded to the research staff, and a letter of consent was sent to each principal.

Principals then sent to the research staff lists of teachers in their school who had agreed to learn more about the study. A letter describing the study and a consent form were then sent to each interested teacher. A $20 honorarium was offered to each teacher who agreed to participate.

Questionnaire Administration. The students, their teachers, and their parents completed the HPI in February, March, and April 1995. Materials for completion

---

f. The researchers were interested in the effect of homework completion and related variables on students' grades, which were assigned by the teacher. If the teacher used the quality and completeness of students' homework as a factor in determining their grades, then grade would simply be another measure of homework rather than an independent measure of students' learning. Because the researchers could not ask teachers to remove homework as a factor in assigning students' grades, they used a statistical technique for this purpose. This technique, while imperfect, helps to remove (or "control") the influence of homework on students' grades.

by parents or guardians of the students were sent home with the child. The packet contained the HPI and a #2 lead pencil inscribed with the words "Thank you from the homework study." About 4 weeks after the initial contact, new surveys were sent to parents who had not returned the survey. Parents who did not respond to the second contact were lost to the study.

To minimize expenses and disruption in classes, school personnel administered the HPI to students. However, a standard, written, procedural description was developed that included a list of students whose parents had agreed to let them participate and instructions on HPI administration and on how to respond to student queries. The procedural description was meant to reduce the variability in how instructions were given and how much time the students were given to answer.

After administering the HPI, the teachers completed an administration survey that asked (a) the name of the administrator; (b) the name of the classroom teacher; (c) the date; (d) how nonparticipating students were treated; (e) whether the instructions were read aloud; (f) which questions, if any, prompted questions by students; (g) the approximate time it took for students to complete the questionnaire; (h) whether all participating students completed the questionnaire; and (i) when the participating teacher completed the questionnaire.

In about 90% of classrooms, the teacher administered the questionnaire. In most classrooms, the HPI was read aloud by the teacher. About 72% of teachers completed the HPI after the students, whereas about 15% completed it while administering it to the students.

Achievement Data Collection. The TCAP was administered to the students in April 1995, roughly concurrent with the completion of the homework surveys. Teacher-assigned grades were collected in June 1995.

Data Analysis

We used the SEM program MPlus (Muthen & Muthen, 1998), using maximum likelihood estimation.[g] We provide chi-square goodness-of-fit tests and also an information criteria fit index, the Bayesian information criterion (BIC; Schwarz, 1978).[h] Standardized regression coefficients are presented in Figure 1.[i] Proportion of variance explained (R^2) is also presented for all endogenous variables.[j] Any time a manifest variable item had two or more reporters (but more than the single item per factor), the errors of those parallel items were correlated within the factor.

RESULTS

Theoretical Model of Homework Completion

We expected that the endogenous factors within the home and community stage of the model (homework environment lacking distractions, parent facilitation, and alternative activities) would all be influenced by the three exogenous factors: student norms, student ability, and parent attitude. Therefore, we estimated the relationships between each of our exogenous factors (student and family background) and each of our home and community factors (see Figure 1, left side).

g. Researchers typically study a sample, but they wish to generalize their empirical findings to the population that the sample presumably represents. Maximum likelihood estimation is a method for estimating population characteristics based on sample data.

h. Chi-square and the Bayesian information criterion are statistical tests of how well the observed relationships between variables fit the hypothesized relationships in a cause-and-effect model (e.g., the model shown in Figure 1).

i. A standardized regression coefficient expresses the relative importance of different variables in structural equation modeling. For example, the variable of student norms in Figure 1 has greater influence on homework environment than on parent facilitation, because the standardized regression coefficient for the former (.27) is greater than for the latter (.18).

j. An endogenous variable is a factor for which hypothesized causes are specified in a theoretical model. For example, parent facilitation in Figure 1 is an endogenous variable because three other variables (student norms, student ability, and parent attitude) that presumably affect it are specified. R^2 (called the coefficient of determination) expresses how much of the variance in the endogenous variable is explained by the presumed causal variables. The larger the R^2, the more influence these causal variables are presumed to have on the endogenous variable.

In terms of the homework outcome constructs (see Figure 1, right side), we hypothesized that homework completion would mediate the relationship between student's attitude toward homework and student's classroom grade. Therefore, we estimated the paths from all student and family background and home and community factors to student's attitude toward homework, and paths from all prior variables, including student's attitude toward homework, to amount of homework the student reported completing. We then estimated the direct paths from student's attitude toward homework and homework completion to classroom grade. In estimating those last relations, we felt it would be important to control for the extent to which teachers gave grades on homework assignments and then used those grades as a portion of the student's class grade.

The full model was estimated, $\chi^2(185, N = 214) = 342.80, p < .001$; BIC = 11,076.82. Figure 1 contains the standardized loadings and only significant ($p < .05$) standardized structural paths between the factors.[k] Table 2 contains a correlation matrix of the observed variables.[l]

Measurement Model. All factor loadings on their respective indicators were significant at least $p < .05$. Standardized factor loadings ranged from .30 to .85 ($M = .56$) for multiple-indicator factors (single-indicator factors each had a factor loading of 1.0).

Paths between Student and Family Background and Home and Community Factors. Positive student norms, measured by the teacher's assessment of the percentage of students in class who completed homework assignments, were positively related to (a) the extent to which the student had a homework environment that was free of distractions, $\beta = .27, p < .01$, and (b) the degree to which the parent's help was viewed as facilitating homework, $\beta = .18, p < .05$. A student norm that favored homework completion was associated with a positive

homework environment and more parent facilitation. Greater parent facilitation was also predicted by higher student ability, $\beta = .55, p < .01$, and parent's attitude toward homework, $\beta = .18, p < .05$. Of the three endogenous factors in this part of the model, the exogenous (student and family background) factors explained more variance in parent facilitation of homework, $R^2 = .39$, than in the homework environment, $R^2 = .10$, or in participation in alternative activities, $R^2 = .03$ (of which there were no significant predictors).

Paths to Homework Outcome Measures. We examined the relationship of student and family background constructs to student's attitude toward homework, homework completion, and final grade. Parent's attitude toward homework was associated with student's attitude toward homework, indicating that parent and student attitudes were consistent, $\beta = .25, p < .01$. No other constructs significantly predicted student's attitude toward homework. Approximately 14% of the variance in student's attitude toward homework was explained by parent's attitude toward homework. Homework completion was not associated with any of the student and family background or home and community constructs. Therefore, we estimated the final model shown in Figure 1 without including any paths from student and family background constructs to homework completion. Student's classroom grade was significantly associated with student ability, $\beta = .22, p < .01$. More positive parent facilitation of homework was associated with higher classroom grades, $\beta = .45, p < .01$.

Homework Outcomes. When other variables were taken into account, student's attitude toward homework did not predict homework completion or classroom grade. In predicting classroom grade, we controlled also for the extent to which homework counted in grade computation (i.e., the teachers report of the percentage of

---

k. Figure 1 shows that certain factors, such as parent facilitation, were assessed by various measures that presumably serve as indicators of the factor. In these cases, a factor analysis was done to determine how well scores on each measure correlated (or "loaded") on the presumed factor. Indicator measures with higher loading are presumed to be more closely related to the factor than indicator measures with lower loadings. The strength of the paths in the hypothesized causal structure in Figure 1 is expressed by standardized regression coefficients (see footnote i).

l. A correlation matrix is an arrangement of correlation coefficients in rows and columns that show the correlation between each pair of variables that were measured by the researchers.

grades that were based on homework). The extent to which homework counted in grade computation fell just short of being significantly associated with classroom grade, $p = .06$. Classroom grade was positively associated with homework completion, $\beta = .20$, $p < .01$, again after controlling for the extent to which homework counted in the final grade. The model explained a great deal more variance in classroom grade, $R^2 = .44$, than in student's attitude toward homework, $R^2 = .14$, or homework completion, $R^2 = .001$.

Although we expected homework completion to mediate the relationship between student's attitude toward homework and final grade, the data suggested otherwise. Student's attitude toward homework was not associated with homework completion, $\beta = .03$, nor did it show a direct path to grade, $\beta = .01$.

Mediational Analysis. We were interested in the mediational linkages from the set of student and family background and home and community factors (i.e., student norms, student ability, parent resources, parent's attitude toward homework, homework environment, parent facilitation, and alternative activities) to the set of homework outcome variables. Specifically, we tested whether the endogenous parent facilitation factor significantly mediated (accounted for) the relationship between the three exogenous student and family background factors (student norms, student ability, and parent's attitude toward homework) and classroom grade, because parent facilitation was significantly related to each of those constructs. As parent facilitation was not significantly associated with student's attitude toward homework, we did not test the mediational linkages between the three exogenous factors and student's attitude toward homework. Neither of the other endogenous student and family background constructs (i.e., homework environment or alternative activities) was considered as a potential mediator, because neither was associated with homework outcome variables.

We tested the significance of parent facilitation as a mediator by calculating the standard error (*SE*) for the mediated (indirect) effect via parent facilitation using the multivariate delta method (MacKinnon, 1994; MacKinnon & Dwyer, 1993; Sobel, 1982, 1986). We found that parent facilitation significantly mediated the relationship between student ability and grade (unstandardized mediated effect = 2.10, *SE* = .70; $z = 2.98$) and the relationship between parent's attitude toward homework and grade (unstandardized mediated effect = .95, *SE* = .31; $z = 3.04$) but not the relationship between student norms and grade (unstandardized mediated effect = 2.39, *SE* = 1.78; $z = 1.34$).

DISCUSSION

Our modeling of the elementary school data revealed several important findings. First, norms of other students, as measured by teacher reports of how likely students in their classes were to complete homework, were positively related to the elimination of distractions from homework by parents. Second, positive classmate norms, higher student ability, and positive parent attitudes toward homework were all related to greater parent facilitation. Third, student's attitude toward homework was unrelated to classmate norms, student ability, and home and community factors but related positively to parent's attitude toward homework. Finally, classroom grades were unrelated to student's attitude toward homework but were predicted by how much homework the student completed (even after the use of homework in grading was controlled); by student ability; and by parent facilitation. More generally, parent facilitation proved to be an important mediator of the relation between student norms, student ability, and parent's attitude toward homework and classroom grades.

Implications for Practice

Several of our findings are important to educators. Most important, the data revealed the critical role of parents in both the homework process and in the success of elementary school students. Positive parent involvement in homework was the strongest predictor of grades. Furthermore, the effect of student norms and parent's attitude toward homework on grades was mediated through the influence those two variables had on parent facilitation. A significant portion of the relationship

TABLE 2   Correlation Matrix for Model (N = 214)

Variable	1	2	3	4	5	6	7	8	9	10
1. Homework norms (T)	—									
2. Student ability (S)	.01	—								
3. Like homework (P)	−.07	.13	—							
4. Help learn (P)	.00	.03	.56	—						
5. Interest (P)	−.12	.09	.46	.50	—					
6. Skills (P)	−.03	.05	.47	.62	.46	—				
7. Manage time (P)	−.07	.23	.37	.39	.44	.63	—			
8. Kid alone (P)	−.01	−.07	.02	−.00	−.09	.04	−.08	—		
9. TV on (P)	.26	−.13	−.08	−.03	−.06	−.04	−.14	.30	—	
10. Quiet time (P)	.09	.07	−.04	−.12	−.12	−.15	−.19	.26	.36	—
11. Ask help (S)	.01	−.08	−.09	−.02	−.19	−.00	−.02	.10	.10	.00
12. Help harder (S)	.24	.30	.02	.03	.07	.01	.10	−.06	.12	−.01
13. Help alone (S)	−.05	.30	−.00	.02	.06	.01	.08	−.10	−.05	−.08
14. Require help (P)	−.07	−.26	−.08	.03	−.05	.01	−.06	.14	.10	−.15
15. Ask help (P)	−.12	−.22	−.04	.02	−.03	.07	−.11	.17	.17	−.04
16. Help faster (P)	−.09	−.22	−.15	−.19	−.26	−.13	−.19	.23	.08	.03
17. Help harder (P)	−.03	.20	.10	.05	.02	.00	.07	.10	−.07	−.00
18. Help alone (P)	.10	.40	.12	.07	.21	.06	.19	−.14	−.10	−.10
19. TV time (S)	.19	−.06	−.04	−.03	−.13	−.08	−.09	−.05	.20	.13
20. Extracurricular (P)	−.01	.00	.00	−.08	−.03	.01	−.01	−.00	.04	.04
21. Student attitude (S)	.03	−.23	.08	.22	.16	.11	.03	.12	.08	−.08
22. Finish homework (S)	.01	.02	−.01	.09	.05	.11	.18	−.11	.05	−.08
23. Grade (T)	.06	.49	.11	.03	.08	−.00	.21	−.14	−.14	−.04
24. % homework counts toward grade	.01	−.17	−.18	−.08	−.08	−.06	.01	−.09	−.02	−.10

Note.   Values beyond approximately .135 in magnitude are significant at $p < .05$, and values beyond approximately .175 in magnitude are significant at $p < .01$.

Legend

Reporter: S = student; P = parent; T = teacher.

Homework norms (T) = how many students finish their homework.

Student ability (S) = Tennessee Comprehensive Assessment Program test of student ability.

Like homework (P) = extent to which parent likes homework.

Help learn (P) = extent to which parent thinks homework helps child learn.

Interest (P) = extent to which parent thinks homework increases versus decreases interest in school.

Skills (P) = extent to which parent thinks homework helps study skills.

Manage time (P) = extent to which parent thinks homework helps child learn how to manage time.

Kid alone (P) = whether child is usually alone or with other people when he/she does homework.

TV on (P) = whether television is generally on or off while child does homework.

Quiet time (P) = how often parent makes child set aside quiet time for doing homework.

11	12	13	14	15	16	17	18	19	20	21	22	23
—												
.19	—											
.23	−.18	—										
.23	−.17	−.18	—									
.01	−.09	−.08	.46	—								
.04	−.11	−.20	.43	.33	—							
.16	−.07	−.21	.13	.08	.10	—						
.14	−.17	−.23	.36	.23	.45	−.29	—					
.11	−.00	−.09	−.05	−.16	−.03	−.17	.05	—				
−.01	.02	−.20	.00	−.05	.07	−.00	−.07	.23	—			
.10	−.09	−.13	.23	.17	.09	.01	.14	−.03	−.05	—		
.09	.24	.03	.02	.00	.01	−.01	−.04	−.10	−.01	.03	—	
.08	.31	.18	−.29	−.38	−.28	.13	−.35	−.03	.03	−.18	.23	—
.02	−.05	.06	−.10	−.11	−.05	−.07	.10	.03	.02	.00	−.13	−.18

Ask help (S) = extent to which student asks for help with homework from a family member.
Help harder (S) = extent to which someone else's help makes it harder for student to do homework.
Help alone (S) = extent to which someone else helps with homework by doing things student should do his/herself.
Require help (P) = how often student's homework requires help from another.
Ask help (P) = extent to which student asks for help with homework from a family member.
Help faster (P) = how often somebody helps so the child can finish faster.
Help harder (P) = extent to which someone else's help makes it harder for the student to do homework.
Help alone (P) = extent to which someone else helps with homework by doing things student should do his/herself.
TV time (S) = how much time student spends watching television.
Extracurricular (P) = composite of number of hours per week that child spends doing extracurricular activities.
Student attitude (S) = Do you think homework helps you learn?
Finish homework (S) = how much of your homework do you finish?
Grade (T) = final grade at the time of the study.
% homework counts toward grade (T) = extent to which homework counted in grade computation.

between student ability and class grades also was mediated by parent facilitation.

That being said, it is also important to distinguish between parent facilitation and other types of parent involvement that might not be salutary. Recall that our measure used a reverse-scored question concerning how often involvement of others makes homework harder. Furthermore, using this data set and another involving secondary school students, we found different types of facilitation had opposite relationships to achievement (Cooper, Lindsay, & Nye, in press). Specifically, parental support for autonomous student behavior showed a positive relationship to achievement, whereas direct instructional involvement showed a negative relationship. We speculated that parent instructional involvement did not actually cause poor performance in students, but instead that poor performance caused parents to get directly involved in instruction. Thus, parents appear to modify their type of involvement with homework depending on the ability level of their child.

The role of positive parent attitudes toward homework also deserves attention. Positive parent attitudes toward homework not only predicted amount of parent facilitation but also directly related to student's attitude toward homework. During the elementary school years, student's attitude toward homework appears not to play a large role in determining classroom success, evidenced by the lack of a significant path in our data. However, when the student moves into secondary school, attitudes become more strongly linked to grades (Cooper et al., 1998). Thus, developing positive attitudes when students are young might help lay the groundwork for later school success.

The finding involving parent facilitation and attitudes suggests that examination of the differences between elementary and secondary models might improve our understanding of the homework process. It seems reasonable to suggest that as students get older, the role of parent facilitation of homework may have a diminishing influence on grades. That would occur because parents become less able to directly instruct students as the material becomes more difficult. We might also expect that the importance of the student's own attitude toward homework would become stronger. Likewise, the importance of student norms would increase as children move into adolescence due to the increasing role of peers in determining behavior.

To examine those developmental changes in model structure, future research on homework's influence on the lives of young children should be longitudinal. There has yet to be a large-scale or in-depth study of homework that follows a cohort of students from the early grades into adolescence. Many of the questions about homework that remain unanswered require such an approach.

Limitations of the Study

The low response rate, approximately 35%, in this study raises the possibility that respondents were not a random sample drawn from the districts. That proved to be the case. Just over 90% of respondents were White, but only about 64% of patrons of the three school districts were White. Similarly, about 40% of all school district students were eligible for free lunch, but only about 12% of respondents were eligible for free lunch. The differences in respondent backgrounds are probably related to their attitudes toward homework and homework practices. On the basis of self-presentation concerns, we could hypothesize that parents and students who responded to the survey had more positive attitudes toward homework and better homework practices than nonrespondents. Certainly then, care must be taken in generalizing our results to populations containing percentages of Whites and disadvantaged families that differ markedly from our sample statistics. However, minorities and low-SES families were already somewhat overrepresented in the three school districts compared with national statistics.

Also, we were unable to obtain data on the reliability of responses from all three groups of participants. Although efforts were made to word questions in a manner that was clear (through pilot testing) and that would lead to consistent responding over time (by asking about typical or average behaviors), that is no substitute for having multiple questions on the same topic or obtaining repeated measurements.

Acknowledgments

This research was supported by Office of Educational Improvement Grant No. R117E40309 to the first author. The views expressed herein are those of the authors and not necessarily those of the granting agency. Thanks are expressed to the staff of the Center of Excellence for Research in Basic Skills for help with the data collection.

Address correspondence to Harris Cooper, Department of Psychology, McAlester Hall, University of Missouri, Columbia, MO 65211. E-mail: cooperh@missouri.edu

References

Bents-Hill, C., Boswell, R., Byers, J., Cohen, N., Cummings, J., & Leavitt, B. (1988, April). *Relationship of academic performance to parent estimate of homework time.* Paper presented at the annual meeting of the National Association of School Psychologists, Chicago.

Cooper, H. (1989). *Homework.* White Plains, NY: Longman.

Cooper, H., Lindsay, J. J., & Nye, B. (in press). Homework in the home: How student, family, and parenting style differences relate to the homework process. *Contemporary Educational Psychology.*

Cooper, H., Lindsay, J. J., Nye, B., & Greathouse, S. (1998). Relationships among attitudes about homework, amount of homework assigned and completed, and student achievement. *Journal of Educational Psychology, 90,* 70–83.

Coulter, F. (1979). Homework: A neglected area of research. *British Educational Research Journal, 5,* 21–33.

CTB. (1988). *Comprehensive Test of Basic Skills: Technical report* (4th ed.). New York: Macmillan/McGraw-Hill.

Epstein, J. L. (1988). *Homework practices, achievements, and behaviors of elementary school students* (Center for Research on Elementary and Middle Schools Report No. 26). Baltimore, MD: Johns Hopkins University.

Keith, T. Z. (1982). Time spent on homework and high school grades: A large sample path analysis. *Journal of Educational Psychology, 74,* 248–253.

Keith, T. Z., & Cool, V. A. (1992). Testing models of school learning: Effects of quality of instruction, motivation, academic coursework, and homework on academic achievement, *School Psychology Quarterly, 3,* 207–226.

Keith, T. Z., Keith, P. B., Troutman, G. C., Bickley, P. G., Trivette, P. S., & Singh. K. (1993). Does parent involvement affect eighth-grade student achievement? Structural analysis of national data. *School Psychology Review, 3,* 474–496.

Keith, T. Z., Reimers, T. M., Fehrmen, P. G., Pottebaum, S. M., & Aubey, L. W. (1986). Parent involvement, homework, TV time: Direct and indirect effects on high school achievement. *Journal of Educational Psychology, 78,* 373–380.

MacKinnon, D. P. (1994). Analysis of mediating variables in prevention and intervention research. In A. Cazeres and L. A. Beatty, *Scientific methods for prevention intervention research* (NIDA Research Monograph 139, DHHS Pub. No. 943631, pp. 127–153). Superintendent of Documents, U.S. Government Printing Office, Washington, DC.

MacKinnon, D. P., & Dwyer, J. H. (1993). Estimating mediated effects in prevention studies. *Evaluation Review, 17,* 144–158.

Mulhenbruck, L., Cooper, H., Nye, B., & Lindsay, J. J. (in press). Homework and achievement: Explaining the different strengths of relation at the elementary and secondary school levels. *Contemporary Educational Psychology.*

Muthen, L. K., & Muthen, B. O. (1998). *MPlus: The comprehensive modeling program for applied researchers.* Los Angeles: Author.

Schwarz, G. (1978). Estimating the dimension of a model. *The Annals of Statistics, 6,* 461–464.

Sobel, M. E. (1982). Asymptotic confidence intervals for indirect effects in structural equations models. In S. Leinhardt (Ed.), *Sociological methodology* (pp. 290–293). Washington, DC: American Sociological Association.

Sobel, M. E. (1986). Some new results on indirect effects and their standard errors in covariance structure models. In N. Tuma (Ed.), *Sociological methodology* (pp. 159–186). Washington, DC: American Sociological Association.

chapter 9

Experimental Research

Greg Evans is in a school psychology doctoral program at a university, and he spends one day a week in an elementary school for his psychology internship. Greg and a teacher at the school want to help one of the teacher's special education students, Manny, who is trying hard to improve his reading skills. However, Manny gets angry whenever he comes to a word that he doesn't know, and then begins acting aggressively toward the teacher or other students.

The teacher told Greg that when Manny is allowed to play a computer game for a few minutes, he seems to calm down and enjoy the game, and then will readily return to his reading. So Greg and the teacher set up an experiment. After establishing a baseline for Manny's aggressive behavior during class, they will introduce the opportunity for Manny to play a computer game for a few minutes following a specified period of reading instruction. If they can reduce Manny's aggressiveness, they think he will learn more, and also be less of a threat to the teacher or other students.

In this chapter you will learn how researchers carry out experiments with groups of research participants, or single-case experiments with individuals like Manny. You will learn about various procedures that researchers can use to demonstrate that the experimental treatment, rather than some uncontrolled variable, caused the desired change in the target behavior that is being studied. You will also learn how to determine whether the findings of an experimental research study can be applied to your local setting. ●

After studying this chapter, you will be able to

1. explain three essential steps involved in conducting an experiment.

2. explain the difference between a true experiment, a quasi-experiment, and a single-case experiment.

3. explain how extraneous variables can threaten the internal validity of experiments.

4. describe three aspects of external validity that affect the extent to which the findings of experimental research can be applied to local settings.

5. describe two common experimental research designs.

6. describe two common quasi-experimental research designs.

7. describe three common designs used in single-case experiments.

THE NATURE OF EXPERIMENTAL RESEARCH

In doing experiments, researchers manipulate one variable (e.g., a teaching technique) to determine its effect on another variable (e.g., students' on-task behavior in class). If the experiment is well done, the researchers can conclude that the first variable caused or did not cause a change in the second variable. No other type of quantitative research (descriptive, correlational, or causal-comparative) is as powerful in demonstrating the existence of cause-and-effect relationships among variables as experimental research.

After research participants have been selected, an experiment typically involves three steps:

1. Research participants are randomly assigned to either the experimental group or the control group. **Random assignment** means that each participant has an equal chance of being in either group. Thus, previously existing group differences are unlikely to be the cause of observed differences in the outcome variable.

2. The **experimental group** is exposed to an intervention—also called the **treatment** or the **independent variable**—while the **control group** either is exposed to an alternate intervention or receives no intervention.

3. A comparison is made of the experimental and control groups' performance on the variable that the experiment is designed to affect. This variable is called the **dependent variable,** because participants' scores on a measure of the variable are presumed to be dependent on the intervention introduced by the researchers. The dependent variable is sometimes called the **target behavior,** because the research intervention typically aims to produce a particular change in the level of that behavior.

Types of Experiments

This chapter covers three related types of research that all are based on the experimental research paradigm. The first type, a true **experiment,** involves all three of the essential characteristics of a good experiment: random assignment, administration of a treatment to an experimental group and an alternative or no treatment to a control group, and comparison of the groups' performance on a posttreatment measure.

The random-assignment feature of a true experiment helps to equate the experimental and control groups on all factors except the intervention, but it is not perfect. For example, suppose that a sample includes an equal number of male and female participants. Even with random assignment, a higher percentage of males or females might wind up by chance in the experimental or control group. Thus, the experimental and control groups will not be equivalent on the factor of gender. Random assignment only ensures that there is no systematic bias in the assignment of participants to the experimental and control groups.

The second type of experimental research, a **quasi-experiment,** approximates the treatment and posttreatment procedures of a true experiment, but it does not involve random assignment. As in other applied disciplines, educational practice often does not permit the random assignment of students, teachers, or other groups to different experimental conditions. As a result, quasi-experiments are probably more common than true experiments in educational research, but they present more problems in the interpretation of the research results.

The third type of research, a **single-case experiment,** involves administration of a treatment to one individual, or to a small number of individuals who are treated one at a time, with each individual's behavior under nontreatment conditions serving as the control for comparison purposes.

Example of an Educational Experiment

Let us consider an example of a simple educational experiment. Suppose that a new program has been developed to reduce ethnic stereotyping among students in ethnically diverse first-grade classrooms. This program is the experimental treatment, so the independent variable is exposure or nonexposure to the treatment.

The first step in carrying out the experiment would be to select a sample of, let's say, twenty ethnically diverse first-grade classrooms and randomly assign ten of them to receive the program on reducing ethnic stereotypes. Students in the other ten classrooms would receive the control treatment, which could be either an alternative program dealing with ethnic stereotypes, or no program.

At the end of first grade, a measure of ethnic stereotyping would be administered to children in all twenty classrooms. This measure is the dependent variable, that is, the variable that the researchers expect will be affected by the experimental treatment. Statistical analyses would be done to determine whether students in the experimental classes showed a lower level of ethnic stereotyping on the measure than students in the control classes. Assume that, at the conclusion of the experiment, the ethnic stereotyping scores of the experimental students and those of the control students were different at a previously selected level of statistical significance. Then the researchers could generalize their findings. That is, they could conclude, with some certainty, that administering the same program to other students who are similar to those who participated in the experiment would have a positive effect on their stereotyping behavior.

Researchers have created many variations of this basic experimental design. For example, in some studies a **pretest** is administered before a program starts, and a **posttest** (the measure of the dependent variable) is administered at the end of the experimental program. The pretest data can be analyzed to check how similar the experimental and control groups were at the outset of the experiment and to measure pretest-to-posttest gains. In some experiments, several treatments might be compared. For example, an experiment might be designed to compare the effectiveness of three different computer-generated test formats.

In some experiments, more than one independent variable is studied. For example, in the experiment described above, the researchers might include both the new program and gender as independent variables. By doing so, the researchers could determine the effect of gender on ethnic stereotyping and whether the new program is more effective for one gender than the other.

Analysis of experimental research data typically involves computing the mean scores of each group on the dependent variable and then comparing the mean scores to determine whether the differences obtained are statistically significant. Table 7.3 presents a summary of the inferential statistics commonly used in causal-comparative, experimental, and quasi-experimental research.

Experiments and Educational Policy

In the field of medicine true experiments constitute the "gold standard" of scientific research and are widely used for determining which medical procedures are effective and therefore should be recommended to medical practitioners. (True experiments in medicine are collected and displayed at this website: <http://Campbell.gse.upenn.edu>.) There are increasing efforts to use a similar standard of scientific research as a basis for educational policy and practice. The National Research Council (Shavelson & Towne, 2002) concluded that true experiments are the most powerful form of scientific research for determining whether a particular educational intervention (e.g., a program or instructional method) is effective:

> [F]rom a scientific perspective, randomized trials (we also use the term 'experiment' to refer to causal studies that feature random assignment) are the ideal for establishing whether one or more factors caused change in an outcome because of their strong ability to enable fair comparisons. . . . Random allocation of students, classrooms, schools—whatever the unit of comparison may be—to different treatment groups assures that these comparison groups are, roughly speaking, equivalent at the time an intervention is introduced (that is, they do not differ systematically on account of hidden influences) and chance differences between the groups can be taken into account statistically. As a result, the independent effect of the intervention on the outcome of interest can be isolated. (pp. 110–111)

THE VALIDITY OF EXPERIMENTS

Some factors affect an experiment's **internal validity,** that is, the extent to which extraneous variables have been controlled and thus the level of certainty that the experimental treatment has a causal influence on the dependent variable. Other factors affect an experiment's **external validity,** that is, the extent to which the experimental findings can be generalized beyond the research sample to other groups. Below we describe both types of validity and the factors that need to be controlled in order to maximize them. These factors have been studied primarily in relation to their effects on true experiments and quasi-experiments, both of which involve groups of research participants. We will refer again to validity when we examine the nature of single-case experiments, because they too are subject to certain threats to their validity.

Internal Validity

The observed effects in an experiment can be caused partly by the treatment variable and partly by extraneous variables. **Extraneous variables** are nontreatment factors that are present while the experiment is in progress. If extraneous variables are present, the researchers will be unable to determine the extent to which any observed difference between the experimental and control groups on the dependent variable is caused by the treatment or by one or more extraneous variables. The practical implication is that educators might implement the treatment in their local situation expecting to achieve the same positive effects that occurred in the experiment, but they might not achieve these effects because the effects resulted from extraneous variables, not from the treatment.

To demonstrate the importance of controlling for extraneous variables, we will consider a research problem that can be studied through a simple experimental design. Suppose that researchers are evaluating the effectiveness of a newly developed reading program for slow learners. At the beginning of the school year, they select one hundred students for participation in the program. All the students meet the selection criterion of scoring at least two grades below the age norm on a standard test of reading achievement. After participation in the program for a school year, the students are once again given a reading achievement test.

Suppose that the researchers find a large, statistically significant gain in reading achievement, as determined by a *t* test. Can the researchers conclude that this achievement gain was caused by the experimental treatment, that is, the new reading program? The answer depends on how well various extraneous variables were controlled.

Donald Campbell and Julian Stanley (1963) identified eight types of extraneous variables that can affect the internal validity of experiments. We will explain how each of these threats to internal validity could affect the results of the experiment described above. Other extraneous variables have been identified, but these eight effects reflect common challenges to researchers in designing and conducting experiments.

1. **History effect.** The fact that experimental treatments extend over a period of time provides an opportunity for other events besides the experimental treatment to cause changes in the experimental group. The students in our example participated in the reading program for an entire school year. Therefore, other factors, such as the students' other instruction from teachers, could have accounted for all or part of their achievement gain in reading.

2. **Maturation effect.** While an experimental treatment is in progress, certain biological or psychological processes occur in the research participants. For example, participants become older, and they might experience increased fatigue, comfort, or some other emotional or physical change, all of which are forms of maturation as defined by Campbell and Stanley. During the year of the experimental reading program, students were developing physically, socially, and intellectually. Perhaps maturation in one of these areas, rather than the reading program itself, enabled students to overcome their reading deficiency.

3. **Testing effect.** In many educational experiments a pretest is administered, followed by the treatment, and concluding with a posttest. If the pretest and posttest are similar or are administered close together in time, research participants might show an improvement on the posttest simply as a result of their experience with the pretest. In other words, they have become "test-wise." It is unlikely that this extraneous variable was operating in the hypothetical experiment on a new reading program. Because of the long period of time between the pretest and posttest, students are not likely to have remembered enough about the pretest for it to have affected their posttest performance.

4. **Instrumentation effect.** An apparent learning gain might be observed from the pretest to the posttest due to changes in the nature of the measuring instrument. Suppose that the students in our example were administered a posttest of reading achievement that was easier than the pretest that they took. The gain in reading achievement then would be caused by differences in the testing instruments rather than by the experimental treatment.

5. **Statistical regression.** Whenever a pretest–posttest procedure is used to assess learning in an experiment, the individuals scoring high or low on the pretest will tend to have scores somewhat closer to the mean on the posttest. This phenomenon is known as statistical regression. For example, suppose that the students in the experimental group on average scored at the 15th percentile on a pretest of reading achievement. When this group of students is tested again on the same or a similar test, they are likely to earn a higher mean score, with or without any intervening experimental treatment. The reason is that their lower initial score likely results from not only lower ability but also chance factors (e.g., they were feeling ill on the day of the test, or they made unlucky guesses on some test items). Upon retesting, these chance factors are unlikely to be present again. Consequently, their test scores will improve independently of the effect of the experimental treatment. Similarly, due to chance factors, when students with very high scores on the pretest are retested, their scores also are likely to regress, that is, move towards the mean.

6. **Differential selection.** In some experiments, participants are selected for the experimental and control groups by a procedure other than random selection. (Such quasi-experiments are discussed later in the chapter.) Because the

participants in the two groups are differentially selected, the effects of the treatment can be distorted. For example, suppose that the students receiving the experimental treatment (the new reading program) came from schools whose principals were instructional leaders and wanted to try the new program. The control group subsequently was formed by recruiting schools opportunistically until the desired sample size was achieved. Their principals might, or might not, be instructional leaders. If the experimental group of students subsequently showed greater achievement gains than the control group, the effect could be attributed to the principals' instructional leadership rather than to the experimental treatment itself. The best way to avoid the difficulties of interpretation caused by differential selection is to assign participants randomly to the two groups, a condition that is essential to a true experiment.

7. **Selection–maturation interaction.** This extraneous variable is similar to differential selection, except that maturation is the specific confounding variable. Suppose that, in our example, first-grade students from a single school district are selected to receive instruction in the new reading program, while the control group is drawn from the population of first-grade students in another school district. Because of different admissions policies in the two school districts, the mean age of students in the control group is six months higher than the mean age of students in the experimental group. Now, suppose that the experiment shows that the experimental group made significantly greater achievement gains than the control group. Do these results reflect the effectiveness of the experimental treatment or the effects of maturation? Due to differential assignment of students to the experimental and control groups, the researchers would not be able to provide a clear answer to this question.

8. **Experimental mortality** (sometimes called **attrition**). Experimental mortality is the loss of research participants over the course of the experimental treatment. This extraneous variable can bias the results, because the participants who discontinue their participation usually differ in important ways from those who remain. For example, suppose that there was a systematic bias in the type of students who dropped out of the reading program during the school year: The students who left the school district happened to be the lowest-achieving students. If the researchers measured the achievement gains of only the students who completed the program, the effectiveness of the experimental treatment would be exaggerated.

External Validity

Experiments are externally valid to the degree to which their results can be generalized to other individuals, settings, and times. Glenn Bracht and Gene Glass (1968) described three aspects of external validity to consider when you wish to apply the findings of an experimental study to your particular conditions.

1. *Population validity.* You will recall from our discussion of sampling in Chapter 5 that **population validity** is the degree to which the results of a research study

can be generalized from the specific sample that was studied to the population from which the sample was drawn. To determine population validity, one must assess the degree of similarity between the research sample that was used in the study, the accessible population from which the research sample was drawn, and the larger target population to which the research results are to be generalized. The more evidence the researcher provides to establish links between the sample, the accessible population, and the target population, the more confident you can be in generalizing the research findings to the target population.

In practice, educators who want to apply research findings to their own setting are interested not so much in the similarity between the research sample and the target population, but rather the similarity between the research sample and the individuals in their local setting. To determine this type of similarity, you should note all relevant information in the research report about the research sample, such as age, gender, academic aptitude, ethnicity, socioeconomic status, and the characteristics of the communities in which they live. You then should compare the resulting profile with information about individuals in the local setting to which you want to apply the research findings.

2. *Personological variables.* Another factor affecting external validity is the possibility that various personal characteristics of the research sample will interact with the experimental treatment. An interaction is present if the experimental results apply to research participants with certain characteristics (e.g., those who have high test anxiety) but not to those with other characteristics (e.g., those who have low test anxiety). For example, the Beginning Teacher Evaluation Study sought to relate specific teaching strategies to the achievement of second- and fifth-grade pupils in mathematics and reading (Fisher et al., 1978). The researchers found that some teaching strategies were significantly related to academic achievement at both grade levels and in both subject areas, but the majority were not. For example, academic feedback was positively related to achievement at both grade levels and for both subject areas. However, academic monitoring was negatively correlated with second-graders' reading achievement, but was positively correlated with second-graders' mathematics achievement. At grade 5, correlations between academic monitoring and achievement in both subject areas were virtually zero.

These results demonstrate that even though a teaching strategy might have merit, it can vary greatly in its effectiveness at different grade levels, in different subject areas, or for students with different personal characteristics. In generalizing from the results of a specific experiment, you need to look carefully at any differences in the findings for different subcategories of research participants.

3. *Ecological validity.* **Ecological validity** is an estimate of the degree to which an experimental result can be generalized to a local setting. It depends on the extent to which the situational conditions that were present during the experiment are similar to the conditions that exist in the setting to which you wish to apply the results. As a rule, you can assume that the larger the difference between the experimental environment and the local environment, the less confidence you can have that the results will apply.

Keep in mind, however, that not all experimental results are situation-specific. Thus, the results of an experiment on the effects of a classroom management program conducted with fifth-grade children in a small town in the South might generalize quite well to small towns, rural communities, and medium-sized cities in other regions. By contrast, suppose that all the classrooms in the study of classroom management included twenty or fewer students, and each teacher had a part-time aide to help with instruction. If your classroom has twenty-eight students and there are no teacher aides, the generalizability of the experimental results is questionable. In this case, you might wish to do a small-scale action research project (see Chapter 15) to determine whether the intervention is effective in your classroom.

Research Tradeoffs

Often the procedures that researchers use to improve an experiment's internal validity tend to reduce its external validity. The reason is that the procedures make the research environment considerably different from a typical educational setting. For example, the best method of ensuring internal validity is random assignment of research participants to different treatments. In practice, however, students seldom can be randomly assigned to classrooms, so if the experimental treatment is administered in classrooms, the internal validity of the experiment is immediately compromised. Yet the solution of randomly assigning students to experimental and control treatments and taking them to a laboratory-like setting for short periods of time is likely to decrease the experiment's external validity.

Researchers must continually weigh the advantages of more rigorous control of extraneous variables against the advantages of doing research in educational environments that are as natural as possible. They often must compromise in their attempts to provide acceptable levels of both internal and external validity.

EXPERIMENTAL DESIGNS

The following symbols commonly are used to describe experimental designs (discussed below) and quasi-experimental designs (discussed in the next section):

R   (represents random assignment of the research participants)
X   (represents the experimental treatment)
O   (represents observation of the dependent variable, by administering either a pretest or a posttest)

Below, we describe two true experimental designs that often are used in educational research. We also discuss the threats to internal validity that each design presents.

Pretest–Posttest Control Group Design

The pretest–posttest control group design is written

$$R \quad O_1 \quad X \quad O_2$$
$$R \quad O_1 \qquad O_2$$

The top line represents the experimental group, and the second line represents the control group. The symbols have these meanings:

R   (Research participants are randomly assigned to the experimental or control group.)
O   (Both the experimental and the control group are given the pretest, O_1.)
X   (The experimental group is given the treatment, while the control group is given no treatment, or receives an alternative treatment.)
O   (Both the experimental and the control group are given the posttest, O_2.)

This design is excellent for controlling the threats to internal validity that were described earlier in the chapter. For example, the effects of differential selection are minimized, because there is no systematic bias in the assignment of individuals to the experimental and control groups. Testing effects are controlled, because the experimental and control groups take the same tests. If the experimental group performs better on the posttest, this result cannot be attributed to pretesting, because both groups had the same pretesting experience.

The only extraneous variable that cannot be ruled out by this design is experimental mortality. Differences in the demands made on the research participants in the experimental and control groups can lead to differences in the number of participants who are lost from each group during the course of the experiment. Thus, posttreatment differences between the groups on the dependent variable could be due to differences in such characteristics as the motivation and ability of the remaining experimental group members compared to the control group members.

Posttest-Only Control Group Design

The posttest-only control group design is written

$$R \quad X \quad O$$
$$R \qquad O$$

which means:

R   (Research participants are randomly assigned to the experimental or control group.)
X   (The experimental group is given the experimental treatment.)
O   (Both the experimental group and the control group are given a posttest that measures the dependent variable.)

This design is useful in studies in which the administration of a pretest could influence the research participants' behavior either during the experiment or on the posttest. For example, suppose that the pretest is a measure of students' attitudes toward students who are developmentally disabled. Right after completing the pretest, the research participants view a film about developmental disabilities. It is possible that the pretest would dispose the participants to respond to the film differently from the way that they would respond if they had not taken the pretest. If so, any differential change between the experimental and control groups can be attributed to both the film and the pretest. By using the posttest-only control group design, the researchers can determine the effect of the film by itself.

QUASI-EXPERIMENTAL DESIGNS

Quasi-experiments are similar to true experiments except that research participants are not randomly assigned to the treatment and control conditions. Researchers do not intentionally avoid random assignment, but often they are unable to assign research participants randomly because of circumstances beyond their control. For example, school administrators generally will not allow students to be randomly assigned to classrooms, even though that is the best way to ensure that students receiving the treatment are not systematically different from those not receiving the treatment. When this happens, researchers usually must consider each class as an intact group. For example, two classes could be randomly assigned, so that students in one class comprise the treatment group, while the students in the other class comprise the control group. This procedure still does not qualify as random assignment, because each student does not have an equal chance of being in either group.

Researchers sometimes select students in one school as the treatment group and students in another school as the control group. School administrators often prefer this arrangement, because the control group is unlikely to know what the treatment group is doing. As a result, teachers and parents are unlikely to question why the students in the control group are not getting the presumed benefits of the experimental treatment. Again, the drawback of this arrangement is that students are not randomly assigned to the treatment or control group. Thus, there is a risk that the two groups may differ on some important variable at the outset of the experiment.

Below we discuss two common designs used in quasi-experimental research.

Pretest–Posttest Design with Nonequivalent Groups

The pretest–posttest design with nonequivalent groups is probably the most widely used quasi-experimental design in educational research. It is represented by the following diagram:

$$O_1 \quad X \quad O_2$$
$$\text{--------------}$$
$$O_1 \qquad O_2$$

The symbols mean:

O$_1$ (Both the experimental group and the control group are given a pretest.)

X (The experimental group is given the experimental treatment.)

--- (The broken line indicates that the experimental and control groups were not formed randomly.)

O$_2$ (Both the experimental group and the control group are given a posttest that measures the dependent variable.)

The pretest scores in this experimental design can be used to determine whether the two groups were initially equivalent on the pretest variable, even though the groups were not formed by random assignment. However, we have no evidence that the groups are initially comparable on other unmeasured variables that could influence the results of the study. For example, some systematic bias of which we are unaware might cause more research participants who score high on variable X to be placed in one group, whereas more participants with low scores on variable X would be placed in the other group.

If researchers must use a quasi-experimental design, they should attempt to draw their experimental and control groups from very similar classrooms, schools, or other situations. Also, they should report as much descriptive data as possible about the experimental and control groups, such as the location and socioeconomic level of the participating schools, teachers' experience level, and mean achievement scores of students in the different classrooms or schools. This kind of information helps clarify the degree of similarity between the experimental and control groups. If the treatment and control groups are demonstrated to be similar, results of a pretest–posttest design with nonequivalent groups can be given nearly as much weight as the results of a true experimental design.

Posttest-Only Design with Nonequivalent Groups

The posttest-only design with nonequivalent groups is similar to the posttest-only control group design that we described earlier, except for the assignment procedure. Assignment of participants to experimental and control groups is random in the former design, but not in this design. The posttest-only design with nonequivalent groups is written:

$$X \quad O$$
$$\text{---------}$$
$$O$$

which means:

X   (The experimental group is given the experimental treatment.)
--- (The broken line indicates that the experimental and control groups
     were not formed randomly.)
O   (Both groups are given a posttest that measures the dependent variable.)

The main threat to internal validity in this design is differential selection. That is, posttest differences between the experimental and control groups can be attributed to characteristics of the groups as well as to the experimental treatment. For example, suppose that the teachers in one school receive an experimental treatment and then are given a posttest, while the teachers in another school simply are given the posttest. If differences on the posttest are found, it can be argued that they are due to initial differences between the teachers in the two schools rather than to the effect of the experimental treatment. Because no pretest was given, it is not possible to determine whether the two groups were similar or different prior to the experimental treatment. For this and other reasons, it is difficult to make strong cause-and-effect inferences from the results of a posttest-only experiment with nonequivalent groups.

Single-Case Designs

Single-case designs are favored over true experimental designs or quasi-experimental designs when researchers want to make a quantitative study of the effects of interventions on specific behaviors of individuals. Using a single-case design, for example, researchers can diagnose a dyslexic student's reading problem, devise an individualized strategy to solve it, and rigorously test the effectiveness of the strategy through repeated phases of data collection.

While both single-case experiments and qualitative case studies (see Chapter 10) focus on one case, they differ greatly in design and purpose. Single-case designs use special procedures to achieve tight control over, and precise description of, the experimental situation: frequent observations of the behaviors targeted for change; description of the treatment in sufficient detail to permit replication; tests of the reliability of observations of the individual's behavior; and replication of treatment effects within the experiment. In contrast, case studies explore much broader phenomena, focus on perceived reality in addition to behavior, usually are carried out in a field setting, and rely heavily on qualitative data.

Because single-case designs involve the treatment and study of individuals one at a time, it is not necessary to form groups of individuals who have the same characteristic before researchers can conduct an experiment. In fact, no matter how unique the individual's concern, a single-case design will permit investigation of the research problem. Also, single-case designs allow teachers, counselors, or others to function simultaneously as both treatment providers and researchers. In contrast, these functions often are handled by different people when a group experiment is conducted.

Some researchers perceive the single-case experiment as a watered-down version of one of the group designs presented earlier in this chapter. However, single-case designs are rigorous and time-consuming, and often they involve as much data collection as a design involving experimental and control groups. Furthermore, researchers who conduct single-case experiments are just as concerned with the issues of internal and external validity as researchers who conduct group experiments.

Single-case designs often lack external validity, that is, the ability to generalize the findings to other individuals in the population of interest. This is because the research participants are not randomly selected, and the experiment involves only one or a few individuals. Replication thus is the best way to increase the external validity of single-case experiments. Replication involves repeating the experiment with other individuals, perhaps with variations in the investigators, the settings, and the measures.

The following symbols are used in describing single-case designs:

A = baseline, meaning that an individual's behavior is observed under normal conditions.

B = treatment, meaning that an individual's behavior is observed under treatment conditions.

We describe three common single-case research designs in the following sections.

A-B-A-B Design

The **A-B-A-B design** for a single-case experiment includes two or more baseline periods (condition A) and two or more treatment periods (condition B). During the **baseline** period, the individual's behavior is observed under normal conditions. The A-B-A-B design was used by Glen Dunlap and his colleagues in the single-case experiment that is reported in their article at the end of this chapter.

Figure 9.1 is a reproduction of Figure 2 in the article by Dunlap and his colleagues. Its five columns, divided by dashed vertical lines, show clearly how the level of on-task and problem behavior changed for the research participant Jill during each phase of the experiment.

The first condition A, or baseline, is shown in the first column in Figure 9.1 (labeled "Standard Outcome"). During these five data points, Jill shows a slight decline in on-task behavior and a slight increase in problem behavior. The first condition B, or treatment, is shown in the second column in Figure 9.1 (labeled "Functional Outcome"). During these eight data points, Jill's on-task behavior shows some variation but tends to be even more consistent, while her problem behavior declines to almost zero.

The second condition A, which involves treatment **reversal,** is shown in the third column of Figure 9.1 (labeled "Standard Outcome"). During this time period the treatment was withdrawn, meaning that Jill was asked to return to performing

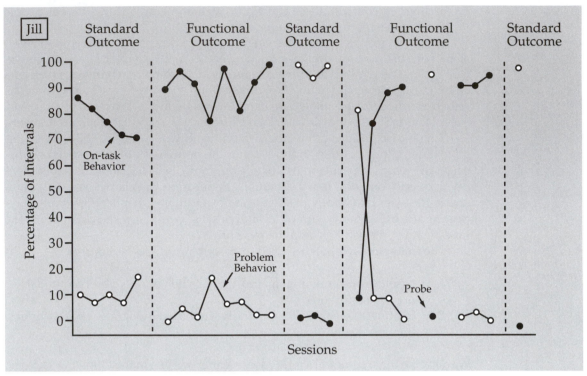

FIGURE 9.1   **Results for Jill Showing the Effects of the Standard versus Functional-Outcome Assignments on On-Task and Problem Behavior: An Example of the A-B-A-B Single-Case Design**

Source. Figure 2 on p. 254 in Dunlap, G., Foster-Johnson, L., Clarke, S., Kern, L., & Childs, K. E. (1995). Modifying activities to produce functional outcomes: Effects on the problem behaviors of students with disabilities. *Journal of the Association for Persons with Severe Handicaps, 20,* 248–258. Reprinted with permission of the Association for Persons with Severe Handicaps.

the original, minimally relevant task. The change in Jill's behavior is dramatic, with all three data points showing a very high level of problem behavior and a near-zero level of on-task behavior.

The second condition B, or treatment, is shown in the fourth column of Figure 9.1 (labeled "Functional Outcome"). During this time period the treatment was reinstated, meaning that Jill again was asked to perform the modified, functional-outcome task. After the first data point, Jill's on-task behavior increases to a high level while her problem behavior drops to a low level. During this second condition B, however, one data point (labeled "Probe") represents a return to condition A, the standard-outcome task. For this data point Jill's problem behavior soars to nearly 100 percent, while her on-task behavior drops to near zero. When condition B is resumed, shown in the last three data points of the fourth column, Jill's on-task behavior returns to near 100 percent and her problem behavior returns to near zero.

As a final check, condition A is again reinstated for one data point, shown in the fifth column of Figure 9.1 (labeled "Standard Outcome"). Once again Jill's problem behavior reaches near 100 percent and her on-task behavior drops to zero.

Figure 9.1 shows a clear pattern of high levels of problem behavior and low levels of on-task behavior during the baseline conditions, and high levels of on-task behavior and low levels of problem behavior during the treatment conditions. This pattern occurs regardless of whether each condition is one, three, four, five, or eight data points in length. This graph is typical of the type used by researchers to report the results of single-case experiments using the A-B-A-B design.

By returning to conditions A and B in turn, this design enables researchers to demonstrate that the individual's behavior is not changing by chance, but varies consistently with the presence or absence of the treatment. The graphic display of the descriptive data obtained in such studies usually is sufficiently clear that no test of statistical significance is needed. Looking at the graph, the researchers would be justified in concluding that instituting the experimental intervention is effective in promoting on-task behavior and reducing problem behavior.

Because research results based on a single individual cannot be generalized to other individuals with confidence, single-case research is weak in external validity. The solution to this weakness is replication, that is, repeating the study with other individuals. This approach was used in the study by Dunlap and his colleagues. The researchers applied a variation of the same treatment (modification of a standard outcome to a functional outcome), to three individuals who differed in age and in the nature of their learning-associated disabilities. All three students showed increased on-task behavior and decreased problem behavior during the treatment phases.

Caution is needed in using the A-B-A-B design, because not all behaviors can be readily reversed (that is, returned to condition A after condition B) during a research study. For example, a teacher's goals for an individual student might include learning various social skills such as cafeteria manners, or academic skills such as taking multiple-choice tests. Learning such skills is similar to learning to ride a bicycle: although individuals may get rusty without practice, once they learn how, they never completely forget. Because these skills are not completely reversible, it is necessary to use a design other than the A-B-A-B design. Two such designs are described in the next sections.

Single-Case Design Involving Multiple Baselines across Behaviors

In this single-case design, baseline measurements are taken on two or more behaviors exhibited by the same individual. After baselines are stable, a treatment condition is applied to one of the behaviors. The treatment is continued until a noticeable change occurs in that behavior. Then the treatment condition is applied to the second behavior until a change is observed.

An important requirement for using the across-behaviors design is the discreteness of the behaviors to be observed. If the occurrence of one behavior is relatively dependent on the occurrence of the other, treatment of one behavior may cause a change in both. If so, explanations other than the treatment could account for the change.

To understand this design further, suppose that you want to train a teacher in using three behaviors designed to provide reinforcement for correct student responses during a question-and-answer lesson. The three behaviors to be learned are as follows:

1. The teacher smiles at the student who gives a correct response.
2. The teacher gives the responding student a token that can be exchanged for free time.
3. The teacher praises the responding student.

Here are the steps a researcher might take in conducting this study:

1. The researcher would first collect baseline data on the number of times that the teacher exhibited each behavior during five half-hour lessons (i.e., one a day for one week) and record the results, as in Figure 9.2.
2. The researcher then would train the teacher to use Behavior 1.
3. Over the subsequent five days the researcher would record the number of times the teacher used each of the three reinforcement behaviors during half-hour lessons. If the training has been effective, the teacher will increase use of Behavior 1 but will not change noticeably on Behaviors 2 or 3 (Days 6–10 in Figure 9.2).
4. The researcher then would train the teacher to use Behavior 2.
5. Again the researcher would record the teacher's use of all three behaviors during five half-hour lessons and record the results (Days 11–15 in Figure 9.2). At this point, Behaviors 1 and 2 should be higher than baseline, but Behavior 3 should stay about the same.
6. The researcher then would train the teacher to use Behavior 3.
7. The researcher again would record the teacher's use of all three behaviors during five half-hour lessons (Days 16–20 in Figure 9.2). If the training has been effective, all three behaviors should occur more frequently than was the case during the baseline condition.

Inspection of Figure 9.2 indicates that the training in all three behaviors was effective. However, notice that Behavior 1 gradually decreases near the end of the study. This decrease might indicate that the researcher's training program for this behavior is weak and needs to be strengthened, or follow-up instruction may be needed to achieve more permanent results. Notice also that the frequency of Behavior 2 never reaches the levels of Behaviors 1 and 3. This result could lead to one of several possible interpretations: (a) the teacher needs more training in Behavior 2; (b) teachers give tokens less frequently as a reinforcement strategy than smiles or praise, perhaps because giving tokens takes more class time; (c) teachers sense that students respond better to smiles and praise than to tokens.

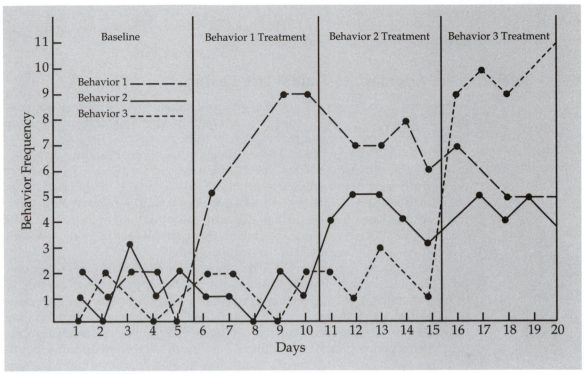

FIGURE 9.2 Results of a Single-Case Experiment Involving Multiple Baselines across Behaviors

Of course, other explanations of the observed results are possible. In many cases, the researcher will conduct additional research to test alternate hypotheses. As alternate hypotheses are supported or rejected in subsequent studies, the researcher learns more about the phenomenon being studied.

Single-Case Design Involving Multiple Baselines across Individuals

In this single-case design, two (or more) individuals are selected for whom the behavioral goal of treatment is the same. After the baseline rates of behavior have become stable for both individuals, a treatment condition is applied with one individual. If a change is noted in the behavior of the individual to whom treatment was applied but the behavior of the other individual remains constant, the researchers can conclude that their treatment has an effect. The treatment then is applied to the second individual to see if that individual's behavior now changes. If change does occur, this result represents a replication of the treatment's effect on that behavior.

The across-individuals design is invalidated if the intervention for one individual influences the behavior of the other individual who still is in the baseline condition. This problem can occur, for example, when an intervention is provided to several children in the same classroom, to members of the same family, or to employees in the same work location.

Selecting the Appropriate Single-Case Design

Just as you learned in our discussion of group experiments and quasi-experiments, the choice of a single-case design depends largely on the researchers' efforts to balance the internal and external validity of the experimental findings.

The A-B-A-B design presents fewer threats to the internal validity of a single-case experiment than the two multiple-baseline designs we discussed. It is a more powerful design, because the reversal phase (the second A condition) demonstrates active control of the individual's target behavior by removing the treatment that is hypothesized to have caused the initial change (the initial B condition). Reinstatement of the treatment (the second B condition) provides additional evidence of the effect of the treatment.

Despite the power of the A-B-A-B design, it cannot be used in all situations. For example, in many counseling situations it is not appropriate to attempt to bring a client back to baseline. For example, if a client's anxiety level has been reduced during the course of treatment, a counselor could not ethically withdraw the successful treatment in order to observe whether the client's anxiety level returned to its pretreatment level. Multiple-baseline designs give educators the advantage of studying the effects of a treatment without having to withhold it from a distressed client, and they allow the study of treatment-induced behaviors that are not reversible or that have a high resistance to extinction. Because they involve experimental procedures that better reflect real-life treatment conditions designed to modify individuals' behavior, these designs tend to improve the external validity of research findings.

EXAMPLE OF OUTLINING A RESEARCH PROPOSAL

This feature of the chapter gives you an example of how to outline a research proposal using the form in Appendix 1. The example, involving a proposal to study curriculum alignment, is introduced at the end of Chapter 2.

The third research question in the example is as follows: "Does students' performance on achievement tests improve after a curriculum-alignment process has been completed in their schools?" This question is best answered by an experiment, because the question specifies an intervention (a curriculum-alignment process) and an anticipated effect of the intervention (improved student performance on tests). The intervention constitutes a deliberate manipulation of individuals' behavior, and manipulation is the essential feature of experiments.

We show below how we filled out the part of the proposal outline pertaining to the research design.

4. RESEARCH DESIGN
    A. *Research design.* The research design is experimental. The independent variable is the curriculum-alignment process, and the dependent variable is student performance on achievement tests.

    We have chosen to form a sample of elementary schools and randomly assign them to an experimental condition in which they will participate in a curriculum-alignment process or to a control condition in which they will continue with their regular curriculum processes. The experimental group consists of the schools participating in the curriculum-alignment process, and the control group consists of schools that receive no intervention. Because the schools are randomly assigned to the experimental and control groups, the research design is a true experiment rather than a quasi-experiment.

    Training of teachers in curriculum alignment will occur over the summer, and teachers also will have the opportunity and resources to align their curriculum for the coming school year. Prior to the start of classes in the fall, students of teachers in the two groups will take a math and reading achievement test. They also will take a math and reading achievement test at the end of the school year. Thus, the experiment constitutes a pretest–posttest control-group design.
    B. *Threats to internal validity.* A pretest–posttest control-group experiment has excellent internal validity. The only threat is experimental mortality. In most schools, some students drop out of school during the year. If different types of students drop out of the experimental and control group, any observed differences between students on the posttests could be attributed to these differences rather than to the experimental intervention. To control for this threat, the characteristics of dropouts in the two groups (e.g., gender, pretest scores) will be compared. If differences are found, procedures such as analysis of covariance will be used to equate the two groups.
    C. *Threats to external validity.* The threats to external validity are the same as those described in the example of outlining a research proposal in Chapter 8. We explained in this example that the accessible population from which the sample will be drawn is school districts in Oregon. High-stakes testing and curriculum alignment are relatively recent movements in education, so different states are likely to have different budgets and strategies for implementing them. Therefore, generalization of findings from the study must be made with caution.

    In reporting the study, we will provide a detailed description of Oregon's state-level context for high-stakes testing and curriculum alignment so that educators in other states can compare it with their context. To the extent that the contexts are similar, they might be more confident about generalizing our findings to their states.

SELF-CHECK TEST

1. A true experiment typically involves all the following steps except for
   a. random assignment of research participants to an experimental or control group.
   b. administration of an intervention to an experimental group.
   c. selection of a control group after the dependent variable has been measured.
   d. comparison of the experimental and control group's performance on the dependent variable.

2. Unlike a quasi-experiment, only a true experiment
   a. involves comparison of a control group with an experimental group.
   b. involves random assignment of research participants to the experimental and control groups.
   c. involves administration of a treatment to some of the research participants.
   d. can produce findings with a high degree of external validity.

3. Unlike single-case experiments, true experiments and quasi-experiments
   a. can establish cause-and-effect relationships.
   b. involve the study of groups rather than individuals.
   c. need to control for possible threats to internal validity.
   d. involve the administration of a treatment designed to affect research participants' behavior.

4. Researchers find that students with the highest pretest scores in the class tend to have more moderate posttest scores. This phenomenon most likely demonstrates the effect of
   a. experimental mortality.   c. maturation.
   b. testing.   d. statistical regression.

5. To determine the generalizability of experimental findings to their local settings, educators should look mainly for evidence of similarity between
   a. the research sample and the target population.
   b. the accessible population and the target population.
   c. the target population and the individuals in the local setting.
   d. the research sample and the individuals in the local setting.

6. $$R \quad O_1 \quad X \quad O_2 \qquad R \quad X \quad O$$
   $$R \quad O_1 \qquad\quad O_2 \qquad R \qquad\quad O$$

   The symbols above represent two different research designs that are commonly used in true experiments. The main difference between the design on the left and the design on the right is whether
   a. a control group is included in the experiment.
   b. research participants are randomly assigned to the experimental and control groups.

    c. a pretest is given to the experimental and control groups.

    d. a treatment is administered to the experimental group and withheld from the control group.

7. Probably the most widely used quasi-experimental design in educational research is the
   a. posttest-only design with nonequivalent groups.
   b. pretest–posttest design with nonequivalent groups.
   c. pretest-only design.
   d. pretest–posttest control group design.

8. Probably the best way to increase the generalizability of the findings of a single-case experiment is to
   a. replicate the experiment with other individuals.
   b. add more baseline and treatment conditions.
   c. end the experiment with reinstatement of the pretreatment conditions.
   d. have the research conducted by someone other than the treatment provider.

CHAPTER REFERENCES

Bracht, G. H., & Glass, G. V. (1968). The external validity of experiments. *American Educational Research Journal, 5,* 437–474.

Campbell, D. T., & Stanley, J. C. (1963). Experimental and quasi-experimental designs for research on teaching. In N. L. Gage (Ed.), *Handbook of research on teaching* (pp. 171–246). Chicago: Rand McNally.

Fisher, C. W., et al. (1978). Teaching and learning in the elementary school: A summary of the beginning teacher evaluation study. San Francisco: Far West Laboratory for Educational Research and Development. (ERIC Document Reference No. ED165322.)

Shavelson, R. J., & Towne, L. (Eds.). (2002). *Scientific research in education.* Washington, DC: National Academy Press. Also available at: www.nap.edu/books/0309082919/html

RESOURCES FOR FURTHER STUDY

Crawford, J., & Impara, J. C. (2001). Critical issues, current trends, and possible futures in quantitative methods. In V. Richardson (Ed.), *Handbook of research on teaching* (4th ed., pp. 133–173). Washington, DC: American Educational Research Association.

    The authors consider important issues in the design of experiments in education. For example, they stress the importance of using random assignment to form experimental and control groups and using psychometrically sound measures to assess intervention outcomes and pretest–posttest changes.

Franklin, R. D., Allison, D. B., & Gorman, B. S. (Eds.). (1997). *Design and analysis of single-case research.* Mahwah, NJ: Lawrence Erlbaum Associates.

    The chapter authors examine single-case experiments from different perspectives. They review the history of single-case research, the types of behavioral phenomena amenable to study by this approach, the range of single-case designs, and methods of statistical analysis.

Martin, D. W. (2004). *Doing psychology experiments* (6th ed.). Belmont, CA: Wadsworth.

> *This book is a basic guide to the logic of experimentation, the various experimental designs available to researchers, step-by-step procedures for conducting an experiment, and ethical considerations.*

Mosteller, F., & Boruch, R. (Eds.). (2002). *Evidence matters: Randomized trials in education research.* Washington, DC: Brookings Institution Press.

> *The contributors to this book present the case for field experiments with random assignment as an important approach to improving educational practice. They review the history of experiments in the evaluation of federally sponsored programs, and they discuss the difficulties of doing experiments involving randomization in schools and possible solutions.*

Shaver, J. P. (1983). The verification of independent variables in experimental procedure. *Educational Researcher, 12*(8), 3–9.

> *This article identifies weaknesses in the conventional research procedures that are used to assess treatment fidelity, that is, whether an experimental treatment was implemented in accordance with the researchers' specifications.*

In the following section of the chapter you will read a research article that illustrates an experimental research study. It is preceded by comments written especially for this book by the authors of the article. Then the article itself is reprinted in full, just as it appeared when originally published. Where appropriate, we have added footnotes to help you understand the information contained in the article.

SAMPLE EXPERIMENTAL RESEARCH STUDY
Early Exposure to Direct Instruction and Subsequent Juvenile Delinquency: A Prospective Examination

Mills, P. E., Cole, K. N., Jenkins, J. R., & Dale, P. S. (2002). Early exposure to direct instruction and subsequent juvenile delinquency: A prospective examination. *Exceptional Children, 69*, 85–96.

● **RESEARCHER'S COMMENTS,** *by Paulette Mills, Philip Dale, Joseph Jenkins, and Kevin Cole*

Quality longitudinal research requires much time, energy, and dedication, and an outstanding researcher team. For eighteen years, the four of us have had the opportunity to collaborate in conducting a study comparing two highly contrasting instructional programs.

When the project began in 1984, we did not plan to conduct an 18-year longitudinal study. Over a period of four years, we operated classrooms representing two distinctly different curricula: an academically based instruction program, Direct Instruction (DI); and a cognitively based interactive program, Mediated Learning (ML). Young students (ages 3–6) with a broad range of mild to moderate developmental disabilities were randomly assigned to one of the two curricula, exposed to their assigned program for at least one year, and evaluated for progress in language and cognition.

By the end of that first grant period, we obtained some extremely interesting results that were in direct opposition to conventional wisdom and research regarding the relationship between program structure and entering student aptitude (aptitude–treatment interaction, or ATI). Friedman and Friedman (1980), in a post hoc analysis of language data, found that students benefited differently from programs based on their cognitive and language skills. The cognitively based program was more successful for the higher functioning students, and the direct instruction program was more effective with children with lower ability levels. In our initial research, by contrast, relatively higher-performing students at pretest gained more from DI, and relatively lower-performing students gained more from the cognitively based program.

The initial grant provided for very limited follow-up testing of each child during the school year after each student left the project. Because of our intriguing results, however, we decided to pursue further funding in order to follow the students and investigate the extent and maintenance of the initial aptitude–treatment interactions.

We have now received a series of three additional grants over a total of eighteen years. The final data gathering for the project was planned as the last students in the project reached 18 years of age, in spring 2003. Part of the reason for the continued support from the U.S. Department of Education is that this is one of the relatively few true experiments, with random assignment to conditions, in early childhood education. Random assignment rules out many confounding factors and provides much more confidence in the results.

Though the original and main focus of this research was the effects of the two curricula on cognitive and language development, the design of the study provided the opportunity to investigate other important questions not evident at the outset. One such opportunity was stimulated by a publication by Schweinhart, Weikart, and Larner in 1986. In their follow-up of students at age 15 (from research on curricula conducted in the late 1960s), questions were raised about the social impact of enrollment in various curricula (Direct Instruction, High Scope, and DARCEE), specifically the subsequent rate of juvenile delinquency behavior. Schweinhart and colleagues had reported significantly higher rates of subsequent juvenile delinquency in students receiving the DI program than in students receiving the other two programs. Though the authors suggested that the information be taken with great caution, their caveat was generally ignored. Much attention was given to these results in both the popular press (Hechinger, 1996; Preschool Pressure, 1986) and academic journals without critical review, and debates have continued.

Since our study also included DI classrooms and our ML curriculum contained many of the same elements of the High Scope program, we were able to address the same issue. We requested the questionnaire given in the Schweinhart et al. (1986) project and started gathering data. Our methods and procedures differed somewhat from their study. We gathered data starting at age 13 and each year after through age 16, and again at 18. We had a potential sample of approximately 100 students per program, in contrast to the much smaller number of students (18 per program) represented in the Schweinhart et al. study. Rather than interviewing students, we gave them the opportunity to respond anonymously, thus increasing the likelihood of honest responses. The study reprinted here is the summary of data gathered from the students at age 15.

Gathering the data presented a number of challenges, including privacy issues. Students received this questionnaire as part of their yearly two-hour appointment each summer at ages 13, 14, 15, 16, and 18. The students completed an achievement test, a cognitive measure, and social measures in addition to the juvenile delinquency (JD) questionnaire. Most often the examiner would leave the student alone in the testing room after the testing to complete the JD form. At the student's request, however, the examiner would remain and read the form to the student (some could not read well enough to complete the form themselves). The examiner always guaranteed anonymity to the student. Several students refused to answer, but no more than two each year. We felt that the data were accurate and representative of the students' behavior. The students had a longstanding relationship with us and trusted us, as evidenced by their behavior in the overall testing situation and their desire to participate in the study. On one occasion, however, we received a form with a clear message written at the bottom: "You'll never know, gov't chumps."

Working with students and their families in a longitudinal study has provided us the opportunity to get to know them in many ways. This familiarity has undoubtedly had an impact on each aspect of the project, and needs to be considered in interpreting the results. Conversely, the students and families have had an impact on each of our lives. An everlasting, unique bond has been formed.

References

Friedman, P., & Friedman, K. (1980). Accounting for individual differences when comparing the effectiveness of remedial language teaching methods. *Applied Psycholinguistics, 1,* 151–170.

Hechinger, F. M. (1986). Preschool programs. *The New York Times,* April 22.

Preschool pressure, later difficulties linked in study. (1986). *Education Week,* April 23.

Early Exposure to Direct Instruction and Subsequent Juvenile Delinquency: A Prospective Examination

Paulette E. Mills
Washington State University, Pullman

Kevin N. Cole
Washington Research Institute, Seattle

Joseph R. Jenkins
University of Washington, Seattle

Philip S. Dale
University of Missouri, Columbia

Abstract

In a widely cited follow-up study of disadvantaged preschool attendees, Schweinhart, Weikart, and Larner (1986a) found that graduates of an early childhood program using direct instruction (DI) methods exhibited higher rates of juvenile delinquency at age 15 than did graduates of two other preschool education models. The present research examined juvenile delinquency outcomes for young children with disabilities in a prospective longitudinal study that tracked the long-term impact of two preschool models—one using DI, the other using a cognitively oriented, child-directed model. We followed 171 children who had been randomly assigned

Mills, P. E., Cole, K. N., Jenkins, J. R., & Dale, P. S. (2002). Early exposure to direct instruction and subsequent juvenile delinquency: A prospective examination. *Exceptional Children, 69*(1), 85–96. Copyright © 2002 by the Council for Exceptional children. Reprinted with permission.

to the two early childhood models. At age 15, the groups did not differ significantly in their level of reported delinquency. Analyses suggest that gender differences in delinquent behavior may provide a more parsimonious explanation than program effects for the earlier Schweinhart et al. findings.

The value and long-term impact of early intervention have been examined extensively over the past 2 decades. Core questions have included whether early intervention increases children's skills (e.g., Casto, 1988; Guralnick, 1988, 1998), whether early intervention models derived from differing theoretical bases have different effects (e.g., Cole, Dale, Mills, & Jenkins, 1993; Yoder, Kaiser, & Alpert, 1991), and whether the effects of early intervention last beyond the early years (Mills, Dale, Cole, & Jenkins, 1995; Schweinhart et al., 1986b). Most studies in these areas focus on cognitive, language, and academic outcomes, but a growing appreciation of the interdependence of cognitive, academic, and social development has prompted researchers to broaden the question of early intervention effects to include social development outcomes (e.g., Caprara, Barbaranelli, Pastorelli, Bandura, & Zimbardo, 2000; Davis, Brady, Hamilton, McEvoy, & Williams, 1994; Odom et al., 1999).

The hypothesis that early childhood programs produce differential effects on social skills and behavior is a plausible one. For example, child-directed, cognitively oriented programs often include a metacognitive component designed to increase self-awareness, self-monitoring, and self-regulation that may improve an individual's ability to control impulsive and antisocial behaviors (Krogh, 1997; Smith, 1997). Alternatively, academically oriented programs may advantage children on academic tasks, increasing children's self-esteem and lessening academic frustration and stress linked to problem behaviors (Calhoun & Beattie, 1987; Lawrence, 1988).

In one of the most striking and provocative studies on the long-term impact of early childhood education, Schweinhart et al. (1986b) found evidence for a relationship between a specific early childhood educational approach and later juvenile delinquency. These researchers followed children from three early childhood education programs, each with a different emphasis. They included High/Scope (Hohmann, Banet, & Weikart, 1979), an "open-framework approach, in which teacher and child both plan and initiate activities and actively work together" with the intention "to promote intellectual and social development" (Schweinhart et al., 1986b, p. 18); Direct Instruction (Bereiter & Engelmann, 1966), an academically oriented program in which teachers use scripted lessons to teach reading, math, and language skills; and DARCEE (National Education Association, 1977), a traditional nursery school program employing a "child-centered approach, in which the child initiates and the teacher responds" and where "the teacher encourages children to actively engage in free play" in a broadly enriched environment of toys, materials, and play activities (Schweinhart et al., 1986b, p. 18).

At age 15, graduates of the three programs responded to a questionnaire on antisocial behavior (see Figure 1). Graduates of the DI preschool reported more antisocial behavior than graduates of the other preschool programs. Schweinhart et al. (1986b) speculated that the relative emphasis on teacher-directed academic learning in the DI approach sacrificed opportunities for the kind of child-directed experiences necessary for learning self-regulatory, prosocial skills. The provocative nature of the finding attracted considerable attention and led to a debate about early childhood education among Schweinhart, Weikart, and Larner (1986a) and proponents of DI (i.e., Bereiter, 1986a, 1986b; Gersten, 1986).

Schweinhart et al. (1986b) acknowledged a need for replication studies, but despite an absence of corroborating findings, the link between DI and juvenile delinquency was widely reported in education journals and in the popular press. Schweinhart et al.'s article has been cited over 600 times (Social Sciences Citation Index), and the findings passed on in thousands of articles reporting the finding as a secondary source. The DI model was characterized in the *New York Times* as an "early education pressure cooker approach" that damages children and leads to violence (Hechinger, 1986). Some researchers accepted the direct instruction-delinquency link at face value and sought to identify causal factors within the model that put graduates on delinquent

- Have you ever argued or had a fight with either of your parents?
- Have you ever run away from home?
- Have you ever hit an instructor or supervisor?
- Have you ever gotten into a serious fight in school or at work?
- Have you ever taken part in a fight where a group of your friends were against another?
- Have you ever hurt someone badly enough to need bandages or a doctor?
- Have you ever used a knife or gun or some other thing (like a club) to get something from a person?
- Have you ever taken something not belonging to you worth under $50?
- Have you ever taken something not belonging to you worth over $50?
- Have you ever taken something from a store without paying for it?
- Have you ever taken a car that didn't belong to someone in your family without permission of the owner?
- Have you ever taken part of a car without permission of the owner?
- Have you ever gone into some house or building when you weren't supposed to be there?
- Have you ever set fire to someone's property on purpose?
- Have you ever damaged school property on purpose?
- Have you ever damaged property at work on purpose?
- Have you ever smoked marijuana?
- Have you ever used any drugs or chemicals to get high or for kicks, except marijuana and alcohol?

FIGURE 1 **Questions Presented to Participants**

paths (e.g., DeVries, Haney, & Zan, 1991; DeVries, Reese-Learned, & Morgan, 1991).

Schwinhart et al. (1986b) speculated that the relative emphasis on teacher-directed academic learning in the DI approach sacrificed opportunities for the kind of child-directed experiences necessary for learning self-regulatory, prosocial skills.

The relationship between the DI model of early childhood education and delinquency reported in a single study has thus had considerable influence on practice and thinking in early childhood education (Schweinhart & Weikart, 1998). The implications of their study are especially relevant to the field of special education. Teacher-initiated direct instruction is often considered an appropriate component of a carefully designed program for young children with disabilities (e.g., Sandall, Schwartz, & Joseph, 2001). However, if early exposure to direct instruction actually leads to later higher rates of juvenile delinquency, then use of the model in early

intervention should be strongly reconsidered. An examination of the long-term influence of early direct instruction on antisocial behavior is warranted for this population. We report in this article an examination of the long-term social effects of direct instruction and child-directed instruction for preschoolers. Employing a substantial sample in a fully randomized experimental design, we assigned children who qualified for special education services to one of two preschool models, DI or a cognitively-based, child-directed model called Mediated Learning (ML), then followed program graduates into adolescence.

METHOD

This study included both an intervention and a follow-up phase. We provide a relatively brief description of the preschool intervention phase (detailed accounts are available in Cole et al., 1993 and Mills et al., 1995), followed by a detailed description of the methods for the follow-up of children at age 15.

Preschool Intervention Phase

Participants. Two hundred and six children between the ages 3 and 7 years ($M = 4.9$, $SD = .96$) participated in the intervention phase of the study. According to state administrative code, all children were eligible for special education services based on developmental delays or on medical diagnoses. On entry into the program, their mean IQ on the McCarthy Scales of Children's Abilities (McCarthy, 1972) was 76.7.

Approximately 80% of the students had delayed language, 50% cognitive delays, 60% fine motor delays, 60% gross motor delays, and 60% social-emotional delays. Approximately 20% also had a medical diagnosis, such as cerebral palsy, Down syndrome, or seizure disorder. The majority of children exhibited a significant delay in more than one of the five developmental domains.

Classes and Assignment for Intervention. Each year for 4 years, new students were randomly assigned to either DI (Engelmann & Bruner, 1974; Engelmann & Carnine, 1975; Engelmann & Osborn, 1976) or to ML (Osborn & Sherwood, 1984) programs. Children participated in the programs for an average of 1.65 years, range 1 to 4 years. Modal length of participation was 1 academic year.[a]

Children attended classes in a university laboratory school for 2 hours per day, 5 days a week for 180 school days. There were six preschool classes per year, three for each program, with 12 students in each. One of the three classes for each program enrolled 4 typically developing students and 8 children with disabilities; other classes enrolled only students with disabilities. We report data only for those students with disabilities. In addition, some children attended a kindergarten class for 5.5 hours per day, 5 days a week for 180 days. There was one such kindergarten class for each program, with 14 students per class.

Across both programs, classrooms were staffed with a head teacher who held a Master's degree in Special Education and one assistant teacher, as well as additional staff including occupational and physical therapists, speech language pathologists, and student interns, resulting in a student-staff ratio of approximately 4:1.

Program Descriptions. DI is derived from an extensive task analysis of academic skills, which serves as the basis for a systematic approach for teaching academic skills. It is based on the educational philosophy of Siegfried Engelmann (e.g., Engelmann & Bruner, 1974; Engelmann & Carnine, 1975; Engelmann & Osborn, 1976) and embodied in curriculum materials published as Distar math, language, and reading. DI is teacher directed and fast paced, utilizing highly structured presentation of material with frequent opportunities for student response and reinforcement or correction.

By contrast, ML emphasizes the development and generalization of cognitive processes rather than specific academic content. The theoretical ancestry of ML is derived from Vygotsky (1962) and Feuerstein (Feuerstein, Rand, Hoffman, & Miller, 1980). The approach was originally brought to the United States and developed by Haywood, Brooks, and Burns (1986). The preschool curriculum was further developed by Osborn and Sherwood (1984). The curriculum is organized around such processes as comparison, classification, perspective changing, and sequencing. Teachers interpret the environment according to students' needs, responding and modeling, rather than teaching directly. Constructivist in theory and design, ML includes problem-solving activities, with children and teachers working together; multiple opportunities for children to select materials and activities; and encouragement of child initiation of interactions. Instruction focuses on promoting generalization of cognitive processes to new environments. At the preschool level, ML did not include formal instruction in reading, math, and language skills. At the kindergarten level, children received developmentally appropriate activity-based instruction including the Mathematics-Their-Way (Baratta-Lorton, 1974) program and the Addison-Wesley "Superkids" reading program (Rowland, 1982).

As reported in Cole et al. (1993) and Mills et al. (1995), graduates of the two programs did not differ on cognitive, language, or academic measures taken at the end of 1 year of intervention and at follow-up testing at age 9. However, at both time points there were several significant aptitude-by-treatment interactions. Children who performed higher on cognitive and language

a. The mode is the most frequently occurring score in a set of scores.

measures at pretest showed relatively larger gains from DI than ML, whereas children who performed lower on pretests demonstrated relatively larger gains from ML than DI. The magnitude of these interactions remained comparable over time.

Further information about DI and ML, including information on teacher training and fidelity of implementation is provided in Cole et al. (1993) and Notari, Cole, Osborn, and Sherwood (1996).

> Teachers interpret the environment according to students' needs, responding and modeling, rather than teaching directly.

Follow-Up Phase at Age 15 Years

Participants. We followed children who had completed at least 1 year of early intervention, conducting annual assessments with a battery of tests that varied according to the age of the student. The distribution of the sample by program, ethnicity, gender, and preschool entry IQ and language performance is presented in Table 1. By age 15 the follow-up sample included 171 students, or 83% of the original sample (77% of DI group and 89% of ML). This included 119 males, 62% European American; 29% African American; and 9% Pacific Islander, Asian, Latino, or Native American. Chi square analyses indicated the follow-up DI and ML groups did not differ significantly on gender or ethnicity ($p > .05$).[b]

Juvenile Delinquency Self-Report Questionnaire. When graduates reached age 15, they responded to Schweinhart et al.'s (1986b) juvenile delinquency questionnaire. The questions are presented in Figure 1. Items seek in-

TABLE 1 — Descriptive Statistics for Follow-Up Phase Participants

	Program			
	Direct Instruction		Mediated Learning	
Characteristics	*n*		*n*	
Gender				
Male	56		63	
Female	25		27	
Ethnicity				
European American	43		63	
African American	29		21	
Other	9		6	
Standardized Measures at Entry into Preschool				
	M	*SD*	*M*	*SD*
McCarthy Cognitive Index	77.82	17.50	76.08	15.91
Peabody Picture Vocabulary Test	78.52	17.36	80.67	16.31

b. Chi-square is used as a test of statistical significance when the variables of interest are categorical. In this case, the ethnic groupings and gender are categories. The chi-square test yielded nonsignificant results. This means that any differences in the distribution of ethnicity and gender across the DI and ML groups are more likely due to chance than to real differences in the populations from which the two groups were drawn.

formation on the frequency of behaviors such as fighting, running away from home, stealing, weapons use, arson, and drug use. Consistent with Schweinhart et al., we scored each item 0 for "not at all," 1 point for "once," 2 points for "twice," 3 points for "three or four times," or 4 points for "five or more times."

Procedures. To assure students' anonymity, neither their names nor other identifying information were linked to their answers. Testers coded only information about students' preschool program assignment, gender, ethnicity, and current living arrangement (i.e., living with a single parent, both parents, or residential placement) on individual response forms. With our relatively large sample size, this set of variables was intentionally insufficient to identify individual participants, thus protecting participants' anonymity. Participants were assured their answers would remain confidential even from testers and could not be tied to them personally. Participants who could not read the questionnaire received assistance from a tester and were assured that no information would be revealed. After completing the paper and pencil questionnaire privately in the testing room, students inserted the interview form into an envelope, which they sealed and placed in a locked box which remained unopened until all testing for that year was completed. Although this procedure prevented analyses relating questionnaire responses to cognitive or academic test scores, it increased the probability that youth would respond truthfully, without fear of social, civil, or criminal recourse.

RESULTS

First, we examined the proportion of respondents from the two programs who left one or more questions unanswered. Rate of incomplete responding was similar for the two groups: DI (4%) and ML (6%). We were also able to determine the number of students who completed the assessment battery (which included several other measures), but declined to answer the delinquency questionnaire. Three DI graduates declined to answer the questionnaire, whereas all ML graduates agreed to participate.

Following Schweinhart et al.'s (1986b) approach, we examined program differences for self-report of delinquency at the level of overall questionnaire score (total delinquent acts), subscale scores (personal violence, property damage, stealing, drug abuse, and status offenses), and individual questionnaire items (Table 2). None of the 25 t-tests were significant (all $p > .08$).[c] Effect sizes ranged from $-.27$ to $.16$, considered to fall in the "small" range (Cohen, 1988; Sedlmeier & Gigerenzer, 1989).[d] Of the 25 effect sizes computed, 20 were negative, reflecting differences that were opposite the predicted direction of higher juvenile delinquency for DI graduates.

We then conducted two sets of analyses of variance (ANOVAs): one for Program × Gender and the other for Program × Ethnicity.[e] Uneven and small cell sizes ruled

c. The t test used to determine whether an observed difference between the mean scores of two groups on a measure is likely to have occurred by chance or whether it reflects a true difference in the mean scores of the populations from which the two groups were drawn. The fact that all 25 t tests were not statistically significant ($p > .08$) means that any differences between the DI and ML groups in delinquent behavior were more likely due to chance than to real differences in the populations from which the two groups were drawn.

d. An effect size is a statistic based on a formula involving both the mean scores and standard deviations of the scores of two groups. It allows a precise calculation of how different the score distributions of two groups are. The fact that small effect sizes were found indicates that the DI and ML groups differed in their self-reports of delinquency but the differences were minor.

e. Analysis of variance is used for several purposes, including determination of the effect of several independent variables (the presumed causes) on a dependent variable (the presumed effect). In the present case, the researchers wished to determine the effect of three independent variables (program, ethnicity, and gender) on the dependent variable of delinquent behavior. Analysis of variance also has the capacity to determine whether the effect of a particular independent variable is mediated by another independent variable. For example, DI might be found to promote more delinquent behavior than ML, but only in males.

| TABLE 2 | Means and Standard Deviations for Delinquent Act Ratings by Curriculum Groups | | | | |

Variable	Direct Instruction (n = 78–81)[a]		Mediated Learning (n = 89–90)[a]		Effect Size
	M	SD	M	SD	
Total delinquent acts	11.05	13.66	12.62	14.27	−0.11
Personal violence subscale	3.01	4.12	3.66	4.70	−0.15
Hit an instructor/supervisor	0.37	0.90	0.41	0.92	−0.04
Had a serious fight in school or at work	1.01	1.37	1.07	1.40	−0.04
Been in a group fight	0.80	1.21	1.13	1.45	−0.25
Seriously injured someone	0.56	1.07	0.80	1.26	−0.21
Used a weapon to get something[b]	0.27	0.84	0.31	0.98	−0.04
Property damage subscale	0.71	2.10	1.06	1.93	−0.17
Committed arson	0.28	0.98	0.20	0.69	0.10
Purposely damaged school property	0.44	1.08	0.78	1.37	−0.27
Purposely damaged work property	0.02	0.46	0.11	0.57	−0.17
Stealing subscale	3.75	5.42	3.98	5.41	−0.04
Stolen something worth under $50	1.04	1.52	1.11	1.57	−0.04
Stolen something worth over $50	0.59	1.24	0.62	1.29	−0.02
Stolen something from a store	1.30	1.53	1.30	1.49	0.00
Stolen a car	0.23	0.81	0.30	0.92	−0.08
Stolen part of a car	0.33	0.97	0.34	1.00	−0.01
Used a weapon to get something[b]	0.27	0.84	0.31	0.98	−0.04
Drug abuse subscale	0.98	2.15	0.90	1.91	0.04
Smoked marijuana	0.57	1.34	0.67	1.40	−0.07
Used other illegal drugs	0.40	1.10	0.24	0.84	0.16
Status offenses subscale	3.32	3.35	3.68	3.30	−0.11
Argued or fought with parents	1.95	1.67	2.10	1.66	−0.09
Run away from home	0.58	1.12	0.51	1.13	0.06
Trespassed	0.79	1.41	1.07	1.57	−0.19

[a]df varied according to the number of students responding to a question.
[b]Weapon use was included in both scales in the original version of the questionnaire.

out Program × Gender × Ethnicity analyses.[f] Our interest in gender effects stemmed from differences in the proportion of males and females between Schweinhart et al.'s (1986b) two groups, which may have affected their findings. We also examined ethnicity and its interaction with program because our sample included proportionally more

f. Analysis of variance enables researchers to look for significant interactions at various levels of complexity. In the present case, the researchers considered looking for a three-way interaction involving program, gender, and ethnicity. For example, DI (program) might be found to promote more delinquent behavior than ML, but only in males (gender) who are Caucasian (ethnicity). The researchers determined that they lacked a sufficient sample size for each subgroup to test the statistical significance of any observed three-way interactions.

European Americans than Schweinhart et al.'s. The two sets of analyses were conducted on the total and the subscale scores, but not on individual items.

Program × Gender Analysis

Program effects were not significant either for number of delinquent acts or for subscale scores. (All $Fs < 1.7$, df in the denominator vary from 159 to 167 depending on the number of students responding to each item.)[g] Table 3 shows that self-report of delinquent acts was similar for DI and ML models.

Gender was significant for total delinquent acts, $F(1, 159) = 4.88$, $p = .03$, and for the subscales measuring personal violence, $F(1, 166) = 9.37$, $p = .003$; property damage, $F(1, 164) = 3.80$, $p = .05$; and stealing, $F(1, 165) = 4.63$, $p = .03$, with males reporting higher delinquency levels than females.[h] However, the

TABLE 3 Means and Standard Deviations for Total and Subscale Scores by Gender and Ethnicity

Delinquent Acts	Direct Instruction				Mediated Learning			
	Male		Female		Male		Female	
	M	SD	M	SD	M	SD	M	SD
Total acts	12.51	15.11	7.56	8.61	14.36	14.80	8.89	12.53
Personal violence	3.72	4.60	1.33	1.81	4.29	5.06	2.22	3.41
Property damage	0.95	2.45	0.13	0.34	1.21	1.98	0.71	1.82
Stealing	4.46	6.06	2.08	2.98	4.44	5.51	2.96	5.14
Drug abuse	1.04	2.23	0.83	1.97	1.08	2.01	0.50	1.67
Status offenses	3.42	3.52	3.08	2.93	4.08	3.48	2.78	2.71

	Direct Instruction						Mediated Learning					
	European American		African American		Other		European American		African American		Other	
	M	SD	M	SD	M	SD	M	SD	M	SD	M	SD
Total acts	11.54	14.62	11.76	14.01	6.00	3.46	9.83	11.65	22.21	18.85	10.17	9.54
Personal violence	3.09	4.36	3.45	4.27	1.22	1.39	2.82	3.71	6.24	6.53	3.33	3.67
Property damage	0.80	2.53	0.76	1.72	0.11	0.33	0.89	1.88	1.75	2.15	0.50	1.22
Stealing	3.86	6.05	3.86	4.97	2.75	3.37	2.55	3.78	8.57	7.45	2.67	1.51
Drug abuse	1.14	2.34	0.86	2.08	0.56	1.33	0.58	1.68	1.74	2.26	1.50	2.34
Status offenses	3.79	3.73	3.00	3.07	2.11	1.69	3.48	3.14	4.67	3.42	2.33	4.32

g. The calculation of analysis of variance for a set of data results in an F value. The magnitude of the F value is examined to determine whether observed differences between groups are statistically significant. The abbreviation df stands for "degrees of freedom." The concept of degrees of freedom has a complex statistical basis. In analysis of variance, the degrees of freedom depend largely on sample size. The more the degrees of freedom, the easier in general it is to determine whether an observed difference between groups is statistically significant.

h. A p value of .05 or less is generally used as the criterion for judging that an observed difference between groups is statistically significant. The fact that all gender comparisons on the measures of delinquency were statistically significant means that the observed differences were not likely due to chance, but rather reflect real differences in the populations of males and females that these samples presumably represent.

Program × Gender interaction was not significant for either total delinquent acts or for any subscales (all $Fs < 1$).

Program × Ethnicity Results

Significant main effects were found for ethnicity on total delinquent acts, $F(2, 157) = 4.08$, $p = .02$, and for the subscales of personal violence, $F(2, 164) = 3.69$, $p = .03$; and stealing, $F(2, 163) = 6.17$, $p = .003$, with African American students reporting more delinquent acts than European American students and students classified as "Other." The Program × Ethnicity interaction was significant for total delinquent acts, $F(2, 157) = 3.15$, $p = .04$, and the stealing subscale, $F(2, 163) = 5.68$, $p = .004$. African American students in DI had significantly lower delinquent acts than did African American students in ML.

Relative Delinquency Levels

We compared our delinquency levels with those of Schweinhart et al. (1986b; see Table 4). The mean number of delinquent acts reported by DI graduates from the two studies were comparable, $t(94) = .54$, $ns.$[i] However, relative to Schweinhart et al.'s High/Scope graduates, ML graduates reported significantly more delinquent acts, $t(105) = 3.70$, $p < .001$.

DISCUSSION

In contrast to Schweinhart et al.'s (1986b) results, the most striking finding of this study is the absence of pro-gram effects on *any* aspect of delinquency, even though both studies focused on children of comparable ages, employed similar preschool curricula, and used the same measure of delinquency. There are several differences between the two studies, however, that may explain the discrepant results. They include design differences, program characteristics, historical context, and sample differences. Each of these four areas is discussed below.

Design Differences

In reporting their seminal study, Schweinhart et al. (1986b) acknowledged that small sample size and incomplete random assignment may have affected their results. We attempted to overcome these problems by substantially increasing sample size (i.e., at least 77 children per group, versus 18 per group in the earlier study) and randomly assigning all of our participants to preschool programs (versus 87% in the earlier study).

The two studies also differed in degree of anonymity provided respondents. Schweinhart et al. (1986b) employed as data collector a former local high school coach "who knew well the neighborhood where the families of the 15-year-olds in the study lived" (Schweinhart et al., 1986a, p. 304). By contrast we provided subjects complete anonymity and visibly handled their survey responses in a manner to assure them of this fact. Validity of results based on self-report rests in large part on the willingness of youth to respond truthfully, without fear of unfavorable social perception or of prosecution for their disclosures. The anonymity provided respondents in our study was designed to encourage honest reporting.

TABLE 4	**Means and Standard Deviations of Total Delinquent Acts Reported in the Two Studies**				
	Present Study		**Schweinhart et al. (1986b)**		
	M	*SD*	*M*	*SD*	*t* value
DI curricula	11.05	13.66	12.83	12.33	0.54
Cognitive curricula	12.62	14.27	5.44[a]	5.15[a]	3.70*

[a]High/Scope.

*$p < .001$.

i. The abbreviation *ns* stands for "not significant," meaning not statistically significant.

Program Characteristics

Although the DI programs used in the two studies were derived from the same general theoretical model, they varied significantly in form and completeness. We were able to use the commercial version of the Distar materials, rather than less specific DI guidelines available at the time of the Schweinhart et al. (1986b) study. Authors of Distar have noted that the nascent DI methods from the earlier study are not a valid representation of their final published Distar materials (even though they were mistakenly referred to as Distar in Schweinhart et al., 1986b). Although earlier and later versions of DI may have differed in inducing juvenile delinquency, the mechanism for such an effect is not apparent.

Could differences among the High/Scope, DARCEE, and ML models explain the different results from the two studies? The ML model, like the High/Scope model and DARCEE, is a developmentally appropriate, child-directed, cognitively oriented approach. In ML children were encouraged to plan, make choices, and solve problems independently. ML incorporates the essential elements of an open-framework and child-directed approach in which creative activities and solutions are supported, and children are encouraged to select activities in a structured environment. Teachers assume the role of facilitator, rather than director. ML bears greater family resemblance to the High/Scope and DARCEE models than to the highly teacher-directed, academically oriented DI model.

> Validity of results based on self-report rests in large part on the willingness of youth to respond truthfully, without fear of unfavorable social perception or of prosecution for their disclosures.

Historical Context

The overall level of delinquent acts reported by both our DI and ML groups were comparable to that of Schweinhart et al.'s (1986b) DI group. The high overall level of delinquent behaviors in the present study is consistent with the national trends that show a 70% increase from the previous decade (Snyder & Sickmund, 1999). However, the relative difference in the rate of juvenile delinquency between the two time periods cannot account for absence of group differences in the present study.

Sample Differences

The principal difference between the research samples in the two studies is that our sample qualified for special education services. This distinction is not as marked as it might appear, however, because the average IQ scores were similar for the children in the two studies (approximately 80), and special education services were not federally mandated at the time of the Schweinhart et al. (1986b) study. It is a reasonable conjecture that many of Schweinhart et al.'s children would have qualified for services under today's eligibility guidelines. Our study probably included more children with characteristics such as Down syndrome, cerebral palsy, and other specific diagnoses. However, children with severe disabilities were not included in our study, allowing a sampling of participants more similar to those in the Schweinhart et al. study.

The two studies also differed on sample ethnicity. The majority of children in the 1986 study were African American versus approximately 30% African American children in our study. This sample difference does not resolve the different findings between the studies. In fact the only significant Program × Ethnicity interactions were due to African American youth in ML reporting higher scores (relative to DI) for total delinquent acts and the stealing subscale.

The most parsimonious explanation for the different results in the two studies lies in the gender differences between the samples. At follow-up Schweinhart et al.'s (1986b) DI group had 57% more boys than their High/Scope group (11 versus 7). Similarly, their DI group had 38% fewer girls than did their High/Scope group (8 versus 11). The balance between males and females in Schweinhart et al.'s treatment groups changed markedly between the intervention phase and the follow-up phase, resulting in substantial difference in males and females between curriculum groups. This is a critical research design problem because males participate in unlawful behavior approximately four times more than females (Office of Juvenile Justice and Delinquency Prevention, 1993). This difference is not a new trend and has been documented in studies specifically addressing the relationship between early education experience and delinquency (e.g., Farnworth, Schweinhart, &

Berrueta-Clement, 1985). The higher proportion of adolescent males in the DI sample relative to the High/Scope sample provides a possible explanation for the higher level of reported delinquent acts for the 1986b DI group.

The confound of program with gender in Schweinhart et al.'s (1986b) study provides a rival hypothesis to their interpretation that preschools using child-initiated learning activities reduce the rates of juvenile delinquency, relative to preschools using teacher-directed approaches. The effect of imbalance in number of males and females between the groups provides an explanation based on a widely researched and consistently documented phenomenon: a higher rate of delinquent behavior for males than females (Bjerregaard & Smith, 1993; Broidy & Agnew, 1997; Burton, Cullen, Evans, Alarid, & Dunaway, 1998; Canter, 1982; Farnworth et al., 1985; Jang & Krohn, 1995; Mears, Ploeger, & Warr, 1998; O'Brien, 1999; Triplett & Jarjoura, 1997). Schweinhart et al.'s apparent program differences may have been the result of gender imbalances in their follow-up groups.

> Our results indicate young children with disabilities can be provided direct instruction as an aspect of intervention without fear that the method will result in later antisocial behavior.

Attributing these differences to gender imbalances rather than program effects reconciles the discrepancy in findings between the Schweinhart et al. (1986b) study and the current study. A gender explanation is also consistent with a large body of research on gender and delinquency, whereas there are no other corroborative findings to indicate that child-directed preschool curricula serve as a protective factor against later delinquency.

IMPLICATIONS FOR PRACTICE

We wish to make it clear that we do not interpret these results as in any way denigrating the value of the High/Scope model or similar child-directed models for young children. In fact, in our original intervention comparison study, we found that the cognitively oriented ML model was more effective than DI in serving preschool-age children who entered the program with greater delays in cognitive and language development. In contrast, we found the DI model was more effective for children who entered the program with relatively higher cognitive and language skills. Based on these findings we see an advantage for both types of early education program for young children who are at risk for school failure. Our results indicate young children with disabilities can be provided direct instruction as an aspect of intervention without fear that the method will result in later antisocial behavior. The findings also suggest that Schweinhart et al.'s (1986b) conclusion that direct instruction results in later juvenile delinquency with typically developing children should be viewed with caution until their data are reexamined for the variable of gender. Gender should certainly be considered in studies of juvenile delinquency. Until this is done, such conclusions lack a scientifically sound empirical base.

About the Authors

Paulette E. Mills, Associate Professor, Department of Human Development, Washington State University, Pullman.

Kevin N. Cole (CEC #1103), Senior Researcher, Washington Research Institute, Seattle.

Joseph R. Jenkins (CEC #28), Professor, College of Education, University of Washington, Seattle.

Philip S. Dale, Professor, Department of Communication Sciences and Disorders, University of Missouri, Columbia.

Correspondence concerning this article should be addressed to Joseph R. Jenkins, University of Washington, Experimental Education Unit, Box 357925, Seattle, WA 98195-7925.

Email: jjenkins@u.washington.edu.

This research was supported by Grant H324C990012 from the U.S. Department of Education to the University of Washington.

Manuscript received October 2001; accepted March 2002.

References

Baratta-Lorton, M. (1974). *Mathematics-their-way.* Campbell, CA: Center for Innovation in Education.

Bereiter, C. (1986a). Does direct instruction cause delinquency? *Early Childhood Research Quarterly, 1,* 289–292.

Bereiter, C. (1986b). Mountains of evidence said to contradict study effects of preschool. [Letter to the Editor]. *Educational Leadership, 5,* 37.

Bereiter, C., & Engelmann, S. (1966). *Teaching disadvantaged children in the preschool.* Englewood Cliffs, NJ: Prentice-Hall.

Bjerregaard, B., & Smith, C. (1993). Gender differences in gang participation, delinquency, and substance abuse. *Journal of Quantitative Criminology, 9,* 329–355.

Broidy, L., & Agnew, R. (1997). Gender and crime: A general strain theory perspective. *Journal of Research in Crime and Delinquency 34,* 275–306.

Burton, V. S., Cullen, F. T., Evans, T. D., Alarid, L. F., & Dunaway, R. G. (1998). Gender, self-control, and crime. *Journal of Research in Crime and Delinquency, 35*(2), 123–147.

Calhoun, M. L., & Beattie, J. (1987). School competence needs of mildly handicapped adolescents. *Adolescence 22,* 555–563.

Canter, R. J. (1982). Sex differences in self-report delinquency. *Criminology: An Interdisciplinary Journal, 20,* 373–393.

Caprara, G. V., Barbaranelli, C., Pastorelli, C., Bandura, A., & Zimbardo, P. (2000). Prosocial foundations of children's academic achievement. *Psychological Science, 11,* 302–306.

Casto, G. (1988). Research and program evaluation in early childhood special education. In S. L. Odom & M. B. Karnes (Eds.), *Early intervention for infants and children with handicaps* (pp. 51–62). Baltimore: Paul H. Brookes.

Cohen, J. (1988). *Statistical power analysis for the behavioral sciences* (2nd ed.). Hillsdale, NJ: Lawrence Erlbaum Associates.

Cole, K. N., Dale, P. S., Mills, P. E., & Jenkins, J. R. (1993). Interaction between early intervention curricula and student characteristics. *Exceptional Children, 60,* 17–28.

Davis, C. A., Brady, M. P., Hamilton, R., McEvoy, M. A., & Williams, R. (1994). Effects of high-probability requests on the social interactions of young children with severe disabilities. *Journal of Applied Behavioral Analysis, 27,* 619–637.

DeVries, R., Haney, J. P., & Zan, B. (1991). Sociomoral atmosphere in direct-instruction, eclectic, and constructivist kindergartens: A study of teachers' enacted interpersonal understanding. *Early Childhood Research Quarterly, 6,* 449–471.

DeVries, R., Reese-Learned, H., & Morgan, P. (1991). Sociomoral development in direct-instruction, eclectic, and constructivist kindergartens: A study of children's enacted interpersonal understanding. *Early Childhood Research Quarterly, 6,* 473–517.

Engelmann, S., & Bruner, E. C. (1974). *Distar reading I and II.* Chicago: Science Research Associates.

Engelmann, S., & Carnine, D. (1975). *Distar arithmetic I and II.* Chicago: Science Research Associates.

Engelmann, S., & Osborn, J. (1976). *Distar language I and II.* Chicago: Science Research Associates.

Farnworth, M., Schweinhart, L., & Berrueta-Clement, J. (1985). Preschool intervention, school success and delinquency in a high-risk sample of youth. *American Educational Research Journal, 22,* 445–464.

Feuerstein, R., Rand, Y., Hoffman, M., & Miller, R. (1980). *Instrumental enrichment: Redevelopment of cognitive functions of retarded performers.* Baltimore: University Park Press.

Gersten, R. (1986). Response to "Consequences of three preschool curriculum models through age 15." *Early Childhood Research Quarterly, 1,* 293–302.

Guralnick, M. (1988). Efficacy research in early childhood intervention programs. In S. L. Odom & M. B. Karnes (Eds.), *Early intervention for infants and children with handicaps* (pp. 75–88). Baltimore: Paul H. Brookes.

Guralnick, M. (1998). Effectiveness of early intervention for vulnerable children: A developmental perspective. *American Journal of Mental Retardation, 102,* 319–345.

Haywood, H. C., Brooks, P., & Burns, S. (1986). Stimulating cognitive development at developmental level: A tested, non-remedial preschool curriculum for preschoolers and older retarded children. *Special Services in the Schools, 3*(1–2), 127–147.

Hechinger, E. M. (1986, April 22). Preschool programs. *The New York Times,* 17.

Hohmann, M., Banet, B., & Weikart D. P. (1979). *Young children in action: A manual for preschool educators.* Ypsilanti, MI: High/Scope Press.

Jang, S., & Krohn, M. D. (1995). Developmental patterns of sex differences in delinquency among African American adolescents: A test of the sex-invariance hypothesis. *Journal of Quantitative Criminology, 11*(2), 195–222.

Krogh, S. L. (1997). How children develop and why it matters: The foundation for the developmentally appropriate integrated early childhood curriculum. In C. H. Hart & D. C. Burts (Eds.), *Integrated curriculum and developmentally appropriate practice: Birth to age eight* (pp. 29–48). Albany: State University of New York Press.

Lawrence, P. A. (1988). Basic strategies for mainstream integration. *Academic Therapy, 23,* 349–355.

McCarthy, D. (1972). *McCarthy Scales of Children's Abilities.* San Antonio, TX: Psychological Corporation.

Mears, D. P., Ploeger, M., & Warr, M. (1998). Explaining the gender gap in delinquency: Peer influence and moral evaluations of behavior. *Journal of Research in Crime and Delinquency, 35,* 251–266.

Mills, P. E., Dale, P. S., Cole, K. N., & Jenkins, J. R. (1995). Follow-up of children from academic and cognitive preschool curricula at age 9. *Exceptional Children, 61,* 378–393.

National Education Association. (1977). *The DARCEE teacher's guide (preschool series) and DARCEE resource unit materials.* (Project on utilization of inservice education R & D outcomes). Washington, DC: Author.

Notari, A., Cole, K., Osborn, J., & Sherwood, D. (1996). Adapting Feuerstein's Theories for Preschool: Teaching cognitive and social strategies to young children with disabilities in integrated settings. *Teaching Exceptional Children, 28,* 12–16.

O'Brien, R. M. (1999). Measuring the convergence/divergence of "serious crime" arrest rates for males and females: 1960–1995. *Journal of Quantitative Criminology, 15,* 97–114.

Odom, S. L., McConnell, S. R., McEvoy, M. A., Peterson, C., Ostrosky, M., Chandler, L. K., Spicuzza, R. J., Skellenger, A., Creighton, M., & Favazza, P. C. (1999). Relative effects of interventions supporting the social competence of young children with disabilities. *Topics in Early Childhood Special Education, 19*(2), 75–91.

Office of Juvenile Justice and Delinquency Prevention. (1993). *Juvenile justice.* Rockville, MD: Juvenile Justice Clearinghouse.

Osborn, J., & Sherwood, D. (1984). Mediated Learning Program for Young Children. Unpublished curriculum, University of Washington at Seattle.

Rowland, P. (1982). *The Addison-Wesley Reading Program.* Menlo Park, CA: Addison-Wesley.

Sandall, S., Schwartz, I., & Joseph, G. (2001). A building blocks model for effective instruction in inclusive early childhood settings. *Young Exceptional Children, 4*(3), 3–9.

Schweinhart, L., & Weikart, D. (1998). Why curriculum matters in early childhood education. *Educational Leadership 55*(6), 57–60.

Schweinhart, L., Weikart, D., & Larner, M. (1986a). Child-initiated activities in early childhood programs may help prevent delinquency. *Early Childhood Research Quarterly, 1*(3), 303–312.

Schweinhart, L., Weikart, D., & Larner, M. (1986b). Consequences of three preschool curriculum models through age 15. *Early Childhood Research Quarterly, 1,* 15–45.

Sedlmeier, P., & Gigerenzer, G. (1989). Do studies of statistical power have an effect on the power of studies? *Psychological Bulletin, 105,* 309–316.

Smith, K. E. (1997). Student teachers' beliefs about developmentally appropriate practice: Pattern, stability, and the influence of locus of control. *Early Childhood Research Quarterly, 12*(2), 221–243.

Snyder, H., & Sickmund, M. (1999). *Juvenile offenders and victims: 1999 national report.* Washington, DC: Office of Juvenile Justice and Delinquency.

Triplett, R., & Jarjoura, G. R. (1997). Specifying the gender-class-delinquency relationship: Exploring the effects of educational expectations. *Sociological Perspectives, 40,* 287–316.

Vygotsky L. (1962). *Thought and language.* New York: Wiley.

Yoder, P., Kaiser, A., & Alpert, C. (1991). An exploratory study of interaction between language teaching methods and child characteristics. *Journal of Speech and Hearing Research, 34*(1), 155–167.

In this section of the chapter you will read a research article that illustrates the use of the single-case experimental research method. It is preceded by comments written especially for this book by Glen Dunlap, the first author of the article. Then the article itself is reprinted in full, just as it appeared when originally published. Where appropriate, we have added footnotes to help you understand the information contained in the article.

SAMPLE SINGLE-CASE EXPERIMENTAL RESEARCH STUDY

Modifying Activities to Produce Functional Outcomes: Effects on the Problem Behaviors of Students with Disabilities

Dunlap, G., Foster-Johnson, L., Clarke, S., Kern, L., & Childs, K. E. (1995). Modifying activities to produce functional outcomes: Effects on the problem behaviors of students with disabilities. *Journal of the Association for Persons with Severe Handicaps, 20,* 248–258.

● RESEARCHER'S COMMENTS, *Prepared by Glen Dunlap*

The analyses presented in this article represent a line of inquiry that our research group has pursued for over six years. The focus of this research is the effects of antecedent and curricular variables on the problem behaviors of students with disabilities. We have attempted to illustrate the impact that curricular and instructional procedures exert on problem behaviors. We also have sought to demonstrate that teachers can reduce students' undesirable behavior patterns by individualizing curricula on the basis of functional assessment information (Dunlap & Kern, 1993; 1996).

Our initial commitment to this line of research occurred in 1990 when we were asked to consult on the extreme behavior problems of a 12-year-old girl with multiple disabilities. Jill (a pseudonym) was in danger of being institutionalized, because her disruptive behaviors were very frequent and intense and had proved resistant to years of multidisciplinary interventions.

We first conducted a thorough assessment of the interactions between Jill's behavior and events in the school environment (Foster-Johnson & Dunlap, 1993; O'Neill et al., 1997). Eventually we were able to identify associations between her most serious behavior problems and certain curricular variables. When we modified Jill's curriculum based on the assessment findings, her problem behaviors were eliminated, her adaptive behavior improved, and she was able to remain in school (Dunlap, Kern-Dunlap, Clarke, & Robbins, 1991). This positive experience convinced us of the untapped power of assessment-based curricular interventions. It led to a series of studies in special education programs for children with developmental, emotional, and behavioral disabilities.

Our research team is based at the Florida Mental Health Institute (FMHI) of the University of South Florida, and we have conducted all these studies in association with local school systems. This research has been supported by FMHI and by several grants from the U.S. Department of Education. For the most part, the data have been collected by members of our team who have worked on a daily basis in partnership with classroom teachers. Together they have sought to solve problem behaviors with approaches that are effective, feasible, and sensitive to the individual student's needs and characteristics.

Some of the studies have involved detailed analyses of a single student, with data being collected over many months. Jill's story was an example of this approach, as was a study with Eddie (a pseudonym), a boy identified as severely emotionally disturbed (Kern, Childs, Dunlap, Clarke, & Falk, 1994). Eddie had above-average intelligence, but during academic instruction he displayed emotional outbursts and occasional self-injury.

The functional assessment process revealed several instructional and curricular variables that affected Eddie's behavior. These included long academic sessions, assignments that required handwriting, the lack of reminders to self-monitor his engagement, and the visible presence of possible distractors. Each of these factors was shown in brief single-subject research designs to produce low levels of task engagement and high rates of problem behaviors. Eddie's three teachers then used this information (with our assistance) to create small changes in the way they delivered instruction to him. Eddie's problem behaviors decreased dramatically, his engagement increased, and he subsequently moved to a regular class, where he continued to succeed.

Another type of study that we have conducted involves collecting data from large numbers of students in order to evaluate the potential relationship between the general quality of a curriculum and the presence of problem behaviors. In one investigation, we obtained data from students in 64 classrooms and measured the quality of the curricular activity as well as the occurrence of desirable and problem behaviors. The analyses showed that each of the quality dimensions that we measured was related to the behavior patterns, indicating that curriculum and student behavior are related to one another (Ferro, Foster-Johnson, & Dunlap, 1996).

We have observed that many students with acting-out behaviors seem to engage in disruption to obtain desired activities, or to exert some control over their environment. Our studies and those of other researchers show that providing students the option of selecting among scheduled assignments, materials, or sequences can reduce problem behaviors significantly, at least for some students in some circumstances. Similarly, we have seen that the provision of preferred activities or materials can reduce behavior problems. In two recent studies (Clarke et al., 1995; Foster Johnson, Ferro, & Dunlap, 1994) we demonstrated that the identification and infusion of curriculum elements matched to students' preference helped decrease behavior problems and produce desirable, successful student performance.

The study that is reprinted here is closely aligned with the investigations on student preference. This set of data has a little twist that we felt was important to convey, and therefore we assembled these analyses to emphasize the similarity of the interventions. That is, in the curricular modifications for each of the three students, the activity was modified such that its natural outcome would be one that the individual student would perceive as meaningful and pleasing. Importantly, the integrity of the instructional objective in each case was not abridged; instead, the manner in which it was addressed was changed. The interventions show how instructional activities can be tailored to individual students in order to produce improved responding and deportment, without compromising the curriculum.

Some features of this study are important. For one, the three students were identified as having different disabilities, including autism, mental retardation, emotional and behavioral disorder, and multiple disabilities. This diversity indicates explicitly that the approach has external validity, meaning that its applicability is not limited to a particular kind of disability or circumstance. Similarly, the interests that were identified for the three students were quite different. What motivated one student would not necessarily have motivated another. Repeatedly, we have confirmed through our observations and systematic analyses that an individualized understanding of a student's interests and characteristics is essential for effective interventions.

Another feature that deserves mention is that none of the interventions required a specific alteration of programmed rewards or other consequences. There is no question that contingency management is an important element of motivational and disciplinary systems. However, it is also important to recognize that significant improvements can be achieved with antecedent manipulations, including carefully designed curricula. In fact, that is a core message of the above-mentioned line of research.

As I write these comments, our group is continuing to pursue applied research issues that involve richer and more effective interventions and supports for children with disabilities. Some members of our team have taken other positions. Lynn Foster-Johnson has moved to Dartmouth College, and Lee Kern is now at the University of Pennsylvania. Others of us remain at the University of South Florida, where we are beginning to work increasingly with students with disabilities in the context of their family lives and community participation. We believe that the same ideas and practices that are expressed in this article will have relevance in these expanded domains.

References

Clarke, S., Dunlap, G., Foster-Johnson, L., Childs, K. E., Wilson, D., White, R., & Vera, A. (1995). Improving the conduct of students with behavioral disorders by incorporating student interests into curricular activities. *Behavioral Disorders, 20,* 221–237.

Dunlap, G., dePerczel, M., Clarke, S., Wilson, D., Wright, S., White, R., & Gomez, A. (1994). Choice making to promote adaptive behavior for students with emotional and behavioral challenges. *Journal of Applied Behavior Analysis, 27,* 505–518.

Dunlap, G., & Kern, L. (1993). Assessment and intervention for children within the instructional curriculum. In J. Reichle & D. Wacker (Eds.), *Communicative approaches to the management of challenging behavior* (pp. 177–203). Baltimore: Paul H. Brookes.

Dunlap, G., & Kern, L. (1996). Modifying instructional activities to promote desirable behavior: A conceptual and practical framework. *School Psychology Quarterly, 11,* 297–312.

Dunlap, G., Kern-Dunlap, L., Clarke, S., & Robbins, F. R. (1991). Functional assessment, curriculum revision, and severe behavior problems. *Journal of Applied Behavior Analysis, 24,* 387–397.

Dunlap, G., White, R., Vera, A. G., Wilson, D., & Panacek, L. (1996). The effects of multi-component, assessment-based curricular modifications on the classroom behavior of children with emotional and behavioral disorders. *Journal of Behavioral Education, 6,* 481–500.

Ferro, J., Foster-Johnson, L., & Dunlap, G. (1996). Relation between curricular activities and problem behaviors of students with mental retardation. *American Journal on Mental Retardation, 101,* 184–194.

Foster-Johnson, L., & Dunlap, G. (1993). Using functional assessment to develop effective, individualized interventions. *Teaching Exceptional Children, 25,* 44–50.

Foster-Johnson, L., Ferro, J., & Dunlap, G. (1994). Preferred curricular activities and reduced problem behaviors in students with intellectual disabilities. *Journal of Applied Behavior Analysis, 27,* 493–504.

Kern, L., Childs, K. E., Dunlap, G., Clarke, S., & Falk, G. D. (1994). Using assessment-based curricular intervention to improve the classroom behavior of a student with emotional and behavioral challenges. *Journal of Applied Behavior Analysis, 27,* 7–19.

O'Neill, R. E., Horner, R. H., Albin, R. W., Sprague, J. R., Storey, K., & Newton, J. S. (1997). *Functional assessment and program development for problem behavior: A practical handbook.* Pacific Grove, CA: Brooks/Cole.

Modifying Activities to Produce Functional Outcomes: Effects on the Problem Behaviors of Students with Disabilities

Glen Dunlap, Lynn Foster-Johnson,
Shelley Clarke, Lee Kern, and Karen E. Childs
University of South Florida and University of Pennsylvania

This article presents three empirical demonstrations of desirable effects that accrued from modifying curricular activities in accordance with individual students' interests. Participants were three elementary students with disabilities and diverse labels including autism, mental retardation, and emotional and behavioral disorder. In each case, the instructional objective was held constant; whereas, the context of the activity was modified so that it produced an outcome that was judged to be meaningful and reinforcing to the student. Reversal designs showed that each student exhibited less problem behavior and more on-task responding when the modified activity was presented. These results are discussed in relation to the applied and conceptual literatures on curricular design, student preference, and the expanding enterprise of positive behavioral support.

DESCRIPTORS: challenging behavior, curricula, developmental disabilities, functional assessment, positive behavioral support, research, school-age subjects, special education

Dunlap, G., Foster-Johnson, L., Clarke, S., Kern, L., & Childs, K. E. (1995). Modifying activities to produce functional outcomes: Effects on the problem behaviors of students with disabilities. *Journal of the Association for Persons with Severe Handicaps, 20,* 248–258. Reprinted with permission of the Association for Persons with Severe Handicaps. Copyright © 1995 by the *Journal of the Association for Persons with Severe Handicaps.*

For some time, curriculum has been acknowledged as a crucial ingredient in the education of students with disabilities (Brown et al., 1979). There has been widespread encouragement to develop curricula that are age appropriate and that develop skills that will be used in students' daily lives in the community (e.g., Falvey, 1986). Some authors have also indicated that curricula should be constructed so that activities are interesting and lead to outcomes that have meaning, or relevance, in the lives of individual students (Neel & Billingsley, 1989). In this regard, there has been some indication that curricula that are designed to meet these criteria will produce improvements in student behavior.

Horner, Sprague, and Flannery (1993) described features of a functional curriculum that they argued should be associated with programs of positive behavioral support. These authors indicated that curriculum should be referenced to activities of peers and to the demands of the local community. They also indicated that curricula should focus on immediate effects and that the content should be functional from a social and from a behavioral (i.e., reinforcement) perspective. In a recent study that investigated several of these features, Ferro, Foster-Johnson, and Dunlap (1994), collected observational data in 64 classrooms to determine possible relationships between curricular characteristics (age appropriateness, social functionality, and student preference) and student behavior. The authors found significant correlations between each of these curricular features and measures of desirable responding and problem behavior.

The past few years have produced a number of within-subject [sic] investigations that have shown empirical associations between instructional and curricular characteristics and the behavior of students who are engaging in the activities (Dunlap & Kern, 1993; Munk & Repp, 1994).[a] For example, one variable that has been studied is the relative preference that a student demonstrates for stimuli that are included in activities (e.g., Green et al., 1988; Pace, Ivancic, Edwards, Iwata, & Page, 1985; Parsons, Reid, Reynolds, & Bumgarner, 1990; Wacker, Berg, Wiggins, Muldoon, & Cavanaugh, 1985).[b] Beneficial effects of student preference have been reported when the stimuli are used as reinforcers or activities (Koegel, Dyer, & Bell, 1987).

Foster-Johnson, Ferro, and Dunlap (1994) used a systematic assessment to determine preferences that individual students with intellectual disabilities showed for activities in their curriculum. In this study, the student responses and the instructional objectives were held constant, while the context and the materials that were used in the activities were adjusted. The results demonstrated that the sessions with the preferred activities contained elevated levels of task engagement and reduced levels of problem behavior for each of the three participants. Clarke and colleagues (1995) also reported data showing that curricular activities that incorporated student interests were associated with reductions in disruptive responding. This latter study was conducted with four participants who were described as having serious emotional and behavioral disorders. In a related line of research, several authors have described positive effects of allowing students to make choices among curricular activities (Bambara, Ager, & Koger, 1994; Dyer, Dunlap, & Winterling, 1990; Guess, Benson, & Siegel-Causey, 1985). This phenomenon has been shown to apply to students who exhibit a diversity of challenging characteristics, including developmental, emotional, and behavioral disabilities (e.g., Dunlap et al., 1994; Dunlap et al., 1993; Seybert, Dunlap, & Ferro, in press; Sigafoos & Dempsey, 1992).

Dunlap, Kern-Dunlap, Clarke, and Robbins (1991), working with an adolescent female with multiple disabilities, eliminated the student's severe problem behavior by thoroughly revising her curriculum. After 5 weeks of a detailed and comprehensive functional assessment, four curricular variables were implicated and then modified for intervention.[c] One of the variables involved the functionality of the curriculum from the point of view of the student. The authors hypothesized and demonstrated that the student would be better behaved if the curriculum was based on the student's interests and if it led to concrete outcomes that were valued by the student. For example, instead of completing typical subtraction problems from a workbook, the student was asked to use methods of subtraction and a bus schedule to calculate times of the day that a bus would pass by a nearby location. This student was fascinated by busses and other forms of transportation and, thus, this manipulation made the activity relevant to her interests and her daily routine. This modification was shown in a process of functional analysis to be associated with improved behavior.

This issue of relevance in an educational curriculum is, of course, a major concern that is being addressed throughout the panorama of instructional efforts, from early childhood through continuing education programs. Although there are surprisingly few data, there have been frequent reports that an instructional content and

a. Within-subjects investigations involve comparisons of an individual's behavior under one experimental condition with the same individual's behavior under another experimental condition.

b. A variable is a behavior or characteristic that varies across individuals and that is measured for the purpose of investigation.

c. Intervention here refers to modifying the standard or baseline condition to determine whether the modification results in changes in the individual's behavior. In this study the variable of functionality of the curriculum was modified for all three students.

educational process that students can relate to their daily lives leads to improved motivation, greater attention, reduced drop outs, and improved performance. Therefore, the concern about this issue appears to transcend special education and the instruction of students with challenging behaviors and severe disabilities.

Aside from the Dunlap et al. (1991) example, there are very few data that relate directly the notion of relevant outcomes to student behavior or motivation. Therefore, in this report, we bring together data from three students whose curricular activities were modified so that the outcomes of the activities would be of relevance to each student's interests and daily lives. As in Foster Johnson et al. (1994) and Clarke et al. (1995), we held the instructional objectives constant and modified only the context and outcome that the activity produced. To extend the external validity of the approach, we included students who were described as exhibiting a diversity of challenges that included developmental, emotional, and behavioral disabilities.[d]

METHOD

Participants

Data obtained from three students are presented in this article. All of the students were described as having severe disabilities; however, they displayed very different characteristics, and their disability labels indicated a range of developmental to emotional and behavioral challenges. All of the participants had been referred for assessment and behavioral consultation because of persistent and extensive problem behaviors in their school settings.

Jary was a 13-year-old boy with autism and mental retardation. Various tests of performance and intelligence estimated his functioning to be more than 3 standard deviations below the mean.[e] Despite his label of autism, Jary enjoyed social interactions with his peers. Jary was enrolled in a self-contained classroom for children with autism and related disabilities. His teachers were concerned with his low level of task engagement and high frequency of inappropriate and disruptive verbalizations and noises.

Jill was a 13-year-old girl who was described with multiple disability labels including severe emotional disturbance, mild mental retardation, schizophrenia, and attention deficit disorder. Test scores showed her intellectual functioning as a 63 full-scale score on the Wechsler Intelligence Scale for Children—Revised (WISC-R), and her performances in reading and mathematics were about 3 years behind grade level.[f] On the Vineland Adaptive Behavior Scales, Jill's adaptive behavior composite was estimated at an age equivalency of 5 years, 4 months. Her teachers were concerned about Jill's extensive history of very severe disruptive behavior, negative and inappropriate affect, and immature social relations. She was enrolled in a classroom for students with severe emotional disturbance; however, her activities were highly individualized, and a personal aide was assigned to her on a full-time basis. Prior to the current analysis, Jill had participated in a functional assessment that had identified the influence of several antecedent variables on her problem behaviors (Dunlap et al., 1991).[g]

Natalie was a 9-year-old girl who was described as having behavioral and emotional challenges and had received a diagnosis of Oppositional Defiant Disorder by

---

d. External validity is the extent to which the experimental findings can be generalized to other similar individuals. By selecting students with a diversity of challenges for their single-case experiment, the researchers hoped to make their findings more widely generalizable.

e. A standard deviation is a measure of the degree to which the scores of a sample vary around the mean score. A student who is performing more than 3 standard deviations below the mean score on a test is at the first percentile of students who have taken such tests.

f. A WISC-R full-scale score of 63 is more than 2 standard deviations below the mean score, because the derived mean score of this test is set at 100 and the standard deviation is set at 15. A score this low signifies that a student is at the first percentile of students who have taken this test.

g. Antecedent variables are characteristics of an individual that have been previously measured. In this experiment they are variables that are presumed to cause the problem behaviors observed in this student.

the public school system. She was a third grader enrolled in a school program for students with severe emotional disturbance. Natalie was given a full-scale score of 71 on the WISC-R.[h] She participated on a daily basis in four elementary school classrooms, each of which was designed to support approximately eight students in special education. Her teachers were concerned with Natalie's noncompliance and acting out behaviors during instructional sessions.

Settings

Data for this study were collected in the context of the students' routines in their school settings. Jary's sessions were conducted in his classroom, by his classroom teacher, during regularly scheduled vocational and prevocational training activities. Jill's sessions were conducted in a separate room by a familiar aide, and Natalie's sessions were held in the ongoing context of a classroom in which she and her classmates were instructed in handwriting and English composition. The majority of the sessions for Jary and Jill were videotaped.

General Procedures

A first step in this investigation was to determine particular tasks that were associated with high levels of problem behaviors. The second step was to identify the instructional objectives that were the purpose of the tasks. Then, assessments were conducted to ascertain interests of the students and, in particular, interests that could be matched with the existing instructional objectives. The tasks were then modified such that they produced outcomes that were functional for the students, in the sense that the results of the activity were relevant to the students' interests. Although the tasks were modified, the instructional purpose of each task was maintained. Reversal analyses were conducted to determine experimentally if the tasks with functional outcomes were associated with more desirable student behavior.[i]

Assessments of Tasks and Interests

Tasks associated with high levels of problem behavior and relatively low levels of on-task responding were identified by interviewing the teachers and confirming the reports by direct observation. When a problematic task was identified, the purpose of the task (i.e., the instructional objective) was determined. These were described by the teachers and included on the students' individual educational plans.

Student interests were assessed in a number of ways. First, teachers were asked in an interview to identify preferred activities, materials, and reinforcers for each student. Second, direct observations of the students were conducted in each setting. These observations were intended to identify those activities and stimuli that were associated with the most positive affect, the highest level of engagement, and the most student initiations (Dyer, 1987; Foster-Johnson et al., 1994). For example, these observations showed that Jary appeared to be highly motivated during snack and lunch time when he was interacting with his peers. A third method of assessing interests for Jill and Natalie was simply to ask the students to identify activities that they favored (e.g., Kern, Dunlap, Clarke, & Childs, 1994). A final method of assessment for Jill and Natalie was to conduct brief probes in which hypotheses regarding preferred, functional outcomes were tested empirically (Dunlap & Kern, 1993).[j] The combination of these assessments yielded a number of identified preferences for each participant. These were then related to the instructional objectives to find an expeditious means of incorporating outcomes that would be functional for the students.

---

h. A full-scale score of 71 on the WISC-R is close to 2 standard deviations below the mean score, because the derived mean score of this test is set at 100 and the standard deviation is set at 15. A score this low signifies that a student is at the second percentile of students who have taken this test.

i. Reversal analyses involve the shift from the treatment condition (condition B) in an A-B-A experiment back to the baseline condition (condition A). Here the functional-outcome task for each student represents condition B, and the standard-outcome task represents condition A.

j. As used here, a probe is a brief intervention to test hypotheses (i.e., hunches or educated guesses) about the students' interests.

Modified Tasks and Functional Outcomes

This process of assessment determined that Jary experienced difficulties when he was asked to assemble component parts of ballpoint pens, in which the instructional objective was to complete a multistep assembly task until a set number of assembled items was completed. The assessment of interests revealed that Jary enjoyed sharing snacks with his peers and, thus, it was determined that an assembly task could be developed from this interest. A functional outcome associated with assembly was established by having Jary prepare cracker sandwiches with peanut butter and jelly. This modified task required a multistep assembling process, and it produced the snacks that Jary and his classmates would consume later in the day.

The assessment for Jill indicated that she experienced tremendous problems when she was asked to complete handwriting assignments, where the objective was to demonstrate correct letter formation and spacing in writing sentences. Among her interests was an activity in which she took photographs of her classmates and teachers in her school environment. She enjoyed looking at and commenting on the photographs. Therefore, the modified task, incorporating a functional outcome, required Jill to use handwriting to prepare captions for her photo album.

Natalie's assessment also implicated handwriting, and her instructional objective was identical to Jill's. The interest assessment for Natalie determined that she enjoyed engaging in activities that were helpful and useful to others. Therefore, the modified task simply required Natalie to use her handwriting period to copy dittos that would later be laminated and used by students as they completed their lessons in another class.

The instructional objectives, standard tasks, and tasks with functional outcomes for each student was [sic] summarized in Table 1 and described in greater detail below.

Procedures

Once the assessment phase was completed, experimental comparisons were conducted to evaluate the effects that the assignments with the standard versus functional outcomes would have on students' behavior. As indicated above, the standard outcome assignments were those activities that had been associated with problem behavior and in which the result of the activity did not relate to the student's interests. The functional outcome assignments addressed the same objectives as the standard outcome assignments, and they were presented to the students in the same fashion. However, the modifications involved the incorporation of functional outcomes as products of the activity.

For Jary, the standard outcome activity consisted of a task composed of the assembly of 18 pens. During the functional outcome conditions, Jary completed an assembly activity, during which he assembled 18 peanut-butter cracker sandwiches for snack time later in the day. Sessions were conducted in the classroom by the classroom teacher and ranged in length from 8 to 15 min. Each session began with the teacher presenting the activity and providing instructions for Jary. During the sessions, the teacher circulated around the classroom providing reinforcement, directions, and feedback for all students in the room on an intermittent schedule. Following every session in both conditions, Jary was given a cracker sandwich as a reward for participation.

For Jill, the standard outcome sessions involved 15 min of handwriting. The sessions began when Jill was given a Merrill handwriting book along with a blank sheet of paper and instructed to copy manuscript from an assigned page (averaging 35 words) to the blank sheet of paper. For sessions in the functional outcome condition, Jill was presented with photographs that she had taken at an earlier time and instructed to develop a caption for each picture, and then to write the caption on blank paper. The task was structured so that Jill was expected to write captions of approximately 35 words during the session. The sessions were 15 min and ended with Jill being given an opportunity to glue the captions and the photos into a photo album. In all sessions, the instructor was available to provide assistance upon request and encouragement on an intermittent schedule.

For Natalie, the standard outcome assignment consisted of copying cursive sentences from a ditto to a blank sheet of paper. The functional outcome assign-

TABLE 1 Descriptions of Instructional Objectives, Standard, and Functional Assignments and Outcomes

Name	Instructional Objective	Standard Assignment	Standard Outcome	Functional Assignment	Functional Outcome
Jary	To perform a multistep assembly task	Six parts of a pen were presented in individual pieces. The student assembled each pen by placing parts of the pen together and then placing completed object in a bin.	Completion of task. Student placed completed task in designated area, indicated completion by checking off activity on board, and continued with another activity.	A five-step task to make peanut butter and jelly cracker sandwiches. Pieces of the task were laid out sequentially, and the student was required to complete the steps and put the finished sandwich on a plate.	The student placed the plate of sandwiches aside to be given to the class for snack later in the day. He then checked off the activity on the board, and continued with another activity.
Jill	To demonstrate the correct use of letter formation and spacing in manuscript handwriting	For 15 min, the student was expected to copy words from a handwriting book onto a blank sheet of lined paper.	After completing the assignment, Jill raised her hand to inform instructor, turned in completed assignment, and went on to next scheduled activity.	For 15 min, Jill developed and wrote captions related to photographs that she had taken earlier in the week, onto a blank sheet of lined paper.	After completing the assignment, Jill added her completed captions to a photo album she was creating.
Natalie	To demonstrate the correct use of letter formation and spacing in cursive handwriting	Copy four to five cursive sentences from a ditto onto a blank sheet of lined paper.	Teacher acknowledged completion of task. Student then placed sheet in a bin. It was later graded and returned by the teacher.	Copy four to five cursive sentences from a ditto onto a blank sheet of lined paper.	Teacher acknowledged completion of task. Then Natalie took the finished product to another teacher's room, where it would later be laminated and used by other students.

ment was identical to the standard outcome assignment in terms of the work that was performed. The only difference was the outcome associated with the assignment. After each of the functional outcome sessions, Natalie took her completed assignment to another teacher, who would use the finished product with his students during the handwriting activities for that class later in the day. During the first five sessions of the functional outcome condition, Natalie was also able to choose which ditto she would copy out of a pool of five dittos. However, this choice option was then removed, so that the conditions then differed only with respect to their outcomes. In all sessions, Natalie was given 15 min to complete the assignment.

In conducting experimental sessions, no changes other than those indicated above distinguished one condition from the other. A behavior management system was in place in all three classrooms with the same schedules of reinforcement and error correction in effect in all phases of the study.

Each participant experienced a reversal design, beginning with sessions in the standard outcome condition and including at least two additional phases (i.e., a minimum of an ABA).[k] In addition, a brief probe was inserted during the second functional outcome condition for Jill. Because of unavoidable scheduling conflicts, the final phase for each participant was limited to a single session.

Dependent Variables—Desirable and Problem Behavior

The principal dependent variables for each participant included categories of desirable and problem behaviors.[l] Definitions for these categories were developed by the participants' teachers and research staff. The behavioral definitions for desirable behavior were the same for all three students. Desirable behavior was scored whenever the student was engaged in the assigned activity according to the teacher's instructions for the majority of an interval. This included eyes on materials during assignments requiring physical manipulation or on the teacher during verbal instruction.

Problem behaviors were defined for each child individually. For Jary, problem behavior consisted of any occurrence of inappropriate vocalizations (e.g., inappropriate giggling, talking about things unrelated to task), inappropriate use of materials (e.g., mouthing, rubbing, or hitting material on the desk), or leaving the instructional area. Problem behaviors for Jill were recorded when she exhibited any of the following behaviors: aggression (e.g., kicking, hitting, spitting, throwing objects), inappropriate vocalizations (e.g., perseverative or delusional speech, cursing), noncompliance (failure to follow instructions within 5 sec), or elopement (running around or out of the room). Natalie's problem behaviors included inappropriate initiations directed at her teacher (e.g., threatening, grabbing, snapping fingers), talking out to peers, noncompliance, and noise making.

Measurement

For all three participants, data for desirable and problem behaviors were collected using a 15-sec partial interval recording system in which the first 10 sec were devoted to observation and the remaining 5 sec were used to record data. Observers were cued using a tape recording that signaled the beginning and ending of each interval. At the end of the interval, observers recorded whether desirable or problem behavior occurred or did not occur. The data on these dependent variables were recorded in vivo for all participants.[m]

Observers and Reliability

All data were collected by observers who had been trained previously to record desirable and problem behaviors of students within special education programs. Observer training involved attaining at least 80% agreement during in vivo classroom practice observations.

Interobserver agreement was calculated for occurrences and nonoccurrences of each dependent variable. Agreements between observers were defined as intervals scored in an identical manner by two observers. Percentage agreement was calculated by dividing the number of agreements by the number of agreements plus disagreements and multiplying by 100.

---

k. A reversal design here involves the standard-outcome task during condition A followed by the functional-outcome task during condition B, and then a reversal back to the standard-outcome task, that is, a repeat of condition A. Thus each student experienced a minimum of an A-B-A single-case design, although the experiment included additional manipulation of the functional-outcome (B) condition and in one case also the standard-outcome (A) condition.

l. Dependent variables are the behaviors or characteristics of individuals that are presumed to be affected by the experimental treatment. The experimental treatment constitutes the independent variable.

m. Recording in vivo means that observers rated the students' behavior live, as it occurred.

Interrater reliability was collected for Jary during 87% of the sessions across all conditions.[n] Reliability estimates for occurrence of desirable behavior averaged 95% (77–100).[o] The reliability for nonoccurrence of desirable behavior was 85% (72–100). Interobserver agreement for problem behavior averaged 89% (84–100) for occurrences and 97% (91–100) for nonoccurrences. For Jill, interobserver agreement was obtained during 71% of the sessions across all conditions of the study. Reliability calculations for Jill produced the following results: occurrences of desirable behavior, 98% (98–100), nonoccurrences, 96% (50–100); occurrences of problem behavior, 92% (0–100), and nonoccurrences, 99% (98–100). For Natalie, interobserver agreement was assessed during 45% of the sessions across all conditions. Agreement on occurrences for desirable behavior averaged 93% (82–100). Reliability for nonoccurrences of desirable behavior averaged 89% (67–100). Interrater agreement for occurrences of problem behavior averaged 93% (67–100), with nonoccurrences averaging 97% (90–100).

Measurement of Student Productivity and Affect

In addition to data on the participants' desirable and problem behavior, other dependent measures were assessed for all three students. Productivity was evaluated in Jary's analysis to determine if the functional outcome condition influenced his rate of responding as compared to the standard outcome task. Prior to recording these data, an empirical comparison of the average time required to assemble a single object (ballpoint pen or cracker sandwich) showed that the assembly generally required similar amounts of time. During the sessions, rate was computed by dividing the number of correctly completed objects (pens or sandwiches) by the time it took to complete each session.

Productivity for Natalie was evaluated in two ways. First, observers noted the percentage of sessions in which she completed her assignment within the expected period of time (15 min). Also, for those sessions in which her assignment was completed within 15 min, a comparison was made of the number of minutes that were required from the time she was presented with the assignment until the assignment was completed.

Productivity was not considered to be a particular problem for Jill; however, her affect was a concern. Therefore, data were obtained on Jill's happiness and interest in the task using six-point Likert-type rating scales (Dunlap, 1984).[p] These data were collected from videotapes. The videotaped sessions were divided into 1-min intervals for scoring purposes. The raters were graduate students who did not know Jill and who were not informed of the purpose of the study. The raters were asked to score each interval according to their judgments of Jill's "interest" and "happiness." Scores ranged from 0 (very unhappy or very uninterested) to 5 (very happy or very interested). Interobserver agreement occurred during 91% of the sessions with agreements defined as either exact number matches or ratings differing by only one number. Mean agreements were 96% (86–100) for interest, and 98% (87–100) for happiness.

RESULTS

Figures 1 through 3 depict the results of the reversal analyses for the three students in this study. The percentage of intervals with on-task (desirable) responding

---

n. Inter-rater reliability, also called *interobserver agreement* in this study, is a measure of the degree to which two or more observers are consistent in their ratings of the same individual. Here the degree of reliability is expressed as the percentage of the total number of ratings that were the same for all observers.

o. The numbers in parentheses (77–100) represent the range of agreements across sessions. In this case, the lowest reliability for a session was 77 percent inter-observer agreement, and the highest reliability for a session was 100 percent inter-observer agreement.

p. A Likert scale is a measure that asks individuals to check the extent of their agreement or disagreement with various statements about a topic (e.g., strongly agree, agree, neither agree nor disagree, disagree, strongly disagree). The scales in this study were a variation of Likert scales (i.e., they were "Likert-type"), because the individuals rated other individuals rather than themselves. Also, rather than rating degree of agreement, they rated degrees of interest and happiness.

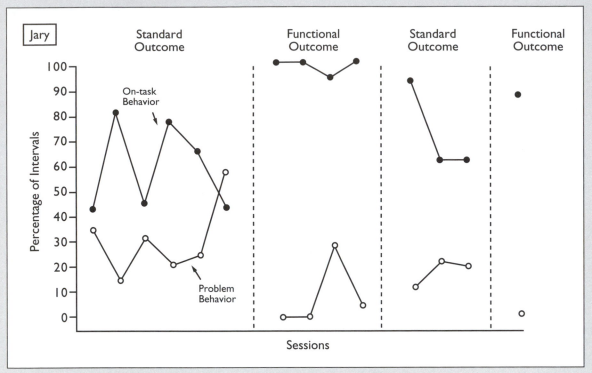

FIGURE 1 **Results for Jary Showing the Effects of the Standard versus Functional Outcome Assignments on On-Task and Problem Behavior**

and problem behavior are shown on the ordinate; whereas, sessions are on the abscissa.[q]

During the first standard outcome condition, Jary (Figure 1) demonstrated variable levels of on-task and problem behavior, averaging 59% and 31%, respectively. The functional outcome condition resulted in an immediate increase in on-task responding that was maintained throughout the condition, averaging 98%. Problem behavior showed a corresponding decrease to an average of 8%. The third phase, returning to the standard outcome condition, produced a reduction in on-task responding ($M = 71\%$) and an increase in problem behavior ($M = 17\%$). The final phase contained only one data point, but that session yielded data that were consistent with the previous data functions.

The data for Jill (Figure 2) show relatively slight improvements from the first standard outcome condition to the first functional outcome condition for on-task and problem behaviors. However, the return to the standard outcome condition resulted in a dramatic reversal of data functions, with extremely low levels of on-task responding and with problem behavior being exhibited during virtually every interval. After an initial session of continued problems, the next phase of the functional outcome assignment restored desirable patterns of behavior. A probe session with the standard outcome assignment, as well as the final phase of the analysis, replicated the effects of the second standard outcome condition.[r]

The data for Natalie (Figure 3) resemble those that were obtained with Jill. That is, the first condition

q. The ordinate is the vertical dimension of Figures 1 through 3, and the abscissa is the horizontal dimension of the figures.

r. The probe was a one-trial reversal from the functional-outcome task back to the standard-outcome task. This reversal is labeled "Probe" in Figure 2.

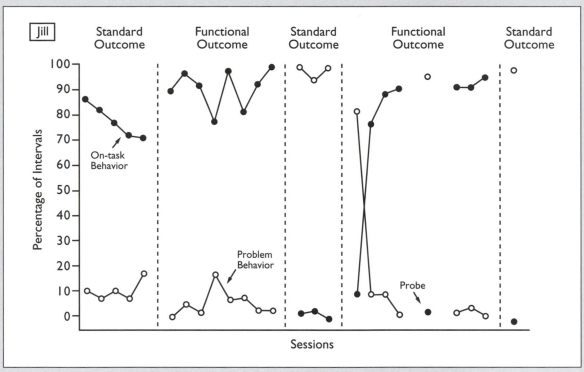

FIGURE 2   Results for Jill Showing the Effects of the Standard versus Functional Outcome Assignments on On-Task and Problem Behavior

change, from the standard to the functional outcomes, produced changes in amplitude and slope, but these initial effects were not as prominent as they were for Jary.[s] However, the subsequent condition changes were associated with very distinct differences, all of which were consistent with the other participants' data.

The data on productivity for Jary and Natalie showed that the functional outcome assignments were accompanied by increased rates of task completion. For Jary, the ballpoint pens were assembled at an average rate of 1.5 pens per minute; whereas, the cracker sandwiches were prepared at an average rate of 2.8 per minute. For Natalie, whose work in the two conditions was essentially identical, completion of her assignment within the expected 15-min period occurred during only 25% of the standard outcome sessions, but it happened during 100% of the functional outcome sessions. Of those sessions in which the task was completed, she required an average of 14.85 min in the standard outcome condition, and only 8.15 min in the functional outcome condition. As noted above, the increased rate of task completion in the functional outcome sessions for Jary and Natalie meant that these sessions were of shorter duration. An analysis of within-session trends for problem and on-task behavior showed no consistent association between these variables and session duration, indicating that the shorter sessions were not responsible for the improved responding depicted in Figures 1–3.

The data on Jill's affect also indicated positive results with the functional outcome assignments. During the

s. The term *amplitude* refers to the height of the data points on the ordinate. Inspection of Figure 3 shows that the data points for the first functional-outcome condition are generally higher than the data points for the first standard-outcome condition. Also, the slopes of the data points in these two conditions go in the opposite direction.

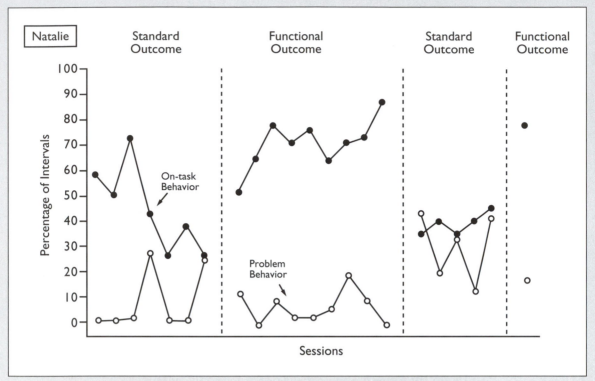

FIGURE 3   **Results for Natalie Showing the Effects of the Standard versus Functional Outcome Assignments on On-Task and Problem Behavior**

standard outcome assignments, the scores for Jill's happiness averaged 2.1, but this increased to an average of 3.5 during the functional outcome sessions. The ratings for Jill's interest averaged 1.94 during the standard outcome condition, and 3.5 during the functional outcome condition.

DISCUSSION

The data reported in this article demonstrate that the behavior of each student improved when a curricular activity was modified such that it produced an outcome that was judged to be in accordance with the student's interests. The procedures were the same across the three students. That is, observations and interviews were conducted to identify classroom contexts and outcomes that

were considered to be more relevant and that might evoke enhanced motivation from the students. These contexts and outcomes were then used to modify existing curricular activities that had been associated with low levels of engagement and relatively high levels of problem behavior. When the activities were modified, the students' behavior improved. This was apparent across different tasks, with students who exhibited a diversity of characteristics and disability labels and with a variety of dependent measures (including task engagement, problem behavior, productivity, and affect).

The applied implications of these data are clear. That is, instructional activities can be modified, or individualized while maintaining the integrity of the instructional objective, and these modifications can produce notable improvements in student behavior.

Although the ultimate value of the particular objectives that were targeted in this study (e.g., handwriting) may be questioned and although it is quite possible that the student's behavior may have been improved by simply eliminating these objectives, the important point is a more general one. Curricula for all students must include instructional objectives, and there is a probability that some agreed upon objectives will be addressed through activities that are considered irrelevant or tedious. Indeed, many people's opinions of typical school activities might very well be characterized in that manner. This study offers an empirical demonstration that modifying curricula to align with students' interests can produce more desirable patterns of responding.

Although the procedural approach that was used in this study is straightforward, the conceptual basis for the effects are less clear. On one hand, it is possible to explain the phenomenon by describing it in terms of reinforcement. Some tasks are more reinforcing than others, and when the task is reinforcing, the student spends time engaged in the task and tends not to engage in problem behavior that is competitive and, quite likely, escape-motivated (Carr, Robinson, & Palumbo, 1990; Horner & Billingsley, 1988). From this perspective, the operations of this investigation are conceptually similar to those described in the literature on preference (e.g., Dyer, 1987; Foster Johnson et al., 1994) and, perhaps, choice making (e.g., Bambara et al., 1994; Dyer et al., 1990; Dunlap et al., 1994).

The notion that tasks differ in their properties of reinforcement does not explain the specific means that determine such distinctions. Tasks can differ along many dimensions including materials, response requirements, outcomes, familiarity, and the social context in which they are performed. Any combination of these variables, as well as their interaction with individual student characteristics, could affect the extent to which a task is reinforcing. Although the procedural operations in this investigation focused on the functionality of task outcomes, other ingredients could have contributed to results. For example, one possibility is that social reinforcers were more distinct in the experimental conditions for two of the participants.

The outcome of Natalie's modified task was that she delivered her product to a second teacher who presumably expressed gratitude and appreciation that was not experienced in the standard activity. Jary's products, the cracker sandwiches, were consumed by his classmates later in the day. At that time, it is likely that some acknowledgement of Jary's role in preparing the sandwiches was announced. It would have been interesting to see if comparable results had occurred if the pens that were assembled in the standard activity condition had been similarly dispensed to the class. Although social reinforcers were not an obvious component in Jill's intervention, this, nevertheless, is an interpretation that must be regarded as partly responsible for the desirable effects. The effects that an activity or response has on the social environment, of course, must be considered as an important component in the relevance of most tasks and, therefore, the possible contribution of social reinforcement is compatible with an explanation that emphasizes curricular congruence with valued, real-life experiences.

The procedural variables in this study may suggest other explanatory perspectives. For example, some investigations involving children with autism have demonstrated that responses leading directly to reinforcers were associated with enhanced performances, compared with more arbitrary response-reinforcer connections (Koegel & Williams, 1980; Williams, Koegel, & Egel, 1981). Although the procedures in this study did not manipulate response-reinforcer relationships explicitly or intentionally, it is reasonable to interpret the activities' outcomes as reinforcing events and, in this way, the tasks with the more functional outcomes could be viewed as being more direct.

It is important to recognize that this investigation was not designed to sort out the conceptual basis for the observed phenomenon. Indeed, when one examines the differences in the tasks and the ways in which they were manipulated, it is clear that a number of different variables might have been responsible for the beneficial effects. Future research on this topic would be well directed if it controlled for all variables (e.g., social reinforcement, preference for materials, etc.) aside from the perceived relevance of the tasks.

The contributions of the present data need to be qualified in certain respects. For example, even though the current participants displayed diverse characteristics including cognitive, emotional, and behavioral challenges, none experienced intellectual disabilities in the severe to profound range. It is not clear how such disabilities might limit the direct applicability of the present strategies. Another limitation may be that the functional assessment in this study did not include a functional analysis of the operant motivations for problem behavior. Although it is probable that the problem behaviors were governed by escape, this is an inference that was not specifically demonstrated. Future research could add a preliminary functional analysis (Iwata, Vollmer, & Zarcone, 1990) to help delineate the functions of individual topographies and, perhaps, help explain some of the response variability. In this respect, additional data would also be useful to substantiate the presence of functional relations, especially with respect to the governance of problem behaviors. Some of the present analyses for this category of dependent variable should be considered suggestive rather than definitive. Another stipulation pertains to the range of dependent variables that were included. In this study, data were collected on those variables (e.g., productivity, affect) that were identified as concerns for the individual students, without a priori consideration for their contribution to a unified research endeavor. Greater consistency across participants could facilitate comparison and synthesis of data across individuals.

The methods from this study produced another phenomenon that might warrant further investigation. In the second phases of the standard activity sessions for Jill and Natalie, the data show levels of problem behavior that were greater amplitude than the first phases. This is similar to a phenomenon described by Parsonson and Baer (1986) as "postreversal intensification," and appears to be a contrast effect (cf., Reynolds, 1961). After Jill and Natalie experienced the modified task condition, they apparently found the standard condition to be even more undesirable, probably because of the contrast with the more desirable condition. Although this particular manifestation of contrast differs from previous reports, in which reinforcement schedules vary across settings (Koegel, Egel, & Williams, 1980), this kind of pattern undoubtedly has many practical analogies and might merit further study.

The central argument that these data have to offer, however, pertains to curriculum design. The findings show that increased relevance contributed directly to improved behavior by three children with severe emotional, behavioral, and/or developmental needs. It should be noted that this verdict most likely applies to all children and, indeed, to all people who find themselves in instructional circumstances that are nebulous, tedious, or seemingly immaterial. It is hoped that further research will document the generality of these data and that educational practice will continue to infuse additional meaning into all instructional endeavors.

This research was supported by Cooperative Agreement No. H133B2004 from the U.S. Department of Education (National Institute on Disability and Rehabilitation Research); however, opinions expressed are those of the authors and no official endorsement should be inferred. Reprint requests should be sent to Glen Dunlap, Department of Child and Family Studies, Florida Mental Health Institute, University of South Florida, 13301 Bruce B. Downs Blvd., Tampa, FL 33612.

References

Bambara, L. M., Ager, C., & Koger, F. (1994). The effects of choice and task preference on the work performance of adults with severe disabilities. *Journal of Applied Behavior Analysis, 27,* 555–556.

Brown, L., Branston, M. B., Baumgart, D., Vincent, L., Falvey, M., & Schoeder, J. (1979). Using the characteristics of current and subsequent least restrictive environments as factors in the development of curricular content for severely handicapped adolescents and young adults. *Journal of Special Education, 13,* 81–90.

Carr, E. G., Robinson, S., & Palumbo, L. W. (1990). The wrong issue: Aversive versus nonaversive treatment. The right issue: Functional versus nonfunctional treatment. In A. C. Repp & N. Singh (Eds.), *Perspectives on the use of nonaversive interventions for persons with development disabilities* (pp. 361–379). DeKalb, IL: Sycamore.

Clarke, S., Dunlap, G., Foster-Johnson, L., Childs, K. E., Wilson, D., White, R., & Vera, A. (1995). Improving the conduct of students with behavioral disorders by incorporating student interests into curricular activities. *Behavioral Disorders, 20,* 221–237.

Dunlap, G. (1984). The influence of task variation and maintenance tasks on the learning and affect of autistic children. *Journal of Experimental Child Psychology, 37,* 41–64.

Dunlap, G., dePerczel, M., Clarke, S., Wilson, D., Wright, S., & Gomez, A. (1994). Choice making to promote adaptive behavior for students with emotional and behavioral challenges. *Journal of Applied Behavior Analysis, 27,* 505–518.

Dunlap, G., & Kern, L. (1993). Assessment and intervention for children within the instructional curriculum. In J. Reichle & D. Wacker, (Eds.), *Communicative approaches to the management of challenging behavior problems* (pp. 177–203). Baltimore: Paul H. Brookes.

Dunlap, G., Kern-Dunlap, L., Clarke, S., & Robbins, F. R. (1991). Functional assessment, curricular revision, and severe behavior problems. *Journal of Applied Behavior Analysis, 24,* 387–397.

Dunlap. G., Kern, L., dePerczel, M., Clarke, S., Wilson, D., Childs, K., White, R., & Falk, G. D. (1993). Functional analysis of classroom variables for students with emotional and behavioral disorders. *Behavioral Disorders, 18,* 275–291.

Dyer, K. (1987). The competition between autistic stereotyped behavior with usual and specially assessed reinforcers. *Research in Developmental Disabilities, 8,* 607–626.

Dyer, K., Dunlap, G., & Winterling, V. (1990). Effects of choice making on the serious problem behaviors of students with severe handicaps. *Journal of Applied Behavior Analysis, 23,* 515–524.

Falvey, M. A. (1986). *Community based curriculum.* Baltimore: Paul H. Brookes.

Ferro, J., Foster Johnson, L., & Dunlap, G. (1994). *The relationship between curricular activities and problem behavior in students with intellectual disabilities.* Manuscript submitted for publication.

Foster-Johnson, L., Ferro, J., & Dunlap, G. (1994). Preferred curricular activities and reduced problem behaviors in students with intellectual disabilities. *Journal of Applied Behavior Analysis, 27,* 493–504.

Green, C. W., Reid, D. H., White, L. K., Halford, R. C., Brittain, D. P., & Gardner, S. M. (1988). Identifying reinforcers for persons with profound handicaps: Staff opinion versus systematic assessment of preferences. *Journal of Applied Behavior Analysis, 21,* 31–43.

Guess, D., Benson, H. S., & Siegel-Causey, E. (1985). Concepts and issues related to choice-making and autonomy among persons with severe disabilities. *Journal of the Association for Persons with Severe Handicaps, 10,* 79–86.

Horner, R. H., & Billingsley, F. F. (1988). The effect of competing behavior on the generalization and maintenance of adaptive behavior in applied settings. In R. H. Horner, G. Dunlap, & R. L. Koegel (Eds.), *Generalization and maintenance: Lifestyle changes in applied settings* (pp. 197–220). Baltimore, MD: Paul H. Brookes.

Horner, R. H., Sprague, J. R., Flannery, K. B. (1993). Building functional curricular for students with severe intellectual disabilities and severe problem behaviors. In R. Van Houten & S. Axelrod (Eds.), *Behavior analysis and treatment* (pp. 47–71). New York: Plenum Press.

Iwata, B. A., Vollmer, T. R., & Zarcone, J. R. (1990). The experimental (functional) analysis of behavior disorders: Methodology, applications, and limitations. In A. C. Repp & N. N. Singh (Eds.), *Perspectives on the use of nonaversive and aversive interventions for persons with developmental disabilities* (pp. 301–330). Sycamore, IL: Sycamore Press.

Kern, L., Dunlap, G., Clarke, S., & Childs, K. E. (1994). Student-assisted functional assessment interview. *Diagnostique, 19,* 29–39.

Koegel, R., Dyer, K., & Bell, L. (1987). The influence of child-preferred activities on autistic children's social behavior. *Journal of Applied Behavior Analysis, 20,* 243–252.

Koegel, R. L., Egel, A. L., & Williams, J. A. (1980). Behavioral contrast and transfer across settings in teaching autistic children. *Journal of Experimental Child Psychology, 30,* 422–437.

Koegel, R. L., & Williams, J. A. (1980). Direct vs. indirect response-reinforcer relationships in teaching autistic children. *Journal of Abnormal Child Psychology, 8,* 537–547.

Munk, D. D., & Repp, A. C. (1994). The relationship between instructional variables and problem behavior: A review. *Exceptional Children, 60,* 390–401.

Neel, R. S., & Billingsley, F. F. (1989). *Impact: A functional curriculum handbook for students with moderate to severe disabilities.* Baltimore: Paul H. Brookes.

Pace, G. M., Ivancic, M. R., Edwards. G. L., Iwata, B. A., & Page, T. J. (1985). Assessment of stimulus preference and reinforcer value with profoundly retarded individuals. *Journal of Applied Behavior Analysis, 18,* 249–255.

Parsons, M. B., Reid, D. H., Reynolds, J., & Bumgarner, M. (1990). Effects of chosen versus assigned jobs on the work performance of persons with severe handicaps. *Journal of Applied Behavior Analysis, 23,* 253–258.

Parsonson, B. S., & Baer, D. M. (1986). The graphic analysis of data. In A. Poling & R. W. Fuqua (Eds.), *Research methods in applied behavior analysis: Issues and advances* (pp. 157–186). New York: Plenum Press.

Reynolds, G. S. (1961). Behavior contrast. *Journal of the Experimental Analysis of Behavior, 4,* 57–71.

Seybert, S., Dunlap, G., & Ferro, J. (in press). The effects of choice making on the problem behaviors of high school students with intellectual disabilities. *Journal of Behavioral Education.*

Sigafoos, J., & Dempsey, R. (1992). Assessing choice making among children with multiple disabilities. *Journal of Applied Behavior Analysis, 25,* 747–755.

Wacker, D. P., Berg, W. K., Wiggins, B., Muldoon, M., & Cavanaugh, J. (1985). Evaluation of reinforcer preferences for profoundly handicapped students. *Journal of Applied Behavior Analysis, 18,* 173–178.

Williams, J. A., Koegel, R. L., & Egel, A. L. (1981). Response-reinforcer relationships and improved learning in autistic children. *Journal of Applied Behavior Analysis, 14,* 53–60.

part IV

QUALITATIVE RESEARCH IN EDUCATION

To grasp fully the findings and methods of educational research, you need to understand both quantitative and qualitative methods of research. The third part of this book emphasizes quantitative methods of inquiry, which dominated educational research until recently. Now we invite you to turn your attention to qualitative methods of inquiry. Part IV describes the typical characteristics of qualitative research and also several specialized qualitative research traditions. Chapter 10 explains how qualitative researchers design and carry out case studies to explore educational phenomena. The chapter also introduces specialized qualitative research traditions.

Chapter 11 describes the qualitative research tradition of ethnographic research. It explains how ethnographers make in-depth studies of individuals in their natural settings in order to explore the cultural context of educational phenomena.

In Chapter 12 we describe the qualitative research tradition of critical-theory research. We show how criticalists' commitment to the emancipation of oppressed groups from dominant power structures operating within a culture contributes to educational research and practice.

Chapter 13 covers historical research, a primarily qualitative research endeavor that involves the study of past phenomena and their relationship to present conditions.

chapter 10

Case Studies in Qualitative Research

After studying this chapter, you will be able to

1. describe the primary characteristics and purposes of case studies.

2. describe how qualitative researchers select cases for study.

3. describe the data-collection methods that typically are used in case study research.

4. compare the purposes and procedures of interpretational, structural, and reflective data analysis.

5. describe criteria that can be used to judge the soundness of case study findings.

6. explain two approaches to determining the applicability of case study findings to other settings.

7. describe the characteristics of a qualitative research tradition.

8. describe three broad areas of investigation with which qualitative research traditions are concerned.

Nitza Goldberg is returning to the university to earn an administrator's license and master's degree so that she can become a school principal. During Nitza's program of studies, she developed an interest in the problems faced by principals of language-immersion schools, which provide some content instruction in English and other content instruction in a second language.

While taking a research course, Nitza decided that for her master's research project she might do a quantitative study of principals of language-immersion schools involving administration of a questionnaire to a nationwide sample of such principals. However, she saw two drawbacks to that approach: (a) there are still only a few language-immersion schools in the country, so her sample would be very small; (b) a questionnaire is poorly suited for some of the questions that interest her, including: What unique problems arise in administering language-immersion schools? What solutions do principals typically try, and with what success? How do principals cope with problems that have no easy solution?

As Nitza's research class proceeded, its focus shifted from quantitative research to qualitative research and the case study method. It was then that she realized that a case study would be an ideal master's project for addressing her questions and promoting her professional development.

In this chapter, you will learn why qualitative research and the case study method is particularly appropriate for Nitza's interests. Also, the chapter will broaden your view of what constitutes educational research and will enable you to comprehend and evaluate case study reports. ●

THE NATURE OF QUALITATIVE RESEARCH

As we explained in Chapter 1, much of qualitative research is based on an **interpretivist epistemology.** In this view of knowledge, social reality is seen as a set of meanings that are constructed by the individuals who participate in that reality. Any social phenomenon, such as a high school football game, does not have an independent existence apart from its participants; rather, it will have different meanings for the individuals who participate in the phenomenon or who subsequently learn about it. A major purpose of qualitative research is to discover the nature of those meanings. The primary method of investigation is in-depth, field-based studies of particular instances of the phenomenon, known as **cases.**

Qualitative research involves a very different world view than positivist epistemology, which characterized most prior investigation in philosophy and science until late in the twentieth century. **Positivism** assumes that there is a real world "out there" that can be known by using similar investigative strategies as those that guide the physical sciences. The growth of qualitative research reflects in part a reaction against the intellectual and scientific constraints of positivism, and an embrace of more naturalistic ways of knowing that typify non-Western cultural perspectives.

We suggest that you review Table 1.1 in Chapter 1, which summarizes the ways in which qualitative researchers characterize and investigate the social environment. Qualitative research sometimes is called **case study** research because of its focus on cases, but not all case studies reflect the interpretivist epistemology. In this book we use the term *qualitative research* to refer to the entire body of research that is guided by interpretivist epistemology.

The Purposes of Case Studies

Researchers conduct case studies in order to describe, explain, or evaluate particular social phenomena. Let us consider each of these purposes as they apply to educational research.

1. *Description.* In many case studies the researchers' main purpose is to depict and conceptualize an educational phenomenon clearly. These case studies usually provide a **thick description** of the phenomenon, that is, a set of statements that re-create the situation and its context and give readers a sense of the meanings and intentions inherent in that situation. The term *thick description* originated in anthropology to refer to a complete, literal description of a cultural phenomenon, but it now is widely used in qualitative research.

2. *Explanation.* The purpose of some case studies is to explain particular phenomena. The researchers look for patterns among phenomena within a case or across cases. For example, researchers might observe that American teachers in international schools vary in (a) their perceptions of teaching in such schools and (b) their perceptions of the local culture. If the researchers find that the teachers' perceptions of teaching are related to their perceptions of the culture, they can say that a pattern has been discovered. If one variation appears to have a causal effect on the others, it is referred to as a **causal pattern.** If the cause is not specified, it is referred to as a **relational pattern.**

3. *Evaluation.* Case study researchers have developed several qualitative approaches to evaluation (see Chapter 14). In each approach, researchers conduct a case study about certain phenomena and make judgments about those phenomena. For example, a historical case study carried out by Larry Cuban (1997) bears a title reflecting the case study's evaluative flavor: "Change without Reform: The Case of Stanford University School of Medicine, 1908–1990."

As we just explained, case studies vary in purpose. They also vary in the degree to which they rely on particular qualitative research traditions. Many case studies are not guided by a specific theoretical framework, nor do they use a particular substantive discipline, such as linguistics or philosophy, in their attempts to clarify the meaning of the case. Other case studies are embedded within one or more qualitative research traditions. Evelyn Jacob (1987) describes a **qualitative research tradition** as "a group of scholars who agree among themselves on the nature of the universe they are examining, on legitimate questions and problems to study, and on legitimate techniques to seek solutions" (pp. 1–2). In this book we use the term *tradition* also to refer to the body of research and theory generated by those scholars. Later in the chapter we introduce the primary traditions that have been used in qualitative educational research.

How Case Studies Can Be Applied

As an educational practitioner, you might ask what you can learn from qualitative research case studies. We would respond by noting that case studies resemble stories in works of literature or "human interest" accounts that enliven news reporting, because they reflect the nature of reality as experienced by those who have been there. Reading about cases that are either similar to or different from your own experience in education can deepen your understanding of the educational phenomena that you experience in your work. Although case studies tend not to make definite claims about preferred courses of action, their insights and speculations can help you develop the capacity to explore and refine your educational practice.

Discovery of Constructs, Themes, and Patterns

Case study researchers often look for constructs to bring order to descriptive data and to help them relate their data to other research findings reported in the literature. A **construct** is a concept that is inferred from commonalties among observed phenomena and that is assumed to underlie those phenomena. For example, Jean Piaget made sense of the case study data that he collected about children's thinking by developing such constructs as assimilation, conservation, and operational thinking.

The discovery of how existing constructs are manifested in qualitative data, or the discovery of new constructs, can be a significant outcome of a case study. In the case study that is reprinted in this chapter, Monica Miller Marsh (2002) studied how the classroom instruction of a teacher named Ms. Nicholi was grounded in particular "discourses," which are ideological frameworks for thinking and acting. Ms. Nicholi taught a kindergarten class consisting primarily of children of color from low-income families. Marsh inferred three discourses from her qualitative data about the teacher's classroom behavior and explanations of that behavior: a discourse of children at risk, a discourse of child-centeredness, and a discourse of normalization. Each of these discourses is a construct that identifies certain commonalties in the teacher's instruction and thinking. Marsh also inferred an alternative construct—a critical, sociocultural discourse—that was not present in her data about the teacher, but was present in the teacher education program from which the teacher graduated.

Case study researchers add further depth to their descriptions by searching for themes present in the phenomena they investigate. A **theme** is a salient, recurrent feature of a case. For example, Marsh observed a consistency in Ms. Nicholi's teaching style: ". . . the majority of the class is teacher directed and skill oriented." Another theme was the pedagogical goal of duplication: "In virtually every activity that I observed, children were asked to duplicate products that Ms. Nicholi had made."

Patterns represent possible relationships among phenomena, some of which may be causal in nature. For example, Marsh observed the following causal pattern in Ms. Nicholi's discourses: Because the teacher perceived that none of the children met the criteria of the "ideal kindergartner" (cause), she resorted to a teacher-directed style (effect) rather than to a learner-centered style. Researchers could test the validity of this causal pattern further by studying a group of teachers who perceive their children as "ideal" and another group of teachers with opposite perceptions. The researchers would collect data to determine whether the groups differed in their teaching style, as predicted by the causal pattern discovered by Marsh.

Key Characteristics of a Case Study

To explain the characteristics of a case study, we will refer to a study by Dona Kagan, Mary Beth Dennis, Mary Igou, Polly Moore, and Karen Sparks (1993). The study involved the effects of a staff development program on the professional lives of the teachers who participated in it. Kagan conducted an audiotaped interview with four teachers who were in or had recently completed the program (Dennis, Igou, Moore, and Sparks), and these teachers subsequently became coauthors of her research report.

In the following sections we show how this study reflects four key characteristics of case study research: (1) study of a phenomenon by focusing on specific instances, or cases; (2) in-depth study of each case; (3) study of a phenomenon in its natural context; and (4) representation of both the researchers' (etic) perspective and the participants' (emic) perspective.

The Study of Particular Instances.   A case study is conducted to shed light on a particular **phenomenon,** that is, a set of processes, events, individuals, or other things of interest to the researchers. Examples of educational phenomena are instructional programs, curricula, staff roles, and school events. The researchers must first clarify the phenomenon of interest before they can select for intensive study a particular instance of the phenomenon, that is, a case.

In the Kagan study, the phenomenon of interest was school–university partnerships, and more specifically partnerships that strengthen the staff-development capacity of local school districts. The case selected for study was the Teacher in Residence (TIR) Program at the University of Alabama. Experienced elementary teachers became teachers in residence at the university for two years, teaching and supervising in the university's preservice teacher education program. They then returned to their districts with knowledge to help them design in-service staff development programs.

A phenomenon has many aspects, so researchers must select a focus for investigation. The **focus** is the aspect, or aspects, of the phenomenon on which data collection and analysis will concentrate. Previous research on school–university partnerships tended to focus on their policies and structures. The focus of the Kagan study was different: It focused on the effects of the partnership program on the professional lives of the teachers.

In some case studies, multiple instances of the phenomenon are studied, and each instance might be analyzed as a separate **unit of analysis.** If Kagan had studied several school–university partnerships around the United States, school–university partnerships would be the unit of analysis. In fact, four teachers from the TIR program at Kagan's university were selected for study. Therefore, the unit of analysis was the participating teacher, and four such units were studied.

In-Depth Study of the Case.   A case study involves collection of a substantial amount of data about the specific case, or cases, selected to represent the phenomenon. These data are mainly verbal statements, images, or physical objects, but some quantitative data also might be collected. Data typically are collected over an extended time period, with several methods of data collection.

In Kagan's study, the researcher conducted ninety-minute interviews with each teacher. Kagan audiotaped, transcribed, and analyzed each interview in order to provide a coherent narrative of the teacher's experience. She returned two preliminary drafts of the narratives to the interviewees for correction, amendment, and editing. Thus, both the researcher and the teachers were involved in "an iterative process of constructing meaning . . . " (p. 428). As coauthors, the four teachers also were invited to modify and edit the entire article.

We can infer from this description that the narratives were developed by the researcher after the interviews, but they then involved continuing dialogue between the teachers and the researcher and among the teachers. The data thus reflect **in-depth study** of the teachers' experience of the TIR program, although involving a relatively brief period of data collection.

Study of a Phenomenon in Its Natural Context.   Jerome Kirk and Marc Miller (1986) define qualitative research as an approach to social science research that involves ". . . watching people in their own territory and interacting with them in their own language, on their own terms . . ." (p. 9). Consistent with this definition, case studies typically involve **fieldwork,** in which the researchers interact with research participants in their natural settings.

The final report of Kagan's case study includes a narrative for each teacher ("Mary Beth's Experience," "Karen's Story," "Mary's Reflections," and "Polly's Story"). These narratives position each teacher's interview statements about her program experience in the context of her past and current life as an elementary school teacher. For example, the segment on Mary reveals that her motivation to serve as a teacher in residence was to give more realism to the university's teacher education preservice program. The narrative describes Mary's positive and negative experiences as a teacher in residence, and how they affected her perceptions of classroom teaching and her plans upon returning to the elementary school classroom. This narrative, and the others, reflect the teachers' language rather than a reconstruction of that language in particular pedagogical or theoretical terminology.

Representation of Both the Emic and Etic Perspectives.   Case studies seek to develop an understanding of a complex phenomenon as experienced by its participants. In other words, the researcher must come to view the phenomenon as the participants view it. The participants' viewpoint is called the **emic perspective.** Typically, researchers obtain the emic perspective through informal conversations with the case study participants, and by observing them as they behave naturally in the field.

At the same time, the researchers maintain their own perspective as investigators of the phenomenon. Their viewpoint as outsiders, which is called the **etic**

perspective, helps them make conceptual and theoretical sense of the case, and to report the findings so that their contribution to the research literature is clear.

The last section of the university–school partnership study ("Dona's Commentary and Analysis") reflects Kagan's use of her own past experience as a professor of education in the analysis and interpretation of the data obtained from the teachers. This commentary provides the etic perspective. The four teachers' involvement in data collection and in the report of the findings ensured that the emic perspective was represented as well.

Selection of Cases for Study

Michael Patton (2001) describes the procedures that case study researchers use to select their cases as purposeful sampling. The goal of **purposeful sampling** is to select individuals for case study who are likely to be "information-rich" with respect to the researchers' purposes. Thus, instead of trying to spend time with every individual in the field setting, case study researchers usually search for **key informants.** These are individuals who have special knowledge or perspectives that make them especially important in obtaining the emic perspective. In Marsh's case study, she selected two first-year teachers, but chose to report on only one of them. She observed the teacher's kindergarten class during fourteen visits over half a school year, conducted interviews with the school staff, attended staff meetings, and also examined historical documents, curriculum guidelines, and syllabi at the school and the university where the teacher completed her teacher education program.

Researchers generally follow a systematic sampling strategy to select the case or cases to be studied. As you read a case study, you should look for information that will help you determine the sampling strategy that was used. Having this information will help you decide whether and how to apply the case study findings to your specific situation.

Table 10.1 summarizes fifteen purposeful sampling strategies described by Patton. All these strategies can be used to select multiple cases for study. If the researchers choose to study just one case, only some of them are appropriate (i.e., the eleven strategies for which the "Cases Selected" listed in column 2 begin with the word *Cases* rather than with the words *Multiple Cases*). In examining Table 10.1, you will see that the strategies are grouped into four categories based on their underlying rationale.

The first category of sampling strategies in Table 10.1 involves selecting cases that represent a key characteristic of the phenomenon that the researchers wish to study. In Marsh's case study, the focus of investigation was the discourses that inform teachers' instruction. Marsh selected Ms. Nicholi because this teacher was recommended by one of her university instructors as ". . . a conscientious and concerned teacher interested in providing each of the children in her care with the best education possible." Ms. Nicholi possessed, then, several key characteristics of interest to the researcher: She had been exposed to several discourses during

TABLE 10.1 Purposeful Sampling Strategies Used in Qualitative Research	
SAMPLING STRATEGY	**CASES SELECTED**
Strategies to Select Cases Representing a Key Characteristic	
1. Extreme/deviant case	Cases that exhibit the characteristic to an extreme high or low extent
2. Intensity	Cases that exhibit the characteristic to a high or low, but not extreme, extent
3. Typical case	Cases that exhibit the characteristic to an average or typical extent
4. Maximum variation	Multiple cases that exhibit the entire range of variation in the characteristic
5. Stratified	Multiple cases that exhibit the characteristic at predefined points of variation
6. Homogeneous	Multiple cases that represent the characteristic to a similar extent
7. Purposeful random	Multiple cases selected at random from an accessible population
Strategies Reflecting a Conceptual Rationale	
8. Critical case	Cases that provide a crucial test of a theory, program, or other phenomenon
9. Theory-based/operational construct	Cases that manifest a particular theoretical construct
10. Confirming/disconfirming case	Cases that are likely to confirm/disconfirm findings from previous case studies
11. Criterion	Cases that satisfy an important criterion
12. Politically important case	Cases that are well known/politically important
Emergent Strategies	
13. Opportunistic	Cases that are selected during data collection to take advantage of unforeseen opportunities
14. Snowball/chain	Cases that are recommended by individuals who know other individuals likely to yield relevant, information-rich data
Strategy Lacking a Rationale	
15. Convenience	Cases that are selected simply because they are available

her teacher education program and she had the opportunity to be exposed to other discourses in her school and also put them into action, if she chose.

Marsh does not explicitly identify one of the sampling strategies listed in Table 10.1 as the basis for selecting Ms. Nicholi. However, Marsh stated that Ms. Nicholi was exposed to two "disparate" and "conflicting" discourses in her teacher education program, which was jointly offered by two university departments. The discourse in one department centered around theories of child development and pedagogy suitable for young children, whereas the discourse in the other department "was renowned for its critical perspectives on curriculum theorizing." These features suggest that the program was not typical, so the strategy could be characterized as intensity or extreme/deviant case sampling.

The second category in Table 10.1 includes five sampling strategies reflecting a conceptual rationale. Researchers choose among these strategies based on the particular rationale that they have chosen to guide their research. The first three strategies involve rationales related to the researchers' theoretical conceptions of the meaning of the case. To return to our example of power among teachers, researchers might select teachers who make it possible to test whether a program designed to empower teachers was effective (critical case sampling), teachers who illustrate a particular conceptualization of power in organizations (theory-based/operational construct sampling), teachers who enable the researchers to test the replicability of previous research findings (confirming/disconfirming case sampling), teachers who satisfy a specific criterion, or politically important teachers.

We describe the next group of two strategies as emergent, because both involve a decision to select cases based on data that already have been collected. For example, the researchers might make initial observations of teachers rated as high, medium, and low in power. They then might decide to focus only on the teachers rated unusually high and low in power because the medium-power group seems unlikely to yield useful data. Thus they have made an opportunistic switch from a maximum variation sampling strategy to an extreme case strategy.

Another emergent strategy shown in the table is snowball sampling, in which researchers ask individuals from whom they already have collected data to recommend others who can provide useful information about the phenomena of interest. Thus, the sample increases in size (i.e., it "snowballs") as individuals mention other individuals as potential key informants.

The final strategy listed in Table 10.1 acknowledges that some researchers might select cases for study based primarily on convenience. For example, they might select teachers at a school where they formerly worked, because they believe that it will be easy to obtain the teachers' agreement to participate in the study. Patton observes that convenience is the least desirable basis for selecting cases to study.

DATA COLLECTION IN CASE STUDY RESEARCH

In collecting data, qualitative researchers use whatever methods are appropriate to their purpose. They might begin a case study with one method of data collection and gradually shift to, or add, other methods. They might use multiple methods to collect data about the same phenomenon in order to enhance the soundness of their findings—a process called *triangulation* (explained later in the chapter). Below we describe the methods of data collection most often used in case studies.

1. *Observation.* In observing field participants, some researchers might tape-record or videotape the sessions, or take extensive field notes. Many researchers strive to become participant observers, meaning that they interact personally with the field participants in field activities in order to build empathy and trust and to further their understanding of the phenomenon. These researchers generally take notes on their observations only after they have left the field.

Case study researchers might also make observations of material culture. For example, Peter Manning and Betsy Cullum-Swan (1994) did a case study of McDonald's restaurants using the qualitative research tradition of semiotics, which investigates how both verbal and configural sign systems convey meaning. They studied the meaning of McDonald's sign systems as conveyed by such elements as the design of the menu board, lighting, outdoor playgrounds, food containers, and utensils, and the use of the prefix "Mc-" to label food items.

2. *Interviews.* Researchers often conduct interviews of field participants in case studies. Usually the questions are open-ended, meaning that respondents can answer freely in their own terms rather than selecting from a fixed set of responses. An open-ended interview can be informal, occurring in the natural course of conversation. If many respondents are being interviewed, or if more than one interviewer is involved, the researchers might choose to use a general interview guide that outlines a set of topics to be explored with each respondent, or a standardized interview format.

Focus groups are a form of group interview in which a number of people participate in a discussion that is guided by a skilled interviewer. Because the respondents can talk to and hear each other, they are likely to express feelings or opinions that might not emerge if they were interviewed individually. Focus groups sometimes are used by researchers to explore such phenomena as individuals' reactions to educational programs and practices.

3. *Document and media analysis.* Case study researchers often study written communications that are found in field settings. Consistent with interpretivist epistemology, many of these researchers believe that the meaning of a text can vary depending on the reader, the time period, the context in which the text appears, and so forth. For example, G. Genevieve Patthey-Chavez (1993) did a document analysis in her case study of the cultural conflict between Latino students and their mainstream teachers in a Los Angeles high school. In one of her analyses, she interpreted a local newspaper article as revealing the schools' mission to assimilate immigrant students into the mainstream, whether the students wanted to be assimilated or not.

Official records and personal documents are widely used in historical research. For example, in the case study involving an evaluation of medical education that we mentioned earlier in the chapter, Cuban (1997) described his main sources as the annual announcements and bulletins of courses published at Stanford University every year since 1910.

4. *Questionnaires.* Case study researchers typically choose to use questionnaires when individual contact with every research participant is not feasible and the research data to be collected are not deeply personal. A well-designed questionnaire also can elicit in-depth information, as illustrated in a study by Ismail

Yahya and Gary Moore (1985). These researchers designed a questionnaire to collect qualitative data that included open-ended questions calling for lengthy replies. They sent the respondents an audiotape with the questionnaire, asking respondents to record their responses on the tape.

5. *Tests and other self-report measures.* While more typical of quantitative research, tests can serve a useful purpose in qualitative research. For example, in a case study of the mismatch between a teacher's expectations and the actual reading achievement of two of her first-grade students, Claude Goldenberg (1992) combined qualitative and quantitative methods of data collection. The researcher made qualitative observations of each child's classroom behaviors, and administered two standardized tests of reading achievement to each child. Data from both types of measures yielded key findings. The teacher's greater involvement with the child about whom she initially had low expectations based on the child's achievement test score actually appeared to help this girl to improve her reading achievement. The other girl, about whom the teacher initially had positive expectations, remained in a low reading group.

Reflexivity in Data Collection

The role of case study researchers in data collection is complex. The researchers themselves are the primary "measuring instruments," relying heavily on personal observation, empathy, intuition, judgment, and other psychological processes to grasp the meaning of the phenomenon as it is experienced by the individuals and groups in the field.

In some case study reports the researchers make explicit their role in the data-collection process by describing their personal experiences and reactions in the field. They might also describe how their beliefs and personal background influence the phenomena that they are studying. The researchers' analysis of their own role as constructors and interpreters of the social reality being studied is called **reflexivity.**

Alan Peshkin (1988) illustrates the process of reflexivity in his case study of a multiethnic high school. In his published report, he describes a number of "I's" that he had listed during data collection to characterize different aspects of himself, and explains how they affected his findings. The *Ethnic Maintenance I,* based on his identity as a Jew, approved of individuals maintaining their ethnic identity. The *Justice-seeking I* was aroused when Peshkin repeatedly heard the community in which the high school was located being criticized by both residents and nonresidents. This aspect of Peshkin's self strengthened his desire to convey the community in a more generous light.

Data Analysis in Case Study Research

Even a modest case study is likely to generate many pages of field notes, interview transcripts, and documents obtained from the field setting. Suppose there are 200 such pages, each containing 250 words. That totals 50,000 words. How do the researchers analyze all those words in order to produce significant, meaningful findings? Several approaches can be used, which Renata Tesch (1990) classified into three types: interpretational, structural, and reflective analysis. Each is explained below.

Interpretational Analysis

Interpretational analysis involves a systematic set of procedures to code and classify qualitative data to ensure that the important constructs, themes, and patterns emerge. These procedures can be carried out manually, but use of a computer software program such as Ethnograph makes the task much more manageable.

The steps of interpretational analysis are: (1) preparing a database containing all the data (field notes, documents, transcripts, records, etc.) collected during the case study; (2) numbering each line of text sequentially and then dividing the text into meaningful segments (e.g., in the analysis of interview data, each question plus the participant's response might be a separate segment); (3) developing meaningful categories to code the data; (4) coding each segment by any and all categories that apply to it; (5) cumulating all the segments that have been coded by a given category; and (6) generating constructs that emerge from the categories.

The case study reprinted in this chapter is an example of interpretational analysis. Marsh analyzed her data using a set of categories that represent different discourses about teaching and learning. For example, she taped and transcribed four hours of conversation with her case teacher, Ms. Nicholi. Then, in Marsh's words: "I analyzed these stories in order to identify and illuminate the discourses that Ms. Nicholi drew upon to make meaning in her personal and professional life." It is not clear from the report how Marsh identified these discourses, or how systematic she was in coding the data for occurrences of each discourse category. Some research reports do not provide this level of detail. If you are interested in it, though, it is legitimate to query researchers about details of procedures mentioned in their report.

Figure 10.1 illustrates the blending of data collection and interpretational analysis that is typical of case study research. It shows a contact summary form used in a case study described by Matthew Miles and A. Michael Huberman (1994). A **contact summary form** is a form qualitative researchers use to summarize the procedures they used to collect and analyze data from a field contact in a case study. This form summarizes eight salient points from the contact. Some points probably were taken from the researchers' field notes, and others might have come to mind when they reviewed the notes. The researchers treated each point on the contact summary form as a data chunk and coded it, using a theme coding system.

The right column in Figure 10.1 shows how each point was coded by the specific "theme/aspect" to which it relates. Some points were coded with more than one theme; e.g., point #6 was judged to relate both to power distribution and to conflict management. Thus the researchers must already have made a list of themes/aspects to describe the phenomenon that they were investigating, from which they obtained these two codes. To code point #7 the researchers invented a

Contact Summary

Type of contact: Mtg. <u>Principals</u>   <u>Ken's office</u>   <u>4/2/76</u>   Site <u>Westgate</u>
           Who, what group   place   date

         Phone _____   _____   _____   Coder <u>MM</u>
           With whom, by whom   place   date

         Inf. Int. _____   _____   _____   Date coded <u>4/18/76</u>
           With whom, by whom   place   date

1. Pick out the most salient points in the contact. Number in order on this sheet and note page number on which point appears. Number point in text of write-up. Attach theme or aspect to each point. Invent themes where no existing ones apply and asterisk those. Comment may also be included in double parentheses.

Page	Salient Points	Themes/Aspects
1	1. Staff decisions have to be made by April 30.	Staff
1	2. Teachers will have to go out of their present grade-level assignment when they transfer.	Staff/Resource Mgmt.
2	3. Teachers vary in their willingness to integrate special education students into their classrooms—some teachers are "a pain in the elbow."	*Resistance
2	4. Ken points out that tentative teacher assignment lists got leaked from the previous meeting (implicitly deplores this).	Internal Communic.
2	5. Ken says, "Teachers act as if they had the right to decide who should be transferred." (would make outcry)	Power Distrib.
2	6. Tacit/explicit decision: "It's our decision to make." (voiced by Ken, agreed by Ed)	Power Distrib./ Conflict Mgmt.
2	7. Principals and Ken, John, and Walter agree that Ms. Epstein is a "bitch."	*Stereotyping
2	8. Ken decides not to tell teachers ahead of time (now) about transfers ("because then we'd have a fait accompli").	Plan for Planning/ Time Mgmt.

FIGURE 10.1   **Contact Summary Form: Salient Points in a Field Contact, with Theme Codes Assigned**

Source. Adapted from Figure 4.2 on p. 54 in Miles, M. B., & Huberman, A. M. (1994). *Qualitative data analysis: An expanded sourcebook* (2nd ed.). Thousand Oaks, CA: Sage. Reprinted by permission of Sage Publications, Inc.

new theme (signified by the asterisk), labeled "Stereotyping." Thus the researchers were continuing to identify themes as they collected and analyzed new data.

Structural Analysis

Structural analysis involves a precise set of procedures for analyzing qualitative data that do not need to be inferred from the data but are inherent features of the discourse, text, or events that the researchers are studying.

To understand the distinction between inherent and inferred patterns, consider this segment of conversation between a Spanish teacher and a student:

Teacher: What does *la casa* mean?
Student: House.
Teacher: That's right. *La casa* means house.

A qualitative researcher conducting a structural analysis of this interaction might note certain features of it, such as:

1. The sequence of speakers within this instructional event was teacher, student, teacher.
2. Each of the teacher's utterances contained more words than the student's utterance.
3. Four Spanish words were uttered.
4. Three words (*la, casa, house*) were uttered twice, and the other six words were uttered once.

You will note that these features are inherent in the data. The researchers need to engage in very little, if any, inference to arrive at these findings. In contrast, researchers using interpretational analysis overlay a structure of meaning on the data. For example, suppose that researchers were conducting an interpretational analysis of how students receive feedback in the classroom. To analyze their data, they might develop several feedback categories, such as informational feedback, praise, criticism, and ambiguous feedback. Using this category scheme, the researchers might code the segment of conversation as an instance of informational feedback, because of the utterance, "That's right. *La casa* means house." This classification is not inherent in the teacher's utterance, but rather it is an inference from the data made by the researchers.

Structural analysis is used in narrative analysis, ethnoscience, and other qualitative research traditions (see Table 10.2). It can be used to investigate a variety of educational phenomena, for example, the sequence of events in children's stories, the organization of the parts of textbooks, and movement patterns within a school building.

Reflective Analysis

The reporting of findings from structural or interpretational analyses of case study findings typically follows a conventional format (introduction, review of literature, methodology, results, and discussion), and the researcher's voice is silent or subdued. This reporting style thus is similar to that used in reporting quantitative research studies (see Chapter 5). By contrast, **reflective analysis** refers to a process in which qualitative researchers rely mainly on their own intuition and personal judgment to analyze the data that have been collected. It does not involve the use of either an explicit category system or a prescribed set of procedures.

One way to understand reflective analysis is to compare it with artistic endeavors. The artist reflects on phenomena and then portrays them so as to reveal both their surface features and essences. Many case study researchers engage in similar reflections and portrayals. Reflective analysis also can involve criticism. Art critics might study a piece of art in order to develop an appreciation of its esthetic elements and "message," but also to make critical judgments about its artistic merit. Some case studies that are carried out as educational evaluations (see Chapter 14) follow a similar process of critical appreciation. These evaluative studies help educators and policy makers understand the features and purposes of educational programs, products, and methods, and also to appreciate their strengths and weaknesses. Just as an art or literary critic develops reflective ability with experience, an educational evaluator must build up a store of experience in order to use reflective analysis wisely.

In reflective reporting, researchers often weave case study data into a story. For example, Harry Wolcott (1990) conducted an extensive case study of a school dropout, whom he called Brad. The story of Brad starts in present time, and then recounts earlier events in his life to clarify the broader and narrower themes around which the story is organized. One theme is "in the chute," a phrase to describe living in a situation that appears to be leading the individual toward prison. Wolcott's voice is heard clearly in the last two sections of the report, where he presents his interpretation of the case. Wolcott (1994) notes that he used this sequence so that, "By the time readers arrive at the point where I offer *my* thoughts as to what might be done [about school dropouts], I want to be sure they have a sufficient background to form their own assessment of Brad and his circumstances . . . " (p. 64).

Much of Wolcott's report consists of direct quotes of Brad's statements, made in informal conversations with the researcher. For example:

> I guess being sneaky means I always try to get away with something. There doesn't have to be any big reason. I used to tell the kid I was hanging around with, "I don't steal stuff because I need it. I just like to do it for some excitement." (p. 77)

Some case study researchers use more dramatic methods to convey findings, including poetry, oral readings, comedy, satire, and visual presentations. Laura Richardson (1992) includes a poem that she wrote to convey her understanding of an unmarried mother whom she had studied. The poem uses only the mother's language, as arranged by Richardson. It begins:

> The most important thing
> to say   is that
> I grew up in the South.
> Being Southern shapes
> aspirations   shapes
> what you think you are
> and what you think you're going to be.

*(When I hear myself, my Ladybird
kind of accent on tape, I think, OH Lord.
You're from Tennessee* (p. 126).

Source. From p. 126 of Richardson, L. (1992). The consequences of poetic representation: Writing the other, rewriting the self. In C. Ellis & M. G. Flaherty (Eds.), *Investigating subjectivity: Research on lived experience* (pp. 125–140). Newbury Park, CA: Sage. Copyright © 1992 by Sage Publications, Inc. Reprinted by permission of Sage Publications, Inc.

Richardson observed that case study researchers who use unconventional reporting genres typically have a postmodern sensibility. As we explained in Chapter 1, postmodernism questions all claims to authoritative methods of inquiry and reporting, including mainstream scientific reports. A postmodernist thus would view poetry as just as legitimate for reporting case study findings as the standard journal-article format used by case study researchers writing in an analytic reporting style.

CRITERIA FOR EVALUATING CASE STUDIES

Researchers who conduct case studies differ in their views about whether case study methods and findings should meet the criteria of validity, reliability, and generalizability that are used to judge the soundness of quantitative research. This chapter focuses on case studies carried out according to **interpretivist epistemology,** which rejects the notion of an external reality that can be discovered through objective means. Interpretivists believe that all the researchers, research participants, and readers of a case study report will have their own unique interpretation of the meaning and value of a case study. Researchers who embrace interpretivism do not judge their case studies using traditional notions of validity and reliability, but instead use criteria that are meant to demonstrate the credibility and trustworthiness of their findings and methods. Below we describe eleven such criteria that will help you evaluate case studies. We have grouped them into three categories: criteria reflecting sensitivity to readers' needs, criteria based on the use of sound research methods, and criteria reflecting thoroughness of data collection and analysis. Appendix 4 contains a list of questions that also can be used in evaluating qualitative research.

Criteria Reflecting Sensitivity to Readers' Needs

1. Strong Chain of Evidence.   The readers of case study reports need to be able to make their own assessment of the soundness of the findings that are reported. Researchers can help readers do so by providing clear, meaningful links between the research questions, the raw data, the analysis of these data, and the conclusions drawn from the data. Robert Yin (1994) refers to these links as a **chain of evidence.** The principle underlying a chain of evidence is that readers of the case study should be able to easily follow the derivation of any evidence from the initial research questions to the ultimate case study conclusions.

Researchers can make the chain of evidence explicit by providing an audit trail in the case study report. An **audit trail** is a complete documentation of the research process used in the case study. The items to document might include: (1) the sources and methods of recording raw data, (2) process notes, (3) the development of the instruments and procedures used to collect data, (4) data reduction and analysis products, and (5) data reconstruction and synthesis products. A case study report would be very long if it included all these materials, but small, representative samples of the most important materials can be provided in a methodology section or appendix.

2. Truthfulness. Readers of a case study report want some assurance that the researchers' descriptions are faithful representations of the phenomena that were studied. The goal is to achieve **verisimilitude,** which Patricia Adler and Peter Adler (1994) describe as "a style of writing that draws the reader so closely into subjects' worlds that these can be palpably felt" (p. 381). As we explained earlier in the chapter, some case study researchers consider literary structures—for example, the telling of tales, one-act plays, or poetry—especially good formats for portraying the emic perspective.

3. Usefulness. An important criterion to consider in evaluating a case study is its usefulness to the reader. A case study can be useful if it enlightens the individuals who read the report of its findings. Another way it can be useful is that it liberates or empowers the individuals being studied. Critical-theory research, a qualitative research tradition described in Chapter 12, emphasizes this aspect of usefulness. Still another aspect of usefulness is that the findings can be applied to the readers' settings and used to make meaningful changes in how they deal with the phenomena that the case study involved.

Criteria Reflecting Use of Sound Research Methods

4. Triangulation. Imagine that you are studying youth gangs, and a gang member tells you that he engages in acts of vandalism because he is bored. Is this a truthful statement of the individual's state of mind? If this person also indicates a habitual state of boredom on a structured questionnaire or personality measure, this evidence would strengthen the truthfulness of his statement. If the researchers report that other gang members make similar statements, this finding would be further evidence of truthfulness. Still another type of evidence would be finding that this causal attribution is consistent with a well-supported theory of aggression.

What has been done in each of these instances is to test the soundness of a case study finding by drawing on corroborative evidence. Case study researchers call this process **triangulation:** it is the process of using multiple data-collection methods, data sources, analysts, or theories to check case study findings.

Triangulation in social science research sometimes does not produce convergence, but instead illustrates inconsistencies or contradictions among findings about the same phenomenon. For example, in studies of controversial, stressful, or illicit phenomena, self-report data might be inconsistent with, or even directly contradict, data resulting from more direct methods of data collection such as observation or document analysis. When this happens, it still may be possible to validate the conflicting data by reconciling them within an explanatory framework.

5. Coding Checks.   In describing interpretational analysis, we explained how researchers develop a category system to code the segments into which interview transcripts, field notes, documents, and other materials have been divided. The reliability of the coding process can be checked with methods similar to those used for determining inter-rater reliability for quantitative measures (see Chapter 5). Because ethnographers rarely rate or code data for enumeration, the form of inter-observer agreement they generally seek is agreement among observers on the nature of the description of, or the composition of, the events that have been observed, not on the frequency of occurrence of events (LeCompte & Preissle, 1993). Besides using multiple observers, they can increase the reliability of their coding schemes by such strategies as using low-inference descriptors and mechanical recording of data.

6. Disconfirming Case Analysis.   Rather than ignoring or explaining exceptions away, Miles and Huberman (1994) recommend using extreme cases as a way to test and thereby strengthen the basic findings: "You need to find the outliers, and then verify whether what is present in them is absent or different in other, more mainstream examples . . . " (p. 269). In quantitative research an outlier is a score at either the high or low extreme of the score distribution. In case study research, an **outlier** is an individual or situation that differs greatly from most other individuals or situations that are studied. Several of the sampling strategies listed in Table 10.1 could lead the researchers to such cases, including extreme/deviant case, maximum variation, critical case, and disconfirming case sampling.

An example of disconfirming case analysis occurred in a case study of school innovation (Miles and Huberman, 1994). In one site a new practice was evaluated by many teachers as a miraculous cure for local ills. The researchers also discovered two outliers among the field participants at this site, that is, individuals who had not adopted the practice or had expressed strong criticism of it. The researchers learned that these individuals had not mastered the innovation as intended, and that their reasons for not adopting the innovation were opposite to those given by adopters. The outliers' comments thus strengthened the researchers' interpretation that technical mastery of an innovative practice by users leads to positive results.

Miles and Huberman also recommend seeking out individuals who have the most to gain or lose by affirming or denying something. If such individuals give an unexpected answer (e.g., a person who has much to gain by denying a statement affirms it), the researchers can be more confident that they are answering truthfully. A related tactic is to look for negative evidence, that is, to actively seek disconfirmation of what the researchers think is true. For example, asking skeptical colleagues to look at the raw data and independently come up with their own conclusions is a good way to test the soundness of the researchers' analyses and interpretations.

7. Member Checking.   A major purpose of case study research is to represent the emic perspective, that is, reality as constructed by the individuals who were studied. Researchers can check their reconstruction of individuals' emic perspective by member checking, which is the process of having individuals review statements in the researchers' report for accuracy and completeness. Member checking was the primary strategy that Kagan and her colleagues used in their study of teachers in residence to ensure the accuracy of the findings.

Member checking might reveal factual errors that are easily corrected. In other instances, the researchers might need to collect more data in order to reconcile discrepancies. It is possible, too, that the opportunity to read the report will cause participants to recall new facts or to have new perceptions of their situation. The report would be rewritten accordingly.

Criteria Reflecting Thoroughness of Data Collection and Analysis

8. Contextual Completeness.   In order for case study phenomena to be fully understood, they must be set within a context. The more comprehensive the researchers' contextualization of the case, the more credible are their interpretations of the phenomena. David Altheide and John Johnson (1994) recommend that case study researchers consider the following contextual features in interpreting the meaning of the phenomena they investigate: history, physical setting, and environment; the number of participants; specific activities; the schedules and temporal order of events; divisions of labor; routines and variations from routines; significant events and their origins and consequences; members' perceptions and meanings; and social rules and basic patterns of order.

Altheide and Johnson stress that thorough contextualization requires collecting data about the multivocality and the tacit knowledge of field participants. **Multivocality** refers to the fact that, in many field settings, participants do not speak with a unified voice; they have diverse interests and viewpoints. **Tacit knowledge** refers to the implicit meanings that the individuals being studied either cannot find the words to express, or that they take so much for granted that they do not refer to them in everyday conversation or in research interviews. Case study findings that reflect multivocality and tacit knowledge are more likely to be complete, and thus more credible.

9. Long-Term Observation.   Gathering data over a long period of time and making repeated observations of the phenomenon can increase the trustworthiness of case study findings. For example, students' perceptions of school are known to vary depending on the time of year due to such factors as tests, the weather conditions, and whether a school vacation is coming or has just passed. Changing conditions in their own lives also affect participants' perspective, such as problems on the job or in personal relationships. If data are collected over an extended time period, the researchers might be able to distinguish situational perceptions from more consistent trends. The researchers' own perceptions of the phenomenon also develop over time, allowing them greater opportunities to reconfirm or refine their interpretations.

10. Representativeness Check.   Researchers should determine whether a finding is typical of the field site from which it was obtained. They can do so by reflecting on whether they relied too much on accessible or elite informants in collecting data. Researchers might also describe how they ensured that unusual occurrences, or the fact that the researchers were present on some occasions but not on others, did not skew the findings.

11. Researchers' Self-Reflection.   Researchers' interpretations are more credible if they demonstrate reflexivity, which, as explained earlier in the chapter, is self-reflection with respect to their qualifications to conduct the study and their relationship to the situation being studied. For example, David Thomas (1993) demonstrated the use of self-reflection in his case study of cross-race relationships between managers and their protégés in a corporation. Thomas described two major concerns he had about conducting the study: the potential impact of his being an African American male of junior rank, and his ability to develop effective interview rapport with Caucasian senior managers. Thomas explained the steps he took to manage these concerns, including asking two Caucasian senior managers with expertise in clinical supervision and race relations research to serve as his research supervisors. This sensitivity to his possible effect on the data-collection and analysis process contributed to the soundness of the research findings.

CHECKING THE APPLICABILITY OF CASE STUDY FINDINGS

In reading a case study, one of the main concerns that an educational practitioner might have is the extent to which the study's findings can be applied to the individuals or situations in the practitioner's setting. **Applicability** thus is similar to generalizability, which is an important goal of quantitative research.

Sampling techniques used in quantitative research (see Chapter 5) allow for precise determination of the generalizability of a study's findings. Determining the applicability of case study findings is less direct. Some researchers argue that the findings of a case study depend on the ongoing interaction between the data and the creative processes of the researcher, and thus are unique to the case that was studied. However, most qualitative researchers believe that case study findings can be applied to other settings besides those that were studied.

One approach to determining the applicability of case study findings is to consider the sampling strategy that the researchers used to select the case. If the researchers studied a typical or extreme case, the results should be applicable to other similar cases. If the researchers used a **multiple-case design,** they usually conduct a cross-case analysis to help readers determine whether there was generalizability of findings among the cases that they studied. The presence of cross-case generalizability is strong evidence that the findings are applicable to other situations and individuals than those studied by the researchers.

Another position on the issue of applicability is to place the responsibility for making this judgment on readers of the case study findings. In this view, it is the responsibility of the readers, not the researchers, to determine the similarity of the cases that were studied to the situation of interest to them. Researchers can help readers make this determination by providing a thick description of the participants and contexts that comprise the case.

QUALITATIVE RESEARCH TRADITIONS

Some case study research in education draws from qualitative research traditions in the social sciences (e.g., anthropology, sociology, psychology), the humanities (e.g., art, literature, and philosophy), and interdisciplinary studies. As we explained earlier in the chapter, a qualitative research tradition represents the work produced by a group of investigators who hold a similar view of the nature of the universe and are in agreement as to legitimate questions to ask and techniques to use in its exploration. The literature of a particular tradition can be searched by using terms and descriptors specific to that tradition (see Chapter 2).

Table 10.2 presents seventeen qualitative research traditions organized into three categories. The traditions in each category involve the study of similar phenomena. Those in the first category seek to understand language and communication phenomena; those in the second category focus on understanding the nature of inner experience; and those in the third category study societal and cultural phenomena. Some have played a major role in educational research, whereas others have been applied to education rarely but clearly have potential for educational application. The list is not exhaustive, because the field of qualitative research is undergoing rapid growth and continual reconceptualization. Also, the list of traditions shown in Table 10.2 does not include historical research, because the subjects of historical research cut across the three categories shown in the table. Historical research is a strong qualitative research tradition, and is the focus of Chapter 13.

Below we briefly explain how investigation of each of the three types of phenomena that these research traditions involve can contribute to the study of education.

Traditions Involving the Investigation of Communication

Instruction in schools and other educational institutions involves verbal and nonverbal communication among teachers and students. Even when individu-

TABLE 10.2 Phenomena Investigated by Qualitative Research Traditions	

RESEARCH TRADITION	PHENOMENA INVESTIGATED
	Communication
1. Ethnographic content analysis	The content of documents from a cultural perspective
2. Ethnography of communication	How members of a culture use speech in their social life
3. Ethnoscience	A culture's semantic systems
4. Semiotics	Signs and the meanings they convey
5. Narrative analysis	Organized representations and explanations of human experience
6. Structuralism	The systemic properties of language, text, and other phenomena
7. Hermeneutics	The process by which individuals arrive at the meaning of a text
	Inner Experience
8. Cognitive psychology	The mental structures and processes used by individuals in different situations
9. Phenomenology	Reality as it is subjectively experienced by individuals
10. Phenomenography	Individuals' mental conceptions of reality
11. Life history	Individuals' life experiences from their own perspective
	Society and Culture
12. Ethnomethodology	The rules that underlie everyday social interactions
13. Event structure analysis	The logical structures of social events
14. Symbolic interactionism	The influence of social interactions on social structures and individuals' self-identity
15. Ethnography	Characteristic features and patterns of a culture
16. Critical-theory research	Oppressive power relationships in a culture
17. Action research	Practitioners' self-reflective efforts to improve their effectiveness

Source. Adapted from Table 15.1 on p. 593 in Gall, M. D., Borg, W. R., & Gall, J. P. (1996). *Educational research: An introduction* (6th ed.). White Plains, NY: Longman.

als engage in self-instruction, some of the time they are interacting with a book, computer screen, film, videotape, or other communication media. Each of these activities involves either reacting to, or generating, language or some other form of communication.

Qualitative research traditions involving the investigation of communication have contributed to educational research in many ways. Researchers have investigated such topics as the philosophy of education conveyed by curriculum guides; the presence of gender bias in textbooks as reflected in the frequency of the use of the terms *he* versus *she* and other pronouns; the symbolic meanings conveyed by physical phenomena in a school building such as school uniforms, sports paraphernalia, and the arrangement of desks in a classroom; and the ways in which teachers exert guidance or control of students through their verbal and nonverbal acts in the classroom. Some researchers study the meaning of texts and artifacts from the perspective of various cultures or subcultures.

Four qualitative research traditions that have focused on communication as it reflects cultural phenomena are ethnographic content analysis, the ethnography of communication, ethnoscience, and semiotics. Three other qualitative research traditions that focus on the investigation of language or other texts are narrative analysis, structuralism, and hermeneutics.

Traditions Involving the Investigation of Inner Experience

All acts of teaching and learning in human beings involve changes in the teachers' or students' inner experience. Thus qualitative researchers who investigate inner experience can shed light on the meaning of education as experienced by various participants.

Quantitative researchers typically ignore the study of inner experience. For example, B. F. Skinner's views of learning had a great impact on educational research, yet Skinner viewed the human mind as a "black box" between a defined stimulus and an observable response, not accessible to scientific study. Qualitative researchers, by contrast, view human thoughts and feelings as phenomena worthy of investigation. They have developed research traditions that focus on the thought processes of individuals and on ways that different individuals apprehend and describe their experiences. These traditions have been used to study the lives of individuals from various subcultures, to explore the life history of exemplary teachers and scholars, and to compare the thinking processes of different types of people (e.g., experts versus novices in a field of inquiry such as art or science).

Four qualitative research traditions that involve the study of inner experience are cognitive psychology, phenomenology, phenomenography, and life history.

Traditions Involving the Investigation of Society and Culture

Here we use the term *society* to refer to the various groups and social categories to which individuals perceive themselves or other human beings as belonging. The term *culture* refers to all the ways of living (e.g., values, customs, rituals, and beliefs) that particular groups of human beings develop, and that are transmitted from one generation to the next, or from current members to newly admitted members, over time. Education is one of the most powerful factors in cultural transmission, and it has profound effects upon the maintenance of, and changes in, the groups and social categories with which individuals identify. Therefore, the qualitative research traditions that directly investigate societal and cultural phenomena have much to offer educational research.

Three qualitative research traditions involving the study of society and culture are ethnomethodology, event structure analysis, and symbolic interactionism. Three other qualitative research traditions that investigate society and culture have influenced many educational researchers, and therefore each of them is the subject of a separate chapter in this book. Specifically, ethnographic research is discussed in Chapter 11, critical-theory research is discussed in Chapter 12, and action research is discussed in Chapter 15.

Example of Outlining a Research Proposal

This feature of the chapter gives you an example of how to outline a research proposal using the form in Appendix 1. The example, involving a proposal to study curriculum alignment, is introduced at the end of Chapter 2.

The second research question in the example is as follows: "What procedures have administrators, teachers, and specialists used to align curriculum content with instruction and test content?" This question can be addressed by the methods of quantitative or qualitative inquiry, or both. For present purposes, we choose to address it by the qualitative methods of case study research. Our rationale for this choice is that we wish to produce a thick description of the curriculum alignment process. We wish to understand in depth the experiences of a few school sites rather than to grasp at a surface level the experiences of many school sites.

To suggest what is involved in the design of a case study, we will fill out various parts of the proposal outline.

4. RESEARCH DESIGN
   A. *Research design.* The research design is a case study. The primary purpose of the case study is to describe the curriculum alignment process rather than explain or evaluate it. The study will be based partly on the research tradition of narrative analysis, because we are interested in identifying whether the unfolding "story" of the curriculum alignment process can be understood in terms of critical incidents (e.g., crises and resolutions) and phases of change. We also will draw on the methods developed by cognitive psychologists to understand thinking processes, because we are interested not only in what educators do during the alignment process, but also in how they think while planning a change, enacting the change, and reflecting on the change.
   D. *Criteria for judging credibility and trustworthiness of results.* We will create a chain of evidence by making a record of all data collected in the study, the individuals involved in the data collection, and the dates of data collection. Constructs and themes identified in the data analysis will be related to specific examples of data sources from which they were inferred.

      We will write detailed vignettes of critical incidents in the curriculum alignment process, so that the process becomes concrete and real for readers of the study. We will have several educational practitioners involved in the process read and evaluate the report in terms of its soundness and usefulness to them. Their feedback will be used to revise the report.

The primary methods of data collection will be interviews, direct observation of critical events, and inspection of documents generated as part of the curriculum alignment process. The collected data will be analyzed to determine whether they provide corroborative evidence for constructs and themes that we identify in the curriculum alignment process.

The soundness of data coding will be checked by having several researchers code samples of the data to determine whether they derive similar constructs and themes from the data.

The soundness of the interview data, observational data, and documents selected for analysis will be checked by having selected participants in the study check them for accuracy, bias, and completeness.

To ensure thoroughness of data collection, we will continually check with participants that we have identified all the individuals involved in the curriculum alignment process and that we have identified all relevant events leading up to initiation of the process and the process itself. The check will involve making a list of the individuals and events we have identified, showing the list to a sample of the participants, and asking them whether any person or event is missing from the list.

5. SAMPLING
   B. *Phenomenon.* The phenomenon of interest to us is the process of curriculum alignment as actually enacted by particular schools. Therefore, our case will be a school involved in this process.
   C. *Sampling procedure.* Because of the intensive data collection required by this study, we will select just one school (the case). The sampling strategy will be to select a typical case, which for us means a school that has a recent history of neither being a district leader in school change nor a reluctant participant. We believe that this sampling strategy will enable us to identify typical (rather than atypical) problems, solutions, and products that result from a curriculum-alignment process. To an extent, sampling also will involve a convenience strategy in that the school will be selected from a district that is near the researchers' work site. The proximity will permit the researchers to make frequent trips to the school to collect data and make validity checks.
   D. *Sampling units.* Participants in the study will be selected to represent all the stakeholders in the curriculum-alignment process. The known stakeholders include district-level specialists, the principal, teachers on the alignment team, and teachers not on the team but affected by the alignment outcomes. If additional stakeholders are identified as the study progresses, they will be invited to participate in the study.

If the number of individuals in a stakeholder group is large, a representative sample will be selected for data collection procedures that are intensive.

6. VARIABLES

   B. *Focus of the case study.* We plan to focus on (a) the problems that occur during the process and how those problems get resolved; and (b) alignment procedures and products for which there is consensual agreement and those for which consensual agreement could not be reached.

7. METHODS OF DATA COLLECTION

   C. *Framework for data collection.* The procedures for data collection will focus on an emic perspective, that is, the perspective of the stakeholders as they experience the curriculum-alignment process. We will observe and take notes on significant events in the process. These notes will provide the basis for interviewing event participants about their perceptions of specific incidents that occurred in the event. If an upcoming event seems particularly significant, efforts will be made to videotape it. We will watch the videotape with the event participants to obtain their perceptions as the event unfolds. Furthermore, we will interview stakeholders who were not directly involved in the event, but who will be affected by it. We also will collect significant documents prepared by stakeholders during the alignment process.

   The framework for data collection described above will provide the basis for developing specific instruments and procedures, for example, interview schedules and content-analysis categories for examining documents.

8. DATA ANALYSIS PROCEDURES

   B. *Method of data analysis.* An interpretational approach to data analysis will be used. The data will be entered into computer files and analyzed using the software program Ethnograph. We will focus on identifying constructs, themes, and patterns relating to problems and problem-resolution processes and also on alignment procedures and products.

Self-Check Test

1. In a qualitative research case study, the researchers strive to do all of the following except
   a. conduct an in-depth study of the phenomenon.
   b. study the phenomenon in its natural context.
   c. maintain a completely objective perspective on the phenomenon.
   d. reflect the research participants' perspective on the phenomenon being studied.

2. Looking for relational patterns in a case study reflects the goal of
   _____ a phenomenon.
   a. describing   c. evaluating
   b. explaining   d. generalizing

3. Qualitative researchers use purposeful sampling in order to
   a. reduce the chances of selecting atypical cases of the phenomenon to
      be studied.
   b. eliminate the need to study more than one case.
   c. select cases that are the most convenient for in-depth study.
   d. select cases that are "information-rich" with respect to the purposes
      of the study.

4. In qualitative research, the main measuring instrument is
   a. the questionnaire or other self-report measure used to collect data.
   b. audiotape or videotape recordings of field events.
   c. the researchers themselves.
   d. the researchers' key informants.

5. In interpretational data analysis, the researchers
   a. search for patterns inherent in the data.
   b. impose meaning on the data.
   c. search for naturally occurring segments in the data.
   d. use categories developed by other researchers.

6. Researchers who wish to rely on their own intuition and judgment in analyzing case study data will most likely use
   a. interpretational analysis.   c. reflective analysis.
   b. structural analysis.   d. narrative analysis.

7. Reflective reporting of a case study tends to involve
   a. an objective writing style.
   b. computer analysis of the data.
   c. a conventional organization of topics.
   d. the strong presence of the researchers' voice.

8. Researcher bias in case studies is best handled by
   a. honest exploration of one's identity and beliefs as possible biasing
      factors.
   b. exclusive use of objective data-collection methods.
   c. using data collectors who are similar to the field participants.
   d. studying phenomena in which one has minimal interest.

9. If researchers want to increase the applicability of their case study findings to other settings, it is not wise to
   a. study an atypical case.
   b. use a multiple-case design.
   c. compare their case to similar cases studied by other researchers.
   d. provide a thick description of their case.

10. Qualitative research traditions
    a. do not typically use case study methods to investigate phenomena.
    b. are grounded in positivism.
    c. use the techniques of various academic disciplines in the study of phenomena.
    d. are based primarily on models from the physical sciences.

11. Ethnography primarily involves the investigation of
    a. inner experience.
    c. language and communication.
    b. society and culture.
    d. historical phenomena.

CHAPTER REFERENCES

Adler, P. A., & Adler, P. (1994). Observational techniques. In N. K. Denzin & Y. S. Lincoln (Eds.), *Handbook of qualitative research* (pp. 377–392). Thousand Oaks, CA: Sage.

Altheide, D. L., & Johnson, J. M. (1994). Criteria for assessing interpretive validity in qualitative research. In N. K. Denzin & Y. S. Lincoln (Eds.), *Handbook of qualitative research* (pp. 485–499). Thousand Oaks, CA: Sage.

Cuban, L. (1997). Change without reform: The case of Stanford University school of medicine, 1908–1990. *American Educational Research Journal, 34,* 83–122.

Goldenberg, C. (1992). The limits of expectations: A case for case knowledge about teacher expectancy effects. *American Educational Research Journal, 29,* 517–544.

Jacob, E. (1987). Qualitative research traditions: A review. *Review of Educational Research, 57,* 1–50.

Kagan, D. M., Dennis, M. B., Igou, M., Moore, P., & Sparks, K. (1993). The experience of being a teacher in residence. *American Educational Research Journal, 30,* 426–443.

Kirk, J., & Miller, M. L. (1986). *Reliability and validity in qualitative research.* Beverly Hills, CA: Sage.

LeCompte, M. D., & Preissle, J. (1993). *Ethnography and qualitative design in educational research* (2nd ed.). San Diego: Academic.

Manning, P. K., & Cullum-Swan, B. (1994). Narrative, content, and semiotic analysis. In N. K. Denzin & Y. S. Lincoln (Eds.), *Handbook of qualitative research* (pp. 463–477). Thousand Oaks, CA: Sage.

Miles, M. B., & Huberman, A. M. (1994). *Qualitative data analysis: An expanded sourcebook* (2nd ed.). Thousand Oaks, CA: Sage.

Patthey-Chavez, G. G. (1993). High school as an arena for cultural conflict and acculturation for Latino Angelinos. *Anthropology and Education Quarterly, 24,* 33–60.

Patton, M. Q. (2001). *Qualitative evaluation and research methods* (3rd ed.). Thousand Oaks, CA: Sage.

Peshkin, A. (1988). In search of subjectivity—one's own. *Educational Researcher, 17*(7), 17–21.

Richardson, L. (1992). The consequences of poetic representation: Writing the other, rewriting the self. In C. Ellis & M. G. Flaherty (Eds.), *Investigating subjectivity: Research on lived experience* (pp. 125–140). Newbury Park, CA: Sage.

Tesch, R. (1990). *Qualitative research: Analysis types and software tools.* New York: Falmer.

Thomas, D. A. (1993). Racial dynamics in cross-race developmental relationships. *Administrative Science Quarterly, 38,* 169–194.

Wolcott, H. F. (1990). *Writing up qualitative research.* Newbury Park, CA: Sage.

Wolcott, H. F. (1994). *Transforming qualitative data: Description, analysis, and interpretation.* Thousand Oaks, CA: Sage.

Yahya, I. B., & Moore, G. E. (1985, March). On research methodology: The cassette tape as a data collection medium. Paper presented at the Southern Research Conference in Agricultural Education, Mobile, AL. (ERIC Document Reference No. ED262098.)

Yin, R. K. (1994). *Case study research design and methods* (2nd ed.). Thousand Oaks, CA: Sage.

Resources for Further Study

Denzin, N. K., & Lincoln, Y. S. (Eds.). (2000). *Handbook of qualitative research* (2nd ed.). Thousand Oaks, CA: Sage.

> *An authoritative, comprehensive overview of qualitative research across various disciplines, including education. Among the topics covered are new directions in qualitative research such as autoethnography, critical race theory, and queer theory.*

Glesne, C. (1999). *Becoming qualitative researchers: An introduction* (2nd ed.). New York: Longman.

> *Covers each stage of a qualitative research study: design methods and the role of theory, pilot studies, interviewing and other techniques of data collection, data analysis, and report writing. The author emphasizes the researchers' personal involvement in the study and the ethics of qualitative research.*

Stake, R. E. (1995). *The art of case study research: Perspectives on practice.* Thousand Oaks, CA: Sage.

> *A primer on how to do case studies in education. The author explains such matters as selection of a case, generalization from one case to another, and triangulation of case study findings.*

Yin, R. K. (2003). *Case study research* (3rd ed.). Thousand Oaks, CA: Sage.

> *Covers key aspects of case study research, including problem definition, design issues, data collection methods, data analysis, and report writing. See also: Yin, R. K. (2003).* Applications of case study research *(2nd ed.). Thousand Oaks, CA: Sage.*

In the following section of this chapter you will read a research article that illustrates a case study based on qualitative research. It is preceded by comments written especially for this book by the author of the article. Then the article itself is reprinted in full, just as it appeared when originally published. Where appropriate, we have added footnotes to help you understand the information contained in the article.

Sample Case Study
The Shaping of Ms. Nicholi: The Discursive Fashioning of Teacher Identities

Marsh, M. M. (2002). The shaping of Ms. Nicholi: The discursive fashioning of teacher identities. *International Journal of Qualitative Studies in Education, 15,* 333–347.

● **RESEARCHER'S COMMENTS,** *Prepared by Monica Miller Marsh*

This study grew out of a desire to better understand how teachers come to think as they do about children, teaching, and learning. When I began my public school teaching in a fifth-grade classroom, over 60 percent of the students were children of color, many from low-income families. (A decade before, the district had taught mainly a white, upper-middle-class, Jewish student body.)

My colleagues were smart, caring, and committed teachers, the majority near retirement age. They struggled with how to teach this "new" population of children, lamenting that the teaching strategies and curricula that they had created for their former students no longer worked with this more diverse population. Rather than rethinking the way that they approached their pedagogy, they argued that the students and their families were not supportive of the school. At school I often heard talk like, "These kids don't want to work . . ." and "I get no support from these parents. . . ."

My decision to return to college for doctoral work was due, in part, to my own struggles as a beginning teacher. I did not have answers for the problems that my district was facing, but I knew that there were other ways of teaching that would better address a diverse student population. Multicultural education was gaining in prominence, and I wanted to explore its methods for instruction and curriculum development. I also wanted to work with teachers who had just entered teacher education programs, whom I believed would be more willing to implement alternative pedagogies.

During my first year in the doctoral program, I taught an early childhood social studies methods course that included a field component. One course requirement for the prospective teachers was to keep a journal of their field experiences in the elementary classroom. I was stunned when I read the first set of entries after they were in the field only three weeks. Their critical words about struggling students, and about many parents with whom they had never personally interacted, reflected the same sentiments that my former colleagues had expressed. Some said that their cooperating teachers had shared information about students' families, but others admitted that they were simply hypothesizing about why the students were behaving in particular ways.

As I looked at the group of white, middle-class, females sitting before me in my course, I began to wonder how my own beliefs and actions about teaching were formed. I began to study the literature on teacher thinking. Eventually I designed my dissertation project to study the thinking of two first-year teachers, one of whom was Ms. Nicholi.

I situate my work with others who have explored the notion of teacher thinking as a social phenomenon rather than an individual enterprise. I am interested in how language about children and their families is negotiated among groups of teachers, and how that leads to decisions about the educational futures of specific children. To study this I turned to the concepts of discourse and ideology.

I engaged in life history work with Ms. Nicholi. I also sought to interview Ms. Nicholi's instructors in her teacher education program and some of her administrators and colleagues at Woodlawn. By identifying the prevailing discourses and ideologies in each of these contexts, I was able to trace the origins of some of the thoughts and ideas that Ms. Nicholi drew upon during her first year of teaching.

At first my efforts to get information from other people at Woodlawn were rebuffed. After I agreed to substitute for a fourth-grade teacher who was ill one day, many of them became much easier to reach. This experience reinforced my understanding that people are much more open and willing to share their time and expertise when they see the research project benefiting them directly. My physical presence as a classroom aide and substitute teacher was perceived as much more valuable than the written report on Woodlawn that I had promised to provide upon completion of my project. It probably increased the staff's trust in me by making me less of an outsider (Kemmis & McTaggart, 2000).

I had offered to serve as both a participant observer and a mentor to Ms. Nicholi during my study. While I gave her my fieldnotes following each school visit, she never commented on them, and as far as I know, never read them. When she received my dissertation draft she seemed clearly unhappy with my portrayal of her. She declined my offer to include her response to my portrayal as part of the final report. In retrospect, I regret not having more dialogue with her throughout the study.

In a subsequent article, titled "The Influence of Discourses on the Precarious Nature of Mentoring," I examined my role as university researcher/mentor for Ms. Nicholi and the other first-year teacher featured in my original study. There I again turned to the concept of discourse to interrogate my own ideological positioning and illustrate ways in which I could perhaps have nurtured richer, more meaningful relationships with both my research participants. I am very grateful to these two teachers for helping me learn not only about them, but about myself as well.

At the university I now explicitly teach the concept of discourse so that prospective and practicing teachers have opportunities to develop awareness of how teachers, children, and families are positioned in relation to one another within particular discourses. The references below include citations for two other pieces I wrote on teacher discourse and the works of four classroom teachers that I mention in the article.

References

Ashton-Warner, S. (1963). *Teacher*. New York: Simon & Schuster, Inc.

Conroy, P. (1987) *The water is wide*. New York: Bantam Books.

Kemmis, S., & McTaggart, R. (2000). Participatory action research. In N. K. Denzin & Y. S. Lincoln (Eds.), *Handbook of qualitative research* (2nd ed., pp. 567–605). Thousand Oaks, CA: Sage.

Miller Marsh, M. (2002). The influence of discourses on the precarious nature of mentoring. *Reflective Practice, 3*, 103–115.

Miller Marsh, M. (2002b). Examining the discourses that shape our teacher identities. *Curriculum Inquiry 32*, 453–469.

Paley, V. G. (2000). *White teacher*. Cambridge, MA: Harvard University Press.

Paley, V. G. (1995). *Kwanzaa and me: A teacher's story*. Cambridge, MA: Harvard University Press.

Weber Gordon, J. (1946). *My country school diary*. New York: Harper and Bros.

The Shaping of Ms. Nicholi:
The Discursive Fashioning of Teacher Identities

Monica Miller Marsh
State University of New York at Binghamton

This article examines how teacher thinking is socially nego-tiated yet individually enacted. Through a case study ap-proach, the author explores how the identities of a first-year kindergarten teacher were fashioned linguistically as she moved through the contexts of her teacher education pro-gram, the elementary school in which she taught and the per-sonal aspects of her life. Using ethnographic techniques, multiple layers of data were gathered in nested contexts. A theoretical framework was developed by juxtaposing the work of the Russian theorists Valentin Volosinov on the con-cept of ideologies and M. M. Bakhtin on his notions of lan-guage to guide the analysis of data. Findings indicate that by providing prospective teachers with the tools for concep-tualizing teacher thinking as social, teacher educators can provide future educators with alternative ways to author their identities and help them to understand that they can create possibilities for all children.

INTRODUCTION

Conceptualizing teacher thought as social in nature is a relatively recent phenomenon (Britzman, 1991; Casey, 1993; Gomez, in press). Traditionally, research on teacher thinking has focused on the individual (Clandinin & Con-nelly, 1987; McCutcheon, 1980; Zahorik, 1970). However, a growing body of literature has shown that schools and families are shaped by the historical, cultural, social, and political forces that surround a given community (Graue, 1993; Graue & Miller Marsh, 1996; Heath, 1983; Lareau,

1989). The juxtaposition of this research with that of the research on teacher thinking would suggest that the na-ture of teacher thought is dialogic (Bakhtin, 1981), in the sense that it is an ongoing dialogue between one's personal history, present conditions, beliefs, values, and the social, cultural, historical, and political forces that surround groups of individuals in a given time and place. From this perspective, teacher thought is socially con-structed yet individually enacted.

In this paper, I draw upon the work of Mikhail Bakhtin (1981) and Valentin Volosinov (1973), two Russian schol-ars, in order to understand better the social nature of teacher thinking. The merging of Volosinov's work on the concept of ideologies with that of Bakhtin's notion of language creates a theoretical framework which explains how ideologies are social constructions that both shape and are shaped by individual and collective thought. I begin by revealing the relevant theoretical contributions of Bakhtin and Volosinov. Using data drawn from a larger research project, I illustrate how the thought and ulti-mately the identities of Ms. Nicholi[1], a first-year teacher, were discursively fashioned as she moved through the contexts of her teacher education program, the elemen-tary school in which she taught and personal aspects of her life.[a] I then examine how the social identities of the children in Ms. Nicholi's care were fashioned by and in relation to their teacher. Finally, I share implications for teacher education by conceptualizing teacher thinking from this perspective.

THEORETICAL CONSTRUCTS

Most prospective teachers enter a teacher education program because they desire to learn how to teach. They are seeking knowledge about how children learn,

---

a. "Discursively fashioned" means that the thoughts and identities of this teacher were shaped by the discourses that the teacher encountered and expressed in various contexts.

strategies for planning and carrying out various types of instruction, and techniques for managing behavior. Upon entrance into a teacher education program, prospective teachers are immersed in specific ways of thinking, speaking, and acting as teachers that are sanctioned by the community of educators to which they aspire to belong. These discourses, or frameworks for thought and action, in which particular notions about teaching and learning are embedded, are appropriated by prospective teachers as they read, discuss, student teach, and are evaluated with and by those who are already members of the teaching profession. As Bakhtin (1981) explains, "One's own discourse is gradually and slowly wrought out of others' words that have been acknowledged and assimilated, and the boundaries between the two are at first scarcely perceptible" (p. 345).

As individuals appropriate fragments of particular discourses they absorb the ideologies inherent in them. Ideologies structure how we visualize the world while simultaneously locating us within it. As we are introduced to different ways of seeing, thinking, and acting through our interactions with others, various ideologies enter into our consciousness and come into contact with those things that we already hold as "true". An ideological struggle ensues as we try to make sense of these multiple "representations of reality" (Shapiro, 1988) in the context of our daily lives. As Bakhtin (1981) explains, "Our ideological development is [just such] an intense struggle within us for hegemony among various available verbal and ideological points of view, approaches, directions and values" (p. 346).[b] This struggle is ongoing. We are constantly in a state of *ideological becoming* (Bakhtin, 1981).

The ideological discourses that enter into an individual consciousness are negotiated on *interindividual territory*. According to Volosinov, this is the space where the consciousness of self and other converge. Ideologies are diffused among individuals as they encounter one another socially. Volosinov (1973) writes, "This ideological chain stretches from individual consciousness to individual consciousness, connecting them together. . . . Consciousness becomes consciousness only once it has been filled with ideological (semiotic) content, consequently, only in the process of social interaction (p. 11).[c]

Ideologies enter into an individual consciousness that is already replete with meaning. This internal ideology or individual consciousness is created in the context of an individual's particular life. It is the whole aggregate of conditions of life and society in which that organism has been set" (Volosinov, 1973, p. 35). According to Volosinov (1973) the individual consciousness is the space where biology, biography, and ideology intersect. It is here that individuals process their understanding of experiences and put their "individual imprint" on their thoughts, actions, and ways of being in the world.

This process of socially negotiating various ideological representations of the self is the act of constructing identities. Identities are created through dialogue on interindividual territory. As Kondo (1990) explains, "Rather than universal essences, selves are rhetorical assertions produced by our linguistic conventions, which we narrate and perform for each other" (p. 307).

As individuals piece together identities from the discourses that are made available to them, they simultaneously create possibilities and constraints for the identities of those with whom they are in relationship. Conceptualizing the construction of the self as relational means that choosing to author one's self-identities in particular ways directly impacts the social identities that can be formed by others. This would seem to be especially significant in a field where adults and children have the power to construct identities with and for one another.

THE STUDY

This article is based on part of a larger investigation into the social nature of teacher thinking. The larger research design comprised two in-depth case studies which ex-

---

b. Hegemony refers to the maintenance of domination by privileged cultural groups over other groups through cultural agencies that exert power (e.g., the government's system of criminal justice).

c. Semiotics is the study of signs and the meanings that they convey.

amined the identity formation of two first-year teachers. Teachers who were considered for the study had attended and been graduated from one of the teacher education programs offered at Midwestern University, a large research institution. They were also currently teaching in the Mayfield City School District, the large racially, ethnically and economically diverse community in which the university was located. Ms. Nicholi, the focal teacher of this article, had been enrolled in the Early Education Program (EEP) at Midwestern and was teaching in a magnet kindergarten classroom at Woodlawn Elementary School. Ms. Nicholi was recommended to me by an instructor in the EEP as a conscientious and concerned teacher interested in providing each of the children in her care with the best education possible. She was also highly regarded by her colleagues at Woodlawn.

Conceptualizing teacher thought and action as socially negotiated and individually enacted meant that research had to be carried out on multiple levels in order to "capture" both the social and the individual aspects of each teacher's identities. At the social level, I attempted to make visible the discourses that surrounded the EEP and Woodlawn Elementary by examining historical documents, curriculum guidelines and syllabi as well as by conducting interviews with faculty and staff at Midwestern and Woodlawn. In addition, I attended staff meetings at Woodlawn. I took on the role of participant observer in Ms. Nicholi's classroom and visited the kindergarten one half-day per week from January 1997 through May 1997 for a total of 14 visits. During these observations I took extensive fieldnotes and returned them to Ms. Nicholi so that she could make additional comments, which were then included as data. Documents such as classroom communications, worksheets, and copies of report cards were also collected and analyzed.

At the individual level, I gathered personal data from Ms. Nicholi using a life history approach. She shared her life story in conversations with me that were taped and transcribed over a period of 4 hours. I analyzed these stories in order to identify and illuminate the discourses that Ms. Nicholi drew upon to make meaning in her personal and professional life. I then shared my analysis with Ms. Nicholi and we discussed the findings.

THE DISCURSIVE FASHIONING OF MS. NICHOLI

The identities of Ms. Nicholi were positioned and repositioned as they were situated within the different discourses that swirled around her teacher education program, Woodlawn Elementary School, her kindergarten classroom, and the personal aspects of her life. While identifying the most prominent discourses in each context, I want to stress that discourses have meaning only in relation to one another (Gee, 1996) and that none of the discourses in a given context is mutually exclusive. I am artificially isolating each discourse in order to make it visible for the purposes of portraying how Ms. Nicholi discursively fashions her identities by drawing on the discourses that were available to her.

Exploring the Personal Aspects of a Life

Ms. Anne Nicholi is a 28-year-old, second-generation Italian-American woman. She grew up in what she described as a "middle to upper class neighborhood with nice yards. Real plain. Real white." Ms. Nicholi's father owned a plumbing business and she described her mother as a "traditional homemaker." Catholicism played a large role in Ms. Nicholi's life and she attended a parochial elementary school and high school. Ms. Nicholi and her younger brother lived with both of her parents until they divorced when she was in high school.

Ms. Nicholi described herself as being a "people person" who "was always rooting for the underdog." She explained, "I think people need help and they need chances. I think you should [help people] for the good of society because if you don't things will be worse instead of better." One of the ways that Ms. Nicholi thought that she might help those who were less fortunate than she was to pursue a degree in juvenile law at Midwestern. As an intern, it was her job to take statements from juveniles who had been involved in misdemeanor cases. It was at this time that she began to think about a career in early childhood education. She explained, "If I could have only talked to them earlier, I could have helped. If they had someone in their life who had showed them, like their mom or someone who cared about them . . . they were just so hard and really lost." Ms. Nicholi made the decision to leave law and enter the field of education. She said:

> I wanted to teach kids at risk. I wanted to make a difference in kids' lives. I wanted a job that was important, that you go to and you're doing good. You're helping, even if it's in a small way you're doing something.

As Ms. Nicholi spoke about the experiences that had led her into teaching she spoke within a discourse of "children at risk."[2] Within this discourse children who are poor, of color, reside in single-parent families, and/or are native speakers of languages other than English are constructed as being "at risk" based on the assumption that they are lacking the cultural and moral resources for success in a dominant white middle-class society (Swadener & Lubeck, 1995). This discourse emerged in the 1980s as part of the conservative backlash against the historically oppressed groups that had made political and economic gains in the 1960s and 1970s (Sleeter, 1995). As Sleeter explains, "the discourse of children at risk deflects attention away from injustices perpetrated and institutionalized by the dominant society and again frames oppressed communities and homes as lacking in the cultural and moral resources for advancement" (Sleeter, 1995, p. x).

This discourse permeated Ms. Nicholi's speech as she shared her reasons for becoming a teacher and as she spoke about her current struggles. For example, Ms. Nicholi and a neighboring teacher switched classes so that they could experience teaching one another's kindergarten class for an afternoon. Later, when I asked Ms. Nicholi about her teaching experience with the other class, she said that "it was a good class much different from mine. It was really fun." I asked why she thought that this class was so different from hers to which she replied, "because her kids have Moms and Dads and mine don't." Within the discourse of "at risk" Ms. Nicholi perceives the children in her care, the majority of whom are poor, of color, and reside in female-headed households, as deficient based on their family circumstances. A further example of how this discourse works in relation with other discourses to position two

boys of color as in need of special education is presented in a later section of this article.

Discourses Surrounding the Teacher Education Program

At Midwestern the EEP is offered jointly by the Department of Child and Family Studies (CFS), housed within the School of Family Resources and Consumer Studies, and the Department of Curriculum and Instruction (C&I), housed within the School of Education. While faculty in the Department of CFS were involved in researching theories of child development and models of pedagogy for young children, the Department of C&I became renowned for its critical perspectives on curriculum theorizing at the elementary and secondary level. Struggling to work across two departments with very different orientations, it is not surprising that faculty and staff members from both schools described the EEP as "disparate," "conflicting" and "polyvocal."

Within the discourse of child-centeredness that permeates the Department of CFS, the child is conceptualized as a unique individual possessing an inner potential that is rooted in biology (Burman, 1994). The concept of development, which is conceived of as always happening in advance of learning, refers to the cognitive, social, emotional, physical, and linguistic stages that each individual child experiences as she/he grows and changes. It is the role of the early childhood teacher to determine each child's level of development in order to present curriculum and instruction appropriate for that child's level of learning. As the Chair of the Department of CFS explained, "If you don't look at each child exactly where they are in their cognitive and language development and where they are in their social and emotional development and exactly where they are today, you're never going to teach them." Once a teacher has identified a child's level of development it is her responsibility to facilitate that child's learning. In the words of one faculty member, "You know, none of us really teach anybody. We facilitate their learning . . . we don't teach them and we don't motivate them, they motivate themselves."

Within a child-centered discourse, differences in ability, race, class, and gender are believed to be situated within children, families, and communities (Burman, 1994). Commented one faculty member, "diversity is just another unique individual trait. If you just teach individuals . . . [y]ou don't need Chinese or Asian or any of that; you just need children." Through this discourse, if the teacher is meeting the needs of her individual students, she will automatically be addressing the issues of diversity that are a part of that child as well.

Within the sociocultural discourse that permeates the department of C&I, relations among children, teachers, and families are configured much differently. When described within this discourse, the child is conceptualized as being a product of the social, cultural, political, and historical forces that are present in any given time and place. Through this discourse, development is conceptualized as being social as well as individual (Berk & Winsler, 1995). As one faculty member said:

> You can be so intent on knowing what that [developmental] map is that you don't pay attention to the scenery in front of you. . . . Those kids aren't just that little body there they're bringing with them a history and a set of connections with their family.

From this perspective, caregivers take into account both the biological and the social aspects of development. Development and learning are conceived of as being recursive and learning is believed to happen through social interaction (Berk & Winsler, 1995).[d] It is the role of the caregiver to structure collaborative learning situations in which children are assisted, by either a more capable peer or an adult, to reach ever more advanced levels of development (Berk & Winsler, 1995). This approach to learning is modeled by the faculty and staff as they assign projects in which students are required to assist and participate in the development and learning of one another.

The juxtaposition of a sociocultural and a critical discourse carries with it a strong critique of capitalism and American society. Within this discourse, knowledge is viewed as being socially constructed and tied to the economic interests of those who are the most privileged in society. Schools are viewed as institutions that perpetuate the status quo by shaping the social identities of

children which reproduce inequities (McLaren, 1989). Within a critical, sociocultural discourse, legitimizing the experiences of all children rather than simply the ones who are members of the dominant culture and teaching children to question the social order are important goals of the early childhood educator.

Prospective teachers in the EEP are positioned and repositioned within these competing discourses as they are placed in student and teaching relationships, have their course work assessed, and are evaluated on their teaching techniques within either one or the other at any given time. As prospective teachers slip in and out of these linguistic creations that are provided by the faculty of the EEP, they piece together different identities for themselves while simultaneously creating possibilities and constraints for the social identities of the young children with whom they work.

The Discourse That Envelops the Elementary School

Unlike the EEP, in which there were two distinct competing discourses, Woodlawn elementary was enveloped by one coherent discourse: a discourse of normalization (Popkewitz, 1993). Embedded within this discourse is a white, middle-class standard, based on a set of "appropriate behaviors," sanctioned by the school, against which everyone is measured. The discourse of normalization grew out of Woodlawn's history as the Wonago neighborhood school that, prior to 1988, catered exclusively to white, middle-, and upper middle-class children and families. Owing to the implementation of several redistricting plans, the demographics of the school had fluctuated wildly over the past 10 years. At the time of the study there were about 500 students attending Woodlawn. The racial/ethnic breakdown was as follows: 0.2% American Indian, 14.02% Asian or Pacific Islander, 33.75% Black, 4.26% Hispanic, and 47.77% white. Forty-six percent of the students received free or reduced lunch. The student population was drawn from five different neighborhoods, yet the staff spoke as if there were only two, referring continually to the "Wonago children" and the "Archer Avenue children."

Archer Avenue comprised a number of heavily populated low-income apartment complexes in which

---

d. "Recursive" in this context refers to the ongoing process of learning and development that occurs through social interaction.

resided a number of poor children of color. In addition to the Archer Avenue children, Woodlawn had been designated as one of the schools in the district to house an English as Second Language program, which also drew in a number of children from other attendance areas in the city who were low income and in need of special services. It was for this reason the kindergarten magnet program in which Ms. Nicholi taught was designed. The four magnet kindergartens are intensive full-day programs. Between 70 and 75% of those attending are Archer Avenue children.

Within the discourse of normalization that permeated Woodlawn, the Archer Avenue children were referred to by the staff as *high needs* children in relation to the Wonago children, while the white, middle-class children bused in from other areas were referred to as *role models*. In fact, Ms. Nicholi shared that when several new children had moved into the area and were going to be assigned to kindergarten classrooms she was asked by the administration if she "wanted one Archer Avenue child or two role models."

Children of non-dominant cultures could become role models once they became inculcated with the norms that surrounded the school. To support this inculcation, Woodlawn had adopted a "progressive developmental multicultural program."[3] The program consisted of multiage classrooms that were developed first and foremost to deal with behavioral issues. Children who were socialized to the norms at Woodlawn could become the role models for those who supposedly were not. "Appropriate behaviors" were defined on both a social and an individual level. On an individual level "appropriate behaviors" were exhibited by children who could regulate their own actions (e.g., sit on rug without touching those nearby, follow directions, raise hands, etc.). On a social level "appropriate behaviors" were those actions carried out by children that showed they were able to cooperate with others (e.g., share materials, solve problems through discussion rather than force, etc.). Most of the children were, indeed, polite and well behaved; however, the children who couldn't always maintain such behaviors were constructed as deficient.

The academic curriculum was described as being developmental in the sense that it was individualized for each child. At the beginning of the year each child was assessed in order to identify her/his developmental level. Once a child's developmental needs had been identified, ideally, the parents would meet with the teacher to discuss the goal for that child's progress over the course of the academic year. Yet, although the goal of the multiage classrooms was to provide teachers with the flexibility to move away from strict grade-level compliances, ability and achievement were always discussed in terms of grade level.

Within the discourse of normalization at Woodlawn, the standards are defined in terms of the white, middle-class children who formerly populated Wonago. The skills, values, and behaviors associated with dominant cultural norms continue to be upheld for all children. The expectation that children should speak, think, and act as white middle-class children created a hierarchy of deficits at the school which were replicated in the classroom of Ms. Nicholi.

The Discourses That Permeate Ms. Nicholi's Classroom

Ms. Nicholi's classroom is warm, colorful, and inviting. Individually or in small groups, 18 children circulate among the dramatic play area, block area, book corner, water table, invention center, computer, and two easels. Demographically the class consists of six African-American children (four boys and two girls), five Southeast Asian children (four girls and one boy), one East Asian boy, and six white children (three girls and three boys). The five Southeast Asian children, who speak primarily Hmong and are enrolled in the English as Second Language Program, spend most of their free choice time together. I am told by Ms. Nicholi that 12 of the 18 kindergartners reside in the Archer Avenue area and that this class contains "some of the neediest kids you've ever seen."

While the physical appearance of the classroom is organized with the children's interests in mind, the pedagogical strategies that Ms. Nicholi draws upon are almost exclusively teacher directed with the heaviest emphasis placed on reading and writing. In the following section, I use a vignette to portray a typical lesson as presented by Ms. Nicholi.

A vignette, is a short, thickly described, recounted version of an event, person, or setting which is used to convey an interpretive theme (Erickson, 1986; Graue & Walsh, 1997). The interactions that occur between and among the children and Ms. Nicholi in this vignette took place in the kindergarten classroom over the period of about an hour. I have also supplemented the vignette with phrases used and actions carried out by Ms. Nicholi and the children which were repeatedly recorded in my fieldnotes over time but did not occur on this particular day.

"THE FIVE LITTLE CARROTS"

The children are sitting in a semi-circle on the large square of gray carpet in the middle of the room. Ms. Nicholi is leading the kindergartners in a chant of "The Five Little Carrots," which is written on chart paper and hanging on the easel in the front of the room. After they finish the chant, Ms. Nicholi passes out the books in which they have been copying and illustrating the chant. She reminds them not to open their books until she is through passing them out to everyone. Using her book as a guide, she opens up the cover and directs the children to do so as well. "I want you to open to page one, two, three, four, five, six," counts Ms. Nicholi as she slowly turns each page. The children follow her lead. Ms. Nicholi picks up the pencils that are in front of her and passes one to each child as she says, "When I give you your pencil put it right on the spot in the book where you are going to start writing."

The children stretch out on their stomachs as they position themselves to write. Most of them have their pencils pointed to the spot where they are going to begin to print. Ms. Nicholi walks around to each child, repositioning the pencils of those who don't seem to have it quite right. Ms. Nicholi then walks back up to the front of the room, points to the sixth line in the chant, and reads, "Do you like to eat carrots?" She then specifies, "This is the sentence that we are working on."

The children are asked to sound out the letters in each word. Ms. Nicholi exaggerates the movement of her mouth as she sounds out the first word, which begins with the letter "d." She asks the children to sound it out. A

few of the children make the "d" sound, but many other sounds are voiced as well. "Did you hear that?" asks Ms. Nicholi. She writes the letter "d" on the dry erase board and directs the children to copy the letter down on their papers. "What's the letter we're writing?" she asks. Some children shout out, "d." Ms. Nicholi nods her head indicating that "d" is correct. Referring to herself in the third person she says, "Look how Ms. Nicholi made her 'd.' Is it sloppy?" The children answer, "No." Ms. Nicholi reminds the children, "Do your best work."

"If you just made a 'd' put your hands on your head," directs Ms. Nicholi. Letter by letter they spell out the word "you." "If you wrote Y-O-U, make a U in the air with your hands so that I know you're done," directs Ms. Nicholi. "I'm done!" shouts Wayne as he throws his arms into the air.

Wayne's "I'm done!" has caught on. As the children write the next letter several of the children shout "I'm done!" Ms. Nicholi asks if anyone wants to write the sentence, "I will not shout when I'm done writing a letter." Maureen says, "Ooh, that's 10 words!" No one shouts after they finish writing the next letter although there are some very softly whispered "I'm dones."

Wayne begins to squirm around on the floor and his foot touches the girl next to him as he waits for Ms. Nicholi to direct him to print the next letter. "Wayne's kicking me!" yells Maureen. "I'm not kicking you girl!" Ms. Nicholi walks over to look at Wayne's paper and points out that his letters are not printed on the line. She turns his pencil over and begins to erase his work as she says, "This is not your best work. You're finishing so quickly because you are not printing neatly." Wayne starts to protest, "I ain't gonna be doin' this over!" As he sits up he begins kicking some books that are on the floor across the room as he shouts, "I hate this stupid old school!" Ms. Nicholi says, "Think about your attitude. Do it over or stay in for recess. It's your choice."

The above vignette illustrates that, although children are provided the opportunity to play and make some choices about the activities that they engage in during their free time, the majority of the class is teacher directed and skill oriented. While Ms. Nicholi does not specifically refer to her curriculum as one that promotes "basic skills," she does emphasize the fact that she is a "traditional teacher." In her words:

> Being a teacher and the traditional view is a big part, especially of the kindergarten years. I'm here to teach them things. I want them to learn. I want them to learn what they need to progress in school. I want them to learn their numbers, their letters and their sounds. I want them to learn work habits, to take pride in their work. I want them to learn how to share, how to be friends, how to be independent. The things that are important to function in society to move on; the rules to live by.

The class is teacher directed in the sense that activities are directed almost exclusively by Ms. Nicholi. I observed this type of lesson being presented to the kindergartners 12 of the 14 times that I visited Ms. Nicholi's classroom. Children rarely have the opportunity, outside of their free choice time, to discover or create on their own. Yet Ms. Nicholi made it clear that she was conflicted by the way that she felt she had to teach. She explained that this highly structured classroom was not how she had originally envisioned her teaching. Drawing on the meaning of development as it was conceptualized within the discourse of child-centeredness, Ms. Nicholi explained how she had turned to a traditionally structured classroom when she found that, as a group, the children in her class were not "developmentally ready" for the types of learning opportunities that she was presenting to them. She explained, "I had manipulatives on the tables; I didn't have journal writing and I didn't have them sit in assigned seats. I gave them choices but they weren't ready for that and it led to a lot of social problems."

Ms. Nicholi's conception of biological readiness was woven through her speech and actions. Issues of development shaped the way that she perceived the individual children who comprised her class and in turn defined the curriculum and instruction that she presented to them. This conception of development that was embedded within the discourse of child-centeredness was strengthened and supported by the discourse of nor-malization that enveloped Woodlawn. When intertwined, these discourses positioned the kindergartners, the majority of whom are poor children of color, as needing a more structured environment because they did not exhibit the "appropriate behaviors" that are sanctioned by the school and reinforced in their classroom. Developmentally, these children were diagnosed as being socially and emotionally unready to make the choices that Ms. Nicholi initially provided for them. This led her to basic skills-oriented and teacher-directed curriculum and instruction. Certainly pedagogy that is basic-skills oriented and teacher directed can lead to positive learning experiences for children (see e.g. Delpit, 1995; Ladson-Billings, 1994). However, Ms. Nicholi was lowering her expectations and promoting conformity rather than working towards the acquisition of higher level thinking skills.

In addition to the discourse of child-centeredness and the discourse of normalization that were visible in Ms. Nicholi's talk and action, a variant of the discourse of behaviorism was present as well. Within a discourse of behaviorism, knowledge is believed to be formed as children make associations between situations and responses (Byrnes, 1996). The actions of children are regulated externally by the teacher rather than being self-regulated.

As is evident from the vignette, Ms. Nicholi asked the children to imitate precisely the way that she shaped the letters with her hand as she wrote and the shape of her mouth as she sounded out each letter. In virtually every activity that I observed, children were asked to duplicate products that Ms. Nicholi had made. When children were asked to complete an activity, Ms. Nicholi gave explicit directions, which she repeated an average of three times. Children were then asked to complete their work by repeating the exact sequence of steps that Ms. Nicholi had articulated. Conformity and work habits were praised as Ms. Nicholi circulated around the room complimenting individual children for such things as "remembering to use pencil first then pen" or "following directions nicely."

This ability to conform to "appropriate behaviors" was recognized and reinforced by two reward systems that Ms. Nicholi had developed. Short-term rewards for behavior usually consisted of snacks such as crackers, cookies, or fruit. These rewards were not immediate, but rather were contingent upon the behaviors of children that were exhibited over a short period of time. Long-term rewards consisted of badges for "best listener," "best hall walker" and "best friend." These were awarded to the children in an elaborate "badge ceremony" at the end of each day.

While presenting children with rewards for appropriate behaviors was a common practice, so also was the use of punishments for "inappropriate behaviors." Punishments included writing sentences, being given a time out, and missing the first 5 to 10 minutes of recess or free choice time, or in extreme cases being physically removed from the classroom. The punishment that Ms. Nicholi used most frequently was assigning the kindergartners sentences to write pertaining to their misbehavior. This was a fairly effective technique because children did not like to take the time to write the sentences and often, as with the case of Wayne in the vignette, the "inappropriate behavior" immediately subsided with the threat to write having been made.

Through a discourse of normalization, Ms. Nicholi worked towards constructing her vision of an ideal kindergartner: one who is between the ages of 60 and 71 months, is well-versed in basic skills and is socialized to the white, middle-class ways of acting that are sanctioned by the faculty and staff at Woodlawn. Variants of the discourses of child-centeredness and behaviorism intermingled in her speech and action as she worked towards realizing this vision.

Fashioning the Identities of Children

Ideologies define the nature of the relationships that are possible within any discourse. The ideology embedded in the discourse of normalization constitutes a "representation of reality" for Ms. Nicholi and the children that defines children relationally—those who were white and middle class were perceived as "normal" while their peers who are members of non-dominant cultures are considered "not normal." Those children (and families) who have difficulty conforming to the norms of the dominant culture are pathologized.

Recall that initially Ms. Nicholi had attempted to position herself as a learner-centered teacher who valued freedom and choice for the children in her care. As she worked with the children, however, she found that they did not possess the ways of thinking, speaking, and acting that would be considered "normal" within the discourse of normalization and deemed them "developmentally unready" to handle the type of teaching that she offered. In response to the children, Ms. Nicholi's identity shifted as she became a much more teacher-directed authoritarian force in the classroom. Since none of the children met the criteria of the "ideal kindergartner," a hierarchy of deficits emerged as children's identities were shaped in relation to Ms. Nicholi and one another.

Take for example, the case of Tim, a white male, whose birthday fell at the end of August. Cognitively, Tim was at the top of the class. He utilized an extensive vocabulary and was extremely knowledgeable about animal and marine life. While Ms. Nicholi acknowledged his intellectual abilities, she continually referred to the fact that he was a "young five" and pointed out his shortcomings, such as his coloring, which she referred to as "scribbles," and his "inappropriate" social interactions with his peers. She explained, "Intellectually he knows a lot, but his birthday is August 22nd. He's a young five. His fine motor and social skills are so behind. I just don't know what to do with him." By February, Ms. Nicholi had spoken with Tim's parents about the possibility of retention.

Lack of appropriate social skills was a concern voiced by Ms. Nicholi pertaining to other children in the class as well. This was especially true of two African-American males, Shawn and Wayne, who lived in households headed by single females. These two boys frequently exhibited angry outbursts in the classroom. The intensity of the outbursts ranged from a loud "No!" when asked to complete a task, to the less frequent kicking and knocking over of furniture. Over the course of my visits to Woodlawn, both boys had been suspended from school more than once.

It is interesting to note that these outbursts were often in response to academic activities in which the children were engaged. As illustrated in the vignette, Wayne, who often began a task with enthusiasm, would become frustrated and then agitated when he was not able to duplicate the model that Ms. Nicholi had provided for the children. Ms. Nicholi did not view her teaching methods or strategies as having anything to do with the actions of the boys. Instead, she described the boys as having needs beyond those of the average kindergartner:

> They get so angry, and it has nothing to do with what you're asking them to do. Nothing with the project that they are working on. I don't feel like I have a lot of strategies on how to help kids overcome all that anger and to feel successful and to deal with their frustration and to help them with their own problems. I mean classroom management, behavior management, and those kinds of issues.

The discourse of normalization becomes braided with the discourses of child-centeredness and children at risk to locate the anger and frustration within individual children such as Shawn and Wayne. Rather than assuming that Shawn and Wayne need more time to mature, as she assumed with Tim, she perceived their behavioral problems as stemming from their family situations and conceptualized these problems as residing within the children themselves. She saw her responsibility in this situation as building up her repertoire of behavior management techniques and when her strategies remained ineffective she shifted the responsibility for educating Shawn and Wayne to special education services. She explained, "I think they are either LD or ED and I think there's been abuse too. It was hard to make a case, but once I did and talked to the team I realized that this was not like other classes."

One must wonder about the correlation between Wayne's emotional outbursts and the way in which he was forced to complete his work. In her attempt to shape the children into "ideal" kindergartners, Ms. Nicholi provided no space for children to perform comfortably the identities that they brought with them from home into school.

While the identities of the Southeast Asian children and the East Asian child were constructed much differently than those of the "young fives" or the African-American children within a discourse of normalization, the ability to fashion positive social identities was limited for this group of kindergartners as well. The "Asian" children often seemed as if they were invisible. They were not reprimanded for "inappropriate behaviors" because the behaviors that they exhibited generally fell within the bounds of what was considered "normal" in the kindergarten. Although Ms. Nicholi did help the children with their work in a limited manner, and rewarded them for their work habits and other "appropriate behaviors," there was little interaction between the "Asian" students and their teacher. The five Southeast Asian children made daily trips to the English as Second Language Program for instruction and a Hmong interpreter traveled in and out of the classroom. Because of this external support, it was possible for Ms. Nicholi to assume that she needed to take no further steps to incorporate culturally relevant pedagogy (Ladson-Billings, 1994). In her mind, she was not experiencing any behavioral problems with this group of children so she just left them to themselves.

Acknowledging Discourses across Multiple Contexts

Ms. Nicholi's approach to teaching is a mélange of discourses that work together in complex and often contradictory ways. Through a discourse of child-centeredness, Ms. Nicholi conceptualizes development as being rooted in the individual child. The practice of diagnosing the development of each child, to which Ms. Nicholi was introduced as a prospective teacher, is nurtured at Woodlawn and supported by her personal philosophy. It is understandable that Ms. Nicholi has appropriated this practice and enacted it in her pedagogy.

As a first-year teacher, her desire to fit into the school and the teaching profession may account for her readily appropriating the discourse of normalization that envelops Woodlawn. In addition, the discourse of normalization is consistent with Ms. Nicholi's personal philosophy of teaching. Ms. Nicholi continues to appropriate a variant of the discourse of child-centeredness, perhaps because it fits with the ideas of normalization practiced at Woodlawn elementary and is recognized and supported by her colleagues. A critical, sociocultural discourse, on the other hand, was not evident at the school and most likely would not have been recognized by the Woodlawn staff.

Like the discourse of normalization, the discourse of "at risk" locates problems within individuals, families, and communities rather than in institutions, such as schools, that produce and maintain inequities. Perhaps this discourse is also comfortable to Ms. Nicholi because it is congruent with her position as a member of the dominant culture. Ms. Nicholi's personal history resonates with the discourse of normalization at the school so there is no need to question it.

CONCLUSIONS

As teacher educators we are in the business of promoting ideologies through the discourses that we choose to use as we work with prospective teachers. According to Bakhtin it would seem that it is in the process of struggling with shaping an identity as teacher that prospective teachers are the most open to being influenced by the discourses of educators at the university as well as at the elementary school level. As Bakhtin (1981) explains:

> The tendency to assimilate others' discourse takes on an even deeper and more basic significance in an individual's ideological becoming, in the most fundamental sense. Another's discourse performs here no longer as information, directions, rules, models and so forth—but strives rather to determine the very bases of our ideological interrelations with the world, the very basis of our behavior. . . . (p. 342)

This openness could be capitalized upon by explicitly discussing the concept of discourse and by introducing the possibility of functioning effectively within multiple discourses.

As teacher educators, we can help prospective teachers develop an awareness of how the discourses of particular fields of education have been, and continue to be, socially, culturally, historically, and politically constructed. Teacher educators need to work with prospective teachers to identify and articulate the ideologies that are alive in discourses. We can do so by providing information that allows prospective teachers to compare how teachers, children, and families are positioned within particular discourses and how these positionings make a material difference in the lives of specific groups of individuals. For example, we could ask prospective teachers to read several personal accounts of classroom teaching with the objective of identifying the discourses through which the authors are thinking, speaking, and acting.[4] Prospective teachers could then analyze how specific discourses limit or create possibilities for children and families. This activity could be carried a step further by asking prospective teachers to explore how identities would shift in each classroom if different discourses were employed.

Prospective teachers also need to be provided with opportunities to examine their own personal biographies in order to scrutinize how discourses of race, class, gender, religion, and sexuality have shaped and continue to shape their lived experiences and worldviews. However, as Britzman (1991) contends, this biographical work cannot be reduced to the "nostalgia of the personal or the rhapsody of the unique" (p. 233). Rather, Britzman argues that teacher educators need to help prospective teachers contextualize their life histories by encouraging them to make connections between their biographies and social structures. Such biographical work provides opportunities for prospective teachers to examine consciously how particular ideologies have worked in their own lives to define their past, present, and future identities.

By providing teachers with the tools for conceptualizing teacher thinking as social we offer them alternative ways to author their identities. Preparing teachers who are well versed in multiple discourses does not ensure that particular discourses will be accepted or rejected. What it does ensure is that prospective teachers will recognize that the discursive choices they make as they construct their identities have ramifications for the social identities of the children and families with whom they work.

Acknowledgments

I thank Ms. Nicholi for her willingness to engage in this research and for her permission to use the stories that are woven throughout this article. I would also like to thank my colleagues Tamara Lindsey, Don Reynolds, Jean Schmittau, Ken Teitelbaum, and Margot Vagliardo for reading and sharing their helpful comments throughout the evolution of this article.

Notes

1. All names are pseudonyms.
2. The discourse of "at risk" has been written about by numerous educational researchers, for example see Cuban (1989), Fine (1990), Polakow (1993), and Swadener & Lubeck (1995).
3. Multicultural education was discussed by the administrators and support staff but was nearly absent in my discussions with classroom teachers. As the principal stated, Woodlawn "had a long way to go" in terms of moving towards a multicultural perspective.
4. Examples would include works by Pat Conroy, Vivian Gussin Paley, Sylvia Ashton Warner, and Julia Weber Gordon.

References

Bakhtin, M. M. (1981). *The dialogic imagination: Four essays by M. M. Bakhtin*. Ed. Michael Holquist. Austin: University of Texas Press.

Berk, L. E., & Winsler, A. (1995). *Scaffolding children's learning: Vygotsky and early childhood education*. Washington, DC: NAEYC.

Britzman, D. (1991). *Practice makes practice: A critical study of learning to teach*. New York: State University of New York Press.

Busman, E. (1994). *Deconstructing developmental psychology*. New York: Routledge.

Byrnes, J. (1996). *Cognitive development & learning in instructional contexts*. Needham Heights, MA: Allyn & Bacon.

Casey, K. (1993), *I ensure with my life: Life histories of women teachers working for social change*. New York: Routledge.

Clandinin, J. D. & Connelly, M. F. (1987). Teachers' personal knowledge: What counts as personal in studies of the personal. *Journal of Curriculum Studies, 19*(6).

Cuban, L. (1989). The "at risk" label and the problem of urban school reform. *Phi Delta Kappan, 70,* 780–801.

Delpit, L. (1995). *Other people's children*. New York: New Press.

Erickson, F. (1986). Qualitative methods in research on teaching. In M. Wittrock (Ed.), *Handbook of research on teaching* (pp. 119–161). New York: Macmillan.

Fine, M. (1990). Making controversy: Who's "at risk"? *Journal of Cultural Studies, 1*(1), 55–68.

Gee, J. P. (1996). *Social linguistics and literacies: Ideology in discourses*. London: Taylor and Francis.

Gomez, M. L. (In press). Learning to speak and teach in a new genre. *World Studies in Education*.

Graue, M. E. (1993). *Ready for what? Constructing meanings of readiness for kindergarten*. Albany, NY: SUNY Press.

Graue, M. E, & Marsh, M. M. (1996). Genre and practice: Shaping possibilities for children. *Early Childhood Research Quarterly, 11*(2).

Graue, M. E. & Walsh, D. (1997). *Researching children in context: Theories, methods, and ethics*. Thousand Oaks, CA: Sage Publications.

Heath, S. (1983). *Ways with words*. Cambridge: Cambridge University Press.

Kondo, D. (1990). *Crafting selves: Power, gender, and discourses of identity in a Japanese workplace*. Chicago: University of Chicago Press.

Ladson-Billings, G. (1994). *The dreamkeepers: Successful teachers of African American children*. San Francisco: Jossey-Bass.

Lareau, A. (1989). *Home advantage*. New York: Falmer Press.

McCutcheon, G. (1980). How do elementary school teachers plan? The nature of planning and the influences of it. *Elementary School Journal, 81,* 4–23.

McLaren, P. (1989). *Life in schools*. New York: Longman.

Polakow, V. (1993). *Lives on the edge: Single mothers and their children in the other America*. Chicago: University of Chicago Press.

Popkewitz, T. (1993). *A political sociology of educational reform: Power/knowledge in teaching, teacher education, and research*. New York: Teachers College Press.

Shapiro, M. J. (1988). *The politics of representation: Writing practices in biography, photography, and policy analysis*. Madison, WI: University of Wisconsin Press.

Sleeter, C. (1995). Foreword. In B. B. Swadener & S. Lubeck (Eds.), *Children and families "at promise"* (pp. 17–50). New York: SUNY Press.

Swadener, B. B. & Lubeck, S. (1995). *Children and families "at promise": Deconstructing the discourse of risk*. New York: SUNY Press.

Volosinov, V. (1973). *Marxism and the philosophy of language*. New York: Seminar Press.

Zahorik, J. A. (1970). The effects of planning on teaching. *Elementary School Journal, 71,* 143–151.

chapter 11

Ethnographic Research

After studying this chapter, you will be able to

1. describe the major characteristics of ethnographic research.
2. explain what ethnographers mean by culture and why they view it as worthy of systematic study.
3. explain how ethnographers collect and analyze data about the phenomena they study.
4. describe the issues that ethnographic researchers face in their efforts to understand and improve educational practice.

Arvella Johnson just completed the requirements for an elementary teaching certificate. Arvella, an African American, grew up in a relatively homogeneous culture in the United States, where she developed a strong commitment to justice. She is now applying for several jobs in a nearby state with a high proportion of immigrant families from Central and South America. To prepare for her job interviews, she decided to do some reading about the cultures of families from different ethnic groups.

By doing a literature review, Arvella located ethnographic research studies that related to her problem. Some are about the cultures of Central and South American countries, while others describe the culture shock and adjustment that students from these countries face as they enter U.S. society and schools. After reading this research, she felt almost as if she had seen and talked with some of the students she expects to encounter in her first teaching assignment. Also, the research stimulated Arvella's reflections on what she might do as a teacher if she learned that some of her students faced the issues that these students faced.

In this chapter you will see how the findings of ethnographic research can help educators understand and respond more effectively to the cultural characteristics of the varied groups they encounter in their work. ●

THE CHARACTERISTICS OF ETHNOGRAPHIC RESEARCH

Ethnography is the firsthand, intensive study of the features of a given culture and the patterns in those features. Readers of ethnographic research reports can expand their awareness of cultures much different from their own, and also develop more understanding of their own culture.

Ethnography was developed by anthropologists, but researchers in other disciplines, including sociology and psychology, have also contributed to this research tradition. Since the 1960s, some educational researchers who became disenchanted with positivism and the methods of quantitative research have turned to ethnography as an alternative approach. The main features of ethnographic research are described below.

1. *Focus on culture or aspects of culture.* Early ethnographies focused on providing a comprehensive description and analysis of the entire culture of a group of people. This research tradition sometimes is called **holistic ethnography.** Most current ethnographies are more modest in scope; they focus on particular aspects of culture. These studies sometimes are called **microethnography** to reflect their narrowed focus. For example, Kathleen Hogan and Catherine Corey (2001) focused their microethnography on one fifth-grade classroom in order to understand science instruction in the context of classroom culture and the culture of professional scientists.

Some ethnographic studies bear labels that characterize the phenomena that were studied or the research methods that were used. For example, **critical ethnography** involves the use of ethnography to study oppressive power relations in a specific culture, while **ethnoscience** involves cataloging the semantic systems used by a culture or subculture (e.g., elementary school children) to describe important social phenomena, such as work and play.

2. *Naturalistic study of individuals in the field.* Many early ethnographers lived in another culture for a period of years in order to investigate the origins of such cultural phenomena as religious beliefs, sexual practices, and the learning of work skills and social roles. They typically sought to provide a holistic description of non-Western cultures, whose presumably more "primitive" cultural practices were expected to reveal universal patterns in the development of such phenomena. Today, ethnographers often study subcultures in their own vicinity, but they still carry out data collection in the natural setting of the members

of the culture. They rely on unobtrusive data collection methods, such as informal observations and conversations, with which field participants will be comfortable. They also seek to immerse themselves in the setting, both to increase participants' trust of them and to deepen their own understanding of cultural phenomena.

3. *Making the familiar strange.* Traditionally, ethnographers have sought to "make the familiar strange" (Spindler & Spindler, 1982). This goal involves analyzing a cultural phenomenon from the perspective of an outsider (to whom it is strange) while seeking to understand it from the perspective of an insider (to whom it is familiar). Therefore, part of the ethnographer's mission is to reflect light on phenomena that members of a culture overlook because they are taken for granted. This research helps us understand the hidden meanings in patterns of language, behavior, and arrangement of physical space that are characteristic of different groups or types of people. For example, an ethnographer studying the culture of college sports teams might notice varied patterns of acceptable and unacceptable behavior beyond those contained in the game rules, such as differences in the way that starters and bench players cluster around the coach during time-outs.

Ethnographers can make the familiar strange either by immersing themselves in a culture far different from their own, by studying a subculture in their own community with which they are unfamiliar, or by investigating a subculture with which they are familiar but looking at it from the perspective of the subculture's members rather than from their own perspective.

4. *Thick description.* In writing their research report, ethnographers typically describe the field setting in great detail and use extensive quotations from field participants. This "thick" description is intended to bring the culture alive for the reader. Also, ethnographers often write their descriptions in the present tense, which creates the impression of permanence or even universality—that is, the sense that the description applies not just to the specific cases that were studied, but to any and all similar cases.

Some of the characteristics of ethnography match those of a qualitative case study, as described in Chapter 10. As in a case study, the ethnographer focuses on a case or cases, which can range from a single individual to an entire community, society, or institution. Likewise, in ethnographic research the researcher makes an in-depth study of the phenomenon of interest (a culture or some aspect of culture); studies the phenomenon in its natural context; and represents both the field participants' (emic) and researchers' (etic) perspectives. For this reason, David Lancy (1993) claimed that ethnography is "the prototype for the qualitative method" (p. 66).

While educational ethnographies are similar to other case studies, they differ in several ways. First, ethnographies focus specifically on aspects of culture, whereas case studies may focus on a wide range of phenomena, such as the life history of a teacher or the effectiveness of an instructional program. Second, ethnographies usually involve a longer, more in-depth period of data collection than a typical educational case study. Third, ethnographers often make cross-cultural comparisons to further explore and explain the phenomena with which they are concerned. The comparative study of cultures, called **ethnology,** is the primary focus of some ethnographers. In contrast, case study researchers usually limit themselves to a single cultural context.

ETHNOGRAPHIC CONCEPTIONS OF CULTURE

Culture is the central concept in ethnographic research. The term originated with the development of efforts to assist the growth of specific organisms, as in agriculture. Early ethnographers viewed "native" cultures as representing earlier stages of cultural evolution than those of supposedly more "civilized" Western cultures. Researchers today view the peoples of the world as being grouped into many cultures, each with positive qualities and unique characteristics.

Culture can be defined as the pattern of traditions, symbols, rituals, and artifacts that characterize a particular group of individuals. Different cultural features are viewed as being systematically related to each other, forming an integrated whole. On close examination, however, the culture of a given group of people might appear more like what Murray Wax (1993) called "a thing of shreds and patches" (p. 101) than a consistent whole. Also, Lancy (1993) notes that today's world is becoming increasingly homogeneous with respect to culture. Wealth, rather than influences unique to their culture, is now the principal force that differentiates individuals' lifestyles.

Ethnographers believe that the influence of culture in human beings' lives is what makes us unique as a species. Culture allows a particular group of people to live together and thrive through a system of shared meanings and values, but that same system also may lead them to oppose or oppress groups with different shared meanings and values.

Ethnographers also believe that certain aspects of human culture have a particularly strong influence on individual and group life. These aspects include patterns of social organization, socialization, learning, family structure, religious practices, and ceremonial behavior. For example, ethnographers might focus on the celebratory rituals marking transitional events in the lives of members of the culture, including school graduations, weddings, and baby showers. Because such aspects of culture are interrelated, ethnographers must study not only one aspect of a culture, but also attend to other aspects to which it is closely related.

The study of culture might be compared to creating a mosaic. Each ethnographic study contributes fragments of information to a broad description of the culture. However, certain parts of the mosaic are likely to be more differentiated and complete than others. For example, with respect to U.S. school culture, more research exists about the culture of teachers than about the culture of school boards and administrators, in part because groups in power often are less inclined to communicate openly to researchers about their cultural life.

Lancy (1993) identified three cultural themes on which educational ethnography has focused: (1) **enculturation,** which is the process by which cultural practices and beliefs are transferred to the youth or other new members of a culture; (2) how communities adapt to or resist the efforts of formal educational institutions to shape and control the learning processes of their youth; and (3) the culture and subculture of individuals in various social roles (e.g., teacher, student, principal) in educational institutions. We give examples of research reflecting each of these themes in the sections that follow.

THE METHODS OF ETHNOGRAPHIC RESEARCH

The following discussion of ethnographic research procedures corresponds closely to the steps in doing a case study, which we described in Chapter 10. These procedures involve formulating a research problem and selecting a case, collecting field data, analyzing and interpreting the data, and reporting study findings.

Formulating a Research Problem

To formulate a research problem for ethnographic research, the researcher must first define the aspect of culture to be explored. Sometimes this step occurs after the culture to be studied has been selected. This selection process sometimes capitalizes on accidental or forced circumstances. For example, a study of the Trobriand Islanders in New Guinea by Bronislaw Malinowski (1922) was occasioned, or at least lengthened, by the advent of World War I and his detention on the islands in the status of an enemy alien. Similarly, a trilogy of studies about the high school dropout "Brad" by Harry Wolcott (1994) began when the researcher discovered the youth living on a corner of his property in the forest outside a small city.

Ethnographers often first formulate their problem and then select a setting that fits it. For example, Margaret Mead (1930) wanted to study the relationship between children's thinking processes and spontaneous animism (i.e., beliefs in the existence of spirits that were thought to develop independently of any external influence). Mead selected Melanesia because it contained many "primitive" groups and had been characterized by previous researchers as a region filled with the phenomena usually associated with spontaneous animism. She then narrowed her focus to the relatively unknown Manus tribe for practical reasons, including the availability of some texts in the native language and a school boy willing to act as an interpreter.

The research study by Kenneth Anderson and Anne McClard (1993) that is reprinted in this chapter involved a team of ethnographic researchers who explored two aspects of university student culture: the meanings that students attributed to the construct of *study,* and the students' perceived and actual use of time. The researchers also explored the effects of computers on these aspects of student culture.

Collecting Field Data

Ethnographers use the full range of qualitative data-collection methods, and also quantitative methods when appropriate. Mead (1930) investigated the Manus children at play, in their homes, and with their parents. She collected spontaneous drawings from the children, who had never before held a pencil in their hands, and asked them to interpret ink blots. Because the entire Manus tribe included only 210 people, Mead was able to follow all current events in the village "with careful attention to their cultural significance and the role which they played in the lives of the children" (p. 291). Records of conversations and interpretations were all taken down in the native language. Mead avoided technical terms, couching her descriptions "in the field of the novelist" (p. 292). She also used detailed record sheets to organize her notes. For example, the household record sheet included headings for the house owner's children by each marriage, who financed his marriages, and what marriages he was financing. Mead made a detailed analysis of the composition of a subculture of the Manus tribe (the Peri population), recording the number of married couples, widows, and widowers and the average number of children per married couple.

In his ethnography of a school principal, Harry Wolcott (1973) shadowed the principal for a period of time while making continuous entries in a notebook. He then collected "time and motion" data, recording what the principal was doing, where, and with whom, at sixty-second intervals over a carefully sampled two-week period at school. The researcher also carried out analyses of official school notices, quantitative records, and census data for the community in which the school was located.

Wolcott engaged in almost constant note taking so that participants in the setting that he studied would become comfortable with it. His longhand notes were typed onto 5" × 8" cards, each describing a single event. The researcher did not return to the school until he had completed his notes from the last visit. To avoid becoming overidentified with the principal, he visited often with teachers and staff members. Wolcott also carried out visits with the principal's family at home and observed the principal's errands and community activities around town and at special social events.

Only after he had spent over half a year at the school did Wolcott add interviewing as a data-collection method. He conducted and taped several one-hour interviews with the principal (e.g., about the principal's forecast of the coming school year, his family life, and what had occurred at the school since Wolcott's last visit). The ethnographic research also included individual interviews with "informants"—thirteen faculty and two staff members—about their perceptions of the principal as a school administrator. All fifth- and sixth-grade students were asked to write brief, anonymous comments about the principal.

Wolcott concluded his fieldwork by distributing a ten-page questionnaire to all faculty and staff: "The questionnaire was particularly valuable in enabling me to obtain systematic data about the staff, as I could see no point in holding a long taped interview with each of the twenty-nine members of the regular and part-time staff" (p. 123).

In the ethnographic study that is reprinted in this chapter, the research team spent an entire academic year investigating the college students living in a freshman residence hall at their university that had just been outfitted with computers. The researchers describe **participant observation** as their chief method of data collection: assuming a meaningful identity within the group while maintaining their role as researchers. One of the researchers actually lived in the residence hall for the entire study year, thus serving as an almost constant participant observer. Other information was obtained from formal and informal interviews and from written questionnaires (referred to in the article as *surveys*).

The questionnaire data included quantitative measures of students' self-reported use of computers and their time allocations to study and other activities. Another quantitative measure was the amount of each student's computer and network use. These data were collected directly by a computer program that tracked the use of computers in the residence hall network.

Thus, although ethnography generally is a qualitative method of inquiry, quantitative measures can contribute to the study of a culture, just as they did to Mead's study of the Manus tribe. In qualitative research, as in quantitative research, researchers are free to use any methods that help them understand the phenomena they are studying.

Analyzing and Interpreting Ethnographic Data

As we explained in Chapter 10, data analysis in qualitative research usually begins while the data are being collected, and affects subsequent data-collection efforts. For example, Mead's (1930) research led her to an emerging sense that the hypothesis guiding her study (i.e., that the concept of animism arises spontaneously in children's thinking) was not going to be supported by the data. Nonetheless, she continued collecting data in order to discover and support an alternate interpretation of what she was observing:

> The results of this research were negative, that is, evidence was found to support the view that animism is not a spontaneous aspect of child thinking nor does it spring from any type of thought characteristic of immature mental development; its presence or absence in the thought of children is dependent upon cultural factors, language, folk lore, adult attitudes, etc., and these cultural factors have their origin in the thought of individual adults, not in the misconceptions of children. (p. 289)

Mead's admission of her failure to support her original hypothesis reflects the requirement that ethnographers look for disconfirming evidence and then modify their hypotheses, theories, and interpretations to reflect whatever they discover in the field.

The use of theory to interpret ethnographic data is illustrated by a study of Christian schooling in a U.S. community that was conducted by Alan Peshkin (1986). Using data obtained by interviews, questionnaires, and observations,

Peshkin examined many aspects of the culture that a fundamentalist Christian high school sought to establish, including how it originated from, and in turn influenced development of, the beliefs of teachers, students, and students' parents. Peshkin applied a particular sociological theory to describe the culture of Bethany Baptist Academy as that of a "total institution." By this he meant that the school had pervasive effects on its members, effects that were "unrestricted in time and space, neither limited to a term or a sentence nor confined to a building or a particular setting" (p. 274).

Reporting Ethnographic Research

Marion Dobbert (1982) described an ethnographic report as having five parts:

1. A statement of the research questions and the situations and problems that led to them
2. A description of the background research and theory used to refine the study's questions and design
3. A detailed review of the research design
4. A presentation of the data
5. An explanation of the findings.

Dobbert described the presentation of data as the "heart and soul" of the report. To her, this presentation should be a detailed description of the cultural scene under investigation, presented in organized fashion and based on a low-level (i.e., descriptive or low-inference) categorical analysis of data.

Dobbert's emphasis on including both detail and theory in ethnographic reports is supported by the anthropologist Murray Wax (2002). He argues that the best ethnographic reports are "two-sided":

On the one hand, the text familiarizes the reader with basic concepts from the discourse of the host people, providing interpretation by situating them within narratives; on the other hand, the text explains the conduct of the hosts using categories and concepts from the social sciences. (p. 122)

In the research report included in this chapter, Anderson and McClard use several long quotes from individual students. Their narrative also explains the meaning of these constructs from the students' emic perspective:

Study breaks were an integral part of study time. Indeed, students often spent more time on study breaks than they spent studying. Because study breaks were a social activity, it appeared to the outsiders that students goofed off a lot. Clearly, the study break, as defined by the student, was actually study time. The academic problems that the students worked out during a break could not be worked out in more formal settings or on their own. The study break was a secure environment for testing ideas. (pp. 165–166 in the original article)

The authors thus paint a sympathetic, but revealing, picture of how typical college students define and use their time, likening it to the time orientation of farmers rather than to that of "9-to-5 workers."

Ethnographic reports often have a story-like flavor, because of ethnographers' concern for thick description and conveying the emic perspective. This story-like quality is illustrated by Mead's (1930) description of an interaction between a six-year-old child, Popoli, and his father:

> [H]e whines out in the tone which all Manus natives use when begging betel nut: "A little betel?" The father throws him a nut. He tears the skin off with his teeth and bites it greedily. "Another," the child's voice rises to a higher pitch. The father throws him a second nut, which the child grasps firmly in his wet little fist, without acknowledgment. "Some pepper leaf?" The father frowns. "I have very little, Popoli." "Some pepper leaf." The father tears off a piece of a leaf and throws it to him. The child scowls at the small piece. "This is too little. More! More! More!" His voice rises to a howl of rage. (pp. 20–21)

The story concludes with the father rationally explaining why he cannot give his son more pepper leaf, accidentally dropping his knife into the water and requesting that his son get it, and the son refusing: "No. I won't, thou, thou stingy one, thou hidest thy pepper leaf from me." The child swims away, leaving his father to climb down and rescue the knife himself. And Mead leaves it to the reader to infer the quality of parent–child relationships in the Manus culture.

APPLYING ETHNOGRAPHIC RESEARCH FINDINGS TO EDUCATIONAL PRACTICE

Ethnography has provided educational researchers a means to explore in depth the various ways in which cultural factors affect teaching and learning. Studies that reveal the cultural milieu in which students find themselves when outside of school, for example, obviously can help teachers better understand the students and hopefully foster their learning. However, you should take care to read ethnographic research reports critically, just as you would any other type of research report, rather than accept their findings at face value.

As we explained in Chapter 10, qualitative researchers use different criteria than quantitative researchers to judge the credibility, trustworthiness, and applicability of their findings. Some of these criteria involve reader judgment, whereas others involve principles of sound research design and thoroughness of data-collection and analysis procedures. These same criteria apply to ethnographic research, which relies primarily on qualitative methodology.

In addition to applying these general criteria, you should know about issues of credibility, trustworthiness, and applicability that are specific to ethnographic research and the ethnography of education. Sensitivity to these issues will help you read ethnographic research reports with greater understanding and a more critical eye. We discuss seven of these issues below.

1. *Equating schooling and education.* Ethnographers of education face the risk of equating schooling and education. In many cultures, formal educational institutions control the provision and validation of learning among the members of the culture. However, many individuals have important learning experiences in other contexts, including family units, peer groups, or the workplace. A holistic ethnography of education would need to include explorations of the teaching-learning process as it occurs in varied contexts.

2. *Learning as a cultural process.* Ethnographers of education face the issue of whether it is better to view learning primarily as a process of cultural transmission or of cultural acquisition. Research on **cultural acquisition** puts the focus on how individuals seek to acquire, or to avoid acquiring, the concepts, values, skills, and behaviors that are reflected in the common culture. In contrast, research on **cultural transmission** puts the focus on how the larger social structure intentionally intervenes in individuals' lives in order to promote or, in some cases, to discourage, learning of particular concepts, values, skills, or behaviors.

This issue plays a central role in efforts to understand differences in educational success among the members of various cultural groups. Lancy (1993) cites a number of research studies that explored the adaptation to public schooling of young people whose cultures were in transition:

> All document persistent "failure" in the sense that one sees little pleasure in either the teaching staff or the children. There is no evidence that students are making satisfactory academic progress, enabling them to "climb out of the ghetto," "leave the reservation," or "become self-sufficient." Increasingly, anthropologists who study minority education now take student failure as their point of departure. . . . (p. 41)

In seeking the cause of many minority students' lower level of academic success compared to that of students in the mainstream culture, John Ogbu (1978) carried out research based on a theoretical model of education and caste. The model focuses on learning as cultural acquisition, and the claim that native-born members of minority groups who have suffered a long history of economic discrimination in the United States tend to withhold their investment in education, because they do not perceive it as having any economic payoff. Other qualitative researchers interested in cultural acquisition have studied individuals' sense of **agency**, which refers to the assumed ability to shape the conditions of one's life, whatever one's cultural situation.

George Spindler and Louise Spindler (1992) observed that the focus on cultural acquisition makes it easy to slip into a "blame-the-victim" interpretation of individuals' learning problems. They argued that ethnography can best contribute to the understanding of learning by showing how societies use their cultural resources to organize the conditions and purposes of learning. Their research focuses on how schools and other agents of cultural transmission (e.g., families) facilitate or hinder specific types of learning by individuals from various cultures.

Still another position is that both cultural acquisition and cultural transmission can figure in a given individual's or group's learning. In this view, the task of educational ethnography is to determine how cultural factors and human agency interact to codetermine what individuals and groups learn.

3. *Conveying culture accurately.* Some educators question the ability of ethnographic research to convey the richness and complexity of cultural phenomena. Clifford Geertz (1973) claimed that ethnographies are "fiction," in that they are not an accurate description of the culture but rather a story told by the researchers using various literary conventions and devices. Critics argue that the genre of writing used in typical ethnographic reports imposes an order on cultural phenomena that might not accurately reflect the variety and ongoing changes occurring in the culture being described. As a result, different role groups (e.g., teachers or administrators) might accept ethnographic findings as applying to the individuals or groups with whom they have contact (e.g., students or parents) without checking their actual applicability to those individuals or groups. As Lancy (1993) notes, "one must be extremely skeptical of the cherished assumption [in ethnography] of cultural homogeneity" (p. 63).

4. *Reflecting privileged discourse.* Some feminist theorists argue that traditional ethnographies reflect a privileged, male discourse that maintains unequal relationships between researchers and the members of the culture who are studied. Such criticisms have prompted some ethnographers to adopt a "dialogic" stance, in which they conduct their research as a collaboration between the researcher and the members of the culture being studied. In fact, some educational ethnographers have sought not just to describe, but also to change, a particular culture to promote student learning and empowerment (e.g., Weisner, Gallimore, & Jordan, 1988).

Educational ethnographers frequently use teachers as informants. Because many teachers have expertise in action research (see Chapter 15) and multicultural approaches to education, they may wonder how their work differs from that of educational ethnographers. The potential for tension exists if teachers feel that their research and approach to culture is perceived as having less value than that of ethnographers. This feeling of inequality can be exacerbated by the nonreciprocity of their roles: ethnographers study teachers, but teachers do not study ethnographers!

Lorie Hammond and George Spindler (2001) suggest that this tension can be relieved if teachers and ethnographers view each other as having important, but different, roles to play in solving problems of schooling. As an example, they consider the problem of how to involve ethnic-minority parents in the schooling of their children and how teachers and ethnographers might solve it by carrying out complementary roles. Teachers might do research to answer a question of interest to them, such as, "How can we incorporate language-minority parents into the school program?" Ethnographers might be interested in doing research on a different, but related question, "Why do misunderstandings between parents and teachers occur?" If ethnographers and teachers respect each others' expertise, they are likely to find that each group can generate knowledge of mutual benefit.

5. *Difficulty in making the familiar strange.* Because educators who become researchers typically valued and did well in school themselves, they may have difficulty in discovering the hidden meanings of school culture as it is experienced by individuals with different values about, and experiences with, education. As Wolcott (1987) puts it:

> Being so totally immersed in and committed to formal education, they are as likely to "discover" school culture as fish are likely to discover water. The cross-cultural and comparative basis that helps ethnographers identify something they are tentatively willing to describe as culture in someone else's behavior—because it is readily distinguishable from their own—is lacking. (p. 50)

Wolcott recommends that students learning ethnographic research methods do their first major fieldwork in a distant society or with a dramatically different microculture before attempting to study the all-too-familiar culture of the school or classroom.

6. *Overidentification with informants.* In their attempt to reflect the emic perspective, ethnographers sometimes overidentify with one or more of the cultural groups from whom they seek their informants. In studying school culture, for example, they might give the impression that the students' perspective is more truthful or ethical than that of the teachers with whom they have contact.

7. *Balancing the emic and etic perspectives.* It is not easy for ethnographers to balance the emic and etic perspectives obtained about a group's culture. The **emic perspective** involves the perceptions and language categories used by members of the culture to describe and explain the culture. That perspective helps readers understand a culture as a unique social reality, but does not always provide a sound basis for discovering regularities of social life that can be used to describe and explain other cultures. Some critics argue that the ethnographers' **etic perspective,** which is based on the researcher's conceptual and theoretical orientation and involves standard categories for describing a culture, might provide a better basis for the discovery of cross-cultural regularities.

Lancy (1993) suggests ethnographers attempt to reconcile the etic and emic perspectives by checking the correspondence between field participants' thoughts about their setting and their actual behavior in that setting. For example, Lancy (1976) conducted an ethnographic study using research methods based on ethnoscience to explore the activities in which students engage while at school, from the perspective of the students themselves. He developed a taxonomy of activities from information obtained in student interviews. The taxonomy included main categories of student activities (working, helping, making, playing, and fooling/messing around), and subcategories for each. He then used the categories derived from the student interview data to develop a behavior observation checklist of students' in-school activities. In subsequent observations of the students in six different school settings, he found a good match between the taxonomy categories and students' actual behavior.

EXAMPLE OF OUTLINING A RESEARCH PROPOSAL

This feature of the chapter gives you an example of how to outline a research proposal using the form in Appendix 1. The example, involving a proposal to study curriculum alignment, is introduced at the end of Chapter 2.

The third research question in the example is as follows: "Does students' performance on achievement tests improve after a curriculum-alignment process has been completed in their schools?" We will take an ethnographic approach by focusing on student culture as it affects the process of preparing for a particular achievement test, let's say, a high-stakes, state-administered test administered during the ninth grade.

By student culture, we mean the distinctive rituals, traditions, symbols, and artifacts that students use among each other and in their interactions with other cultures, such as teacher culture and parent culture. We want to understand how aspects of student culture relate to preparing for and taking a high-stakes test. Although we will report data on test gains for the year before and after a curriculum-alignment process, our focus is on how aspects of student culture might explain the presence or absence of test gains.

To suggest what is involved in the design of an ethnography, we filled out various parts of the proposal outline.

4. RESEARCH DESIGN
    A. *Research design.* The research design is an ethnography, which is a qualitative research tradition. Our purpose is to understand relevant aspects of student culture in a particular time frame—the weeks leading up to a high-stakes test. We will not draw strong causal inferences from the study (e.g., aspects of student culture that "cause" students to do well or poorly on a high-stakes test). However, the ethnographic study might suggest variables for research designs that allow for strong causal inferences (e.g., causal-comparisons and experiments).
    D. *Validity and reliability criteria.* Our major concern will be to select sufficient data that we can create a "thick description" of typical features of the particular student culture we selected for ethnographic investigation. We will accomplish this goal by collecting data from a representative group of students on a frequent basis as they respond to the upcoming achievement test.

    We will write detailed vignettes illustrating representative aspects of student culture, so that the process becomes concrete and real for readers of the study. We will have several educational practitioners evaluate the ethnographic report in terms of its validity and usefulness to them. Their feedback will be used to revise the report.

    The validity of the interview data, observational data, and documents selected for analysis will be checked by having some of the research participants check them for accuracy, bias, and completeness.

5. SAMPLING

   B. *Phenomenon.* The phenomenon of interest to us is student culture related to an upcoming high-stakes achievement test.

   C. *Sampling procedure.* Because of the intensive data collection required by this study, we will select just one class taught by a particular ninth-grade teacher. We will select one of his classes the year preceding the curriculum alignment and another, similar class after he has realigned his curriculum based on school-district guidelines and training.

   D. *Sampling units.* All students in one class (e.g., ninth-grade English taught by Mr. Hamlin) will be selected for study. We expect that students occasionally will interact with each other in pairs and small groups and will also act independently in class or in study settings (e.g., their private space at home). Each of these groupings of students will constitute a sampling unit of interest.

6. VARIABLES

   B. *Focus of the case study.* Of particular interest will be any discourse or behavior that reflects how students value the test, the particular rituals they perform to get ready for the test either by themselves or in interactions with other students, their interactions with other cultural groups (in particular, members of the teacher and parent cultures), and their use of any special materials or technology. We will take special note of students' reactions to anything that reflects a curriculum alignment procedure introduced by the teacher, such as reviewing state curriculum standards with students, highlighting particular textbook content, or giving test-taking tips.

7. METHODS OF DATA COLLECTION

   C. *Framework for data collection.* The procedures for data collection will focus on an emic perspective, that is, the perspective of the students as they prepare for the achievement test.

   To get a sense of the aspects of student culture that change as a high-stakes test approaches, we will observe and interview students intensively for two weeks leading up to the test, and also a month preceding that period of time in order to get a sense of students' typical culture.

   We will sit in on class during the six weeks preceding the test, taking notes on student behavior that we observe. We also will select a small sample of student informants to interview intensively in person or by phone each day.

8. DATA ANALYSIS PROCEDURES

   B. *Method of data analysis.* A reflective approach to data analysis will be used. We will study other ethnographies of student culture (such as the journal article included in Chapter 11) to develop a sense of how other ethnographic researchers have investigated similar aspects of student culture.

SELF-CHECK TEST

1. When researchers study a subculture in their own vicinity with which they are unfamiliar, they are fulfilling the intent of ethnographic research to
   a. carry out naturalistic observations of participants in the field.
   b. make the familiar strange.
   c. provide a thick description of a cultural phenomenon.
   d. do a cross-cultural comparison.

2. Ethnographers focus on the study of culture because they believe that
   a. the influence of culture in human beings' lives is what makes them unique as a species.
   b. the study of primitive cultures can show how Western cultures evolved.
   c. an increasing number of distinct cultures are emerging in the world.
   d. the similarities observed between people from different parts of the world are best explained in terms of enculturation.

3. Ethnographers
   a. rely exclusively on qualitative methods of data collection.
   b. begin analyzing their data only after concluding their fieldwork.
   c. sometimes present their findings in a story-like format.
   d. continue collecting data until they have confirmed their hypotheses.

4. In providing a holistic description of a culture, ethnographers generally seek to
   a. compare the culture to other cultures.
   b. give primacy to the views of high-status members of the culture.
   c. use their own perspective to reconcile conflicting views of the culture.
   d. balance the emic and etic perspectives.

5. Some educational ethnographers consider the main reason for minority students' lower academic performance than mainstream students to be their tendency to withhold their investment in education because they do not perceive it as having any economic payoff. This viewpoint focuses on the effects of _____ on students' performance.
   a. cultural acquisition   c. school organization
   b. cultural assimilation   d. teacher bias

6. Referring to ethnographies as "fictions" reflects primarily the view of some scholars that
   a. ethnographers can never reflect the emic perspective; they can only reflect the etic perspective.
   b. ethnographers are biased toward conveying cultural aspects in the most negative terms.
   c. ethnographies are stories told by researchers using various literary conventions and devices.
   d. only holistic ethnography can truly represent the characteristics of a culture.

CHAPTER REFERENCES

Anderson, K. T., & McClard, A. P. (1993). Study time: Temporal orientations of freshmen students and computing. *Anthropology and Education Quarterly, 24,* 159–177.

Dobbert, M. (1982). *Ethnographic research: Theory and application for modern schools and societies.* New York: Praeger.

Geertz, C. (1973). *The interpretation of cultures: Selected essays.* New York: Basic Books.

Hammond, L., & Spindler, G. (2001). Not talking past each other: Cultural roles in education research. *Anthropology and Education Quarterly, 32,* 373–378.

Hogan, K., & Corey, C. (2001). Viewing classrooms as cultural contexts for fostering scientific literacy. *Anthropology and Education Quarterly, 32,* 214–243.

Lancy, D. F. (1976). The beliefs and behaviors of pupils in an experimental school: Introduction and overview. *Learning Research and Development Center Publication Series 3.* ERIC Document Reference No. ED 127301.

Lancy, D. F. (1993). *Qualitative research in education: An introduction to the major traditions.* White Plains, NY: Longman.

Malinowski, B. (1922). *Argonauts of the Western Pacific.* New York: Dutton.

Mead, M. (1930). *Growing up in New Guinea: A comparative study of primitive education.* New York: William Morrow.

Ogbu, J. U. (1978). *Minority education and caste: The American system in cross-cultural perspective.* New York: Academic Press.

Peshkin, A. (1986). *God's choice: The total world of a fundamentalist Christian school.* Chicago: University of Chicago Press.

Spindler, G., & Spindler, L. (1992). Cultural process and ethnography: An anthropological perspective. In M. D. LeCompte, W. L. Millroy, & J. Preissle (Eds.), *Handbook of qualitative research in education* (pp. 53–92). San Diego: Academic.

Wax, M. (1993). How culture misdirects multiculturalism. *Anthropology and Educational Quarterly, 24,* 99–115.

Wax, M. (2002). The school classroom as frontier. *Anthropology and Education Quarterly, 33,* 118–130.

Weisner, T. S., Gallimore, R., & Jordan, C. (1988). Unpackaging cultural effects on classroom learning: Native Hawaiian peer assistance and child-generated activity. *Anthropology and Education Quarterly, 19,* 327–353.

Wolcott, H. F. (1973). *The man in the principal's office: An ethnography.* New York: Holt, Rinehart, & Winston.

Wolcott, H. F. (1987). On ethnographic intent. In G. D. Spindler & L. Spindler (Eds.), *Interpretive ethnography of education* (pp. 37–57). Hillsdale, NJ: Erlbaum.

Wolcott, H. F. (1994). *Transforming qualitative data: Description, analysis, and interpretation.* Thousand Oaks, CA: Sage.

RESOURCES FOR FURTHER STUDY

Chambers, E. (2000). Applied ethnography. In N. K. Denzin & Y. S. Lincoln (Eds.), *Handbook of qualitative research* (2nd ed., pp. 851–869). Thousand Oaks, CA: Sage.

> *The author discusses recent trends in ethnographic research. One trend is to use ethnographic methods to guide policy making and decision making. Another trend is for ethnographers to study how cultures are constructed and change over time and what happens when different cultural groups interact with each other.*

LeCompte, M. D., & Preissle, J. (1993). *Ethnography and qualitative design in educational research* (2nd ed.). San Diego: Academic Press.

> *Describes how to design and carry out ethnographic research in education. Traces the origins of ethnography from anthropology as well as more recent influences on educational ethnography from sociology, psychology, and other fields.*

Levison, B. A. U., Cade, S. L., Padawer, A., & Elvir, A. P. (Eds.) (2002). *Ethnography and education policy across the Americas.* Westport, CT: Praeger.

> *This book includes chapters by U.S. and Latin American researchers who use ethnographic methods for studying and influencing education policy.*

Wolcott, H. F. (1997). Ethnographic research in education. In R. M. Jaeger (Ed.), *Complementary methods for research in education* (2nd ed., pp. 327–362). Washington, DC: American Educational Research Association.

> *The author offers a perspective on the meaning of ethnography and culture and the tradition of ethnographic research in education. He also describes four research strategies as they are used in the context of ethnographic work: participant observation, interviewing, making use of existing records and making one's own records of cultural phenomena, and the transformation of fieldwork into a report.*

In the following section of this chapter you will read a research article that illustrates an ethnographic research study. It is preceded by comments written especially for this book by the authors of the article. Then the article itself is reprinted in full, just as it appeared when originally published. Where appropriate, we have added footnotes to help you understand the information contained in the article.

SAMPLE ETHNOGRAPHIC RESEARCH STUDY

Study Time: Temporal Orientations of Freshmen Students and Computing

Anderson, K. T., & McClard, A. P. (1993). Study time: Temporal orientations of freshmen students and computing. *Anthropology and Education Quarterly, 24,* 159–177.

● **RESEARCHERS' COMMENTS,** *Prepared by Kenneth Anderson and Anne McClard*

Background

We wrote the article that is reprinted here when we were both predoctoral graduate students in anthropology at Brown University, employed by the Institute for Research in Information and Scholarship (IRIS). Before this study we were involved in IRIS's three-year research project on the effectiveness of using an early network-based, hypermedia educational software product (Intermedia) in the classroom. (The World Wide Web is an example of this technology as it has evolved.)

On the IRIS project we had done extensive ethnographic work in school classrooms and computer laboratories, under the direction of William Beeman. We focused on the question of whether and how the Intermedia technology was changing the way students learned. Although we found this work interesting, we also felt that we were missing "the big picture" concerning the nature of students' knowledge acquisition. It seemed to us that much of what the students were learning came through informal means, and was more related to social networks than to computer networks. As a consequence, we and two colleagues who had also worked on the Intermedia project decided to redirect our research on technology.

Some of the questions that compelled us to undertake this research were: (1) How do students go about learning on a day-to-day basis? (2) What practices do students employ to mediate their college experience? (3) What "interpretive lenses" do students use to navigate through college, both socially and academically? We wanted to explore through ethnography the less formal learning environment of the university, where students live, work, and spend the majority of their time. The college dormitory provided us with a naturally occurring social unit to study. Although residential life studies were numerous at the time of our research, we knew of none that focused on the social aspects of learning.

We were also interested in the effects of technology on learning, but not in a conventional sense. Instead, we sought to look at technology from the perspective of a cultural anthropologist. With a few notable exceptions (Blomberg, 1987; Orr, 1987a, 1987b; Suchman, 1983a, 1983b, 1986; Suchman & Trigg, 1986), cultural anthropologists had not done much research on technology in the United States. Most technology studies in the 1980s focused on evaluation: Researchers sought to test the hypothesis that technology has an impact on human behavior. By contrast, our focus was on the *human process of making sense of something*—in this case, network-connected computers as part of the university living experience.

We were interested in how students construct meaning—how their experience of technology is shaped through their mediated understanding of what it is and how they can use it. To put it another way, people's use of technology relies upon their understanding, which is culturally constructed and contextually situated. Technologies do not have meaning apart from the ways that they are used and experienced in a particular context.

This said, the end product of such cultural inquiry is not meant to be a dictionary-like treatment that implies it conveys the "true" meaning of things. Rather, the result of an ethnographic analysis should serve as an arbiter of what meaning the members of a particular culture are likely to construe. We feel that our article failed in this regard. People often read it and conclude that *study time* is X, Y, or Z. Instead we viewed study time as a "native category," that is, a conceptual framework that had many different hooks on it. We wanted to convey the point that students understood, interpreted, and enacted study time in many different ways. Study time is an acknowledged and even institutionalized part of the student experience, but it is not an instance of "shared meaning."

Perhaps our extensive use of the present tense and various authoritative and declarative statements in the article gave readers the impression that we were making statements of fact, but that was not our intention. Were we to write the article today, the tone would be considerably different. Rather than conforming to the positivistic style of scientific writing, we would make more extensive use of stories in order to reflect the diversity of perspectives that were represented among the students living in Ford Hall.

Our Research Experiences

The Dorm Project field study, as we called it, lasted for one year. Each of the four team members had differing experiences and roles. There were three ethnographers: the two of us, and Gail Bader. Anderson lived in the dormitory for the entire academic year. Bader and McClard were itinerant participant observers, and they each played a key role in interviewing and in the ethnographic data analysis. The fourth member of the team, Jim Larkin, was responsible for quantitative data collection (electronic tracking and scoring of questionnaires), data management, and computer-based data analysis. He spent very little time in the dorm or talking with its residents.

People often refer erroneously to "the ethnographic method," as if it were a single research approach. In fact ethnographers typically use a variety of approaches to conduct a research study. The key tools of ethnographic research are participant observation and interviewing, but ethnographers use whatever data-collection tools are the most appropriate to answer the questions at hand. In the case of the Dorm Project, we used both qualitative and quantitative approaches, but it was participant observation that served as the "glue" that helped us piece together the sometimes incomprehensible results churned out by our structured interviews, questionnaires, and electronically collected data.

"Doing ethnography," which in the 1990s has come into vogue in many disciplines beyond anthropology, is often equated with participant observation. To many, participant observation appears to be little more than "hanging out," watching what people are doing, and taking a few notes. We believe strongly that good participant observation is never just "hanging out." Participant observation requires the active, systematic collection of information. The participant observer must constantly reflect on the data that have been collected to develop new directions of inquiry. Additionally, because it is a reflexive process, seemingly irrelevant information that is noted at one time often turns out to be critical at a later time. Ethnographic inquiry is not an unmediated process; one cannot simply take notes, type them up, stick some pseudonyms in, and summarize events in an impressionistic way. Ethnographic research requires complex social, practical, and personal skills to sustain a role in the field.

We approached the dorm just as we would have approached a village in a foreign country. After all, the youngest of us was ten years older than the oldest freshman in Ford Hall. At the outset we felt culturally quite distant from the students and their everyday experiences. For the most part we did not share common cultural references with them. As a result, we needed to find our way into their "village," to learn how to be accepted and gain their confidence so that we could understand the village from *their* perspective. Participant observation was the approach to data collection that allowed this to happen.

As the name implies, the participant observer must find a means to participate in a meaningful way. He or she cannot simply stand by passively as a witness to things that are happening, but must become a part of the social context. Anderson's role as an older dorm resident was critical to gaining a depth of understanding of the students' experiences. Having multiple ethnographers of different genders and ages was also important, because ethnography is "perspective based." We felt that it was important to capture a wide range of perspectives among the freshmen.

Each ethnographer on the project interacted with the dorm residents in a unique way. Where one ethnographer had difficulty developing rapport with a particular resident or group of residents, another did not. The students in the dorm became a significant and integrated part of our lives, and we became a part of theirs. In this way we were able to gain a breadth of understanding that would not have been possible had only one participant observer been on the job. On the other hand, we soon learned that participant observation, done right, is neither easy nor quick.

In retrospect, we wish we had focused less on some of our other data-collection activities and more on the qualitative side of the work. The structured interviews and questionnaire instruments provided the least interesting information, simply documenting what people said they believed or said they did. We gained a much better understanding of the unspoken, inchoate, and taken-for-granted aspects of peoples' lives that underlie their beliefs and behaviors from computer-generated behavioral data (collected electronically), daily informal conversations, observations, and contextually elaborated interviews.

Aftermath

After the Dorm Project was completed, the computers were distributed to various campus locations, and the freshmen moved on to other places. The project had been funded because it was a technology initiative—a hot topic—not because of its focus on the nature of social learning. One of the things we had hoped was that the university would see the educational value of network computing, and that this would lead to all the residential halls on campus getting "wired." While this did not happen immediately, Brown was on the forefront in providing computer networks in residential halls. We do not know if the Dorm Project informed these decisions or not.

Soon after we completed our study, IRIS folded and the team disbanded. Bader, who was then a postdoc, now holds a faculty position in educational anthropology at Ball State University. Larkin started a consulting company that specializes in technical writing and Web publishing.

We (Anderson and McClard) got married and embarked on our dissertation research. While we could have used the data from our previous two studies for our dissertations, we wanted to have the "traditional" anthropological experience of doing research in a foreign country. We therefore went to the Azore Islands, an autonomous region of Portugal. Anderson's work focused on another aspect of technology—television and its meaning in that culture. McClard studied the annual cycle of festivals in the region. We are currently employed in a research division of a Regional Bell Operating Company, where we are involved with ethnographic studies of technology and education.

Implications

A decade has passed since we carried out the Dorm Project research described in this article. Since then we have been involved with numerous studies of innovation in society. Themes and issues raised in our analyses from the Dorm Project continue to be relevant. The tentative conclusions we drew have been validated in multiple contexts. While we can't say with any degree of certainty that this work has been enormously influential for educators or technologists, we do know that it was tremendously important for our own development as professional anthropologists.

References

Blomberg, J. (1987). Social interaction and office communication: Effects on users' evaluation of new technologies. In R. Kraut (Ed.), *Technology and the transformation of white collar work* (pp. 195–210). Hillsdale, NJ: Lawrence Erlbaum Associates.

Orr, J. E. (1987a). Narratives at work: Story telling as cooperative diagnostic activity. *Field Service Manager: The Journal of the Association of Field Service Managers International, 11*(6), 47–60.

Orr, J. E. (1987b). Talking about machines: Social aspects of expertise. Contract Report No. MDA903-83-C-0189. Alexandria, VA: Army Research Institute.

Suchman, L. (1983a). Office procedures as practical action: Models of work and system design. *ACM Transactions on Information Systems, 1*(4), 320–328.

Suchman, L. (1983b). The role of common sense in interface design. In D. Marschall & J. Gregory (Eds.), *Office automation: Jekyll or Hyde? Highlights of the International Conference on Office Work and New Technology.* Cleveland, OH: Working Women Education Fund.

Suchman, L. A. (1987). *Plans and situated actions.* Cambridge: Cambridge University Press.

Suchman, L., & Trigg, R. (1986, December). A framework for studying research collaboration. In the *Proceedings of Conference on Computer Supported Cooperative Work,* Austin, TX.

Study Time: Temporal Orientations of Freshmen Students and Computing

Kenneth T. Anderson
Brown University

Anne Page McClard
Brown University

This article presents an ethnographic examination of the student domains of "study" and "time," and how these domains relate to a technological innovation in a freshman residence hall. We argue that technological innovations in education warrant attention as part of the more general movement toward reform in higher education. We believe that a closer examination of student life is necessary before discussing effects of educational reform. In this article we point out some of the ways in which students' conceptions and configurations of time differ from those of others, including university administrators and professors, and the implication of their differing perspectives on the way they use personal computing facilities in a residence hall.

COMPUTER USE, EDUCATIONAL REFORM,
UNIVERSITY STUDENT CULTURE

Anderson, K. T., & McClard, A. P. (1993). Study time: Temporal orientations of freshmen students and computing. *Anthropology and Education Quarterly, 24,* 159–177. Reproduced by permission of the American Anthropological Association.

Americans are once again clashing over the goals and methods of higher education. At the time we were doing the research for this article there was a proliferation of exchanges on the topic of educational reform. During the intervening five years, interest has continued to grow. Two critiques of higher education, Allan Bloom's *Closing of the American Mind* (1987) and E. D. Hirsch, Jr.'s *Cultural Literacy* (1987), became best-sellers. Beyond the popular press, many people in the field published critiques of education, such as Ernest Boyer's *College* (1987) and reports by former Secretary of Education William Bennett. Furthermore, a survey conducted by the American Council on Education (ACE) in 1987 indicated that 95 percent of all two- and four-year higher education institutions in the United States either had overhauled their curricula in the last few years or intended to do so in the near future (Ottinger 1987).

Across the country, universities and colleges have been scrambling to computerize their campuses. Increasingly, courses are being taught with the computer as an integral component. Technical innovations, however, have not drawn the amount of attention that ideological innovations have. Although technical innovation is perceived as revolutionizing education and educational possibilities, it has not been seen or studied as part of the general movement toward reform.

Although this article is neither a call for educational reform nor an essay refuting the need for it, it is a call for a close examination of the population that will be most affected by both technological and ideological reforms: students. We are asking, in short, for more ethnographic research in educational situations in which the student is viewed as a vital element who actively shapes the educational community and institution.

This article contains an analysis of our research at Brown University as it relates to the addition of technical innovations. Specifically, we will deal with the domains of "studying" and "time"—the way that students categorize their time (study and non-study)—and discuss some of the ways in which the computer has fit into their lives as students.[a]

METHODS

The analysis presented here is based on data collected over the course of the 1987–88 academic year. For this project we placed IBM Model 30 computers in 33 of the 34 rooms at Ford Hall, a freshman residence hall at Brown University. During the project, Ford was home to 63 students. Of these, 61 agreed to participate in the project. The rooms were fairly spacious by Brown standards, and most rooms had two windows. The halls were dark and narrow, perhaps because the residence hall was built in 1925. The dorm was coed by room; that is, each room was occupied by same-sex roommates, but both males and females lived on the same floor. Only the more senior class counselors were allowed to have individual rooms. In Table 1 we compare the Ford Hall population with the 1987 freshman class as a whole with respect to sex and race.[b]

TABLE 1	Sex and Race of Ford Hall Residents Compared to All Freshmen					
Ford Hall Residents	47	53	73	10	6	10
All Freshmen	53	47	81	7	3	9

Each computer came with a word processing package, a presentation manager, a relational database, and a number of games. In addition, each computer was linked to an IBM PC AT—the server for a laser printer (IBM 3813) that was placed in a common area. Along with the server, an IBM Model 30 and a PC AT were available as "public machines." The local area network (Novell Netware 2.0) allowed the students to send and receive electronic mail (e-mail), exchange files, and play the network game "Snipes." Finally, a terminal emulation package (N3270) was available that allowed the students to reach the campus mainframe via BRUNET using mainframe facilities. The equipment and software were set up for the students before they arrived, and support was provided by two members of the residence hall who were hired by the project as consultants.

We used a variety of ethnographic methods to collect data for this project: surveys, computer and network use data, time and task diaries, informal and formal interviews, and participant observation.

We conducted three surveys during the academic year to gain a broad perspective on the project. The questions we asked in the surveys emerged from our interviews, participant observation, and the other mentioned sources of data, allowing us to draw on a large number of the res-

---

a. The authors' reference to the domains of "studying" and "time" means that studying and time both are constructs about which a good deal of research and theoretical work has been carried out.

b. Table 1 does not include the information about gender and race to which the authors refer in the article. At our request, the authors provided the following interpretation: The numbers in each data column of the table are percentages, with those in data columns 1–2 representing students' gender and those in data columns 3–6 representing the main racial groupings of Brown students. The similarity between the two numbers in each data column indicates that Ford Hall residents (row 1) are fairly representative of all freshmen at Brown University (row 2) with respect to their gender and race.

idents of Ford Hall to substantiate ideas that may have originated with just one student. Response rates were 85 percent, 62 percent, and 62 percent for the first, second, and third surveys respectively. In addition to the project-specific surveys, all incoming freshmen were asked to complete a brief computing questionnaire the summer before they arrived at Brown. The response rate for this survey was 85 percent. Furthermore, a shorter version of the third Ford questionnaire, which had been administered in the spring, was administered to a sample of all students at Brown. These two non–Ford Hall surveys served as a comparative frame for certain measures. The analysis of these quantitative data also provided us with broad parameters within which our ethnographic endeavors were framed.

We collected computer use data in two ways: (1) from student use logs (self-reported use) and (2) from an automated network use tracking system. These sources had to be interpreted carefully. Self-reported computer use data are not the same as actual use data. Some students discovered ways to defeat the network tracking devices by breaking out of the menu system supplied by the project. Consequently, those users, who naturally were among the heaviest and most sophisticated users, were not fully represented in our tracking data.

Given these limitations, however, the data are still useful if treated not as absolutely descriptive but as relatively descriptive. For example, although we cannot provide an exact figure for the amount of time students spent using their computers on weekday mornings, we can with confidence say that they used them in the mornings substantially less than they did in the afternoons and evenings. Furthermore, we can say they used them more for word processing (as opposed to games or electronic mail) during the mornings than at any other time.

To understand how computers fit into student work and life patterns, we first had to understand those patterns. The time and task sheets were designed to provide an "insider's" perspective. A group of student volunteers recorded their activities for several one-week periods during the academic year. A wide range of students kept the time and task self-reports. Each report was organized into half-hour sections. The students were asked to describe for each time frame what they were doing and where they were doing it. We tried also to monitor different weeks in the semester so that we would not overlook important pattern shifts during the academic year.

The research staff conducted formal and informal interviews. On a regular basis we held formal interviews with standardized questions about computing attitudes, behaviors, educational goals, and work habits. Twenty-three students were interviewed during the first semester of the academic year. Ten of these students were interviewed in the third and fourth weeks of the semester, and 13 others were interviewed just before final exams. During the second semester, we changed our approach to interviewing: we developed a third interview protocol based on discussions and findings from the interviews in the first semester. Instead of interviewing all students at specific points, as we did in the first semester, we interviewed students at different times throughout the final semester. This allowed us to ask a "core" set of questions and to amend the interviews quickly to trace the changes in dorm life as they occurred over time. By the end of the second semester, we had formally interviewed all but four residents of Ford Hall at least once.

In addition to the formal interviews, the staff conducted informal interviews in a variety of contexts. These sometimes took the form of conversation over coffee, a discussion with a student about a recent exam while walking to class, or a few quick questions to students while they were watching television. Although formal interviews provided standardized data from which generalizations could be drawn, informal interviews were a valuable means of gathering complementary information on student life. In other words, scheduled, formal interviews with specific questions may have elicited informant responses that were deliberate and calculated, but less than candid. Informal interviews occurred in a variety of contexts and elicited spontaneous and situationally relevant responses.

Participant observation was the most central research activity of the project. A male participant observer lived in the residence hall throughout the year. Two female observers visited Ford Hall on a regular basis, noting what students were doing, what they said they were doing, and how they talked about what was going on.

Participant observation was used to obtain information on the social context of computing in the residence hall. It allowed us to get a firsthand look at how students go about work and play, and enabled us to create a detailed picture of student life in a freshman dormitory. The ethnographer's understanding and experience of the complex web of social life in the dorm was critical to this research and ultimately provided an interpretive framework for all other forms of data.[c] For example, without the ethnographer we could not have seen the subtle way in which residents established rules of appropriate computing. In watching the process by which the rules were developed, we could see how group pressure was exerted to "move" other students to comply.

This article is organized to give the reader an ethnographic perspective on student life at Ford Hall. In the first section, we discuss how student categories of time relate to student patterns of leisure and work. We point out some of the ways in which time was configured differently for students at Ford Hall than it is for the average working American. In the second section, we examine several time events over which the students have little control. These events are tied to institutional time (i.e., the semester and the day). In the third section, we explore student orientation toward time. Here we discuss attitudes toward the present and future, student goal setting, and choices. Finally, we show how the computer, an example of educational innovation, was subsumed under student categories of time, work, and leisure, and how it was integrated into student living patterns.

FRESHMEN CATEGORIES OF TIME

A freshman walks along the green, returning from a double feature at the movie theater, and into her dorm. A few minutes later a friend drops by her room and asks "What have you been up to?"

She answers, "I've been studying all day."

"Well," responds the friend, "let's take a study break then and go get some coffee."

"Sure," she agrees.

Later in the evening a computer consultant helps the same woman print a letter to her mother. She writes to apologize for not writing sooner. She says "she has been busy studying."

The scenario above is fictional, but it is similar to incidents that took place at Ford Hall. The young woman who claimed that she had been studying all day had been at the movies for several hours, had socialized over coffee, and had written a letter to her mother. The observer might be inclined to think that the woman was lying or irrational. To her way of thinking, however, she was studying, as we explain below.

Differing concepts of time across cultures have been of long-term interest to anthropologists from Benjamin Whorf to Edward T. Hall. Cultures, like individuals, are in some sense time bound, and, like individuals, each of them has a slightly different attitude toward, and configuration of, time. In an attempt to understand the students at Brown we began with their notion of time.

Much of daily life in any society consists of necessary habitual activities. For some people, in the United States for instance, this involves planning social and other activities around an eight-hour work day, a five-day work week, and a two-week paid vacation. For others, the structuring of time revolves around cultural interests. For example, Hallowell reported that the Andamanese developed their calendar on the basis of a succession of dominant smells of flowers and trees, and used the plants as reference points for activities (Hallowell 1937). The Ford Hall story is not as exotic as that of the Andamanese. However, the freshman concept of time is quite different from the American 9-to-5 worker's concept of time.

The first-year students we studied at Brown had two general time-planning categories under which all of the others were subsumed: study time and free time (social time). Study time, taken in the most general way, was from Sunday afternoon through Friday morning. Free time was from Friday afternoon through Sunday afternoon. Free time was the primary "social time." We will argue that it was free not in terms of task completion, but by definition.

---

c. This reference to *the ethnographer* means the male participant observer who was a member of the research team and who lived in the freshman residence hall where the research was carried out.

One might guess, based on the two categories, that the primary activity of these students from Sunday afternoon through Friday morning was studying, and that from Friday afternoon through Sunday afternoon the primary activity was socializing. Surprisingly, the activities that took place Sunday afternoon through Friday morning were not all that different from the activities that took place during the remainder of the week—at least as viewed by an outsider. Brown students, however, perceived and acted on them as being fundamentally different.

The category of "social time" on Friday night and Saturday night included such activities as going to sports events, going to movies, going to parties, "hanging out," going to eat. The category of "study time" during the rest of the week was divided into three segments: "studying," "time spent in class," and "study breaks." "Studying" consisted of such activities as "reading on my bed," "reading at my desk," "reading in the library," "studying in the library," "doing a problem set," "reviewing for an exam," and "writing a paper." We found that, on the average, students spent about ten hours a week on such "studying" activities. Additionally, students said that they did two kinds of study: "serious" study and "social" study. The distinction drawn here is best exemplified by one student's response when asked how much studying she did.

> How much actual studying, or how much time do I sit at my desk daydreaming and pretending to study? . . . [I study at my desk] maybe like five hours a day, but I don't [really] study that much. I write letters, and I listen to music, and then sometimes I study. . . . When I am in my room studying, like if I study in my room for two hours, I might actually get 45 minutes of studying done, because people come in and talk so you are sitting at your desk pretending to study but you are really socializing.

Oddly, freshmen did not generally see the time that they spent in class as being an integral part of studying, and they frequently skipped classes, especially discussion section.

"Study breaks," which seemed to take up the most time from Sunday night through Friday, included all of the same activities that are included in the category of "social time." Students took study breaks when they were "fed up" with working, had "had it," or were just "tired." Also, a study break was something earned by working hard. Such phrases as "I deserve to take a study break" or "I have gotten to the point where I need to take a study break" were not unusual. On several occasions students were known to have spent the whole night on a study break. The next day, when asked what they did the night before, they answered, of course, "I studied." During "study time" students are supposed to study. To their way of thinking, they do.

On just about any day of the week, students went to parties, to the movies with friends, out to eat, over to friends' rooms to "hang out," but the way they framed these activities on different days varied. For example, going to a movie on a Wednesday evening might have been considered a "study break," whereas going to a movie on a Saturday would not be considered a study break because Saturday was designated for social activities.

Students performed two different acts in "going to the movies" on Wednesday or "going to the movies" on Saturday, although to the outsider it appeared as the same act done on different days. "Study time" had meaning to them in the sense that it directed the action. "Going to the movies" meant different things during "social time" and "study time." If the student went to the movies during study time, then the action of going to the movies was viewed as a short-term respite from the ongoing action of studying. The action of going to the movies was seen as having the function of bringing the student back to a place where it was possible to study. The explicit aim of "free time" was to relax, which in most cases means avoiding study. In this context, movie-going is seen as a part of relaxing, "having fun," "hanging out" with friends.

Study breaks had another important function: they were a frame within which students could discuss academic subjects informally with one another. For example, during a pizza study break students covered a variety of topics related to their current class assignments. One student discussed a political science paper, another tried to figure out how to approach a paper topic in a literature course, and yet another student discussed topics in a geology course. Oddly, students did not view this informal discussion time as studious activity in the way that they did "sitting at their desks."

Students discussed academic problems informally all semester. They seemed continually aware of their assignments, and they used the informal and social nature of the study break to play with ideas and to develop their thoughts for a later time, when they would actually use them in either an examination, a formal discussion, or a paper.

Study breaks were an integral part of study time. Indeed, students often spent more time on study breaks than they spent studying. Because study breaks were a social activity, it appeared to the outsiders that students goofed off a lot. Clearly, the study break, as defined by the student, was actually study time. The academic problems that the students worked out during a break could not be worked out in more formal settings or on their own. The study break was a secure environment for testing ideas.

During "social time," however, the student avoided studying. Indeed, those who tried to study during this time were pressured by peers not to study—particularly on Friday and Saturday nights. People caught studying at these times were verbally forced into non-study behavior by "dorm mates." This is exemplified by a conversation that was overheard at Ford Hall:

Student A: What are you doing studying on a Friday night. Let's go out and party.

Student B: No I can't. I have this paper due on Monday and I'll never get it done if I go with you over to Ellen's and party.

Student A: Oh come on! You don't really have that much to do. I wrote a five-page paper last Sunday night for Philosophy with no problem so I know that you can do it too. Chip and Fluffy are coming too and they'll be disappointed if you don't come. At least come up and have a quick beer and then you can decide.

In the end, Student B decided to go have a beer, and she never went back to her room to work on the paper. If one person did not succeed at talking the student into partying, reinforcements were sometimes brought in to convince the student to go to the party. In other instances, students even started a party in the violator's room to prevent him or her from studying.

There were several factors operating in these situations. As an example, take the first instance in which the student was coerced into partying. First the student was challenged because she was working on a Friday night—she was violating a time category. Second, we can see by her response that she had calculated her time and felt that she needed the extra time afforded by the weekend—"non-study" time in the student's mind—to complete the task. The response of the other student illustrated that she was wrong in her expectation about the amount of time required to write the paper. He claimed to have written a five-page paper the previous Sunday. Furthermore, he went on to say that it was for his Philosophy class. In their world this translated as an assignment for a "hard" class, not a "B.S." class. He then brought in another dimension—significant others. He told the woman that her friends Chip and Fluffy would be there. Without allowing the woman to say "no," the young man took yet another tack by offering a compromise: he suggested that she take only a short break for a drink. The implication was that she could then just drift back downstairs. Once upstairs with her peers, however, she would not stand much chance of escaping.

Conversely, people who attempted to disrupt the residence hall environment during the week with loud music, games, and partying faced another set of problems. Although it was recognized that most of these activities constituted a "study break" for the student, the atmosphere in which they were done was extremely different. On weekends, such activities were usually open and loud. During the week, however, the tendency was to keep these activities under control. Through the social network, most people knew when and where things were happening (who was going to the movies when, who might have been polishing off a case of beer or smoking marijuana). Study-time parties were not advertised, nor were they usually in violation of another person's rights to study. On the rare occasion when studying rights were violated, a request by the studying student to the violator was usually sufficient. If it wasn't, the resident counselors were called in.

There was another set of activities that crosscut the two major time categories: "extracurricular" activities, which could be both educational and social, but did not necessarily fall neatly into either study or social time. Freshman year at Brown is largely a time for experimentation. Many of the students were involved with a variety of nonacademic and academic clubs, which ran the gamut from the sailing club to the Society for Creative Anachronism to CIAO (keeping the CIA off campus). Some of these activities took up an enormous amount of time.

There are a few possible explanations for why freshmen saw their time divided into study time and social time, even though the activities during the different periods were not inherently different. One obvious explanation derives from the course schedule. There were no classes held on Saturday or Sunday, so there was no pressure on Friday and Saturday nights for the students to get work done.

Another explanation may lie in expectations of what college is supposed to be like. Most come to college thinking that they should study all the time. This view is represented in statements made by students, such as "I'm not exactly sure what I am going to do when I get done with my education at Brown. All I know is for now I have to study and study hard. I mean, that is why I am here." People come to college to get an education for the unknown future. Typically, the way that one achieves this desired goal is to study. Because students think they ought to be studying all the time, they sometimes say they are studying when they aren't.

A third possible explanation may be found in the way the students categorized their time in high school. Most said that there were several things that were different about college life: (1) their mother wasn't there, (2) they weren't in classes all day long, (3) they had classes at all hours of the day, and (4) college work was more difficult and more interesting than the work they did in high school. In short, they had much more freedom in college than they did in high school.

To give us a better idea of what he meant about the differences, one freshman gave us an example of how he spent his time when he was in high school:

In high school I would be in school from nine in the morning until three. Here, I am in school from nine to twelve. And I would have class everyday, and it was less work every night but more tedious during the day in class and stuff. Here, the work, if you let yourself get behind in the work, it seems like a lot of quantity, but I guess if you do it when you are supposed to do it, it is not that much. . . . It is a lot different socially. I guess the big difference is that on week nights in high school you are isolated and you did whatever it is that you do after school. I was involved in a couple of things after school in high school, and then you go home. And then from say 6 o'clock until you go to bed you are by yourself. Here you have say 49 people of your own age around and that is the social environment. There is always somebody around if you want to take a break from studying. . . . On the weekends I guess there is not much difference. A lot of people here like to go out and drink on weekends and a lot of people in high school like to go out and drink on weekends.

The striking feature of this passage is that it reveals the same time categories that we have found among the freshmen at Ford Hall—parties on the weekends, studying during the week. What has been introduced since high school is an enhanced social environment that allows "study breaks." Therefore, perhaps freshmen time categories are a carry-over from high school.

OTHER TIME EVENTS

Although "study time" and "social time" are two of the primary structuring time frames within which the students operate, there are others that affect the students' strategies of organization and pacing within these two time units. These are the semester and the day.

The Semester

The semester is the imposed time frame within which the student operates. At Brown, the semester is 16 weeks. The semester has a cycle of its own over which the student has little control. There is a beginning, a middle, and an end. Within this framework students have to choose, plan, and prioritize their activities. Assignment due dates largely regulate the flow of the semester for students and directly affect the "study time" and "study break" process. Many classes require that work be handed in regularly, whereas others require it sporadically. Usually, the most time-consuming assignments are due at the end of the semester.

The events that lie between the beginning and the end of the semester are somewhat random. Aside from classes there are no regularly recurring events. Assignment due dates and exams drive the time frame. This in turn is determined by which courses the students have chosen. Additionally, the students must juggle time and resource demands.

Most freshmen are not semester planners; they plan for the student week. As a consequence, they end up working intensively in spurts around mid-semester and at the end of the semester.

The Day

The final unit of time is the day. The structure of the day is highly dependent on how it fits into "study time" and "social time." Each day is then framed by these notions. "Social study" (studying with other people) and "study breaks" are fluid components of "study time" that occur randomly during the course of the day. Freshmen are not very good at estimating how much time any one studying activity will take, so they are not as skilled as they might be at apportioning time.

Within the day there are better times to study than others. Most social study occurs in the evening, whereas individual study occurs in the afternoon and late night. Classes, a daytime activity primarily, are not a primary time frame within which the students operate. Classes can be turned into study break time for any number of reasons, including "I worked hard last night, I don't need to go to class today" or "I don't feel like going— I think I will just read the material instead."

These explanations embody two important concepts that were mentioned earlier. In the first, we can see evidence of the notion of deserving a study break. After a large effort has been put into an assignment, a break is deserved. We saw this on smaller scale when we discussed regular reading assignments. After reading so many pages, the person can justify taking a study break. On larger assignments where a product is due, the reward is greater. We can also see the importance placed on critical due dates as opposed to classes. Classes are not necessarily critical for students to complete their assignments, and as such, they can be missed. Students do only what is necessary; they read only what they have to; they attend class only if it is necessary to. The necessity of an activity is directly related to whether the students will be evaluated on the basis of their performance.

Related to this, we can see in the second explanation that replacement strategies are in operation. If a lecture is the same as a reading, then it is possible, depending on how the person is evaluated in the course, to skip one or the other.

The student day is not one that is governed by a clock; rather, the number and type of activities that a student has to do govern its flow. Certain amounts of text have to be read, papers written, exams reviewed for, and classes attended, but these are not time-bound events—they are activities that shape the day.

Study can occur in the morning, afternoon, evening, or late night; it doesn't matter to the student. Their concept of when a day begins or ends is not dependent on a clock, but on what they have to do. Consequently, when they are studying, they are in many ways unaware of hours of the day or night, but they are aware of tasks that must be accomplished—tasks that are often done at the expense of sleep.

Many students find themselves "cycling" through days. Cycling refers to being completely off a "normal" schedule; that is, their work and sleep patterns do not reflect those of the outside world (i.e., working until 4 a.m., getting up at 8 a.m., sleeping again from 2 to 4 p.m., then working again until 3 or 4 a.m., and repeating the cycle). The pattern most often develops during crisis times, although some students operate on this kind of schedule more or less all the time. By examining the temporal orientation, we can see the effects of living by "study time."

TEMPORAL ORIENTATION

In the previous section we discussed some of the overarching categories and units of time for the student, but we have neglected to discuss their temporal orientations. Temporal orientations often pique the interest of anthropologists. A classic example of temporal orientation is found among the Iroquois; they see themselves as servants to the past and the future. Any decision made in the tribe requires asking, "How does the decision that we make today conform to the teaching of our ancestors and to the yearnings of our grandchildren?" (Lyons 1980). Thus, temporal orientation refers here to attitudes toward time—the value a people places on events occurring in the present and their relationship to events that took place in the past or that will happen in the future.

The students' temporal orientation differs dramatically from that of the Iroquois, as one might suspect. Students orient their activities to the present, the near future, and the distant future. The past is not very important when they are deciding how to spend their time. Their perspective arises from the time structure of the semester and from their educational goals for the distant future. Student orientation to the future is reflected by goal setting and the means by which goals are achieved—both short-term and long-term—whereas orientation to the present is reflected in what must be done right now to get the grades that will allow long-term goals to be realized.

First, there is the immediate goal of getting a grade. Although Becker et al. (1968) formulated the idea that all student life revolves around the grade, this is not true for the students at Brown, at least not in terms that Becker described. Instead of the grade being the currency of the campus, as Becker suggests, the grade has other meanings. At Brown there is no grade lower than a C. It is impossible to have a failing grade. Yes, a student can "flunk," but then that course is dropped from the record. To get above a C is the driving force. The search for the B shapes the student's attitude toward the present. Students do what has to be done "now" to get the B at the end of the semester, which will in turn give them passage to their professional careers in the distant future.

The quest for the B had ramifications for interaction in the residence hall. Because as we mentioned earlier, the events of the semester are somewhat randomly dispersed, with pockets of crisis, students in the residence hall developed an interactional style that allowed them to ask other residents for help. Crises for students led to the need for help "right now." "Right now" could be at three o'clock in the morning or at one o'clock in the afternoon. A crisis could be needing help retrieving something on the computer, needing to work out an idea for a paper that was due the next day, getting information that could help on an exam, or getting assistance with a problem set. By "knowing" everyone in the residence hall students were able to seek help or just talk to anyone they came into contact with in the building. Other students were important academic resources when it came to periods of or even moments of crisis.

Students at Ford Hall lived in a present-oriented world, like the pioneers of old—facing unknown hardships each day that seemed to emerge from no place. And like pioneers, they did not cross the wilderness (college) alone, but in a "wagon train" (the residence hall) with others who were going through the same experience, who helped when they were able, and who, in return, asked for help when they needed it.

Is every moment a crisis time, a time when students need help? No. Students are, in many ways, much more like farmers in their time orientation than the 9-to-5 workers we mentioned earlier. The farmer, like the student, sometimes has to work from dawn until dusk, and at other times hardly at all. His clock, like the student's clock, depends on tasks that have to be done. Crises often hit farmers all at once, and so too for students; they are barraged at times with crises—papers, exams, and so forth.

The future is what comes at the end of the semester and lies beyond school. The student's orientation toward the future goes far beyond school, but it relates to the courses chosen in school. In choosing courses, students ask themselves two future-oriented questions: (1) "Does this course make me a more well-rounded person?" and (2) "Will this course assist me in fulfilling my career choices?" The second question is secondary to the first for freshmen. Students use these long-term goals to select courses. Once courses are selected, these goals determine the amount of time students will spend working on course-related activities. The amount of time allotted to a particular course-related activity depends primarily on the course's importance to career goals, and then on the student's personal interest in the course and desire to get a good grade.

INTERVENTION OF THE COMPUTER

Because we did not have a control group residence hall, and because this was not a pre-test/post-test situation, we are unable to make conclusive claims about changes brought about by the computer. The data we present here about possible changes in how students use and view "time" and "studying" are based on what students reported themselves about how the computer changed their work and play patterns. Primarily, the computer, as it was integrated into the residence hall during the course of the year, provides another example of how students understood and manipulated the fundamental categories of time.

The computer is potentially valuable to students, especially because of their particular orientation toward time. The computer can increase the amount of work that students do within bounded periods of time. When students are under a crunch and have to work in crisis mode, they need a tool that allows them to increase the rate at which they work. Just as pioneer farmers needed better plows at planting time, and better equipment at harvest time, when more intensive labor was required, students need tools that allow them to complete their work more efficiently at times of crisis. Unfortunately, at Ford Hall, the computers were not as helpful to students during crisis times as they might have been.

For example, a primary crisis time in the residence hall came during midterms and finals. Students "crammed" the night before an exam so that the information learned would be recalled more easily at the time of the exam. At Ford Hall, the computer did not facilitate studying for exams. Only when computers are an integrated feature of a course are they used as tools for study in this way (Beeman et al. 1988).

The computer was useful for routine writing assignments and major term papers. As described previously, students "talked through" their papers and developed their ideas long before they wrote them. We found out that this informal talking often took place while students were in their rooms studying with friends or during meals. Having the computer immediately available, or available soon after a late night "study break," allowed students to write things down in an unstructured form that could later be included or developed into a larger corpus.

Furthermore, in the actual production, our data show that students usually had papers done further in advance than they did formerly, so they had time to revise. One of the most common claims students made was that it allowed them to redistribute time from one stage of writing to another. The time they used to spend typing the final draft of a paper could now be used for editing and revising:

> Let's say that I write my rough draft and it has been five hours recopying that paper. That is absolutely busy work. . . . I can spend those five hours . . . actually going over the paper . . . rereading it . . . going away from it for a while, coming back and rereading it. I can do that and make minor adjustments.

Students felt that revisions were less laborious when done on the computer. Even students who wrote their first drafts by hand (because they did not feel comfortable composing on the computer) liked rewriting on the computer and felt that it saved an enormous amount of time. A paper was no longer finished once the assigned number of pages had been typed. To further illustrate this point, when students' papers were a page longer than was assigned, with only a couple hours left before it was due, they were able to (1) edit it easily or (2) play with the type style and formatting. Over the year, students became increasingly interested in making their papers good in form as well as in content.

As we have mentioned, student schedules are erratic in many ways. The personal computer is useful for students because it can be used at any time of the day or night. As we have described, students tend to write at night, and often late into the night. Unlike students using the public areas at Brown, the students at Ford Hall were able to use the computer whenever they wished; they were not tied to the institutional restrictions that apply at the clusters. The advantages of this situation were explained by a student from Ford:

> Well, for writing papers, having a computer in your room, you can use it at any time, at any time of night and not have to worry about going over and walking some place, worrying about whether or not you are going to get a computer or have to wait for a computer. And with the printer downstairs, you just print out and you can go. A lot of times it is ten minutes before you have to get to class and you finish up the last thing and you print it out and go, which wouldn't be possible otherwise.

Accessibility to computers is important. Crises tend to come up for groups of students at the same time; they are not spread out. Personal computers in individual rooms reduce the competition for resources. Nothing is more detrimental to students than not having access to the materials necessary for writing a paper. Often, there are long waits to use equipment at computer clusters on campus. Even when the student finally gets on the computer, he or she has a limited amount of time. As a consequence, computers are often used only as typewriters at the clusters, rather than as tools for writing.

We have focused on how the computer is useful for the students at the residence hall when they are in "crisis mode," but the computer has served several other important purposes as well. As we pointed out, "study time" includes "serious study," "pretend study," "study breaks," and "classes." The computer has played a role for the students in each of these categories.

In discussing the computer with respect to "crisis times" in the residence hall, we have touched on some of the ways it has entered into serious study time and the ways that it integrated with classes, but there are several other aspects of computer use.

One curious phenomenon that we discovered is that students used the computer as a "warm-up" for doing "serious study." Warming up to study consisted of reading and sending electronic mail or playing a quick computer game. These two activities also fall under the category of "pretend study"—those occasions when students sit at their desks intending to study, but end up daydreaming, writing notes, and so on. Being occupied at the desk gives the activity a feeling of studying. The computer activities also appear under the category of "study break." The student has been studying and takes a break on the computer. One student explained:

> Sometimes when I get tired of studying I just sit and make pictures [on the computer]. I need a break from work. . . . I love being able to sit at my own desk in my own room to create them. It's one of the best things about having the computer here.

Computer games were a primary way to take a "study break" at Ford Hall. They were much less time consuming and expensive than a movie or a pizza. As such, the computer provided the student with a valuable new tool for study breaks. One did not have to spend large amounts of time on it, although some computer games were more involved than others. Regardless of what game the student played, he or she had control over the duration. The types of computer games with which students took breaks generally required little thought, and yet they were engaging enough to constitute actual breaks. These breaks differed considerably from the formally held breaks in which the students worked out their academic problems with others. Playing a computer game is genuinely a break from thinking about academic subjects.

In the previous section we discussed how an ethic of "knowing others" arose at Ford. It was important for students in the residence hall to get to know one another. The computer arrangement at Ford Hall, rather than having an isolating effect, promoted different types of social behavior; it opened a new avenue for meeting, communicating, and playing with other students in the residence hall.

As we mentioned, Snipes was one of the games on the computer network. It is a group game requiring a certain amount of coordination. Six players play at once, all logging on to their computers at the same time. Students at Ford created a communication network in their building that facilitated this process. "Runners" were stationed at the stairwell entries. They would count down so that the individual players could log on to the computer at the same time. One student explained how it worked:

> Snipes was fantastic, I mean, just the idea of six people playing each other, you know, in a hunt-chase, hunt-and-kill game throughout the dorm. It's like, we used to yell down the hall, "Okay, we're starting now! Everybody log on . . . Go!" And it was it was, like, you could hear yells down the hall, and it was a lot of fun.

Students played other games together too—games that were not on the network. Not only did they compete with one another at these games, but they also worked together to develop strategies to win, or they just sat with a person who was playing for the vicarious thrill it provided. The ultimate goal was not to beat your friends, but to beat the machine.

Besides the games, another social component was provided to the student through the new medium of electronic communication. Students used the mail system at Ford Hall in a variety of ways. Some people were "heavy" users, using the system every day for sending and receiving personal messages from friends in the building. Others used computer mail only to check on "happenings" in the residence hall through postings or announcements on the mail system. The kinds of things that could be posted varied from the sale of bicycles (public notices) to people seeking rides (requests for assistance) to debates about political candidates (opinion forums).

Although all the students had access to the campus-wide mainframe computing system that has a mail system of its own, only four freshmen had used it by the end of the first semester. Even then, they were not using it extensively, but on a weekly basis. Here, once again, we feel that the "knowing others" ethic comes into play. Although the campus-wide mailing service offered the student access to every person on campus, and through BITNET and ARPANET access to people around the world, it was not used much.[d] The reason is clear—most of the people to whom they wanted to send e-mail were in their residence hall. These people were the people they needed to "know" to survive.

Aside from communication channels opened by e-mail, other new communication channels were spontaneously opened with the presence of computers in Ford Hall. For example, an unexpected consequence of having a common area for the printers was that students would run into one another when picking up printed material. This time allowed just one more opportunity, which did not exist before, to "get to know" others in the residence hall. The following example illustrates this phenomenon:

> I was working on a paper that was due at 9 a.m. and I didn't want to stay up all night. I just wanted to get the thing done. I shut my door, I worked on the machine as stand alone until I had to print so no one knew I was there. I didn't even turn on my stereo. Then I printed and headed down to pick up my output to see what I had done. I went out the door and made it as far as the printer before I was compelled into conversation. Normally it probably takes about three minutes to make it from my room down to the printer. That night it was like running a gauntlet because I ran into so many people. It ended up taking me an hour. I was waiting for the paper [to come out of the printer]. My paper was behind a couple others. One of them was Robin's. Robin and a couple others convinced me to go credit [go get a snack] and then come back. Since my paper wasn't coming out right away I did. But I have never made it down to the printer and back without seeing someone.

Another spontaneous channel of communication sprang up. The friends of students who did not live in Ford Hall frequently came to use the facilities there.

---

d. The acronym *BITNET* stands for the *Because It's Time/Because It's There Network*. This network was created in 1981 to connect IBM computing centers around the world. It was a cooperative network in which members could pass traffic to other sites for free, and software developed by one was made available to all. By 1994 BITNET encompassed over 1,400 organizations in 49 countries around the world. The acronym *ARPANET* stands for the *Advanced Research Projects Agency Network*. The precursor to the Internet, this network was developed in the late 1960s and early 1970s by the U.S. Department of Defense as an experiment in wide-area-networking that was intended to survive a nuclear war. Neither of these networks is currently in operation.

The examples we have shown here illustrate that the computers in Ford Hall were used by the students in ways that were consistent with their fundamental understandings of "time" and "studying." For the students, having a computer in the room was as a beneficial tool, allowing them maximum flexibility in their work schedules. The computer has come to be more than a neutral tool that sits on students' desks; it has come to have social meaning as an object that is understood and used in the social context of the residence hall.

CONCLUSIONS

In this article we have drawn some conclusions about the way that students categorize their time and the strategies they use in accomplishing academic goals. We have presented the freshmen as sharing a particular orientation toward time and having specific strategies for dealing with it. Furthermore, we have drawn some conclusions about the ways that the computer fits into these time constructs.

We have argued that technological innovations in education warrant the attention that ideological innovations have received, and that the resulting changes must be considered if we are to understand student life from the student perspective. As we have shown, the student perspective differs markedly from the outsider's perspective. We have discovered that there are problems with implementing technical innovations when it is assumed that students operate on a schedule that is the same as the rest of the world's. People in the world do not necessarily share a concept of "time" or "work"— not even all Americans share such concepts.

The student world is one full of randomly interwoven events over which students have little control. Students must respond and develop specific time strategies that will allow them to accomplish immediate tasks and long-term goals. Personal computers fit well into the student world when implemented appropriately. We have attempted to show that students' concepts of time and studying result in certain types of actions, and that their categories are not merely linguistic. Understanding the meaning of these categories and their resultant actions may allow us to understand the process of the adaptation of innovations by society.

Kenneth T. Anderson and Anne Page McClard are doctoral candidates at Brown University.

Notes

Acknowledgments. The research reported here was supported by a Joint Study Grant from Brown University and IBM. We gratefully acknowledge their support. We also thank the 1987–88 freshmen of Ford Hall who invited us into their lives.

References Cited

Becker, Howard S., Blanche Geer, and Everett C. Hughes. 1968. Making the Grade: The Academic Side of College Life. New York: John Wiley.

Beeman, W. O., K. Anderson, G. Bader, J. Larkin, A. McClard, and P. McQuillan. 1988. Intermedia: A Case Study of Innovation in Higher Education. Final Report to The Annenberg/CPB Project on A Network of Scholars Workstations in a University Environment: A New Medium for Research and Education. Providence, RI: Office of Program Analysis, Institution for Information and Scholarship, Brown University.

Bloom, Allan. 1987. The Closing of the American Mind: How Higher Education Has Failed Democracy and Impoverished the Souls of Today's Students. New York: Simon & Schuster.

Boyer, Ernest L. 1987. College: The Undergraduate Experience in America. New York: Harper & Row.

Hallowell, A. Irving. 1937. "The Temporal Orientation in Western Civilization and in Preliterate Society." American Anthropologist 39(4):647–670.

Hirsch, E. D., Jr. 1987. Cultural Literacy: What Every American Needs to Know. Boston, MA: Houghton Mifflin.

Lyons, Oren. 1980. "An Iroquois Perspective." In American Indian Environments: Ecological Issues in Native American History. Pp. 171–174. Christopher Yecsey and Robert Venables, eds. New York: Syracuse University Press.

Ottinger, Cecilia A., Comp. 1987. Fact Book on Higher Education. New York: Macmillan.

Critical-Theory Research

Paula Corrado teaches language arts at a culturally diverse middle school in Chicago. In a graduate course on bilingual and multilingual education, she explored the complexities involved in helping children from different cultures honor their own language while learning another language. She also learned about the efforts of a group of educators who, by insisting on challenging oppression, are day by day striving to make schools and society better places for all.

Paula devised a project to modify her teaching strategies. She shared with a colleague that although she felt she couldn't solve the world's problems, she could start with herself and the students in her class.

As part of her project, Paula made up a list of "will do's" and "won't do's" for herself. It included these ideas:

WILL DO:
Respect the culture of each student by encouraging students to write about their own families and cultural traditions.
Post assignments and class rules in multiple languages all around the classroom.
Provide activities each day in which all students can speak in their own language.
Provide books in all the languages of my students.

WILL NOT DO:
Not make assumptions about "language difficulties" for bilingual students who are in the process of acquiring English.
Not use labels for students who are not yet able to learn in English.
Not make judgments about any student based on any test that is not in the student's native language.

Paula has asked another teacher in her school to help her critically observe and collect data to see whether her action

OBJECTIVES

After studying this chapter, you will be able to

1. describe the goals and underlying assumptions of critical theory as applied to educational research.

2. explain the meanings of hegemony, voice, and internalized oppression from the critical-theory perspective.

3. list the various bases of cultural oppression on which criticalists have focused in their research.

4. describe one way in which the cultural context of capitalist production and consumption has affected U.S. students' education.

5. give an example of how the educational system has tended to reproduce the cultural oppression of nonprivileged groups.

6. describe the methods of inquiry used by researchers who work within the critical-theory framework.

7. explain the unique perspective that critical theory offers to the study of educational phenomena.

8. give possible reasons why critical theory has not had a greater impact on educational research and practice.

commitments will help her students whose first language is other than English become more engaged and successful learners. She also wants to discover what other questions she needs to ask and changes she needs to make to counter her own and her students' stereotypes about their capacity to learn.

Educators who learn about critical theory often find that new light has been shone on their professional practice, revealing tensions and possibilities that may have been only dimly felt before. In this chapter you will learn how critical theory can be applied to both educational research and practice, and the benefits of doing so. ●

KEY TERMS

agency	dialogical data generation	norms
anti-oppressive education	emancipation	objective truth claims
border pedagogy	feminisms	postmodernism
conscientization	hegemony	privilege
critical ethnography	hidden curriculum	reconstructive analysis
critical pedagogy	instrumental rationality	reproduction
criticalist	internalized oppression	subjective truth claims
cultural studies	monological data collection	text
deconstruction	normative-evaluative	troubling
	truth claims	voice

THE PURPOSE OF CRITICAL-THEORY RESEARCH IN EDUCATION

Critical-theory research involves a broad range of methods aimed at uncovering the detrimental effects of unequal power relationships in cultures and in the global community. Through critical inquiry it seeks to emancipate individuals from the many forms of oppression that exist in the world. Developed primarily in Europe and Latin America, critical-theory research has much to contribute to educational research and practice in the United States.

Anti-Oppressive Education

Critical-theory research in education can be regarded as one form of the broader field of **anti-oppressive education.** As Kevin Kumashiro (2002) asserts, anti-oppressive education "involves constantly *looking beyond* what we teach and learn" (p. 6). It thereby serves the critical purpose of **troubling** education and educational research by exposing the assumptions underlying widely accepted but oppressive cultural practices that traditional educational practices help maintain.

ASSUMPTIONS OF A CRITICALIST

Joe Kincheloe and Peter McLaren (1994) list seven basic assumptions that are accepted by a **criticalist,** that is, "a researcher or theorist who attempts to use her or his work as a form of social or cultural criticism" (p. 139). We explain these assumptions below, paraphrasing them to foster understanding and giving examples of their implications for educational research and practice.

1. *Every society systematically gives privileges to certain cultural groups and oppresses other cultural groups.* If a cultural group is **privileged,** this means that its members enjoy greater power, resources, and life opportunities than the members of other cultural groups. Such privilege is reinforced through both hegemony and internalized oppression. **Hegemony** refers to the ways in which privileged cultural groups maintain domination over other groups through various cultural agencies that exert power, in particular the political, criminal justice, and educational systems, according to McLaren (2003).

Internalized oppression refers to the phenomenon by which individuals unwittingly help maintain their lack of privilege through thoughts and actions consistent with their lesser social status. Through this process, **reproduction** of their oppression occurs as new members who are born to or join the culture accept the preexisting patterns of cultural inequity. McLaren (1998) argues that hegemony involves "a struggle in which the powerful win the consent of those who are oppressed, with the oppressed unknowingly participating in their own oppression" (p. 182).

Critical theory seeks to disclose the true interests (i.e., the needs, concerns, and advantages) of different groups and individuals. Those who are privileged always have an interest in preserving the status quo in order to protect their advantages. Critical theory strives to highlight the sense of frustration and powerlessness that nonprivileged groups feel with respect to their opportunities to realize their potential, and to provide insight to guide them toward greater autonomy and, ultimately, emancipation. **Emancipation** is a process of generating actions and changes in consciousness of and toward the members of oppressed cultural groups that help free them from their oppression.

2. *The oppression experienced by an individual is an interactive combination of the various oppressions generated in response to all that individual's nonprivileged identities.* Criticalists argue that the tendency to focus on one basis of oppression (for example, racism) obscures the connections among different forms of oppression and the weight of their joint operation in a given individual's life. To understand and combat oppression, they believe it is necessary to examine all the cultural categories that operate to separate and oppress people and to examine their joint effects.

In his book *Troubling Education,* Kumashiro (2002) uses the stories of queer activists whom he interviewed to illustrate this phenomenon by "reading" their multiple identities, cultures, and experiences of oppression. Through a poetic rendering of the story of Pab, a teenage activist born in Nepal who now lives in the

United States and identifies as a lesbian, Kumashiro demonstrates the "impossibility of identity" that queer Asian American women experience. Caught up in the conflicting cultural expectations involving Asian, Asian American, female, and heterosexual identities, Pab, like other Asian American women who are queer, is "often invisible both in Asian American communities and mainstream society" (p. 95).

3. *Cultural texts (including but not limited to language) are probably the most powerful means of expressing and maintaining differences in privilege.* Criticalists view any discourse, object, or event as having communicative value and thus able to be analyzed as a **"text"**: comic books, songs on the Internet, or product packaging; signs such as the flagpole outside a school; and events as perceived by others, such as a gay rights march or a confrontation between a traffic cop and a car driver.

Individuals' awareness can be either expanded or constrained by the language they use to encode their experience. The formal and informal language in classrooms, or instructional programs involving different forms of discourse (such as bilingual education or whole-language instruction) are examples of how educators use language to maintain or contest hegemony.

Criticalists use the concept of voice to study particular expressions of domination or oppression in the educational system (Giroux, 1992). **Voice** refers to the degree to which individuals occupying particular social categories or identities are privileged, silenced, muted, or empowered through the operations of discourses that maintain or contest dominant and subordinate cultures in a society.

In her book on critical pedagogy, Joan Wink (2000) gives dozens of examples of how teachers' use of language empowers or disempowers certain individuals every day. Wink's explanation of **conscientization,** namely, "knowing we know and [having] the voice and the courage to question ourselves and the role we are playing in maintaining educational processes that we do not value" (p. 37), provides the following example.

Rainey and Carmen, two teachers in a school with a high proportion of Latino students, were discussing family involvement. Rainey was a new teacher who had never been around Mexican kids before, but who really wanted to learn and help her kids learn. Carmen taught in Spanish and had been around Mexican kids all her life. During their talk Rainey said she would be willing to do a computer search of the university library holdings about what Latino families need. Carmen nodded and added, "Or, we could ask the families." At the next family meeting, the teachers asked, and the families told them their needs.

4. *Every human act, creation, or communication can be interpreted in relation to the cultural context of capitalist production and consumption.* Criticalists believe that the form and content of most texts reflect the values of the dominant culture and are consistent with standards derived from a capitalist value framework. Viewing most of the texts in education and research as problematic (that is, tending to misrepresent individual's lived experience) they subject such texts to **deconstruction.** In deconstructing a teacher's letter to parents, for example, they would examine the connotations of each term, opening the text to multiple interpretations, with none privileged over any other.

Take professional sports as another example of a cultural text to be deconstructed. Most of us regard football games and golf tournaments on television as a form of entertainment or a break from work. Now consider this deconstruction by Pierre Bourdieu (1991):

> More than by the encouragement it gives to chauvinism and sexism, it is undoubtedly through the division it makes between professionals, the virtuosi of an esoteric technique, and laymen, reduced to the role of mere consumers, a division that tends to become a deep structure of the collective consciousness, that sport produces its most decisive political effects. (p. 364)

Criticalists are at the forefront in investigating educational influences in society beyond those of schools, particularly the products of popular corporate culture. Increasingly, the common discourse and interests of young people (and perhaps most people) lie in what is loosely called the "entertainment media," including movies, songs, and even advertising. In *Kinderculture: The Corporate Construction of Childhood,* Shirley Steinberg and Joe Kincheloe (1997) argue that the prevailing economic and technological climate in the United States has created a "crisis of childhood." They document, and preview, the increasing role of corporations as educators of children through the permeation of corporate products, images, and messages within as well as outside the schools. *Kinderculture* makes a strong case that the impact of corporate culture on education requires a new response from educators who have clung to traditional forms of cultural transmission (see Chapter 11) in the design of curriculum and pedagogy.

Criticalists even question the authority of their own emancipatory agenda by deconstructing the statements used to express that agenda. They emphasize that there is never one essential, universal answer to any issue, but that a key role of education is to encourage continual questioning and discussion of the meaning and impact of such issues.

5. *All thought is mediated by socially and historically constructed power relations.* In the context of education, this assumption implies that the beliefs and activities of students, teachers, and the other groups involved in education are inevitably affected by their experiences with power and dominance, both within and outside the educational system. Thus, the particular beliefs and activities of such groups or individuals can only be understood in reference to the unique context in which they occur. For example, say that a student ignores a teacher's command to stop talking in class. Depending on students' views of the teacher, their history of experience with that particular classmate, and what is occurring in the classroom at the moment the teacher utters his command, some students might regard the student who keeps talking as a trouble maker, while others might see the student as a buddy or a hero.

Any text can be subjected to contextual analysis to determine how it reflects power relations. For example, McLaren (2003) argues that multiculturalism (a movement aimed at improving relationships among students of different cultures and their conformance to society's educational expectations) is still largely a mainstream, progressive agenda, exceedingly important but conceptually and politically compromised from the start.

6. *Facts can never be isolated from the domain of values and prevailing assumptions about what is valued.* Critical-theory research rejects the notion that research about teaching and learning can ever be a neutral or value-free process. Indeed, criticalists question the notion of objective reality itself. Like other qualitative researchers, criticalists believe that all so-called facts about human nature and behavior are socially constructed, thus open to many interpretations, and modifiable through human action.

Critical theory is often associated with postmodernism. In Chapter 1 we explained that **postmodernism** is a philosophy based on the assertion that no one approach to developing knowledge about the human world is privileged over (that is, better than) any other. Criticalists are skeptical of any theory or method that claims to have timeless or universal application to understanding or improving the human condition. However, they remain committed to forms of social inquiry and action that promote the emancipation of nonprivileged individuals and groups, thereby affirming what Kincheloe and McLaren (1994) call "resistance postmodernism" (p. 144).

Criticalists also argue that ideas about how teaching and learning operate always involve preformed systems of values and beliefs, which usually reinforce the power of dominant groups in society. Criticalists like Michael Apple (2003) show that even the most seemingly "common-sense" educational concepts, such as achievement, reform, innovation, and standards, are categories constructed by, and serving the interests of, certain privileged groups in the educational hierarchy.

7. *Mainstream research practices help reproduce systems of oppression that are based on class, race, gender, and other cultural categories.* The majority of educational research has been carried out by middle- or upper-class white males using positivist epistemology. This research rests on assumptions about science, truth, and good that such researchers accept as universal. According to criticalists, such research has actually served to maintain the oppression of groups who represent other cultural categories. Criticalists particularly oppose educational research that focuses on prediction and control for the purpose of maximizing educational productivity. In their view, such research reflects the operation of **instrumental rationality,** a preoccupation with means over ends or purposes. Rex Gibson (1986) views the IQ testing movement as a key example of the shortcomings and injustices that this preoccupation involves:

> Instrumental rationality is the cast of thought which seeks to dominate others, which assumes its own rightness to do so, and which exercises its power to serve its own interests. Coldly following its narrow principle of efficiency and applying a crude economic yardstick, its results are all too obvious . . . the interests least served are those of comprehensive schools and pupils from working class homes. (pp. 8–9)

Criticalists thus spotlight problems that affect the members of nonprivileged groups at a much more personal and pervasive level than other groups. Yet they also help clarify the ways in which the members of other groups also suffer from the same problems. Education is meant to address the needs of every student. Educators therefore must attend to the increasingly negative consequences experienced by all the members of a culture, even those belonging to privileged groups, from cultural practices that privilege some and oppress others. For example, in his study of suburban youth, Ralph Larkin (1979) observed that:

> [Middle-class] students experience a two-fold alienation: from adult society wherein lies the power, and from each other as invidious competition and mobility undercut authenticity and understanding of each other. They are isolated as a class and as monadic individuals. Most lives are characterized by lack of depth. . . . They live at the surface, fearful yet desirous of what might happen should they "bust out" of their not quite Edenic existence . . . [they] are terrorized by their fears. (p. 210)

Despite the widespread effects and taken-for-granted nature of much cultural oppression, criticalists seek to balance their criticism with hope, and a deep belief that the emancipation of nonprivileged groups will improve the life conditions of all groups and individuals.

Some individuals denounce critical theory because of its critical view of capitalism, the worldwide spread of the market culture, and a politics in the United States and other Western societies that equates national well-being with domination of the global marketplace. However, critical theory stands "in opposition to crude material or economic determinism" (Seymour-Smith, 1986, p. 59). Thus, while it shares with Marxism a critique of the inequities of the capitalist system, it promotes democratic principles as the best way to discover and correct those inequities. The scholarship based on critical theory can stimulate much critical reflection about dominant forms of educational practice and research.

METHODS OF INQUIRY

Perhaps the only method common to the research and theory building of criticalists is critique—of the phenomenon being studied, of methodology, and of the researchers' own perspective and values. Philip Carspecken (1996) states:

> Criticalists find contemporary society to be unfair, unequal, and both subtly and overtly oppressive for many people. We do not like it, and we want to change it. (p. 7)

Below we describe several specific approaches to critical-theory research and practice that vary in their focus, goals, and level of structure: critical ethnography, based on Philip Carspecken's model; cultural studies; and three versions of critical pedagogy, which we label as (1) critical pedagogy in "the real world," (2) revolutionary critical pedagogy, and (3) grass-roots critical pedagogy.

Critical Ethnography

Critical ethnography is a structured approach to critical-theory research that uses the research methods of ethnography to investigate power relationships and forms of oppression in a culture. Thus it builds on, and seeks to build bridges with, other, more traditional research methods.

Philip Carspecken and Geoffrey Walford (2001) describe how critical ethnography seeks to critically explore cultural phenomena in ways that increase the likelihood of generating "validity truth claims" that are supportable.

Carspecken (1996) explains his use of critical ethnography in the evaluation of a program (Project TRUST) intended to develop inner-city elementary students' self-esteem and conflict-resolution skills. He states the overall research goal: "Making your research project as democratic as possible, from start to finish, is the best way to help rather than harm" (p. 207). He describes critical ethnography as involving preliminaries and five stages, summarized below.

Preliminaries.   Researchers first specify their research questions and make a list of items for study. For Project TRUST these included how student selection was handled and what the existing relationships were between project participants and the school and community in which the project was housed. Items to study included the ordinary social routines of Project TRUST participants. Researchers also need to explore their value orientations at the start of the study, in order to raise awareness of their biases and how to counter them.

Stage One: Compiling the Primary Record through Monological Data Collection.   **Monological data collection** means that only the researchers "speak" at this stage, writing the primary record from the perspective of uninvolved observers. They seek to be unobtrusive, observe passively, and produce a thick description of field participants' verbal and nonverbal behavior from the researchers' perspective. By using low-inference vocabulary, frequent time notations, and bracketed observer comments, they aim to produce objective data that are similar to what other observers would be likely to obtain and that thereby support **objective truth claims.**

Stage Two: Preliminary Reconstructive Analysis.   Now the researchers begin analyzing the primary record to determine interaction patterns and their apparent meaning. They "reconstruct" the information obtained in Stage One by specifying the cultural themes and system factors that can be derived from the primary record but are not usually articulated by the research participants. Researchers speculate about participants' **subjective truth claims** (what the participants themselves would say about what's going on). Researchers also ask participants to generate positions about their own **normative-evaluative truth claims** (claims involving assumptions about the world as it is or should be). In this stage participants often express new or unanticipated comments compared to their comments during Stage One.

Stage Three: Dialogical Data Generation.   Now the researchers engage in interviews and discussions with the research participants in order to test the validity of the participants' subjective and normative-evaluative truth claims. These new data often challenge information from previous stages, and give the people under study more control over the research process. A six-step typology of responses ranges from "bland encouragement" (low) to "high-inference paraphrasing" (high), corresponding to the extent to which the interviewer seeks to direct the participant's next response.

Stage Four: Discovering System Relationships.   During this stage researchers compare the findings from the specific site being investigated with findings from other sites involving a similar research focus. In Project TRUST one such system relationship involved the ways that individual students sought to "renegotiate" stressful classroom settings by their expressed dominance of or subordination to other students.

The type of system relationships that critical ethnography can discover is illustrated by Paul Willis's classic study (1977) of working-class "lads." Willis discovered correspondences, which he termed a *reproductive loop,* between the lads' behavior in three different social sites—the school, the home, and the job setting. He reported that the lads sought to avoid activities in school (e.g., doing the assigned work) that could conceivably help them to move out of the working class into the middle class, but which they viewed as a rejection of their home-based culture. In the home site, the lads' fathers had stayed within the working class in seeking work. The lads in turn moved into jobs involving physical labor when they left school.

Stage Five: Seeking Explanations of the Findings through Social-Theoretical Models.   The level of inference rises as the researchers seek to explain the findings from earlier stages by referring to existing or emerging system theories. The interests and power relations discovered at Stage Four now serve as explanatory factors. Researchers reflect on the symbolic and cultural meaning of the cultural products that affect the participants—for example, the video games, TV shows, and popular music that the Project TRUST students favored. Carspecken (1996) describes the difficult living conditions of the students and their families. He concludes: "Schools end up keeping children like those in the TRUST study off the streets, but the students [are] ill prepared to do anything but unskilled labor" (p. 206).

Cultural Studies

Cultural studies is a qualitative research tradition that cuts across traditional disciplines and invents new ones to explore the varied economic, legal, political, and other socially constructed underpinnings of cultural phenomena (Nelson, Treichler, & Grossberg, 1992). Although much of its effort has been devoted to cultural phenomena as expressed in literature, art, and history, the field of education has increasingly captured the attention of cultural studies scholars. Some of it is descriptive and highly polemic, journalistic, or even autobiographical. Cultural studies is a growing field in higher education, in which criticalists representing various disciplines and academic orientations explore and deconstruct many aspects of capitalist culture that other researchers trivialize or ignore. Many of the writings of cultural studies researchers are quite abstract and do not appear to involve any fieldwork as such.

At the same time, cultural studies' descriptive analyses often involve critique of the educational settings (schools, universities) in, or genres (conferences, journals) through which criticalists carry out their work. Thus their descriptions have direct applications to educational practice. For example, in a presentation on the theoretical underpinnings of cultural studies, Stuart Hall (1992) speaks autobiographically, from his own experience as a "critical intellectual" (p. 277).

Greg Dimitriadis and Dennis Carlson (2003) see cultural studies as having had a particularly strong influence on three subfields in education: the reconceptualist curriculum movement, critical pedagogy, and the social foundations of education. Their edited book, *Promises to Keep,* includes eleven chapters exploring the possibility of keeping "the promises of public education in the construction of an autonomous democratic public sphere and revitalized political system" (Morrow & Torres, 2003, p. xi).

Gender and race as cultural categories have each formed the basis for specialized fields of study within cultural studies. Feminist research involves such varied foci and methods that Virginia Olesen (1994) describes it in the plural, as **feminisms.** According to Olesen, critical work in feminist studies has had two main foci: (1) the study of females' lived cultures and experiences and how they are shaped by the cultural meanings that circulate in everyday life; and (2) the production and meaning of cultural objects as texts.

Critical feminists have done much work to identify and deconstruct cultural texts, such as those in film and popular literature, that contain and circulate depictions of women primarily or only as: (1) sexual objects for men; (2) responsible for domesticity, housework, child rearing, and care giving; (3) the weaker or secondary sex; and (4) normally as well as normatively heterosexual (Agger, 1992). Later in the chapter we discuss an example of critical feminist research concerning the depiction of young women's sexuality in an education context.

With respect to race, critical research on each of the commonly identified racial or ethnic groups is being carried out, some conducted by members of the groups being studied but still a good deal by Caucasian researchers. John Stanfield II (1994) argues that the more empowering and normality-revealing aspects of African American intellectuals "have been ignored, marginalized, or reinterpreted to fit into the more orthodox norms of social scientific communities" (p. 177). Such **norms** are unstated sets of rules and assumptions that guide mainstream intellectuals' beliefs and actions.

Stanfield suggests that indigenous qualitative methods that draw from the cosmos of people of color will diverge from previous mainstream forms of investigation. He recommends "the collection of oral histories that allow the examined people of color to articulate holistic explanations about how they construct their realities" (p. 185), and that U.S. researchers engaged in such research discard their own notions of time, space, and spirituality in order to grasp the meaning of indigenous people's stories.

A form of oppression rarely mentioned in the research literature is ageism. Aside from their market value as potential consumers or workers, both youth and elders are particularly subject to devaluation and exploitation. Youth are oppressed because their behavior is perceived as immature, while elders are oppressed because, over time, their capacity to contribute through work tends to diminish while their need for social services increases.

Critical Pedagogy

Because of its commitment to foster emancipation from oppression, critical-theory research in education is very closely connected to educational practice. Here we define **critical pedagogy** as any applied system of teaching and learning that is based on the goals and values of critical-theory research. Below we describe three approaches to critical pedagogy that vary widely in the extent to which they accept or reject the educational system as currently structured, seek to work within it or to bypass it in their efforts to promote the emancipation of young people, and focus on local or global issues and communities of practice.

1. *Critical pedagogy in "the real world."* For Joan Wink (2000), critical pedagogy involves a wedding of a caring heart ("Love trumps methods!," p. 168) and a critical eye ("Why should kids critically reflect if we don't?," p. 169). She puts her focus on transforming individual kids into learners through a three-step process: to name, to reflect critically, and to act. In this process "the practitioners' voice . . . must be as strong as the theorists' voice" (p. 120).

To name means problem posing. In the case of Joan's young friend Jonathan, who bloomed late as a reader, "to name would be to say that he could not decode and encode; he could not read and write" (p. 135). In Joan's process of reflecting critically she listened, watched, talked, thought, read, called specialists, and tried many methods to help Jonathan read. Her third step, to act, occurred after Jonathan's parents enrolled him in an expensive reading program based on teaching methods the opposite of those Joan favors. Jonathan began to have success and pleasure from reading and writing. Joan's action then involved arriving at the realization that she had to give up her assumptions that her favored mode of teaching reading was best for all students. "At this enlightened—and often uncomfortable—educational space, relearning and unlearning begins" (p. 16) for the critical-theory researcher/practitioner, followed by a new phase of learning.

2. *Revolutionary critical pedagogy.* Peter McLaren and Ramin Farahmandpur (2001) argue that through the expanding globalization of capitalism, education has been reduced to a subsector of the economy. They give many examples of the growing disastrous effects of "free-market" trends on human beings who work for a living. They sketch the fundamental requirements for developing revolutionary critical pedagogy, based on Marxist theory, to encourage critical con-

sciousness among students and teachers and to build working-class solidarity and opposition to global capitalism.

As to specifics, E. S. Weinbaum (in McLaren and Farahmandpur, 2001) suggests three conditions necessary for this development. (1) Critical educators must facilitate dialogues among workers and students about everyday labor practices and teaching practices. (2) Teachers and workers must link their individual interests and issues to broader social and economic relations at the global level. (3) Critical educators must play an active political role in labor unions and schools.

One of the authors of this book (Joy) had the good fortune to attend a workshop at the University of Oregon at which McLaren (2003) spoke. He described work by some of his graduate students at UCLA, who joined the bus drivers' union in Los Angeles and were doing their dissertations on that experience. McLaren's talk was full of exciting ideas, which Joy had never encountered in the mainstream media and only rarely in educational circles. McLaren argues that instead of putting their focus on difference and identity politics, teachers, students, and workers must honor the need for collective action to transform schools and society at large.

3. *Grass-roots critical pedagogy.* In a recent paper, Grace Lee Boggs (2003a) argues that "We must be the Change" that we want to see in the world. She states:

> Children need to be given a sense of the unique capacity of human beings to shape and create reality in accordance with conscious purposes and plans. Learning . . . is not something you can make people do in their heads with the perspective that years from now they will be able to get a good job and make a lot of money. . . . (p. 5)

At the workshop mentioned above at which McLaren spoke, the keynote speaker was Grace Lee Boggs (2003b). She described the work of the James and Grace Lee Boggs Center to Nurture Community Leadership, based in Detroit, Michigan. The center sponsors community-building activities designed to motivate all the community's children to learn and at the same time reverse the physical deterioration of its neighborhoods. These efforts include community gardening and mural painting programs, and build systems change from that foundation. An activist for more than sixty years, Boggs finds hope in her observation that "the new generation, which is beginning to discover its mission, is more open than the generation that led the movement in the 1960s" (1998, p. 272).

THE IMPACT OF CRITICAL-THEORY RESEARCH ON EDUCATION

Perhaps the most unique contribution of critical-theory research to the field of education is its conception of the causes and effects of the academic "achievement gap" between students from different cultural backgrounds. A great many educational researchers and practitioners have publicly addressed the problem of the disproportionate levels of school failure among low-income and ethnic "minority" cultural groups. Whereas the majority of explanations attribute this problem to psychological and personal causes, criticalists who focus on this problem view it as reflecting reproduction of the hegemonic oppression experienced by these groups.

As described earlier, Paul Willis (1977) explored how lads from working-class backgrounds expressed values consistent with their class identity and resisted school activities that challenged those values. Jean Anyon (1980) showed how cultural oppression operates in the other direction, namely, how schools shape nonprivileged and privileged individuals' educational experiences differently in ways that maintain hegemony. Anyon studied the **hidden curriculum** in schools—the implicit instruction in attitudes and habits that schools continually transmit by their structure and the way that they organize activities. Anyon found that schools with students primarily from working-class families tend to teach skills and values that prepare students for working-class lives (mindless obedience, tolerance for repetitive tasks, and respect for authority). In contrast, Anyon found that schools serving mainly students from upper socioeconomic classes tend to teach skills and values that prepare students for middle- and upper-class lives (leadership, problem solving, critical thinking, and creativity).

Although research like that of Willis and Anyon is enlightening, the criticalist Michael Apple (1997) argues that it is not possible to understand the reasons for educational inequity in U.S. society without considering the interaction of race or ethnicity with social class. Criticalists question much of the research that has been done to investigate or address the social and cultural conditions that affect "minority" students' learning, claiming that it is based on middle-class Caucasian values and perspectives.

In his discussion of the need for ethnic modeling in qualitative research, Stanfield (1994) comments that "only recently have people of color in some disciplines, the humanities in particular, been allowed to speak in different legitimated voices" (p. 180), citing bell hooks as one such scholar. In her writings hooks (1992) refers openly to her personal experience and uses literary discourse, rather than strictly research discourse, to critique educational research and practice.

Criticalists also are interested in the role of schools and other institutions in silencing or muting the voices of nonprivileged groups and thereby perpetuating hegemony. Michelle Fine (1988) did a critical ethnography of sex education and school-based health clinics. This research illustrates critical feminists' exploration of how educators' views of gender and class issues jointly conspire to limit females' preparation for adulthood. Fine interviewed high school girls, observed sex education programs, and analyzed curriculum materials in U.S. schools. She sought to explore the desires, fears, and fantasies that shape female students' silences and voices concerning sex and sex education.

Fine found that female students, particularly those from low-income families, had minimal access to school-based health clinics or courses providing information relevant to their developing sexuality. Where such clinics and courses were provided, their prevailing discourse and practice tended to discourage rather than encourage students to use their services.

Fine defined three discourses of female sexuality that prevail within the public school system. Sexuality is (1) described as violent and coercive, (2) associated with victimization, with males cast as potential predators, and (3) cast in terms of premarital abstinence as the preferred sexual behavior of all female students. Fine saw all these discourses as designed to discourage adolescent females from sexual activity, even though the research findings she reviewed indicate that they generally engage in responsible sex practices (for example, ensuring the use of contraceptives).

Fine argued for a fourth possibility: the discourse of desire. This discourse would acknowledge the possibility of desire, pleasure, and sexual entitlement among female students. She concluded that this discourse "remains a whisper inside the official work of US public schools" (p. 33). As a result, many of the students she studied viewed school-based sex education programs and health clinics as largely irrelevant or opposed to their perceived needs. Fine concluded that such educational practices actually hinder females' development of sexual responsibility, thereby contributing to their continued disempowerment: "How can we ethically continue to withhold educational treatments we know to be effective for adolescent women?" (p. 50).

A more recent treatment of Fine's research involving female sexuality is included in a chapter in *Promises to Keep* by Lois Weis and Michelle Fine (2003). In honoring the two school sites they studied as representing "instances of forceful pedagogy that deliberately and directly challenge inequity," the authors describe how "schools are promoting extraordinary conversations for and by youth," creating "buried moments" of "interruption . . . within deeply reproductive educational settings" (p. 121).

Other criticalists have examined how the voices of teachers are silenced, or at least muted, by the prevailing structure of public and private educational systems. The research article reprinted in this chapter describes how Nancy Kraft (1995), a staff development specialist, uses concepts and procedures based on critical theory in an effort to empower the teachers with whom she works.

In her workshops, Kraft shares her perceptions of her role as a facilitator of teachers' learning and structures their learning experiences on the principles of adult education theory. She helps participants examine their own beliefs, values, and assumptions about teaching and learning and actively fosters teachers' reflection on, and sharing of, their experience and the "rich knowledge of their craft" (p. 34). By first analyzing why their own voices are not part of most debates about school reform, teachers gain more understanding of the sources of student resistance and disempowerment. In the process they rediscover their own **agency,** which means the belief that they are able to shape the conditions of their lives. Thus Kraft attempts to help teachers deconstruct traditional models of school change and become empowered as real change agents.

THEORY BUILDING IN CRITICAL-THEORY RESEARCH

Critical-theory research emphasizes the value of theory in explaining society and contributing to the emancipation of its participants. Giroux (1988) is among those scholars who have played a major role in developing a body of critical theory that is applicable to education in the United States and other western cultures.

Giroux starts his development of a theory of critical pedagogy with the assumption that U.S. public education is in crisis. He sees this condition reflected most clearly in the contrast between the hegemonic rhetoric that equates U.S. culture with democracy in its ultimate form and numerous indicators of the falsity of this rhetoric: low voter participation, growing illiteracy rates among the general population, and the increasingly common opinion among U.S. citizens that social criticism and social change are irrelevant to the maintenance of U.S. democracy.

Giroux proposes a liberatory theory of **border pedagogy** to replace what he describes as the "politics of difference" that characterizes much of the current dialogue about educational problems and solutions. For Giroux the term *border* reflects the notion of permeable, changing boundaries to describe differences between individuals and groups, as opposed to the rigid, "either–or" nature of conventional social categories.

In Giroux's theory, difference is linked to a broader politics, and schools and pedagogy are organized around a sense of purpose that makes difference central to a critical notion of citizenship and democratic public life. This concept of difference is postmodern (see Chapter 1) in that it recognizes the need to acknowledge the particular, the heterogeneous, and the multiple; and it views the political community as a diverse collection of subcommunities in flux. Giroux envisions a pedagogy in which educators at all levels of schooling engage in redefining the nature of intellectual work and inquiry itself, so that educators and their students can "become knowledgeable and committed actors in the world" (1988, p. 208).

Applying Giroux's theory to schools requires that students no longer study unified subjects. Instead, students explore the "borderlands" between diverse cultural histories as sites for critical analysis and a potential source of experimentation, creativity, and possibility. Power is explicitly explored, both to help students understand how forms of domination are historically and socially constructed and to explore how teachers can use their authority to aid students in their emancipation from such domination. Finally, students are educated to read critically, not only how cultural texts are regulated by various discursive codes, but also how such texts express and represent different ideological interests.

Wink (2000), in her chapter, "Critical Pedagogy: Where in the World Did It Come From?," provides brief summaries of the work of many other theorists in the critical-theory tradition.

OPPORTUNITIES AND CHALLENGES IN APPLYING CRITICAL-THEORY RESEARCH

The assumptions and methods of critical theory have provoked considerable criticism from educators and researchers representing other traditions. For example, Charlene Spretnak (1991) argues that criticalists' preoccupation with the deconstruction of every possible form of rhetoric or other text leads to groundlessness being "the only constant recognized by this sensibility" (p. 13). In other words, their critics view criticalists as hypercritical! Such critics argue that deconstruction, if taken to an extreme, can lead to a sense of hopelessness rather than to hope for emancipation.

In practice, however, at least some researchers in the critical theory tradition fulfill its emancipatory agenda. The work of criticalists such as Henry Giroux and Michelle Fine suggests promising directions for educators to explore in order to better meet the needs of traditionally underserved students.

Another limitation of critical theory is the complicated terminology of many researchers who work in this tradition. Rex Gibson (1986) described this problem:

> The writings of criticalists do not exactly help their cause. Turgidness, unnecessarily complex sentence structures, a preference for their own neologisms (newly-coined words), and an almost wilful refusal to attempt to communicate directly and clearly with the lay reader, characterise many of their books and articles. The impression conveyed is of "cliquishness," or exclusion; of insiders writing only for insiders. (pp. 16–17)

If one assumes that understanding is a part of what emancipation involves, the inaccessible language of many criticalists limits understanding, by not only educational practitioners but also by members of oppressed cultural groups, thereby hindering its efforts to foster emancipation of all human beings. A writing style that is more accessible to educators and others interested in emancipation is definitely desirable, especially in light of the continual "speeding up" of communicative messages in Western cultures. To their credit, some criticalists make considerable effort to translate their ideas into familiar language. In this chapter we have aimed to summarize work that, while challenging in its conceptions and implications, is relatively free of neologisms and unnecessarily complex sentence structure.

EXAMPLE OF OUTLINING A RESEARCH PROPOSAL

This feature of the chapter gives you an example of how to outline a research proposal using the form in Appendix 1. The example, involving a proposal to study curriculum alignment, is introduced at the end of Chapter 2.

    2. RESEARCH QUESTIONS
        A. The third research question in the example in Chapter 2 is as follows: "Does students' performance on achievement tests improve after a curriculum-alignment process has been completed in their schools?" Previous research involving black students has found that black

students tend to use a writing and speaking style in school that reflects their cultural heritage and diverges widely from what has been called "majority-standard English." A critical ethnography conducted by Judith Hansen (2001) found that black students who wanted to do well on a standard test of writing felt they had to abandon an important part of their cultural identity.

    B. Based on this research, we will pose a more specific question for our research proposal. It is: How have efforts to align the schools' curriculum and instructional practices with standard tests of writing affected black students' motivation to do well on a subsequent state test of writing achievement?

4. RESEARCH DESIGN
    A. We will use the qualitative methods of critical-theory research, specifically Carspecken and Walford's model of critical ethnography, to explore this topic. Our rationale for this choice is that we wish to examine critically certain aspects of black culture that may affect black students' motivation in preparing for the state writing test, and the possible effects of curriculum alignment on their motivation.
    D. The types of validity criteria that are relevant to our research design are those that best support the objective, subjective, and normative-evaluative truth claims made by researchers and research participants in a critical ethnography.

5. SAMPLING
    B. *Phenomenon.* The phenomenon of interest to us is black students' beliefs and behavior in the weeks before a high-stakes writing achievement test.
    C. *Sampling procedure.* We will select a high school by the critical-case form of purposive sampling. This particular high school received much positive publicity about three years ago for its approach to language arts instruction. The school was known for fostering culturally diverse students' oral literacy through classroom activities in which students were encouraged to speak and write in their own language and communication style. We will ask black students at this high school to participate in informal conversations with us individually or in groups of two or three students. To encourage participation, we will offer each participant a gift certificate for the school bookstore.
    E. *Sample size.* We plan to study about ten black students in this school, where black students constitute about one-fourth of the student population. If more than ten black students show interest, we will use a purposeful random sampling strategy to select among the volunteers.

6. VARIABLES
    B. Data collection and analysis will focus on black students' attitudes and beliefs about their culturally based language patterns and about "majority-standard English" patterns. We will focus on how partic-

ipants perceive the relevance and fairness of the state writing test, the types of communications they have had with other black students who are planning to take it, and what they are doing to prepare for the test. We will attempt to discern students' emic perspective of the test's appropriateness to assess their writing ability and of its degree of alignment with the instruction they have received related to writing and speaking.

We will also seek to develop an objective description of the strategies used to teach writing in this school three years ago and the strategies used to teach writing since curriculum alignment was carried out.

7. METHODS OF DATA COLLECTION

     A. To encourage participation and to discover the common student culture, we will first talk with students informally in small groups (two to four students) containing one or more black students. Then we will conduct more focused interviews with individual black students.

     We also plan to examine school materials and interview a few long-term teachers to develop a record of the nature of the classroom activities that existed in the school three years ago. Our questions will concern the activities' focus on oral literacy, their impact on black students' writing skills, and the extent to which they may have been reduced since the curriculum-alignment process was carried out.

     We will seek to obtain data that support objective truth claims by using low-inference vocabulary and bracketing observer comments.

8. DATA ANALYSIS PROCEDURES

     B. We will first compile a primary record, that is, a thick description of the study participants' verbal and nonverbal behavior, obtained through informal interviews of small groups of students (two to four).

     To analyze our data, we will use the procedures for validating objective truth claims and generating core cultural themes specified in Carspecken and Walford's model of critical ethnography.

     B. We will check the validity of our data by generating a strong chain of evidence, member checking, writing a record with contextual completeness, and making representativeness checks by reflecting on whether the research participants we studied were typical of black students at this high school. We will generate dialogical data with the participants in order to test the validity of their subjective and normative-evaluative truth claims. Next we will analyze the primary record, speculate about the participant's subjective truth claims, and ask them to describe their normative-evaluative truth claims about the world as it is or should be.

     Finally, we will specify the cultural themes and system relationships that emerge from our research.

SELF-CHECK TEST

1. What most clearly distinguishes critical theory from other research traditions is its
   a. focus on cultural phenomena.
   b. commitment to an emancipatory agenda.
   c. attention to societal problems.
   d. examination of the positive aspects of culture.

2. In the view of critical theory proponents, mainstream research practices have maintained cultural oppression primarily by
   a. neglecting the study of racial and ethnic minorities.
   b. upholding hegemonic assumptions about truth, science, and good.
   c. questioning the meaning of all texts.
   d. not distinguishing between the effects of class, race, and gender on individuals' cultural attainments.

3. Criticalists refer to the tendency of certain researchers to become preoccupied with means over ends or purposes as
   a. instrumental rationality.   c. cultural assimilation.
   b. voice.   d. deconstruction.

4. Hegemony refers to
   a. emancipatory methods as conceptualized by criticalists.
   b. a conception of social justice advocated by criticalists.
   c. differences among the emic perspectives of members of a nonprivileged cultural group.
   d. the domination of nonprivileged cultural groups by privileged cultural groups.

5. Deconstruction of a text involves
   a. rephrasing it in language that culturally oppressed groups can understand.
   b. specifying the cultural themes and system factors reflected in it.
   c. asking the members of the culturally dominant group to clarify its meaning.
   d. examining its connotations and various possible meanings.

6. In a critical ethnography, it is desirable to
   a. involve field participants in all phases of data collection.
   b. demonstrate consistency between the data collected through passive observation and data collected through dialogue with field participants.
   c. analyze the findings from the specific research site in terms of existing or emergent theory about system relationships.
   d. collect primarily data that meet objective truth claims.

7. An example of the schools' reproduction of cultural oppression is
   a. teaching students from poor backgrounds skills associated with obedience and students from affluent backgrounds skills associated with achievement.
   b. designing sex education programs centered on premarital abstinence.
   c. teaching history in a way that characterizes the portrayals in textbooks as factual.
   d. all of the above.

8. One reason for the limited impact of critical theory on educational research to date is its relative
   a. neglect of issues of central importance to educational practice.
   b. preference for everyday mundane language over scientific terminology.
   c. emphasis on deconstructing any form of rhetoric or text.
   d. lack of a foundational theory.

CHAPTER REFERENCES

Agger, B. (1992). *Cultural studies as critical theory.* Washington, DC: Falmer.

Anyon, J. (1980). Social class and the hidden curriculum of work. *Journal of Education, 162,* 67–92.

Apple, M. W. (1997). Introduction. In M. W. Apple (Ed.), *Review of Research in Education,* vol. 22 (pp. xi–xxi). Washington, DC: American Educational Research Association.

Apple, M. W. (2003). *The state and the politics of knowledge.* New York: RoutledgeFalmer.

Boggs, G. (1998). *Living for change: An autobiography.* Minneapolis: University of Minnesota Press.

Boggs, G. L. (2003a, January). *We must be the change.* Paper based on a presentation at the University of Michigan 2003 Martin Luther King Symposium, Ann Arbor, MI. Retrieved February 18, 2003 from www.boggscenter.org

Boggs, G. L. (2003b, February). A paradigm shift in our concept of education. In the Center for Critical Theory and Transnational Studies, *Transnationalism, ethnicity, and the public sphere.* Workshop presented at the University of Oregon, Eugene, OR.

Bourdieu, P. (1991). Sport and social class. In C. Mukerji & M. Schudson (Eds.), *Rethinking popular culture: Contemporary perspectives in cultural studies* (pp. 357–373). Berkeley: University of California Press.

Carspecken, P. F. (1996). *Critical ethnography in educational research: A theoretical and practical guide.* New York: Routledge.

Carspecken, P. F., & Walford, G. (Eds.) (2001). *Critical ethnography and education.* Oxford, United Kingdom: Elsevier Science.

Dimitriadis, G., & Carlson, D. (Eds.) (2003). *Promises to keep: Cultural studies, democratic education, and public life.* New York: RoutledgeFalmer.

Fine, M. (1988). Sexuality, schooling, and adolescent females: The missing discourse of desire. *Harvard Educational Review, 58,* 29–53.

Gibson, R. (1986). *Critical theory and education.* London: Hodder & Stoughton.

Giroux, H. A. (1988). Critical theory and the politics of culture and voice: Rethinking the discourse of educational research. In R. R. Sherman & R. B. Webb (Eds.), *Qualitative research in education: Focus and methods* (pp. 190–210). New York: Falmer.

Giroux, H. A. (1992). Resisting difference: Cultural studies and the discourse of critical pedagogy. In L. Grossberg, C. Nelson, & P. A. Treichler (Eds.), *Cultural studies* (pp. 199–212). New York: Routledge.

Hall, S. (1992). Cultural studies and its theoretical legacies. In L. Grossberg, C. Nelson, & P. A. Treichler (Eds.), *Cultural studies* (pp. 277–294). New York: Routledge.

Hansen, J. (2001). Testing white culture: African American students and standardized testing. In P. F. Carspecken & G. Walford (Eds.), *Critical ethnography and education* (pp. 199–222). Oxford, United Kingdom: Elsevier Science.

hooks, b. (1992). *Black looks: Race and representation.* Boston: South End.

Kincheloe, J. L., & McLaren, P. L. (1994). Rethinking critical theory and qualitative research. In N. K. Denzin & Y. S. Lincoln (Eds.), *Handbook of qualitative research* (pp. 138–157). Thousand Oaks, CA: Sage.

Kraft, N. P. (1995). The dilemmas of deskilling: Reflections of a staff developer. *Journal of Staff Development, 16,* 31–35.

Kumashiro, K. (2002). *Troubling education: Queer activism and anti-oppressive pedagogy.* New York: RoutledgeFalmer.

Larkin, R. W. (1979). *Suburban youth in cultural crisis.* New York: Oxford University Press.

McLaren, P. (1998). *Life in schools: An introduction to critical pedagogy in the foundations of education* (3rd ed.). New York: Longman.

McLaren, P. (2003, February). Critical pedagogy in the age of neoliberal globalization: The domestication of political agency and the struggle for socialist futures. In the Center for Critical Theory and Transnational Studies, *Transnationalism, ethnicity, and the public sphere.* Workshop presented at the University of Oregon, Eugene, OR.

McLaren, P., & Farahmandpur, R. (2001). Teaching against globalization and the new imperialism: Toward a revolutionary pedagogy. *Journal of Teacher Education, 52*(2), 136–150.

Morrow, R. A., & Torres, C. A. (2003). Between unthinking modernism and rethinking postmodernism. Series editors' foreword in G. Dimitriadis & D. Carlson (Eds.), *Promises to keep: Cultural studies, democratic education, and public life* (pp. ix–xi). New York: RoutledgeFalmer.

Nelson, C., Treichler, P. A., & Grossberg, L. (1992). Cultural studies: An introduction. In L. Grossberg, C. Nelson, & P. A. Treichler (Eds.), *Cultural studies* (pp. 1–22). New York: Routledge.

Olesen, V. (1994). Feminisms and models of qualitative research. In N. K. Denzin & Y. S. Lincoln (Eds.), *Handbook of qualitative research* (pp. 158–174). Thousand Oaks, CA: Sage.

Seymour-Smith, C. (Ed.) (1986). *Dictionary of anthropology.* Boston: G. K. Hall.

Spretnak, C. (1991). *States of grace: The recovery of meaning in the postmodern age.* New York: HarperCollins.

Stanfield, J. H. II (1994). Ethnic modeling in qualitative research. In N. K. Denzin & Y. S. Lincoln (Eds.), *Handbook of qualitative research* (pp. 175–188). Thousand Oaks, CA: Sage.

Steinburg, S. R., & Kincheloe, J. L. (1997). *Kinderculture: The corporate construction of childhood.* Boulder, CO: Westview.

Weis, L., & Fine, M. (2003). Extraordinary conversations in public schools. In G. Dimitriadis & D. Carlson (Eds.), *Promises to keep: Cultural studies, democratic education, and public life* (pp. 95–123). New York: RoutledgeFalmer.

Willis, P. (1977). *Learning to labour: How working class kids get working class jobs.* London: Gower.

Wink, Joan. (2000). *Critical pedagogy: Notes from the real world.* (2nd ed.). New York: Addison Wesley Longman.

Resources for Further Study

Carspecken, P. F., & Walford, G. (Eds.) (2001). *Critical ethnography and education*. Oxford, United Kingdom: Elsevier Science.

> *Describes distinct features of critical ethnographies from qualitative educational researchers at the University of Houston. Seven such ethnographies are presented, including studies of standardized testing in a predominantly African American university, the hidden curriculum of a constructivist charter school, and constructions of meaning from student discussions of literature.*

Dimitriadis, G., & Carlson, D. (Eds.) (2003). *Promises to keep: Cultural studies, democratic education, and public life*. New York: RoutledgeFalmer.

> *Provides twelve chapters that represent counternarratives in the project of reinventing and reimagining democratic education and public life. They show how broad shifts occurring in the United States are influencing education, and how school curricula are being reconceptualized in relation to those shifts.*

Kumashiro, K. (2002). *Troubling education: Queer activism and anti-oppressive pedagogy*. New York: RoutledgeFalmer.

> *The author provides guidelines to help schools address the multiple, interconnected, and ever-changing forms of oppression operating within and beyond schools. He explains why educators' traditional assumptions and curricular "facts" need to be "troubled," that is, subjected to questioning and the examination of varied interpretations.*

McLaren, P. (2003). *Life in schools: An introduction to critical pedagogy in the foundations of education* (4th ed.). Boston: Allyn & Bacon.

> *Summarizes the author's experiences as a school teacher, professor of education, and a leading theorist and activist in critical pedagogy.*

Wink, J. (2000). *Critical pedagogy: Notes from the real world* (2nd ed.). New York: Addison Wesley Longman.

> *The author tells many stories about her own and others' experience in questioning and transforming the relationships among classroom teaching, knowledge production, the structures of schooling, and the social and material relations of the wider world.*

In the following section of this chapter you will read a research article that illustrates research based on critical theory. It is preceded by comments written especially for this book by the author of the article. Then the article itself is reprinted in full, just as it appeared when originally published. Where appropriate, we have added footnotes to help you understand the information contained in the article.

Sample Critical-Theory Research Study
The Dilemmas of Deskilling: Reflections of a Staff Developer

Kraft, N. P. (1995). The dilemmas of deskilling: Reflections of a staff developer. *Journal of Staff Development, 16*, 31–35.

● RESEARCHER'S COMMENTS, *Prepared by Nancy Kraft*

Critical theory has been highly influential in shaping the way I facilitate the professional development of other educators. It has provided a means to critically reflect on my role in educational systems and how I perform it.

Viewing the world critically was always part of my life, having been raised in a household with a grandmother who was a socialist from Finland and with a father who encouraged me to question everything. However, it was not until I began facilitating seminars for agricultural extensionists from developing countries, and working toward a Ph.D. in educational policy studies at the University of Wisconsin–Madison (UW), that I was able to name the philosophical orientation that reflects my way of looking at and participating in the world. These experiences enabled me to view the world from a new perspective, built upon a critical awareness of how government and economic systems perpetuate an inequitable distribution of power and monetary resources. Through my own work and my interactions with peers who had critical perspectives, I came to know and value the work of criticalists, especially Jürgen Habermas's theory of knowledge-constitutive interests (Held, 1980).

Critical theory also influenced my work as an educational consultant for a statewide evaluation consortium that was connected with an outreach department at UW. The culmination of this five-year experience was my dissertation research: a critical analysis of the role of external change agents in facilitating change in schools (Kraft, 1997). This research was grounded in a critical social science paradigm and an action research philosophy and methodology. Briefly, I discovered the difficulties of facilitating change in situations where a propensity exists for maintaining the status quo. My study showed the power of hegemony in hindering school educators from critically reflecting on their own beliefs, values, and assumptions and how this negatively impacts their practice.

Ironically, this critical perspective generally was not valued or welcomed in the work I did at UW. Critical theory, which at its core involves questioning the basis of power relations, was perceived as threatening by some people in positions of power at UW.

It wasn't until I began working for a private educational research firm, where I am now employed, that this perspective and the concomitant passion I had in situating my practice within it was acknowledged, tolerated, and even valued by my colleagues and peers. In my current role, I have been asked to organize and facilitate professional development internally for my colleagues. This has afforded me the opportunity to integrate a critical perspective in selecting readings and structuring dialogue around important educational issues that confront us in schools.

In the present study my goal was to assist a group of Chapter 1 (now Title I) educators to critically question their own beliefs, values, and assumptions about teaching and learning. More specifically, I wanted to help them understand how their perceptions of Title I children and parents influence the ways they interact with and structure learning experiences for these children.

Children who qualify for Title I traditionally come from lower socioeconomic backgrounds and are often children of color. These facts alone often lead teachers to assume that instructional practices for such children should be remedial in nature. The focus is generally on memorization of mathematics facts and vocabulary, not on engaging the children in analytical or critical thinking and giving them a voice in their own learning program. Also, their instruction is rarely grounded in the kinds of accelerated learning practices that are commonly used in instruction for students in talented and gifted programs. Critical theory provides a means to reveal to educators that some of their beliefs and attitudes may be ideological illusions that perpetuate an inequitable status quo.

As in all my work, my intent at the workshop described in the study that is reprinted here was to help teachers understand the negative effects of power relationships within schools, including the relationship between teachers' limited voice in decision-making processes and the lack of students' voice and ownership in instructional decision making. While I rarely name social science theories such as positivism, interpretivism, critical theory, or postmodernism in my workshops, I do describe how these different philosophical orientations influence the ways that we educators look at the world, and our practices in schools. I try to show that a critical world view permits individuals to better understand why the conditions under which they operate are often frustrating, and that it can foster discoveries of the kinds of actions that may be required to eliminate the sources of those frustrations.

I use participatory and structured dialogue to involve educators in the tasks of critical analysis of their own situations, with a view to transform them in ways that will improve educational situations for students, teachers, and society. My goal in these professional development experiences is to help participants come to realize their collective potential as the active agents of history and change. According to Carr and Kemmis (1986):

> . . . critical educational science has a view of educational reform that is participatory and collaborative; it envisages a form of educational research which is conducted by those involved in education themselves. It takes a view of educational research as critical analysis directed at the transformation of educational practices, the educational understandings, and educational values of those involved in the process, and the social and institutional structures which provide frameworks for their action. (p. 156)

Focusing on entitlement programs that serve marginalized and disenfranchised groups in society makes it generally easy to introduce concepts of power relationships in schools and society. If we first address the way that teachers' own voices are silenced, it then becomes easier for them to acknowledge and talk about the silenced voices of students.

Another technique that I utilize to encourage discussion of such issues is to include exercises that challenge participants to identify their own beliefs, values, and assumptions about teaching and learning, knowledge and curriculum, and children's capabilities. I expose participants to critical literature such as *Rethinking Schools,* a journal published by teachers in Milwaukee, Wisconsin, which focuses on issues of social justice and equity.[1] I also cite books on educational issues that present an alternative perspective to the linear, rational models that form the basis of much of the mainstream literature on educational reform and change processes.

Critical educational science requires that teachers become researchers into their own practices, understanding, and situations. Because I consider my role as a staff developer congruent with that of a teacher, I have always researched my own practice as a staff developer. While the participant whom I quote at the beginning of my research report indicated on the reflection sheet that her attendance was required, I didn't want to brush off her comment as merely that of a disgruntled teacher. Instead, her negative comments confirmed to me that I always need to look for meaningful ways to validate participants' knowledge and involve them in their own learning. Therefore I used her comments as an opportunity to critically reflect on the content and process of this three-day workshop and the way that I try to structure learning for adults. I reread several books that had shaped my practice as an educator. I then wrote an extensive reflection paper that was included in my professional portfolio. This paper formed the basis for the present article.

Interestingly, I had an opportunity to present another workshop to the same group of educators one year later. Because I wanted to stress the value of teachers engaging in reflective practice as well as to model what that looked like, I read portions of my article on the dilemmas of deskilling to these teachers. I explained to them how I had used negative participant feedback from the previous year's workshop to critically reflect on my own practice. I indicated how analysis from a broader socioeconomic, political, historical, and cultural perspective helped me examine power relations in schools. I also noted that outside consultants typically are afforded expert status, whereas teachers themselves have expertise but few forums in which to share it. I explained that as a result of this individual's comments, I had incorporated an activity in which the participants would generate strategies for having a greater voice in effecting needed change in the schools.

I continue to find critical theory a useful framework to guide my own understanding of the ways that schools silence both teachers' and students' voices in identifying directions for meaningful educational reform. It is much more than a framework or an analytical tool, however. It has become a way of life and thinking that provides me a lens to look at and deconstruct the world. Using critical theory, I can continually analyze and reflect on how the broader socioeconomic, political, historical, and cultural context impacts my life and the lives of those with whom I interact on a professional and personal basis.

Recent Discoveries

Critical theory continues to guide my practice as an educator. More than a framework or an analytical tool, it has become a way of thinking that provides a lens through which I look at and deconstruct the world.

In 1999 I began three years at the University of Kansas (KU), teaching curriculum theory to teachers pursuing graduate degrees, educational philosophy to Ph.D. candidates, and action research to entry-level teacher candidates. All my courses examined educational issues from the perspective of race and class. In the curriculum course, which I taught six times while at KU, my goal was to address critical questions, including: "What counts as curriculum knowledge?," "How is curriculum knowledge produced and transmitted in the classroom?," "Who has access to legitimate forms of knowledge?," and "Whose interests does curriculum knowledge serve?". Many of my students, who taught in suburban schools with few students of color, often questioned the need to look at curriculum from multiple and critical perspectives. At the same time, others shared their appreciation for their first exposure to the larger cultural, historical, political, and socioeconomic context within which schooling and education are positioned.

In 2002 I accepted the position of director of the Kansas Parent Information Resource Center. Here I continue to find ways to integrate a critical agenda in the Center's work as we try to make sense of the No Child Left Behind Act. I am committed to help schools move beyond traditional, limited modes of parent involvement to a model grounded in principles of empowerment, in which even the most marginalized parents and families can find and express their voices.

References

Carr, W., & Kemmis, S. (1986). *Becoming critical: Education, knowledge and action research*. London: The Falmer Press.

Held, D. (1980). *Introduction to critical theory: Horkheimer to Habermas*. Berkeley: University of California Press.

Kraft, N. P. (1997). A critical analysis of the role of change agents in facilitating change. *Dissertation Abstracts International, 57*(12), 5018A. (University Microfilms No. AAG97-11786).

Note

1. *Rethinking Schools: An Urban Education Journal* is edited by Robert Lowe, Bob Peterson, and Rita Tenorio and is available from Ed Press in Milwaukee, WI.

The Dilemmas of Deskilling:
Reflections of a Staff Developer

Nancy P. Kraft

Effective staff development programs need to minimize teacher deskilling practices and instead engage participants in critical, democratic, and participatory learning experiences.

I have been a staff developer for the past 10 years working with teachers and educators to help them learn about their teaching through the processes of self-study, reflective practice, and action research. I believe that staff development should encourage educators to be more critical, self-analytical, and reflective.

Unfortunately, much of today's staff development consists of giving teachers the "nuts and bolts" and the "how-to's" rather than creating learning opportunities for teachers to examine the nature and processes of educational change and reform initiatives. In effect, these practical staff development approaches without self-

Kraft, N. P. (1995). The dilemmas of deskilling: Reflections of a staff developer. *Journal of Staff Development, 16,* 31–35. Reprinted with permission of the National Staff Development Council. Copyright © 1995 by NSDC.

study and reflection actually cause teachers to be deskilled, to limit their improvement.

The deskilling approaches separate the conception of curriculum from execution of curriculum; these approaches have experts do the "thinking" while teachers are reduced to doing the "implementing." Giroux (1988) concludes that "the effect is not only to deskill teachers, to remove them from the processes of deliberation and reflection, but also to routinize the nature of learning and classroom pedagogy" (p. 124). If one major outcome of education for children is to create individuals who are critical thinkers and problem solvers, how will teachers be successful in doing this if they, themselves, aren't given opportunities to engage in critical discourse about educational issues.

As a professional who has devoted many years to thinking through educational processes through inquiry into my own practice, and as a person who adamantly resists my own deskilling, I refuse to perpetuate a model of staff development for others which ultimately contributes to their deskilling as well. Thus, this article presents a story about a recent dilemma that I confronted regarding deskilling practices. In addition to sharing my journal reflections from this workshop, I describe a set of strategies that I use as a staff developer to encourage teachers to actively participate in their own learning.

THE EMPEROR IS WEARING NO CLOTHES

"The emperor's new clothes are here. There she is parading before the audience. No one is telling her she got nothing." As I read these words written on the reflection sheet I received from one participant during the second day of a three-day workshop, I suddenly felt very dejected and extremely discouraged. I was facilitating learning for 35 Chapter 1 teachers in a workshop which covered a broad array of topics ranging from "getting in touch with your beliefs, values, and assumptions about knowledge and learning" to "how to get meaningful parent involvement in Chapter 1 programs."

In my own journal, I had noted resistance from some of the participants who were expecting the traditional "sit and get" type of workshop, but I thought that by the end of the first day I had been rather successful in presenting a different kind of staff development opportunity—one that required the participants to think and engage in critical discourse. After all, I reflected in my journal, attendees had been actively participating in their own learning, exploring their beliefs about education and assumptions of Chapter 1 students, and willingly sharing their craft knowledge and expertise with each other. Even though I had encouraged critical reflection on the events of the workshops, the criticism by this participant hurt me.

I questioned the source of this participant's criticism: Was it my style or the content of my workshop? Was it because I was requiring her to think and become more analytical about her own teaching situation (something she may not have had to do in a long time)? I wondered how I could find ways to validate her feelings, but at the same time find ways to help her reconceptualize staff development as an opportunity to reflect and engage in critical discourse.

APPROACHES TO STAFF DEVELOPMENT

I see two approaches to staff development—the traditional approach which essentially tells teachers what to do and the critical theory approach which has teachers engage in critically reflective analyses of educational constructs and their beliefs, values, and assumptions.[a]

The Traditional Approach

So much of staff development has traditionally focused very narrowly on effecting change through telling teachers what to do and how to do it. Teachers haven't been involved in either conceptualizing what change should look like or in deciding how best to initiate and implement that change. They are typically relegated to technician status in implementing others' ideas or "recipes" for change. In a critique of the process of educational reform, Giroux (1988) says:

> Many of the recommendations that have emerged in the current debate either ignore the role teachers play in preparing learners to be active and critical citizens or they suggest reforms that ignore the intelligence, judgment, and experience that teachers might offer in such a debate. Where teachers do enter the debate, they are the object of educational reforms that reduce them to the status of high-level technicians carrying out dictates and objectives decided by experts far removed from the everyday realities of classroom life. The message appears to be that teachers do not count when it comes to critically examining the nature and process of educational reform. (p. 121)

The Critical Theory Approach

The critical theory approach allows teachers to examine society from the perspective of power relationships within that society; it allows staff developers to engage participants in questioning power relationships within schools. Thus the critical theory approach allows teach-

---

a. Educational constructs are concepts (e.g., hyperactivity, intelligence) that are inferred from observed phenomena and then are used as explanations of other instances of such phenomena.

ers to deconstruct traditional models for enacting school change (i.e. questioning why their voices aren't part of the school reform debate, engaging in historical analyses of teacher roles in school change, and understanding feelings of teacher resistance and alienation in school change efforts).[b]

Reaching this understanding helps teachers to collectively generate strategies which might bring about meaningful change. This deconstruction, generally, also provides them with the means to understand sources of student resistance, alienation, and disempowerment, as well.

Carr and Kemmis (1986) and Apple (1983), who ground their work in critical theory, criticize the traditional model of teacher involvement in staff development that views teachers as mere "operatives" in an education factory, carrying out the dictates of others. In the traditional model, the outside expert or consultant is brought in, often as an extension of administrative control, with the charge of "telling" others how to go about effecting change.

While it has become popular in recent years to involve teachers in staff development focused on action research, teacher research, reflective practice, and collaborative inquiry processes, most of these efforts have perpetuated a deficit model of teachers' knowledge in that the emphasis of these efforts is often on the development of teachers' skills as the sole means of school improvement. These collaborative processes, however, are detrimental to teachers' perceptions of their own abilities and possibilities (Miller, 1990).

A common belief is that teachers only need to change their behavior to improve schools. Staff development based on the critical theory paradigm, however, allows teachers to look more critically at their own practices and also to become more analytical and critical about the conditions which shape their lives as professionals and impact student learning.

My Approach with Critical Theory

While I strongly believe that teachers, for too long, have not been treated as intellectuals, I continue to be frustrated by teachers, themselves, who prefer to participate in their own deskilling, who want to go away from an inservice session with a "bag of tricks" or ideas for "what to do on Monday morning" in the classroom.

Myles Horton, an adult educator instrumental in using adult education for social change, maintains that teachers sometimes prefer the traditional approach because they have had limited opportunities to make important decisions in their professional lives and thus come to the workshop expecting to be taught rather than be challenged to create solutions to their own problems (Kohl & Kohl, 1991).

As a staff developer who relies on a critical theory framework to inform and guide my own practice, I have tried to become more cognizant of the broader social, political, economic, historical, and cultural context which shapes teachers' lives and their professional practice. Thus, the staff development that I plan is heavily influenced by constructs of knowledge and power emanating from a critical theory social science paradigm.[c]

Consequently, I take deliberate steps to negate the power afforded me in the privileged role of the external consultant. These steps include: (a) sharing perceptions of my role as a facilitator of learning with the participants; (b) structuring the learning experience to reflect adult education theory; (c) assisting participants in examining their beliefs, values, and assumptions about teaching and learning, knowledge and curriculum, and learners; and (d) providing opportunities for reflection throughout the staff development experience.

Sharing Perceptions of My Role

Regardless of the topic of my workshop, I always begin by sharing with participants my own philosophy of

---

b. To deconstruct a concept or model involves analyzing it as though it were a "text." Deconstruction is based on the assumption that no text has a definite meaning, but rather any text can have multiple interpretations, with no single interpretation privileged over any other.

c. A social science paradigm is a particular model of inquiry based on agreed-upon concepts, procedures, and standards of judgment. Chapter 1 described two major paradigms in social science, the positivist and interpretivist paradigms. Some scholars view critical theory as a third paradigm.

learning which is consistent with constructivism. I explain this concept as involving others in constructing meaning through acknowledging participants' histories and experience and validating them as capable and thinking beings. Thus the program will not be a "make it and take it" workshop, but will instead involve them in critical thinking and reflection. I share with participants who I am (my own background as an adult educator with an interest in school change/reform) and how I see my role (as a facilitator of a learning experience for them).

Even though I am designated presenter or speaker, I also share with them that I view myself as a learner and that I will use this opportunity with them to become more reflective, myself, on my role as a staff developer. My own journal keeping is visible throughout the workshop with my recording of incidents as they occur. Killion and Harrison (1991/1992) refer to this as reflection-in-action, or the mental processing of actions as they occur. I believe that the most effective way to present reflective practice is to model, that is to "walk my talk."

I relate the connections I see between theory and practice, sharing with them I believe there is nothing as practical as a good theory—that theory guides everything we do and believe as educators. I tell them that, as part of my role, I will be using theory as the bases for both the process and content of our shared learning experience.

Structuring the Learning Experience

At this point in my workshops, I usually share with participants adult learning theory delineating the following characteristics of adult learning as identified by Smith (1982):

- adults bring a different orientation to education and learning than children (which results from adults having multiple roles, tasks, responsibilities, and opportunities);
- adults have an accumulation of experience (deriving from their vast range of roles and responsibilities) which I make integral to the workshop content;

- adults pass through developmental phases that are different from those experienced by children and youth; and
- adults bring a degree of anxiety and ambivalence to learning (given multiple roles and responsibilities).

I also share with participants the theory (Smith, 1982) regarding conditions for adult learning:

- adults feel the need to learn and have input into what, why, and how they will learn;
- adults' previous experiences are taken into account when designing both the process and content of the new learning experience;
- what is to be learned is related optimally to the individual's developmental change and life tasks;
- the learning experience provides the learners with the necessary training to adequately complete the task (i.e., making learners more independent for self-directed learning and interedependent for collaborative learning);
- adults learn best in a climate that minimizes anxiety and encourages freedom to experiment; and
- adult learning styles are taken into account.

By realizing that adults have an accumulation of experience, I often begin my workshops with an acknowledgement of this experience. During the initial introductions, I generally ask participants to share how many years of experience they have as educators, and then systematically provide opportunities for them to share their experience throughout the workshop. I believe that one of my roles as a staff developer is to create the conditions (e.g., a climate that minimizes anxiety and provides encouragement for experimentation) that will foster their willingness to share their vast array of experience, wisdom, and expertise.

Barth (1990) says that adults who work in schools carry around with them extraordinary insights about curriculum, staff development, community relations, leadership, and other issues; the challenge is to create the conditions under which they will reveal this rich knowledge of their craft so that it may become part of the discussion.

In this particular workshop (where one participant reflected about the "emperor's new clothes), the 35 educators had 611 years of collective experience, wisdom, and knowledge. I made a point at that workshop, as [sic] all others, that their collective experience would be the basis for examining and critiquing the designated content together. Given the vast experience of these particular participants, one of the unplanned activities became a "teacher exchange" where participants had a formal opportunity to share ideas with each other.

Participants appreciated the teacher exchange, as reflected by several who commented, "Thank you for opening up to teacher idea exchanges," and "I was impressed with the presenter and how she took the time to listen to *our* concerns instead of being a presenter and filling us with all kinds of material that you might forget two days after. It was useful because it opened my eyes to new ideas for my classes. Also the ideas from the other teachers were very, very helpful!" and "Allowing lots of interaction between the teachers and sharing of ideas and concerns was very helpful."

As a means to give them input into the what, why, and how they will learn, we generally co-construct a list of ground rules for how the learning will be structured throughout the workshop. As a co-participant, in addition to being the facilitator of their learning, I list my expectations of their participation in the workshop. Ground rules include such things as:

- the experience of all participants is valued and drawn upon;
- people share/debate/discuss what they are learning with others;
- participants feel respected/listened to;
- participants have input into how teaching and learning happens;
- the learning experience models democratic relations between learner and leader;
- the learning experience includes both reflection and action; and
- the learning experience will be an enjoyable one.

While participants are always given the opportunity to co-construct ground rules, I find that generally few

take me up on this offer. For the most part, participants are surprised that they can have direct control over their learning, as this has not been the norm of past staff development experiences. Common sense procedures, such as mutually developed ground rules, establishes [sic] a climate that is conducive to learning and supports participants' willingness to share and interact with each other.

Assisting Participants

I always encourage participants to get in touch with their own beliefs, values, and assumptions about teaching and learning and the knowledge and curriculum they hold as educators. This establishes a precedent of critical thought for the entire workshop.

Brookfield (1987) believes that such a process entails much more than the skills of logical analysis and should involve, "calling into question the assumptions underlying our customary, habitual ways of thinking and acting and then being ready to think and act differently on the basis of this critical questioning" (p. 1).

I believe that only through this kind of reflection, we are able to imagine and explore alternatives. But at the same time, it can be threatening to call into question the values and beliefs that shape the ways in which we look at the world. Consequently, we use nonthreatening activities, such as personal reflection with small-group sharing or a graffiti exercise wherein participants write down and share their reactions to a series of questions, as a means to explore personal values, beliefs, and assumptions.

Coming to grips with this part of themselves enables participants to better understand their own resistance and frustrations regarding change. These exercises generally provide an excellent means to redirect those negative feelings into positive strategies and action.

Participants willingly engage in these activities and found it to be valuable as reflected by one teacher who said, "This (workshop) was like a retreat in that we took time from the busy work of teaching to reflect on 'why' we do what we do and/or why and what can be improved. It has helped me get in touch with myself as a professional." Or another, who commented, "A belief, value, or view that is presented should be reflected on and experimented with, but not taken as 'etched in stone' simply because someone presents it as such." And a final comment, "Reflection through journaling, discussion with other teachers, reflective thought, etc. can enable me to evaluate my teaching at present as well as new teaching ideas, to see if I am/can be teaching at the standard of my beliefs and ideals."

Providing Opportunities for Reflection

Frequent check-ins and opportunities for feedback from the participants are incorporated throughout the workshop. Participants are encouraged to challenge and question continuously, and are given opportunities to anonymously share their perceptions. One such strategy asks participants to reflect on the positive points, the negative points, and the interesting or intriguing points about the ideas, opinions, or activities discussed and conducted as part of the workshop. Participant feedback at the end of the workshop generally invites participants to reflect critically, practically, and artistically on any of the ideas discussed during the workshop (Gage & Berliner, 1989).

In reflecting critically, participant comments included: "(The workshop) caused me to identify and analyze my beliefs/values/assumptions regarding teaching and learning," "For one thing, it makes sense to say that educational reform begins in the classroom with the teacher rather than with a state or federal mandate most often designed by others who have no real working knowledge of what goes on in classrooms today," and "I need to be more aware of the research, its applicability to our situation or to that of individual children either before buying into something or as a guide in designing action research for evaluating current practices."

Practical reflections encompassed, "I'm going to start using my computer to document student progress," and "Using journals seems very practical and of great value for sorting thoughts and feelings and planning action." Viewing new learning artistically included comments such as: "I now take notes on each class and student— what we did, special notes I want to remember about a student, things I want to do with them. With a little more time, perhaps I can expand this into a journal with

anecdotal records, my response, notes on my reactions, feelings, kids, etc;" "I think journaling has a wide variety of uses. For me personally, it would probably give me a feeling of continuity with my students. My day is spent doing a variety of jobs. I finish the day feeling disconnected sometimes. It would help me take time to reflect;" and "I would set up an educational tracking plan for my students that includes opportunities for his or her discussion and reflection of the worth of what is being learned."

RECOMMENDATIONS FOR STAFF DEVELOPERS

The adage, "The more things change, the more they stay the same," comes to my mind as I reflect on the stories I have heard, witnessed, and recorded about the ways schools operate and use staff development to effect change. If staff developers ever hope to have an impact in facilitating meaningful change, there are several lessons that can be learned from my narrative.

First, we should be aware of our own ideological positioning and theoretical framework which guides and shapes our work as staff developers. This framework will influence the way we view educators and their capacity to change as well as the nature of change itself. Grounding my work in critical theory has assisted my understanding of teacher resistance to change and provided ways that I can counter that resistance to engage teachers in more meaningful processes to facilitate change. Therefore, staff developers need to understand how social science paradigms affect and influence our own practice.

Second, starting points for staff development experiences should take into consideration the four points outlined in this article. I establish a tone for staff development that actively involves participants in engaging in their own learning by assuming a facilitator role versus role of "expert"; structuring workshops on adult education theory; encouraging critical examination of participants' beliefs, values, and assumptions; and providing ample opportunities for participant reflection. This engagement has generally led to participants' willingness to at least consider trying the new ideas which were the basis of the staff development experience in the first place.

Third, personal reflection via journaling has been a powerful tool for me to become more reflective about my own successes and failures in facilitating others' growth and change. My journal entries have been the basis for writing stories which I often share with participants in other workshops. I use these stories as a means to assist participants in analyzing and understanding their own feelings towards change. If we as staff developers aren't ourselves reflective, how can we expect others to become more reflective.

As this narrative has shown, positive teacher comments serve as a validation that what I am doing is on the right track. But negative comments, such as those of the participant alluding to the "emperor's new clothes," have caused me to think and critically reflect on ways that I can involve even the most resistant person in actively participating in his or her own learning.

My reflections about this experience have shown me that I need to look for ways to validate these feelings and discern their sources. Part of my own growth as a staff developer needs to focus on understanding resistance and continuing to look for ways to encourage active participation on the parts of all learners.

Nancy P. Kraft is a research associate, RMC Research Corporation, Writer Square, Suite 540, 1512 Larimer St., Denver, Colorado 80202, (303)825-3636.

References

Apple, M. W. (1983). Curricular form and the logic of technical control. In M. W. Apple & L. Weis (Eds.), *Ideology and practice in schooling* (pp. 143–165). Philadelphia, PA: Temple University Press.

Barth, R. (1990). *Improving schools from within: Teachers, parents, and principals can make the difference.* San Francisco, CA: Jossey-Bass Publishers.

Brookfield, S. (1987). *Developing critical thinkers: Challenging adults to explore alternative ways of thinking and acting.* San Francisco, CA: Jossey-Bass Publishers.

Carr, W., & Kemmis, S. (1986). *Becoming critical: Education, knowledge and action research.* London: The Falmer Press.

Gage, N. L., & Berliner, D. C. (1989). Nurturing the critical, practical and artistic thinking of teachers. *Phi Delta Kapan, 71*(3), 213–214.

Giroux, H. A. (1988). Teachers as transformative intellectuals. In H. A. Giroux, (Ed.), *Teachers as intellectuals: Toward a critical pedagogy of learning* (pp. 121–128). Granby, MA: Bergin & Garvey Publishers, Inc.

Killion, J., & Harrison, C. (1991/1992, December/January). The practice of reflection: An essential learning process. *The Developer.*

Kohl, H., & Kohl, J. (1991). *The long haul: An autobiography of Myles Horton.* New York: Doubleday.

Miller, J. (1990). *Creating spaces and finding voices: Teachers collaborating for empowerment.* Albany, New York: State University of New York Press.

Smith, R. (1982). *Learning how to learn: Applied theory for adults.* New York, NY: Cambridge.

13

Historical Research

After studying this chapter, you will be able to

1. describe several ways in which the study of history figures as a central concern for educators.

2. explain the major steps of a historical research study.

3. explain the role and relative value of primary and secondary sources in historical research.

4. describe the types of primary sources that historical researchers might study.

5. describe the procedures used by historical researchers to determine the authenticity of primary sources.

6. describe the procedures used by historical researchers to determine the accuracy of primary sources.

7. explain the unique contribution that quantitative records make to historical research.

8. explain several key issues that are involved in interpreting and applying historical research findings.

Conrad Timms is a curriculum coordinator for a large urban school district. Sandy du Vall, head of the science department at one of the district's high schools, has asked Timms for help in writing a grant proposal to try out a new constructivist-based curriculum for teaching science.

Timms remembers the new science programs that were introduced in the 1960s following Sputnik, and the widespread perceptions back then that students needed better science instruction. He wonders how the assumptions and techniques of the new science program differ from those of the earlier ones, so he tells du Vall: "Fine, but first let's do a literature search on the history of science education." Together they conduct a search of the ERIC database, entering the descriptor *Science Education History* and related terms. They locate several useful journal articles, including a special issue of the *Journal of Research in Science Teaching* on "Science Curriculum Reform." One article gives suggestions for undertaking science reform today in light of some of the errors made during the curriculum reform efforts of the 1960s. After reading this and other articles, Timms and du Vall feel prepared to write a strong grant proposal, in which they will cite several historical studies that support their ideas for implementing the proposed science program.

Historical research helps educators improve education by its insights into the past, present, and future. This chapter explains the methods used by historical researchers so that you can draw on their studies to understand educational phenomena of interest to you from a historical perspective. ●

THE NATURE OF HISTORICAL RESEARCH

The education literature is rich with historical studies of educational leaders, institutions, policies, and procedures. The range of issues and subjects investigated by historical researchers is suggested by the following list of published studies:

Hill, I. (2002). The beginnings of the international education movement; Part IV; The birth of the IB diploma. *International Schools Journal, 22,* 17–30.

Johnson, L. (2002). "Making democracy real": Teacher union and community activism to promote diversity in the New York City public schools, 1935–1950. *Urban Education, 37,* 566–587.

Rudolph, J. L. (2003). Portraying epistemology: School science in historical context. *Science Education, 87,* 64–79.

Walton, A. (2000). "Scholar," "Lady," "Best man in the English Department"?—Recalling the career of Marjorie Hope Nicolson. *History of Education Quarterly, 40,* 169–200.

Historical research is the process of systematically searching for data to answer questions about a past phenomenon, in order to better understand the phenomenon and its likely causes and consequences. Historians have engaged in this process for thousands of years, using methods of inquiry that today we might call *qualitative.* With the rise of positivism in the twentieth century, historical research shifted toward the compilation of historical "facts" and causal interpretations of the relationship between such facts. Today historical research continues to undergo further shifts. For example, some historians now use computer technology to retrieve and analyze data about the past.

Contemporary historians tend to dismiss much of the historical literature of bygone eras as mere chronicles of events and lives. Their own writings generally are shorter, and they subordinate historical facts to an interpretive framework within which those facts are given meaning and significance. In this chapter we treat historical research as a qualitative research tradition because of its reliance on, although not exclusive use of, interpretivist approaches to data collection and analysis.

The types of research that we describe in other chapters of this book involve the creation of data. For example, researchers create data when they make observations or administer tests to determine the effectiveness of an instructional program. In contrast, most historical researchers primarily discover already existing data in such sources as diaries, official documents, and relics. On occasion, though, historical researchers interview individuals to obtain their recollections of past events. This form of historical research, called **oral history,** does involve data creation.

The Role of History in Education

The past is of great interest to both educational researchers and educational practitioners, although not necessarily for the same reasons. In the following sections, we describe various ways in which educators use historical research methods and findings in their work.

A Subject in the Curriculum.   History is a standard component of the social studies curriculum in most schools in the United States and many other countries (Downey & Levstik, 1991). The emphasis on history in the curriculum reflects the belief of policy makers and the general public that students need to learn a great many facts about previous political leaders, wars, economic shifts, and technological advances involving their own and other countries in order to become well-informed, contributing citizens as adults.

Presumably, historical knowledge of their country's culture gives students an appreciation of their cultural heritage and a commitment to fostering and maintaining that heritage. Robert Bellah and his colleagues (1985), for example, argue that the individualism and scientific rationalism that permeate society today provide little guidance to help individuals make sense of life and form moral judgments. In their view, study of the past provides a reminder of traditions that involved a defined moral and social order to which most members of a community subscribed. In fact, many religious and ethnic groups seek to keep their collective past alive through ritual and documentation in an attempt to preserve a sense of moral and social order.

A Foundation for Developing New Knowledge and Policies Relating to Education.   Educational researchers must reflect on past findings and methods of investigation in order to develop fruitful ideas for new research. In fact, almost every research report includes a review of the literature related to the topic that the researchers addressed. If educational researchers did not conduct these reviews of past research, they would be much more likely to test hypotheses that had been shown to be unproductive, to reinvent research methodology, to "discover" what was already known, and to continue making the same methodological errors as their predecessors.

The study of the past also is important for educational practitioners. The creation of the many educational activities and institutions that exist in society today reflects particular values and views of society that have a long history.

Study of that history can inform the way in which teachers and other educational practitioners view present and proposed educational practices. For example, research into the past can shed light on current approaches to science instruction, bilingual education, educational standards, parent involvement, student assessment, and teacher certification.

There is debate about whether and how educational historians should participate in school policy making. Some historians believe that that they should influence policy making directly, whereas others believe that historians might corrupt the integrity of their discipline by becoming too closely involved with the policy-making process. Rubén Donato and Marvin Lazerson (2000) reviewed these differing views and made their own recommendation:

> [E]ducational policies are proposed and implemented in the context of historical moments. Invariably, the policies rest on assumptions about the past; they rest on the stories people believe about the past. Educational historians have an obligation to thrust their stories into the policy arena for if they do not, the stories that become the common view will be told by others who often have little stake in the integrity of historical scholarship. Or, even worse, their stories will go unnoticed altogether. (p. 10)

When you carry out a literature search you might want to include *History* as a descriptor, connected by *and* with your subject descriptors (see the discussion of computer searching in Chapter 3). In this way, you can locate possible historical studies on the topic that you are investigating. Obtaining a historical perspective on your topic can prove invaluable in furthering your understanding of current educational practices and in designing a research study.

A Tool in Planning the Future.   Thomas Popkewitz (1997) observed that researchers disagree in their conceptions of such history-related notions as time, development, and progress. Nonetheless, they generally agree that knowledge of the history of educational phenomena can help us predict, and to some extent plan, what the future of those phenomena will be. In fact, a type of research called **futurology** specifically examines what the future is likely to be. Some futurology studies are based on surveys of current trends, while others use simulation and gaming involving various imagined future scenarios. The predictions are based largely on statistical logic or rational reasoning derived from the study of past events.

Another purpose of historical research, then, is to assist educators in defining and evaluating alternative future scenarios involving a particular educational phenomenon. If we know how certain individuals or groups have acted in the past, we can predict with a certain degree of confidence how they will act in the future. For example, we can make a good prediction of how specific legislators will vote on an upcoming education bill by doing research on their past voting records.

As in other types of educational research, however, prediction rarely is perfect. New social, political, and economic conditions continually arise, and they create discontinuities in educational practices. For example, Oregon voters in 1991 passed Measure 5, a voter-approved initiative, which fundamentally changed the basis for funding public schools. Thus, pre-1991 practices in Oregon education no longer serve as a reliable guide for projections concerning schools' budget allocations, organization, or educational programs.

Some historical researchers, generally called **revisionist historians,** carry out research to point out aspects of a phenomenon that they believe were missed or distorted in previous historical accounts. Their larger goal is to sensitize educators to past practices that appear to have had unjust aims and effects, but that have continued into the present and thus require reform. For example, Michael Katz (1968) studied educational innovation in mid-nineteenth-century Massachusetts and demonstrated how it functioned to serve dominant economic interests and thwart democratic aspirations. As another example, Gilbert Gonzalez (1990) studied schooling in the Southwest in the first half of the twentieth century and found widespread practice of separate schooling for Mexican American children. He concluded that this practice was encouraged by the economic interests of white communities in this part of the United States. These studies alert educators to the possibility of similar problems with current educational practices and innovations so that they can be avoided or corrected.

Methods of Historical Research

Historiography is the study of the procedures that historians use in their research. In a discussion of historiography, the historian E. H. Carr (1967) described how he carries out research:

> For myself, as soon as I have got going on a few of what I take to be the capital sources, the itch becomes too strong and I begin to write—not necessarily at the beginning, but somewhere, anywhere. Thereafter, reading and writing go on simultaneously. The writing is added to, subtracted from, re-shaped, cancelled, as I go on reading. The reading is guided and directed and made fruitful by the writing: the more I write, the more I know what I am looking for, the better I understand the significance and relevance of what I find. (pp. 32–33)

Educational researchers conducting historical research often use procedures similar to those Carr described. In the next sections of this chapter we describe these procedures as a series of steps. Keep in mind, though, that many researchers skip back and forth between steps, or modify their procedures based on the particular research questions being asked, the circumstances of their search for historical data, and the interpretive framework they use to understand the data.

SELECTING HISTORICAL SOURCES

As we explained previously in the chapter, historical researchers primarily seek to discover, not create, the data that are relevant to their research problem. Those data are available in various existing sources. However, before researchers begin an active search for sources, they first must reflect on the types of sources that are likely to exist. They then can consider what kinds of individuals or institutions are likely to have produced the types of sources they need, whether those sources would have been saved, and if so, where they are most likely to be stored. As their interpretive framework develops, or as sources point them toward still other sources that deserve exploration, researchers can revise their tentative search plan.

In searching for sources, historical researchers use the three basic types of sources that we described in Chapter 3—preliminary, secondary, and primary sources. Below we describe sources of each type that are relevant to historical research.

Preliminary Sources

A literature search for historical research studies usually begins with the use of a preliminary source. You will recall from Chapter 3 that a **preliminary source** is an electronic or hard-copy index to secondary and primary sources on various topics. Most preliminary sources related to history are indexes of secondary sources, but some list primary sources as well.

Many of the general preliminary sources listed in Appendix 2 are useful for doing a search of historical literature. This appendix also lists specialized preliminary sources for historical research.

Secondary Sources

A **secondary source** in historical research is a document or other type of recorded information, such as a videotape, in which the author describes an event or situation at which the author was not present. Authors of secondary sources base their accounts on descriptions or records of events generated by other individuals who witnessed or participated in the events. For example, many newspaper articles and TV news broadcasts are secondary sources, because the reporters relied on interviews with eyewitnesses in order to obtain the information. Annual reports of educational programs and school operations also can be considered secondary sources if they are prepared by individuals who relied on data collected from other individuals, such as school administrators and teachers.

Most historical researchers read a number of secondary sources early in their research study in order to clarify their research problem and determine the types of primary sources that are relevant to the problem. Sometimes researchers decide to accept the information given in a secondary source about a relevant primary source, rather than tracking down the primary source itself. In other cases, they might decide that they need to examine the primary source directly. In making their decision, they consider the reputation of the author of the secondary source, the degree of compatibility between that author's interpretive framework and their own, and the feasibility of gaining access to the primary source.

Primary Sources

A **primary source** in historical research is any source of information (e.g., a diary, a song, a map, a set of test scores) that has been preserved from the past, or that is created to document a past phenomenon by someone who witnessed or participated in it. Virtually any object or verbal account can be a primary source in historical research.

Four main types of primary sources are studied by historical researchers.

1. *Text and other media.* **Text materials,** whether written or printed, are the most common type of primary source for historical research. Yvonna Lincoln and Egon Guba (1985) classify such materials as either **documents,** which are prepared for personal use only (e.g., a letter to a friend or a private diary), or **records,** which have an official purpose (e.g., a legal contract, a will, or a newspaper article). Documents and records might contain handwritten, typed, or computer-generated text, be published or unpublished, and use various genres (e.g., newspaper articles, poetry, or novels).

The text materials examined by historical researchers might include both materials that were intentionally written to serve as a record of the past (e.g., a memoir or a school yearbook), and materials that were prepared only to serve an immediate purpose (e.g., school memoranda or a teacher-prepared test), with no expectation that they might be used as a historical source at a later time.

Increasingly, visual media are used to communicate information, for example, TV, film, CDs, DVDs, digitized photos, and Internet "streaming videos." Ian Grosvenor and Martin Lawn (2001) claim that these media can yield important evidence about historical events and practices in education.

2. *Oral history.* Many cultures use ballads, tales, and other forms of spoken language to preserve a record of past events for posterity. Some historical researchers make recordings of these oral accounts. Others conduct interviews of individuals who witnessed or participated in events of potential historical significance, recording and transcribing the interviews to produce a written record. The tapes and transcripts of research informants' recollections are primary sources, but when historical researchers summarize and comment on the information obtained from informants, the summaries become part of a secondary source (the historical research report).

An example of oral history is *Missing Stories,* a book by Leslie Kelen and Eileen Stone (1996). These researchers studied eight cultural communities in the state of Utah. They conducted lengthy interviews with 352 individuals, taped the interviews, and transcribed them. The book presents the stories of 88 of the individuals, who share recollections of their past as it relates to the community that each represents. For example, the epilogue to the chapter on the Chicano-Hispano community is the story of a Chicano woman who is an assistant principal of an intermediate school. She describes her father's struggle to obtain an education and become a teacher, and how she as an educator continues his commitment to "reject rejection," despite living in an environment still tempered with racial stereotypes.

3. *Relics.* **Relics** include any object whose physical or visual properties provide information about the past. School supplies, computers, a blueprint of a school building, textbooks, worksheets, and instructional games are examples of relics that researchers could examine for information about historical educational practices.

4. *Quantitative materials.* Materials that provide quantitative information about educational phenomena are another important primary source. Like documents and records, they are recorded and preserved in some print form or as computer files. Census records, school budgets, school attendance records, teachers' grade sheets, test scores, and other compilations of numerical data can provide useful data for historical researchers. Later in the chapter, we discuss the unique value of **quantitative materials** in historical research.

Some primary sources used by historical researchers fit more than one of the four types of sources that we have listed. For example, a school memorandum might include a discussion of plans based on the results of a survey of teachers (documenting the number of teachers for, against, and having no opinion) concerning a proposed change in the intramural sports program. This memorandum is both a written record and a quantitative record, because it includes numerical information as well as text.

Other primary sources might be classified as both text materials and relics, depending on how they are used in a historical study. For example, in a study of the printing methods used in producing textbooks, a specific textbook would be classified as a relic, because one of its physical properties is being examined. The same textbook would be considered a record in a study of how textbooks of different periods explained a particular mathematical operation, because the content of the textbook now is the focus of study.

Written primary sources such as diaries, manuscripts, or school records, and relics such as old photographs or classroom paraphernalia might be found in regional museums or **archives** (also known as **repositories**). Archives are special locations for storing primary sources in order to preserve them in good condition and control access to them.

Historical researchers must learn and follow any required procedures for getting access to a primary source, such as making a written request to an archive for permission to study the records, indicating the length of time they will need the records, how they will record information, and perhaps even the use to which they plan to put the information.

VALIDATING HISTORICAL EVIDENCE

Educators who wish to apply the findings of historical research need assurance that the historical sources that were used by the researchers as a basis for their interpretations are valid. Otherwise, their views of present practices will be distorted by incorrect perceptions of past events. The disturbances in contemporary society created by Holocaust-denial stories, presumably based on "sound" historical evidence, provide a cautionary tale about the need for strong validation procedures in historical research.

Historical sources are valid to the extent that they are authentic and contain accurate information. In the following sections, we describe procedures for validating historical sources against these criteria.

Procedures for Determining the Authenticity of Historical Sources

Determining the authenticity of primary sources in historical research sometimes is called **external criticism.** The process of external criticism is concerned not with the content of the primary source, but whether the apparent or claimed origin of the source corresponds to its actual origin. The term *origin* refers to such matters as the primary source's author, place, date, and circumstances of publication.

The citation for a primary source should include its author, place of origin, date of publication, and publisher or sponsoring institution. While the author of a primary source usually is listed in the source itself, this indicator may not be reliable. Some primary sources, such as recorded speeches, are ghostwritten by someone other than the individual who is identified as the author. In other cases, authors use pseudonyms to conceal their identity. If a primary source has multiple authors, it might be impossible to determine who wrote the parts of it that are relevant to a historical research problem. Still another issue relating to authorship is the possibility of forgery. A forgery is a fabrication that is claimed to be genuine—for example, a diary written by someone other than the person whose experiences are described.

The place of origin of a primary source often is apparent from where it is stored, or from indications in the source itself. The date of origin might be more difficult to ascertain. If no date is given, it might be possible to infer the date from references in the primary source, or from its sequential location in a file cabinet. Dates on primary sources should be viewed critically, because people often make innocent errors. For example, at the start of a new year it is not uncommon for someone to make the mistake of recording the previous year.

The possible existence of variant sources is another problem in judging the authenticity of a primary source. **Variant sources** are materials that have been altered in some way from the original version. For example, in going through the files of an educational institution, researchers might discover file copies (i.e., copies stored in the organization's official records) of internal memoranda that relate to their study. However, it is possible that the file copy was not distributed in exactly that form to all its intended receivers. Perhaps the author of a memo added a personal note to one receiver's copy of the memo. In this situation, both versions of the memo could be considered primary sources, each of which reveals different information about a past event.

Typewriters were not available before about 1880. Before then, most documents were written in longhand, and copies were prepared in the same manner. In working with pre-1880 documents, then, researchers need to determine whether more than one copy was made, and if so, compare their content for errors.

To determine the authenticity of a primary source, researchers must generate and test alternative hypotheses about each aspect of its reputed origin. For example, they might hypothesize that a particular primary source was written by a subordinate in the organization rather than the person designated as the author. As they collect information showing that this and other hypotheses are untenable, they increase the probability, although never to the point of absolute certainty, that the source is genuine. Any doubts that a researcher has about the authenticity of a source should be noted in the research report.

Procedures for Determining the Accuracy of Historical Sources

The process of determining the accuracy of information in a primary historical source is called **internal criticism.** In doing internal criticism, researchers ask such questions as: Is it likely that people would act in the way that the writer described? Is it physically possible for the events described to have occurred this close together in time? Do the budget figures mentioned by the author seem reasonable? However, a researcher's sense that an event or situation described in a historical source seems improbable might not be sufficient basis for discounting the source. Most people can recall highly improbable events that actually occurred during their lifetime.

Internal criticism requires researchers to judge both the reasonableness of the statements in a historical source and the trustworthiness of the person who made the statements. Criteria that are used to judge the trustworthiness of a source's author include: (1) the author's presence or absence during the events being described; (2) whether she was a participant in or an observer of the events; (3) her qualifications to describe such events accurately; (4) her level of emotional involvement in the situation; and (5) whether she might have a vested interest in the outcomes of the event.

Even competent and truthful witnesses often give different versions of events that took place. When researchers discover widely differing accounts of an event, they need not conclude that all are equally true or false. As Carr (1967) notes, "It does not follow that, because a mountain appears to take on different shapes from different angles of vision, it has objectively either no shape at all or an infinity of shapes" (pp. 30–31). Carr argues that the historical researchers' task is to combine one or more witnesses' accounts, admittedly subjective, and to interpret them (also a subjective process) in an attempt to discover what actually happened.

Accounts of historical events need to be checked carefully for bias. A bias is a set to perceive events in such a way that certain types of facts are habitually overlooked, distorted, or falsified. Individuals with strong motives for wanting a particular version of a described event to be regarded as "the truth" are likely to produce biased information. For example, if a school memo describing a dispute between the superintendent and members of the school board was written by the superintendent, researchers might suspect that the superintendent's side of the argument would be presented in the most favorable light.

Many biased reports of events can be traced to people's tendency to make a story more dramatic, or to exaggerate their role in events. Historical researchers examine such factors as the ethnic background, political party, religious affiliation, and social status of those whose views are conveyed in a historical source, in an effort to appraise the likelihood of bias. They also examine use of emotionally charged or intemperate language, which can reflect commitment to a particular position on an issue.

Biased reports are especially likely when the social or political position of individuals requires them to make socially acceptable statements, even if they do not honestly feel that way. For example, a school principal we know was questioned about internal difficulties with particular teachers and classified staff at her school. The principal made claims about high staff morale and cohesiveness at her school. Such claims probably were made to avoid compounding the problem, and to guard against putting the speaker in a negative light. For similar reasons, some people in public life make mild statements about a colleague or rival, even when those statements do not reflect their true feelings. Recently the opposite trend has emerged in political campaigns, that is, a tendency to "blast" one's opponent regardless of the verifiability of one's statements.

If researchers discover a difference between someone's public and private statements, the discrepancy does not necessarily mean that the public statements have no value as historical evidence. Rather, the discrepancy itself is evidence about the person making the statement, and about the social environment in which the person functioned.

INTERPRETING THE INFORMATION OBTAINED FROM HISTORICAL SOURCES

In explaining internal criticism, we noted that witnesses to an event report different impressions based on their competence, personal position, and relationship to an event. Historical researchers are in a similar position. Historians will write different histories about the past depending on the evidence that they have chosen to collect and how they have interpreted it.

Because history inevitably involves interpretation, historical researchers continually reconstruct the past as their interests and knowledge change. In recent decades, revisionist historians (also known as **reconstructionists**) have become prominent voices in education. As we explained earlier in the chapter, these researchers take a different view of educational history than the conventional or popular view. Revisionist historians tend to believe that past educational practices reflect particular political, economic, or other social forces and motivations more than they reflect rationality, good will, or pedagogical considerations. As a result, Sol Cohen (1976) notes that historians of education ". . . are now disclosing phenomena long hidden by official pieties: the maltreatment of immigrants and ethnic groups, the discriminatory treatment of women and minority groups, the connections between schools and politics and between education and social stratification" (p. 329).

In Chapter 12 we discussed critical-theory research, which is similar to revisionist history in that both take a critical stance toward much educational practice, and seek historical explanations for many practices that they view as negative or problematic. Critical theory also is aligned with recent historical research on the importance of investigating nonschool influences that affect the socialization and learning of young people and adults. This research reflects critical theory's resistance to "essentializing" one definition of education over any other.

Historical researchers need to be especially careful to avoid a type of interpretive bias known as presentism. **Presentism** is the interpretation of past events based on concepts and perspectives that originated in more recent times. Historical researchers need to discover how various concepts were used in the time period and setting that they are investigating, rather than attach present meanings to them.

For example, there has been much interest in school choice, which refers to such phenomena as allowing parents to send their children to any public school in the district in which they reside, or providing tuition vouchers so that parents can send their children to private schools instead of state-supported public schools. Researchers interested in the history of school choice during the nineteenth century might look for data on the choices then available to parents about their children's education. Educators at that time might have used a term similar to *school choice*, but it might have meant something quite different—for example, whether children whose parents kept them home to work during harvest season would be considered absent from school and thus responsible for making up missed schoolwork.

The Importance of Concepts to Interpret Historical Information

As in other types of qualitative research, researchers doing historical research develop concepts to organize and interpret the data that they have collected. **Concepts** are terms that can be used to group individuals, events, or objects sharing a common set of attributes. For example, without a concept such as *progressive education*, a great many past phenomena that share common characteristics might be seen as separate and lacking historical significance.

Concepts, however, also place limits on historical researchers' interpretation of the past. For example, a researcher conducting a historical study of teaching might consider the defining attribute of the concept of *teaching* to be paid work done by someone who holds a state certificate that signifies completion of a college-level teacher education program. This definition of teaching will cause the researcher to study some individuals from a certain historical period but to exclude others (e.g., teacher aides and school volunteers) who would have been considered to be teaching if a different definition of the concept were used.

Historical researchers should determine whether the definition of each concept used in their research applies to the historical phenomena that they wish to study, and if necessary, provide definitions of important concepts in their research report. Many educational terms (e.g., *intelligence, distance learning, multicultural education*) have become part of people's everyday vocabulary, but readers need to understand how such terms are used in the context of a research study.

Historical researchers have made increasing use of concepts from the social sciences and other disciplines. In their investigation of historical studies that had won awards during a certain time period, T. C. R. Horn and Harry Ritter (1986) found that all the studies that were judged to be outstanding had drawn on conceptual frameworks from other disciplines. Interdisciplinary concepts are useful tools. For example, in applying the concept of *bureaucracy* to the public school system that developed in the United States during the mid-nineteenth century, Michael Katz (1987) defined it with reference to the definition set forth by Carl Friedrich, a sociologist.

Using Quantitative Materials in Historical Research

One reason for the growing use of quantitative materials in historical research is that conclusions based on large amounts of carefully selected quantitative data are considered to be more generalizable than conclusions based on case studies. Another benefit of quantitative materials is that they allow researchers to characterize the historical views and experiences of many people, which sometimes is referred to as the *common-man approach* to historical research. By contrast, older historical studies tend to focus on a few prominent individuals.

H. Warren Button (1979) referred to the common-man approach as "history from the bottom up—grassroots history" (p. 4). Because historical records typically give minimal attention to grassroots perspectives, Button argued that historical researchers must mine every source in order to reflect those perspectives:

> For instance, for a quantitative study of Buxton, a black antebellum haven in Ontario, it is necessary to assemble data from perhaps fifteen thousand entries in the census manuscripts of 1861, 1871, and 1881; from town auditors' accounts, and church records. . . . The research necessity for compilation and statistical treatment, by unfortunate paradox, produces history almost without personalities, even without names. Still, this new history has and will produce new understandings and will counterweight our long-standing concern for "the better sort." (p. 4)

Thus, a historical research study that includes the analysis of quantitative materials (sometimes referred to as *quantitative history*) provides information beyond that available from a purely qualitative historical research study. In turn, it requires the researchers to use sampling techniques, to define and measure variables, and to conduct statistical analyses.

Causal Inference in Historical Research

An essential task of historical research consists of investigating the main causes of past events. Examples of causal questions that could guide historical studies are: What were the forces and events that gave rise to the intelligence-testing movement? Why did U.S. educators adopt so readily the British open-classroom approach several decades ago? How did the role of school principal originate in this country?

Causal inference in historical research is the process of reaching the conclusion that one set of events brought about, directly or indirectly, a subsequent set of events. Historical researchers cannot prove that one past event caused another, but they can make explicit the assumptions that underlie their causal inferences concerning sequences of historical events.

Some historical researchers make the assumption that humans act similarly across cultures and across time. Thus, they might use a currently accepted causal pattern to explain an apparently similar pattern in the past. For example, a researcher might find an instance in nineteenth-century U.S. education when students at a particular college stopped attending classes and began making public protests against some college administrators. Suppose that the researcher also discovered that this event was preceded by administrative rulings at the college that diminished students' rights and privileges. He might infer—perhaps correctly—that these rulings led to the student revolt, his reasoning being that a similar chain of events precipitated student protests in many U.S. colleges during the 1960s.

Historians generally believe, however, that historical events are unique, and therefore that history does not repeat itself. In this view, occurrences at one point in time can illuminate, but do not explain, occurrences at another point in time. Even historians who see past occurrences as a harbinger of later events must be wary of presentism, which we described previously as the use of concepts that now have different meanings to interpret events from an earlier time period.

Historical researchers have emphasized various types of causes in their attempts to explain past events. They might attribute past educational occurrences to the actions of certain key persons, to the operation of powerful ideologies, to advances in science and technology, or to economic, geographical, sociological, or psychological factors. Some historians take an eclectic view and explain past events in terms of a combination of factors. For example, David Tyack (1976) studied the rise of compulsory education in the United States. He concluded that until about 1890, Americans built a broad base of elementary schooling that attracted ever-growing numbers of children. During that period most states passed compulsory attendance legislation, but did little to enforce those laws. Tyack calls this phase the *symbolic* stage of compulsory schooling.

Tyack concluded that a second stage, which he calls the *bureaucratic* stage, began in the United States shortly before the turn of the twentieth century. He notes that during this era

> . . . school systems grew in size and complexity, new techniques of bureaucratic control emerged, ideological conflict over compulsion diminished, strong laws were passed, and school officials developed sophisticated techniques to bring truants into schools. By the 1920s and 1930s increasing numbers of states were

requiring youth to attend high school, and by the 1950s secondary school attendance had become so customary that school-leavers were routinely seen as dropouts. (p. 60)

The question arises, why did schooling in the United States gradually become compulsory under force of law? Tyack examined five causal interpretations to see how well each answered this question. For example, the ethnocultural interpretation argues that compulsory education came about because of the belief that it would inculcate a single "correct" standard of behavior. This interpretation is based in part on a recognition of efforts then being made to address challenges to the U.S. economy and culture resulting from the influx of immigrants from southern and eastern Europe, which provoked considerable concern among some religious and ethnic groups already established in this country. Another interpretation, drawn from the economic theory of human capital, states that compulsory schooling grew out of a belief that education would improve the productivity and predictability of the workforce.

Each of Tyack's interpretations of the main reason for the growing strength of compulsory schooling in the United States explains some historical evidence, leaves other evidence unexplained, and suggests new lines of research. Tyack notes that such alternative interpretations help historians "to gain a more complex and accurate perception of the past and a greater awareness of the ambiguous relationship between outcome and intent—both of the actors in history and of the historians who attempt to recreate their lives" (p. 89).

The more researchers learn about the antecedents of a historical event, the more likely they are to discover possible alternative causes of the event. Therefore, it probably is more defensible to identify an earlier event as *a* cause, rather than *the* cause, of a later event. Moreover, by their choice of language in the research report, researchers can convey their interpretation of the strength of the causal link (e.g., "It was a major influence . . . " or "It was one of many events that influenced . . . ") and of its certainty (e.g., "It is highly likely that . . . " or "It is possible that . . . ").

Hopefully, such clarification of the ambiguity involved in causal interpretation of past events will also contribute to a richer, more nuanced understanding of history when students study it in school.

Generalizing from Historical Evidence

Like other qualitative researchers, historical researchers do not seek to study all the individuals, settings, events, or objects that interest them. Instead, they usually study only one case or a few instances of the phenomenon of interest. The case that is chosen is determined partly by the availability of sources. For example, suppose that a historical researcher wished to examine the diaries, correspondence, and other written records of elementary school teachers in the 1800s in order to understand teaching conditions during that time. The study necessarily would be limited to teachers whose writings had been preserved, and to which the researcher could gain access. The researcher also would need to consider the possibility that teachers who kept written records of their work might not be typical of teachers in general.

Before generalizing the study's findings to other teachers of the period, the researcher should consider whether other teachers would have provided similar data. One way to determine whether similar results would be found for other types of teachers would be to examine how teachers in different circumstances viewed their teaching experience. For example, the researcher might ask: Did teachers who wrote about their work for publication describe similar conditions as did teachers who wrote about their work in private diaries and correspondence?

Another potential problem in historical interpretation involves the generalizability of historical data relating to a single individual. For example, a historical researcher might discover a primary source in which an educator stated an opinion about a particular educational issue. The statement does not prove that this educator held the same opinion at a later or earlier time. The researcher must look for more data that will help her decide whether the expressed opinion was characteristic of this educator.

As in any research project, historical research findings are strengthened by increasing the size of the data set on which they are based. Conducting an extensive search for primary and secondary sources relating to the topic will help historical researchers expand their data set. If the evidence is limited to only a few sources, the researchers should exercise restraint in asserting the generalizability of their interpretations. For example, they might phrase a generalization about teaching as "Teachers in rural schools of fifty or fewer students during the period 1860 to 1870 . . . " rather than "Teachers during the period 1860 to 1870. . . ." Historical researchers wishing to make the latter generalization could strengthen their case by presenting statistical analyses based on representative quantitative data.

Reporting of Historical Research Findings

The presentation of findings in a historical research report varies. Some historical reports present historical facts in chronological order. Another method of presentation involves organizing historical facts according to topic or theme. Benjamin Justice, the author of the research article reprinted at the end of this chapter, predominantly followed a chronological approach to ordering his historical facts. Each of the main headings covers a different time period:

> Nineteenth-Century Rehabilitation: The Work of Punishment (1870–1900)
> Inmate Education and "Ethical Evolution" (1900)
> "Like Other Men": A Humanitarian Basis for Education (1904–1912)
> Social Efficiency and the Ascendancy of the School (1913–1920)

Within each time period Justice identified educational reform themes that characterized it, reflected in the headings above.

Example of Outlining a Research Proposal

This feature of the chapter gives you an example of how to outline a research proposal using the form in Appendix 1. The example, involving a proposal to study curriculum alignment, is introduced at the end of Chapter 2.

In introducing this example, we noted that educators increasingly are turning to curriculum alignment in response to new federal and state policies holding them accountable for student learning. Many educators believe that curriculum alignment will help them meet these accountability requirements.

Taking a historical perspective, we find ourselves asking two questions: What events, individuals, and groups in the recent past initiated the curriculum-alignment movement and helped it gain momentum? Were there other, similar movements in the history of U.S. education?

Undoubtedly, additional interesting questions about the history of curriculum alignment can be posed. For present purposes, we will focus on our question about the recent past of the curriculum-alignment movement. In the next section, we fill out various parts of the proposal outline to show how a research study might be designed to answer this question.

4. RESEARCH DESIGN
    A. *Research design.* The research design involves historiography, which is predominantly a qualitative research tradition. Our purpose is to understand the events, organizations, individuals, and societal trends that were influential in bringing curriculum alignment to prominence as an educational practice at the local, state, and national levels. We will not draw strong causal inferences from the study, but instead will seek to understand curriculum alignment as a historically situated phenomenon. In particular, we seek to understand how the curriculum-alignment movement reflects the values, goals, needs, and knowledge of particular individuals and stakeholder groups in the recent past.
    D. *Validity and reliability criteria.* We expect to make extensive use of secondary sources, but also plan to search for relevant primary sources. To the extent possible, we will subject both types of sources to internal and external criticism.
5. SAMPLING
    B. *Phenomenon.* The phenomenon of interest to us is the recent history of the curriculum-alignment movement. To determine the time period encompassed by "recent history," we will determine the number of ERIC citations for the descriptor "curriculum alignment" for the current year and then go back year by year. We expect to find the number of citations to start ascending from a more-or-less level plateau. We will select a year near the end of the plateau to be the starting year of the "recent past" and the current year to be the ending year of the time period encompassed by our historical study.

C. *Sampling procedure.* Our search for primary and secondary sources will be grounded in the documents indexed by ERIC for the selected time period. We will look for patterns in the documents, for example, the individuals and groups prominently associated with the curriculum-alignment movement, and the types of publications in which their views were expressed (e.g., conference proceedings, journals, working papers). As we find such patterns, we will use them to search for additional primary and secondary sources.

6. VARIABLES
   B. *Focus of the case study.* Of particular interest will be factors that shaped the views of key individuals and groups. We are open to the possibility that these factors might arise within the education profession or from outside forces, such as legislative acts or groups representing special interests in society.

7. METHODS OF DATA COLLECTION
   C. *Framework for data collection.* The primary data will be the content of the documents identified through our ERIC search. For documents of peripheral importance to the study, the ERIC abstract might be sufficient. For many documents, however, an actual copy of the document will need to be obtained. Document-procurement services available through ERIC, the local university library, and other organizations will be used.

8. DATA ANALYSIS PROCEDURES
   B. *Method of data analysis.* Interpretational analysis will be used initially to identify recurrent themes in the primary and secondary sources. Of particular interest will be influences on particular individuals and groups associated with the curriculum-alignment movement. Also of interest will be actions taken by individuals and groups to advance or thwart the movement. Following the interpretational analysis, we will move toward reflective analysis. That is, we will use our personal judgment to weave together our findings into a coherent story of how particular events, individuals, and groups in the recent past initiated the curriculum-alignment movement and helped it gain momentum.

SELF-CHECK TEST

1. All educational researchers can be regarded as historians in the sense that they generally
   a. review past research as a basis for designing their own research studies.
   b. seek causes for present-day phenomena by investigating past phenomena.

     c. interpret the practical significance of their research findings.

     d. suggest desirable directions for future research on the topics they have studied.

2. In historical research, the literature review typically
   a. is a relatively minor part of the research process.
   b. provides the research data.
   c. is conducted after the data have been analyzed.
   d. focuses on secondary sources.

3. Historical researchers typically read secondary sources relating to their research problem in order to
   a. gain an overview of historical information relevant to their problem.
   b. obtain the most accurate information possible about a past event.
   c. identify relevant preliminary sources.
   d. eliminate the necessity of examining primary sources.

4. In historical research, a private journal written by a nineteenth-century school principal most likely would be considered
   a. oral history.   c. a document.
   b. a relic.   d. a secondary source.

5. In historical research, physical objects preserved from the period being studied are called
   a. records.   c. repositories.
   b. secondary sources.   d. relics.

6. The procedure for determining whether a source of historical data is authentic sometimes is called
   a. internal criticism.   c. historiography.
   b. external criticism.   d. revisionism.

7. Internal criticism of documents is used to
   a. detect forgeries.
   b. determine the accuracy of the information in the bibliographic citations for documents.
   c. locate variant sources.
   d. determine the accuracy of the information in the text of documents.

8. In historical research, presentism refers to the
   a. belief that the present is more important than the historical past.
   b. use of contemporary concepts to interpret past events.
   c. belief that the present cannot be understood by the study of past events.
   d. set of assumptions underlying revisionist history.

9. Historical researchers generally consider quantitative materials superior to other types of primary sources for
   a. exploring the unique aspects of a historical phenomenon.
   b. investigating the history of nonliterate cultures.
   c. writing grassroots historical accounts.
   d. describing prominent individuals of past periods.

10. Causal inference in historical research is a process by which researchers
    a. narrow the cause of a historical phenomenon to one set of factors.
    b. explain past events in terms of contemporary concepts.
    c. take a critical view of past practices that previously were viewed positively.
    d. use interpretation to ascribe causality to a sequence of historical events.

*C*HAPTER REFERENCES

Bellah, R. et al. (1985). *Habits of the heart: Individualism and commitment in American life.* Berkeley: University of California Press.

Button, H. W. (1979). Creating more usable pasts: History in the study of education. *Educational Researcher, 8*(5), 3–9.

Carr, E. H. (1967). *What is history?* New York: Random.

Cohen, S. (1976). The history of the history of American education, 1900–1976: The uses of the past. *Harvard Educational Review, 46,* 298–330.

Donato, R., & Lazerson, M. (2000). New directions in American educational history: Problems and prospects. *Educational Researcher, 29*(8), 4–15.

Downey, M. T., & Levstik, L. S. (1991). Teaching and learning history. In J. P. Shaver (Ed.), *Handbook of research on social studies teaching and learning* (pp. 400–410). New York: Macmillan.

Gonzalez, G. (1990). *Chicano education in the era of segregation.* Philadelphia: Balch Institute Press.

Grosvenor, I., & Lawn, M. (2001). Ways of seeing in education and schooling: Emerging historiographies. *History of Education, 30,* 105–108.

Horn, T. C. R., & Ritter, H. (1986). Interdisciplinary history: A historiographical review. *The History Teacher, 19,* 427–428.

Katz, M. B. (1968). *The irony of early school reform: Educational innovation in mid-nineteenth century Massachusetts.* Cambridge, MA: Harvard University Press.

Katz, M. B. (1987). *Reconstructing American education.* Cambridge, MA: Harvard University Press.

Kelen, L. G., & Stone, E. H. (1996). *Missing stories.* Salt Lake City, UT: University of Utah Press.

Lincoln, Y. S., & Guba, E. G. (1985). *Naturalistic inquiry.* Beverly Hills, CA: Sage.

Popkewitz, T. S. (1997). A changing terrain of knowledge and power: A social epistemology of educational research. *Educational Researcher, 26*(9), 18–29.

Tyack, D. B. (1976). Ways of seeing: An essay on the history of compulsory schooling. *Harvard Educational Review, 46,* 55–89.

Resources for Further Study

Barzun, J. (1998). *The modern researcher* (6th ed.). Belmont, CA: Wadsworth.

> *Provides a comprehensive description of historical researchers' work, including strategies for fact finding, criticism, interpretation, and reporting.*

Darcy, R., & Rohrs, R. C. (1995). *A guide to quantitative history.* Westport, CT: Greenwood.

> *The authors describe statistical techniques suited to the needs of historians.*

Kaestle, C. F. (1997). Recent methodological developments in the history of education. In R. M. Jaeger (Ed.), *Complementary methods for research in education* (2nd ed., pp. 119–131). Washington, DC: American Educational Research Association.

> *The author compares traditional and revisionist research on the history of education. Also, he explains the methods of quantitative historical research, the role of theory in historical research, and pitfalls to be avoided in conducting a historical study.*

Tuchman, B. W. (1982). *Practicing history: Selected essays.* New York: Ballantine.

> *A collection of essays on the uses of history and the craft of doing historical research. Examples of the author's historical studies are included.*

Yow, V. R. (1994). *Recording oral history: A practical guide for social scientists.* Thousand Oaks, CA: Sage.

> *The author explains interviewing strategies and the ethical issues involved in oral history. Includes an in-depth description of three types of oral history projects—community studies, biographies, and family histories.*

In the following section of this chapter you will read a research article that illustrates a historical research study. It is preceded by comments written especially for this book by the author of the article. Then the article itself is reprinted in full, just as it appeared when originally published.

Sample Historical Research Study
"A College of Morals": Educational Reform at San Quentin Prison, 1880–1920

Justice, B. (2000). "A college of morals": Educational reform at San Quentin Prison, 1880–1920. *History of Education Quarterly, 40,* 279–301.

● RESEARCHER'S COMMENTS, *Prepared by Benjamin Justice*

Why are there schools in prisons? This question started me off on a research paper I wrote for a graduate history seminar at Stanford University. That paper eventually became the article, "A College of Morals," that you will read here. I must confess that at first I thought the question was too simple, and that the literature relevant to answering it would be overwhelming. My professor felt the same way. As I dug, though, I found quite the opposite. Very few historians had looked at the history of prisons at all; those interested in my question I could count on one hand. The challenge I faced thus switched from trying to say something new in a crowded conversation to trying to say anything meaningful at all!

Getting Started

Usually the secondary source literature offers guidance for a new research project—it is certainly the first place to start. I began by writing an annotated bibliography of books in three fields: prison history, prison education, and educational history. Because there was so little on prison education per se, I turned instead to what I knew well: the literature on the history of education. In that literature, the Progressive era stands out as a major reform period. Its emphasis on social reform in general made it a good candidate for prison reform too. Likewise, the few works on prison history pointed to the Progressive era as a major period of reform, including many programs targeting education and "correction" over mere punishment.

Secondary literature can also point to sources, but in this case there was little to go on. The most famous example of prison educational reform—Elmira State Penitentiary—was too far away to be useful, and had, in any case, already been studied. I began my own search by looking at the history of all prisons in the state of California. I very quickly realized that San Quentin and Folsom were both close to where I lived and exciting possibilities because of their fame.

Finding Sources

As it turned out, I never had to visit either prison, and I found many of their documents in my own library. The annual reports of the administration of both institutions were microfilmed and easy to find through a computer search. So were other related documents, including reports from prison reform associations and children's reformatories. These all provided a good glimpse of the long-term developments at both Folsom and San Quentin. The latter prison quickly proved to be the best option for my purposes, because it was older and more specifically designed to offer an educational program.

Annual reports and other official publications have obvious limitations, however. Such sources tell an extremely biased story, and they tend to exaggerate the success of innovations and hide the failures of their authors. These sources alone would have not been enough for a deep analysis of prison reform. Fortunately, I was able to find others that breathed life—and credibility—into my story. The first trove included several books written by officials and former inmates at San Quentin during the very period that I hoped to study. Second, I unearthed a fascinating archive in the Bancroft Library at the University of California, Berkeley, which included the personal papers and correspondence of several San Quentin wardens during the Progressive era. Among these were the letters and personal papers of inmates. The third find was an early-twentieth-century scrapbook someone at San Quentin had kept of newspaper articles about the prison. (I found it by chance at the California State Archives in Sacramento.) Scrapbooks like this are often worth hundreds of hours of newspaper scouring.

Together, the books and archival materials from Berkeley and Sacramento allowed me to see educational reform at the prison from many different points of view, and to better understand the biases and motivations of individual actors in the evidence they left behind.

Interpretation

In the early stages of my career, I have found historical writing to be a two-stage process. The first stage is figuring out what happened. Experienced historians already have a good sense of this part of the writing. For beginners like myself, it involves a complicated, but fun, process of piecing together various sources, making decisions about where the story begins and ends, and assembling evidence into paragraphs. The second part of the process is every bit as hard for the veteran as the novice: explanation. Coming up with a reason for why things happened proves to be the most challenging part of the historical research process. My paper on San Quentin was no exception.

Most good historical explanations fit into a broader conversation among scholars. The researcher needs to understand how others have explained similar historical phenomena and then situate her explanation within that context. The few historians who have studied prison education have left a sparse landscape. The best-known writer on prisons-as-educators, Michele Foucault, wasn't much of a historian. More to the point, he used far too ephemeral an explanatory model for my taste. (Reviewers pressured me to discuss Foucault, and I relented enough to put him in a footnote.) Others had studied prisons to understand social attitudes about gender, childhood, and crime. None of these said much to me about why San Quentin had developed its program, or why this particular program went so much further than those in other prisons. In the end, I decided that changing ideas about schooling, morality, and crime guided the actions of reformers at San Quentin. Where did these ideas come from, and why did reformers find them so appealing?

The unusual politics of Progressive-era California provided one explanation; broader patterns in American life offered another. I turned to the work of historians of public education, who have shown the role that the socioeconomic context has played in shaping school policy and practice. Tying these ideas together allowed me to reach the conclusion that schools ended up in prisons because of a widespread perception on the part of the middle and upper classes that attending school improved a person morally.

Revision

Explanation in hand, I revisited my original narrative and began to rebuild. To do so I had to cut its size—perhaps sculpting would be a better description—by nearly 30 percent. I lopped off a detailed history of criminal anthropology and broke up discussions of other institutions within the California state prison system. Even the master escape artist, Harry Houdini, could not evade my chisel. (He performed for inmates during the period, and his handcuffs escape drove them wild!) In the end I had a tight enough argument to send the paper off to the *History of Education Quarterly* and await their reply.

The reviews were favorable, though they diverged widely in their suggestions for revision. The trouble, it seemed, was that each reviewer was an expert in either prison history or educational history, but not in both. One called for a greater emphasis on race and ethnicity, another wanted me to discuss children and juvenile justice, while the third called on me to frame the discussion in terms of Foucault. All agreed that I should put more literature review into the article, and some of this now appears in the first three pages or in footnotes.

The editor proved very understanding and supportive, helping me identify helpful criticism and urging me to stick to my guns when I felt the suggestions were inappropriate. A year and a half after I first wrote "A College of Morals," *HEQ* agreed to publish it. The experience was truly a pleasure!

"A College of Morals": Educational Reform at San Quentin Prison, 1880–1920

Benjamin Justice

Since the early nineteenth century, the idea of American prisons, like the idea of common schools, has reflected a faith in public institutions for effecting social reform through individual transformation. With this goal in mind, penal theory has been a type of educational theory, making a systematic, sustained effort to "correct" the behavior and ideas of inmates.[1] What has set penal theory apart from educational theory—and prisons apart from schools—are other social functions of imprisonment: retribution for crimes committed, custodial control that separates the inmate from society, and deterrence. The goal of punishment has dominated the evolution of American prisons; nevertheless, as "total" institutions prisons have had their own *paeadia* and this *paeadia*—along with its relationship to punishment—has changed significantly over time.

Formal schooling played a negligible role in the nineteenth-century prison *paeadia*. Prison schools (where they even existed) were small, mediocre, and served mainly juveniles.[2] The progressive movement, by contrast, ushered in new paradigms for penal theory and practice that rested squarely on the idea of formal schooling. Using the much-touted school at San Quentin State Penitentiary as a case study, this essay examines forty years of educational change, in theory and practice, at one of the nation's largest—and, by World War I, most progressive—prisons. In particular, this essay considers the evolution of the prison school as a part of the institution's overall correctional agenda and in the context of broad changes in penal theory. The dramatic change in penal theory that led to San Quentin's formal education program reflected a larger movement in progressive social theory and reform. Moreover, the relatively sudden growth of schooling within the prison mirrored an increase in the theoretical and social value of schooling in society.

There has been little scholarly work on the history of prisons as educational institutions (especially on schools

Justice, B. (2000). "A college of morals": Educational reform at San Quentin Prison, 1880–1920. *History of Education Quarterly, 40*, 279–301. Reprinted with permission of the *History of Education Quarterly*. Copyright © 2000 by the History of Education Society.

1. For such a view of education I rely on Lawrence Cremin's expansive definition: "the deliberate, systematic, and sustained effort to transmit, evoke, or acquire knowledge, values, attitudes, skills, and sensibilities, as well as any learning that results from that effort, direct or indirect, intended or unintended," as cited in *American Education: The Metropolitan Experience* (New York: Harper and Row, 1988), *x*. I also thank Cremin for the term *paeadia*.

2. The one significant exception is The New York State Reformatory at Elmira, under Zebulon Brockway. See David J. Rothman, *Conscience and Convenience* (Boston: Little Brown, 1980), 32–36.

within prisons) except in terms of children's institutions, juvenile justice systems, and women's reformatories.[3] The formal education of adult male inmates—most of the prison population in the nineteenth and twentieth centuries—remains underexplored. This essay bridges the gap in the fields of penal and educational history by analyzing the rise of formal schooling as an aspect of progressive penal theory and practice. Informal and unintended, education has also been a critical aspect of the prison experience (attracting much scholarly attention), and this essay points to some of the ways in which actual education in the prison fell far short of theory. Nevertheless, even viewed from the perspective of most inmates, the changes at San Quentin were substantial, if incremental. By 1920 more than half of all inmates were enrolled in some kind of school. From the point of view of the prison administration, the rise of the prison school at San Quentin marked a new era in corrections. For them, and for enthusiastic observers, San Quentin State Penitentiary became nothing short of a "College of Morals."

NINETEENTH-CENTURY REHABILITATION: THE WORK OF PUNISHMENT

For advocates of prison reform in California, 1880 was a seminal year. The recently revised state constitution of California created a Board of Prison Directors, composed of lay citizens, as an attempt to take the prison out of politics and to help streamline the process of reform. A new law also consolidated the power of the warden by ending the contract labor system, which had allowed the prison to "hire out" its inmates as laborers. Finally, in July of 1880, the second state prison officially opened at Folsom, accepting forty-four transfers from San Quentin.[4] The administrative restructuring of California's prisons convinced officials that a new era was at hand. Leading penologist Enoch Wines confirmed this optimism, writing that the new board of directors placed California "in the forefront of all States on the North American continent in the matter of prison reform."[5] Reformers hoped that administrative restructuring would lead to substantive improvement in corrections.

The emphasis on a prison administration that was above politics stemmed from a larger agenda of nationwide prison reform known as the New Penology. At an 1870 meeting of prominent penal reformers in Cincinnati, and later at the First International Prison Congress in London, advocates of the New Penology recommended revitalizing the penitentiary ideal of prisons—that is, making prisoners penitent through rigid routines and hard labor—by refocusing prison administration away from punishment and towards rehabilitation. Their program focused on alleviating overcrowding, building separate institutions for juveniles and women, and instituting probation, parole, and the indeterminate sen-

3. See in particular, Robert M. Mennel, *Thorns and Thistles: Juvenile Delinquents in the United States, 1825–1940* (Hanover: University Press of New England, 1973), which links institutional reform to changing conceptions of childhood and Steven L. Schlossman, *Love and the American Delinquent: The Theory and Practice of "Progressive" Juvenile Justice, 1825–1920* (Chicago: University of Chicago Press, 1977). From 1880–1920, the number of inmates under 18 years of age at San Quentin fluctuated between 1 and 2 percent of the total. On women's institutions, see Estelle B. Freedman, *Their Sister's Keepers: Women's Prison Reform in America, 1830–1930* (Ann Arbor: University of Michigan Press, 1981), and Nicole Hahn Rafter, *Partial Justice: Women in State Prisons, 1800–1935* (Boston: Northeastern University Press, 1985). Although there was a tiny women's department at San Quentin, its inmates were kept separate from the rest of the population—virtual prisoners within the prison. While their story is valuable in its own right, this essay only includes the women's department as it touched on the more general educational reforms at the prison, which was seldom. Anne Butler's *Gendered Justice in the American West: Women Prisoners in Men's Penitentiaries*, (Urbana: University of Illinois Press, 1997) offers a gendered Analysis of the type of experience that women had at San Quentin, though it does not specifically cover California prisons.

4. California State Board of Prison Directors. *Annual Report for Fiscal Year 1880* (Sacramento: State Printer, 1880), 1.

5. Shelley Bookspan, *A Germ of Goodness: The California State Prison System, 1851–1944.* (Lincoln: University of Nebraska Press, 1991), 37–40; Enoch Wines, *The State of Prisons and Child-Saving Institutions in the Civilized World* [1880] reprint (Montclair: Patterson Smith, 1968).

tence.[6] This last reform aimed at fixing no length onto an inmate's sentence; prison authorities would judge, based on the inmate's behavior while incarcerated, when (if ever) he would be released. Wines summed up the foundation of this rehabilitation: "Work—steady, active, honorable work," he wrote, "is the basis of all good, and especially all reformatory systems of prison discipline."[7]

Income and occupation most clearly separated middle-class reformers from the working-class inmates in their care. Since the early decades of the nineteenth century, school and prison reformers had pointed at the interconnection between lawbreaking and poverty. As historian Michael Katz, among others, has shown, middle-class social reformers used this correlation as proof that the poor were morally depraved.[8] San Quentin's Warden Ames believed that criminals were lazy, writing in 1880 that "There is a class whose aversion to work is so great that, rather than labor, they will resort to unlawful means to obtain the necessaries of life." Moreover, he asserted that "There is no cure for this class but enforced labor, and after being compelled to labor for a term of years, such prisoners may acquire the habit of work." Ames believed that most inmates lacked any skilled trade, which partly accounted for their criminal behavior. Thus the work that they did in prison was to be productive and would give the inmate skills to use when released. Unproductive labor "provide[d] no mental exercise, and simply serve[d] to degrade the convict."[9]

The year 1880 may have marked a new era in administrative design, but in educational matters the traditional policy of San Quentin changed little. Though the warden espoused the New Penology's emphasis on rehabilitation through skilled work, his first annual report (1880) laid out an agenda that reflected the penitentiary's usual emphasis: punishment. The purpose of the prison, wrote Ames, was "the suppression of crime." The means was a combination of punishment (will-breaking) and reformation but definitely favored the former. "The criminal should not only be restrained of his liberty," he wrote, "but he should be subjected to a discipline so thorough as to prevent his again committing crimes." Rigid discipline, including uniforms, marching in step, and silence, would not only deter the inmate from committing crime in the future but would also help him to contemplate the error of his ways. In fact, Ames recommended that in the future the incoming prisoner be subjected to solitary confinement for a few weeks or even a few months to give him time to "reflect upon his past career" and "to make him penitent."[10] Once San Quentin had broken the prisoner's will, then reformation through hard labor could begin.

In this context, it is not surprising that formal schooling had little place in the prison. Schooling was for juveniles only (there were nineteen inmates under age eighteen), and in 1880 Ames reported excusing these "youths" and other "young men" from work detail to receive "the benefits of a good, plain schooling." By law, the "moral instructor" took charge of inmates under the age of eighteen and segregated them as much as possible from the older inmates. The Moral Instructor H. Cummings grouped the boys and some slightly older illiterate young men by ability into four classes led by inmate instructors, each in a corner of the prison chapel. There were no textbooks, chalkboards, or few other resources. The curriculum was an "English education," but the moral instructors' reports specified nothing beyond reading, writing, spelling, and discipline. The school was too small (average monthly attendance sank from 42 to 11 in one year) and too paltry to reflect any central role in the general reformatory function of the prison. That was left to the prison labor system.[11]

6. Lawrence Friedman, *Crime and Punishment in American History* (New York: Basic Books, 1993), 77–80, 159–166.

7. As cited in Charles R. Henderson (ed.), *Correction and Prevention* (New York: Charities Publication Committee, 1910), vol. I, 24.

8. Michael B. Katz, *The Irony of Early School Reform* (Cambridge: Harvard University Press, 1968), chapter 3.

9. Prison Directors, *Report for 1880*, 17–18.

10. Ibid.

11. "Report of the Moral Instructor" in Prison Directors, *Report for 1880*, 51–52.

In fact and at the Warden's suggestion, Cummings's successor, William Hill, took the majority of the students *out* of school in order for them to work. These students "care[d] little or nothing for the advantages of the school," and Hill reported that he and they found their work at caning chairs and in the prison jute mill quite beneficial. Like Warden Ames, Hill believed that manual labor was the road to reformation for young inmates. By July of 1883, Hill had disbanded the school altogether, citing the "idleness and carelessness" of the boys in their studies and offering to oversee an evening school for the few men and boys who wished to continue their studies in prison. "If the choice must be made between . . . work and schooling without work," he wrote to the warden, "I would choose the former."[12]

Prison labor also provided income for the state, and it is likely that the theory of prison labor did not spring from the minds of reformers *ex nihilo.* Despite any lip service to reform, fiscal pressures outweighed rehabilitative intentions for the rest of the nineteenth century and on into the twentieth. While the population at Folsom Prison grew rapidly through the 1880s and 1890s, the population at San Quentin, after an initial decrease, remained fairly level (roughly 1300–1400 men, and 20 women) throughout the period. So did the number of available cells (696).[13] Under pressure from trade unions, San Quentin dropped all other industries except the jute sack mill, a business that coincided with the rising agricultural sector and competed only with Chinese jute sack manufacturers (who in this period of California's history lacked the support not only of the unions, which resented competition, but of the state government itself). Thus the job skills that would ostensibly aid prisoners in finding employment outside of the prison were virtually useless everywhere in California except within the prison itself—a fact that the prison board eventually admitted.[14]

Until the twentieth century the prison school would continue to languish in an atmosphere of retribution and neglect, suffering from the doubts of even reform-minded administrators that schooling inmates was appropriate. In 1890 August Drahms replaced William Hill (the title changed from moral instructor to chaplain) and reorganized a small prison school for young inmates. Two years later there were only forty inmates per month enrolled, and by the following year, that school closed, not to reopen until 1907.[15] Year after year the legislature rejected requests for more funding and reform legislation. Likewise, the prison board and San Quentin administrators themselves made little effort at expanding or enhancing the rehabilitative aspects of the prison.

There were a few notable exceptions to the dearth of legislative and administrative action from 1880–1900, though none fundamentally changed the institution or brought it much closer to its ostensible goal. Each offered new opportunities for specific populations of the prison. In 1885 a matron replaced abusive male prison guards in the tiny women's department, and the warden purchased sewing machines and put the women to work sewing uniforms for the entire prison. Now the women of the prison engaged in their own, gender-specific labor toward rehabilitation.[16] The legislature built a separate institution, the Whittier State Reform School in Los Angeles, for child offenders in 1892—an institution that, like others of its day, sought to inculcate middle-class values in a "family-like" environment.[17] Finally, the legislature passed a parole law in 1893.[18]

---

12. "Report of the Moral Instructor" in Prison Directors, *Report for 1882,* 67–68; "Report of the Moral Instructor" in Prison Directors, *Report for 1883,* 49.

13. Bookspan, *A Germ of Goodness,* 119–120.

14. Prison Directors, *Report for 1894,* 7. On anti-Chinese discrimination, see Kenneth Lamott, *Chronicles of San Quentin: The Biography of a Prison* (New York: D. McKay Co, 1961), 139. Alexander Saxton, *The Indispensable Enemy: Labor and the Anti-Chinese Movement in California* [1971] reprint (Berkeley: University of California Press, 1995).

15. "Report of the Moral Instructor" in Prison Directors, *Report for 1892,* 40.

16. Prison Directors, *Report for 1886,* 6. There is no evidence of any formal education for female inmates in this period.

17. Mennel, *Thorns and Thistles,* chapter two; Schlossman, *Love and the American Delinquent,* 105–123.

18. As a later governor would note, in the first thirteen years after the passage of the parole law only 304 prisoners enjoyed the privilege. See California State Senate, "Biannual Address of the Governor of California," *Senate Journal* (1907), 23.

But none of those reforms confronted the fundamental problem highlighted by the New Penology: whether San Quentin could live up to its promise of rehabilitating the inmates who did "belong" there, and if so, how that rehabilitation could be accomplished. Neither the legislature nor the prison administration was willing to commit the energy or resources necessary to make San Quentin something new. For those inmates who were old enough to know better, the administration considered the penitentiary to be the appropriate environment, with hard work and punishment being the correctives to the criminal class.

INMATE EDUCATION AND "ETHICAL EVOLUTION"

The first significant argument for formal education as a means of prisoner rehabilitation came not from moralistic arguments, but from scientific ones. Early in the nineteenth century, phrenologists like George Combe had used science to explain criminal behavior. By 1867 C. L. Brace had linked social class and crime to evolution in his widely read *The Dangerous Classes of New York and Twenty Years' Work Among Them,* which argued that crime was both heritable and socially conditioned. In 1900 San Quentin Chaplain August Drahms published his own account, *The Criminal: His Personnel and Environment,* which applied the theories of criminal anthropology to the problems of American penology. The book included data collected at San Quentin and featured an introduction written by the founder of the field, Cesare Lombroso, whose belief that criminals were evolutionary throwbacks enjoyed decades of prominence in America.[19]

Drahms argued that human behavior was genetically based and that it existed at different evolutionary stages in different individuals. "The criminal," Drahms wrote, "is an anomaly in civilization, because he represents primitive conditions under modern forms and an instinctive savagery not yet eliminated in past racial evolution through the process of evolution." Criminals revealed atavistic behaviors—a lack of remorse, vanity, low intelligence, and an inability to blush—that were not as common in more highly evolved "normals." Even those criminals who demonstrated high intelligence did so in base and savage ways.[20] (Criminals also tended to exhibit certain atavistic physical traits, such as the criminal ear, which was "voluminous and projecting," and the hair, in which "there [was] no propensity to turn gray among criminals, except in the case of swindlers.")[21]

Given Drahms's emphasis on heredity, it may seem paradoxical that he also placed great emphasis on social reform in general and prison reform in particular. Yet this emphasis corresponded with two of his scientific beliefs. The first was that criminal propensity, not simply criminal behavior, was genetic. The social and spiritual context of an individual *stimulated* his or her latent criminal tendencies, especially in the case of the habitual criminal. For failing to create a better context, society shared the criminal's guilt. Drahms also justified reform with his belief in Lamarckian evolution, in which individuals supposedly pass down characteristics acquired in their lifetimes. "Habit fixes itself in the organic and psychological constitution of the individual," Drahms wrote; "heredity perpetuates it in the race."[22] Thus the genetic material of criminals, indeed of whole races, could be brought up to evolutionary code over time.

Drahms's cure for the disease of crime was formal education. Rigorous moral and mental training could ingrain the proper civilizing influences into the genetic "germ-plasm" of the individual or group. In the case of the instinctive criminal, education could at least provide the opportunity to bridge the civilization gap: "The psychology of the child is the psychology of the Man plus the educative and repressive agencies that go in modification of innate tendencies." Since criminals were the evolutionary equivalent of children, criminals needed to be educated just as children did. For the habitual criminal, a solid education could teach him or her

19. Mennel, *Thorns and Thistles,* 78–80. August Drahms, *The Criminal: His Personnel and Environment* (New York: Macmillan, 1900).

20. Drahms, *The Criminal,* 59; 64–81.

21. Ibid., 59–81; 103.

22. Ibid., 136.

to avoid temptation and bad company. For the potential single offender, education could at the least lessen the likelihood of future crimes of passion. As Drahms wrote, "Education is the equivalent for selection in the ethical evolution."[23]

Drahms was expressing a nineteenth-century, middle-class Protestant faith in the civilizing role of education for the lower classes. In fact, his argument did not entirely divorce itself from the ideas expressed by the social reformers of the 1870s who argued that class *behavior*, not class *biology*, was the root of crime. Concluding his chapter on the "instinctive criminal," Drahms wrote that he had never known an instance of a habitual criminal or recidivist as being a member in good standing in a Protestant Evangelical church.[24] Thus Drahms was willing to promote the role of biology in crime, but not at the expense of his class prejudices, his belief in the wickedness of the criminal, and his resentment at their rejection of his idea of proper habits and proper religion. As a result, although he was in charge of education at San Quentin, Drahms did nothing to implement the sweeping reforms he recommended in his book. By treating inmates as children, Drahms foreclosed the possibility of inmate enthusiasm for his educational program. Paradoxically, the unwillingness of inmates to partake in Drahms's school surely confirmed his suspicions that they were incorrigible. In fact, after his brief revival of the prison school for young inmates in 1891, Drahms did little except acquire more books for the library and facilitate the sparsely attended religious programs on Sundays, and he earned the intense dislike of inmates and administrators alike.[25]

Neither the prison board nor the warden ever commented on Drahms's work in their annual reports—let alone initiated any of his theoretical reforms—probably as a result of Drahms's personal unpopularity. But Drahms's book is an important representative of the cutting edge of penology at San Quentin and in general. *The Criminal* marks a bridge between the nineteenth and twentieth centuries, continuing to rely on the belief in a criminal class, but using science, not morality or philosophy, to buttress the argument. If anything, with the exception of his opposition to the death penalty, Drahms's arguments only reinforced the legislature's unsympathetic view of criminals. Still, his book also represented a challenge to traditional theories of crime. The criminal was vicious but was also scientifically proven to be a product of both nature *and* nurture. Most importantly, Drahms's assertion that formal education could produce moral capital among adult inmates (even though it infantilized them to do so) foreshadowed the rise of adult education at San Quentin. As the new century progressed, prison reformers would enjoy newfound political support from Sacramento which acknowledged nurture's dominance in the formation and rehabilitation of criminals.

"LIKE OTHER MEN": A HUMANITARIAN BASIS FOR EDUCATION

"It is no exaggeration," lamented the California State Board of Charities and Corrections (BCC) in 1904, "to say that our state prisons in their present condition are simply schools for crime." Only one year earlier the California state legislature had created the board to monitor the conditions of orphanages, hospitals, asylums, and prisons. (The BCC remained separate from, and much less powerful than, the Board of Prison Directors.) Now, in its first report, the BCC blasted the state's prison system. Inspectors found the conditions at California's two state prisons abysmal. Approximately fourteen hundred prisoners squeezed into less than half that number of cells; some cells housed as many as six inmates. With no system of classification or differentiation among inmates, young first offenders, a few in their early teens, mixed with "hardened criminals." Violent and nonviolent

---

23. Ibid., 62.

24. Ibid., 81.

25. Donald Lowrie, *My Life in Prison* (London: John Lane, 1912), 111. One inmate described Drahms as "a parasitical sniveling hypocrite, a grafter and traducer of hopes of unfortunate convicts" (cited in Lamott, *Chronicles of San Quentin*, 129). There is also some evidence that the administration had wanted to fire Drahms for years but could not because of his status as a Civil War veteran. See Lowrie, 111.

offenders lived, worked, and socialized together. In the BCC's opinion, San Quentin had become a place where relatively innocent inmates learned to be "incorrigibles." "The wonder," the report continued, "is that any prisoner can serve a term and become a good man. As a matter of fact, almost none do achieve this end."[26]

The BCC's efforts were the product of a new humanitarianism, both on the part of the prison administration and the more general public.[27] The view of the prisoner as a more or less normal human being represented the continuing evolution of nineteenth-century penology—finding its justification in the social responsibility argument of men like August Drahms, but rejecting his emphasis on the evolutionary inferiority or juvenilism of the criminal. The BCC advocated many of the reforms first proposed by nineteenth-century New Penologists: the indeterminate sentence, classification, separate facilities for women and first offenders, and expanded parole and probation. But unlike their nineteenth-century counterparts, the BCC strongly emphasized the inherent humanity of the criminal. In its 1906 report to the governor, the BCC approvingly quoted a recent speech by the Honorable D. E. Meyers, which asserted that:

> It is too often assumed that because a man is sentenced to prison he is wholly bad. That all criminals belong in the same grade or class; that they are to be shunned like evil wild beasts, that they are to be treated so by the state. . . . All men are more or less criminal; . . . the difference between the criminal and the honest man is not a question of fact but of degree; thus the only index to a man's character are the habits he has acquired.[28]

Like Drahms, Meyers saw habits, acquired through education and honest work, as the measure of a person. But Meyers saw habit as the *only* factor separating the criminal from everyone else. For Drahms, education would fill the yawning evolutionary gap between the criminal and the civilized person, controlling the atavistic and protecting the normal. For Meyers, education was even more vital, since anyone could turn to crime without it. Moreover, the fact that criminals were like other people made them more deserving of a chance at reform.

Meyers's speech indicated the spreading influence of progressive reform in California. One of the most eloquent connections between progressive theory and the idea of the criminal came in sociologist Edward Alsworth Ross's book, *Sin and Society* (which included a prefatory letter from progressive giant Teddy Roosevelt). For Ross, the biggest threat to society in the industrial age came not from petty criminals but from corporate ones, and the old forms of moral judgment no longer applied. "The public," he wrote, "is childishly naive and sentimental. It is content with the surface look of things. It lays emphasis where emphasis was laid centuries ago. It beholds sin in a false perspective, seeing peccadillos as crimes, and crimes as peccadillos. It never occurs to the public that sin evolves along with society, and that the perspective in which it is necessary to view misconduct changes from age to age."[29] As individual sins in the marketplace became more dangerous to more people than ever before, Ross argued, morals needed to evolve to a higher level to keep apace. By emphasizing corporate and indirect criminals ("criminaloids"), Ross deemphasized the petty criminal as the worst type of humanity. After all, if the best men in society were capable of the greatest harms, than all people were potentially criminal.

In California the changing conception of crime and criminals gained increasing prominence as part of a wider movement toward political reform in the battle against the corrupt Southern Pacific political machine. Prominent

---

26. California. State Board of Charities and Corrections, *Report to the Governor for Fiscal Years 1903–1904,* (Sacramento: State Printer, 1904), 12.

27. A. C. Hill, "Prison Schools" in United States Bureau of Education, *Bulletin,* 1913, No. 27, 7. For humanitarianism in Southern prison reform, see Jane Zimmerman, "The Penal Reform Movement in the South During the Progressive Era, 1890–1917," *Journal of Southern History* 17 (1951): 462–492.

28. Board of Charities, *Report for 1905–1906,* 31–32. The Board did not identify Meyers beyond his title, and I have had no success learning more.

29. Edward Aisworth Ross, *Sin and Society* (Boston: Houghton Mifflin, 1907), 11.

California newspapers began to take an active role in pushing for changes in the prisons, publishing graphic exposes and "insider" accounts of life in the state prisons. The reform spirit that infected the press and civic organizations swept a progressive legislature and Governor Hiram Johnston into office in 1911. The Progressive Party made penal reform a plank in its platform.[30]

Although the legislature later balked on a number of proposed reforms, particularly in the face of a recession in 1913, the spirit of humanitarian reform had already penetrated the walls of San Quentin in the unlikely person of Warden John Hoyle, appointed by a conservative Republican board of directors in 1907. Hoyle had no prior experience in prison work, and his appointment appears to have been a political favor more than an expression of a new penal philosophy.[31] The governor wrote to him shortly after Hoyle's appointment with clear instructions: "There are two things you will have to look carefully after, and that will be, proper discipline and a proper and economical expenditure of money."[32] With such a conservative agenda to carry out, Hoyle could have continued the prison's traditional emphasis on punishment and economy. Instead, he embarked on a six-year administration that would significantly change the day-to-day operation of the prison, as well as pave the way for future prison reform bent on educating, not only punishing, inmates.

Hoyle's administration departed from those of the past most dramatically in its opinion of the criminal. In an interview with the *Saturday Evening Post,* Hoyle said, "Convicts are pretty much like other men. I'll handle them along these lines."[33] He increased privileges, phased out the straitjacket, and replaced the hated striped uniform with a plain blue one—helping to ensure that inmates even looked "like other men."[34] On Christmas Eve, 1907, Hoyle noticed that many inmates hung socks outside their cells, a tradition which they apparently followed each year for either ironic or sentimental reasons. The warden immediately sent a guard into town to buy all the candy he could find and that night secretly filled the prisoners' stockings. As inmate Donald Lowrie would later write, "Next morning when the prisoners awoke and found that they had at last been remembered it struck deeply. It was not the first instance of the warden's humanitarianism, but it made a deeper impression than anything else he had done." On New Year's Eve, for the first time in Lowrie's memory, the prisoners refrained from their annual riot.[35]

Hoyle placed unprecedented emphasis on the education and training of inmates. The warden's first significant reform, in concert with the prison directors, was to replace Chaplain August Drahms with the more tolerant, reform-minded W. H. Lloyd.[36] In 1910 Rev. Lloyd surveyed all inmates under the age of twenty-four and placed those he considered to be educationally deficient (112 of 455 in that age cohort) into a day school, which was held in the chapel. He divided the group into two sessions, each meeting once a day, Monday through Friday, for two hours. The class covered a condensed version of first through eighth grades in public school and used the few books provided by the State Superintendent of Instruction. For those inmates deemed too old for day school but in need of special instruction, Lloyd established a night school. This he also divided into two cohorts: one for "colored" inmates and one for whites, each meeting for two hours nightly. Inmate assistants taught both of the classes. The chaplain also established a night school class for Spanish- and Italian-speaking inmates, taught by a multilingual inmate, for English instruction and basic academics. Hoyle and Lloyd en-

30. "A Record of Progressive Achievements" (ca. 1913), Arlett Papers, Bancroft Library, University of California at Berkeley, Box 5.

31. Lamott, *Chronicles of San Quentin,* 177.

32. John E. Hoyle, Papers relating to San Quentin Prison (hereafter Hoyle Papers], Box 1, University of California at Berkeley, Bancroft Library (ca. 1907–ca. 1913).

33. Frederick R Bechdolt, "Honor Among Thieves," *The Saturday Evening Post,* May 7, 1910, 6.

34. Ibid., 6–7; "Hoyle Glad It Came" and other clippings in *Hoyle Papers,* Box 1.

35. Donald Lowrie, *My Life in Prison,* 391.

36. Lamott, *Chronicles of San Quentin,* 179.

couraged a number of inmates not in need of basic education to take correspondence courses, of which the most popular were trades classes.[37] In the following two years, Lloyd and his successor, William Call, expanded the prison school into a program covering the first through eighth grades, including the appropriate public school curriculum for each.[38]

Although the prison school represented a major administrative attempt at the rehabilitation of inmates and resembled prison education programs that had emerged elsewhere in the nation, by the educational standards of the day it was inadequate.[39] Individual classes did not meet in classrooms, but rather crowded together in the chapel. (The night school met in a small, spare room, a constraint that limited enrollment.) The students did not sit at individual desks, but crowded shoulder to shoulder along benches, and their teachers were other inmates. Moreover, those who did enroll "voluntarily" in the prison school were excused from two hours of work in the jute mill—a strong incentive to attend class without necessarily intending to study or participate. Even for motivated students, the two-hour school day was not long enough to approximate the typical public school day it was meant to replicate. In fact, the concept of replicating the age-graded school—the norm for children—in classes for adults may have struck inmates as insulting. One inmate artist, Charles Dorsey, depicted a prison school class as a bored, smart-alecky group of men more interested in the weekend's baseball game and Dick Turpin, the highwayman, than in the seemingly irrelevant

instructor (see Figure 1, "Advancement of Education"). The BCC was equally unimpressed, writing in 1912 that, "There are no schoolrooms, no equipment, and few textbooks. . . . The instruction here can hardly be dignified by the name of school."[40]

The Board of Charities and Corrections also reprimanded the prison administration for not offering manual training or "hand work" in its school program, reflecting the increasing emphasis of the day on vocational training in public schools.[41] But in fact, the Hoyle administration had expanded that aspect of the prison

FIGURE 1   Advancement of Education within the Walls of San Quentin

Inmate Charles Dorsey depicted a Hoyle-era classroom in one of his "souvenir" books, commemorating his stay at San Quentin (Hoyle Papers, Box 1, BANC MSS 88/139c. Reprinted with permission of Bancroft Library, University of California, Berkeley).

37. The chaplain never specified whether these were through the University of California or the letter-box courses described below.

38. "Prison Directors, *Report for 1910*, 10, 110–111; Prison Directors, *Report for 1912*, 125–128.

39. Hill, "Prison Schools." By Hill's standards, no existing system was adequate. Nevertheless, though more developed than most prison "schools," San Quentin did not measure up to existing programs in New York State, for example, which had better resources and full-time civilians as head instructors.

40. "Chaplain's Report" for 1911 and 1912 in Prison Directors, *Report for 1912*, 125–128; Board of Charities, *Report for 1912*, 51.

41. Ibid. For vocational education in the Progressive era, see W. Norton Grubb and Marvin Lazerson, "Education and the Labor Market: Recycling the Youth Problem," and Harvey Kantor, "Vocationalism in American Education: The Economic and Political Context, 1880–1930," both in Harvey Kantor and David B. Tyack (eds.) *Work, Youth, and Schooling. Historical Perspectives on Vocationalism in American Education* (Stanford: Stanford University Press, 1982).

considerably, both with the trade-oriented correspondence courses and through the "state-use" system approved by the legislature in 1911, whereby San Quentin would manufacture materials, such as desks and uniforms, required by other state institutions. Now prisoners could develop skills that might translate into jobs on the outside. These new industries included a clothing shop to make prisoner uniforms and "citizen suits" for discharged inmates, a shoe shop, a furniture factory, a tin shop to make pots and pans, a print shop, and a machine shop to make iron beds and (ironically enough) fireproof safes. For perhaps the first time in San Quentin history, some inmates learned a useful trade. The prison directors were also happy to note that thanks to the new revenue generated by these industries, San Quentin required no fiscal appropriation from the legislature in 1912. The inmates continued to "pay" for their incarceration.[42]

Hoyle's reforms were by no means universally appreciated, and charges both of coddling criminals and inhumane treatment abounded in the northern California press.[43] Although it would be misleading to suggest that Hoyle's administration made life in San Quentin pleasant, the educational changes in the prison were undeniable. The legislature's adoption of the state-use system had given inmates the opportunity to learn skills that they could actually use on the outside—reflecting the growing national emphasis on vocational education. The prison also offered inmates a chance for a basic education in reading and writing. But Hoyle's administration made formal education only a small piece of an overall program to make prison life more tolerable. His reforms emphasized many mainstream middle-class values: prisoners should wear nicer clothes, attend lectures, and engage in wholesome sporting events; the female prisoners should be released for springtime walks on Mount Tamalpais to pick wildflowers. Remedial classes for young men and night classes for adults—meager as

they were—reflected the increasing importance that education played in the middle-class view of normal life, not an exclusively education-based agenda.

SOCIAL EFFICIENCY AND THE ASCENDANCY OF THE SCHOOL

The faith that many progressives placed in social evolution led them to conclude that while industrial society was inherently superior to what had preceded it, its rapid development had outstripped the public's ability to develop an equally advanced intellectual and moral framework for living in it. For progressive leaders like Roosevelt and Ross, the cure for poverty, child labor, pollution, and corruption lay not with leftist policies empowering factions within society, or in social programs that would later characterize the New Deal, but rather with an informed citizenry. Properly socialized individuals acting reasonably and working efficiently, not fractious groups, would cure the ills of modernity. Thus the institutions of the press and the school—particularly through compulsory education—were the linchpins of progressive theory.[44]

Though they shared a common concern for social progress, however, progressive reformers did not agree on much else. Hoyle's administration revealed one strand of progressive reform—humanitarianism. But as charges of coddling criminals spread, humanitarian fever cooled even while the Progressive Party ascended to power, with reformers increasingly locating the source of social chaos in individuals themselves.[45] In public education, historian David Tyack has identified a variety of strands of progressive reform but notes that those who carried the day, particularly in urban systems, were advocates of social efficiency. These "administrative progressives" pushed a program of consolidation, specialization, compulsion, and scientific efficiency in the public schools, hoping to model school administration on the corpora-

42. Prison Directors, *Report for 1912*, 8; *The Sacramento Union*, Dec. 8, 1912, from the *Corrections Scrapbook* (1912–1925), California State Archive, Sacramento.

43. Oakland _____. [Source is damaged and second word of title is unrecognizable], Monday, June 10, 1912, and "Foot the Bill of Coddling," *The Times*, June 19th, 1912, from the *Corrections Scrapbook*.

44. Ross, *Sin and Society* and *Social Control* [1901] reprint (New York: Johnson Reprint Corp, 1970).

45. Mark Colvin, *Penitentiaries, Reformatories, and Chain Gangs* (New York: St. Martin's Press, 1997), 173.

tion. The educational aim of the social efficiency move-ment was to train students for their likely position in the economy, basing this judgment on IQ tests and other measures of "aptitude."[46]

The educational theory of social efficiency reflected, in part, a change in the actual role that education played for the middle class as the rise of industrial society brought profound changes and insecurities to their lives. In cities, as management positions sprang up to mediate between large numbers of increasingly low-skilled work-ers and their employers, small family businesses gave way to impersonal bureaucratic corporations. Middle-class families turned to formal education in high school and college for the training and credentials necessary for ac-cess to good jobs.[47] As a result, the number of high school graduates nationwide jumped from 2.5 per cent of all seventeen-year olds in 1880 to 16.3 per cent by 1920.[48] High schools themselves attended to the demands of the middle class—both for credentials and training—through the creation of career-specific (and generally class-specific) tracks, preparing students for ex-cellence in blue-, pink-, and white-collar professions. As far as middle-class reformers were concerned, school was evolving into the literal—as well as the theoretical—foundation of modern society.

As the theoretical and practical value of education for workers and citizens alike increased, a new adult ed-ucation movement rose to meet the demand. Ten state colleges and universities had established extension di-visions by 1920, including the University of California in 1914. The adult education movement was especially

healthy in California where, explained Stanford's David Starr Jordan, "the pressure of education to the square inch is greater . . . than anywhere else in the world." In addition to forming the Extension Division (which was available to and free for prison inmates), the legislature also encouraged adult education by authorizing junior colleges in 1911, evening high schools in 1914, and spe-cial adult day high schools in 1917. The evening schools were the most successful of these programs, growing in enrollment by 450 percent in the first five years to nearly 77,000 in 1919. As America entered the Great War, the resulting intense nationalism reemphasized the need for an educated citizenry and no doubt contributed to the success of these programs.[49]

Total institutions like the prison were particularly suited, in theory, to the social efficiency agenda. David Snedden—Columbia professor of education and leading advocate of social efficiency—even suggested that chil-dren's reform schools were superior to public schools, offering "the most persistent, comprehensive, and ef-fective experiment in the domain of education that is available to the student."[50] Warden James A. Johnston, former warden of Folsom Prison and Hoyle's successor at San Quentin in 1913, shared Snedden's belief in educa-tion for social efficiency and reoriented San Quentin to-ward the general trend of secondary and post-secondary education. Johnston saw the prison as a dutiful educa-tional institution. He later recalled,

To take hate-filled, mentally warped men into prison and just let them serve their sentences

46. David B. Tyack, *The One Best System* (Cambridge: Harvard University Press, 1974), 182–216.

47. Harvey Kantor "The Economic and Political Context," 15–22; for the credentialing function of progressive era high schools, see David Labaree, *How to Succeed in School Without Really Trying* (New Haven: Yale University Press, 1997), 102–109. David Hogan "'To Better Our Condition': Education Credentialing and 'the Silent Compulsion of Economic Re-lations' in the United States, 1830 to the Present," *History of Education Quarterly* 36:3 (Fall 1996): 243–270.

48. United States, Bureau of the Census, *Historical Statistics of the United States, Colonial Times to 1970*, (Washington, DC: U.S. Government Printing Office, 1970), Vol. 1, 207.

49. University of California Extension Division, *The Spokesman*. February, 1923, 91; Statistics on extension divisions Ibid, 92; Jordan as cited in John R. Nichols, "State Educational Policy in California During 1910–1915" (Ph.D. diss., Stanford University, 1930), 186–187; California, State Board of Education, *Fourth Biennial Report of the State Board of Education, 1918–1920* (Sacramento: State Printer, 1920), 78–79, 117.

50. David S. Snedden, *Administration and Educational Work of American Juvenile Reform Schools* (New York: Columbia Uni-versity, 1907), 8.

without making earnest effort to correct their wrong notions and replace their anti-social tendencies with better ideas, seemed to me a sure guaranty that they would leave the prison worse than when they entered. In such an event, the prison would be a menace to the society it presumed to protect.[51]

Johnston made no apologies for criminal behavior, but at the same time did not believe in a criminal type or class. He claimed to treat every inmate as an individual and tried to design a prison administration that effected individual reform. To meet this end, Johnston would appeal to the most advanced forms of education available in his day, using "science" to efficiently place incoming inmates in their appropriate training track. While Johnston, like Hoyle, used all aspects of prison life as tools for reformation, he emphasized formal education, both academic and vocational. His ultimate goal, as he succinctly put it, was "to turn social liabilities into social assets."[52]

In Johnston's San Quentin, the resocialization process began as soon as a new inmate entered the gate. First, he or she was taken to the physician, who administered a complete physical examination, looking for evidence of disease and drug addiction, and inquiring into the inmate's family history—next, to the dentist for a thorough checkup. Finally, the inmate was taken to the chaplain–education director (the title changed from chaplain in 1915, suggesting an increasing emphasis on scientific, not just moralistic, methods of rehabilitation) for a mental examination that sought to determine "mental measure and moral status, amount of schooling, degree of moral training in youth, habits, tendencies, and something of the circumstances that led to the commission of the crime." The inmate was then placed into the academic and vocational program considered appropriate to his (or her) individual needs.[53]

The primary function of San Quentin prison under Johnston was education—especially vocational education. To a degree this emphasis on vocationalism reflected the traditional belief that work cured crime. But the curative was work skills, not just a work ethic. Since the initiation of the state-use system under Hoyle, the prison industries had continued to grow. By 1916, less than half the men at San Quentin worked in the jute mill; an increasing number assisted in the growing prison bureaucracy or worked in the more skilled trades (carpentry, metal work, etc.) established under Hoyle. During the war, the prison added a flag factory to put flags in every classroom in the state—an act, Johnston claimed, that made the prisoners proud.[54] The warden also encouraged the addition of vocational courses through an inmate-initiated agricultural club and through correspondence courses including agriculture, typing and shorthand, and "The Gas Engine and its Application to Automobiles and Tractors," taught on a volunteer basis by a professor from the University of California.[55]

Johnston believed vocational education would fit each inmate to "take a useful place in the world when he is released" and become an "economic asset" to society.[56] Because the jute mill earned most of the prison's budget, Johnston was forced to keep it operating despite its lack of educational value.[57] He generally assigned new men to this duty and rotated them out after six months to a year and used the assignment as punishment for old-timers.[58] Once finished with the jute mill, men were to be trained according to their preexisting occupations. To those prisoners who had white-collar careers on the out-

51. James A. Johnston, *Prison Life is Different* (Boston: Houghton Mifflin, 1937), 61.

52. Ibid., 335.

53. Prison Directors, *Report for 1916*, 143. This emphasis on individualized treatment of the inmate was a common Progressive-era reform. (See Rothman, *Conscience and Convenience*, ch. 2).

54. Johnston, *Prison Life*, 125.

55. Prison Directors, *Report for 1918*, 10–11.

56. Prison Directors, *Report for 1920*, 14, Johnston, *Prison Life*, 187.

57. For finances, see "Clerk's Report" in Prison Directors, *Report for 1920*, 21.

58. Johnston, *Prison Life*, 113–121.

side, Johnston gave white-collar jobs within the prison bureaucracy on the inside, and some men he never assigned to the mill. Such men had "talent, a trade, or ability that indicated that [their] employment in some other department of the prison would be better for [them] and for the state."[59] Every prisoner was to be rehabilitated, but it was rehabilitation for success in his own station. Johnston, a student of social efficiency, was not in the business of undoing social stratification.

The machinery of socially efficient education rested on sorting individuals into the appropriate programs through testing. In 1916 Johnston collaborated with Lewis Terman, a Stanford Professor of Education who worked at the forefront of intelligence testing. As part of a large-scale study of school children, orphans, and inmates, Terman came to San Quentin for two months in 1916 to test all incoming inmates. After administering a battery of tests (seven in all) to 155 men, Terman concluded that feeble-mindedness was sixteen times higher among the prison population than among the public at large. He "proved" a staggering 30 percent to be feeble-minded (mental age of 10 years or less) or borderline feeble-minded. Not surprisingly, Terman also "proved" that feeble-mindedness was much more common among "Mexicans, Negroes, and foreign-born than among native white Americans." Terman's tests must have reassured the middle-class white males who administered them. In an informal experiment, Warden Johnston, the chaplain–education director, and the captain of the guard found that they could accurately predict a man's performance on the test from just a short interview. None of them thought to question whether the tests, which so easily corresponded with their own guesses, were biased.[60]

The test results produced strong reactions from the prison directors and the Board of Charities and Correc-

tions. In fact, the BCC was sufficiently alarmed to recommend "strengthening the law of sterilization to include feeble-minded inmates of state prisons." (The existing law, first passed in 1909 and revised in 1913, only allowed for the sterilization of "idiots" and "sexual offenders," and had been used, in the BCC's view, too sparingly.)[61] But at the same time, the BCC continued to advocate educational programs at the state prisons. Johnston recalled that when he saw the result, he actually "took heart" at the large percentage of men, 70 percent, who "had natural mental ability and capacity to learn and understand.[62] At last prison reformers had scientific proof that many prisoners were, at least in terms of their educability, just like other men. An appropriate symbol of the changing use of science in criminology was a medical program initiated a few years later, in which the prison physician used plastic surgery to correct "flat noses, cauliflower ears and other criminal stigmata." The criminal might be marked, but he could at last be fixed.[63]

Johnston sorted inmates into academic, as well as vocational, tracks expanding the prison school into a comprehensive, three-tiered education department: the prison school, the "letter box" courses, and the University Extension program. He directed incoming inmates into the appropriate level, encouraging each to acquire a minimum level of academic education (although schooling remained voluntary) and urging all to follow their interests beyond that point if they wished. The prison school grew on the foundation built in Hoyle's day and, thanks to the legislature, now received an adequate stream of free textbooks (for adults) from the state superintendent of schools. All inmates under twenty-five-years of age and in need of primary education qualified for the day school, which offered a half-day rotation out of work duty. For older inmates, the

59. Johnston, *Prison Life,* 120 and 127.

60. Johnston, *Prison Life,* 167–169; Board of Charities, *Report for 1918,* 56.

61. Board of Charities, *Report for 1918,* 56; Wendell Huston, *Sterilization Laws: Compilation of the Sterilization Laws of the Twenty-four States* (Des Moines: Wendell Huston Co., 1930–), p. 3.; Paul Popenoe, "Eugenic Sterilization in California," reprinted from *Journal of Social Hygiene* 13:6 (June 1927) as cited in Human Betterment Foundation, *Collected Papers on Eugenic Sterilization in California* (Pasadena: Human Betterment Foundation, 1930), 321.

62. Johnston, *Prison Life,* 174.

63. Board of Charities, *Report for 1910,* 39.

night school continued five nights per week. By 1920, Johnston discontinued the day school in favor of a more comprehensive night school, which met for an hour and a half five nights per week. The prison school continued the special class for Spanish speakers, taught by a bilingual inmate, and a primary class, which met for an hour before regular night school for particularly needy students. Increased space because of a decreased population (World War I briefly increased employment opportunities and decreased crime rates, shrinking San Quentin's inmate population 17 per cent between 1916 and 1920) allowed these classes to meet in their own rooms.[64] This improved the efficiency and specialization of the prison school and put it more directly in line with public education.

In addition to expanding classes, the education department also developed the "letter box" courses, a dozen individual correspondence courses designed and printed within the prison and distributed to the inmates for work in their cells. These included a range of courses in traditional academic fields such as English, history, and government.[65] For educationally advanced inmates, San Quentin offered correspondence courses through the University of California's extension program, though the warden wrote that often "Men who wanted to enroll for university courses in some 'ology,' 'osophy,' 'ism,' or 'pathy' had to be guided into taking spelling, grammar, and arithmetic."[66] In 1916 the warden estimated that two-thirds of the population was enrolled in one of these three branches of the education department (the latter two of which were even open to women).[67] (See Table 1.)

By 1920 the chaplain–educational director wrote with confidence that San Quentin was "capable of satisfying the needs of every inmate—no matter at what stage of educational progress he may have arrived." In all, the educational department consisted of a principal and eleven inmate teachers, covering public school grades one through five, a bilingual class, a basic literacy class, and the "letter box" courses, not to mention

TABLE 1 Prison School Enrollment at San Quentin, 1920		
Program	**Enrollment**	**Percent of Total Population (n = 1924)**
Night School		
Primary (English reading & writing)	50*	3
Elementary (5 grades)	98*	5
Letter Box	437*	23
University Extension		
Academic Department	252**	13
Agricultural Division	134**	7
Total enrolled	971	51

*daily attendance as of June 30, 1920.

**enrollment estimated by Education Director for Sept. 1, 1919 through June 30, 1920. The Academic and Agricultural Divisions of the University Extension Programs had completion rates of 85% and 90% respectively.

Source. Prison directors, *Report for 1920,* 102–105.

64. Ibid., 15; Prison Directors, *Report for 1920,* 5.

65. Prison Directors, *Report for 1916,* 15.

66. Johnston, *Prison Life,* 177.

67. Prison Directors, *Report for 1916,* 15.

its connection to the university. A new filing system and new equipment allowed the growing bureaucracy to function smoothly. Inmate participation in 1920, even by a conservative estimate, amounted to half of the total prison population.[68]

In 1917, the legislature passed two acts that enhanced the role of the educational program. The first, drafted by Johnston himself, separated San Quentin and Folsom inmates into two categories. First-timers were placed in San Quentin, safe from the influence of the hardened criminals, who went to Folsom. All incoming inmates would henceforth be placed based on their previous records. To facilitate the envisioned reformatory aspects of San Quentin, the legislature also passed the Indeterminate Sentence Act, placing minimum and maximum incarceration limits on particular types of crime.[69]

The separation of first offenders and recidivists and the passage of an indeterminate sentence law gave the prison administration the power to segregate adult inmates and the power to discharge or hold them depending on their compliance with the administration's plans for rehabilitation—in other words, gave prison officials the ability to punish the criminal and not the crime. The justification for indeterminate sentences would come from the facility's greatly expanded educational programs. Prisoners now had the opportunity to prove their willingness to mend their ways. Even before the 1917 legislation, Johnston had transformed San Quentin into a highly organized education machine, at least in theory. The machinery rested on scientific measurement and individualized programming. Now that the state prison system had adopted its own tracking system, San Quentin's educational program was truly progressive.

CONCLUSION: A COLLEGE OF MORALS

By 1920 the California State Prison at San Quentin stood as a national model for prisoner education, housing the largest and most comprehensive prison school in the nation. Although not representative of prison practice in its size and scope, the school was indicative of cutting-edge reform theory and embodied the best hopes of advocates of inmate rehabilitation at the time.[70] Even skeptical prison reformer Frank Tannenbaum singled out San Quentin as the only prison in the nation "making a real attempt" to educate inmates.[71] A southern California newspaper went further, hailing the program as a "College of Morals."[72]

In fact, the word "moral" and other normative judgments appeared consistently in the official reports of the prison administration and the BCC, clustering like moths around the bright descriptions of the educational program. In 1916, San Quentin's Chaplain–Education Director, A. C. Sheppard, reported confidently that "The better moral impulse that has been imparted, the awakening of worthy aspiration, the stimulating of the best that is in the nature of men, cannot be written down in figures."[73] Four years later, in 1920, Sheppard's successor tried to offer more quantitative data to support the view that the programs were successful. He reported that 85 per cent of the inmates taking University of California academic courses passed, while even more, 90 percent, of those taking university agricultural courses did so. Those who passed their courses within San Quentin ("letter box" and night school) received an average grade of 92.1.[74] Such data must have pleased Johnston, but his faith in the inherent value of education was such that "the mere statement [that so many inmates were

---

68. Prison Directors, *Report for 1920,* 102–104.

69. Ibid., 50; Prison Directors, *Report for 1918,* 12.

70. David J. Rothman argues that the use of such models throughout the history of the prison led to the continuing survival of the prison ideal despite the overwhelming evidence that it was a failure. The reformatory at Elmira is a particularly strong example of this phenomenon (*Conscience and Convenience,* 32–36).

71. Frank Tannenbaum, "Prison Facts," *The Atlantic Monthly* 128:5 (November 1921), 577–588.

72. "San Quentin Prison—A College of Morals," newspaper article cited in *The Bulletin* (published at San Quentin), Vol. 6, No. 1, Oct. 1918, 9. The title of the Los Angeles paper was not given.

73. Prison Directors, *Report for 1916,* 116.

74. Prison Directors, *Report for 1920,* 103–104.

enrolled in classes] is sufficient to impress any thinking person with the importance of the work, and to induce the belief that material, mental, and moral improvement is bound to result."[75] The assumption is telling. Neither Johnston nor his educational directors offered any concrete data that correlated participation in prison education and reduced rates of recidivism, nor did the BCC request it. The efficacy of the school went unquestioned because the answer was taken for granted.

The creation of a school at San Quentin as the centerpiece of adult rehabilitation reflected the great shift in schooling for the middle class—both in its practical and theoretical social value. It also indicated a consequence of that shift. On a practical level, Johnston and other advocates of social efficiency believed that modernity required more schooling for every class of society. The school was the best tool for the nation's march toward progress and one that the middle class increasingly used as the foundation of its own status. On a theoretical level, schooling took a central place in middle-class identity, as well as in the progressive vision of social reform. As the school took on the responsibility of sorting and training the next generation, it donned the mantle of morality once worn exclusively by work. School attainment, like the possession of a job, emerged as a yardstick of character. Together, the practical and theoretical significance of schooling gave it an unprecedented moral weight. The blind faith of Johnston and others implied that an upright man was not only employed, he was educated. Public school policy buttressed this view. Compulsory education laws, largely ignored in the nineteenth century, found new strength in the twentieth. As administrative progressives redoubled efforts to enforce these laws, it became clear that the real crime—literally as well as metaphorically—was staying out of school.[76]

Benjamin Justice is a graduate student in history of education at Stanford University and a Charlotte W. Newcombe Fellow. He wishes to thank David Kennedy, David Tyack, and especially Jennifer K. Justice for their suggestions in the initial stages of this essay, and the Quarterly's *anonymous reviewers and editorial staff for their patience.*

75. Prison Directors, *Report for 1916*, 15.

76. David B. Tyack, "Ways of Seeing: An Essay on the History of Compulsory Schooling," *Harvard Educational Review* 46 (August 1976): 355–389.

part V

APPLICATIONS OF RESEARCH METHODOLOGY

This part of the book examines two major uses of educational research to directly improve educational practice. These applications—evaluation research and action research—can involve either, or both, quantitative and qualitative research methods.

Chapter 14 describes the uses of evaluation research in education and the major features of different models of evaluation research.

Chapter 15 explores how action research enables educational practitioners to conduct research studies in their own setting. We describe how action research fosters the professional development of educators and helps them improve their effectiveness.

Evaluation Research

After studying this chapter, you will be able to

1. describe the advantages of using published research findings to evaluate educational phenomena about which educators need to make decisions.

2. describe several types of educational phenomena that have been the subject of evaluation research.

3. describe the difference between formative and summative evaluation and the value of each.

4. describe how needs assessment, educational research and development, and objectives-based evaluation can contribute to the evaluation of educational phenomena.

5. describe the similarities and differences between responsive evaluation and educational connoisseurship and criticism.

6. describe four criteria that a good evaluation research study should satisfy.

Amy Tanner is the assistant superintendent of instruction for her school district. Her superintendent notes that many parents in the district have expressed concerns about whether their children are developing the science skills that they will need for life in the Twenty-first Century. He has asked her to determine what changes should be made to the science curriculum to help students understand and apply scientific knowledge.

From a literature search Amy finds an article that reviews curriculum programs based on recently established national standards for science education. She learns that the programs have been evaluated to varying degrees. One of the programs integrates mathematics and science teaching, which Amy thinks might appeal to many of the school district's stakeholders.

Amy reports to the superintendent that she wants to review the evaluation data and costs for these programs to determine which of them have the features that her district values. Then she will submit a report of her findings and recommendations to the district's stakeholder groups.

The superintendent believes that Amy's approach to evaluating science curriculum programs will result in a sound adoption decision, and so he gives her approval to proceed.

This chapter describes the advantages of using published research findings to evaluate curriculum programs and other aspects of educational practice about which educators make judgments and decisions. We explain the aspects of educational practice that evaluators commonly examine, major types of evaluation research, and quantitative and qualitative approaches to evaluation. We also describe criteria for judging an educational evaluation. ●

THE VALUE OF USING EVALUATION RESEARCH IN EDUCATIONAL DECISION MAKING

Educational evaluation is the process of making judgments about the merit, value, or worth of any component of education, such as the eight aspects of educational practice described in the next section of the chapter. The conduct of educational evaluations has greatly expanded in the past forty years, and it continues to grow. The importance of evaluation research is evidenced in various ways, including the fact that all educational programs receiving federal funding must undergo formal evaluation, the presence of evaluation teams on the staff of many school districts and state departments of education, and the employment of institutional researchers to evaluate the operations of most colleges and universities.

Some educators rely primarily on personal experience or expert advice to make such decisions as the determination of educational goals, the selection of textbooks, and the design of needed instructional programs. However, those sources of information may contain bias and error and, in any case, are incomplete. A well-done evaluation study is a valuable aid because it helps educators and policy makers weigh a wider range of factors that are relevant to a major decision. Additionally, a carefully designed evaluation can yield persuasive evidence that makes educators less vulnerable to protests by individuals or groups who might disagree with their decisions, and that helps them justify the costs associated with a decision.

Various individuals and groups have a stake in the decisions that involve schools and students. Therefore, it is important to identify relevant stakeholders at the outset of an evaluation study. **Stakeholders** are the individuals who are involved in the phenomenon that is being evaluated or who may be affected by or interested in the findings of an evaluation. For example, stakeholders in the evaluation of a school career guidance program might include career education teachers, parents whose students might participate in the program, school counselors, and employees of businesses that are likely to hire graduates of schools where the program is offered.

Some stakeholders want input into the design of an evaluation, the collection and analysis of information, the interpretation of the findings, and the decisions based on the evaluation. However, different types of stakeholders often hold conflicting positions on the value of a given educational phenomenon. Thus, evaluators face challenges in conducting evaluations ethically, and in reflecting and reconciling the varied views of relevant stakeholders. The reconciliation of stakeholders' views is one of the most helpful aspects of good evaluation research, but it is not easy to perform.

ASPECTS OF EDUCATIONAL PRACTICE INVESTIGATED BY EVALUATORS

Evaluation research is conducted on many different aspects of the educational enterprise. Below we describe eight aspects of educational practice that frequently are the focus of evaluation research.

Instructional Programs

An instructional program can be defined as a reproducible sequence of activities that is designed to produce particular learning outcomes for a particular population of students. Head Start, the language arts curriculum in a high school, and the sequence of courses and field experiences that preservice teachers must complete in order to be certified are examples of instructional programs. Programs often are evaluated to determine whether they have been implemented as intended, and to assess their effectiveness in promoting the learning of students.

Richard Dukes, Jodie Ullman, and Judith Stein (1996) carried out an evaluation to determine the long-term effectiveness of the Drug Abuse Resistance Education (D.A.R.E.) program in one district. D.A.R.E. involves a trained police officer delivering a curriculum to fifth or sixth graders once a week for one semester. The curriculum is designed to build students' self-esteem and resistance to peer pressure, increase peer bonding, and delay the onset of experimentation with alcohol, tobacco, and other drugs.

Three years after the D.A.R.E. program was first offered in the school district, a questionnaire survey was administered to a random sample of ninth graders, most of whom would have had the opportunity to take the program, if they chose. Survey responses of the 497 students who reported they had received D.A.R.E. and the 352 students who reported that they had not received the program were compared.

The evaluators carried out statistical analyses to identify target outcomes that were presumed to reflect the long-term effectiveness of D.A.R.E.: (a) age of onset of use of marijuana and current use of drugs; (b) age of onset of drinking and current use of alcohol; and (c) two items from a measure of self-esteem. The presumed predictor variable, participation in D.A.R.E., did not significantly predict any of the D.A.R.E. target outcomes. The evaluators concluded that D.A.R.E., like most drug-use prevention programs, manifests its strongest effects shortly after program implementation, with a decay over time. They suggest approaches that might improve the program's long-term effectiveness.

The D.A.R.E. follow-up study is unusual, because it reports nonsignificant results. Most evaluation studies in which the tests of statistical significance show no support for the study's hypotheses are never published. Over time this publication bias tends to skew the education literature toward an overestimate of the effectiveness of particular programs. D.A.R.E.'s continuing popularity, despite such nonsignificant findings, also illustrates the fact that many educational programs remain in existence for reasons other than their demonstrated effectiveness. For example, some schools might continue an ineffective program because parents or politicians support it.

Instructional Methods

Educators want to know which instructional methods are most effective, for example, the lecture versus the discussion method of teaching, the whole-language approach to reading instruction, or the use of manipulatives in teaching English as a Second Language (ESL). Kevin Miller (1995) evaluated a well-known instructional method, cooperative learning, to determine its value in stimulating conversational interaction between mainstreamed deaf and hard-of-hearing students and their hearing peers and teachers at the middle school level. Three general-education teachers of social studies with a hard-of-hearing student in their class participated in the research, which involved a single-case experimental research design using the A-B-A format (see Chapter 9).

During the first A phase (days 1–3), the teachers used a traditional teaching style, in which each teacher lectured to his or her entire class, students functioned independently of one another, and the teacher determined which students spoke at various points in the lesson. During the B phase (days 4–6), each teacher established a cooperative learning group that included the hard-of-hearing student, and used a cooperative learning style (which the teachers had learned during a pre-intervention workshop). During the second A phase (days 7–9), the teachers again used a traditional teaching style.

Each teacher's class was videotaped for about an hour on each of the nine days of the experiment. The dialogue of the teacher and of each student during the first ten minutes of each videotape was later transcribed and coded. Then the number of conversational turns, conversational initiations, requests for information, and informational comments for each hard-of-hearing student was calculated for each day.

Miller found that both the hard-of-hearing students and other students who had displayed low levels of conversation during the first A phase (baseline) tended to increase their participation during the B phase (cooperative learning treatment). Having the hard-of-hearing student play the role of recorder was particularly effective in stimulating their increased conversation with hearing peers and the teacher. Thus the study resulted in a positive evaluation of cooperative learning as a method of fostering conversational interaction among hard-of-hearing students and their hearing peers and teacher.

Instructional Materials

Educators and students spend large amounts of money each year on textbooks and other curriculum materials. Educators count on these materials to help students achieve intended learning objectives. However, reviews of the textbook publishing industry indicate that publishers focus far more on market conditions than on evidence of effectiveness to promote their products (Apple, 1991; Lockwood, 1992). Evaluation research can reveal the relative effectiveness of textbooks and other instructional materials.

The research article that is reprinted at the end of this chapter, by Roberta Ogletree, Barbara Rienzo, Judy Drolet, and Joyce Fetro, involves a comparative evaluation of twenty-three school-based sexuality education curricula. The authors summarize the philosophy, content, skill-building strategies, and teaching strategies of each curriculum, point out general strengths and weaknesses of the curricula, and suggest strategies for overcoming major weaknesses. A similarly designed evaluation of K–8 science curriculum materials by Dana Johnson, Linda Boyce, and Joyce Van Tassel-Baska (1995) is described later in the chapter, where we use its design to illustrate a set of professional standards for evaluation research.

Specific Groups or Organizations

Any educational group or organization (e.g., a support group for minority students, or an organization for parents who home-school their children) can be evaluated, and its operations can be compared to its own organizational goals or to the operations of other organizations. For example, David Porretta, Michael Gillespie, and Paul Jansma (1996) conducted an evaluation of the Special Olympics organization that was commissioned by the organization directors. The authors note that, with over 1 million athletes participating, Special Olympics currently is the largest sports organization in the world for athletes with mental retardation.

The evaluation involved a questionnaire mailed to 232 respondents representing various agencies throughout the United States (e.g., Special Olympics executive directors, parent organizations, state directors of special education, university-affiliated programs) that provide services to individuals with disabilities. The questionnaire addressed four research questions involving: (1) the prevailing philosophy of agencies servicing individuals with mental retardation, (2) the terminology used by agencies to describe mental retardation, (3) strategies employed by leading agencies in the United States to attract people with disabilities to service delivery systems, and (4) agency professionals' prevailing perception of the Special Olympics' mission.

The research report shows the percentage of respondents giving various responses to each question or its component subquestions. For example, in response to the question, "What is your agency/organization's philosophy related to servicing people with disabilities?" 66 percent indicated, "Least Restricted Environment Based," meaning that the majority of agencies/organizations provide their services in an environment characterized as least restrictive. The researchers summarized the responses as showing that

> (1) the mission of Special Olympics should be to place more emphasis on inclusion opportunities, (2) there appears to be a trend away from the term "mental retardation" toward other terms, (3) Special Olympics should provide opportunities to a wider variety of individuals with disabilities, and (4) Special Olympics should examine its mission statement in order to stay abreast with current philosophies being espoused by other agencies/organizations that serve individuals with disabilities. (p. 44)

Educators

Teachers and many other types of educators must take tests or demonstrate certain competencies in order to obtain certification or employment. Performance appraisals in relation to salary reviews and promotions also may occur. These forms of evaluation focus on an individual's merits in comparison to other individuals or to some standard. The personnel evaluation standards set by the **Joint Committee on Standards for Educational Evaluation** (1988) are meant to guide such evaluations.

Educators who must make decisions about educational programs, materials, and methods also need general information about the qualifications of the educators who will administer such programs, materials, and methods. Therefore, many evaluation research studies evaluate educators not in comparison to each other, but more generally to determine the quality of human resources available to carry out specific educational activities. For example, Kenneth Sirotnik (1983) described an observational study of over 1,000 school teachers that was conducted by John Goodlad and his colleagues. Sirotnik notes that the researchers were startled by the low level of corrective feedback that teachers provided in any of the classrooms observed:

> . . . in the elementary classes observed, on the average, just under 3 percent of the instructional time that the teacher spent interacting with students involved corrective feedback (with or without guidance). At the secondary level, this estimate is less than 2 percent. . . . Thus, one of the most touted pedagogical features of classroom instruction—immediate corrective feedback—rarely occurs. (p. 19)

Sirotnik concludes from the evaluation findings that teachers in U.S. school systems need better supervision and staff development in order to provide effective instruction to students.

Students

Students in schools and other educational institutions are assessed regularly to guide decisions about their school grades and awarding of diplomas or degrees. Many students also periodically take various placement and aptitude tests that affect their access to higher education and employment opportunities.

Teachers are given the responsibility for designing, administering, and scoring many of the tests used to assess student performance. National organizations, such as the Educational Testing Service, focus on standardized assessments that allow for comparisons of student performance to national norms. Increasingly, states are administering assessments to determine whether their students are achieving state-level standards of academic performance in different content areas.

Tests and Assessment Procedures

Because so many decisions about students hinge on their test performance, the tests themselves must be evaluated as to their validity, reliability, fairness, and other relevant factors. In Chapter 5 we described the procedures used to assess the validity and reliability of tests and other measures.

Evaluations

Because of the major impact that evaluation studies have on both individuals and institutions, it is important that the studies themselves meet quality standards. The process of evaluating an evaluation study (sometimes called **meta-evaluation**) is illustrated later in the chapter, where we describe a set of standards that were developed to assess evaluations of educational programs.

COMMON FORMS OF EVALUATION RESEARCH IN EDUCATION

In this section we describe different types of evaluation research. They vary in purpose, stakeholder involvement, and extent of reliance on quantitative and qualitative methodologies.

Needs Assessment

Needs assessment is a set of procedures for identifying and prioritizing needs related to societal, organizational, and human performance (McKillip, 1987). A *need* usually is defined as a discrepancy between a desired and an existing state or condition. For example, evaluators might seek to obtain data concerning the current quality or level of success of an educational program, and to compare those data to what is desired or expected of the program.

When needs are carefully analyzed, proposed solutions are more likely to address the real needs of program participants. For example, one of the authors (Joy) coordinated an educational program for parents of at-risk middle school students. The students participated in an intensive personal growth course and then were assigned mentors for a year-long follow-through program. Soon after the intensive course, all the parents received a telephone call asking about their relationship with the student since the course and about the kinds of support that the parent would like as the student made the transition to high school. Parents also were asked to rate their level of interest in several topics that speakers planned to address in subsequent meetings. Based on the results, certain aspects of the parent program were redesigned.

Educational Research and Development

Evaluation is central to the educational research and development (R&D) process, which is a systematic process involving the development and refinement of educational programs and materials (referred to hereafter as **R&D products**).

Walter Dick and Lou Carey (2001) advocate the **systems approach** model of educational R&D. The ten steps of this model are shown in Figure 14.1. You will note that step 1 involves needs assessment, which we described in the previous section. In this model, a needs assessment is carried out in order to identify the goals of the product to be developed. Step 2, instructional analysis, involves identification of the specific skills, procedures, and learning tasks that are involved in reaching the instructional goals identified by the needs assessment. Step 3 is designed to identify the level of entry behaviors (sometimes called **enabling**

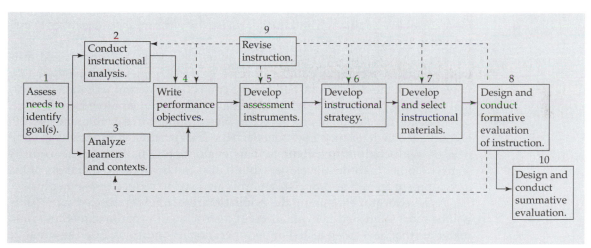

FIGURE 14.1   **The Steps of the Systems Approach Model of Educational Research and Development (R&D)**

Source.   Adapted from figure on pp. 2–3 in Dick, W., Carey, L. & Carey, J. (2001). *The systematic design of education* (5th ed.). Boston: Allyn and Bacon. Copyright © 2001 by Pearson Education. Reprinted by permission of the publisher.

objectives) that learners bring to the learning task, as well as other characteristics of the learners (e.g., specific personality traits such as test anxiety), or of the settings in which instruction will occur and the learned skills will ultimately be used.

During step 4, the developers write specific statements (called **performance objectives**) of what the learners will be able to do after instruction. Then assessment instruments to test achievement of the objectives are developed (step 5); the appropriate instructional strategy is formulated (step 6); and instructional materials are developed, or possibly selected from available materials (step 7).

Steps 8, 9, and 10 of the systems model involve the distinction between formative and summative evaluation, which was formulated by Michael Scriven (1967). Scriven found that, in practice, evaluation serves two different functions. **Formative evaluation** (step 8) involves collecting data about an educational product while it is under development, in order to provide information to guide the developers in revising the product or deciding to discontinue development, if appropriate. In contrast, **summative evaluation** (described below) is conducted to determine the final product's worth in an operational setting, when compared to other available products.

Formative evaluation occurs throughout the development process. The results of formative evaluation then are used to revise (step 9) any of the work carried out during steps 1 to 7. For example, the developers might carry out a formative evaluation of the product's objectives during step 4, examining such issues as the clarity and comprehensiveness of the objectives. Based on the results, they might eliminate some objectives, rewrite others, and add new objectives. Once they have developed instructional materials (step 7), they might do more formative evaluation and further revise the performance objectives to better match the product content.

Formative evaluation is conducted under field-test conditions. Field tests usually involve a smaller number of research participants, more hands-on involvement of the developers, and a more controlled environment than the normal operating conditions in which the final product is meant to be used.

Once the development process is completed, summative evaluation (step 10) is conducted to determine how beneficial the final product is, especially in comparison with competing products. This evaluation usually is carried out by someone other than the developers, but it also can be done by members of the development team if appropriate controls are used to reduce researcher bias.

As an educator examining the evaluation research literature, you probably will be most interested in evaluations of instructional programs, methods, and materials that have been tested under operational conditions. Such summative evaluations will help you determine whether the programs, methods, or materials are effective under conditions similar to your own situation. Sometimes, though, it may be worthwhile to examine studies that involve only formative evaluation. If you must implement a solution to your problem quickly, you might want to know about new products that have not yet been the subject of summative evaluation, but for which formative evaluation results are promising. Learning about a promising product while it still is under development will give you a head start on determining its suitability as a solution to your problem. You might even be able to volunteer your local setting as a field-test site to participate in its evaluation.

Objectives-Based Evaluation

National Assessment of Educational Progress. Quantitative approaches to evaluation usually focus on the extent to which an educational program or method helps students achieve the intended learning objectives associated with it. The **National Assessment of Educational Progress** (NAEP), a congressionally mandated project of the National Center for Education Statistics of the U.S. Department of Education, is a large-scale, continuing assessment of what a representative sample of students in the United States know and can do in various subject areas (Campbell et al., 1997).

The NAEP is based on the model of **objectives-based curriculum evaluation** developed by Ralph Tyler (1949). Tyler claimed that school instruction should be organized around specific objectives and that the success of such instruction should be judged on the basis of how well students reach those objectives. The NAEP involves quantitative analysis of the percentage of youth at various age levels who are competent in performing tasks that reflect skills viewed by subject matter experts as necessary for effective functioning in school and society.

Many research studies, particularly those involving experimental designs, involve quantitative evaluation of how well research participants who receive an innovative instructional program perform on a criterion measure compared to participants receiving a traditional program or no program.

Cost Analysis. Cost analysis (Levin & McEwan, 2000) is another type of objectives-based evaluation. In a **cost analysis,** evaluators determine how well an educational program achieves its objectives (i.e., its benefits) relative to its costs. In one type of cost analysis, a monetary value is placed on the benefits and on the costs (e.g., the salaries of educators who provide the program). The monetary value of the benefits is then compared to the monetary costs. In another type of cost analysis, different educational programs are compared against the criterion of effectiveness. The most *cost-effective* program is the one that yields the greatest benefits for each unit of cost.

An example of cost analysis is the study of school size conducted by Tyler Bowles and Ryan Bosworth (2002). These researchers were interested in the problem of equality of school funding and the equity of such equal funding for schools of different sizes. It might seem reasonable that a good way to achieve equity would be for school districts to allocate the same amount of money for each student in the district's schools. This resource-allocation model ensures that students from poorer families receive the same amount of dollars for their education as students from wealthier families. However, Bowles and Bosworth questioned whether this funding model is truly equitable, because schools vary in size (i.e., number of enrolled students). There might be an economy of scale, such that it costs less per student in a large school than in a small school to provide the same learning opportunities.

The researchers answered this question by doing a cost analysis using expenditure data for the schools in seventeen Wyoming school districts. The schools varied substantially in size and per-student expenditures. The cost analysis revealed that the smaller the school, the greater the per-student expenditure. For example, a school with seventy students spent approximately $7,400 per student, whereas a school with 429 students spent approximately $5,200 per student. If we assume, as the researchers did, that district administrators distribute monies in an effort to provide equal learning opportunities to all students, these results show that it costs substantially more for a small school than for a large school to provide the same opportunities.

Context-Input-Process-Product (CIPP) Model.   Daniel Stufflebeam and his colleagues (1971) developed the **CIPP model** to help practicing educators evaluate both instructional and noninstructional programs.

During context evaluation, needs and problems are identified, including both those associated with the program and those that the program is intended to alleviate. Input evaluation involves making judgments about the resources and strategies needed to accomplish the intended program goals and objectives. Process evaluation involves the collection of evaluative data concerning the program in operation. Finally, product evaluation involves the assessment of the extent to which program goals have been achieved.

In the CIPP model, evaluators work closely with the client in determining what types of information are needed for each phase of the evaluation, and in synthesizing the information so that it can be used for decision making. Because the collection and analysis of evaluative data are viewed primarily as technical activities, these aspects of the evaluation usually are delegated to the evaluator. Although the CIPP approach has been used primarily in quantitative evaluation research, it also appears suitable for evaluation research based on a qualitative orientation.

Qualitative Approaches to Evaluation Research

Qualitative approaches to evaluation research are based on the assumption that judgments of worth depend heavily on the values and perspectives of the individuals doing the judging. Various qualitative approaches have been developed (see Mary Anne Pitman and Joseph Maxwell, 1992), including the two that we describe here.

Responsive Evaluation.   Robert Stake (1991) developed one of the first qualitative approaches to evaluation, called **responsive evaluation.** It focuses on being responsive to stakeholders' issues (i.e., points of contention among different stakeholders) and concerns (i.e., matters about which stakeholders feel threatened or that they want to substantiate). Concerns and issues tend to provide a much wider focus for evaluation study than the goals and objectives that are central to quantitative approaches to evaluation.

The four phases of responsive evaluation are (1) initiating and organizing the evaluation, (2) identifying key issues and concerns, (3) gathering useful information, and (4) reporting results and making recommendations (Guba and Lincoln, 1981). During the first phase, stakeholders are identified; also, the evaluator and client negotiate a contract to specify such matters as the phenomena to be evaluated, the purpose of the evaluation, rights of access to records, and guarantees of confidentiality and anonymity.

In the second phase, key issues and concerns are identified through direct involvement with a variety of stakeholders. The evaluators seek to clarify the values of different stakeholders that underlie the issues and concerns expressed. For example, in an evaluation of a particular school system's governance structure, the evaluators might discover that some stakeholders value a high-quality curriculum and accountability, whereas others place greater value on equality of representation in decision making and a rational decision-making process.

In the third phase of the evaluation, the evaluators collect more information about the concerns, issues, and values identified by the stakeholders, descriptive information about the phenomena being evaluated, and standards to be used in making judgments about it.

The final phase of a responsive evaluation involves preparing reports of results and recommendations. Frequently a case study format (see Chapter 10) is used to describe the concerns and issues identified by stakeholders. The evaluators, in negotiation with stakeholders, then make judgments and recommendations based on the information that has been collected.

In doing a responsive evaluation, evaluators do not specify a research design at the outset of their work. Instead, they use an **emergent design,** meaning that the design of the evaluation changes as evaluators gain insights into stakeholders' primary issues and concerns. Consistent with the purposeful sampling methods described in Chapter 10, responsive evaluators continue obtaining information from stakeholders until the information they are receiving becomes redundant with information already collected.

Advocates of responsive evaluation claim that after sufficient communication, stakeholders can be guided to consensus on the evaluation outcome, despite their differing values and needs. However, Pitman and Maxwell (1992) view this claim as unrealistic, given "that constructions are *socially situated* and, thus, unlikely to come to be shared by individuals in very different social positions" (p. 742).

Educational Connoisseurship and Criticism.   Elliott Eisner (2002) developed an approach to qualitative evaluation research called **educational connoisseurship and criticism.** This approach depends heavily on the evaluator's professional expertise. The first part of this approach, connoisseurship, involves appreciating (in the sense of becoming aware of) the qualities of an educational program and their meaning. The educational connoisseur is assumed to be aware of more nuances of the program being evaluated than a typical educator or lay person would be. The evaluator thus must have expert knowledge of the program being evaluated, as well as of other comparable or competitive programs. The second part of the approach, criticism, is the process of describing and evaluating what has been appreciated. The evaluator needs to be sensitive to both the strengths and the weaknesses of the program.

While Eisner's approach to evaluation is explicitly artistic in nature, he does not discount the value of scientific and quantitative approaches to evaluation. Instead, he asserts that both artistic and scientific evaluation strategies contribute to the understanding of complex phenomena. Because the evaluation methods used in educational connoisseurship and criticism are defined entirely by the individual evaluator, this approach to evaluation is not easy to validate or disconfirm. However, when this approach is used by a talented and well-trained evaluator, it illuminates the unique nature and value of a program in ways that are less likely to occur with other evaluation approaches.

In seeking to determine the validity of the findings of educational connoisseurship and criticism, we recommend that you look for other studies, ideally carried out by different evaluators, to determine whether they obtained similar findings. You also should determine how similar the evaluator's experience and values are to your own, or to those of the stakeholders whom you must consider in making an educational decision.

CRITERIA FOR JUDGING AN EDUCATIONAL EVALUATION RESEARCH STUDY

In reading evaluation research, educators need guidelines for judging the adequacy of the study. The **Joint Committee on Standards for Educational Evaluation** (1994) created a set of standards for this purpose. The Joint Committee defined **program evaluation** to include the evaluation of most of the aspects of educational practice that we described earlier as the subjects of evaluation research. However, the Joint Committee excluded the evaluation of educators from their consideration of the domain of program evaluation. The reason for this decision is that the Joint Committee previously had developed a separate set of personnel evaluation standards (Joint Committee, 1988). More recently, the Joint Committee developed a separate set of standards for assessing evaluation practices in elementary and secondary classrooms (Joint Committee, 2002).

The standards for program evaluation were developed by a committee consisting of representatives from twelve major educational organizations in the United States, including the American Association of School Administrators, the American Federation of Teachers, and the American Educational Research Association. You can use these standards to judge the adequacy of evaluation research studies that you read, or to design your own evaluation research.

The Joint Committee specified thirty standards for program evaluation and grouped them under four criteria: seven standards for the criterion of utility, three standards for the criterion of feasibility, eight standards for the criterion of propriety, and twelve standards for the criterion of accuracy. Below we explain the four criteria by applying them to an evaluation of K–8 science curriculum materials (Johnson, Boyce, & Van Tassel-Baska, 1995).

Utility

The Joint Committee's utility standards are intended to ensure that an evaluation study is informative, timely, and influential.

Johnson and his colleagues conducted their evaluation of K–8 science curricula for high-ability learners under the auspices of the National Science Curriculum Project for High-Ability Learners. They describe the project's mission as to merge (a) curriculum reform principles advocating high-level standards in all traditional curricular areas, (b) the recommendations of recent national standards projects, and (c) key principles of appropriate curriculum for gifted learners.

To address this mission, the members of the review team (the study authors) needed to bring varied competencies to the evaluation. The report describes one reviewer as a materials specialist with a background in library science and gifted education, the second as a scientist with research experience in university and pharmaceutical laboratories, and the third as an educator with expertise in curriculum and gifted education. In their report, the researchers describe how they located materials for possible review and then narrowed their review to twenty-seven sets of K–8 science curriculum materials "based on breadth of use, likelihood of appropriateness for high-ability students, or reputation as innovative or prototypical materials" (p. 37).

Because their article's citations involve recent work on standards and curriculum for gifted learners, the evaluation by Johnson and his colleagues (1995) appears to be timely. The article's description of reviewers' competencies, clear organization of review procedures and findings, and publication in the *Gifted Child Quarterly* confirm that this study is an informative evaluation that is likely to be influential, particularly among educators in gifted education.

Feasibility

The Joint Committee's feasibility standards are intended to ensure that an evaluation study is realistic, prudent, diplomatic, and economical.

The evaluation process used by Johnson and his colleagues appears realistic in that they first categorized the twenty-seven curricula by what appeared to be their primary function: (a) basal stand-alone texts intended for a particular age or grade level; (b) modular curricula packaged into independent units organized around large concepts; or (c) supplementary materials with a precise focus, and comprised of either loosely connected activities or fully developed units to enrich an existing curriculum.

The reviewers concluded that the sets of materials classified as basal textbooks failed to meet new science curriculum standards for all students, but were especially weak for high-ability learners. The sets of materials that were classified as modular programs or supplementary materials were found to be superior to basal textbooks on most dimensions. For example, with one exception, the modular programs tended to be rated the highest in their ability to meet the different needs of high-ability learners, because of their in-depth emphasis on important concepts and their flexibility in use that allowed for faster pacing. The basal stand-alone texts are not identified by name, which one could argue is a prudent and diplomatic treatment of those curricula rated lowest.

Although no mention of the cost of the review is given, it probably was considerable. A note on the first page of the article, entitled "Putting Research to Use," indicates that the evaluation process was developed and carried out over an eighteen-month period. The review procedures (independent ratings, followed by preparation of a narrative review of each rated curriculum) probably took a great deal of time to complete. However, given the potential benefits of improving science instruction for not only high-ability students but for all students, the evaluation study appears to be economical (i.e., cost-effective).

Propriety

The Joint Committee's propriety standards are intended to ensure that an evaluation study is conducted legally, ethically, and with due regard for the welfare of those involved in the evaluation, as well as those affected by its results. In the example we are considering, the evaluators describe positive features of each of the twenty-seven recommended curricula rather than endorse specific programs. They suggest that both pull-out programs and self-contained classes should draw from a number of the available modular and supplementary curricula to meet the needs of gifted students adequately.

In their report, the authors make clear their reasons for advocating the use of these materials over the basal texts. The review thereby conveys a sense that the evaluators acted legally and ethically in judging the curricula and in giving specific recommendations to educators.

Accuracy

The Joint Committee's accuracy standards are intended to ensure that an evaluation will convey technically adequate information about the features that determine worth or merit of the program being evaluated.

Johnson and his colleagues cite two other published reports about the K–8 science curriculum evaluation that describe the evaluation procedures and findings in greater detail. Although their report appears to be fairly comprehensive, it is reassuring to know that additional information about the study is readily available.

Johnson and his colleagues independently assessed features of the general curriculum design, classroom design, and technology of each set of K–8 science curriculum materials that were deemed appropriate for review. They also independently rated each curriculum for its treatment of science content and process, and examined its responsiveness to the needs of intellectually gifted learners, science-prone students, girls, minorities, and students with disabilities. The article includes information on the percentage of agreement among the reviewers' ratings during each of three phases of review and for each of five major features on which each curriculum was rated. The review thus appears to be sensitive to the technical need for inter-rater reliability. Another technical safeguard is that readers who question the conclusions, or wish further information about specific curricula, have the option of referring to the other reports that are cited.

EXAMPLE OF OUTLINING A RESEARCH PROPOSAL

This feature of the chapter gives you an example of how to outline a research proposal using the form in Appendix 1. The example, involving a proposal to study curriculum alignment, is introduced at the end of Chapter 2.

One of the research questions that we proposed to answer is this: What procedures have administrators, teachers, and specialists used to align curriculum content with instruction and test content? If we take the perspective of program evaluation, we might ask a related question: What do various stakeholders see as the strengths and weaknesses of procedures used to align curriculum content with instruction and test content? Conducting an evaluation study to answer this question can yield useful findings that can strengthen the alignment procedures in the future.

In the next section, we fill out various parts of the proposal outline to show how a research study might be designed to answer the evaluation question that we posed.

4. RESEARCH DESIGN
   A. *Research design.* The research design is descriptive, with all data to be collected at one point in time. The participants will be asked to recall particular phases of the curriculum-alignment process. For each phase, they will be asked to identify strengths and weaknesses of its procedures and also to make recommendations for improving them.
   C. *Limitations to generalizability.* Because of resource limitations, we will limit the sample to three nearby school districts that are diverse, but not necessarily representative of the population of school districts nationally. This limitation on the study's generalizability will be noted in the report of findings.
5. SAMPLING
   A. *Characteristics of the population.* Our population of interest consists of all school districts that have made a systematic effort to align curriculum, instruction, and assessment at one or more levels of schooling (elementary, middle, and high school).

C. *Sampling procedure.* We will select a volunteer sample, that is, a sample of school districts that have undergone a systematic curriculum-alignment process and that volunteer to participate in the study. We will document key features of each district (e.g., size, student population, resources for school improvement) and define our target population as districts having similar characteristics. For stakeholder groups that have a substantial number of members (e.g., teachers in a particular school), we will select a random sample to participate in the study. If a selected individual chooses not to participate, another individual from the sample will be randomly selected.

D. *Sampling unit.* The sampling unit will be the individual respondent to the interview protocol that will be used to collect data. It is reasonable to consider each respondent as a sampling unit, because respondents will be interviewed individually and not as a group.

E. *Size of sample.* We will strive to identify all stakeholder groups. We believe that these groups will include district administrators, school administrators, teachers, parents, the school board, and consultants. If other groups are identified as the study proceeds, they will be added to the sample. If the number of individuals in a stakeholder group is small (for our purposes, small is an N of 5 or less), each individual will be included in the sample. If the N is greater than 5, members from the stakeholder group will be randomly selected to yield an N of 5. Because the study does not aim to achieve a high level of population validity, we believe this sample size is sufficient. It should yield an accurate description of the primary perceptions of each stakeholder group.

6. VARIABLES
   A. *Variables to be measured.* There will be three sets of variables: (1) effective procedures used in the curriculum-alignment process; (2) ineffective procedures; and (3) recommendations to improve the process. Each effective procedure, ineffective procedure, and recommendation will constitute a separate variable.

7. METHODS OF DATA COLLECTION
   A. *Measurement of the variables.* An interview protocol will be developed to elicit effective procedures, ineffective procedures, and recommendations. The protocol will be semistructured, so that the interviewer can follow up on participants' responses and also encourage them to remember as much of the alignment process as possible.
   B. *Validity and reliability issues.* We will select interviewers who are not affiliated with any of the school districts, so that the participants will not feel that they need to give socially desirable responses. Participants will be told that their responses will be kept anonymous; this promise of anonymity will help to ensure valid responses to the interview questions. Interviewers will be trained prior to data collection to help ensure that they understand the interview protocol and can use it to collect reliable data. Reliability in this context refers to inter-rater reliability: two interviewers using the interview protocol

independently of each other should be able to collect the same data from a particular participant. Also, the interviews will be tape recorded and transcribed in order to ensure accuracy and completeness of data collection.

8. DATA ANALYSIS PROCEDURES

B. *Method of data analysis.* The interview transcripts will be subjected to content analysis. The researchers will develop a category system that organizes all the effective and ineffective curriculum-alignment procedures identified and all the recommendations mentioned by the interviewees. This category system will be used to code each transcript. For each transcript, the rater will simply record whether each category was mentioned. The raters will be trained in use of the category system to ensure inter-rater reliability. After the transcripts have been coded, tables of descriptive statistics will be constructed. For example, we will show the number of teacher stakeholders within and across districts who mentioned a particular effective procedure, ineffective procedure, or recommendation.

SELF-CHECK TEST

1. In evaluation research the term *stakeholder* refers to
   a. the individual who initiates the request for an evaluation.
   b. anyone who will be affected by the evaluation findings.
   c. an evaluator who uses cost analysis to evaluate a phenomenon.
   d. an evaluator who uses personal interpretation to evaluate a phenomenon.

2. Published evaluation research studies generally help education practitioners make better decisions because usually they
   a. widen the range of factors for educators to consider in making the decision.
   b. provide conclusive evidence of the effectiveness of instructional programs, methods, and materials.
   c. confirm decision preferences that are based on personal experience.
   d. reduce the costs associated with specific decisions.

3. A research study shows the number of students expressing interest in pursuing advanced math before and after viewing a series of videotapes about well-paying careers that require advanced math skills. This research study most likely involves the evaluation of
   a. tests and assessment procedures.
   b. educators.
   c. specific groups or organizations.
   d. instructional materials.

4. A meta-evaluation is
   a. a synthesis of evaluation studies on a particular topic.
   b. an evaluation of an evaluation study.
   c. an evaluation to determine the worth of a fully developed program in operation.
   d. a large-scale evaluation study that follows a series of small-scale evaluation studies.

5. Needs assessment typically involves
   a. measurement of the discrepancy between an existing condition and a desired condition.
   b. interviews of everyone with an opinion about the phenomenon being evaluated.
   c. estimation of the costs and benefits of a proposed intervention.
   d. development and evaluation of a product designed to meet an identified need.

6. The primary purpose of formative evaluation in educational research and development is to
   a. demonstrate the effectiveness of the product under operational conditions.
   b. obtain information to guide revision and further development of the product.
   c. evaluate the product once development has been completed.
   d. test the extent to which learners have achieved the product objectives.

7. Unlike formative evaluation, summative evaluation of an educational R&D product generally
   a. occurs throughout the development process.
   b. is conducted to determine whether development of the product should be discontinued.
   c. determines the effectiveness of the final product.
   d. does not reveal whether the product is effective under conditions similar to a practitioner's situation.

8. Objectives-based approaches to evaluation usually focus on
   a. comparisons of the relative importance of different objectives.
   b. evaluators' interpretations of the inherent value of a program's objectives.
   c. the extent of agreement or disagreement among stakeholders about a program's value.
   d. the extent to which a program helps students achieve the intended learning objectives.

9. Context-Input-Process-Product (CIPP) evaluation emphasizes the
   a. refinement of a product to prepare it for operational use.
   b. evaluation of a product by external evaluators.

   c. evaluators working closely with the client to determine information needs and synthesize evaluation results.
   d. clients' involvement in data collection.

10. A central feature of responsive evaluation is its
    a. focus on identifying the issues and concerns of stakeholders.
    b. specification of the evaluation design prior to data collection.
    c. concern with the goals and objectives of the phenomenon being evaluated.
    d. specification of procedures for reconciling the different perspectives of various stakeholders.

11. Educational connoisseurship and criticism differs from other approaches to evaluation research primarily in its
    a. precise specification of the qualifications that evaluators must possess.
    b. efforts to demonstrate the validity of the evaluators' judgments.
    c. use of artistic methods of perceiving and representing the phenomenon that is evaluated.
    d. reliance on humanities scholars to judge the worth of educational programs in literature and the arts.

12. Some of the program evaluation standards of the Joint Committee on Standards for Educational Evaluation are concerned with the technical adequacy of an evaluation. These standards are intended to ensure an evaluation's
    a. utility.
    b. feasibility.
    c. propriety.
    d. accuracy.

*C*HAPTER REFERENCES

Apple, M. W. (1991). The culture and commerce of the textbook. In M. W. Apple & L. K. Christian-Smith (Eds.), *The politics of the textbook* (pp. 22–40). New York: Routledge.

Bowles, T. J., & Bosworth, R. (2002). Scale economies in public education: Evidence from school level data. *Journal of Education Finance, 28,* 285–300.

Campbell, J. R., Voelkl, K. E., & Donahue, P. L. (1997). NAEP 1996 trends in academic progress: Achievement of U.S. students in science, 1969 to 1996; mathematics, 1973 to 1996; reading, 1971 to 1996; writing, 1984 to 1996. Washington, DC: National Center for Education Statistics. (ERIC Document Reference No. ED409383)

Dick, W., & Carey, L. (2001). *The systematic design of instruction* (5th ed.). New York: Longman.

Dukes, R. L., Ullman, J. B., & Stein, J. A. (1996). Three-year follow-up of Drug Abuse Resistance Education (D.A.R.E.). *Evaluation Review, 20,* 49–66.

Eisner, E. W. (2002). *The educational imagination: On the design and evaluation of school programs* (3rd ed.). Upper Saddle River, NJ: Prentice Hall.

Guba, E. G., & Lincoln, Y. S. (1981). *Effective evaluation.* San Francisco: Jossey-Bass.

Johnson, D. T., Boyce, L. N., & Van Tassel-Baska, J. (1995). Science curriculum review: Evaluating materials for high-ability learners. *Gifted Child Quarterly, 39,* 36–43.

Joint Committee on Standards for Educational Evaluation. (1988). *The personnel evaluation standards: How to assess systems for evaluating educators.* Thousand Oaks, CA: Corwin.

Joint Committee on Standards for Educational Evaluation. (1994). *The program evaluation standards: How to assess evaluations of educational programs* (2nd ed.). Thousand Oaks, CA: Sage.

Joint Committee on Standards for Educational Evaluation (2002). *The student evaluation standards: How to improve evaluations of students.* Thousand Oaks, CA: Corwin.

Levin, H. M., & McEwan, P. J. (2000). *Cost-effectiveness analysis: Methods and applications* (2nd ed.). Thousand Oaks, CA: Sage.

Lockwood, A. (1992). Whose knowledge do we teach? *Focus on Change, 6,* 3–7.

McKillip, J. (1987). *Need analysis: Tools for the human services and education.* Thousand Oaks, CA: Sage.

Miller, K. J. (1995). Cooperative conversations: The effect of cooperative learning on conversational interaction. *American Annals of the Deaf, 140,* 28–37.

Pitman, M. A., & Maxwell, J. A. (1992). Qualitative approaches to evaluation: Models and methods. In M. D. LeCompte, W. L. Millroy, & J. Preissle (Eds.), *The handbook of qualitative research in education* (pp. 729–770). San Diego: Academic Press.

Porretta, D. L., Gillespie, M., & Jansma, P. (1996). Perceptions about Special Olympics from service delivery groups in the United States: A preliminary investigation. *Education and Training in Mental Retardation and Developmental Disabilities, 31,* 44–54.

Scriven, M. (1967). The methodology of evaluation. In R. E. Stake (Ed.), *Curriculum evaluation,* American Educational Research Association Series on Evaluation, No. 1 (pp. 39–83). Chicago: Rand McNally.

Sirotnik, K. A. (1983). What you see is what you get: Consistency, persistency, and mediocrity in classrooms. *Harvard Educational Review, 53*(1), 16–31.

Stake, R. E. (1991). Retrospective on "The countenance of educational evaluation." In M. W. McLaughlin & D. C. Phillips (Eds.), *Evaluation and education: At quarter century* (pp. 67–88). Chicago: University of Chicago Press.

Stufflebeam, D. L., Foley, W. J., Gephart, W. J., Guba, E. G., Hammond, R. L., Merriman, H. O., & Provus, M. M. (1971). *Educational evaluation and decision making.* Itasca, IL: Peacock.

Tyler, R. W. (1949). *Basic principles of curriculum and instruction: Syllabus for Education 360.* Chicago: University of Chicago Press.

RESOURCES FOR FURTHER STUDY

Altschuld, J. W., & Witkin, B. R. (1999). *From needs assessment to action: Transforming needs into solution strategies.* Thousand Oaks, CA: Sage.

The authors explain how to conduct a needs assessment and how to use the results to create an action plan for organizational change.

Baker, E. L., & Niemi, D. (1996). School and program evaluation. In D. C. Berliner & R. C. Calfee (Eds.), *Handbook of educational psychology* (pp. 926–944). New York: Macmillan.

The authors trace the development of educational evaluation as a discipline, classify evaluation models, and discuss the role of evaluation in educational policy making and practice. They also offer their predictions about the future of educational evaluation.

Evaluation Center at Western Michigan University. (n.d.). *Evaluation checklists.* Retrieved August 20, 2003 from www.wmich.edu/evalctr/checklists

> *This website provides refereed checklists that evaluators can use to design and conduct evaluation projects of various sorts. Each checklist is accompanied by a supporting rationale grounded in the evaluation literature and lessons learned from practice.*

Stufflebeam, D. L. (2001). *Evaluation models.* San Francisco: Jossey-Bass.

> *The author analyzes twenty-two evaluation models that have been developed and used over the past forty years or so to judge the quality of programs and services. After applying the standards of the Joint Committee on Standards for Educational Evaluation to each model, he recommends nine of them as particularly worthy.*

Worthen, B. R., Sanders, J. R., & Fitzpatrick, J. L. (2003). *Program evaluation: Alternative approaches and practical guidelines* (3rd ed.). Boston: Allyn & Bacon.

> *The authors discuss the purposes, origins, and likely future of program evaluation and provide detailed treatment of seven different approaches to program evaluation. The book gives practical guidelines for planning, conducting, and using evaluations.*

In the following section of this chapter you will read a research article that illustrates an evaluation research study. It is preceded by comments written especially for this book by the authors of the article. Then the article itself is reprinted in full, just as it appeared when originally published. Where appropriate, we have added footnotes to help you understand the information contained in the article.

SAMPLE EVALUATION RESEARCH STUDY
An Assessment of 23 Selected School-Based Sexuality Education Curricula

Ogletree, R. J., Rienzo, B. A., Drolet, J. C., & Fetro, J. V. (1995). An assessment of 23 selected school-based sexuality education curricula. *Journal of School Health, 65,* 186–191.

● **RESEARCHERS' COMMENTS,** *Prepared by Roberta Ogletree, Barbara Rienzo, Judy Drolet, and Joyce Fetro*

The following research report is the result of a collaborative effort among four Certified Health Education Specialists (CHES)[1] with a long-standing interest in sexuality education. Judy Drolet and Barbara Rienzo have taught the professional preparation courses in human sexuality education at their respective universities for many years. Joyce Fetro, a curriculum specialist for a school district, has participated in several research and evaluation studies examining the effectiveness of sex education programs in preventing pregnancy and the spread of the human immunodeficiency virus (HIV). Roberta Ogletree's primary focus has been the study of sexual coercion. As a result of our shared interest in sexuality education, we have presented numerous papers and coauthored dozens of articles on this topic.

Our decision to undertake an evaluation of published, school-based curricula for sexuality education resulted in the report that follows. We believed that this evaluation would give teachers, curriculum specialists, administrators, parents, and caregivers information that could help them identify published curricula to better meet the needs of children, youth, and families concerning sexuality. All of us became acquainted through our membership in the American School Health Association, and more specifically, on the Council on Sexuality Education. Three of us have been recognized as Fellows of the American School Health Association (FASHA).

Initial analysis of the curricula described in this assessment resulted in the publication by ETR Associates of *Sexuality Education Curricula: The Consumer's Guide* (Ogletree et al., 1994). This publication offered, in the chart style of *Consumer Reports,* an evaluation of each individual curriculum, with no analysis or comparison made. In addition, we included sexuality education curricula designed specifically for special education.

ETR Associates provided financial support for two author meetings and clerical support for preparing the *Consumer's Guide.* While working on the *Consumer's Guide,* we also decided to carry out a more detailed and comparative assessment of the most recent and comprehensive school-based sexuality education programs, which resulted in the present article.

While this assessment does not include special education curricula, it extends well beyond the scope of the *Consumer's Guide.* In it we examine the overall results for 23 curricula that met our selection criteria. For each curriculum covered in the assessment, we sought to provide a description of the curriculum focus, the lesson format, and the contents of the curriculum package, along with publisher and cost information. We designed a matrix to show the presence or absence of specific content characteristics that we considered appropriate for the age/grade levels that each curriculum addressed. Finally, we used an evaluation matrix to rate each curriculum on each of the evaluation criteria that we had established.

The major challenge to our collaborative process was the physical distance between us. One author was located on the West Coast and another on the East Coast, while the remaining two were at the same university in the Midwest. We were aware that we could meet in the same location for only two days on two different occasions during the course of the project. Although we knew that two or more of us would be able to meet periodically at professional meetings, we could not count on all four of us being together for more than the two scheduled work sessions. As a result, we had to clearly define each of our roles and ensure tight coordination of our efforts.

Rienzo had the original idea for the evaluation, having heard many requests from school personnel for information about and access to "quality" sexuality education. Teachers often report that they do not have access to suitable materials for this purpose. Because we located numerous materials that appeared questionable in terms of their effectiveness, we felt that an evaluation of existing curricula was critical.

Fetro conceptualized what the final product would look like, and her vision and coordination efforts with ETR Associates guided the project. Fetro and Rienzo took on the task of developing the curriculum attributes and evaluation criteria to be used in the actual evaluation of the curricula. They decided that the key elements necessary for an effective sexuality education program were twofold: prevention (that is, promotion of individuals' delay of the initiation of sexual intercourse), and protection (that is, provision of information to foster individuals' adoption of appropriate practices to protect themselves and others from such effects as unintended pregnancy or sexually transmitted diseases).

Ogletree and Drolet were responsible for the identification, collection, and description of available curricula that met our criteria for inclusion in the assessment. Responsibilities for all tasks were clearly defined and assigned, which helped promote smooth, timely progress.

By the time of our first authors' meeting, we had determined the curriculum attributes and evaluation criteria and had developed easy-to-use matrices to simplify the evaluation process. The goal of our first meeting was to assess the contents of the curricula. Fetro and Rienzo worked together as a team, as did Ogletree and Drolet. Each pair examined about half the 23 curricula to identify the philosophy and content of each. Next we switched and reviewed the other half, and then we compared the results for a reliability check.

A noteworthy aspect of the project was our solicitation of teacher input as a part of the evaluation. We believed that teachers would be the group most able to offer a pragmatic evaluation of each curriculum based on their experience in actually implementing sexuality education in schools. Therefore, we each identified teachers at the four different curriculum levels (early elementary, upper elementary, middle/junior high school, and high school) who had experience in teaching sexuality education. We recruited eight teachers from Florida, seven from California, and seven from the Midwest. Each teacher reviewed the curricula at his or her teaching level for developmental appropriateness, cultural sensitivity, and ease of implementation.

At our second authors' meeting, we compiled the individual teacher evaluations and rated each curriculum on the evaluation criteria. Again we paired up. Each pair evaluated half the curricula, then the other half, and compared the results for a reliability check.

The advantages of this collaborative effort were many. All of us are members of the same profession (health education), with a similar interest in sexuality education. Our shared interests and experience ensured sufficient professional knowledge and skill to increase the soundness of our effort. Furthermore, because as a group we represent two different educational settings (public school and university), we brought different perspectives to the process, which strengthened the usefulness of the finished product. We all attacked our responsibilities with relish and maintained progress on our tasks and timeline. Our ability to collaborate on the project itself also paid off in preparing these comments.

When we created the *Consumer's Guide,* we had voiced to each other several concerns that did not appear in the *Guide* but that we articulated in the "Assessment Implications" section of the report reprinted here. We are well aware of the fact that sexuality education is teeming with controversial issues, yet they are issues that we felt should be addressed explicitly, not kept hidden.

The report expressed our concern with the lack of clear philosophies in most of the curricula that we reviewed. A curriculum's philosophy needs to be responsive to community beliefs and values regarding sexuality. Perhaps most of the authors chose not to clarify the philosophy of their curricula in order to increase the acceptability of the curricula to a broad range of potential users. However, it is important that a sexuality education curriculum reflect local community values.

In study after study, support for sexuality education in the schools is reported to be over 80 percent, and more often about 90 percent. That is overwhelming support. Committees that help make decisions regarding which curriculum is to be used must truly be representative if students are to get the education that parents want them to have, instead of something that is dictated by small numbers of individuals or groups who happen to be vocal but who do not truly represent the overall community.

We also feel that it is desirable for a sexuality education curriculum to promote not only abstinence but also responsibility and protection. Some youth will hear and heed the messages encouraging abstinence. Those who do not heed those messages, however, must hear messages that promote responsible decision making and protection. Exclusive emphasis on abstinence would neglect the need to convey messages regarding safer sex practices, and might fail to portray sexuality in a positive light.

It was clear to us that the curriculum developers gave inadequate attention to evaluation of the curricula. We know that many people are fearful of or uncomfortable with the notion of program evaluation. Even so, evaluation is an essential component of curriculum development, and it should be addressed early in the process rather than as an afterthought (or with no thought at all).

Sexuality educators run risks when they address controversial issues in their attempts to help youth sort out the wide range of information about sexuality available in our modern world. But wouldn't they run even graver risks by not addressing these issues? For example, sexual orientation is highly controversial, yet there is a need for all youth, as well as their teachers and counselors, to understand this issue. All the problems caused by myths and misunderstanding (including harassment and violence) make this an issue that needs to be addressed in a sexuality education curriculum.

We also feel strongly that sexuality education should affirm the positivity of sexuality and contribute to helping learners adopt health-enhancing behaviors. The Sex Information and Education Council of the United States published *Guidelines for Comprehensive Sexuality Education* (National Guidelines Task Force, 1991). These guidelines promote six key concepts that sexuality education should address: human development, relationships, personal skills, sexual behavior, sexual health, and society and culture. Under each concept, specific age-appropriate developmental goals are recommended. As we stated in the article, acquiring the necessary knowledge, attitudes, and skills to achieve these goals can best occur within a comprehensive school health program.

Our recommendation would dictate the inclusion of sexuality education in a planned, sequential, developmentally appropriate, and culturally relevant prekindergarten through twelfth-grade curriculum. Such a curriculum needs to integrate the mental, social, emotional, and physical dimensions of health, develop personal and social skills (for example, decision making and communication), and provide opportunities for students to demonstrate appropriate knowledge, attitudes, and behaviors. With this approach, human sexuality would be placed within the context of related events, rather than treated as a separate life entity. It would require programs beyond classroom instruction, including peer education and efforts to educate and involve parents, community organizations, and religious institutions. Through such efforts, the interrelationships among various risk behaviors of youth could be demonstrated, while at the same time reinforcing positive sexuality messages.

Notes

1. The designation of Certified Health Education Specialist (CHES) is a nationally recognized certification in health education offered through the National Commission for Health Education Credentialing, Inc.

References

Ogletree, R. J., Fetro, J. V., Drolet, J. C., & Rienzo, B. A. (1994). *Sexuality education curricula: The consumer's guide.* Santa Cruz, CA: ETR Associates.

National Guidelines Task Force. (1991). *Guidelines for comprehensive sexuality education: Kindergarten–12th grade.* New York: Sex Information and Education Council of the United States.

An Assessment of 23 Selected School-Based Sexuality Education Curricula

Roberta J. Ogletree, Barbara A. Rienzo, Judy C. Drolet, Joyce V. Fetro

Abstract

While quality sexuality education curricula are available, those responsible for selecting a curriculum may not feel confident to choose one to meet the needs of their students and community. This paper presents a method to guide in selecting sexuality education curricula as well as results from an evaluation of 23 school-based sexuality education curricula. School administrators, curriculum specialists, health educators, school nurses, teachers, and parents involved in curriculum adoption or development can use the process described to select or develop a sexuality education curriculum to meet the needs of their school and community. (J Sch Health. 1995;65(5):186–191)

During the past two decades, increases in sexuality-related behavior among teen-agers and young adults prompted development of numerous sexuality education curricula. As school administrators, curriculum specialists, health educators, school nurses, and classroom teachers make decisions about sexuality education curriculum selection, a number of questions arise. Is the curriculum content developmentally appropriate for students? Does the curriculum include skill-building strategies proven effective? Do the instructional strategies address individual needs and learning styles? Can the curriculum be implemented easily and without additional teacher training?[1]

While teachers seek to assist students in acquiring the information and skills they need to avoid the negative consequences of undesired or unprotected sexual activity, many teachers do not feel adequately prepared to do so. Specifically, teachers claim they need more information on many topics, better instructional materials, and better teaching strategies.[2-4] Although quality sexuality education curricula exist, many teachers and administrators may not feel confident in their ability to select a curriculum to meet the needs of their students and community.

CURRICULUM ASSESSMENT

This project developed a method to guide selection of appropriate sexuality education curricula to meet school and community needs, and evaluated existing published and marketed school-based sexuality education curricula.

Ogletree, R. J., Rienzo, B. A., Drolet, J. C., & Fetro, J. V. (1995). An assessment of 23 selected school-based sexuality education curricula. *Journal of School Health, 65,* 186–191. Reprinted with permission of the American School Health Association. Copyright © 1995 by ASHA.

This information was intended for use by school administrators, curriculum specialists, health educators, school nurses, teachers, and parents involved in curriculum adoption or development.

Curricula Identification

School-based sexuality education curricula were identified through a computerized library search using the Education Resources Information Center and referring to Publisher's Guides. In addition, resource lists were obtained from the Sex Information and Education Council of the United States (SIECUS) and the Comprehensive Health Information Database (CHID).

From the above sources, 68 curricula were identified for possible inclusion in the assessment. Selected curricula were limited to those that met the four following criteria: school-based, published and/or revised since 1985, did not focus on a single sexuality issue such as HIV infection or pregnancy prevention, and available for review by [sic] the publisher.

Twenty-three curricula met the requirements and were reviewed for this assessment. The 23 curricula were classified into age/grade levels, according to SIECUS guidelines.[5] Figure 1 lists the SIECUS levels, number of curricula at each level that were evaluated, grade classification, age range for the level, and developmental stage.

Most of the 23 curricula were designed to stand alone, although some encouraged individual instructors to add or delete material to meet student needs. Variability existed with regard to the amount of time allotted for the curricula with as few as five lessons to as many as 43, with a mean of 18 lessons.

Assessment Process

The curricula were assessed in two ways: by evaluating the attributes of the curriculum for inclusion of key elements, and by evaluating potential quality of curricula based on how well each met criteria associated with effectiveness. Two matrices were developed to assess these aspects of curricula—the Attributes Matrix and the Evaluation Matrix.

Attributes Matrix. Fetro's[6] analysis of effective prevention programs determined that certain key elements are necessary for sexuality education program success: accurate information about the short-term and long-term physical, psychological, social, and legal consequences or risks of sexually related decisions, internal and external influences on personal health practices and the normative behavior of the peer group, activities to enhance self-esteem, opportunities to build personal and social skills, a peer helper component, and parent/guardian involvement. "Newly developed or adopted curricula should be carefully examined to determine if they include these key elements."[6] Evaluation of published curricula for inclusion of these elements would assist school personnel in identifying those that best meet their needs and thereby provide better educational offerings for students.

To identify components of an individual curriculum, an Attributes Matrix was developed with four categories: philosophy, content, skill-building strategies, and teaching strategies. The underlying philosophy of each curriculum was identified/extrapolated from the purpose, goal statements, and/or objectives. Develop-

SIECUS Level	Number of Curricula	Grade	Age Range	Developmental Stage
Level 1	1	Early Elementary	5–8	Middle childhood
Level 2	3	Upper Elementary	9–12	Preadolescents
Level 3	9	Middle/Junior High	12–15	Early adolescents
Level 4	10	High school	15–18	Adolescents

FIGURE 1 Summary Description of Curricula

mental messages and student activities included in the curriculum were reviewed for consistency with the philosophy statements.

Age-appropriate content was identified based on the SIECUS *Guidelines for Comprehensive Sexuality Education: Kindergarten-12th Grade*[5] and *Sexuality Education Within Comprehensive School Health Education.*[7] Since all content areas are not appropriate at all age/grade levels, certain content areas were not expected to be addressed at different levels.

Two sources were used to identify key skill-building strategies that should be included. The SIECUS *Guidelines for Comprehensive Sexuality Education*[5] was consulted, and a review was completed of evaluations of prevention programs.[8-14]

A variety of teaching methods were identified for use in both elementary and secondary health education curricula.[15-17] Variety in teaching techniques is important due to the variety in objectives, student needs and interests, and different senses used in learning.[18]

To assure reliability in the assessment of age-appropriate content attributes in each curriculum, the four authors worked in pairs to determine if each attribute was addressed in a specific curriculum. Both sets of assessments were compared. If discrepancies occurred between pairs, the curriculum was reviewed a third time to resolve the discrepancy.

Evaluation Matrix. The Evaluation Matrix consisted of criteria based on related literature describing components of effective sexuality education and health education curricula.[5,7,19-22] These criteria generally are accepted in the profession as the most relevant. Twelve distinct categories were identified for evaluating potential effectiveness of sexuality education curricula. A brief overview of these categories follow.

Comprehensiveness was measured by the *breath* [sic] and *depth* of inclusion of developmentally appropriate concepts and subconcepts as outlined in SIECUS *Guidelines for Comprehensive Sexuality Education.*[5] *Content accuracy/currency* was based on presentation of information from current research. *Skill-building variety* (*breath* [sic] and *depth*) was judged based on variety of personal and social skills included, sequential development of those skills, and opportunities for practice and rehearsal. The curriculum's use of a variety of instructional strategies to meet the diverse needs and learning styles of students was examined to assess *methods variety*. *Developmental appropriateness* was assessed as to whether material was related to the cognitive, emotional, and social development levels of the targeted groups.

Bias in terms of race or ethnicity, sex or gender roles, family types, sexual orientation, and/or age as well as whether a variety of social groups and lifestyles were depicted in the text and pictures were examined to evaluate *cultural sensitivity*. *Ease of implementation* determined "user friendliness" based on inclusion of all materials needed to implement the curriculum. The *evaluation* component considered whether the curriculum provided methods and/or instruments for evaluating student knowledge, attitudes, and skills consistent with the goals and objectives of the curriculum. *Appearance/production quality* was judged based on print quality and layout as well as likelihood of stimulating and maintaining student interest. Finally, an *overall quality* rating was given based on the 11 preceding components.

To rate curricula components for the Evaluation Matrix, the authors worked in pairs using a five-point, Likert-type scale.[a] Ratings included unacceptable, inadequate, fair, good, and excellent. In addition to comparing the authors' assessments, classroom teachers and health educators from across the country evaluated each curriculum for developmental appropriateness, cultural sensitivity, and ease of implementation. A minimum of four reviewers with teaching experience at the appropriate grade level examined each curriculum. When discrepancies occurred between the authors' ratings and the curriculum reviewers' ratings, the authors again examined the curriculum in question to resolve differences in ratings.

---

a. A Likert-type scale is a measure that asks individuals to check the extent of their agreement or disagreement (often on a five-point scale) with various statements about a topic. Here the authors are using the term simply to signify the use of a five-point rating scale.

ASSESSMENT RESULTS

Philosophy

The percentages of curricula at each level and the type of underlying philosophy are listed in Table 1. Of the 23 curricula, 43% had an underlying philosophy of "healthy sexuality." Such a philosophy promotes sexuality as a natural and healthy part of life. Physical, psychological, emotional, social, ethical, and spiritual dimensions of healthy sexuality were addressed.

The Level 1 curriculum was determined to have a "healthy sexuality" philosophy. Of the Level 2 curricula (N = 3), 33% promoted healthy sexuality, 33% promoted abstinence only, and the philosophy of 33% of the curricula could not be determined.

Most (74%) of Level 3 and 4 curricula (N = 19) promoted abstinence as the safest and most effective means of preventing sexually transmitted diseases, HIV infection, and pregnancy. Sixty-eight percent recognized that some adolescents will have sexual intercourse and discussed using protection, if adolescents were sexually active. Sixty-eight percent also supported each individual's right and responsibility to make decisions about their sexuality. Forty-two percent expressed a philosophy of healthy sexuality.

Content

Content attributes of the selected sexuality education curricula and the percentages of curricula that addressed those attributes based on SIECUS levels are listed in Table 2.

The single Level 1 curriculum included in the study contained 75% of the 12 content attributes considered appropriate for the Level 1 age group. However, body image, sexual identity and orientation, and STD transmission issues were not addressed.

Puberty, relationships, and sexual exploitation were covered in all Level 2 curricula (N = 3). Sixty-seven percent included gender roles, reproductive anatomy and physiology, and HIV transmission and prevention. Content areas missing from all three Level 2 curricula included body image, sexual identity and orientation, parenting, STD transmission and prevention, and pregnancy prevention.

As expected, Level 3 and 4 curricula (N = 19) covered the greatest number of content attributes. All but four content attributes were covered by at least half of the Level 3 curricula (N = 9). Forty-four percent addressed sexual exploitation and 33% included reproductive health issues. However, only 22% included body image or sexual identity and orientation.

TABLE 1 **Percentages of Sexuality Education Curricula with Underlying Philosophy by Level**

	Level			
	1	2	3	4
Underlying Philosophy*	(n = 1)	(n = 3)	(n = 9)	(n = 10)
Promotes healthy sexuality	100	33	44	40
Promotes responsibility for decisions	0	0	67	70
Promotes abstinence	0	33	78	70
Promotes using protection, if sexually active	**	0	56	80
Philosophy not clear	0	33	0	0

*A curriculum may have more than one underlying philosophy.

**Not developmentally appropriate for this level.

TABLE 2	Percentages of Sexuality Education Curricula with Content Attributes by Level			
	Level			
	1	**2**	**3**	**4**
Sexuality-Related Content	(n = 1)	(n = 3)	(n = 9)	(n = 10)
Puberty	*	100	67	*
Body image	0	0	22	10
Gender roles	100	67	78	40
Reproductive anatomy and physiology	100	67	89	70
Conception and birth	100	33	78	60
Sexual identity and orientation	0	0	22	40
Relationships	100	100	78	80
Parenting	100	0	56	40
Sexual expression	100	33	56	50
STD transmission	0	0	89	80
HIV transmission	100	67	89	90
Abstinence	*	33	78	80
Pregnancy prevention	*	0	67	90
STD prevention	*	0	78	70
HIV prevention	*	67	78	80
Sexual exploitation	100	100	44	60
Reproductive health	100	33	33	40

*Not developmentally appropriate for this level.

Seventy-five percent of the content areas considered developmentally appropriate for high school students were included in 50% of Level 4 curricula (N = 10). However, only 10% addressed body image. Forty percent discussed gender roles, sexual identity and orientation, parenting, or reproductive health.

Skill-Building Strategies

In the category of skill-building strategies, 78% (18) of all 23 curricula including [sic] decision-making skills and identifying consequences of decisions. Also 17 (74%) addressed accessing community resources and 16 (70%) included building general communication skills. Ten (44%) included goal-setting skills, but only seven (30%) included activities to examine perceived risk. Four curricula (17%) addressed peer norms or goal-setting skills, while two (9%) included conflict management. The percentages of curricula at each level that included skill-building strategies are identified in Table 3.

Specifically, the Level 1 curriculum did include self-esteem building skills, skills for examining the consequences of decisions, accessing community resources, building assertiveness, conflict management, and decision-making skills. Skill-building strategies omitted included examining personal values, influences on decisions, perceived pregnancy risk, and perceived STD/HIV risk, addressing peer norms, building refusal skills, and planning/goal-setting skills.

TABLE 3   Percentages of Sexuality Education Curricula with Skill-Building Strategies by Level

Skill-Building Strategy	Level			
	1	2	3	4
	(n = 1)	(n = 3)	(n = 9)	(n = 10)
Examining personal values	0	0	67	50
Increasing self-awareness/building self-esteem	100	33	67	40
Examining influences on decisions	0	67	89	80
Identifying consequences of decisions	100	67	89	90
Addressing peer norms	0	0	22	30
Examining perceived pregnancy risk	0	0	33	40
Examining perceived STD/HIV risk	0	0	56	50
Accessing community resources	100	67	78	70
Building general communication skills	100	67	78	60
Building assertiveness skills	100	33	100	60
Building refusal skills	0	33	78	20
Building conflict-management skills	100	0	11	0
Building decision-making skills	100	67	78	80
Building planning/goal-setting skills	0	0	44	60

None of the Level 2 curricula (N = 3) included all of the skill-building strategies. Sixty-seven percent examined influences on and consequences of decisions, how to access community resources, and building general communication and decision-making skills. Six skill-building strategies were not addressed in any Level 2 curricula: examining personal values, perceived pregnancy risk, perceived STD/HIV risk, addressing peer norms, building conflict management skills, and planning/goal-setting skills.

Most skill-building skills were included in 67% of Level 3 curricula (N = 9). Building assertiveness skills was included in 100% of curricula in this level. Eighty-nine percent included examining influences on decisions and consequences of decisions. Four skill-building strategies were addressed in less than half the curricula: building planning/goal-setting skills (44%), examining perceived pregnancy risk (33%), addressing peer norms (22%), and building conflict-management skills (11%).

Level 4 curricula (N = 10) tended to include fewer skill-building strategies than those in Level 3. Less than half included strategies to build self-esteem (40%), examine perceived pregnancy risk (40%), address peer norms (30%), and build refusal skills (20%). None addressed conflict-management skills.

Teaching Strategies

All 23 curricula include large-group discussion, lecture, and case studies. Ninety-one percent of curricula at all levels include skill practice and rehearsal as well as cooperative learning/small-group activities. Only 9% included a peer helper component. These results are reported in Table 4.

In the Level 1 curriculum, seven of the 13 (54%) teaching strategies were included. In Levels 2 and 3 (N = 12), five strategies were included in all curricula: lecture, large-group discussion, case studies/scenarios, skills practice and rehearsal, and audiovisual materials.

TABLE 4	Percentages of Sexuality Education Curricula with Teaching Strategies by Level			
	Level			
	1	**2**	**3**	**4**
Teaching Strategy	(n = 1)	(n = 3)	(n = 9)	(n = 10)
Groundrules	0	67	78	80
Anonymous questions box	0	67	67	40
Teacher lecture	100	100	100	100
Large-group discussion	100	100	100	100
Student worksheets	0	67	89	100
Journals/story writing	100	0	56	20
Cooperative learning/small group	100	67	89	100
Case studies/scenarios	100	100	100	100
Skills practice and rehearsal	100	100	100	80
Audiovisual materials	0	100	100	80
Community speakers/involvement	100	0	44	30
Peer helper component	0	0	22	0
Parent guardian involvement	0	67	67	70

In Level 2 (N = 3), three strategies—journals/story writing, community speakers/involvement, and peer helper component—were not used. All Level 4 curricula (N = 10) included lecture, large-group discussion, student worksheets, and case studies/scenarios. The peer helper component was missing from all 10.

Evaluation Attributes

The Level 1 curriculum earned ratings of "good" or "excellent" on all attributes with the exception of evaluation. Those attributes receiving "excellent" ratings were content accuracy/currency, developmental appropriateness, cultural sensitivity, and appearance/production quality.

All Level 2 curricula (N = 3) merited an overall quality rating of "fair." They were strong in content accuracy/currency, developmental appropriateness, ease of implementation, and appearance/production quality. Sixty-seven percent were rated "unacceptable" on evaluation, while 33% rated "inadequate."

Thirty-three percent of Level 3 curricula (N = 9) merited an "excellent" overall quality rating. Four oth-ers (44%) were rated "good" while the remaining two (22%) earned "fair" ratings. Fifty-six percent received "excellent" ratings in methods variety, developmental appropriateness, and appearance/production quality. Again, evaluation was weak with only one curriculum assigned an "excellent" rating, while five were rated as "unacceptable."

Of the Level 4 curricula (N = 10), seven (70%) were given an overall quality rating of "good" and three (30%) were "fair." The single attribute for which at least half of the curricula merited an "excellent" rating was appearance/production quality. Other strong areas were content accuracy/currency, methods variety, and ease of implementation. Consistent with other levels, the evaluation component was noticeably weak with 60% of curricula receiving "unacceptable" ratings.

ASSESSMENT IMPLICATIONS

Most authors designed their curricula to stand alone as the sexuality education curriculum for students. However, sexuality education should be a part of a comprehensive school health education program.[7] A resolution adopted by the American School Health Association recommends that sexuality education occur within a comprehensive school health program so the interrelationship of health behaviors can be examined.[23]

Within the curricula examined in this assessment, variability existed with regard to time allotted for the curriculum lessons. While it was not within the scope of this project to assess length of time for sexuality education units, nor to prioritize content within curricula, the variation found within these curricula confirms a need for research on how these characteristics affect districts' programs. For example, are these components related to districts' ability to implement programs, how programs are incorporated, and to their effectiveness? At this point, school district personnel should strive to provide a program of sufficient length and content to meet identified needs and community standards, ideally within a comprehensive health education program.[7, 23]

Few school-based curricula have been developed and published for Level 1 children, although young children at the early elementary level have sexuality education needs.[24] Only one curriculum was identified for this age group. Most curricula were developed for Level 3 and 4 (middle and high school students), perhaps due to a perception that prepubescent children have no need for sexuality education or that sexuality education is more acceptable at higher grade levels.

In most cases, the underlying curriculum philosophy had to be extrapolated from curriculum goals and objectives statements. This omission is disturbing because philosophy provides the blueprint for sexuality education curricula that should "reflect a community's beliefs about sexuality, sexuality education, and how sexuality education should be taught."[25] Philosophy provides the guiding framework, offers a rationale and justification, and can protect a curriculum from attack by opponents.[15]

For a curriculum to be identified as one with a philosophy of healthy sexuality, sexuality had to be presented as a natural and healthy part of everyday living and the curriculum had to address all dimensions of sexuality including physical, emotional, ethical, and social. Only 53% of curricula were classified in the "healthy sexuality" philosophy category. While this fact raises

some concern, it may be due to failure of curriculum authors to see the need for a clearly stated philosophy. When healthy sexuality was missing as an underlying philosophy, the areas of sexual expression and reproductive health usually was missing from curriculum content.

Upon careful examination of the content of the 23 school-based curricula, it was apparent that many curricula do not provide knowledge and skills consistent with their underlying philosophy. Some curricula with philosophy statements purporting to promote responsible decision-making did not offer skills-building activities in decision-making.

The breadth and depth of content areas covered tended to be acceptable. However, body image and sexual identify [sic] and orientation were two areas that seldom were addressed. No attention was given to these topics in any Level 1 and 2 curricula (N = 4) and very little in Level 3 and 4 curricula (N = 19). Body image is one topic area that falls under the SIECUS National Task Force Guidelines' six key concepts (key concept: human development) in a comprehensive sexuality education program. Body image should be addressed at all four levels because "people's image of their bodies affect [sic] feelings and behaviors."[5] "Positive responses lay the foundation for sexual health and self-esteem by helping children feel good about their bodies, good about being male or female . . ."[24]

At the same time, sexual identity and orientation is another content area recommended for inclusion under human development and for which developmental messages are appropriate at all four levels.[5] According to one sexuality education expert, exclusion of sexual orientation from so many of these curricula likely reflects its history of being "considered inappropriate."[26] Research also demonstrates that students and teachers have inadequate knowledge about and high levels of discomfort with the topic of homosexuality.[4] Recent resolutions at the national level by professional organizations, such as the American School Health Association, Association for Supervision and Curriculum Development, and the National Education Association, along with some educators, assert the need for schools to address the needs of gay, lesbian, bisexual, and questioning youth.[27-30] Curricula that include education about sexual orientation, particularly those with a teacher training component, will help schools meet these identified needs.

More recently published curricula are focusing greater attention on building personal and social skills. General skills for building communication, assertiveness, and decision-making capacity were given ample attention in the selected curricula. Although the depth of skill-building strategies was acceptable, the breadth of skill-building strategies was weak because specific skills, such as refusal skills and conflict-management skills, need greater attention and inclusion.

Although several skill-building strategies are appropriate for Level 1 and 2 students, they were not addressed by those curriculum authors. Given current concern with violence, conflict-management skills were noticeably absent. This absence, particularly violence in relationships, may be a reflection on the curriculum publication date since date rape and domestic violence are relatively recent public concerns.

A variety of teaching strategies should be employed to meet individual needs and learning styles of students. The selected curricula (N = 23) used at least seven different teaching strategies. However, 91% need to be revised/updated to include a peer helper component. It is important for curriculum developers to incorporate skills and teaching strategies that reflect current research findings related to effectiveness.[15,18]

Upon evaluation of the curricula, areas of strength were developmental appropriateness and appearance/production quality. Curriculum authors are writing for their levels and are producing visually appealing curricula. Content accuracy/currency and ease of implementation are additional strengths. It is apparent that evaluation, a critical component of curriculum development, is not being addressed despite its usefulness and value as a tool for measuring the effectiveness of a curriculum.

CONCLUSIONS

Although the curricula assessed in this project were generally rated "good" overall, a need exists for improvement. The upper elementary curricula (Level 2), in particular, need much improvement related to comprehensiveness, skill-building and teaching strategies, cul-tural sensitivity, and evaluation. Most of the selected curricula should be revised to include current, accurate information and additional skill-building strategies as well as evaluation.

While many schools and districts select prepared sexuality education curricula, many elect to develop their own. The process and instruments developed for this assessment should be helpful with such efforts. Local school districts should incorporate the process and matrices developed to examine their existing curricula [sic] for comprehensiveness and inclusion of key elements related to its potential effectiveness. In addition, school districts planning to develop their own sexuality education curricula should consider using the matrices to guide development. Another potential use of this process is for curriculum adoption, particularly if specific curricular attributes are desired such as an abstinence-based curriculum or a strong skills-building component.

Roberta J. Ogletree, HSD, CHES, Assistant Professor; and Judy C. Drolet, PhD, FASHA, CHES, Professor, Dept. of Health Education and Recreation, Southern Illinois University, Carbondale, IL 62901; Barbara A. Rienzo, PhD, FASHA, CHES, Professor, Dept. of Health Science Education, University of Florida, FLG-5, Gainesville, FL 32611-2034; and Joyce V. Fetro, PhD, FASHA, CHES, Supervisor, School Health Programs Office, San Francisco Unified School District, 1512 Golden Gate Ave., San Francisco, CA 94115. This article was submitted November 24, 1994, and revised and accepted for publication April 13, 1995.

References

1. Ogletree RJ, Fetro JV, Drolet JC, Rienzo BA. *Sexuality Education Curricula: The Consumer's Guide*. Santa Cruz, Calif: ETR Associates; 1994.

2. Allen Guttmacher Institute. *Risk and Responsibility: Teaching Sex Education in America's Schools Today*. New York, NY: Allen Guttmacher Institute; 1989.

3. Forrest JD, Silverman J. What public school teachers teach about preventing pregnancy, AIDS, and sexually transmitted diseases. *Fam Plann Perspect*. 1989;21(2): 65–72.

4. Richards CL, Daley D. Politics and policy: Driving forces behind sex education in the United States. In: Drolet JC, Clark K, eds. *The Sexuality Challenge: Promoting Healthy*

Sexuality in Young People. Santa Cruz, Calif: ETR Associates; 1994:47–68.

5. National Guidelines Task Force. *Guidelines for Comprehensive Sexuality Education: Kindergarten-12th Grade.* New York, NY: Sex Information and Education Council of the United States; 1991.

6. Fetro J. Evaluating sexuality education programs. In: Drolet JC, Clark K, eds. *The Sexuality Challenge: Promoting Healthy Sexuality in Young People.* Santa Cruz, Calif: ETR Associates; 1994:555–581.

7. Neutens JJ, Drolet JC, DuShaw ML, Jubb W, eds. *Sexuality Education Within Comprehensive School Health Education.* Kent, Ohio: American School Health Association; 1991.

8. Bell CS, Battjes RJ, eds. *Prevention Research: Deterring Drug Use Among Children and Adolescents.* Rockville, Md: National Institute on Drug Abuse; 1987. NIDA research monograph 63, US Dept of Health and Human Services publication ADM 87-1334.

9. Botvin GJ, Wills TA. Personal and substance use prevention. In: Bell C, Battjes R, eds. *Prevention Research: Deterring Drug Use Among Children and Adolescents.* Rockville, Md: National Institute on Drug Abuse; 1985:8–49.

10. Eisen M, Zellman GL, McAllister AL. Evaluating the impact of a theory-based sexuality and contraceptive education program. *Fam Plann Perspect.* 1990;22(6):261–271.

11. Fetro J. *Personal and Social Skills: Understanding and Integrating Competencies Across Health Content.* Santa Cruz, Calif: ETR Associates; 1992.

12. Howard M, McCabe JB. Helping teenagers postpone sexual involvement. *Fam Plann Perspect.* 1991;22(1):21–26.

13. Kirby D, Barth RP, Leland N, Fetro JV. Reducing the risk: The impact of a new curriculum on sexual risk-taking. *Fam Plann Perspect.* 1991;23(6):253–263.

14. Schaps E, DiBartolo R, Moskowitz J, Palley C, Churgin S Primary prevention evaluation research: A review of 127 impact studies. *J Drug Issues.* 1981;11:17–43.

15. Ames EE, Trucano LA, Wan JC, Harris MD. *Designing School Health Curricula,* 2nd ed. Dubuque, Iowa: William C Brown: 1995.

16. Creswell WH, Newman IM. *School Health Practice.* St. Louis, Mo: Times Mirror/Mosby; 1989.

17. Pollock MB, Middleton K. *Elementary School Health Instruction.* St Louis, Mo: Times Mirror/Mosby; 1989.

18. Fodor JT, Dalis GT. *Health Instruction: Theory and Application.* Philadelphia, Pa: Lea and Febringer; 1989.

19. Association for Sexuality Education and Training. *What Criteria can be used to Assess Sexuality (or HIV/AIDS) Curricula.* Oak Harbor, Wash: Association for Sexuality Education and Training.

20. Cassidy DC. *Family Life Education Curriculum Guidelines.* Minneapolis, Minn: National Council on Family Relations; 1990.

21. English J, Sancho A, Lloyd-Kolkin D, Hunter L. *Criteria for Comprehensive Health Curricula.* Los Alamitos, Calif: The Southwest Regional Educational Laboratory; 1990.

22. Rogers T, Howard-Pitney B, Bruce BL. *What Works? A Guide to School-Based Alcohol and Drug Abuse Prevention Curricula.* Palo Alto, Calif: Health Promotion Resource Center, Stanford Center for Research in Disease and Prevention; 1990.

23. ASHA takes a stand. *The PULSE of the American School Health Association.* 1995;16(1):4.

24. Brick P. Sexuality education in the early elementary classroom. In: Drolet JC, Clark K, eds. *The Sexuality Challenge: Promoting Healthy Sexuality in Young People.* Santa Cruz, Calif: ETR Associates; 1994:105–122.

25. LaCursia NL, Beyer CE, Ogletree RJ. What's behind the curriculum? The importance of a philosophy in sexuality education. *Fam Life Educator.* 1994;13(1):4–9.

26. Yarber WL. Past, present and future perspectives on sexuality education. In: Drolet JC, Clark K, eds. *The Sexuality Challenge: Promoting Healthy Sexuality in Young People.* Santa Cruz, Calif: ETR Associates; 1994:3–28.

27. Blumenfeld WJ. Gay, lesbian, bisexual and questioning youth. In: Drolet JC, Clark K, eds. *The Sexuality Challenge: Promoting Healthy Sexuality in Young People.* Santa Cruz, Calif: ETR Associates; 1994:321–341.

28. Lipkin A. The case for a gay and lesbian curriculum. *The High Sch J.* 1993–1994;77(1–2):95–107.

29. Remafedi G. The impact of training on school professionals' knowledge, beliefs, and behaviors regarding HIV/AIDS and adolescent homosexuality. *J Sch Health.* 1993;63(3): 153–157.

30. Sears JT. The impact of culture and ideology on the construction of gender and sexual identities: Developing a critically based sexuality curriculum. In: Sears JT., ed. *Sexuality and the Curriculum: The Politics and Practices of Sexuality Education.* New York, NY: Teachers College Press; 1992:139–156.

chapter 15

Action Research

After studying this chapter, you will be able to

1. describe the purposes and benefits of action research.

2. describe the seven steps in the model of action research that is presented in this chapter.

3. describe ten differences between formal research and action research.

4. describe the conditions that facilitate action research projects.

5. describe how insider–outsider collaboration and action science can contribute to action research.

6. describe several criteria for increasing the validity of an action research project.

Tom Eppler teaches in a state that requires all public school teachers to earn continuing professional development (CPD) units in order to retain their teaching credentials. He has decided to take an in-service course on motivational techniques to earn some of the CPD units that he needs.

The course instructor has asked that each teacher do a project of his or her own design as the major assignment. Some teachers plan to write a paper based on library research; some are developing curriculum units. Still others, like Tom, want to try out some of the motivational techniques that the course covered to determine their effectiveness for their students. They would like to document their efforts in a way that is useful for them and their colleagues.

Action research is an ideal method of investigation for teachers in Tom's situation. As you will find in this chapter, action research enables teachers, administrators, school counselors, and other education practitioners to investigate and improve their performance in systematic, personally meaningful ways. You will learn that action research draws upon the techniques of investigation that you have studied in other chapters of this book, but for the purpose of improving local practice rather than producing theory or scientific generalizations. ●

Purposes and Benefits of Action Research

Action research involves systematic investigation of new actions by practitioners in order to improve their effectiveness. To master any of the other types of research described in this book, conduct a research study, and report it at a conference or in a research journal would require considerable training. However, action research is well within the reach of education practitioners. This is because the quality of an action research project depends on how well the project serves a practitioner's immediate, local needs, not on how well the project fulfills scientific criteria of sound research design and interpretation. The steps of an action research project are fairly simple, and they are grounded in the practitioner's interests and workplace.

The term *action research* can be traced back to social psychologist Kurt Lewin (1946). Lewin was concerned that the methods and findings of academic researchers could result in scholarly publications that had little effect on society or the work of practitioners. Therefore, he developed action research as a type of investigation that could be used by community members and professional practitioners to promote positive social change. For example, in a study conducted during World War II, Lewin brought together groups of housewives to discuss the possible use of organ meats in meal preparation. This was during a time when the U.S. government wanted to promote cheaper cuts of meat because of a shortage in normal meat supplies. The study demonstrated the value of group discussion in changing people's attitudes about, and subsequent actions toward, a significant social issue.

Action research was widely used in the 1940s and 1950s, but its use in the United States declined thereafter as the term *research* came to be equated primarily with laboratory-based experimentation and statistical significance testing. Australian and British educators brought action research back to the fore in the 1960s, and they continue to use this approach extensively. Today action research is becoming increasingly popular in the United States, especially among teacher educators.

Professional, Personal, and Political Purposes

Over time, various researchers have developed different approaches to action research, depending on their goals and values. Kenneth Zeichner and Susan Noffke

(2001) describe most action research studies as having one or more of the following three purposes.

1. *Professional purposes.* Some action researchers emphasize the value of action research in the professional development of educators in school settings (Burnaford, Fischer, & Hobson, 2001; Noffke, 1992) or in higher education (Zuber-Skerritt, 1992). One focus of this type of action research is the enhancement of practitioners' reflection on their practice so that they become more sensitive to discrepancies between their intentions and their actions (Dadds, 1995; Whitehead, 1993).

2. *Personal purposes.* Other approaches to action research focus on encouraging practitioners to undertake investigations to help build a knowledge base for their own practice and for other practitioners, or in the service of school reform (Hollingsworth & Sockett, 1994). A growing number of journals (for example, *Educational Action Research, Teaching and Change, Focus on Basics*) specialize in reporting action research projects conducted by teaching practitioners.

3. *Political purposes.* Still other approaches emphasize the use of action research to promote democratic forms of education and collaboration among teachers, students, and others in the educational community. Joseph Fischer and Norman Weston (2001), for example, describe teacher research aimed at major school reform in Chicago, Brazil, and Chile. Some of these approaches (for example, Carr & Kemmis, 1988) look to critical theory as a source of inspiration and concepts for framing action research projects (see Chapter 12).

Benefits of Action Research

Action research has at least five benefits for education professionals, described below.

1. It contributes to the theory and knowledge base needed for enhancing practice. When educators carry out their own action research, they learn to reconstruct educational theory and findings in terms that are understandable to them, and to develop more effective practices in their work settings. They then might read formal research reports about similar practices with more comprehension and insight. Furthermore, action research can serve as a wellspring of creativity for new practices. For example, Stephen Jobs and Steve Wozniak were not trained as researchers, but their tinkering in a spare garage—a type of action research—led to the development of the personal computer. Closer to home, Madeline Hunter was the director of the laboratory school at UCLA when she began informally experimenting with ways to improve teachers' classroom instruction. Her individual creativity resulted in the development of a method of instruction called ITIP (Instructional Theory into Practice—Hunter, 1994). This method had a major impact on teaching practice, and it stimulated various formal research studies of its effectiveness.

2. Action research supports the professional development of practitioners by helping them become more competent in understanding and applying research findings, and in carrying out research themselves when appropriate. By carrying out action research, practitioners not only develop needed skills in doing research, but also improve their ability to read, interpret, and apply the research of others.

3. Action research can build a collegial networking system. Action research often involves several educators working together; students, parents, and others also may be involved. The communication network that develops during the research project helps reduce the isolation often experienced by the individual teachers, administrators, or specialists working in the education field. The improved communication patterns foster support and sharing of information among practitioners, and thus continue to benefit both staff and students over time.

4. Action research helps practitioners identify problems and seek solutions in a systematic fashion. It requires practitioners to define problems clearly, to identify and try out possible solutions systematically, and to reflect on and share the results of their efforts. Thus, action research shows practitioners that it is possible to break out of the rut of institutionalized, taken-for-granted routines and to develop hope that seemingly intractable problems in the workplace can be solved.

5. Action research has the advantage that it can be used at all levels and in all areas of education. It can be carried out in specific classrooms or departments, throughout an educational institution, or at the regional or national level.

The benefits of action research have been documented in various projects reported in the literature. Martha Stevens (2001) carried out action research while teaching mainstreamed sixth graders with learning disabilities. To ensure her students' equal status with the neighboring gifted class, called TAPS (Teaching Advanced Placement Students), Stevens named her special education resource class the Language Arts Program on Thinking, Organizing, and Practicing for Success (LAPTOPS). She made curriculum modifications based on a number of research-based learning and self-management approaches. For example, she scaffolded the information in the regular education texts for her students by recording it on audiotape and rewriting the assignments at a simpler reading level.

Stevens reports that six years of data showed good student progress in both reading and writing skills, including test score and grade improvements both in her classes and in mainstreamed settings. Stevens wrote her research report during class, stopping to share comments with her students. She notes, "They seemed delighted that their learning story was receiving such a place of importance" (p. 168).

Barbara Levin and Tracy Rock (2003) studied five pairs of pre-service and experienced teachers who engaged in collaborative action research projects during the pre-service teachers' professional development internship in the experienced (mentor) teachers' classrooms. Levin and Rock analyzed interviews with, and written and audiotaped reports from, the participants. They described the pre-service teachers' perspectives on the costs of collaboration (for example, time pressures, dependence on someone else to fulfill one's responsibilities, or limited access to one's mentor) and its benefits (for example, the mentor's perspective, support, and feedback).

Elizabeth Soffer (1995), a school principal, experimented with ways to reduce serious discipline problems at her school. She concluded that

> . . . my project has benefited both me and the school. Not only did my disciplinary practice improve, but the overall disciplinary climate improved. (p. 124)

Anchalee Chayanuvat and Duangta Lukkunaprasit (1997), two English-language instructors at a university in Thailand, conducted action research to design a course for enhancing the English-language skills of gifted students entering their university. Their findings included recommendations for a special English class for gifted students, with:

> . . . more emphasis on speaking and writing, inclusion of external reading materials which are more difficult and challenging, and exploitation of students' learning activities outside class in our English program, e.g., an oral discussion following the watching of an assigned film. (p. 164)

These few examples illustrate the range of action research projects that can be undertaken and the benefits that they can yield. We recommend that you conduct your own review of the literature, using the methods that we described in Chapters 2, 3, and 4, in order to identify successful action research projects in areas of professional practice that are of interest to you. Robin Marion and Ken Zeichner (2001) have produced a practitioner resource guide for action research that identifies many hard-copy and online resources for learning about, designing, obtaining funding for, and reporting on action research. In secondary sources such as their guide, the listed web addresses may no longer be current, so we suggest you use a comprehensive search engine (for example, Google or Webcrawler) to search for each site name or title in which you are interested.

TYPICAL STEPS OF AN ACTION RESEARCH PROJECT

In this chapter we describe an action research model that includes seven steps. The text authors generated this model, which includes steps of action research that its various proponents have identified. This model puts greater emphasis on the design and data collection/analysis steps of action research than some models. We also recommend the models of Jeffrey Glanz (1998) and of Gail Burnaford, Joseph Fischer, and David Hobson (2001), which put special emphasis on the key role of reflection in action research. **Reflection** is a process in which practitioners step back from the world of practice and ponder and share ideas about the meaning, value, and impact of their work. Because we recommend reflection by action researchers throughout the research process, we do not include it as a step in our model. The seven steps of the action research model are: (1) defining the problem, (2) selecting a design, (3) selecting research participants, (4) collecting data, (5) analyzing data, (6) interpreting and applying the findings, and (7) reporting the findings.

We consider the collection and analysis of data (steps 4 and 5) to be the most important aspects of action research. Most practitioners periodically reflect on their work or try new strategies. However, they rarely collect systematic data to determine the problems that their clients are experiencing, what discrepancies might exist between their intentions and their practices, or whether their strategies are working. Effective, credible action research involves a process of collection, analysis, and interpretation of local data that clearly demonstrates the validity of the research findings.

Geoffrey Mills (2000) provides an excellent chapter on qualitative data collection techniques for action research, with numerous examples of their use in three categories of data collection: experiencing (through observation and field notes), enquiring (when the researcher asks research participants directly or though written measures), and examining (making use of existing educational records as a data source).

We will now explain the steps of the model by presenting examples of actual action research projects. The examples illustrate the different contexts in which action research can be used, the various types of educators who do it, and the wide range of problems in professional practice that can be addressed. We encourage you to explore the many books, websites, and journals that report on action research in education for other examples. For example, *Networks*, the source of the action research article by A. W. Lehmann reprinted in full at the end of the chapter, is available online. Other online and hard-copy sources are cited in Marion and Zeichner (2001). Be sure to check which sources are still in operation when you conduct your literature review.

EXAMPLES OF THE SEVEN-STEP ACTION RESEARCH PROCESS

Example 1. Determining Common Student Concerns in Studying

Summary. Two of the authors of this book (Joy Gall & Mark Gall, 1995) asked the teachers who participated in our study skills instruction workshops over a one-year period to administer a checklist of student concerns when they returned to their classrooms, and to send us the results. Responses were tallied for each classroom, and the concerns most commonly checked by elementary, middle/junior high, and high school students were identified.

1. *Define the problem.* We offered teacher workshops on study skills instruction for many years. In our workshops we gave teachers a fourteen-item checklist that they could use to assess their students' most common concerns about study and schoolwork. We wished to determine what concerns were most common among

elementary, middle, and high school students who responded to the checklist. We thought that it would be useful to include this information when presenting the checklist to teachers in later workshops, and that it would help us decide which aspects of study skills instruction to emphasize in the workshops.

2. *Select a design.* In every workshop that we conducted, we administered the checklist to participants (primarily teachers) and recommended that they in turn administer the checklist to their own students. We decided to conduct a survey by asking the teachers to send us their results. We promised to compile the results for students at each school level—elementary, middle/junior high, and high school—and to forward them to all teachers who participated in the survey.

3. *Select research participants.* The volunteer sample consisted of all teachers who participated in our workshops over a one-year period and who accepted our invitation to send us the results of their administration of the checklist to their classes. After about eight months we had received usable responses from five classrooms in four elementary schools, nine classrooms in four middle schools, and seven classrooms in three high schools. Most of the schools were in Oregon, where we live, but there were also schools in Canada and Panama.

4. *Collect data.* The primary measuring instrument in this project was the Checklist of Student Concerns from the *Study for Success Teacher's Manual* (Gall & Gall, 1995), which is shown in Figure 15.1. Each student who responds to the checklist is asked to check the five items (of the fourteen that are listed) of greatest personal concern. Each teacher had received a copy of the checklist in our workshops and had been encouraged to make copies to administer to students. We gave the teachers self-addressed return envelopes. We asked them to send us their students' responses to the checklist and information about the number of students, their grade level, and the subject of the class in which the checklist was administered.

5. *Analyze the data.* To analyze the data, we calculated the percentage of students in each classroom who checked each of the fourteen items, dividing the number of students checking that item by the total number of students who had filled out the checklist. We ranked the items for each classroom, with the item checked most often receiving a rank of 1, the item checked next most often receiving a rank of 2, and so forth. We then made a master ranking of the items checked most often by elementary, middle, and high school students by averaging the rankings across all the classrooms at each level, weighted by the number of students responding in each classroom.

The top three concerns for elementary students were getting nervous about a test coming up (#13), not understanding what the teacher talked about in class (#6), and coming across words in their reading that they don't understand (#10). The top three concerns for middle or junior high school students were feeling too tired to study (#1), getting nervous about a test coming up (#13), and knowing the answer to the teacher's question but not feeling comfortable in speaking up (#8). The top three concerns for high school students were procrastinating instead of studying (#3), feeling too tired to study (#1), and when they write something, feeling it is not as good as it could be but not knowing how to make it better (#12).

Check the FIVE (5) items below that most concern you about schoolwork. (If any of your top concerns aren't listed, write them in the blank spaces below item #14.)

_____ 1. Feeling too tired to study.

_____ 2. Feeling like I'm wasting my time in school.

_____ 3. Procrastinating instead of studying.

_____ 4. Handing in my assignments late.

_____ 5. Misplacing materials I need for doing my schoolwork.

_____ 6. Not understanding what the teacher is talking about.

_____ 7. Not remembering what the teacher talked about in class.

_____ 8. Knowing the answer to the teacher's question but not feeling comfortable to speak up.

_____ 9. Forgetting what I read soon after I read it.

_____ 10. Coming across words in my reading that I don't understand.

_____ 11. Can't seem to get ideas for my writing assignment.

_____ 12. When I write something, feeling it's not as good as it could be but not knowing how to make it better.

_____ 13. Getting nervous about a test coming up.

_____ 14. Running out of time before I finish a test.

_____ 15. _____

_____ 16. _____

_____ 17. _____

_____ 18. _____

_____ 19. _____

FIGURE 15.1   Checklist of Student Concerns from the *Study for Success Teacher's Manual*

Source. Unit 1, Lesson 1, p. 2 of Gall, M. D. & Gall, J. P. (1995). *Study for success teacher's manual* (5th ed.) Eugene, OR: M. Damien Educational Services. Copyright © 1995 by M. Damien Educational Services. Reprinted by permission of M. Damien Educational Services.

6. *Interpret and apply the findings.* Our interpretation was that students at different school levels have somewhat different concerns about study and schoolwork, corresponding to the new challenges that confront them at each level of schooling. We concluded that teachers could help their students deal with these concerns more effectively if they explicitly taught the students study skills that address those concerns.

In a middle school class of talented and gifted students to which we taught a study skills lesson, the top three concerns did not correspond to the average rankings described above. This result led us to question whether students in special or gifted education, or in other relatively homogeneous groupings of students, might report different study concerns.

After doing this survey we routinely presented these results to teachers in our workshops. We pointed out, however, that each classroom in our sample had somewhat different results. Therefore we continued to recommend that teachers carry out their own action research by administering the checklist to their students and collecting data as they tried out classroom procedures and instructional activities to help students with various study concerns.

7. *Report the findings.* We prepared tables showing the rankings of the checklist items for each classroom in the sample. We wrote a three-page letter summarizing the study and sent it, along with the tables, to all teachers who had sent us data for our survey. As mentioned above, we also presented the findings in each workshop we offered thereafter.

Example 2. Shared Teaching and Learning in a Middle School Industrial Arts Classroom

Summary. Wallace Shilkus (2001), an industrial arts middle school teacher, had recently returned to higher education after seventeen years to earn his master's degree. His action research involved the design and construction of CO_2-powered race cars with his seventh- and eighth-grade "veteran" students, fourth-grade "rookies" with whom the veterans were teamed, and his own graduate education classmates.

1. *Define the problem.* Shilkus was "curious about the ways in which the industrial arts were relevant to middle school students" (p. 143). He wanted to explore teaching methods to activate students' multiple intelligences; explore different ways to reach all students, including hard-to-motivate students; and demonstrate the contribution of industrial arts to students' development, especially in middle school.

2. *Select a design.* Shilkus wanted to help others become aware of the importance of this endangered subject, industrial arts. He decided to use both cross- and peer-tutoring approaches to teach the nine-week race car course, having his seventh- and eighth-grade students tutor first the fourth graders and then the adults in his graduate education class.

3. *Select research participants.* As stated above, his middle school students in the race car class, their fourth-grade "rookie" partners, and Shilkus's graduate education classmates were the research participants. They all engaged in providing data for the research and in sharing their discoveries to learn and help others learn.

4. *Collect data.* Based on his review of Howard Gardner's (1983) theory of multiple intelligences, Shilkus utilized a variety of data-collection techniques. To assure positive student pairings he consulted with the fourth-grade teacher, who knew all the rookies and had taught many of the veterans. "Student journal keeping assisted me . . . in identifying students' strengths and weaknesses" (p. 145). Shilkus continually observed the classroom activity and did pre- and postsurveys of all three groups of research participants. After analyzing each set of data (see below), he added other data-collection strategies: the adults' journal entries describing the classroom atmosphere, a videotape of a two-hour lab

in which the middle school students tutored the adults in design and construction of their race cars, and a videotape of a subsequent elimination car race for all participants.

5. *Analyze the data.* Shilkus gives descriptions of students' design, construction, and tutoring activities in class, with specific examples:

> In many cases, I saw a marked improvement in class participation and behavior. Students were forming a tutoring system in the classroom too, not just with their tutees. I observed many students who asked for additional work; they wanted and enjoyed helping someone else. I was witnessing a form of community being born. (p. 146)

At the elimination car race, "some members of my middle school class commented that the fourth-grade sketches were better than the adult sketches" (p. 148). A postactivity survey revealed that participants liked making the cars more than designing them. Adults reported insights they gained from being in the role of student in an unfamiliar context.

6. *Interpret and apply the findings.* A quote from a home economics teacher in Shilkus's graduate education class confirmed for him the importance of teachers being able to put themselves in their students' shoes when they design instruction:

> I know now some of the frustrations my kids must feel in my sewing class. . . .
> As much as I like to think I can see things through a student's eyes, it's refreshing to be proved wrong on this point!

Shilkus concluded from his research project that basing his class teaching activities on the multiple-intelligences framework helped him reach more of the hard-to-motivate students, promoted socialization skills, and appealed to students' varied learning styles.

7. *Report the findings.* Shilkus's action research report is one of a number of detailed examples of "Teachers Doing Research" in a book of the same title (Burnaford, Fischer, & Hobson, 2001).

DIFFERENCES BETWEEN FORMAL RESEARCH AND ACTION RESEARCH

Both formal research and action research aim to increase knowledge and understanding, but they differ in important ways. G. Mettetal (2001) identifies ten ways in which action research typically differs from formal research.

1. *Training needed by the researchers.* Most researchers need extensive preparation before they are able to use formal research methods skillfully. Individuals who conduct quantitative research studies need to be skilled in using various measurement techniques and inferential statistics. Those who conduct qualitative research studies need specialized skills in collecting and interpreting intensive data on selected cases. By contrast, most education practitioners can carry

out action research, whether on their own, in collaboration with colleagues, or with the aid of a research specialist. They do not need advanced skills in research design and interpretation. In the second case example described earlier, a middle school teacher was the researcher. In the study that is reprinted in this chapter, A. W. Lehmann, a teacher of high school English, designed and conducted action research with his secondary English class.

2. *Goals of the research.* The goals of formal research are to develop and test theories, and to produce knowledge that is generalizable to a broad population of interest. Action research, by contrast, is aimed at obtaining knowledge that can be applied directly to the local situation. It also has the goal of contributing to the preparation, and hence the competence, of education practitioners. In the second case example, Shilkus's primary goal was to improve his teaching of industrial arts for middle school students. His purpose in publishing the study was primarily to encourage other teachers to use action research to improve their own teaching, rather than to present generalizable findings about teaching strategies in industrial arts.

3. *Method of identifying the problem to be studied.* In formal research, problems for investigation usually are identified through a review of previous research. Researchers often study problems of personal interest, but they are not necessarily problems that relate directly to the researchers' work responsibilities. In action research, however, educators investigate precisely those problems that they perceive to be interfering with their effectiveness, or that involve important goals they want to achieve in their work.

4. *Procedure for literature review.* In formal research, an extensive literature review, focusing on primary-source materials, is necessary. The review is needed in order to give the researchers a thorough understanding of the current state of knowledge about the problem being investigated. This knowledge enables them to build on the knowledge accumulated by others in designing and interpreting their own research. For action research, researchers need only to gain a general understanding of the area being studied. Hence, a more cursory literature review, focusing on secondary sources, usually is adequate. In the second case example, Shilkus gives only one reference, to one theory of multiple intelligences (Gardner, 1983). If he had intended his study to be a formal study of multiple intelligences, he would have needed to do a thorough review of research in this area before conducting the study.

5. *Selection of research participants.* In formal research the researchers aim to investigate a representative sample of the population, so as to increase the generalizability of their findings and to eliminate sampling bias as a factor confounding the meaning of the findings. Action researchers, however, do their research with the students or other individuals with whom they typically work. In the first case example, our research participants were teachers who participated in our workshops and courses and chose to send us the results of their use of the Checklist of Student Concerns.

6. *Research design.* Formal research emphasizes detailed planning to control for extraneous variables that can confuse the interpretation of the results. For

example, quantitative researchers give major attention to maintaining similar conditions in experimental and control groups, except for the variable being compared. Rigorous controls also are used in qualitative research, especially in checking the credibility and trustworthiness of the data that are collected. Thus the time frame for carrying out formal research typically extends over a period of many months. Action researchers, by contrast, plan their procedures less extensively, freely make changes that appear desirable during the action phase of the research, and move quickly between data collection, interpretation, and modification to their practice. They may use **narrative,** such as folktales, poems, or anecdotes, to describe their research. Little attention is paid to control of the situation or elimination of sources of error or bias. Because the researchers are personally involved, bias typically is present. However, unless extreme, it is not generally viewed as a problem, because the results are intended for use primarily by those very researchers.

Sometimes an action researcher also wants to encourage other practitioners to undertake their own action research on the same problem, so as to foster more general and more rapid improvements to education practice. Such researchers are likely to use a more rigorous research design, and to produce a publishable report of their work.

7. *Data-collection procedures.* Researchers who do formal studies, particularly quantitative researchers, attempt to collect their data using valid and reliable data-collection methods. As a result, they might first evaluate available measures and conduct a pilot study of the measures prior to conducting the main study. Action researchers, instead, often use convenient methods of data collection (e.g., observing or talking with students) and available measures, such as those routinely administered during classroom instruction (e.g., conventional classroom tests). In the case examples presented above, the only measure utilized was the Checklist of Student Concerns. This measure has not been subjected to extensive testing to determine its reliability or validity.

8. *Data analysis.* Formal quantitative research often involves complex analysis of data, but raw data rarely are presented and tests of statistical significance are usually emphasized. In formal qualitative research, the researcher engages in careful, reasoned analysis of case data to determine their consistency with the theory in which the research is grounded. Most action research, however, involves simpler analysis procedures, with a focus on practical significance rather than statistical significance. Also, the subjective opinion of the researchers often is weighted heavily. The examples of action research in this chapter involve only descriptive statistics (means and percentages in Gall and Gall's research) or general observations that are not quantified or grounded in theory (in the Shilkus study and in Lehmann's reprinted article).

9. *Application of results.* Researchers who do formal research emphasize the meaning and the theoretical significance of their findings and possible directions for further research. They may discuss the practical implications of their results, but this is not a requirement or a reflection on the study's merit. In action research, however, the practical significance of the results is of foremost importance. Ac-

tion researchers report their findings mainly in an effort to clarify how the findings might affect their own work and to inform their colleagues about the possible implications for professional practice. Colleagues may adopt strategies found to be effective in someone else's action research project. They usually do so without reference to theory or concern for careful replication of the original research procedures.

10. *Reporting of the research.* Formal research is usually written, professionally reviewed, and, if accepted, published in a report or journal or presented at a conference. While some action research is reported in similar contexts, it is commonly made available through online networks or shared informally with colleagues.

FACILITATING CONDITIONS FOR ACTION RESEARCH

For action research to be successful, practitioners should have sufficient time, the opportunity to collaborate with colleagues, an openness to change, and both the opportunity and commitment to write about the research process and outcome. In addition, they should value data collection and analysis as a guide to improving professional practice. Below we expand on these facilitating conditions.

1. *Time.* Educators usually need release time from some of their normal work responsibilities to carry out an action research project. The time is needed for designing the project, doing it, reflecting on and sharing the findings, and modifying one's work practices according to what has been found. Educators who enroll in graduate degree programs often find it desirable or necessary to obtain a leave from their regular positions during their period of study. Thus it is not surprising that much action research by educators occurs as a part of university coursework.

2. *Collaboration.* As we explained in the preceding section, some approaches to action research emphasize the desirability of collaboration among education practitioners in conducting an action research project. Such a **collaborative action research** group can also extend to include the clients for whom the research activities are intended. Richard Schmuck (1997), a social psychologist and educational scholar who has done extensive work in organization development, describes many helpful techniques (e.g., positive social support, critical friendship, probing conversation) to develop the type of collaborative relationships that facilitate this approach to action research.

In their guide for teacher-researchers, Marian Mohr and Marion MacLean (1987) describe their experience in helping teacher-researchers form small groups (four or five teachers) based on common interests. Each group typically included teachers from various grade levels and disciplines. They met regularly; got to know one another and one another's work; and discussed their individual research logs, data, analysis, findings, and drafts of reports. Through this process, both individual and joint action research projects were defined, applied, refined, and reported. Mohr and MacLean documented the positive effects of this process on both teachers' classroom instruction and their planning and research skills.

3. *Openness.* Another type of support needed by educators is an openness to modifying their daily routines. This means that administrators, school staff, and clients should feel sufficient trust and freedom to acknowledge and confront workplace practices that need improvement. Once consensus on action has been reached, all stakeholders need to give the teachers or other implementers support for trying it. Verbal support might be sufficient, but depending on the action research project, implementers also might need materials, facilities, assistants, and release time.

4. *Valuing of data.* Action researchers need to respect data as a guide to action. Practitioners who rely exclusively on their personal belief systems as a guide to their practice are not likely to undertake or support action research projects. Such practitioners will be reluctant to challenge those belief systems by comparing them with diagnostic data at the start of an action research project, or with data collected after a new practice has been tried. On the other hand, administrators and staff members who respect data as a guide to practice will encourage each other to engage in ongoing action research projects. When this happens, the organization as a whole improves.

5. *Sharing.* Finally, action researchers should have the opportunity to share their projects and findings with other educators and with education stakeholders (for example, their students' parents). Stephen Tchudi (1991), describing the teacher-as-researcher model of action research, notes:

> The teacher-as-researcher is, above all, a writer. Such a teacher designs questions about curriculum and teaching, creates trials or experimental lessons and activities, collects a variety of evidence, and writes up the findings. The data collected by this teacher/writer/researcher are wide-ranging. . . . While gathering these data, the teacher keeps a learning log, recording and analyzing in the manner of the ethnographic researcher, as a participant observer. (p. 86)

As we explained in the preceding section, various journals publish action research projects conducted by education practitioners. Also, the findings of such projects increasingly are reported at professional conferences.

USE OF THEORY TO INCREASE THE IMPACT OF ACTION RESEARCH

Some educational researchers tend to view action research as a lesser form of research, precisely because it rarely refers to theory or meets the design criteria of formal research. Others see it as having more promise than any other current educational strategy to reconstruct the education of students (Fishman & McCarthy, 2000) by building practice more firmly on both theory and on valid, local research findings about what promotes learning and other desired outcomes for students.

Below we discuss three aspects of educational theory that have particular bearing on action research. Not every action research topic requires a specific theoretical framework, but any project built on an awareness of the theories discussed below would be stronger as a result.

Collaboration and the Insider–Outsider Issue

Whether the promise of action research is realized depends to a great extent on the participants in action research projects. Some practitioners (typically, K–12 teachers) view themselves as **insiders** and may argue against involving **outsiders** (typically, academics from a university or research organization) as collaborators in, or even reviewers of, one's action research. Stephen Kemmis and Robin McTaggart (2000) point out that reliance on the interpretations of "outsider" observers could disempower teachers and convey that "outsider" research is more valid than teacher research.

McTaggart (2002) recently addressed the insider–outsider issue from a different perspective, arguing that one of the surest ways for academics such as university professors to add value to K–12 educators' practice is through participatory action research endeavors.

McTaggart makes the case that educational practice involves not only teaching but all the major educational functions of an educational system. He argues that to be effective, the *action* undertaken through action research must impact all the critical aspects of educational practice: curriculum, administrative practice, teacher education, and educational research practice. He makes it clear that all educators are practitioners with respect to the particular aspect(s) of practice in which they engage, and all can impact other aspects of practice through collaborative efforts.

McTaggart identifies three ways in which academics can best contribute to action research in their work with K–12 educators and other research participants.

1. *The objectification of experience.* McTaggart explains that action research must involve a collaborative process of testing the credibility of evidence and the relevance of the theoretics that make it possible, rather than deference to positivist principles of "objectivity." Such objectification derives both from "an ongoing sociopolitical process . . . in situ with participants" (p. 9) and from systematic data collection and analysis.

2. *The disciplining of subjectivity with respect to affect.* McTaggart suggests that, as part of the research collective, academics must support research participants' expression of affect, while at the same time helping them sort out in the larger context which of their feelings are justified and which are better reframed or set aside.

3. *The disciplining of subjectivity with respect to political agency.* In McTaggart's view, by joining a collective research endeavor, academics can contribute critical support for the development of personal political agency, and provide critical mass for a commitment to change.

McTaggart admits that academics' privileged institutional settings may have deskilled them for these collaborative roles. He nonetheless asserts that if they will "insinuate themselves into political life" (p. 14), they will gradually be able to become equal players with others in a truly participatory action research process.

Action Science

The theory of action developed by Chris Argyris and Donald Schön (1974) provides a foundation for designing action research that produces real change. **Action science** provides an opportunity to discover and address (1) the various **theories-in-action** (the actual behavior of practitioners as they engage in their work) held by different collaborators in an action research endeavor, as well as (2) possible discrepancies between practitioner's **espoused theories** (practitioners' beliefs about how they deal with problems of practice) and their theories-in-action.

1. *Differences in collaborators' theories-in-action.* Collaborative action research presents challenges no matter who the collaborators are. Some collaborative action research endeavors are done by researchers who can all be considered "insiders"—for example, several K–12 teachers, or a number of university researchers, or work teams from several educational research and development agencies working on a joint project. Despite their similar status, different members of the research collective may nonetheless have different theories-in-action. In that situation, the challenge in arriving at shared or consensual approaches to solving specific educational problems is greater.

A study by Thomas Hatch (1998) illustrates this phenomenon. Following a request for proposals issued by the New American Schools Development Corporation in 1991, four large-scale school-improvement organizations formed a collaborative effort called the Authentic Teaching Learning and Assessment for All Students (ATLAS) Communities Project, to effect change in schools nationwide. Hatch shows how differences in the theories-in-action advocated in the writings and expressed by the leaders of these organizations contributed to different approaches to basic schooling dilemmas and "made it extremely difficult to make decisions and to carry out the collaborative work that school improvement required." (p. 24)

Clearly, more attention must be paid up front, and throughout the process of collaborative effort, to resolving or accommodating differences in participants' theories-in-action.

2. *Discrepancies between one's espoused theory and one's theory-in-action.* A second problem addressed by action science is the situation in which a practitioner's espoused theory (what she believes is the basis for her practice) differs significantly from her theory-in-action (how she actually behaves in practice). For example, suppose that Shirley, a ninth-grade history teacher, believes that she fosters higher-order thinking when questioning her students. If in fact she actually

asks mostly knowledge and comprehension questions, she is not tapping the higher-cognitive levels of Bloom's taxonomy of educational objectives.

Action research could help demonstrate this discrepancy and the problems it causes. Shirley could do action research to improve her questioning strategies. She could collect data on both her specific actions and students' responses to them. Then she could involve colleagues and academics in the analysis and interpretation of those data. This process would help Shirley see the discrepancies between her espoused theory and her theory-in-action. Then she could take new actions to bring her behavior closer to what she says she believes. (She could also change her espoused theory to better reflect her actual behavior, but unless this somehow improves students' learning of higher-cognitive thinking skills, it might not be the most appropriate action on Shirley's part.)

Increasing the Validity of Action Research

Action research is time-consuming, and its basic purpose is to improve an educator's practice. Thus it is important to consider ways to design and carry out the research that increase its *validity*, that is, the extent to which the interpretations that action researchers make from the data they collect are appropriate, meaningful, and useful.

From our review of action research studies in the literature, it appears that some projects pay very little attention to the systematic collection of data. Some reports of practitioner research simply include subjective generalizations that students "responded positively" or "did better" after a new action was undertaken, with no examples or data indicating to what extent, or to which students, such statements apply. While such generalizations are very common in education, action research is most worthwhile when it moves practitioners beyond their traditional ways of doing and seeing things. Effective action research should give both the researchers themselves, and those affected by the research, a clear understanding of (1) the actions taken, (2) the results achieved, and (3) the processes of data collection, analysis, and interpretation on which those results are based.

Validity basically has to do with truthfulness or value, and there are many views about how to define it in practice. Many researchers subscribe to a positivist epistemology (see Chapter 1), meaning they believe that obtaining objective knowledge about the world is not only possible but is the ultimate goal of research. In evaluating action research (or any other type of research), they apply standards of validity based on positivist criteria (Yin, 2000).

Because most action research is based on interpretivist epistemology and collects only or mainly qualitative data, interpretivist criteria for determining the trustworthiness and credibility of case study findings (see Chapter 10) are usually more relevant to action research. Gary Anderson and Kathryn Herr (1999) proposed five such validity criteria to evaluate action research studies: (1) outcome validity, (2) process validity, (3) democratic validity, (4) catalytic validity, and (5) dialogic validity. We describe each validity criterion below. For each criterion we also refer to specific strategies used in one or more of the action research studies discussed in this chapter that, in our view, increased that type of validity in the corresponding study.

1. *Outcome validity.* **Outcome validity** concerns the extent to which actions occur that lead to a resolution of the problem that prompted the action research study. Thus it reflects how successful the action research project was in achieving its purpose. Rigorous practitioner research, of course, is not concerned simply with solving a specific problem. Instead, its aim is to help researchers reframe the problem in a more complex way, which often leads to a new set of questions/problems. Thus this criterion also addresses the importance of reflection and the continuing introduction of new actions to address ongoing or emerging problems.

In our own action research on study skills (Gall & Gall, 1995), our survey results solved the problem of identifying the most common concerns reported by students at different school levels. Of course, we recognize that changes might occur over time or in different sites. The discrepant findings from the gifted and talented middle school class, for example, led us to question whether the same study concerns would be reported in homogeneous groupings of students. That is a question we could pursue in future work on study skills instruction.

2. *Process validity.* **Process validity** concerns the adequacy of the processes used in different phases of the action research project. The extent to which problems are framed and solved in a way that permits the researchers' ongoing learning is an aspect of process validity. Triangulation (the inclusion of multiple perspectives or data sources) also contributes to process validity. If the action research is reported through narratives such as poems, folktales, or anecdotes, readers need to know whether they depict accurately what occurred, rather than being purely subjective accounts or interesting exaggerations. Stevens's (2001) study showed how action researchers can use available school data, including grades and test scores, to assess the effect of the actions implemented in a research project. She also tells stories of particular students' breakthroughs, as perceived by her, students themselves, and their parents, that demonstrate their learning.

3. *Democratic validity.* **Democratic validity** refers to the extent to which the action research project is done in collaboration with all parties who have a stake in the problem being investigated. It also involves a determination of whether their multiple perspectives and material interests are taken into account. Here "multiple voices" are viewed not as a basis for triangulation of data sources (as in the criterion of process validity), but as an issue of ethics and social justice.

Shilkus's action research (2001) provides an outstanding example of including multiple voices in the problem of making industrial arts instruction an active learning process for all participants. He included as data sources, and actually as coresearchers, not just his middle school students but also the fourth-grade "rookies" and then his graduate education classmates.

4. *Catalytic validity.* **Catalytic validity** involves examination of the extent to which an action research project reorients, focuses, and energizes participants, opening them to a transformed view of reality in relation to their practice. Action researchers strengthen this aspect of validity by keeping a research journal

to record their reflections and changing perceptions. This criterion also addresses the extent to which practitioner research realizes an emancipatory potential. It evaluates action research in relation to its success in fostering the widespread engagement of educators and education stakeholders in an active quest for ending oppression and promoting social justice.

Lehmann's action research (2000), reprinted in full in this chapter, involves a high school teacher's efforts to encourage classroom discussion that allows all students a greater role in directing and participating in discussions. He used group work, asked all students to generate potential discussion questions, and did surveys to determine students' attitudes about class discussion before and after implementing these actions. His quote of one student's comment illustrates the emancipatory potential of this work:

> . . . here we get to have a say in the way that we are learning . . . it's us getting to be us and learning through the best way we see fit. (Further Research section, paragraph 3)

5. *Dialogic validity.* **Dialogic validity** reflects the value of dialogue with peers in the formation and review of the action researcher's findings and interpretations. It can be met by doing action research collaboratively, or by the researcher engaging in critical and reflective dialogue with other practitioner researchers or with a "critical friend" who serves as a devil's advocate for alternative explanations of research data. It helps ensure the "goodness-of-fit" of the action research problem and findings with the intuitions of the practitioner community.

Mohr and MacLean's (1987) report of teachers' group work while conducting individual action research projects illustrates the ongoing dialogue among teacher-researchers to help them each define, implement, modify, and report their projects. According to Mohr and MacLean, this dialogue positively affected both the teachers' classroom instruction and their planning and research skills. Stevens's (2001) action research also involved a good deal of dialogue between her and her students, the students' other teachers, and the students' parents. The other teachers' positive responses to her program outcomes and materials also reflects "goodness-of-fit" with the teaching community in her middle school.

In summary, each of these validity criteria reflect different aspects of an action research project's perceived credibility and trustworthiness. However, no typology is exhaustive. We encourage you not only to apply the above criteria to your own or others' action research, but also to identify other criteria that you consider important.

To judge the quality of an action research project, you might have little information available to you. Such a project typically is not presented in a complete, formal report. This limitation can be overcome by interviewing the action researcher—and perhaps colleagues and clients, too—in order to learn how the steps of action research that we described earlier in the chapter were carried out. It might also be possible to examine some of the data that the action researcher collected.

EXAMPLE OF OUTLINING A RESEARCH PROPOSAL

This feature of the chapter gives you an example of how to outline a research proposal using the form in Appendix 1. The example, involving a proposal to study curriculum alignment, is introduced at the end of Chapter 2.

In Oregon a state test of social sciences skills is to be introduced in 2004. We, the writers of this proposal, are two of our school's five eighth-grade teachers of social studies. We plan to do action research in our own school. We have seen very different approaches to social studies curriculum and instruction among the five teachers in our department. We wonder if our different theories-in-action might be hampering our schools' curriculum alignment efforts. We want to clarify differences among the five eighth-grade teachers in our school, whose students will be the first to take the eighth-grade-level state social sciences test. We want to get the five of us to closer agreement about the social studies curriculum and teaching methods we use to prepare all our eighth-graders for the state test.

2. RESEARCH QUESTIONS
    B. Our research proposal will focus on question 2 of the example in Chapter 2: "What procedures have administrators, teachers, and specialists used to align curriculum content with instruction and test content?" We suspect that there is a split among the teachers of social studies in our school. Some teachers appear to focus on teaching the facts (names, dates, places, terminology) of social studies. Other teachers appear to focus on developing students' understanding of the ways in which social scientists construct concepts and meanings based both on data and on their personal values and life experiences. Depending on what the state test will cover, we think that not all five of us may have aligned our curricula as much as we should.
    C. Our study builds on the theoretical framework of Argyris and Schön (1974). Their theory states that each practitioner has an espoused theory, corresponding to what she believes is the basis for her practice, and a theory-in-action, corresponding to how she actually behaves in practice. Our speculation is as follows. Even if all the teachers in our school were to express the same espoused theory about the way they should teach in order to align their instruction with the new state test, their theories-in-action might differ considerably. If so, some students would not be receiving the best instruction to prepare them for the state test.
4. RESEARCH DESIGN
    A. We will use action research to study and attempt to solve the problem we have described.
    E. We want to maximize the validity of our findings in relation to all five of the validity criteria that Anderson & Herr (1999) posed for action

research: outcome, process, democratic, catalytic, and dialogic. We will do so by careful data collection and analysis, frequent reflection and ongoing dialogue, considering everyone's point of view, defining new actions as we go along, and trying to remember our ultimate purpose, which is to help all our students learn and grow.

5. SAMPLING
   B. The phenomenon we wish to study is the degree of similarity between the theories-in-action of the five eighth-grade social studies teachers at our school, and its effect of any dissimilarity on curriculum alignment. These five teachers together are the case that we need to study.
   C. The two of us and our three colleagues represent a sample of eighth-grade social studies teachers from the same school. We will describe this sample carefully, so that readers can decide whether the findings for this sample are likely to apply to their local situation.

6. VARIABLES
   B. Data collection and analysis will focus on the curriculum and the teaching methods each teacher uses to teach social studies to eighth graders.

7. METHODS OF DATA COLLECTION
   A. We will ask each teacher to allow herself or himself to be observed by one or more teacher colleagues while teaching a social studies class. Each observer will take notes and make a thick description of the curriculum materials, teaching strategies, and student social sciences competencies that each teacher's lesson involved. Also, the observer will interview the teacher after class and record her reflections about what choices she made and why she took particular actions while teaching the lesson. Our colleague at the university, who does research and teaching in history and social sciences, will help us identify themes to describe each teacher's theory-in-action as reflected in the descriptions.
   B. Our university collaborator will also obtain information from the state department of education about the anticipated content of the eighth-grade social sciences state test.

8. DATA ANALYSIS PROCEDURES
   B. We will use reflective analysis to analyze the data. We will assess the degree of agreement between our five theories-in-action, and the potential impact of any observed disagreement on our students' learning. Our analysis of the match between our school's curriculum and teaching strategies and the state test will also clarify the level of curriculum alignment our school has achieved. We believe our action research will help us better understand and promote curriculum alignment, both in the subjects already covered by the state tests and in any to be added in the future.

SELF-CHECK TEST

1. Action research has all the following purposes except
   a. supporting the professional development of practitioners.
   b. building theory and generalizable knowledge.
   c. building a collegial networking system among educators.
   d. helping practitioners identify problems and seek solutions systematically.

2. The quality of an action research project is *least* dependent on its
   a. use of well-designed methods of data collection and analysis.
   b. promotion of collaboration between the researcher and his or her colleagues.
   c. contribution to the knowledge base for education.
   d. impact on the researcher's practice.

3. Reflection by action researchers
   a. is particularly important at the start of an action research project.
   b. occurs primarily during data analysis and interpretation.
   c. involves pondering the meaning, value, and impact of one's actions.
   d. involves dialogue with the research participants.

4. The problem to be addressed by an action research project typically is identified by
   a. practitioners' consideration of obstacles that exist to achieving their work goals.
   b. reviews of the education literature.
   c. a systematic needs assessment.
   d. consultation with outsiders.

5. Action researchers who publish their studies in the research literature are primarily motivated by the desire to
   a. present generalizable findings to the widest possible audience.
   b. encourage other educators to undertake action research on problems of practice.
   c. demonstrate the rigor that action research can involve.
   d. enhance their status in their local educational context.

6. For an action research project to be considered a success, it is important that the researchers
   a. receive extensive preparation to develop their research knowledge and skills.
   b. review the education literature before designing the action to be taken.
   c. discuss the theoretical implications of their results.
   d. apply the findings to their own practice.

7. According to Robin McTaggart, academics can best contribute to collaborative action research with K–12 educators by
   a. promoting adherence to positivist principles of objectivity.
   b. providing structure for the research design.
   c. providing critical mass for a commitment to change.
   d. all of the above.

8. Considering the multiple perspectives and interests of all stakeholders in an action research project is a strategy that directly increases its _____ validity.
   a. democratic
   b. catalytic
   c. dialogic
   d. process

CHAPTER REFERENCES

Anderson, G. L., & Herr, K. (1999). The new paradigm wars: Is there room for rigorous practitioner knowledge in schools and universities? *Educational Researcher, 28*(5), 12–21, 40.

Argyris, C., & Schön, D. A. (1974). *Theory in practice: Increasing professional effectiveness.* San Francisco: Jossey-Bass.

Burnaford, G., Fischer, J., & Hobson, D. (Eds.) (2001). *Teachers doing research* (2nd ed.). Mahwah, NJ: Lawrence Erlbaum.

Carr, W., & Kemmis, S. (1988). *Becoming critical: Educational, knowledge and action research.* London: Falmer.

Chayanuvat, A., & Lukkunaprasit, D. (1997). Classroom-centered research at Chulalongkorn University Language Institute. In S. Hollingsworth (Ed.), *International action research: A casebook for educational reform* (pp. 157–167). London: Falmer.

Dadds, M. (1995). *Passionate enquiry and school development.* London: Falmer.

Fischer, J. C., & Weston, N. (2001). Teacher research and school reform: Lessons from Chicago, Curitiba, and Santiago. In G. Burnaford, J. Fischer, & D. Hobson (Eds.), *Teachers doing research* (2nd ed., pp. 345–366). Mahwah, NJ: Lawrence Erlbaum.

Fishman, S. M., & McCarthy, L. (2000). *Unplayed tapes: A personal history of collaborative teacher research.* Urbana, IL: National Council of Teachers of English, and New York: Teachers College.

Gall, M. D., & Gall, J. P. (1995). *Study for success teacher's manual* (5th ed.). Eugene, OR: M. Damien Educational Services.

Gardner, H. (1983). *Frames of mind.* New York: Basic Books.

Glanz, J. (1998). *Action research: An educational leader's guide to school improvement.* Norwood, MA: Christopher-Gordon.

Hatch, T. (1998). The differences in theory that matter in the practice of school improvement. *American Educational Research Journal, 35,* 3–31.

Hollingsworth, S., & Sockett, H. (1994). *Teacher research and educational reform,* the ninety-third yearbook of the National Society for the Study of Education, Part I. Chicago: NSSE.

Hunter, M. (1994). *Enhancing teaching.* New York: Macmillan.

Kemmis, S., & McTaggart, R. (2000). Participatory action research. In N. K. Denzin & Y. S. Lincoln (Eds.), *Handbook of qualitative research* (2nd ed., pp. 567–605). Thousand Oaks, CA: Sage.

Lehmann, A. W. (2000). Student-generated discussion in the senior secondary English classroom. *Networks: An On-line Journal for Teacher Research, 3*(2). Retrieved March 3, 2003, from www.oise.utoronto.ca/~ctd/networks

Levin, B. B., & Rock, T. C. (2003). The effects of collaborative action research on preservice and experienced teacher partners in professional development schools. *Journal of Teacher Education, 54,* 135–149.

Lewin, K. (1946). Action research and minority problems. *Journal of Social Issues,* 2(4), 34–46.

Marion, R., & Zeichner, K. (2001). *Practitioner resource guide for action research.* Oxford, OH: National Staff Development Council.

McTaggart, R. (2002). Action research scholar: The role of the scholar in action research. In M. P. Wolfe & C. R. Pryor (Eds.), *The mission of the scholar: Research & practice* (pp. 1–16). New York: Peter Lang.

Mettatal, G. (2001). Research about teaching and learning. Retrieved March 1, 2002, from Indiana University South Bend website: www.iusb.edu/~gmetteta/Research_about_Teaching_and.htm#Comparison

Mills, G. E. (2000). *Action research: A guide for the teacher researcher.* Upper Saddle River, NJ: Prentice-Hall.

Mohr, M. M., & MacLean, M. S. (1987). *Working together: A guide for teacher-researchers.* Urbana, IL: National Council of Teachers of English.

Noffke, S. E. (1992). The work and workplace of teachers in action research. *Teaching and Teacher Education, 8,* 15–29.

Schmuck, R. A. (1997). *Practical action research for change.* Arlington Heights, IL: IRI/Skylight.

Shilkus, W. (2001). Racing to research: Inquiry in middle school industrial arts. In G. Burnaford, J. Fischer, & D. Hobson (Eds.), *Teachers doing research* (2nd ed., pp. 143–149). Mahwah, NJ: Lawrence Erlbaum.

Soffer, E. (1995). The principal as action researcher: A study of disciplinary practice. In S. E. Noffke & R. B. Stevenson (Eds.), *Educational action research: Becoming practically critical* (pp. 115–126). New York: Teachers College Press.

Stevens, M. C. (2001). Laptops: Language arts for students with learning disabilities: An action research curriculum development project. In G. Burnaford, J. Fischer, & D. Hobson (Eds.), *Teachers doing research* (2nd ed., pp. 157–170). Mahwah, NJ: Lawrence Erlbaum.

Tchudi, S. (1991). *Planning and assessing the curriculum in English language arts.* Alexandria, VA: Association for Supervision and Curriculum Development.

Whitehead, J. (1993). *The growth of educational knowledge: Creating your own living theories.* Bournemouth, England: Hyde.

Yin, R. K. (2000). *Case study research: Design and methods* (3rd ed.). Thousand Oaks, CA: Sage.

Zeichner, K. M., & Noffke, S. E. (2001). Practitioner research. In V. Richardson (Ed.), *Handbook of research on teaching* (4th ed., pp. 298–330). Washington, DC: American Educational Research Association.

Zuber-Skerritt, O. (1992). *Action research in higher education: Examples and reflections.* London: Kogan Page.

Resources for Further Study

Burnaford, G., Fischer, J., & Hobson, D. (Eds.) (2001). *Teachers doing research* (2nd ed.). Mahwah, NJ: Lawrence Erlbaum.

Presents guidelines for the conduct of teacher research in local, university, and national or international settings. The many detailed examples of teachers doing research are well designed, clearly written, and inspiring.

Fishman, S. M., & McCarthy, L. (2000). *Unplayed tapes: A personal history of collaborative teacher research.* Urbana, IL: National Council of Teachers of English, and New York: Teachers College.

> *Summarizes the authors' experiences in conducting, and guiding others in the conduct of, "insider–outsider" collaborative teacher research.*

Marion, R., & Zeichner, K. (2001). *Practitioner resource guide for action research.* Oxford, OH: National Staff Development Council.

> *A compilation of resources for practitioner research, including information about practitioner research networks, journals and online sites presenting action research studies, funding sources, and a bibliography on sources for designing action research.*

In the following section of this chapter you will read a research article that illustrates an action research study. It is preceded by comments written especially for this book by the author of the article. Then the article itself is reprinted in full, just as it appeared when originally published online.

SAMPLE ACTION RESEARCH STUDY
Student-Generated Discussion in the Senior Secondary English Classroom

Lehmann, A. W. (2000). Student-generated discussion in the senior secondary English classroom. *Networks: An On-line Journal for Teacher Research, 3*(2). http://www.oise.utoronto.ca/~ctd/networks/

● **RESEARCHER'S COMMENTS,** *Prepared by A. W. Lehmann*

It was my good fortune a few years ago to pursue a master's degree from the University of Northern British Columbia. Of the courses in the stream through which I personally navigated, several focused on the pragmatics of speech in the classroom. Some investigations were devoted to habits of instruction that can so easily become paradigms of classroom management. Others explored the differences between didactic instruction and narrative. Constructivist literature emphasized the significance of student engagement and participation in classroom activity, and so on.

Overall, these courses' most lasting impression on me was the conviction that the common discourse of classrooms, including both the oral interchanges between instructors and students and conversations among students themselves, is of exceptional importance to learning that lasts. In constructing my own learning about this issue, I wished to explore further, by examining my own teaching, the kinds of departures from habitual practices that might more effectively generate student engagement. I wanted to see the effects of meaningful oral activities that were both student-driven *and* productive toward curricular goals, a combination that can prove elusive. Teachers love to promote curricular aims, but often students' interests lie elsewhere. Students love to talk, but frequently not as enthusiastically about classwork as about their personal lives and social priorities.

Discourse dynamics are extremely complicated, despite their surface simplicity. Before one even begins to assess or interpret the denotations of the messages being exchanged, there are numerous elements to consider. The nature of the venue, the participants' ages and genders, the relative social power of the speakers and listeners, and all the tacit understandings implicit in culture, tradition, and social expectation combine to provide the framework in which messages are exchanged.

Then, once such verbal exchange is under way, other considerations arise. For example, whose agenda is being served (is the conversation aimless or directed, and if the latter, by whom)? Is there an understood common purpose to the interchange? Is there mutual understanding of vocabulary and idiom? Of course, if each time we teachers began a lesson in a classroom situation we tried to attend to all these concerns, we would probably stop up our mouths and ears and cower in despair. The priorities of getting on with the job prevent most such analysis.

Despite such a daunting truth, the challenge of improving student speaking and listening in class and developing the participation and utility of student discourse in positive directions is one that doesn't go away. For teachers to rely on the occasional "teachable moment" in an effort to generate student involvement in curricular goals through class discussion has always seemed too haphazard and too inadequate for professional practice. However, if and when such moments occur, we naturally embrace them strongly. Can we, though, devise useful strategies that are more consistently successful? This is a useful question, and perhaps it is natural that we recognize that questioning itself is key.

Although we all use questions quite naturally in our daily lives—asking directions, trying to locate products, investigating details in personal relationships, and so on—in education questions often have a kind of delayed utility. For example, if one asks a store clerk in which aisle one can find the canned tuna and the clerk responds "Aisle 4," the answer fulfills the question's purpose, and the episode is finished. Some questions in the language arts classroom are of just that sort, pragmatic tools for helping youngsters learn to use both the jargon and the concepts of grammar, syntax, composition, analysis, and criticism. However, in the open-ended universe of literary study, it often seems as if our queries never cease, with one question leading to the next in a continual chain toward an elusive goal of more comprehensive understanding—of what? Of ourselves? Of society? Of the world?

Such open-ended questions, the ones with no easy answers, are often, paradoxically, both the most frustrating and the most satisfying. As Leonard Cohen once sang, "I never had a secret chart/to get you to the heart/of this or any other matter." The world of literature is mysterious not only because it reflects a mysterious world, but also because our continual wrestling match with language often leaves us unsatisfied as to the delivery of completely definitive meanings. It is our questions, though, that create the boundaries and forms of our exploration.

Teachers, naturally, direct a great deal of the questioning in classrooms, sometimes to wonderfully beneficial effect. It is to be expected, though, that although curricular purposes will shape much of the direction and form of their questions, teachers' personal biases, judgments, and values will also mold them. By contrast, students may have questions whose boundaries are not necessarily congruent with those of the instructor, or of their peers.

Adventures in English Literature is one of the common texts used in British Columbia to teach a historical overview of English literature. Surely if teachers expect students to participate in this adventure in a whole-hearted way, we must encourage the exploration of literature *as an adventure,* and encourage, embrace, and address genuine student questions about it. I use the adjective "genuine" in contrast to the "red herring" questions youngsters sometimes ask in the hope of drawing the class away from its intended purposes.

In addressing the puzzle of the role of questions amid the greater discourse in senior secondary language arts, I decided to pursue the theory that perhaps student questions have been insufficiently appreciated and underutilized. Teachers have always valued genuine questions from their students. Our difficulty has been, however, to design into our classroom planning successful, systematic, and reliable methods of encouraging such questions, of allowing them a respected place on the floor of discussion, and of using them to enhance overall learning.

To that end I devised the strategy outlined in the paper that follows. It is to be hoped that the methods outlined may prove useful as guides toward more successful approaches, to the ultimate benefit of the whole learning community.

Student-Generated Discussion in the Senior Secondary English Classroom

A. W. Lehmann

The purpose of this research study was to devise and test a method of encouraging, and subsequently managing, student-generated discussion of English literature within a senior secondary classroom. The students would provide not only the discussion itself, but also a "client's-eye" evaluation of the process. Accordingly, students were engaged in part of the initial clarification of the study's purposes and procedures, produced the bulk of the discussion which constituted the content for the method being examined, and provided a post-discussion evaluation which could be compared to earlier comments. A simple qualitative analysis of written comments provided by the students and of my own notes and reactions to the discussion allowed me to define more clearly some observations about the dynamics of discussion and to select some directions for further investigation. It would be premature to draw any definitive conclusions based on this study alone, but some of the observations are constructively suggestive.

Lehmann, A. W. (2000). Student-generated discussion in the senior secondary English classroom. *Networks: An On-line Journal for Teacher Research, 3*(2). www.oise.utoronto.ca/~ctd/networks. Reprinted with permission of *Networks: An On-line Journal for Teacher Research.* Copyright © 2000 by A. W. Lehmann.

PRELIMINARY CONSIDERATIONS

Classroom discussions can be wonderfully valuable for constructing and sharing knowledge. Often, however, the origin of these discussions and their movement toward the success described above is haphazard and fortuitous. I hoped to be able to prompt students to generate discussion that accomplished the valuable goals mentioned, in addition to ameliorating two main problems that are common in classroom activity. The first is that in many classroom discussions three or four voices dominate the interchange of ideas, and at least as many students never participate at all. The second is that many discussions are focused upon issues or ideas that the instructor has defined rather than upon considerations and questions which the students might find more significant or personally meaningful. Thus, the method that I adopted was meant to obviate these problems by requiring at least the limited participation of each student at one or more levels of the discussion and by having the students set the questions for the discussion's foci.

There were several questions that I hoped the project would illuminate. First, I desired a clearer profile of student attitudes to discussion in an average class. Second, I wished to discover students' feelings about teacher evaluation of their discussions; that is, should student discussions be graded and if so, how? Third, I wished to supplement my observations of the success or failure of the method of discussion with those of the students. Do they like the method, and do they find it educationally productive? Do their comments as participants describe much the same features that a teacher might observe?

A limiting factor was the brevity of the actual research period. The learning that needs to be negotiated by any class trying a new procedure is one that cannot be mastered immediately. Consequently, the limited success of the method we tried is probably not clearly indicative of the successes or failures that use of such a method might obtain over a longer period. Nonetheless, some constructive information was obtained.

Several authors and researchers provided useful ideas for the direction of the project. Sara Allen's (1992) paper on student-sustained discussion explored the limits to allowing students to manage a discussion without teacher interference. Her method of non-evaluative analysis of her classroom discussions influenced some of my questions. Douglas Barnes (1991) provided some interesting observations on the methods of and reasons for using small group discussions. Particularly useful were the chapters on learning in small groups (pp. 34–70) and the teacher's control of knowledge (pp. 108–134).

Neil Mercer (1995) makes extensive reference to Barnes. In some ways he recapitulates Barnes' observations, particularly in his support of Barnes' argument that there is a difference between discussion in a classroom and educationally appropriate discussion, the lat-

ter being characterized by "learners (a) sharing the same ideas about what is relevant to the discussion; and (b) having a joint conception of what is trying to be achieved by it" (p. 96).

Borich's (1992) comprehensive text includes a chapter on cooperative learning and the collaborative process. It examines in detail the rationale for cooperative learning strategies; discusses the roles of both student and teacher; and outlines methods for specifying the goal of such activities, structuring the student task, teaching and evaluating the process itself, monitoring group performance, and subsequent debriefing (pp. 320–333). These ideas were particularly useful in designing my project. As well, Borich's explanations about the appropriate times for direct instruction supported my own decision about using direct instruction in part of the project's method (p. 187).

Two other texts, Richmond and McCroskey's (1992) *Power in the Classroom,* and Stewart's (1985) *How to Involve the Student in Classroom Decision Making,* provided insights into problems that might accrue due to disciplinary anomalies. Morgan and Saxton (1994) provided valuable comments on the nature of questioning, whether by instructor or by student. Although I didn't use their specific categories, their text was helpful in clarifying my own approach, which follows.

METHOD

Before beginning this project, I followed the consent/assent procedures that are standard protocol within the school district (School District #82 has in policy a comprehensive procedure to deal with any research efforts in the district that involve children in any way, to ensure their privacy and safety). University ethics approval procedures were followed, as well. These completed, I turned to the project itself.

I first "floated" the idea of doing research in the classroom with my twelfth grade English class to see how they would feel about having their work made the subject of research. They were a normally inquisitive group of youngsters with a fairly equal spread of ability, ambition, gender, and so forth. They seemed interested in the idea, and when I submitted the information letter and the consent/assent forms for them to examine and sign or have signed, nearly every one of them immediately signed and returned the assent forms. Within about a week and a half we were prepared to proceed. Those students who failed to obtain permission to participate went to the library to finish reading the novel which was subject of the discussion, *A Prayer for Owen Meany* by John Irving, under the supervision of the librarian.

My first step was to try to obtain an informal overview of student attitudes toward classroom discussion in general, based on their previous experience. I asked them to compose brief responses, three or four sentences long, to the following clusters of questions. (a) How would you characterize yourself as a participant in classroom discussions: As an eager participant; as an occasional participant; as one who prefers to listen and observe; or as one who commonly "tunes out," for whatever reason? (b) Is classroom discussion, in your experience, a good place to develop skills in listening and speaking, and to develop critical tolerance toward others' points of view? Why or why not? (c) If these learning outcomes are important, as the Ministry of Education believes, should student participation in discussions be graded, and if so, how? (d) Is classroom discussion an effective means for taking responsibiity for your own learning, that is, for generating questions and seeking out their answers? Why or why not? Students were asked to identify themselves with pseudonyms or to leave the papers unsigned altogether, in the expectation that anonymity would encourage honesty in their responses.

I was moderately surprised at the energy with which the students tackled these questions. Time that I had scheduled for this phase of the project had to be extended so that students could get down all their ideas, and I suspect some of them had more to say but were directed forward onto the next question before they could completely explore their own thinking. Nonetheless, their responses presented an interesting spectrum of student experience, including personal descriptions, confessions and opinions.

I created a summary form loosely based on ideas presented by Miles and Huberman (1994) for compiling the student responses to these questions along with some of their more germane quotes. I read all of the student submissions and transferred, usually by quotation but occasionally by paraphrase, their attitudes and ideas to the summary form. One weakness of this method is that I served as editor of their thoughts, only pulling out their more insightful or well-stated contributions to be included. It may be that something important was omitted, although I went through their responses more than once in order to be reasonably rigorous. As well, had I had the time to interview each of the students orally, I could have asked for clarification of some of the ideas they presented. Some statements were either contradictory or so poorly stated grammatically that they were unusable. I didn't like leaving too much out, but some of the data either repeated things that had previously been said or were so general or clichéd as to be relatively valueless for the purposes of the summary.

I randomly assigned students to numbered small groups. The groups were numbered one through six to match the chapter numbers of our novel with which I wanted each group to deal. Thus group one would work on the first chapter, group two on the second chapter, and so on.

As part of preparation for their discussions, I provided the class with some brief direct instruction on the nature of questions and questioning. I explained to them three categories of questions: literal questions, inferential questions, and elaborative questions. Literal questions are those that can be answered by simple reference to the text. For example, how did Johnny Wheelwright's mother die? An inferential question requires both information from the text and knowledge or speculation on the part of the person seeking an answer in order to deal with it satisfactorily. An example, based on clues from the story, is what might some reasons be for Owen's attitudes toward his parents? Here students might provide ideas from their own family relationships and relate them to evidence available in the text. An elaborative question is one that requires synthesis or evaluation to address it fully. It, too, should have some referents in the text to tie it to the rest of the discussion. A suitable example is, did Dan exhibit the characteristics of a good father? Why or why not? (The three samples above are based upon *A Prayer for Owen Meany*.)

I provided them with examples of those distinctions so that, within the context of the exercise, they could explore several dimensions of questioning, and also so that they could be directed toward creating more complex questions for discussion purposes. I wanted to avoid a discussion based solely or even primarily on literal level, search-type questions, which tend to simplify and deaden discussion rather than to encourage it.

Each student was given the same assignment, which was to compose a question from each level of complexity, based on the chapter his or her group had been assigned. A few students asked brief questions of clarification regarding the levels of question described above, but within a few minutes all seemed to understand. I allowed them a full weekend to read any necessary material (some students were still behind in the reading) and to compose their questions.

On the following Monday, we divided into our groups by chapter. Each small group (the largest had four students, the smallest two) was instructed to select a spokesperson by consensus. Then the groups were to share their questions, one level at a time (literal level first, then inferential, then elaborative). At this stage we ran into a small but annoying difficulty. Only about half the class had actually prepared their questions. Thus, those reliable students who were prepared had to wait patiently while their less reliable group partners hastily cobbled together something to contribute to the day's activity. (This particular hazard of group work, the differential reliability of students, is a common detraction from the success of group activities at the secondary level.) After fifteen minutes or so we were once again under way. Students shared and discussed their questions well, appearing to be on topic and on task, and requiring little in the way of instructor intervention to get the job done. I circulated among the groups, noting the progress of their discussion, which lasted twenty to thirty minutes. At the end of their discussions each group was instructed to select, by consensus, one question from either the inferential or elaborative level to present to the full class group discussion to come. They spent ten minutes or so debating the relative merits of the questions they had discussed and selected their questions for the full class discussion by the end of the period.

The following day we gathered as a large group and began sharing the questions. The discussion went well, with rarely a lapse of energy. Some of the questions were more challenging or appealing to the group than others, and the time devoted to them reflected this. Others were a little obscure and "fizzled out" in the large-group discussion.

During the last twenty minutes of the class we did a post-discussion evaluation, or debriefing, as Borich (1992) would have termed it (p. 331). Once again, this was done through soliciting written answers from the students to specific questions about the discussion as well as the process we used to approach it and carry it out. They were as follows: (a) Do you think a two-level discussion (first small group, then larger group) encourages broader participation by students in the discussion? (b) Are student-generated questions superior or inferior to questions generated by your instructor or that emerge by chance? Explain. (c) Was it useful to you to have a knowledge of various levels of questioning? (d) How would you evaluate the successes or failures of the discussion method we used? (e) If we could eliminate the bureaucratic impedimenta (permission slips, etc.) would you like to use this method again? Why or why not?

The participating students readily addressed these questions, providing on average a page to a page and a half of commentary in response. I analyzed their responses in much the same way as I did the pre-discussion responses. I devised a summary form onto which I mapped student responses into categories. Again, I included quotations or paraphrases which seemed most to characterize or explain the reasons behind their attitudes.

RESULTS

Pre-Discussion Attitudes

The pre-discussion background research led to some useful anecdotal information. The class divided itself almost evenly among three categories of participation in discussion: eager participants, occasional participants and listener/observers. Only one student admitted to habitually tuning out, stating that "wonderland is a good place to be if the topic's boring." Eager participants made such statements as, "I love to argue." "I actively participate and then sit back . . . to get a feel of how people react to my opinions." "It's exciting." Even one student who was a self-described avid participant admitted, "I try to zone out . . . it never lasts very long." Apparently the lure of discussion was far stronger to this student than the appeal of day-dreaming.

Others who described themselves as occasional participants seemed, in some ways, more thoughtful. One stated, "I like to feel I have something really relevant to say before I say anything." Another commented, "I prefer to think out my arguments [so as not] to look stupid." Several would speak based on the immediacy and power of their emotions. "If [my] opinion is challenged I will speak up and defend it." "[I participate] when I have something really important to share." Two students wanted to defend personal identity and beliefs: "I try to be my own voice [rather than] go with what the majority thinks." "I'll speak out quite loudly . . . when it has something to do with my faith."

Listener/observers had a third cluster of perspectives. Some were simply shy. "I don't like the attention I bring myself." "I don't want people to judge me for something I said in class." Others claimed uncertainty or lack of knowledge. "Usually I am quite unsure of myself." "[Sometimes] I don't fully understand what is being discussed." Another group remained quiet because they felt other, more aggressive, students would have covered the topic adequately by the time they felt like contributing. "The issue is usually burnt out before I voice my opinion."

A sizable majority of students, whatever their own proclivities toward contributing to a discussion, felt that the classroom is a good place to learn listening and speaking skills, and critical tolerance toward others' ideas. There were many caveats, though. One observed that classroom discussion works because it is "mostly controlled." Another felt that discussions are excellent, but only useful if the class is "mature enough and tolerant enough to allow this to happen." Discussions could, in this student's view, be quite destructive when they became personal, "cruel," with "insults." A student who professed to love discussion also confessed that

"after a discussion I'm often mad, unable to listen, and during and after the discussion I can be quite mean," which rather reinforces the previous student's comments. Some students complained about others' lack of attention. One stated, "I don't think teachers push hard enough to get those few involved and they fall behind." And one blunt student averred that "some people just don't have the know-how to say what they think." Many students, though, recognized that discussions are an excellent forum in which to "widen your understanding of [a] topic" or to be "exposed to many ideas," to get "less nervous," to "develop confidence in speaking and get better at taking 'mental notes.' " One claimed, "That is the way I learn things best" (giving support to theories about preferential learning styles), and another went so far as to make the claim that "in a Utopian classroom all class would be is discussions."

The question about grading discussions generated many interesting and somewhat contradictory ideas. Those in favour of grading them outnumbered those opposed by about three to two, but there were very few constructive ideas about how their contributions to discussion should be graded. There were some astute comments on the problem. As one person put it, "Some [students] are active, some are not; some make themselves heard a lot when they don't have much to say," an observation that shows an awareness not only of the quantity of someone's participation, but also of the quality. Another very clearly pointed out that inopportune timing "makes late speakers' contributions less 'valuable,' thus penalizing shy students," who presumably might speak up later when they got their courage up. One student noted that students are more likely to "speak their minds when they're not worried about a grade," suggesting that some students feel that their opinions might be vulnerable to a low grade due to a teacher who holds a counter-opinion, or that the process of public evaluation inhibits their expressive ability due to a kind of performance anxiety.

Many other unanswered questions about grading discussion activity were raised, either as direct questions or as pithy observations. "How can you put weight on a particular aspect of a discussion [as opposed to another aspect]?" "People [who are] above . . . the activity . . . should be penalized for it." Presumably losing the grade would be the penalty for not participating. "Teacher input would be much more useful [than a number]." Apparently this student would prefer verbal feedback. "It's hard to put a mark on a statement." "A mouthy person should not be marked on the same level as a quiet person." One student made a useful connection between discussion and written activities, suggesting that we "grade essays on the same topic after discussion, or look at notes taken during the discussion," which is quite insightful and pragmatic.

Addressing the problem of personal responsibility for learning and its relation to discussions is a considerably more difficult question. One student expressed the idea that in discussion "your mind doesn't have a chance to wonder [wander?]. This almost forces you to have self-responsibility of your own learning." Another felt it is "good for finding personal answers." A third made the connection that shy students fail to participate, which in turn leads them to devalue the activity because the greatest benefits accrue to those who do participate. "We can ask questions about what we don't understand," said one, indicating a willingness for self-direction. Another acerbically remarked, "The best way to gain knowledge is to shut your mouth and listen, [and] ask questions when you don't understand."

These students showed an alert sensitivity to the problems inherent in classroom discussion. They were able to describe vividly their own strengths and weaknesses as well as to put themselves imaginatively into others' positions, for example, that of another student who might be shy or aggressive, or that of the instructor trying to evaluate the whole process. They also demonstrated strong approval of discussions as learning tools, even if not all students wanted to be actively involved.

Post-Discussion Research

One aim of this research was to evaluate the method we used in our discussion of a novel. Was the division of the discussion into two levels helpful? Was the instruction on levels of questioning useful? How effective was the student-generation of questions? These considerations were to lead to decisions whether or not to try this

method again, or to modify it in some ways and then try again.

In answer to the first question regarding whether or not the two-tier discussion process was effective in broadening the discussion, the students were generally of agreement that it was, though three respondents disagreed. One felt that the small groups "pressured [shy students] into stating an opinion; later in the big group their opinion was more likely to come up [than if they had remained silent]." Students felt that in the small group they did not "have to worry about being judged," because "in the small group you formed similar ideas . . . in the large group . . . you felt . . . the small group supported your ideas. It was not like you were alone." Group solidarity can lend confidence. "It gives a chance to organize thoughts," "you can compare and contrast more easily with [the] smaller group before taking the idea to the larger group," and it probably allows "for more involvement." A more avid participant observed that "a couple of shy people in my small group were actively participating." Nonetheless, of the three who felt there was not any real difference between this method and other discussions, one felt that only "the group that made up the question" really benefited, and another felt that often the student "didn't really have [his] own voice."

On the value of student-generated questions, students were fairly evenly divided. Many felt such an approach clearly superior. Students could "focus on the things that interest us" and could "ask about things we did not understand." "Student questioning gives the students a feeling of importance and acknowledgment." However, a considerable number felt student questions were worse, especially if "major points are missed." "Usually the instructor has a firmer grasp on the material in discussion and can therefore focus the questions on the more important aspects." "Sometimes the teacher seems to ask a question on the more difficult concept which most people need to discuss to understand it better." A few felt there was little difference between student-generated and teacher-generated questions, and questions that emerge organically or by hazard from the story were admired by a few. "Chance allows a discussion to flow. If students are thorough, [missing important points] shouldn't be a problem." "Questions due to chance are probably the best. Some teachers feel that they [must] have specific answers and some students cannot make up good questions." The final word by one was, "A question is a question." Does it matter whose question it is if it is a good one, one that generates reflective discussion?

There was a mixed evaluation of the direct instruction on questioning strategies (the division of questions into literal, inferential, and elaborative levels). Several suggested that it was not important. "I don't think it made much of a difference." "My life hasn't been changed too much by the new knowledge." "I don't think you need to have a knowledge of questions." One held the middle ground. "It is useful . . . in a limited way . . . [it] allows one to organize thoughts and questions for writing in a more orderly fashion . . . beyond this [it is] little more than trivia." Positive responses included, "I learned something new." "The knowledge of these levels will affect the end result in the long run." "It expands your knowledge . . . forcing you to really think about the chapter and its connections to the rest of the world."

There was little consensus as to the success of the exercise. Some felt it was very useful; others had serious reservations. On the positive side, students had a chance "to see what things interest others . . . and maybe have things pointed out to us that we might otherwise have missed." It was "an excellent example of two heads being better than one." "Getting in groups was good." In a more ambiguous response, one student rated the process "a 6 out of 10." "Some people weren't done the book," which limited the participation. "It could have been better. Many people . . . weren't really interested in the questions being discussed." "It took two classes and we were still rushing to get through it all, so the efficiency can be questioned. The student questions were not very effective." And as usual, there were complaints about those few "who don't know when to stop or be quiet," or who "ramble incoherently."

Most students wanted to try again, and they provided some interesting suggestions. One was "to post the questions a day or two before the discussion." Another, from a student who likes discussions to be "fast and fight-like," was a request for a little more freedom. "Do the questions have to be about the novel?" asked one. Several pointed out that the bureaucratic problems to do with consent shrank our class, and recommended trying again with "more people." Only one student said, "No. This method just won't work for me, anyway."

DISCUSSION

It must be noted that a few students chose not to provide assent or neglected to get parental consent for this project; this factor probably skewed my classroom sample to include a greater proportion of students who are actually interested in English discussion or in academic pursuits in general. Nonetheless, for the majority who were involved, the following findings are suggestive.

The purpose of this project was to get a clear profile of student attitudes to discussion in a twelfth grade English class. This was accomplished. Its results were heartening, although they may have been somewhat sanitized by student efforts to please their teacher or to prevent getting a low reputation that might eventually affect their marks. (I made it clear that this project would have nothing to do with the calculation of their English 12 grade, but students are occasionally somewhat skeptical of authority and some may have decided to "play it safe.") I consider the results heartening because of the relatively high level of attention to discussion that was reported by students. There was only one student who confessed to enjoying "tuning out," and even that was in response to topics that are "boring." There may have been a few more such students, but they were not evident in the responses submitted, for whatever reasons.

The second consideration of importance was whether and how to evaluate this activity. The dominant ethos in senior secondary tends toward the evaluation of everything. Anything done for its own sake is usually extra-curricular. It is very common for students to ask, "Do we get marks for this?" in a tone of voice as if to suggest, "If we don't, why should we bother?" And indeed, unless the fear of poor marks threatens, a significant number of students will not participate. Further, as we well know, even this does not motivate a considerable minority of students. As a teacher somewhat habituated to this state of affairs, I would likely try to connect this activity in the future to some form of evaluation, and some of the student suggestions mentioned above are good ideas. The students raised some good objections to grading, though, and evaluation of this kind of activity often seems either "fuzzily" inexact or somewhat pointless. It is difficult enough to distinguish reliably between A and B, let alone between 73% and 74%. If the instructor spends all his/her time filling out some kind of checklist monitoring who was talking, how many times, how forcefully, how many comments were questions, how many were answers, and so on, what kind of contribution is he/she likely to make to actually encouraging the discussion through immediately constructive feedback? Perhaps one student comment is most pragmatic. He claimed that we should not mark discussion directly because participation, whether as a speaker or a listener, would lead to better grades anyway, indirectly. Students who "tuned out" would not learn, and their work that was graded (essays and so on) would suffer accordingly. Those who participated would improve their thinking and, by extension, the content and style of their written work.

Finally, did the students find the exercise a successful one, that they would readily repeat? Many students, especially shy ones, found the two-level discussion liberating, and that it enhanced their participation. Less important to them was the theoretical nature of questioning. Rather they preferred to attend to questions that grew organically from their discussions, to focus on their content and meaning as opposed to their level of abstraction. As for the source of the questions, it appears that students were engaged by the process of questioning, but that they also were attuned to the importance of instructor expertise.

Did student perceptions mirror my own? I, like several of my student critics, found some of the questioning to be weak. I, too, was irked by one or two students who had little of significance to say but who "rambled incoherently" before I could tactfully grant someone else the floor. I agree with the youngster who felt that classroom discussion works best when it is controlled to prevent cruelty and insults, and although some increased freedoms from one-speaker-at-a-time decorum might result in greater entertainment value, I think that we should not aspire to model the classroom on Jerry Springer. I do not think that "fast" discussions characterized by "fights" are educationally defensible.

FURTHER RESEARCH

Like most of the student respondents, I would like to try this method again. Further useful observations could be made toward refinements that would improve discussion considerably and make it a more predictable process than simply capitalizing on what used to be labeled "the teachable moment."

The comparatively high level of student attention drawn to discussion, as shown by the student responses in this project, is fascinating in that it is almost surely higher than that given to lecture-style presentations by the instructor or to most presentations by their fellow students. There is something in the spontaneous give-and-take of discussion, an element of unpredictability and challenge, that is absent in the other forms of discourse cited above, and this feature might account for the higher attention. If this is true, then any methods that we can utilize to energize and foster productive discussion in our classrooms should be pursued.

I was particularly struck by the following final message by one of the students.

I really liked this experiment, not quite chemistry, but very fun. I really like the fact that here we get to have a say in the way that we are learning, we get more emotionally involved and therefore we can take it more seriously. It's not just a marks thing, it's us getting to be us and learning through the best way we see fit.

With such a positive endorsement, it would be difficult not to pursue this method further.

A. W. Lehmann is a teacher in School District No. 82, Terrace, BC, Canada. Correspondence concerning this article should be addressed to A. W. Lehmann, English Department, Caledonia Senior Secondary School, 3605 Munroe Street, Terrace, British Columbia, Canada, V8G 3C4.

References

Allen, S. (1992). Student-sustained discussion: When students talk and the teacher listens. In N. A. Branscombe, D. Goswami, & J. Schwartz (Eds.), *Students teaching: Teachers learning* (pp. 81–95). Portsmouth, NH: Boynton/Cook.

Barnes, D. (1991). *From communication to curriculum* (2nd ed.). Portsmouth, NH: Boynton/Cook.

Borich, G. (1992). *Effective teaching methods* (2nd ed.). Toronto: Maxwell MacMillan Canada.

Irving, J. (1989). *A prayer for Owen Meany.* New York: Random House.

Mercer, N. (1995). *The guided construction of knowledge: Talk amongst teachers and learners.* Philadelphia, PA: Multilingual Matters.

Miles, M. B., & Huberman, A. M. (1994). *Qualitative data analysis: An expanded sourcebook* (2nd ed.). Thousand Oaks, CA: Sage.

Morgan, N., & Saxton, J. (1994). *Asking better questions: Models, techniques and classroom activities for engaging students in learning.* Markham, ON: Pembroke.

Richmond, V. P., & McCroskey, J. C. (1992). *Power in the classroom: Communication, control and concern.* Hillsdale, NJ: Lawrence Erlbaum.

Stewart, W. J. (Ed.) (1985). *How to involve the student in classroom decision making.* Saratoga, CA: R & E Publishers.

Self-Check Test Answers

CHAPTER 1:   Using Research to Improve Educational Practice
1. c   2. b   3. d   4. b   5. d   6. d   7. c   8. c   9. a   10. a

CHAPTER 2:   Conducting a Review of the Research Literature
1. b   2. b   3. d   4. c   5. a   6. c   7. a   8. d

CHAPTER 3:   Using Preliminary Sources to Search the Literature
1. d   2. c   3. d   4. b   5. c   6. a   7. a   8. b   9. b

CHAPTER 4:   Reading Secondary Sources
1. d   2. c   3. a   4. c   5. b   6. a   7. d   8. c   9. d

CHAPTER 5:   Reading Reports of Quantitative Research Studies
1. b   2. c   3. d   4. c   5. a   6. b   7. d   8. d   9. a

CHAPTER 6:   Statistical Analysis of Research Data
1. b   2. a   3. d   4. b   5. d   6. c   7. c   8. a   9. a   10. b   11. d

CHAPTER 7:   Descriptive and Causal-Comparative Research
1. a   2. b   3. c   4. d   5. d   6. a   7. c   8. b   9. c   10. b   11. a   12. d

CHAPTER 8:   Correlational Research
1. b   2. d   3. b   4. c   5. c   6. a   7. a   8. d   9. a   10. c

CHAPTER 9:   Experimental Research
1. c   2. b   3. b   4. d   5. d   6. c   7. b   8. a

CHAPTER 10:   Case Studies in Qualitative Research
1. c   2. b   3. d   4. c   5. b   6. c   7. d   8. a   9. a   10. c   11. b

CHAPTER 11:   Ethnographic Research
1. b   2. a   3. c   4. d   5. a   6. c

CHAPTER 12:   Critical-Theory Research
1. b   2. b   3. a   4. d   5. b   6. d   7. d   8. c

CHAPTER 13:   Historical Research
1. a   2. b   3. a   4. c   5. d   6. b   7. d   8. b   9. c   10. d

CHAPTER 14:   Evaluation Research
1. a   2. d   3. b   4. b   5. a   6. b   7. c   8. d   9. c   10. a   11. c   12. d

CHAPTER 15:   Action Research
1. c   2. b   3. c   4. a   5. b   6. d   7. c   8. a

Form for Outlining a Quantitative or Qualitative Research Proposal

This form consists of a list of items in the form of questions and directions. By completing each item, you can create an outline of a research proposal. Once you complete the outline, you can use it as the basis for preparing a formal proposal for a dissertation or thesis proposal or research grant.

1. PURPOSE OF STUDY
   A. The purpose of this study is to _____. (A good test of your understanding of your proposed test is whether you can state its purpose clearly in one or two sentences.)
   B. What studies is your study most directly based on? (Even if you find many studies and theoretical works that are related to your proposed study, there generally are only a few that are absolutely central.)
   C. How does your study build on previous research? (Another way to think about this question is to ask yourself how you plan to extend a particular study or line of research to address unsolved issues, improve on previously used methodologies, or generalize to new populations or contexts.)
   D. How will your study contribute to knowledge about education? (Another way to think about this question is to ask yourself how your findings will advance educational practice, research, and/or theory.)

2. RESEARCH QUESTIONS, HYPOTHESES, OR OBJECTIVES
   A. In what form are you stating your research purposes? (Check one or more.)
   ____ Questions
   ____ Hypotheses
   ____ Objectives
   B. List your research questions/hypotheses/objectives.
   C. Does your study relate to an existing theoretical framework? If it does, describe the framework, and indicate how your research questions, hypotheses, or objectives relate to it.

3. LITERATURE SEARCH
   A. List the descriptors that you will use initially in your literature search.
   B. List the preliminary sources (i.e., databases such as ERIC) and published literature reviews that you will use in your literature search.

4. RESEARCH DESIGN
    A. Describe the research design that you selected for your study: descriptive, causal-comparative, correlational, experimental, case study, particular qualitative research tradition, evaluation, or action research.
        * Descriptive
        * Causal-comparative
        * Correlational
        * Experimental
        * Case study
        * Particular qualitative research tradition
        * Evaluation
        * Action research
    B. If your study is quantitative in nature, what are the threats to the internal validity of your research design? (Internal validity means the extent to which extraneous variables are controlled, so that observed effects can be attributed solely to the independent variable.) What will you do to minimize or avoid these threats?
        * Causal-comparative designs
        * Correlational designs
        * Experimental designs
    C. If your study is quantitative in nature, what are the limitations to the generalizability (i.e., external validity) of the findings that will result from your research design? What will you do to maximize the generalizability of your findings?
    D. If your study is qualitative in nature, what criteria do you consider to be relevant to judging the credibility and trustworthiness of the results that will be yielded by your research design?
    E. If your study involves action research, what will you do to establish the credibility and trustworthiness of your design?

5. SAMPLING
    A. If your study is quantitative in nature, describe the characteristics of the population that you will study.
    B. If your study is qualitative in nature, describe the phenomenon you wish to study and the cases that comprise instances of the phenomenon.
    C. Identify your sampling procedure, and explain why you selected it.
    D. Indicate the sampling unit (e.g., individual students or a class of students).
        * Quantitative research
        * Qualitative research
    E. Indicate the size of your sample, and explain why that sample size is sufficient.
        Quantitative research
        Qualitative research
    F. Indicate whether the sample will be formed into subgroups, and if so, describe the characteristics of the subgroups.
    G. If your study will involve the use of volunteers, explain whether their characteristics will affect the generalizability of the research findings.

6. VARIABLES
    A. If your study is quantitative in nature, list the variables that you will study. For each variable, indicate whether it is an independent variable, a dependent variable, or neither.

    B. If the study is qualitative in nature, describe the aspects of the cases on which data collection and analysis will focus.

7. METHODS OF DATA COLLECTION
    A. Indicate how you will measure each of the variables that you plan to study.
        • Tests and self-report measures
        • Questionnaires and interviews
        • Observation and content analysis
    B. For each measure stated above, indicate which types of validity and reliability are relevant and how you will check them.
        • Tests and self-report measures
        • Questionnaires and interviews
        • Observation and content analysis
    C. If your study is qualitative in nature, indicate whether your data collection will focus on etic or emic perspectives, or both; what aspects of the context will be studied; whether data collection will focus on description, explanation, or evaluation; what data-collection instruments will be used; and the nature of your involvement in the data-collection process.

8. DATA ANALYSIS PROCEDURES
    A. What descriptive and inferential statistical techniques, if any, will you use to analyze each of your research questions, hypotheses, or objectives? (It is helpful to answer this question separately for each question, hypothesis, or objective; it might also be helpful to show the analysis for simulated data if the statistical procedure is complex.)
    B. If your study is qualitative in nature, indicate whether you will use an interpretational, structural, or reflective method of analysis.

9. ETHICS AND HUMAN RELATIONS
    A. What threats, if any, does your study pose for your research participants? What steps will you take to minimize these threats? Will the study need to be approved by an institutional review board?
    B. How will you gain entry into your proposed research setting, and how will you gain the cooperation of your research participants?

10. TIMELINE
    A. Create a timeline listing in order all the major steps of your study. Also indicate the approximate amount of time that each step will take.

Preliminary Sources That Index the Education Literature

Preliminary sources are essential resources for locating educational literature on any topic of interest. They can help you identify books, journal articles, technical reports, or other types of materials.

Many preliminary sources specialize in a particular topic area, such as the *Applied Science & Technology Index* (1958 to date), *Art Index* (1929 to date), and *International African Bibliography* (1971 to date), all published by H. W. Wilson. Too many exist to include them all in the following list, but you can identify them by using your library catalog and the *Bibliographic Index* (see section 1A below).

Part 1 provides bibliographic citations for preliminary sources that educators can use to locate sources covering various topic areas. The information was current at the time we prepared this appendix, but keep in mind that publishers occasionally change the format of indexes, transfer them to a new publisher, or cease publishing them.

Because so many indexes are now published electronically, we cite the Web address for the index or publisher of the index, even if a print version is available. You can go to this Web address to determine the current status of the index. If the Web address no longer exists on the Internet, you can use a search engine such as Google to check whether the index has a new Web address. Also, you can ask a librarian to determine the current status of a particular index and how you can access it locally in electronic or print form.

In Part 2 of this appendix, we provide a brief list of preliminary sources that are useful for locating historical research sources.

PART 1. GENERAL PRELIMINARY SOURCES

A. Indexes to Bibliographies

Bibliographic index. Web address: www.hwwilson.com/newdds/wn.htm.
This preliminary source indexes bibliographies that have been published separately or as parts of books or journals.

B. Indexes to Book Reviews

Book review digest. Web address: www.hwwilson.com/newdds/wn.htm.
Provides citations to and excerpts from reviews of English-language books. Government publications, textbooks, and technical books in the sciences and law are excluded.

Book review index. (1965 to date). Detroit: Gale.

Provides citations to reviews of books, periodicals, and books on tape in a wide range of popular, academic, and professional interest areas.

Contemporary psychology. (1956 to date). Washington, DC: American Psychological Association.

This journal specializes in reviews of books (excluding textbooks) and other publications that are relevant to psychology.

Education review: A journal of book reviews. Web address: www.ed.asu.edu/edrev.

This on-line journal, established in 1997, is designed to publish reviews of important books across the range of current scholarship in the field of education.

C. Indexes to Books

Books in print. Web address: www.booksinprint.com/bip.

Children's books in print. (1969 to date). New York: Bowker.

El-hi textbooks and serials in print. (1985 to date). New York: Bowker. For earlier editions, see: *El-hi textbooks in print.* (1927–1984). New York: Bowker.

D. Indexes to Curriculum Materials

ASCD curriculum materials directory. (1992 to date). Alexandria, VA: Association for Supervision and Curriculum Development.

Film and video locator. Web address: www.nicem.com.

E. Indexes to Directories

AERA membership directory. Available from American Educational Research Association website: www.aera.net/member/directory.

Directories in print. (1980 to date). Detroit, MI: Gale.

Encyclopedia of associations. (1956 to date). Detroit, MI: Gale.

Klein, B. T. (Ed.). (1999). *Guide to American educational directories* (8th ed.). (1999). West Nyack, NY: Todd.

National faculty directory. (1970 to date). Detroit, MI: Gale.

F. Indexes to Dissertations and Theses

Dissertation abstracts international. Web address: www.umi.com.

This index provides abstracts for doctoral dissertations submitted by hundreds of institutions, mostly in the United States and Canada, but also including a few institutions from other countries.

Master's theses directories. (1993 to date). Cedar Falls, IA: H. M. Smiley. For earlier editions, see: *Master's theses in education* (vols. 1–39). (1951–1990). Cedar Falls, IA: Research Publications.

G. Indexes to Journal Articles, Papers, and Reports

Catalog of U.S. Government publications. Web address: www.gpoaccess.gov/cgp/index.html.

Current index to journals in education (CIJE). Web address: www.askeric.org/Eric.
This index is described in detail in Chapter 3.

Education index. Web address: www.hwwilson.com/Databases/educat.htm.
Unlike *CIJE,* no abstract is provided for each citation, but *Education Index* covers journal articles (and books as well) published since 1929.

Educational administration abstracts. (1966 to date). Thousand Oaks, CA: Sage.

Exceptional child education resources. (1977 to date). Reston, VA: Council for Exceptional Children. For earlier editions, see *Exceptional Child Education Abstracts,* vols. 1–8 (1969–1977) by the same publisher.

Feather, J., & Sturges, P. (Eds.). (2003). *International encyclopedia of information and library science* (2nd ed.). New York: Routledge.

MEDLINE. Web address: www.nlm.nih.gov/libserv.html.
This is an index to the biomedical literature.

Physical education index. Web address: www.csa.com/csa/factsheets/pei.shtml.

Psychological abstracts. Web address: www.apa.org/psycinfo.
This index covers most of the world's literature in psychology and related disciplines. The *Thesaurus of Psychological Index Terms* is available to assist the use of this index.

Resources in Education. Web address: www.askeric.org/Eric.
This index is described in detail in Chapter 3.

Sage family studies abstracts. (1979 to date). Thousand Oaks, CA: Sage.

Science citation index. Web address: www.isinet.com/isi.
This index covers the literature of medicine, agriculture, technology, and science, including the natural, physical, and biomedical sciences. For an explanation of its purpose and use, see the following entry for *Social Sciences Citation Index.*

Social sciences citation index. Web address: www.isinet.com/isi.
This index covers the literature of the social and behavioral sciences. Most articles about education are covered in this index, but depending on their topic, articles about psychology may be covered in this index or in *Science Citation Index.*

To understand the purpose of these indexes, suppose that your literature search identifies a key research report that was published some years ago, and you wish to trace its effects on subsequent research. Or, suppose you identify an article that expresses a controversial opinion, and you wish to know what later authors wrote in support of or opposition to it. By looking up the author of a given document, you can find where it has been cited by authors of subsequent articles and other documents.

Sociological abstracts. Web address: www.csa.com/csa/factsheets/socioabs.shtml.
This index covers the international literature in sociology and related disciplines.

SPORT discus. Web address: www.sportdiscus.com.
This index covers literature on sport, physical education, physical fitness, sport medicine, and related topics.

Women studies international. Web address: www.nisc.com/factsheets/qwri.asp.

H. Indexes to Magazines and Newspapers

Proquest newspaper abstracts. Web address: www.umi.com/products/pt-product-NewsAbstracts.shtml.

Readers' guide to periodical literature. (1900 to date). New York: H. W. Wilson.

I. Indexes to Tests and Test Information

Educational testing service (ETS) database. Web address: http://testcollection.ets.org.
This electronic database provides information on tests designed for research purposes or that are not commercially available.

Maddox, T. (2003). *Tests: A comprehensive reference for assessments in psychology, education, and business* (5th ed.). Austin: PRO-ED.

Mental measurements yearbook: Test reviews online. Web address: http://buros.unl.edu/buros/jsp/search.jsp.
This electronic database is an index to information about almost 4 thousand commercially available tests. The information is taken from the *Mental Measurements Yearbooks,* which have appeared in print form since 1938.

PART 2. PRELIMINARY SOURCES ON THE HISTORY OF EDUCATION

A. Bibliographies of Bibliographies

Fritze, R. H. (2003). *Reference sources in history: An introductory guide* (2nd ed.). Santa Barbara, CA: ABC-CLIO.

Norton, M. B. (1995). *Guide to historical literature* (3rd ed.). New York: Oxford University Press.
This preliminary source contains a bibliography of bibliographies and also historiographical essays on each section topic.

B. Bibliographies of Biographies

Biography and genealogy master index. Web address: www.gale.com.
This is an index to biographical sketches of over 4 million contemporary and historical figures from around the world.

Biography reference bank. Web address: www.hwwilson.com/Databases/biobank.htm.
This is an electronic index to biographical information about more than 450,000 individuals.

C. General Indexes to Historical Publications

America: History and life. Web address: http://serials.abc-clio.com.
This source indexes articles, dissertations, and reviews of books, films, videos, and documents in microfilm/microfiche format covering the history and culture of the United States and Canada from prehistoric times to the present.

Historical abstracts. Web address: http://serials.abc-clio.com.
This source is an index to historical literature about the world (excluding the United States and Canada) from 1450 to the present.

D. Newspaper Reference Source

United States newspaper program. Web address: www.neh.gov/projects/usnp.html.

E. Indexes to Nonpublished Primary Sources

Directory of genealogical and historical libraries, archives and collections in the US and Canada. (2002). Boulder, CO: Iron Gate.

National union catalog of manuscript collections. Web address: www.loc.gov/coll/nucmc/nucmc.html.

Smith, A. (1988). *Directory of oral history collections.* Phoenix, AZ: Oryx.

Secondary Source Reviews of the Education Literature*

Secondary sources are articles, books, and other publications written by individuals to describe other individuals' research studies, theories, and opinions. Many such secondary sources are reviews of the literature on a particular topic. In Part 1 we list secondary sources covering various topic areas in education. In Part 2 we provide a brief list of secondary sources on the history of education.

The bibliographic information for each source was current at the time we prepared this appendix, but sources are subject to change. Keep in mind, too, that some of the handbooks possibly will appear in a new edition. You can check *Books in Print* for the latest edition.

PART 1. GENERAL SECONDARY SOURCES

A. Annual Reviews

Annual review of psychology. (1950 to date). Stanford, CA: Annual Reviews.

Review of research in education. (1931 to date). Itasca, IL: Peacock.

Yearbook of the National Society for the Study of Education. (1902 to date). Chicago: National Society for the Study of Education.

B. Encyclopedias

Alkin, M. C. (Ed.). (1992). *Encyclopedia of educational research* (6th ed.). New York: MacMillan.

Husén, T., & Postlethwaite, T. N. (Eds.). (1994). *International encyclopedia of education* (2nd ed.). New York: Elsevier.

Entries relating to certain subjects (e.g., educational technology, economics of education, teaching and teacher education) have been cumulated and published as separate volumes.

Kazdin, A. E. (Ed.). (2000). *Encyclopedia of psychology.* Washington, DC: American Psychology Association; New York: Oxford University Press.

Levinson, D. L., Cookson, P. W., & Sadovnik, A. R. (Eds.). (2002). *Education and sociology: An encyclopedia.* New York: RoutledgeFalmer.

Lopez, C. (Ed.). (2001). *World education encyclopedia: A survey of educational systems worldwide* (2nd ed.). Farmington Hills, MI: Gale.

*From Meredith D. Gall, Walter R. Borg, & Joyce P. Gall. Educational Research: An Introduction, 6/e. Published by Allyn and Bacon, Boston, MA. Copyright © 1996 by Pearson Education. Adapted by permission of the publisher.

Mitchell, B. M., & Salsburg, R. E. (Eds.). (1999). *Encyclopedia of multicultural education* (2nd ed.). Westport, CT: Greenwood.

Reynolds, C. R., & Fletcher-Janzen, E. (Eds.). (2000). *Encyclopedia of special education* (2nd ed.). New York: John Wiley & Sons.

C. Journals Specializing in Literature Reviews

Psychological bulletin. (1904 to date). Arlington, VA: American Psychological Association.

Psychological review. (1894 to date). Washington, DC: American Psychological Association.

Review of educational research. (1931 to date). Washington, DC: American Educational Research Association.

D. Handbooks

Anfara, V. A., Jr. (Ed.). (2001). *Handbook of research in middle level education.* Greenwich, CT: Information Age Pub.

Banks, J. A., & Banks, C. A. M. (Eds.). (2002). *Handbook of research on multicultural education* (2nd ed.). San Francisco: Jossey-Bass.

Berliner, D. C., & Calfee, R. C. (Eds.). (1996). *Handbook of educational psychology.* New York: Macmillan.

Biddle, B. J., Good, T. L., & Goodson, I. F. (Eds.). (1997). *International handbook of teachers and teaching.* Boston: Kluwer.

Bishop, A. J., et al. (Eds.). (1996). *International handbook of mathematics education.* Boston: Kluwer.

Cawelti, G. (Ed.). (1999). *Handbook of research on improving student achievement* (2nd ed.). Arlington, VA: Educational Research Service.

Firth, G. R., & Pajak, E. F. (Eds.). (1998). *Handbook of research on school supervision.* New York: Macmillan.

Flood, J. (Ed.). *Handbook of research on teaching the English language arts* (2nd ed.). Mahwah, NJ: Lawrence Erlbaum.

Flood, J., Heath, S. B., & Lapp, D. (Eds.). (1997). *Handbook of research on teaching literacy through the communicative and visual arts.* New York: Macmillan.

Fraser, B. J., & Tobin, K. G. (Eds.). (1998). *International handbook of science education.* Boston: Kluwer.

Hargreaves, A., et al. (Eds.). (1998). *International handbook of educational change.* Boston: Kluwer.

Heller, K., Mönks, F. J., Sternberg, R. J., & Subotnik, R. F. (Eds.). (2000). *International handbook of giftedness and talent.* Boston: Kluwer.

Jonassen, D. H. (Ed.). (2004). *Handbook of research for educational communications and technology* (2nd ed.). Mahwah, NJ: Lawrence Erlbaum.

Murphy, J., & Louis, K. S. (Eds.). (1999). *Handbook of research on educational administration* (2nd ed.). San Francisco: Jossey-Bass.

Neuman, S. B., & Dickinson, D. K. (Eds.). (2001). *Handbook of early literacy research.* New York: Guilford Press.

Pearson, P. D., Barr, R., Kamil, M. L., & Mosenthal, P. (Eds.). (1996–2000). *Handbook of reading research* (Vols. 1–3). Mahwah, NJ: Lawrence Erlbaum.

Richardson, V. (Ed.). (2001). *Handbook of research on teaching* (4th ed.). Washington, DC: American Educational Research Association.

Sikula, J., Buttery, T., & Guyton, E. (Eds.). (1996). *Handbook of research on teacher education* (2nd ed.). New York: Macmillan.

Singer, R. N., Hausenblas, H. A., & Janelle, C. M. (Eds.). (2001). *Handbook of sport psychology* (2nd ed.). New York: Wiley.

Teddie, C., & Reynolds, D. (Eds.). (2000). *International handbook of school effectiveness research.* New York: Falmer.

appendix **4**

Questions for Evaluating Quantitative Research Reports

The following questions can be used to help you evaluate each section of a quantitative research report. For each question we indicate the type of information that you will need to identify in the report to answer the question, and we provide a sample answer. The examples are drawn from our experience in evaluating quantitative research studies.

INTRODUCTORY SECTION

1. Are the research problems, methods, and findings appropriate given the researchers' institutional affiliations, beliefs, values, or theoretical orientation?

    Information needed. The researchers' institutional affiliation often is given beneath the title of a published research report, or it might be at the end of the report or at the end of the journal in which the report appears. Also look for any information in the report that indicates the researchers' beliefs, values, or theoretical orientation with respect to education, and how that affected their research.

    Example. Most of the researchers' prior work has focused on cognitive models of learning. Therefore, they designed their research to show the advantages of cognitively oriented teaching methods compared to behaviorally oriented teaching methods.

2. Do the researchers demonstrate any favorable or unfavorable bias in describing the subject of the study (e.g., the instructional method, program, curriculum, etc., that was investigated)?

    Information needed. Identify any adjectives or other words that describe an instructional method, program, curriculum, and so forth, in clearly positive or negative terms.

    Example. The researchers described the group of students who served as research participants as difficult to handle, unmotivated, and disorganized. No evidence was presented to support this characterization. In the absence of evidence, this description might indicate a negative attitude toward the children who were studied.

3. Is the literature review section of the report sufficiently comprehensive, and does it include studies that you know to be relevant to the problem?

    Information needed. Examine the studies mentioned in the report. Note particularly if a recent review of the literature relevant to the research problem was

534

cited, or if the researchers mentioned an effort to make their own review comprehensive.

Example. The researchers stated the main conclusions of a previously published comprehensive literature review on the instructional program that they intended to study. They demonstrated clearly how their study built on the findings and recommendations of this review.

4. Is each variable in the study clearly defined?

Information needed. Identify all the variables (also called *constructs*) that were studied. For each variable, determine if and how it is defined in the report.

Example. One of the variables studied is intrinsic motivation, which is defined in the report as the desire to learn because of curiosity. This definition is not consistent with other definitions in the research literature, which state that intrinsic motivation is the desire to learn because of the satisfaction that comes from the act of learning and from the content being learned.

5. Is the measure of each variable consistent with how the variable was defined?

Information needed. Identify how each variable in the study was measured.

Example. The researchers studied self-esteem but did not define it. Therefore, it was not possible to determine whether their measure of self-esteem was consistent with their definition.

6. Are the research hypotheses, questions, or objectives explicitly stated, and if so, are they clear?

Information needed. Examine each research hypothesis, question, or objective stated in the report.

Example. The researcher stated one general objective for the study. It was clearly stated, but it did not provide sufficient information concerning the specific variables that were to be studied.

7. Do the researchers make a convincing case that a research hypothesis, question, or objective was important to study?

Information needed. Examine the researchers' rationale for each hypothesis, question, or objective.

Example. The researchers showed how the hypothesis to be tested was derived from a specific theory. They also showed that if the hypothesis was confirmed by the study it would add support to the validity of the theory, which is currently being used in the design of new reading curricula.

Method Section

8. Did the sampling procedures produce a sample that is representative of an identifiable population, or generalizable to your local population?

Information needed. Identify the procedures that the researchers used to select their sample.

Example. The researchers selected several classes (not randomly) from one school. The only information given about the students was their average ability and gender distribution. I cannot tell from this description whether the sample is similar to students in our schools.

9. Did the researchers form subgroups to increase understanding of the phenomena being studied?

    Information needed. Determine whether the sample was divided into subgroups, and if so, why.

    Example. The researchers showed the effects of the instructional program for both boys and girls; this information was helpful. However, they did not show the effects for different ethnic subgroups. This is an oversight, because the program might have a cultural bias that could have an adverse effect on some ethnic subgroups.

10. Is each measure appropriate for the sample?

    Information needed. Determine whether the researchers reported the population for whom the measure was developed.

    Example. The ABC Reading Test was developed twenty years ago for primary grade students. The current study also involves primary grade students, but the test may no longer be valid, because students and the reading curriculum have changed considerably over the past twenty years.

11. Is each measure in the study sufficiently valid for its intended purpose?

    Information needed. Examine any evidence that the researchers presented to demonstrate the validity of each measure in the study.

    Example. The XYZ Test was used because it purportedly predicts success in vocational education programs. However, the researchers presented evidence from only one study to support this claim. That study involved a vocational education program that was quite different from the one they investigated.

12. Is each measure in the study sufficiently reliable for its intended purpose?

    Information needed. Examine any evidence that the researchers presented to demonstrate the reliability of each measure in the study.

    Example. The researchers had observers rate each student's on-task behavior during Spanish instruction in a sample of thirty classrooms. Inter-rater reliability was checked by having pairs of observers use the rating system in the same five classrooms. The pairs typically agreed on 90 percent of their ratings, which indicates good reliability.

13. If any qualitative data were collected, were they analyzed in a manner that contributed to the soundness of the overall research design?

    Information needed. Determine whether the researchers report qualitative information about the research participants, procedures, or findings.

    Example. In seeking to explain the absence of differences between the experimental and control groups' classroom behavior, the researcher mentioned information shared by the students' teacher that students in the control group classroom had reacted positively to the observer's presence.

14. Were the research procedures appropriate and clearly stated so that others could replicate them if they wished?

    Information needed. Identify the various research procedures that were used in the study and the order in which they occurred.

    Example. The researchers administered three types of pretests during one class period the day before the experimental curriculum was introduced. The pretests, though brief, might have overwhelmed the students, so that they could not do their best work. Also, some aspects of the experimental curriculum (e.g., the types of seatwork activities) were not clearly described in the research report, and the researchers did not indicate how soon the posttests were administered after the curriculum was completed.

Results Section

15. Were appropriate statistical techniques used, and were they used correctly?

    Information needed. Identify the statistical techniques described in the report.

    Example. The researchers calculated the mean score for students' performance on the five tests that were administered. However, they did not give the range of scores (i.e., lowest score and highest score). This would be helpful information, because they studied a highly heterogeneous group of students.

Discussion Section

16. Do the results of the data analyses support what the researchers conclude are the findings of the study?

    Information needed. Identify what the researchers considered to be the major findings of the study.

    Example. The researchers concluded that the experimental treatment led to superior learning compared to the control treatment, but this claim was true for only two of the four criterion measures used to measure the effects of the treatments.

17. Did the researchers provide reasonable explanations of the findings?

    Information needed. Identify how the researchers explained the findings of the study and whether alternative explanations were considered.

    Example. The researchers concluded that the narrative version of the textbook was less effective than the traditional expository version. Their explanation was that the story in the narrative version motivated students to keep reading, but that it also distracted them from focusing on the factual information that was included in the test. They presented no evidence to support this explanation, although it seems plausible.

18. Did the researchers relate the findings to a particular theory or body of related research?

    Information needed. Identify any theory or body of related research to which the researchers refer in discussing their findings.

    Example. The researchers discussed the conceptual implications of their findings in relation to theories of reinforcement on learning and task performance.

19. Did the researchers draw sound implications for practice from their findings?

    Information needed. Identify any implications for practice that the researchers drew from their findings.

    Example. The researchers claimed that teachers' morale would be higher if administrators would provide more self-directed staff development. However, this recommendation is based only on their questionnaire finding that teachers expressed a desire for more self-directed staff development. The researchers are not justified in using just this bit of data to claim that teachers' morale will improve if they get the kind of staff development that they prefer.

20. Did the researchers suggest further research to build on their results, or to answer questions that were raised by their findings?

Information needed. Identify any suggestions that the researchers make for further study of the topic, and the questions that such study might answer.

Example. The researchers noted that students showed greater levels of problem behavior during the reversal phase of the experiment than during the baseline phase. They recommended further research to explore the conditions under which such "postreversal intensification" tends to occur.

Questions for Evaluating Qualitative Research Reports

The following questions can be used to help you evaluate each section of a qualitative research report. For each question we indicate the type of information that you will need to identify in the report to answer the question, and we provide a sample answer. The examples are drawn from our experience in evaluating qualitative research studies.

INTRODUCTORY SECTION

1. Are the research problems and methods appropriate given the researchers' institutional affiliations, beliefs, values, or theoretical orientation?

   Information needed. The researchers' institutional affiliation often is given beneath the title of a published research report, or it might be at the end of the report or at the end of the journal in which the report appears. Also look for any information in the report that indicates the researchers' beliefs, values, or theoretical orientation with respect to education, and how that affected their research.

   Example. The researchers taught in inner-city schools for many years before doing this study. This experience would give them knowledge of the issues facing inner-city students and teachers.

2. Do the researchers demonstrate any favorable or unfavorable bias in describing the subject of the study (e.g., the instructional method, program, curriculum, etc., that was investigated)?

   Information needed. Identify any adjectives or other words that describe an instructional method, program, curriculum, and so forth, in clearly positive or negative terms.

   Example. The researchers used a qualitative research method known as *educational connoisseurship and criticism* to study a high school football team. This method is inherently evaluative, so it is no surprise that the researchers made many judgments—both positive and negative—about the impact of the team on individual players.

3. Is the literature review section of the report sufficiently comprehensive? Does it include studies that you know to be relevant to the problem?

   Information needed. Examine the studies mentioned in the report. Note particularly if a recent review of the literature relevant to the research problem was cited, or if the researchers described their efforts to make their own review comprehensive.

539

Example. The researchers completed their literature search prior to beginning data collection. This procedure is not desirable in qualitative research, because questions and hypotheses are bound to arise as the data are collected. They should have done an ongoing literature search to discover what other researchers have found concerning the emerging questions and hypotheses.

RESEARCH PROCEDURES

4. Did the sampling procedure result in a case or cases that were particularly interesting and from which much could be learned about the phenomena of interest?

   Information needed. Identify the type of purposeful sampling that the researchers used to select their sample.

   Example. The researchers used intensity sampling to select a high school principal who had received several awards and widespread recognition for "turning her school around." She was a good case to study, given the researchers' interest in administrators' instructional leadership.

5. Were the data-collection methods used in the research appropriate for the phenomena that the researchers wanted to explore?

   Information needed. Examine any evidence that the researchers presented to demonstrate the soundness of their data-collection methods.

   Example. The researchers' primary data-collection method was participant observation. Several quotations suggest that they were accepted as honorary members of the groups they observed. Thus, it appears that they had good access to the kinds of events and behavior about which they wished to collect data.

6. Was there sufficient intensity of data collection?

   Information needed. Identify the time period over which an individual, setting, or event was observed, and whether the observation was continuous or fragmented. If documents were analyzed, identify how extensive the search for documents was and how closely the documents were analyzed. If interviews were conducted, did the researchers build sufficient rapport with field participants before asking in-depth questions, and did they reexplore sensitive topics in subsequent interviews in order to check their data?

   Example. The researchers' goal was to learn how elementary school teachers established classroom routines and discipline procedures at the beginning of the school year. They observed each teacher every day for the first three weeks; this is a good procedure. They assumed, however, that routines and discipline procedures would be explained at the start of the school day, and so they observed only the first hour of class time. The validity of this assumption is questionable.

7. Were the data collected in such a way as to ensure a reflection of the field participants' emic perspective?

   Information needed. Examine any information that the researchers present to demonstrate that they sought to reflect the emic perspective of field participants.

   Example. The researchers wished to learn about children's views of preschool, but noted that children in the culture they studied often become uncomfortable when adults ask them questions in a formal setting. The researchers made the children more comfortable by setting up a playlike environment and asking questions unobtrusively as the interviewer and children played.

8. Did the researchers triangulate their data sources and data-collection methods to test the soundness of the findings?

Information needed. Examine such information as whether the data obtained from two or more data-collection methods were compared for evidence of confirmation or of meaningful discrepancies.

Example. The researcher obtained both observational data on students' self-references when with their peers and interview data about students' self-perceptions from one-on-one conversations with the researcher.

9. Were the research procedures appropriate and clearly stated so that others could replicate them if they wished?

Information needed. Identify the various research procedures that were used in the study and the order in which they occurred.

Example. The researchers' main data-collection procedure was to ask students questions as they attempted to solve mathematics problems. The problems and questions are available upon request, so it seems that the study could be replicated.

RESEARCH FINDINGS

10. Did the report include a thick description that gives a thorough sense of how various individuals responded to the interview questions and how they behaved?

Information needed. Identify the amount of vivid detail that is included about what the individuals being studied actually did or said.

Example. The researchers identified ten issues that mentor teachers faced in working with beginning teachers. Unfortunately the issues were described in rather meager detail, with no examples of what they looked like in practice.

11. Was the research report written in a style that brings to life the phenomenon being studied?

Information needed. Identify any use of visual or literary structures (e.g., drawings, use of similes or metaphors) or unusual genres (e.g., poetry, songs, story telling) that are meant to convey the unique perspective of individuals in the field.

Example. The historical research report included photographs to convey what one-room schools and their teacher and students looked like at the turn of the century. A typical school song of the period was included, and a harrowing newspaper account of a boy who became lost in the woods while on his way to school during the winter.

12. In summarizing the findings, did the report present any specific questions or hypotheses that emerged from the data that were collected?

Information needed. Identify each research hypothesis or question that is stated in the report, and how they are based on the study data.

Example. The researchers focused almost entirely on writing a narrative account of the events leading up to the teachers' strike. There was no attempt to develop hypotheses about why these events happened, which could be tested in subsequent research.

13. If any quantitative data were collected, were they described and analyzed appropriately?

    Information needed. Identify any quantitative data in the report.

    Example. The researchers studied three teachers' aides and made such comments as, "They spent most of their time helping individual children and passing out or collecting papers." Time is easily quantified, so the researchers could have collected some time data and reported means and standard deviations.

14. Did the researchers establish a strong chain of evidence?

    Information needed. Identify information in the report that explains the researchers' reasoning with respect to their decisions from the beginning to the end of the study.

    Example. The researchers wanted to study how recent immigrants adapted to the manner in which students interact with each other in inner-city high schools. They trained high school students from each immigrant culture to collect observational and interview data. They explained that they chose this method of data collection because they assumed that the students would be able to obtain more valid data than adult researchers could obtain. This explanation appears reasonable, and therefore it contributes to the chain of evidence supporting the soundness of the study's findings.

15. Did the researchers use member checking to ensure that the information they presented about field participants was accurate and reflected field participants' perceptions?

    Information needed. Identify information indicating that the researchers asked individuals to review statements in drafts of the researchers' report for accuracy and completeness.

    Example. The researchers asked several members of each of the groups they studied—students, teachers, and parents—to review drafts of the report. An individual who spent considerable time on that task and provided helpful feedback was listed as one of the report authors.

Discussion

16. Did the researchers reflect on their own values and perspectives and how these might have influenced the study outcomes, or steps that were taken to minimize their effect?

    Information needed. Look for information in which the researchers describe their own thoughts or feelings about the phenomenon being investigated, and how they took their personal reactions into account in collecting and analyzing the data.

    Example. The report referred to a discussion among the researchers about their personal disappointment at the ways in which some students treated other students during the research observations. It noted the researchers' agreement to behave in a respectful and friendly manner toward every individual in the field, and then to journal about their personal feelings after each field session.

17. Were multiple sources of evidence used to support the researchers' conclusions?

    Information needed. Identify the researchers' conclusions and how each of them was supported by the data analyses.

    Example. The researchers concluded that textbook adoption committees were frustrated by the paucity of written information provided by publishers and their inability to question publishers' representatives in person. This frustration was documented by analysis of interviews with selected members of the textbook adoption committees, field notes made by the researchers during committee meetings, and letters written by the chair of the committee to the director of textbook adoption in the state department of education.

18. Did the researchers provide reasonable explanations of the findings?

    Information needed. Identify how the researchers explained the findings of the study and whether alternative explanations were considered.

    Example. The researchers found that peer coaching did not work at the school they studied, and they attributed its failure to the lack of a supportive context, especially the lack of a history of collegiality among the teaching staff. Another plausible explanation, which they did not consider, is that the teachers received inadequate preparation in peer coaching.

19. Was the generalizability of the findings appropriately qualified?

    Information needed. Identify whether the researchers made any statements about the generalizability of their findings. If claims of generalizability were made, were they appropriate?

    Example. The researchers made no claims that the results of their case study could be generalized to anyone other than the teacher who was studied. It is unfortunate that they did not discuss generalizability, because the findings have significant implications for practice, if in fact they apply to other teachers. There are not enough data about the teacher's professional education for readers to generalize on their own.

20. Did the researchers draw reasonable implications for practice from their findings?

    Information needed. Identify any implications for practice that the researchers drew from their findings.

    Example. The researchers found that students who volunteer for community service derive many benefits from the experience. Therefore, they encourage educators to support community service programs for their students. This recommendation seems well grounded in their findings about the benefits of community service that students in their study received.

GLOSSARY

A-B-A-B design a type of single-case experiment in which the researchers institute a baseline condition (*A*), administer the treatment (condition *B*), institute a second baseline condition (the second *A*), and re-administer the treatment (the second *B*), while measuring the target behavior repeatedly during all conditions.

abstract a brief summary of the information contained in a publication, usually written either by the author or by an indexer who works for the publisher of a preliminary source.

accessible population the immediate population from which a sample is drawn for a research study.

action research research that is carried out by practitioners to improve their own practice.

action science in action research, a theory of action that provides an opportunity to discover and address possible discrepancies between professionals' espoused theories and their theories-in-action.

age equivalent a derived score that represents a given raw score on a measure as the average age of the individuals in the norming group who earned that score.

agency in qualitative research, individuals' assumed ability to shape the conditions of their lives.

analysis of covariance a procedure for determining whether the difference between the mean scores of two or more groups on a posttest is statistically significant, after adjusting for initial differences between the groups on a pretest.

analysis of variance a procedure for determining whether the difference between the mean scores of two or more groups on a dependent variable is statistically significant.

***and* connector** in an electronic search of a preliminary source, use of the term *and* between two descriptors in order to retrieve only entries that have been coded for both descriptors.

anti-oppressive education a field of educational inquiry and practice that involves questioning traditional educational practices in order to expose and correct assumptions underlying forms of cultural oppression maintained by such practices.

applied research research that is designed to develop and test predictions and interventions that can be used directly to improve practice.

archive (also called *repository*) a facility for storing documents so that they are preserved in good condition and access to them can be controlled.

artifact in quantitative research, an atypical variable or condition that affects the outcome of a research study.

attrition (also called *experimental mortality*) in experiments, the loss of research participants over the course of the experimental treatment.

average variation a measure of the average amount by which the individual scores for a sample deviate from the mean score.

baseline in single-case experiments, the *A* condition or conditions, during which the individual's behavior is observed under natural conditions.

basic research research that is designed to understand basic processes and structures that underlie observed behavior.

bibliographic citation   a statement that describes and locates a publication; it typically includes the publication's author, title, publisher, publication date, page numbers if an article or book chapter, and a brief abstract.

bivariate correlational statistics   a set of statistics that describe the magnitude of the relationship between two variables.

border pedagogy   a critical theory of education that conceives the differences between individuals and groups as permeable and changing, as opposed to the more rigid, "either-or" nature of conventional social categories.

bulletin board   networks by which computer users post information to other computer users or carry on electronic discussions on topics of common interest.

canonical correlation   a type of multiple regression analysis that involves use of two or more measured variables to predict a composite index of several criterion variables.

case   in qualitative research, a particular instance of a phenomenon that is selected for study.

case study   a type of qualitative investigation that involves the in-depth study of instances of a phenomenon in its natural context and from the perspective of the participants involved in the phenomenon.

catalytic validity   a judgment about the credibility of an action research project based on the extent to which the project causes stakeholders to transform their view of reality in relation to their professional practice.

categories   variables that yield values that are discrete and nonordered when measured.

causal-comparative research   a type of quantitative investigation that seeks to discover possible causes and effects of a personal characteristic or behavior pattern by comparing individuals in whom it is present with individuals in whom it is absent or present to a lesser degree.

causal pattern   in case study research, a systematic relationship that is observed between particular phenomena within a case or across cases that is presumed to be causal.

cause-and-effect relationship   a causal relationship between two variables for which research has definitely determined which variable is the cause and which variable is the effect.

ceiling effect   a situation in which the range of difficulty of a test's items is so restricted that too many research participants earn the maximum score or a score close to it.

central tendency   the score that reflects the most representative or typical score in a distribution.

chain of evidence   in qualitative research, a judgment of the soundness of a study's findings based on clear, meaningful links among the study's research questions, the raw data, the data analysis procedures, and the findings.

chart essay   a visual presentation that focuses the audience's attention on particular findings from a research study or research review.

chi-square (χ^2) test   a nonparametric test of statistical significance that is used when the research data are in the form of frequency counts for two or more categories.

CIPP model   see *Context-Input-Process-Product (CIPP) model.*

citation   see *bibliographic citation.*

coding check   a method for determining the reliability of the process used to develop the categories for coding qualitative data.

collaborative action research   a type of investigation in which different types of professionals in a field of study collaborate to collect data about a problem of practice, analyze the data, report the results to stakeholders, and implement a plan of action intended to solve the problem.

comparison groups   the two groups that are selected for comparison in a causal-comparative study, because they naturally possess differing levels of the independent variable under study.

concurrent evidence of test validity (also called *concurrent validity*)   the extent to which individuals' scores on a new test correspond to their scores on a more established test of the same construct, which is administered shortly before or after the new test.

concurrent validity   see *concurrent evidence of test validity.*

connoisseurship and criticism   see *educational connoisseurship and criticism.*

conscientization   in critical-theory research, a process of coming to know what one knows, so that one finds voice and courage to question and change one's role in maintaining educational processes that one does not value.

consequential validity   the extent to which the values implicit in the constructs measured by a test and in the intended uses of the test are consistent with the values of test takers, those who will use the test results to make decisions, and other stakeholders.

constant   a construct that is part of the design of a research study but does not vary.

construct   a concept that is inferred from commonalties among observed phenomena and that can be used to explain those phenomena.

construct validity   the extent to which a test can be shown to measure a particular psychological characteristic.

contact summary form   a form used to summarize the procedures that were employed to collect and analyze data obtained from a field contact in a case study.

content analysis   the study of various aspects of the information contained in a document, film, or other communication.

content-related evidence of test validity (also called *content validity*)   the extent to which the items in a test represent the domain of content that the test is designed to measure.

content validity   see *content-related evidence of test validity.*

Context-Input-Process-Product (CIPP) model   a form of evaluation research used to help practicing educators evaluate the context, input, process, and product of an educational program.

continuous score   a value of a measure that forms an interval or ratio scale with an indefinite number of points along its continuum.

control group   in an experiment, a group of research participants receiving no treatment or an alternate treatment, to whose performance the experimental group's performance is compared.

convergent evidence of test validity   the extent to which individuals' scores on a test correlate positively with their scores on other tests that are hypothesized to measure the same construct.

correlational research   a type of quantitative investigation that seeks to discover the direction and degree of the relationship among variables through the use of correlational statistics.

correlational statistic   a measure of the extent to which the scores on two or more variables covary.

correlation coefficient   a mathematical expression of the direction and degree of the relationship between two measured variables.

cost analysis   in evaluation research, an estimation of the relationship between the costs of a program and its benefits.

criterion measure   in experimental research, the test or other instrument used to assess the dependent variable that the treatment is intended to affect.

criterion variable   in correlational research, the variable that researchers seek to predict by the measurement of predictor variables.

critical ethnography   a qualitative research tradition in which researchers focus on the study of power relationships and forms of oppression in a culture.

criticalist   a researcher or theorist who attempts to use her or his investigations as a form of social or cultural criticism.

critical pedagogy   any applied system of teaching and learning that is based on the goals and values of critical-theory research.

critical-theory research   a qualitative research tradition that involves uncovering the nature of power relationships in a culture and seeks through its inquiries to help emancipate members of the culture from the forms of oppression that operate within it.

cross-sectional research   a type of research in which changes in a population over time are studied by collecting data at one point in time from samples that vary in age or developmental stage.

cultural acquisition   the process by which individuals seek to acquire, or to avoid acquiring, the concepts, values, skills, and behaviors that are reflected in the common culture.

cultural studies   an interdisciplinary research tradition that involves critical investigation of cultural phenomena as expressed in literature, art, history, and other disciplines.

cultural transmission   the process by which the larger social structure intentionally intervenes in individuals' lives in order to promote, or sometimes to discourage, learning of particular concepts, values, skills, or behaviors.

culture   the pattern of traditions, symbols, rituals, and artifacts that characterize a particular group of individuals and that are transmitted from one generation to the next or from current members to newly admitted members.

Current Index to Journals in Education (*CIJE*)   an index to articles in hundreds of education-related journals, published by ERIC.

database   in an electronic preliminary source, the citations to all the publications that it indexes.

deconstruction   the critical analysis of texts, based on the assumptions that a text has no definite meaning, that words can refer only to other words, and that "playing" with a text can yield multiple, often contradictory interpretations.

democratic validity   a judgment about the credibility of an action research project based on the extent to which the perspectives and interests of all stakeholders were taken into account.

dependent variable   a variable that researchers hypothesize occurred after, and as a result of, another variable (called the *independent variable*).

derived score   a transformation of a raw score in order to indicate an individual's performance relative to a norming group.

descriptive research   a type of quantitative investigation that seeks to portray characteristics of a sample or population by measuring prespecified variables; also, research that focuses on making careful, highly detailed observations or measurements of educational phenomena.

descriptive statistics   mathematical techniques for organizing, summarizing, and displaying a set of numerical data.

descriptor   in a literature search, a term that the searcher uses to locate publications that have been classified by that term in a preliminary source.

dialogical data generation   a stage of a critical ethnography project in which researchers collect data by engaging in dialogue with field participants.

dialogic validity   a judgment about the credibility of an action research project based on the extent to which colleagues shared in the development of the practitioner/researcher's findings and interpretations.

dichotomy   a categorical variable that has only two values.

differential analysis   a form of multivariate correlational analysis that involves identifying moderator variables to improve the correlation between a predictor variable and a criterion variable.

differential selection   in quasi-experiments, the selection of participants for the experimental and control groups by a procedure other than random selection.

direct observation   the collection of data while the research participants are engaged in some form of behavior or while an event is occurring.

discriminant analysis   a form of multivariate correlational analysis that involves determining the correlation between two or more predictor variables and a dichotomous criterion variable.

document   in historical research, a type of text material that is prepared for personal use only, as contrasted with material having an official purpose.

document analysis   a type of qualitative investigation involving the study of written communications that are found in field settings.

ecological validity   an estimate of the extent to which an experimental result can be generalized to the naturally occurring conditions of a local setting.

educational connoisseurship and criticism   a type of expertise-based evaluation involving an appreciation of the phenomenon being evaluated (i.e., connoisseurship) and assessment of the strengths and weaknesses of the phenomenon (i.e., criticism).

educational research   the systematic collection and analysis of information (sometimes called *data*) in order to develop valid, generalizable descriptions, predictions, interventions, and explanations relating to various aspects of education.

educational research and development   a systematic process involving the development and refinement of educational programs and materials through formative and summative evaluation.

Educational Resources Information Center (ERIC)   a federally funded agency that maintains the *Current Index to Journals in Education (CIJE)*, *Resources in Education (RIE)*, and other information sources for educators.

effect size   an estimate of the magnitude of a difference or relationship in the population represented by a sample.

electronic preliminary source   a computer-based index to publications of a certain type or on a certain topic; it includes citations for the publications and the software for searching them.

emancipation   a process of generating actions and changes in consciousness of and toward the members of oppressed cultural groups that free them from their oppression.

emergent design   a form of evaluation in which the focus of evaluation changes as evaluators gain insights into stakeholders' primary issues and concerns.

emic perspective   in qualitative research, the research participants' perceptions and understanding of their social reality.

enabling objective   an entry behavior that learners are expected to have in order for a program or set of materials to reach its objectives.

enculturation   the process by which cultural practices and beliefs are transferred to the youth or other new members of a culture.

entry   a citation for a publication indexed in the *Current Index to Journals in Education (CIJE)*.

epistemology   the branch of philosophy that studies the nature of knowledge and the process by which knowledge is acquired and validated.

ERIC   see *Educational Resources Information Center.*

ERIC clearinghouse   one of a number of ERIC-sponsored institutions that until recently prepared citations related to particular topic areas for inclusion in ERIC preliminary sources and also produced their own publications.

espoused theory   in the theory of action, professionals' beliefs about how they deal with problems of practice.

ethnography   the first-hand, intensive study of the features of a given culture and the patterns in and possible meanings of those features.

ethnology   the comparative study of different cultures.

ethnoscience   the study of a culture's semantic systems for the purpose of revealing the cognitive structure of the culture.

etic perspective   in qualitative research, the researchers' conceptual and theoretical understanding of the research participants' social reality.

evaluation research   a systematic process of making judgments about the merit, value, or worth of an intervention.

experiment   a type of quantitative investigation that involves the manipulation of a treatment variable to determine the effect on one or more dependent variables.

experimental group   in an experiment, a group of research participants receiving the treatment that is presumed to affect the dependent variable, to whose performance the control group's performance is compared.

experimental mortality   see *attrition*.

experimental research   a type of quantitative investigation in which at least one independent variable is manipulated, other relevant variables are controlled as much as possible, and the effect on one or more dependent variables is measured.

exploratory case study method   a method for synthesizing qualitative research studies (as well as quantitative studies and nonresearch accounts of a phenomenon) that acknowledges the unique characteristics of each case, but also identifies concepts and principles present across cases.

external criticism   in historical research, the process of determining the authenticity of a historical source, that is, whether the apparent or claimed origin of the source corresponds to its actual origin.

external validity   the extent to which the results of a research study can be generalized to individuals and situations beyond those involved in the study.

extraneous variable   in experiments, any aspect of the situation that, if not controlled, can make it impossible to determine whether the treatment variable is responsible for any observed effect on the dependent variable.

face validity   the extent to which a casual, subjective inspection of a test's items indicates that they cover the content that the test is claimed to measure.

factor   a mathematical expression of a feature shared by a particular subset of quantitative variables that have been correlated.

factor analysis   a correlational procedure for reducing a set of measured variables to a smaller number of factors (also called *latent variables*) that consist of variables that are moderately or highly correlated with each other.

feminisms   various forms of study of females' lived experiences and the manner in which those experiences are shaped by cultural phenomena.

fieldwork   in qualitative research, the researchers' collection of data while interacting with research participants in their natural settings.

focus   the aspect, or aspects, of the phenomenon to be studied in a case study on which data collection and analysis will concentrate.

formative evaluation   a type of evaluation that is carried out while a program or set of materials is under development, in order to improve its effectiveness or to make a decision to abort further development.

free-text search   a search of an electronic database that involves requesting every citation in which a particular word or set of words appears anywhere in the citation.

frequency   the total number of individuals in a sample who fit a particular category.

fugitive literature   publications that are not easy to obtain (e.g., conference proceedings).

futurology   a type of research that examines what the future is likely to be.

f **value**   an inferential statistic that reveals whether the difference between two or more sample means is generalizable to the populations from which the samples were drawn.

gain score a measure of an individual's score on a posttest minus that individual's score on a pretest.

grade equivalent a derived score that represents a given raw score on a measure as the average grade level of individuals in a norming group who earned that score.

hard-copy preliminary source the paper version of an index to publications of a certain type or on a certain topic.

hegemony the maintenance of privileged groups' dominance over subordinate groups through the cultural agencies that they control.

hidden curriculum the knowledge, values, and behaviors that are taught tacitly by a school's structure and organization of activities.

high-inference variable a variable that requires the observer to make an inference from behavior to a construct that is presumed to underlie the behavior.

historiography the study of the procedures that historians use in their research.

history effect in experiments, the possible effect of events that occur while the treatment is in progress on the dependent variable.

holistic ethnography a qualitative research tradition that involves efforts to provide a comprehensive description and analysis of the entire culture of a group of people.

hypothesis the researchers' prediction, derived from a theory or from speculation, about how two or more measured variables will be related to each other.

identifier any term (e.g., a proper noun, test name) used to classify publications in ERIC preliminary source citations that is not listed as a descriptor in the *Thesaurus of ERIC Descriptors*.

independent variable a variable that researchers hypothesize occurred before, and had an influence on, another variable (called the *dependent variable*).

indexer an individual who classifies publications for citation in a preliminary source.

inferential statistics a set of statistics that enable researchers to make inferences about a population based on the descriptive statistics that are calculated from data for a sample drawn from the population.

insider in educational action research, a practitioner who is viewed as having an internal perspective on the problems of practice being studied; this term typically is used to refer to K–12 teachers.

instrumental rationality a preoccupation with means over ends; this term is used by criticalists to characterize educational research that focuses on prediction and control and the maximization of educational productivity.

instrumentation effect in experiments, a change from the pretest to the posttest that is due to changes in the nature of the measuring instrument rather than to the experimental treatment.

interaction effect in experiments, a situation in which the effect of one variable on another variable is influenced by one or more other variables.

internal criticism in historical research, the process of determining the accuracy and worth of the information contained in a historical source.

internalized oppression the process by which individuals help to maintain their disempowered status in society through thoughts and actions that are consistent with that status.

internal validity in experiments, the extent to which extraneous variables have been controlled by the researchers such that any observed effects can be attributed solely to the treatment.

inter-observer agreement (also called *inter-rater reliability*) the extent to which the scores given by one observer or rater on a measured variable correlate with the scores given by another observer or rater.

inter-observer reliability the extent to which the scores assigned by one observer of events agree with the scores assigned by other observers of the same events.

interpretational analysis   the process of examining qualitative data to identify constructs, themes, and patterns that can be used to describe and explain the phenomenon being studied.

interpretivism   an epistemological position that regards aspects of the human environment as constructed by the individuals who participate in that environment, and thus asserts that aspects of social reality have no existence apart from the meanings that individuals construct for them.

interpretivist epistemology   the view that social reality is a set of meanings that are continually constructed by the individuals who participate in that reality.

inter-rater reliability   see *inter-observer agreement, inter-observer reliability.*

interval scale   a measure that lacks a true zero point and for which the distance between any two adjacent points is the same.

interview   the collection of data through direct interaction between the researcher and the individuals being studied.

item consistency   the extent to which all the items on a test measure the same construct, as determined by one of several correlational methods.

item response theory   an approach to test construction designed to increase test reliability, in which the difficulty level of the items presented to each testee are matched with the testee's ability level as determined by performance on earlier test items.

key informant   in qualitative research, any of the various individuals who have special knowledge or status that make them especially important in obtaining an emic perspective of the social reality being studied.

Kruskal-Wallis test of significance   a nonparametric test of statistical significance that is used to determine whether the observed difference between the distribution of scores for more than two groups on a measured variable is statistically significant.

latent variable   see *factor.*

latent variable causal modeling   see *structural equation modeling.*

line of best fit   in correlational research, the line on a scattergram that represents the best prediction of each Y score from the corresponding X score.

literature search   the process in which individuals identify the publications in a preliminary source that are relevant to their information needs.

longitudinal research   a type of quantitative investigation that involves describing changes in a sample's characteristics or behavior patterns over a period of time.

low-inference variable   a variable that requires little inference on the part of an observer to determine its presence or level.

Mann-Whitney U test   a nonparametric test of statistical significance that is used to determine whether the observed difference between the distribution of scores for each of two groups on a measured variable is statistically significant.

maturation effect   in experiments, a change from the pretest to the posttest that is due to changes in the research participants during the course of an experiment rather than to the treatment.

mean   a measure of central tendency corresponding to the average of a set of scores.

measurement error   the difference between an individual's true score on a test and the scores that the individual actually obtains on it when it is administered over a variety of conditions.

median   a measure of central tendency corresponding to the middle point in a distribution of scores.

member checking   a procedure used by qualitative researchers to check their reconstruction of the emic perspective by having field participants review statements in the researchers' report for accuracy and completeness.

meta-analysis   a method for combining the results from different quantitative research studies on the same phenomenon into a single statistic called an *effect size.*

meta-evaluation the process of evaluating an evaluation research study in order to assess the soundness of the research findings.

microethnography the study of specific aspects of the culture of a group of people.

mode a measure of central tendency corresponding to the most frequently occurring score in a distribution of scores.

moderator variable in correlational research, a variable, Z, that affects the extent to which variable X predicts variable Y, such that the correlation between X and Y for some values of Z is different from the correlation between X and Y for other values of Z.

monological data generation the initial stage of a critical ethnography project, in which only the researchers "speak," compiling a thick description of field participants' activities that is written from the perspective of an uninvolved observer.

multiple-case design the study of two or more cases in order to determine the generalizability of findings across cases.

multiple regression a statistical procedure for determining the magnitude of the relationship between a criterion variable and a combination of two or more predictor variables.

multivariate correlational statistics a set of statistics that describe the magnitude of the relationship between three or more variables.

multivocality a situation in which the participants in a culture or societal group do not speak with a unified voice, but express diverse interests and viewpoints.

narrative a form of reporting a qualitative research study that uses poems, stories, folktales, anecdotes, or other literary genres to describe research procedures or findings.

narrative summary a method for synthesizing qualitative research findings that involves using a consistent writing style to create a brief description of each study.

National Assessment of Educational Progress (NAEP) a congressionally mandated, large-scale, continuing assessment of what a representative sample of students in the United States know and can do in various subject areas.

needs assessment a set of procedures for identifying and prioritizing discrepancies between desired and existing conditions (i.e., needs).

negative correlation a correlation between two measured variables such that the higher the score obtained for variable X, the lower the corresponding score for variable Y.

nonparametric statistics mathematical techniques for analyzing scores that do not involve assumptions about their distribution or form.

nonparametric test of significance a type of test of statistical significance that does not depend on assumptions about the distribution or form of scores on the measured variables.

normal curve see *normal probability distribution*.

normal probability distribution a distribution of scores that forms a symmetrical, bell-shaped curve when plotted on a graph.

normative-evaluative truth claims in critical ethnography, assertions by field participants that are intersubjective and based on sets of norms that operate conjointly in the social setting.

norming sample a large sample that represents a defined population and whose scores on a test provide a set of standards to which the scores of individuals who subsequently take the test can be referenced.

norms unstated background sets of rules and assumptions that influence individuals' social acts.

null hypothesis the prediction that an observed result for a sample is a chance finding.

objectives-based evaluation an approach in which evaluators focus their data collection and analysis on how well a program or method helps learners achieve its purported goals.

objective truth claims in critical ethnography, assertions by the researchers about details of the culture to which there is multiple access, meaning that other observers would generally agree with the researchers' assertions.

observer bias   an observer's mental set to perceive events in such a way that certain events or behaviors are overlooked, distorted, or falsified.

oral history   a type of historical research in which individuals who witnessed or participated in past events produce recollections of those events.

or **connector**   in an electronic search of a preliminary source, use of the term *or* between two descriptors in order to retrieve entries that have been coded for either of the descriptors.

outcome validity   a judgment about the credibility of an action research project based on the extent to which new actions lead to a resolution of the problem that prompted the project.

outlier   an individual or situation that differs greatly from other cases that are studied.

outsider   in educational action research, a practitioner who is viewed as having an external perspective on the problems of practice being studied; this term typically is used to refer to academics from universities or research organizations.

panel study   research in which the same sample is surveyed at more than one data-collection point in order to explore changes in specific individuals and possible reasons for those changes.

paper-and-pencil test   an instrument that involves measurement of a variable based on individuals' responses to printed text or graphics.

parameter   a statistic that applies to the entire population rather than just to a sample.

parametric statistics   mathematical techniques for analyzing scores that involve particular assumptions about their distribution and form.

parametric test of significance   a type of test of statistical significance that depends on certain assumptions about the distribution and form of scores on the measured variables.

participant observation   in qualitative research, researchers' assumption of a meaningful identity within the group being studied while maintaining their role as observers, systematically collecting data and using complex social, practical, and personal skills to sustain their roles in the field.

path analysis   a statistical method for testing the validity of a theory about causal links between three or more measured variables.

percentage   the frequency of individuals in a particular category divided by the total number of individuals in the sample.

percentile score   a type of rank score that represents a given raw score on a measure as the percentage of individuals in the sample or norming group whose score falls at or below that score.

performance measure   a test that involves evaluating individuals by examining them as they carry out a behavior that involves a complex, real-life task.

performance objective   a specific statement of what learners will be able to do after the instruction provided by a program or set of materials.

phenomenon   a broad set of processes, events, individuals, or other things of interest to researchers.

population validity   the extent to which the results of a study can be generalized from the sample that participated in it to a particular population.

positive correlation   a correlation between two measured variables such that the higher the score obtained for variable X, the higher the corresponding score for variable Y.

positivism   an epistemological position that asserts that there is a social reality "out there" that is available for study through scientific means similar to those that were developed in the physical sciences.

postmodernism   a broad social and philosophical movement that questions assumptions about the rationality of human action, the use of positivist epistemology, and any human endeavor (e.g., science) that claims a privileged position with respect to the search for truth.

posttest   in experiments, a measure that is administered following the treatment in order to determine the effects of the treatment.

practical significance   the meaning of a research finding in terms of its potential usefulness in professional practice or other real-world settings.

prediction research   research that involves the use of data collected at one point in time to predict future behavior or events.

prediction study   a type of correlational investigation that seeks to predict future behavior or achievement from variables measured at an earlier point in time.

predictive evidence of test validity (also called *predictive validity*)   the extent to which the scores of individuals who take the test at one point of time predict their scores on a criterion test administered at a subsequent point in time.

predictive validity   see *predictive evidence of test validity.*

predictor variable   a variable that researchers measure at one point in time and then correlate with a criterion variable that is measured at a later point in time.

preliminary source   an index or bibliography that lists and provides information about publications of particular types or on particular topics.

presentism   a type of bias in historical research that involves interpreting past events with concepts and perspectives from more recent times.

pretest   in experiments, a measure that is administered prior to a treatment in order to provide a basis for comparison with the posttest.

primary source   a publication or other original source of information that was written or preserved by the individuals who actually conducted the research or witnessed the events presented in the source.

primary source analysis   a synthesis of quantitative or qualitative research findings based on the reviewers' reading of reports prepared by the researchers who obtained the findings.

privilege   in critical-theory research, the disproportionate power, resources, and life opportunities that are granted to members of culturally dominant groups in a society; also, to grant such power to a specific group or individual.

probability value (*p*)   a mathematical expression of the likelihood that a statistical result was obtained by chance.

process validity   a judgment about the credibility of an action research project based on the adequacy of the processes used in different phases of the project.

product-moment correlation coefficient (*r*)   a mathematical expression of the direction and magnitude of the relationship between two measures that yield continuous scores.

professional review   a synthesis of quantitative or qualitative research findings related to a particular topic that is targeted primarily to practitioners.

program evaluation   a general term to describe the various aspects of educational practice that are the focus of evaluation research in education.

progressive discourse   the prevailing scientific view that anyone at any time can offer a criticism about a particular research study or research methodology and that if it proves to have merit, it will be listened to and accommodated.

proportional random sampling   a variation of stratified random sampling that is designed to ensure that the proportion of individuals in each subgroup in the sample is the same as their proportion in the population.

publication   any communication that has been prepared for dissemination, whether in print, on microfiche, on the Internet, or in other forms.

purposeful sampling   in qualitative research, the process of selecting cases that are likely to be "information-rich" with respect to the purposes of a particular study.

***p* value**   see *probability value.*

qualitative research inquiry that is grounded in the assumption that individuals construct social reality in the form of meanings and interpretations, and that these constructions are transitory and situational; the dominant methodology is to discover these meanings and interpretations by studying cases intensively in natural settings and by reflecting the researchers' own experiences in what they report.

qualitative research tradition a group of qualitative researchers and scholars holding a similar view of the nature of the universe and of legitimate questions to ask and techniques to use in its exploration; also, the work of such individuals.

quantitative materials materials containing quantitative information that are preserved and can be used as a primary source in historical research.

quantitative research inquiry that is grounded in the assumption that features of the social environment constitute an objective reality that is relatively constant across time and settings; the dominant methodology for studying these features is to collect numerical data on the observable behavior of samples and subject them to statistical analysis.

quasi-experiment an experimental study in which research participants for the experimental and control groups are selected by a procedure other than random selection.

questionnaire a set of written questions that typically measure many variables.

random assignment in experiments, the process of assigning individuals or groups to the experimental and control treatments such that each individual or group has an equal chance of being in either treatment condition.

range a measure of the amount of dispersion in a score distribution, equal to the difference between the highest and the lowest score plus 1.

rank score the position of an individual's score on a measure relative to the positions of other individuals' scores.

raw score an individual score on a measure as determined by the scoring key, without any further statistical manipulation.

r & d product an educational program or set of materials that is developed through the process of educational research and development (R & D).

reconstructionist (also called *revisionist historian*) a historian who engages in reinterpretation of past events, usually with the intent of demonstrating that past practices reflect particular political, economic, or other social forces and motivations more than they reflect rationality, good will, or professional considerations.

reconstructive analysis the process by which critical ethnographers analyze the data collected during monological data generation in order to describe interaction patterns among field participants and the apparent meaning of those patterns.

record in historical research, a type of text material that is prepared with an official purpose, as contrasted with material prepared for personal use only.

reflection in action research, the process by which practitioners step back from the world of practice and ponder and share ideas about the meaning, value, and impact of their work.

reflective analysis the process in which qualitative researchers rely on their own intuition and personal judgment to analyze the data that have been collected.

reflexivity in qualitative research, the researchers' act of focusing on themselves as constructors and interpreters of the social reality that they study.

refutation the process of submitting the knowledge claims of science to empirical tests that allow them to be challenged and disproved.

relational pattern in case study research, a systematic relationship that is observed between particular phenomena within a case or across cases that is not presumed to be causal.

relationship research any type of quantitative investigation, including causal-comparative and correlational research, that explores observed relationships among variables.

relationship study   a type of correlational investigation that seeks to explore the direction and degree of the relationship between two or more variables that are measured at about the same time.

reliability   a measure of the extent to which a test or other measure is free of measurement error.

relic   in historical research, any object whose physical properties provide information about the past.

replication   the process of repeating a research study with different research participants under similar conditions in order to increase confidence in the original study's findings.

repository   see *archive*.

representativeness check   in qualitative research, a procedure used to determine whether a finding is typical of the field site from which it was obtained.

reproduction   in critical theory, the view that many of the learning problems experienced by members of low-income and ethnic "minority" groups result from educational practices that maintain and reinforce the cultural oppression of such groups.

research and development   see *educational research and development*.

Resources in Education **(RIE)**   an index to papers presented at education conferences and reports of studies involving ongoing research, research grants, and local education projects, published by ERIC.

response-processes evidence of test validity   the extent to which the processes used by testees in taking a test are consistent with the particular construct or constructs underlying the test.

responsive evaluation   a type of evaluation research that focuses on stakeholders' issues and concerns.

resume   a citation for a publication indexed in *Resources in Education* (*RIE*).

reversal   in single-case experiments, the process of withdrawing the treatment (condition *B*) so as to reinstitute the baseline condition (*A*).

reviewer bias   with respect to secondary sources, the omission or distortion of research findings that reflect the reviewers' own mental set to perceive events in a certain way.

revisionist historian   see *reconstructionist*.

r **value**   see *product-moment correlation coefficient*.

sampling bias   the use of any procedure to select a research sample that results in a sample that is not representative of the population from which it is drawn.

sampling error   the difference between a statistic for a sample and the same statistic for the population.

scale   an instrument that measures personal characteristics by totaling the individual's responses to items having a fixed number of response options.

scattergram   a graph depicting the correlation between two variables, with the scores on one variable plotted on the *x* axis and the scores on the other variable plotted on the *y* axis of the graph.

Scheffé's test   a type of t test for multiple comparisons.

search engine   a type of computer software that helps users sort through a database to identify documents or other items that satisfy user-specified criteria.

secondary source   a publication in which the author reviews research or other work that was carried out or witnessed by someone else.

selection-maturation interaction   in experiments, a change from the pretest to the posttest that is due to differential changes in the research participants in the experimental and control groups during the course of the experiment rather than to the experimental treatment.

self-report   a form of data involving individuals providing information about themselves at the researchers' request.

simple random sampling   a procedure in which all the individuals in the defined population have an equal and independent chance of being selected as a member of the sample.

single-case experiment   a type of experiment in which a treatment is administered to a single individual or group in order to determine the effect of the treatment on one or more dependent variables.

stakeholder   an individual who is involved in a phenomenon that is being evaluated or who may be affected by or interested in the findings of the evaluation.

standard deviation   a measure of how much a set of scores deviates from the mean score.

standard deviation unit   a measure of the position of a score in a score distribution relative to the standard deviation of the score distribution.

standard error of measurement   a statistic that is used to estimate the probable range within which an individual's true score on a test falls.

standard score   a derived score that uses standard deviation units to indicate an individual's performance relative to the norming group's performance.

statistic   any number that describes a characteristic of a sample's scores on a measure.

statistical regression   the tendency for research participants who score either very high or very low on a measure to score nearer the mean when the measure is re-administered.

statistical significance   an inference, based on a statistical test, that the results obtained for a research sample can be generalized to the population that the sample represents.

stratified random sampling   a procedure involving the identification of subgroups (i.e., strata) with certain characteristics in the population and drawing a random sample of individuals from each subgroup.

structural analysis   the process of examining qualitative data to identify patterns that are inherent features of discourse, text, events, or other phenomena.

structural equation modeling (also called *latent variable causal modeling*)   a statistical procedure for testing the validity of a theory about the causal links among variables, each of which has been measured by one or more different measures.

subjective truth claims   in critical ethnography, assertions by field participants about their state of being, to which there is privileged access, meaning that only the individual has access to the experience on which the claim is based.

summative evaluation   a type of evaluation that is conducted to determine the worth of a fully developed program in operation, especially in comparison with competing programs.

survey research   a form of descriptive investigation that involves collecting information about research participants' beliefs, attitudes, interests, or behavior through questionnaires, interviews, or paper-and-pencil tests.

systems approach   a model of educational research and development that includes various aspects of product development, formative evaluation throughout the development process, and summative evaluation after development is completed.

tacit knowledge   implicit meanings that the individuals being studied either cannot find words to express or that they take so much for granted that they do not refer to them.

target behavior   in experiments, the dependent variable that is measured to determine the effects of the treatment.

target population   the population to which researchers want to generalize or apply their research findings.

test   a measure of an individual's knowledge, depth of understanding, or skill within a curriculum domain, which typically yields a total score for the number of items answered correctly.

testing effect   in experiments, the effect of the administration of a pretest, rather than of the treatment, on research participants' posttest performance.

test-retest reliability   the extent to which individuals' scores on one administration of a test correspond to their scores on another administration of the test after a delay.

test stability   see *test-retest reliability.*

test of statistical significance   a mathematical procedure for determining whether the researchers' null hypothesis can be rejected at a given probability level.

test validity   see *validity.*

text   in critical-theory research, any example of a cultural discourse, object, or event that possesses communicative value; it is viewed as the most powerful means of expressing and maintaining differences in privilege among cultural groups in society.

text materials   in historical research, materials intentionally written to record past events, and materials originally prepared to serve an immediate purpose that yield important evidence about historical events and practices.

theme   in qualitative research, a salient, recurrent feature of the case being studied.

theory   an explanation of particular phenomena in terms of a set of underlying constructs and a set of principles that relate the constructs to each other.

theory-in-action   in the theory of action, the actual behavior of professionals as they engage in their work.

thick description   in qualitative research, a richly detailed report that recreates a situation and as much of its context as possible, including the meanings and intentions inherent in the situation.

treatment   in experiments, the intervention that is administered to the experimental group to determine its effect on the dependent variable.

triangulation   the use of multiple data-collection methods, data sources, analysts, or theories to increase the soundness of research findings.

troubling   in anti-oppressive education, the process of questioning widely accepted but oppressive cultural practices.

true score   the actual amount of the characteristic measured by the test that the test taker possesses, if it were possible to administer a perfect measure of the characteristic.

truncation   a procedure for searching an electronic database for any word that contains a given sequence of letters; for example, searching for the "trunk" *s-i-g-n* to retrieve all instances of such terms as *signify, insignificant,* and *resign.*

t **test**   a test of statistical significance that is used to determine whether the null hypothesis that two sample means come from identical populations can be rejected.

Tukey's test   a type of *t* test for multiple comparisons.

t **value**   the computation that results from a *t* test; it can be checked in a table of the *t* distribution to determine the statistical significance of the difference between two sample means.

unit of analysis   in case study research, the aspect of the phenomenon that will be studied across a sample of cases.

validity   the appropriateness, meaningfulness, and usefulness of specific inferences made from test scores; also the soundness of research findings based on the satisfaction of specific design criteria for various types of research.

variability   the amount of dispersion in a set of scores.

variable   a quantitative expression of a construct.

variance   a measure of the extent to which scores in a distribution deviate from the mean; it is equal to the square of the standard deviation.

variant source   in historical research, a primary source that has been altered from the original version.

verisimilitude   a style of writing that seeks to draw readers emotionally into research participants' world view and leads them to perceive a qualitative research report as credible and authentic.

voice in critical-theory research, the extent to which individuals occupying particular social categories or identities are privileged, silenced, muted, or empowered through the operation of discourses that maintain or contest dominant and subordinate cultures in a society.

volunteer sample a sample based on individuals' expression of willingness to participate in a research study rather than on a systematic sampling strategy.

vote counting a method of synthesizing the findings of quantitative research studies, whereby the studies are classified into four categories based on the direction (positive or negative) and statistical significance (significant or non-significant) of the reported results.

Wilcoxon signed-rank test a nonparametric counterpart of the *t* test of statistical significance.

NAME INDEX

SUBJECT INDEX